PRISCA MUNIMENTA

A.E.J.H.

Prisca Munimenta

STUDIES IN ARCHIVAL & ADMINISTRATIVE HISTORY

PRESENTED TO

Dr A. E. J. Hollaender

EDITED BY FELICITY RANGER

UNIVERSITY OF LONDON PRESS LTD

ISBN 0 340 17398 X

First published 1973

University of London Press Ltd
St Paul's House, Warwick Lane, London EC4P 4AH

Printed and bound in Great Britain
by W & J Mackay Ltd, Chatham

The Archivist

Simplex eius prandium,
  margarina, panis;
modicum stipendium,
  domus haud immanis,

Vultu tamen hilari,
  inscius pudoris
ridet, quia proprii
  avidus laboris.

Collocat in ordine
  prisca munimenta,
forsan ex origine
  squalida obtenta.

En! scripta veterrima
  diligenter purat;
tenere lacerrima
  pergamena curat.

Si nocent humiditas
  ignis et rodentes,
sint aer sedulitas
  felis avertentes.

Dum Clius benignitas
  ei det quod licet,
opera posteritas
  eius benedicet.

Verses composed by Dr G. Herbert Fowler, sometime County Archivist of Bedfordshire, and a great friend of Sir Hilary Jenkinson, among whose papers the original copy (unsigned, but in Dr Fowler's hand) was found by Roger H. Ellis, June 1961. Reprinted from *Essays in Memory of Sir Hilary Jenkinson*, ed. A. E. J. Hollaender (Society of Archivists, 1962).

Preface

To criticize openly a tyrannical government, and to go into exile rather than submit, needs courage of a high order. To make a new career in a new country, speaking and writing a new language (and learning to do so better than most of the natives), and to become a leader there of a learned profession, requires intelligence, tenacity and scholarship of a quality to which few can even aspire. To do all this, and in the course of it to acquire and hold the affectionate regard of all his colleagues, is something that probably only Albert Hollaender could have done.

Albert Hollaender's friends and colleagues (and all his colleagues are his friends) have long watched for an opportunity to show to the world, and to Albert himself, what they feel for him and what they owe to him. At last that opportunity has arrived. At the end of this year Albert Hollaender will hand over to younger colleagues the two offices – Keeper of Manuscripts at the Guildhall Library, and Editor of the *Journal of the Society of Archivists* – which for so long he has filled – and which indeed he created – with such distinction and success. To mark not the end, but the culmination of his work as an archivist, Albert Hollaender's colleagues have borrowed both a term and a custom from Albert's own native land. In gratitude and in affection, and with every good wish for many happy years to come, they dedicate to him this *Festschrift*.

ROGER H. ELLIS

Editorial Note

Success can be measured in many ways. A universally recognized measure for publications is whether or not they sell. By this criterion alone the *Journal of the Society of Archivists* under Dr Hollaender's editorship has been an outstanding success. Almost every issue of volumes I to III (1955–69) is now out of print. This fact, combined with recognition of the quality of many of the articles published in it, suggested that a volume which made some of the best of them available once more would be welcome to archivists and historians alike as well as constituting a fitting tribute to Dr Hollaender's editorial policy and achievement. No better demonstration of his editorial genius could be given than a collected volume of seminal articles on archives and administrative history by authors of acknowledged authority and distinction. In presenting this volume to Dr Hollaender, the Society of Archivists hopes to serve archivists and historians as well as to acknowledge its debt to the Editor of its *Journal* for the past twenty-three years.

The selection and editing of the volume has been the work of a small subcommittee of the Publications Committee of the Society, composed of some of Dr Hollaender's close friends and colleagues. They have been fortunate in the generous cooperation of all the authors whose articles have been reprinted. Several have taken the opportunity to make slight revisions to their original texts in the light of further research or subsequent developments. Without their collaboration this volume would not have been possible. Nor would it have been possible had Mr Paul Hodder-Williams of Matthew Hodder Limited not agreed to publish it. The Society of Archivists is deeply indebted to him and to the other directors of the Hodder Group, especially University of London Press.

In addition to those authors whose articles are here reprinted, grateful acknowledgments are also due to Mrs Maud Corderoy for permission to reprint the article by her sister, Miss Ida Darlington, to the Director of the Tithe Redemption Office of the Department of Inland Revenue and the Controller of Her Majesty's Stationery Office for permission to reprint the article by the former Secretary of the Tithe Redemption Commission, to the Trustees of the British Museum, the Dean and Chapter of Chichester Cathedral and the Controller of Her Majesty's Stationery Office for permission to reproduce the plates, and to Mr G. F. Osborn for the photograph of Dr Hollaender.

FELICITY RANGER

Contents

Illustrations

The Contributors

Roger H. Ellis sometime Secretary of the Royal Commission on Historical Manuscripts, President of the Society of Archivists since 1961

Philip E. Jones OBE sometime Deputy Keeper of the Records of the Corporation of London

The late **Sir Hilary Jenkinson** CBE sometime Deputy Keeper of the Public Records, President of the Society of Archivists 1955–61

Peter Walne County Archivist, Hertfordshire County Council

Peter Gouldesbrough Assistant Keeper, Scottish Record Office

Pierre Chaplais Reader in Diplomatic, University of Oxford

Norman E. Evans Assistant Keeper, Public Record Office

Maurice F. Bond OBE Clerk of the Records, House of Lords

Thomas G. Barnes Professor of History, University of California, Berkeley

Walter C. Richardson Professor of History, Louisiana State University

Neville Williams Deputy Keeper of Public Records

Athol L. Murray Assistant Keeper, Scottish Record Office

Valerie Cromwell Lecturer in History, University of Sussex

Rupert C. Jarvis sometime Librarian and Archivist, H.M. Customs and Excise

Henry S. Cobb Senior Assistant Clerk of the Records, House of Lords

Jean M. Imray Archivist to the Mercers' Company

E. J. Robinson sometime Archivist to the Church Commissioners

H. G. Richardson sometime Secretary of the Tithe Redemption Commission

The Reverend **Francis O. Edwards** SJ Archivist of the English Province of the Society of Jesus

A. E. B. Owen Under-Librarian in charge of the Department of Western Manuscripts, Cambridge University Library

The late **Ida Darlington** sometime County Archivist, London County Council, and Head Archivist, Greater London Council

A.E.J.H.

It is probable that the disruptive and destructive war of Adolf Hitler helped to provide the impetus for the establishment in 1947 of the Society of Local Archivists in England. Perhaps he must also be given credit for endowing the Society with a learned and enthusiastic editor of its *Journal*. In effect he sent to the Society a man trained in one of the most important archival centres in Europe, who by his editorial policy was to help in no mean degree to establish the international reputation of the British Society.

Albert Edwin Johannes Hollaender, 'Doc' to his Guildhall colleagues, was born in Vienna and was educated at the local grammar school and university. Having obtained a degree of Doctor of Philosophy in medieval and modern history, he was employed in the National Library and State Archives in his native city. As a Staff Reporter and Editorial Assistant he travelled to many of the important archival centres in Europe and his work in that capacity may have encouraged him in later years to undertake editorial responsibilities in England. He remained in Austria for some time after Hitler's invasion but constant threats and persecution caused him to emigrate to England on 24 May 1939. Not surprisingly this period in his life has left its mark upon his character in a tendency to react strongly, and to assess things as superlatively good or frightful. It caused him to rate history and archives as a fundamental aspect of civilization, and gave his life purpose and direction. He lives for archives, his evenings and his holidays are no escape, rather a chance to catch up.

On the outbreak of war he left the Catholic Cathedral and Seminary Library at Leeds, where he had found useful employment, and joined the British Army, serving with the Expeditionary Force in 1940, later in the Pioneers and from March 1943 with the Intelligence Corps. Far from robust in physique, but strong in character, he became a Company Sergeant Major, a rank that most of his subsequent colleagues would find strangely out of character. After the war his Major wrote of him 'he is a tireless worker who never counts the hours', an assessment to the truth of which all his associates will vouch.

At the age of thirty-seven he was appointed a temporary assistant in the Guildhall Library, London, and he has been eternally grateful to the then Librarian for giving him the opportunity to establish himself in the service of archives in England. His ability was unquestionable and although his voice retains a suggestion of his continental upbringing his integration with English archivists was rapid. By 1953 his anglicization was so complete that he felt constrained to protest in an editorial against the sale of a page of a marriage register of special interest to America concluding with the words 'Our archives, national and local are in their entirety our heritage'. Yet still he refers to himself as a foreigner!

More surprising was his success in persuading London authorities, ecclesiastical, commercial and civic, that they had a duty, and that it would be good for their souls, to deposit their records in Guildhall Library. On such occasions his tact and bonhomie was sometimes reinforced by a little necessary bullying, all in a good cause. That he had no present accommodation for a vast intake from St Paul's, or from an insurance company, was immaterial, for he could infiltrate the rooms of his colleague in the Corporation Records Office and gradually take them over. Such was his enthusiasm that opposition would have been churlish. From a mere handful of records he has built up a major collection and his bold black handwriting fills many an accession register. His knowledge of the records in his care, particularly the ecclesiastical archives, is immense and he takes endless pains to help those whose researches are most difficult.

He was elected a member of the Society of Local Archivists in its earliest days, and became editor in succession to Miss Amy Foster in 1950 of the then cyclostyled *Bulletin* of the Society. To his utter chagrin he numbered his first issue in April 1951 No. 7, being quite unaware of a No. 7 issued before his appointment, of which no copy had reached him. This is adequate commentary on the immature project which with regular issues and ever increasing size he has developed into an international journal with world-wide subscribers. Like his predecessor he contributed an editorial to each number of the *Bulletin*. Although he constantly reminded the Society that he was only its servant and that the *Bulletin* was theirs, not his, he felt able on occasions to express strong views. He attacked the editor of *Burke's Peerage* for lack of any reference to sources for genealogy in local record offices. In the *Bulletin* of October 1954 he could 'only make suggestions tactfully and cautiously, but in his modest opinion the *Bulletin* ought to be printed', the next word his modesty allowed him to print in large capitals–'NOW'. He had his way. In April 1955 the *Bulletin* became the printed *Journal* of the Society. Henceforth he did not allow himself an editorial, nor could the editor contribute an article, and only occasionally did he enjoy the luxury of writing a review, then usually because the book under review was in German. Not that his pen was idle, for he remained deeply interested in central European history and contributed articles to continental journals. Even during the war he found time to write on topics of local history in Wiltshire and an article for the *Bulletin of the John Rylands Library* on the coronation of Edward I. Although early reviewers saw some competition between *Archives* and the Society's *Journal* Hollaender wrote several essays for the British Records Association and rightly saw no conflict. To him, as to most archivists, but especially to him, Sir Hilary Jenkinson was a man of great eminence, and nothing gave him more pleasure than editing a volume of essays in Jenkinson's memory for publication by the Society of Archivists.

Perhaps Hollaender's most remarkable attribute as an editor is his ability to persuade eminent historians, as well as archivists, to produce, often within a time limit, scholarly writings on basic sources. He seems to know everyone worth knowing in his field, yet he will always welcome an article, maybe technical or statistical, from the junior assistant in the Mercia record office. His circle of contacts is so extensive that he is also able to commission historical articles for the *Guildhall Miscellany* which he has assembled and edited for the Librarian for the past twenty years. For the Society he has always endeavoured to produce a *Journal* balanced as between modern and medieval, historical and archival, administrative and technical. Content, above all, demonstrates the vitality of his editorship. The number of pages in each issue was not limited by lack of manuscript but by the amount of money he could persuade the Council to authorize for the *Journal*. Quinquennial volumes increased from 296 pages to 493 to 595, while a single issue in the current volume extended to 100 pages, a *magnum opus* to celebrate the twenty-fifth anniversary of the founding of the Society.

Hollaender has not only been editor of the *Journal* for the long period of twenty-three years, but he has also been manager, for he has negotiated printing contracts, he has sought advertisers and let space, and he has sought and won subscribers. While the *Journal* itself is a monument to his work, the Society felt that a reissue of some of the important articles in the earlier numbers now out of print would afford Hollaender great satisfaction, and would go some way to express its gratitude to him for his editorial work over so long a period. But Hollaender will derive most satisfaction from the fact that the Society is proud of its *Journal* and accepts his concept that it is a window through which the world views the archive scene in Britain.

PHILIP E. JONES

General

The Future of
Archives in England

The present occasion[1] (if I may be personal for a moment) comes very near to coinciding with the fiftieth anniversary of my first entry into a Record Office–into *the* Record Office, I may say; for at that time it had, I think, no competitors for the title. For me therefore it is almost inevitably an occasion either for retrospect or for anticipation; and of the two I prefer anticipation. Looking back, though it may be interesting for the looker, is apt to be boring for his audience: they have to have so much explained to them–to be reminded, for instance, that fifty years ago motor transport as a general means of conveyance for Records or other commodities not only did not exist but had not been thought of; that ordinary people (including the present witness) had seldom if ever used a telephone or thought of writing with anything except their hand and a pen;[2] and that the word 'Archives', if it had occurred to anyone to employ it, would have been dredged from the depths of a Dictionary, with perhaps a quotation from Charles Lamb or Mrs Howitt adhering to it but with little else to explain its significance. On the other hand, having spent fifty years (barring the interruptions due to a couple of Wars) almost entirely upon Record Work of one kind or another, I find it interesting to speculate upon the novelties of experience which await my successors: and they too may perhaps think it not unprofitable to look forward from the standpoint of the present (even a little from that of the past) and induce some kind of prevision of what is in store for them in future years.

What then is, in the most general terms, the question that suggests itself? I suppose it is the question whether in the future our conception of Archives, and arising from that our conception of the part Archivists are to play in the work of the world–whether these are to alter. Basically, I think they are not. I see from the review in *Archives* of a little book in 561 pages on *Archivkunde* recently published in Germany that a Manual of my own is 'beginning to show signs of age; experience, practice and archive-theory are overtaking' it. I am to some extent consoled by observing that my book shares that disability with the work of Fruin and Casanova: but while admitting that practice and experience can hardly have failed to advance quite far (perhaps even so far as to overtake me!) in a period of over thirty years I find myself wondering whether, if what I said about Archive Theory (that is about the fundamentals of Archives and Archive-keeping) was true in 1922, it is not true still.

---

[1] This paper was given as a Presidential Address to the Annual General Meeting of the Society of Archivists on 15 December 1955.

[2] The Record Office possessed, I believe, one typewriting machine, but the Secretary's official letters were written normally by his own hand or that of a clerk.

There are, of course, people who say in effect 'The whole position in regard to Archives – both their material character and their importance – is changing and will continue to change. Archives began with the discovery that if a sufficient number of people could read and write the bounds of administrative activity might be enormously extended by the substitution of written for oral communications: the implementing of that discovery went on for centuries and with it went the development of Archives. But now development is proceeding in the reverse direction: equipped with telephones, motor-cars and aeroplanes we are getting back to the oral, substituting it for written communication. Moreover, Writing itself, when it is used, thanks to stenography and typewriters and photographic reproduction and the rest, is quite a different thing from what it used to be. Surely all these considerations must make it necessary to revise our views about the nature and treatment of Archives?'

People who say that forget, I think, that the mere manufacture of documents is only one element in the creation of Archives: another and a much more potent one is their preservation for reference; that is to say their substitution not merely for the spoken word but for the fallible and destructible memory of the people who took part in whatever the transactions may have been that gave rise to them. *Recordari* still means, as it meant in the twelfth century, to remember. So long as memory is a necessary part of the conduct of affairs so long will it be necessary to put that memory into a material form, and so long as that is necessary so long will you have Archives; whether they take the form of writing on paper or parchment or palm-leaves by hand or that of steel tape (shall we say) engraved by mechanical means with microscopic grooves which enable you to reproduce at will the voices of men who forget or have been themselves forgotten. No one denies that the technical problems of the Archivist, and the equipment required for dealing with them, have changed, will change in our own day, and must be expected to go on changing; the steel tape will require quite different conditions for its storage and use from those appropriate to paper. But the principles on which the Archivist must base his treatment of these new problems and new materials remain, I submit, unaltered because Archives will still be, as they have always been, the Documents in the Case: requiring, before we can be sure that we have their significance correctly, a full knowledge of their administrative background, but entailing, for the Archivist, no primary duties other than those he has always had – the duties of *Conserving the Evidence* and of *Communicating it to the Student Public*; with anything in the way of special technique which the material and nature of the Evidence, and the circumstances of the Public's enquiries, may render necessary.

I may perhaps be allowed (it is indeed the main theme of my Address) to come back to this later, if only by way of peroration. For the moment I turn to a consideration in more detail of some of the changes which our own age is witnessing or which may be readily and reasonably predicted. In doing so I shall assume, if you will allow me, that you are all potentially, as many of you are in fact, so closely connected with the active conduct of affairs that you must be prepared to receive more or less regular accruals of Documents no longer required for current business: and in describing the changes which these may entail in your existing procedure and equipment shall not, for the moment, consider the question how those changes are to be effected.

The most obvious are those which are and will be resulting from the vast increase in bulk, the decrease in quality, of many of the existing classes of Archives: with which we may couple changes in the form of well-known classes (*Ledgers*, to take a sad example) which retain their old titles but not their old character; largely as a result of mechanization. Apart from accentuating, so far as it may be considered to affect the Archivist, the importance of the all-but-insoluble problem of Elimination, these changes will induce in time, if they have not already done so, modifications in every section of your work. In the Repository there will probably be alterations in your established system of make-up, packing and racking; and there will certainly be recurrent demands for more space. In the Repairing Room new methods will be necessary to enable you not only to deal with quantities hitherto unthought of but also to defeat the menace of that sheeted saw-dust which now so often passes for paper: something like the American system of lamination (mistrusted hitherto–perhaps unjustly–in this country) will certainly have to be considered–indeed it is urgent that this matter should be the subject of fresh investigation:[3] and later perhaps (who knows?) you may have to add to the qualifications of your operatives devices borrowed from the metal-worker or the cinema industry. In Search Rooms the time may not be far off when space and equipment must be provided not only for the use of microphotographs but also for the examination (has not Bernard Shaw predicted it?) of pictorial and sound recordings in the shape of discs, strips and reels of strange materials; and allied to these requirements is the immediate need for photographic equipment which will enable all Repositories to cater in modern fashion for that familiar (and rather tiresome) client, the 'student at a distance'. Already, when I left the Public Record Office, the photographic Staff, though it had been in existence for less than ten years, had swelled to the proportion of nearly ten per cent of the total personnel.

    That last remark raises in turn the whole question of the effect of modern quantities and modern types of Document upon the policy of Publication. Clearly the old methods of providing by means of printed Transcripts, Calendars and so forth for the needs of the Student who could not or would not make personal search–the method which in the case of the Public Records has proved inadequate to deal in reasonable time even with the relatively small survivals of medieval material[4]–must be far more insufficient when confronted with the sheer quantity of modern Archives. We are driven more and more to look for, and content ourselves with, methods of 'making public' which will rely much less on printing; giving the Student no more in that form (save in exceptional cases) than will enable him to embark economically and intelligently on the task of personal examination, with such additional aids as Photography and other mechanical devices can now supply.

    Altogether, you will say, an ambitious programme: and please do not think I am unaware of that fact, and of the difficulties (financial ones, for example) that must be overcome before such developments as I have sketched can be realized, because in a short address I merely summarize uncompromisingly the new duties and new fashions that lie ahead of you. When I say that the same process of patient endeavour which has brought you so far will be required to carry you so much further it is with a strong conviction that that endeavour, and that patience, will be forthcoming.

    But we are verging here upon major problems; and the first of them–from which indeed the others all stem–is a question not merely of numbers but of relative numbers: I mean the growing preponderance of Modern over Ancient Archives. We are faced–you will be faced, if I am not wrong–not only with the technical problems I have just described as resulting from the spate of modern Documents and development of modern techniques but with problems of policy resulting from the fact that the proportion of Modern to Ancient is constantly changing, to the disadvantage of the Ancient. The numbers of these last–though we are all doing our best to increase the tale of those known and cared for–are in a sense static, whereas those of the Modern are continually increasing: and (what is more) a like ratio is to be observed in the numbers of Students using the one or the other. When I entered the Record Office the intrusion of comparatively modern Documents from Public Departments had of course begun–it began in fact in the early nineteenth century so soon as it came to be known that there was now a place where such things could be dumped– but they were little regarded: to say that a Student was working in the Search Rooms was to assume, with only a few well-marked exceptions, that the documents to be produced to him or her

---

[3] In this connexion the work of Mr W. J. Barrow, of Richmond, Virginia, may be commended to the attention of any who have not already studied it.

[4] Sixty years of work and something like two hundred large volumes have not quite finished dealing with the medieval Enrolments and a few other classes of the Chancery; have barely touched the six great series of the Exchequer (not to mention important subsidiaries); and have only begun on the vast Records of the Courts of Law.

were, at the latest, of the seventeenth or very early eighteenth centuries. I need hardly say that the position now is very different and since such influences as the London School of Economics and Ph.D. degrees in all the Universities began to make themselves felt the number of Students who, for their researches, choose the primrose path that is not embarrassed by the initial obstacles of Court Hand, Latin and the like has grown enormously while that of the medievalists has sensibly declined.

You may say that from the point of view of the Archivist, whose business it is (as I have myself so often insisted) to minister to the researches of others rather than to conduct, or even suggest them himself, this tendency (however regrettable) is not a matter of great moment: but we are threatened by two other results of this unwieldy growth of Modern Archives which touch us more nearly. The first is the suggestion that the care of the Modern ought to be divorced from that of Ancient Records. This is not altogether a new idea – I heard it advocated many years ago as a solution to the housing problem of the Public Record Office – but recently it has been sometimes advanced as a serious theory of Archive Organization; with special reference to the alarm which began to be felt at high levels (not before it was time) about the monstrous accumulations of paper in Public Departments and to the Report of Sir James Grigg's Committee on that subject recently presented to Parliament by the Chancellor of the Exchequer.[5] Any proposals which may ensue would of course affect directly only the Public Records: but accepted theories touching the conduct of these are bound to have ultimately (it is natural and proper that they should) some repercussion at the level of Local Government; and the question is therefore one upon which all Archivists should have clear views. I ought not, within the limits which I have set myself for this Address, to attempt to influence your opinions by expression of my own: but there are two or three permissible and even desirable observations to be made which are of a factual nature. I will make them as briefly as possible.

In the first place, then, in any case where a single Authority is the natural custodian of Ancient Archives and also the regular producer of Modern ones it would almost certainly be found uneconomical to administer the two separately, because that would mean doubling staff and accommodation in certain sections. Secondly, it would be inconvenient for Students, whose period of research would frequently transcend any artificially fixed boundary between old and new. Also since presumably any Authority which adopted the plan would fix its own date for the division, and since in addition many Authorities having Archives of a like standing but not large enough to make action imperative would not adopt it at all, there would be confusion as to where Archives of certain types were to be found in any given case. A third objection, and perhaps the most serious though it is not easy to express in few words, is that the plan not only imposes upon natural accumulations of Archives purely artificial (i.e. unnatural) divisions but also involves breaches of that continuity which is one of the most precious attributes of English Administration and Archives, Central, Local and Private alike. Even if the actual breaking of long continuous series were barred there would still be a breach when modern series were separated (as could hardly be avoided) from their predecessors in function under the same Authority. Imagine (to take an obvious example) the deterioration in the Public Records as Archives of the Central Government, if the Records of the Chancery, the Privy Seal Office, the Secretaries of State and Modern Departments, successive holders of the chief executive control, were sundered. It would be almost as disastrous as lopping off a fine tree a few feet from its roots: and that remark is not merely sentimental; for in numerous cases the significance of the later Records in a long series (such as those of the Exchequer or the Justices of the Peace) can only be appreciated by a scholar who is familiar with the earlier ones in the same series, or even in a different series, out of which they have developed; nor, *per contra*, are there wanting cases where the key to what has puzzled us in the earlier is to be found in the later.

[5] *Report of the Committee on Departmental Records* (Cmd. 9163), 1954.

I am afraid I have rather extended myself over these points of danger: but there is a final and a very serious one which must not be omitted–the potential danger to the professional standards of the Archivist; for (to speak quite frankly) there will be a tendency (no one who has had experience of dealing with Finance Divisions over questions of Staff can doubt it) to employ for the administration of Modern Archives, if that is made a separate affair, persons of a lower educational grade, or, at least, persons not qualified by special training to act as Archivists.

That last remark brings me to one more branch–the last, I think–of what I have to say about the changes which the future may hold for you: the possibility of changes in what I must call, for lack of a better word, the set-up of the Archivist's profession. I have said much of the dangers and embarrassments arising from that modern multiplication of Archives the prospect of which–more than the prospect, the fact; for it is already in being–we all view with some dismay: but what of the multiplication of Archivists, which is (we must all agree) a consummation devoutly to be wished?

I have spoken of the danger of the un-trained Archivist: but we have to face the fact that what are in effect Archive Repositories (though they may not themselves realise it) number, if we include such items as the Church Chest, or, at the other end of a long scale, the strong-room of an Industrial or Commercial or Professional Body, many thousands; or, taking only the more important, many hundreds. What is to be the provision of Archive Services for these? In many cases they do not want, or cannot afford, or have not work for an individual Archivist: yet their Archives should certainly have the benefit of skilled organization; and the case cannot always be met by offers on the part of larger Repositories to take over their older Documents when these are no longer wanted for current work. Even if we leave aside this awkward problem and consider only the case of the really large modern organizations which may be converted (as indeed a few have been) to the view that their establishment should include a trained Archivist we have still to consider the question how that Archivist should be trained. There is, of course, no reason why they should not have one trained to deal with Documents of all periods even though their own are purely modern: indeed it would be a very good thing both for them and for us if they did. But there will be cases–probably many cases–in which, while agreeing that their Archivist should have high educational qualifications, they will press, and not without reason, in view of the very nature of their Archives, for persons whose earlier academic training has been in Science rather than in the Humanities: and for such our present system of Graduate training for Archive work has little room. I am aware that we approach here a problem, or series of problems, of considerable difficulty: but there is no doubt that it will have to be faced. There are in fact signs already of a demand for Archivists with a knowledge of such subjects as Metallurgical Chemistry comparable to your own knowledge of Latin and History; and even a suggestion of the way in which the further requirements of such Students might be met in the tentative proposals which have been made for the setting up, parallel with the existing Diploma Courses in Librarianship and Archives, of a third intended for the training of Information Officers, especially those of large Industrial and Commercial Concerns. If a suitable measure of Archive Science were included in that training our desire that persons charged with the care of Archives of that kind should be properly qualified might be fulfilled. On the other hand it is easy to see troubles arising from the importation of such a new element into the Archivist's profession.

I must not on the present occasion attempt to deal with this complex problem in more detail: but it will arise–is arising already–and who, we may wonder, is going to set about solving it? As you know there have been in preparation, since 1943, proposals for Legislation which, among other things, would set up a National Council of Archives; and it would be an obvious and early task for such a body. But I fear we must face the fact that the prospects of our Bill are at the moment not good: and, failing the Bill, what can–what ought–to be done? The interests involved are directly interests of members of this Society: but the Society, though the progress it has made in a very short time is truly remarkable, is not as yet strong enough to shoulder by itself such a responsibility; nor is it in some respects suitable that it should do so: and indeed in securing for existing Repositories some of the improvements in staff and equipment (not to mention conditions of employment) which are implicit in what I said earlier of the changes produced by the increasing bulk of modern accruals, and in exploring all kinds of technical matters such as the policy to be pursued in elimination, the possibility of common action in the Listing of Maps or seals, and in general the establishment of stronger relations between Repository and Repository – in such tasks as these it will have for many years to come very sufficient employment. Yet the future welfare not so much of Archivists as individuals but of the Archivists' Profession is deeply concerned in the matter and I cannot conceive this Society being blind to that fact or failing in any effort it can usefully make. Moreover you have powerful allies: the National Register of Archives has also in a very short time achieved a wonderful success – greater than is generally realized – and its unofficial parent, the British Records Association, in a longer, but still remarkably brief, space of time, has carried the work of peaceful penetration for the ideas of its founders much further than they themselves ventured to hope when they founded it. If you need one more heartening illustration of the progress that has already been made you need only take the fact, which I ventured to stress in the Catalogue of that Exhibition at Grocers' Hall to which so many of you contributed, of the creation within that same short period, without any legislative or official encouragement, of properly equipped and staffed Archive Repositories in a large majority of the Counties of England and Wales, in a considerable number of other units of Local Government (not forgetting the great Libraries) and in various Academic institutions.[6]

Twenty years ago I remember G. H. Fowler, the founder of that first County Archive organization at Bedford which has been the model of so many others, lamenting to me that he 'had not founded a school'. I wish he could have lived to see how wrong was his prediction as to the result of his own work in his own field: but I think he would have joined me in projecting further extensions of that field. For I believe that if close co-operation between our Society, the Society of practising Archivists, and the two bodies I have named, the National Register and the Records Association, can be secured (and I welcome very heartily – as the Master of the Rolls did at the Records Association's Conference – the steps that have been taken towards that end during the past year), and if those three can be reinforced by further co-operation with the great Commercial, Industrial and Professional Bodies who at present stand to a large extent outside our orbit but whose Archives engage so frequently the attention of modern Students – if that can be achieved we may go forward (with or without statutory recognition) towards a new goal: the goal of an Archive Service for this country not only complete within its present cadre but extending to all the fields in which human effort produces Records that can be used for the furtherance of human knowledge.

I have tried elsewhere to put into a few words a clear and simple conception of what it is the Archivist's public service to do: a kind of Philosophy of Archives hammered out first while I was waiting for bombs to fall on Chancery Lane in 1940. Perhaps you will allow me in concluding this Address to use the words once more though they have now seen print three times – first in a wartime article in the *Contemporary Review*, then in an Inaugural Address for the Diploma Course in Archives at University College, and last at The Hague when I used them in winding up a discussion in which speakers from various countries gave various views about the training of the Archivist. On that occasion I was told that a distinguished foreign Archivist remarked that what I had said made unnecessary what had gone before. I quote that not (please believe me) because it tickled my vanity

---

6 Even while I was writing this I received a letter from one of the older Universities speaking of the satisfactory development and increasing use of 'The University Department of Archives'.

but because I believe it to be true and the words in question to be applicable to all manner of Archives, past, present and to come. I said, then, that *the Creed of the Archivist was the Sanctity of Evidence; his Task, the Preservation in the Documents committed to his charge of everything that was Evidential; his Aim, without prejudice or afterthought, to make available for all who wished to know the Means of Knowledge.* You may find better wording: but if you can adopt that Creed, accept that Task, achieve that Aim, then I may wish you, with complete confidence that the wish will come true (whatever the Archives which Fate may send you), Success in this new Profession of ours, for which you have already done so much and may do so much more; Good Fun (why not?) with Good Fortune; Good Luck and Good Hunting.

HILARY JENKINSON

The
Record Commissions
1800–37

To both historian and archivist, the work of the six Record Commissions between 1800 and 1837 is of interest.[1] The historian's interest springs from the fact that the results of the Commissions' work bore fruit in the opening up of the public archives to his predecessors and so made available the vast mass of documents, accumulated naturally over the centuries by the central organs of justice, finance and administration. The archivist's interest lies in the picture presented to him of the incredible chaos existing in the complex of repositories of public archives scattered up and down the country, with a heavy preponderance of them within the cities of London and Westminster, and in the light thrown on archival theories and practices of the day. For both, the ultimate outcome of the Commissions, the establishment of the Public Record Office in 1838, represents an event of unequalled importance in the practice and growth of the two professions.

No Royal Commission issues without preliminary agitation or motivation, and the first of the Record Commissions, dated 19 July 1800, was no exception. On 9 October 1799, Charles Abbot (later 1st Baron Colchester), M.P. for Helston, gave notice of his intention to move the setting up of a Select Committee of the Commons to inquire into the state of the Public Records. All who have an interest, either professionally or as users, in the national archives of the United Kingdom and of the now Republic of Eire, must always regard Abbot with some large measure of gratitude, for it was his initiative which set in train the sequence of events which ultimately led to the Public Records Act of 1838 and all that has since flowed from that. On 18 February 1800, seconded by the then Master of the Rolls, Abbot's motion was agreed to by the Commons, and a Committee of 15 members, of which Abbot was Chairman, was appointed 'to inquire into the State of the Public Records of this kingdom, and of such other Public Instruments, Rolls, Books and Papers as they shall think proper; and to report to the House the Nature and Condition thereof; together with what they shall judge fit to be done for the better Arrangement, Preservation and more convenient Use of the same'. Barely four and a half months later, on 4 July, Abbot's Committee presented its report, which was ordered to be printed and this folio volume contains within its covers the results of the first large scale investigation into the public records, properly so called, and into many other groups of archives and manuscripts not so strictly, if at all, public records, using the two words as the conventional English synonym for the national archives.

---

[1] This is a slightly amended text of a public lecture delivered at University College, London, on 9 March 1959, under the auspices of the School of Librarianship and Archives.

[See also Lester J. Cappon, 'Antecedents of the Rolls Series: issues in historical editing', *Journal of the Society of Archivists*, vol. 4 no. 5 (April 1972) for a discussion of the work of the Record Commissions. Ed.]

Although the 1800 Committee and the subsequent Commissions concerned themselves with Scottish records, this phase of their activities is one which could more aptly and profitably be told by someone with a more detailed knowledge of Scottish law and administration than the present writer would pretend to.[2] For similar reasons, the work of the Irish Record Commission after its establishment in 1810, which has added value as a result of the disastrous losses in Dublin during 'the Troubles', awaits treatment by others more skilled and knowledgeable.

Both for its own sake and for a proper understanding of what followed, the Report of the Select Committee of 1800 is deserving of more than cursory attention. Whereas previous investigations into the public records had been chiefly *ad hoc* inquiries relating to particular offices or collections of documents, as for example the inquiry into the disastrous Cottonian fire or the Exchequer records, or at the most a limited inquiry into a relatively small number of London repositories, as was the case with the Lords' Committees of the 1720s, the inquiry of 1800, carried out chiefly by questionnaire, probed into some three to four hundred repositories of records from the greater warehouses of the Tower and the Chapter House at Westminster, to the offices of Clerks of the Peace of counties, from the British Museum to the Inns of Court, from the chapters of cathedrals to, by passing reference, the parish chests of rural England. From the returns to the questionnaire and with the aid of personal visits to repositories in London, the Committee compiled a report, remarkably searching and far-seeing in its recommendations, considering the drawbacks of its method of working and the limited time spent on its investigations. The principal restrictions which it placed on its inquiries were the refusal to deal with documents relating to revenue or war – hardly to be wondered at in view of the struggle with Napoleon – and their 'forbearing to enquire into the Existence of any Public Documents contained in private collections, the local situation of which must always be uncertain, and the Possession transitory'. The work of a later Royal Commission, that on Historical Manuscripts, still happily energetically fulfilling its terms of reference, shows in one sense how wise Abbot was in his forbearance, but how mistaken as to the uncertainty of location and transitoriness of possession his Committee has proved to be.

The Committee's Report deals first with the actual buildings in which the records were housed and a bewildering variety of repositories came to light. The Clerk of Assizes, Home Circuit, kept his records in his chambers in the Temple although, until he received the questionnaire from the Committee, all records earlier than 1780 had been kept in the Haberdashers' Hall, his father having been Clerk to the Company as well as Clerk of Assize. Chancery records were scattered through numerous offices and repositories, likewise Exchequer records; in both cases, in buildings of uneven quality. Chests, presses, cupboards, linen bags, bundles, chaotic piles of paper and parchment were all scattered throughout these buildings, in which damp, fires, candles and even gunpowder were potential sources of destruction. The Committee, finding that many of these courtesy 'repositories' were private buildings, recommended that these should, if convenient, be purchased or else the contents moved to public buildings. Some repositories required extensive repair, even rebuilding; the Exchequer of Receipt adjoining Westminster Hall should be rebuilt and secured from 'the Hazards of Fire', the State Paper Office in Scotland Yard, and the Heralds' Office likewise should be rebuilt.

In an attempt to prescribe certain standards for archival preservation, the Committee obtained special reports from Thomas Astle, Keeper of Records at the Tower, John Topham, a Commissioner at the State Paper Office, Joseph Planta, Principal Librarian at the British Museum, and John Caley, Keeper of Records at the Augmentation Office. All show differences of opinion on the best ways of storing records – in chests, presses or bags on open shelves, on the need for air circulation and on the materials and format for archival documents and writing materials. Astle's views,

---

[2] [See below, pp. 19–26, 'The Record Commissions and Scotland', Peter Gouldesbrough. Ed.]

sounder perhaps than the others, may serve to show one professional's opinion. Whilst favouring parchment he saw no objection to paper volumes, provided they were kept free of damp and dust. Both books and rolls were 'proper for records'. He disapproved of bags or chests as storage receptacles, preferring presses, set three inches from the wall, with air holes front and back. Racks admitted air too much, in his view. The Royal Society should be asked to draw up a specification for a permanent archival ink.

For the better arrangement and use of the public records, the Committee recommended that the very considerable number of calendars and indexes of record classes, which were the private property of individual keepers of records, should be purchased for public use. In those many offices with incomplete or defective means of reference, work should immediately be begun to remedy the defects and bring the finding aids to a state of completeness. This was to be done either by the present staff or by way of separate commissions for individual offices after the model of the existing State Paper Commission. Particularly in need of attention were the records of Clerks of the Peace, especially documents relating to inclosure, highways, gaols. A completely revised catalogue to the Harleian MSS. in the British Museum was needed. Generally, however, the Committee, on the information before it, felt that means of reference to the records were adequate, a view which is a little hard to reconcile with the statement elsewhere in the report that, from personal observation, they found much confusion in and lack of knowledge of the contents of repositories.

The Committee did not favour proposals to gather together in one repository all records of a particular series, since this would upset the present arrangement of the records to which many finding aids were closely tied. It did, however, suggest that steps be taken to urge upon parochial clergy the need for a more regular transmission of the annual transcripts of parish registers to diocesan or peculiar registries. Whilst not in favour of piecemeal transfers, the Committee did favour a wholesale transfer to a central repository on the lines of the General Register House in Edinburgh, 'a useful model for Imitation', and included plans of the Register House as an appendix to the Report should the idea be taken up and pursued.

The establishment of the various repositories required regulation, in the Committee's opinion. Where no one was officially in charge of the custody and arrangement of a department's records, then an officer should immediately be made responsible, the defects in the Lord Treasurer's Remembrancer's Office being singled out as an example of defective arrangements. Payment by fees rather than salary was the general rule and the Committee, wishing to see the records more easily and cheaply available to the public, recommended that in these cases payment should be partly by salary and partly by fees, and that the general level of fees should be greatly reduced.

Since the only way to make the contents of any repository known and generally available to enquirers, as all historians and archivists know, is to publish guides, lists, indexes, calendars and even texts in extenso, it is no surprise to find the Committee recommending as a 'most essential measure' the printing of some of the principal calendars and indexes and such unpublished records 'as are the most important in their Nature and the most perfect of their kind'. Having taken the advice of experts, the Committee suggested the publication, amongst others, of the Index to Domesday Book, the calendars to the early Curia Regis and King's Bench Rolls, indexes to the Patent, Close, Charter and Fine Rolls and to the Chancery series of Inquisitions Post Mortem, to the Conventual and Crown Leases of the Augmentation Office. Printed in a similar format to the Journals of Parliament, these finding aids would, the Committee estimated, fill some 16 or 17 volumes. Original records which the Committee considered worth publishing in extenso were the Hundred Rolls, Nonae Rolls, Testa de Nevil, Red Book of the Exchequer, Statutes of the Realm in a complete and authoritative edition, the Dialogus de Scaccario and a continuation of Rymer's Foedera to 1688 or 1714, that most ill-starred of all the projects of both Committee and Commissions.

Two further recommendations are worth notice. The first, still not fully implemented, was the need for a general registry of deeds on the lines of the existing Middlesex Registry. More important and a forerunner of later action was the expressed wish for authority to destroy documents, which it would be useless or inconvenient to preserve. One can only attribute the Committee's unfortunate choice of the Exchequer Port Books to illustrate this recommendation to a lack of technical knowledge and to the rudimentary state of archival theory at the period, if any theory can be said to have existed.

To carry out its recommendations, the Select Committee of the Commons suggested the appointment of a Royal Commission, to which the House assented. On 11 July 1800 they addressed the King for directions towards the 'better preservation, arrangement and more convenient use of the public records of the Kingdom'; any such directions would be 'chearfully provided for and made good by the faithful Commons'–cheerfulness which by 1836 had soured somewhat. On 19 July, with commendable speed, the first of the series of Commissions was issued and the work of implementing to a greater or lesser degree the various recommendations of Abbot's Committee began. It began with enthusiasm and a sense of high endeavour, largely due to Abbot's leadership. On his retirement in 1816 from the Speakership of the Commons and after his tour abroad in 1819–22, he played a lesser part in the Commissions' affairs, and the period between 1819 and 1831 is marked by little of significance as compared with the years before and after. The sixth and final Commission of 1831, despite the heated controversy surrounding its activities and the person of the Secretary, Joseph Purton Cooper, did much to create a better informed and consequently more highly critical opinion on matters archival in England. From the furore which surrounded its endings came the Public Record Office, and that in itself would have been a sufficiently worthwhile conclusion to the labours of the Record Commissioners.

The idea of one central repository for all the records of the departments of central government was mooted in 1800, but it was not until the Act of 1838 that the idea became legislative reality, and a further decade and a half was necessary to see the reality of a building into which the central archives of England were gathered. Each successive report of the Commissioners served to underline and emphasize with increasing force the need for centralization. Apart from any reasons of administrative economy, the virtual denial of justice to litigants, poor and rich alike, and the inaccessibility of the records to gentlemen of literary and historical bent were echoed in succeeding reports and cogently argued in favour of a single repository. Eventual financial economy was strongly pressed as a reason in favour in the General Report of the Commissioners in 1837.

The confusion and scattering of repositories throughout London and Westminster is only too obvious from the successive enquiries made on behalf of the Commissions. From Westminster to the Tower, the archives of the kingdom were scattered in penny numbers, the archives of any one department being rarely all in one repository.

Not merely were repositories scattered, but the great bulk were unsuitable as places for the permanent storage of archives. The principal Chancery repository at the Tower was too near the gunpowder in the main magazine for the liking of the Commission–or for the liking of the Master-General and Board of Ordnance for that matter. The records in the Chapter House at Westminster were exposed to the danger of kitchen fires, and the Pipe Rolls were, at one stage, exposed to the noisome damp of the cellars at Somerset House. The disastrous fire of 16 October 1834, which destroyed the Houses of Parliament, was a painful reminder and pointed example of the dangers to which the records were directly exposed and, as the damage to the records of the Augmentation Office shows, indirectly exposed. Examples could be multiplied of the shocking conditions in which the records were kept.

In the 1830s, the criticism was levelled at the Commission that it had done nothing positive to remedy either the confusion or the buildings, but no Commission had the power to do anything practical in the way of rebuilding from its own funds. They could only advise and recommend.

Others had to find the money, and this was no easy task in time of war and post-war stringency. Some improvements were made, a new State Paper Office came into being, repairs and amendments were made in various places but, as the 1837 Report says, such piecemeal scratchings of the surface in no appreciable way contributed either to the better preservation of, or improved access to, the records themselves. The only radical solution was one office for all. Cooper's pamphlet of 1832, approved by the Commission, with its plans for a General Record Office, heralded the one concrete plan produced by any of the Commissions to solve the problem. In 1833, with the cooperation of Sir John Leach M.R., the Commission procured plans and estimates for a repository, to be built on the Rolls Estate and financed by a £20,000 subvention from the Chancery Suitors' Fund. In 1834, a Bill was drawn up for introduction in Parliament to establish this central repository, which was to be controlled by the Record Commissioners. The Bill was badly drawn and ill conceived, and it is perhaps as well that its sponsor, John William Ponsonby, M.P. for Nottingham, was translated to the Lords as Lord Duncannon before he could introduce it. Considerable difficulties over the diversion of money from the Suitors' Fund would in no way have made its passage easier. In 1837 Charles Buller, M.P. for Liskeard, introduced yet another Bill into the Commons to carry out this scheme, but was thwarted by the death of William IV and the subsequent expiry of the last Record Commission. Eventually, the basic Act of 1838, superseded only in 1958, was passed and the Record Office was established.

As temporary palliatives to bad storage conditions, the Commissioners from time to time resorted to ill-conceived transfers from place to place in attempts to provide better physical preservation of the records. At various times, the records of King's Remembrancer, Common Pleas and Auditor of the Land Revenues had been moved from Westminster Hall to Charing Cross Mews, whence they were displaced by the National Gallery to Carlton House Riding School. Not merely had this and other moves cost the Commissioners, over the years, some £28,000, which would have provided a central repository, but they resulted in considerable losses of records themselves, to the profit of the labourers employed to move them and the glue-makers to whom they were sold. So great indeed did some feel the losses to have been that Sir Thomas Phillipps–of all people–told the 1836 Committee of Inquiry that he was of the opinion that greater losses had been suffered since the Record Commissioners began work than had occurred in the preceding 400 years. Such moves were hardly conducive to the 'better arrangement' of the records either, since every move only made chaos worse confounded.

Not that, by 1837, anyone had, as a general statement, anything to be proud of as far as arrangement of records in permanent repositories went. Space was lacking and the bulk of records was daily increasing, so that they were subjected to ever-changing expedients and shifts. Workmen in the employ of the Commission were put to re-arrangement in various repositories from time to time, but despite the £10,000 spent, the 1837 Report speaks of this as but a fraction of the sum needed. In 1831, for example, at the expiry of the fifth Commission, work of arrangement was going on in the Chapter House at Westminster, in the Augmentation Office, the Duchy of Lancaster Offices and the Rolls Chapel. Work was continued after 1831 at the Rolls Chapel, the Chapter House and the Augmentation Office. In the latter case, the fire of 1834 undid all that had been done and made it necessary to do it over again. The records of the King's Remembrancer were found in the utmost confusion at Carlton House and were taken into the Commission's own custody and re-arranged and repaired under the superintendence of Henry Cole, one of the best of the clerks employed by Cooper, with whom he quarrelled (not unnaturally) over the confusion in his terms of appointment and remuneration. The Pipe Rolls were sorted and re-arranged and, in preference to the enrolment series, the Chancery Miscellanea at the Tower were methodized and dealt with under the superintendence of Thomas Duffus Hardy. Despite the work reputedly done in the Rolls Chapel, the 1836 Committee found that the records were in a chaotic condition and that the quaint habit of pasting into volumes, from which they were detached by damping if required, still per-sisted. But the work of re-arrangement and sorting was not entirely without profit and the Com-missions' recommendations were not always unheeded. At the Tower, Parliamentary Writs were found from the reigns of Henry VI to Charles II, and in the Lord Treasurer's Remembrancer's Office the earliest known Pipe Roll of 26 Henry II came to light, whilst at Durham the only known text of Henry III's *Carta de Foresta* was discovered. As a result of the Commission's recommenda-tions, the Barons of the Exchequer ordered a more regular keeping of records and the annual pro-duction in court of a certificate by the keepers of the Court's records that all was well. The 1837 Report acknowledges that the progress had been, on the whole, small.

For this reason, there is ground for the criticisms voiced by the 1836 Committee about the lack of work and achievement towards the second objective of the Record Commissions–that of making the records more available by the compilation of calendars and indexes. So long as the docu-ments themselves were badly housed and in confused order, the production of calendars and indexes was always sadly in arrear or even neglected. Almost without exception, the work of calendaring and indexing, whether done by clerks in the employment of the Commission or by the existing staff of public offices, was confined to the larger repositories. If the various reports are to be believed, the Chapter House records must have been dealt with at least twice. The Chancery records in the Tower and the records of the Lord Treasurer's Remembrancer's Office were extensively worked on during the period 1800–1819, and in 1837 the Commission reported that work was still in progress on the Tower records. In lesser offices and repositories, where the need for even rudimentary finding aids was greatest, virtually nothing appears to have been done. The early Commissions went so far as to print a number of their calendars–to the Chancery enrolments, the Lord Treasurer's Remem-brancer's Originalia rolls, and to inquisitions post mortem and ad quod damnum. But subsequent work of re-arrangement rendered some of these useless. Nonetheless, the early Commissioners achieved something, whilst the sixth Commission failed to complete a single calendar or index to official records, producing instead lists, of doubtful value, of papers in private hands or of foreign archives bearing on English history. The 1800 Committee strongly recommended the purchase for public use of calendars and indexes, which were the private property of keepers of records. Useful though this might have been, none were purchased though negotiations were in some cases started and then broken off because the price asked was too high. As producers of primary finding aids to the vast accumulations of records into which they were inquiring, the Record Commissioners were singularly unproductive.

Not merely were the records inaccessible in the early 19th century by reason of their pro-fusion and confusion and because of the lack of adequate finding aids, they were virtually in-accessible for legal and historical purposes by virtue of the fees charged for inspection and the evils resulting from the completely non-uniform system then in force. Each Commission was charged to inquire into this and to effect reforms where possible. The 1812 Report blandly says that the Com-missioners had been unable to do anything, the 1819 Report is diplomatically silent. The 1831 Commissioners, more fortunate than their predecessors in having available the facts disclosed by the Fee Commission of 1818–22 and having the recommendations of that Commission behind them, were at least able to make some cogent comments and recommendations in their Report. Agreeing with their brother Commissioners of the Fees, they condemned the irregularities of the system, which amounted virtually to a tax on those who had cause to consult the records. Being largely, if not solely, paid by fees, many keepers of records charged exorbitant fees for inspection and copying, or for production in court, and that not on any uniform system. Seventy-two words made up a folio for copying purposes in one office, ninety in another, charges for production in various courts varied from office to office, even hours of inspection varied. Not only were the keepers maintained from the income from fees, but the records themselves; and in some cases, the fees were so small or the records so unproductive of revenue that there was little to spend on their preservation. The Commissioners were able to contribute a mite to improving matters, when certain minor reforms as a result of their advice were adopted at the Tower and when Palgrave was appointed sinecure keeper at the Chapter House. But the only possible way to bring order to chaos was to do away with the system completely and replace it either by some more regular and uniform method or by a system in which fees played a minor part and were not the sole source of revenue out of which staff and records alike were maintained.

In its report to the Commons, the Select Committee of Inquiry of 1836 into the affairs of the sixth Commission of 1831 pointed out that the order of the objects for which the various Commissions had been established was, in each case, set out in what could only be read as an order of relative importance; not a chance order but an accurate estimation of the value of each object. The Commissions were first to provide for better arrangement and preservation by methodizing and digesting the records and by repairing such as were in need of repair. Having seen to the physical care and control of the records, the next object was to provide for their more convenient use by the production of calendars and indexes, in the modern idiom, to establish intellectual control over the records. With the order, importance and necessity of these objects of all archival operations, no archivist–and one hopes, no historian–will today disagree. The third object of the Commission was to superintend the printing of such calendars and indexes and original texts as they might decide to print 'of the more ancient and valuable' from amongst the public records.

What the Commissioners did, or neglected to do in the views of their critics, in furtherance of their first two objects, has been dealt with in some small measure so far.

To the printing of original records, the Commissioners from the start devoted a considerable part of their energies and their parliamentary grant. And the severest criticisms of their activities were levelled against their publishing proclivities. In fairness to them, it should be said that the words of the 1800 Committee report–'a most essential measure would be to print some of the principal calendars and indexes and such original unpublished records as are the most important in their Nature and the most perfect in their kind'--could be pleaded in justification. And it is but a small step from understanding an indefinite 'a' to mean a very definite 'the'. If the first part of the measure had been heeded more closely, the Commissioners might not have been so open to criticism, for increased publication of calendars and indexes rather than a flow of record type texts would have been a fitting tribute to their labours.

The first two Commissions come out best, printing indexes to Domesday, calendars of Chancery enrolments and proceedings and inquisitions, and new or revised catalogues to the Cottonian, Harleian and Lansdowne MSS. in the British Museum. Although the imperfections and incompleteness of these do not exempt them or their compilers from criticism on these grounds, they do exempt them from any criticism of unproductiveness. The remaining Commissions, the sixth in particular, produced neither printed calendar nor index.

Increasingly as the Commissions' work proceeded, the publication of full texts took precedence over all other forms of archival guide. Indeed, one witness in 1836 somewhat pessimistically said that their efforts were likely to result in the substitution of an unfathomable sea of print for the unfathomable sea of manuscript. The sixth Commission employed four sub-Commissioners–Hunter, Palgrave, Stevenson and, for a time, Caley–in the work of editing for publication, a number of *ad hoc* editors, and a considerable number of clerks, whom Cooper misguidedly and loosely called sub-Commissioners to his subsequent discomfiture, when T. D. Hardy and Henry Cole quarrelled with him over their exact terms of appointment. Certainly the sixth Commission's publications are of a higher standard than those of their predecessors, but, as the 1836 Committee observed, they gave no great works to the world as their predecessors had done, but rather continued series begun in previous years–Curia Regis rolls and Inquisitions post mortem–or else began new series of a similar kind–the various Chancery enrolled series and the Privy Council Acts. The appendixes to the 1836 Inquiry report give some interesting figures about the cost of publications– Sir Harry Ellis' *Introduction to Domesday* in two volumes, of which in common with all publications, except the *Statutes of the Realm*, 500 copies were printed, cost in all £644 14 0, the editor's fee being £300 and the remainder going on costs of production; Harris Nicolas's five volumes of *Privy Council Proceedings* cost in all £2,132 2 11 of which £750 was Nicolas's fee as editor, the rest production costs. A revised Rymer was one of the desiderata listed by the 1800 Committee and an attempt was made to comply with this by the earlier Commissions. The 1831 Commission soon suspended work in progress after investigating what their predecessors had done. They had found little new material to print, they had reprinted badly and without adequate collation texts already in the earlier *Foedera* and could hardly be said to have done more than republish what was already in print. Entrusting the work to Cooper, the sixth Commission determined to comply with the recommendation that an extended and revised work be issued and, with typical energy and verve, Cooper set about the task. He employed clerks in England to search for and transcribe new materials, he corresponded widely with European archives and manuscript centres and employed transcribers in most major countries on the Commission's behalf. He drew up schemes and had them printed for the Commissioners, but in the end less was accomplished in the way of publication than before. £3,000 was spent and nothing printed. Yet the transcripts from Europe still have use. The exact value of some of these various publications to the historian is perhaps debatable. What can be said is that they served the extremely valuable purpose of opening up to the English academic world the national archives of the kingdom at a time when systematic editing of series of public records was a novelty indeed. Whether the Commissions chose wisely in their selection of records to publish is open to question, but they had to choose and with no great experience or experienced body of users behind them. Two interesting sidelights on Cooper's management of the publishing side of the Commission's affairs are his attempt to establish an English *École des Chartes* and the considerable library he built up, on which he spent some £1,600. On the first of these, Cooper's own statement to the Committee in 1836 and the Commissioners' Report of 1837 are both somewhat vague. Unlike preceding Commissions, that of 1831 had taken a wider view of the purpose and value of transcripts, at least in their early days. Not only did they look upon them as essential preliminaries to printing and as one means of possible safeguard against loss of originals, but also for a time, under Cooper's urging, as a cheaper means than printing of making records available by depositing the transcripts in the British Museum. In order to create a trained supply of young transcribers, Cooper set up an embryonic course for young clerks taken on by the Commission, which, had it been more systematically run and encouraged, might have resulted an English equivalent of the French *École des Chartes*. It soon died of inanition and, unfortunately, little came of it but criticism. To help both the School of Transcribers and editorial staff generally, Cooper built up an impressive library of reference works ranging from a dictionary of abbreviations in documents emanating from civil and ecclesiastical courts, published in Cologne in 1577, catalogues of European collections of manuscripts and 19 folio volumes of the *Magnum Bullarium Romanum* to four copies of the 1776 edition of Wright's *Court Hand Restored*, Kelham's French dictionary and several copies of the 1719 Lords' Committee's Reports. Indeed, some 16 close printed pages of the 1836 Report are taken up with Cooper's catalogue of this library.

It was never expected that publication would pay for itself. From sale of the first Commission's publications between 1810 and 1822, some £3,354 9 6 was received, a rough average of £300 a year. The income from the publications of the sixth Commission between 1831 and 1835, according to the return of Baldwin and Craddock, the official retailers, was in all £774 3 0 from which was deducted £258 1 0 as commission, trade expenses and allowances, leaving a total of £516 2 0 accounted for. Of the works issued in these years, only two could be said to be best sellers–

Cooper's two-volume account of the Public Records, which sold 144 copies at 30/- each, bringing in £216 and 87 copies of Ellis' *Introduction to Domesday* bringing in £130 10 0 at 30/- a copy.

The widespread free distribution of copies, whilst obviously working against an economic return, did not entirely preclude a better income. This distribution was from time to time the subject of Treasury inquiry and regulation. In 1810, the maximum permissible free distribution was fixed at 200, when the total number of copies printed was fixed at 1000 with the exception of the Statutes and *Foedera*. In 1822, this was reduced to 122, a figure which by 1831 had reached 161 by the addition of new recipients. Between 1831 and 1836, Cooper worked up the free list to 511 – although only 500 copies of each work were printed – selective distribution in London and the Universities being held to be one way of allowing supply to exceed demand, but the margin for sale was rarely very great. Cooper not only extended his domestic distribution, but brought the colonies and foreign states into his net. At home, 77 local authorities received sets or part sets of the publications – it would be interesting to know how many local archivists can put their hands on their authority's set today. That Cooper, unauthorized and unbidden by the responsible committee of the Commissioners, should have disposed of 16 tons of unsold copies of the earlier Commissioners' publications as waste paper is an interesting sidelight on his own estimation of their value – and perhaps explains some prices charged by booksellers today!

What has been said of the distribution of the Commissioners' works and their publishing activities is symptomatic of the general conduct of the affairs of the last Commission – a heavy concentration of executive power in the hands of their salaried secretary who, whatever one may say of his motives, enthusiasm and undoubted ability and drive, assumed too much authority and showed too few business-like qualities in his work. It was almost entirely Cooper who ran the sixth Commission, with the consent of Lord Chancellor Brougham and the help of a very small number of the named Commissioners. It was Cooper's activities which primarily unleashed the violent pamphlet war which preceded and helped to precipitate the 1836 Select Committee, and it was Cooper's activities, directly and indirectly, which figured overwhelmingly in the evidence taken by the Committee. From the start he conducted the Commission's finances in a most unsatisfactory way. The sixth Commission inherited a £15–£16,000 debt from its predecessors and, having paid off the major part of this, proceeded to run up a debt of £24,000 on its own account. The whole matter of publication and engagement of staff was in Cooper's hands, subject to the most perfunctory formal approval of the Commissioners. Editors were engaged and work begun without authority and even, in the case of Ellis's *Introduction to Domesday*, finished and printed before a formal minute authorizing the work was passed by the Commissioners. Strictly, only sub-Commissioners were authorized by the terms of the Commission to edit materials for publication, a rule more honoured in the breach than the observance. Even editors so extra-legally appointed had little safeguard against Cooper's attempting to welsh on their agreements, since none was ever given a formal contract or even saw an order of the Board of Commissioners authorizing their employment. The disputes which arose from this and from Cooper's loose designation of editors as sub-Commissioners are abundantly clear in the pamphlets and evidence given before the Committee.

Anyone who reads the 1836 Report and evidence can hardly blame Buller's Committee for so severely criticising and castigating the efforts of the last Commission, although they must in fairness agree with the Committee's view that, defects notwithstanding, the Commission had done much of value. They would agree, too, that some drastic reforms not only in the conduct of the affairs of the Commission itself, but in its whole *modus operandi* and objects were necessary. It is perhaps fortunate that both Buller's Bill and the Commission of 1831 were nullified by William IV's death.

Despite their considerable achievements and their many admitted failings, the Record Commissions of 1800–37 proved that only a radical remedy could cure the ills which beset the public records of the kingdom. That they themselves could not effect such a remedy *mere motu* was a defect inherent in their terms of appointment and cannot be held against them. What they did may be the subject of academic controversy today as it was the subject of violent and practical controversy in their own day, the rights and wrongs of what they did and how they did it can, with some cogency, still be argued. We may view their theories on archive administration with tolerance and occasional surprise, and we may disagree with some of the treatment they would mete out to the records themselves, but all this must be set against the fact that out of their work arose a climate of opinion favourable to the establishment of a national archives of England and for that historian and archivist alike owe them a debt.

PETER WALNE

The
Record Commissions
and Scotland

In Peter Walne's article on the Record Commissions, 1800–37,[1] he deliberately excluded from consideration the activities of the Commissioners in connection with Scottish records. It is the aim of this article to fill that gap.

The Select Committee of the Commons to inquire into the state of the Public Records made a number of recommendations on Scottish records and the appendix to its report of 1800 gives an interesting picture of the state of the records at the time. There was no lack of a central repository, the General Register House in Edinburgh having been in use since 1789. In addition to the General Repository under the supervision of the Lord Clerk Register, it contained a number of rooms occupied by clerks of courts or keepers of various registers. In these were kept the records of the particular offices concerned. In a number of cases only the most recent records were kept in these separate rooms, the earlier records having been transmitted to the General Repository. The Keeper of the General Minute Book of the Court of Session complained of his basement room that 'the Keeper, his Clerk, and those making Searches, cannot, owing to its Dampness, continue in it for any length of time'. Some officers kept most of their records in their rooms in the Register House, but their current records in another public office elsewhere.

Some groups of records in Edinburgh were kept outside the Register House. This applied particularly to the Court of Exchequer, which had some rooms in the Register House, but kept most of its records in its chambers in Parliament Square. The officials of the four Exchequer offices made a very detailed return which has been found most useful when their records were being listed in recent years in the Scottish Record Office. The records of the Lyon Office were kept in the Lyon Clerk's house in St Andrew's Square. He admitted having been offered a room in the Register House, but had refused it 'because it was not to his Taste'.

The Select Committee found in general that the situation in Scotland left 'very little Room for Improvement'. It did, however, recommend a number of changes. The heads under which these were arranged corresponded to those in England, but with one addition. Under this additional head of 'Registration' the Committee suggested some improvements in the framing of certain records, particularly local registers. It pointed out the unsatisfactory nature of the accommodation for the Exchequer records and that only a quarter of the Sheriff Courts throughout Scotland housed their records in buildings which were public property. It proposed the compilation of a general repertory of the contents of the Register House and indexes for certain records there and elsewhere in Edinburgh. It recommended the earlier transmission of records to the custody of the Clerk Register and

[1] [Originally published in the *Journal of the Society of Archivists*, II, 1, pp. 8–16. See above, pp. 9–18 Ed.]

the transmission of certain records not previously sent in. Under this head also it found it 'obviously proper that the Proceedings upon Special Commissions for the Trial of High Treason in Scotland, and all other Records now lodged in His Majesty's Offices of Record in England, which exclusively regard the internal Policy and Laws of That Part of the United Kingdom, should be transferred to the General Register House at Edinburgh'. It advised that the records of the Parliament of Scotland be printed, and perhaps also the earliest of the royal charters.

The Commissioners appointed under the first Record Commission first directed their attention to the last of these proposals. William and Alexander Robertson, Deputy Keepers of the Records, had reported to the Select Committee the existence of 'The Records of Parliament from the Year 1210 to the Year 1707'. On 4 November 1800 the Commissioners requested the Clerk Register to cause these records to be printed and also the 'antient Royal Charters'. On 19 December they appointed the Robertsons and James Ferrier as Sub-Commissioners to carry out the work. The Robertsons set to work and by early 1804 a volume of 826 folio pages entitled *Parliamentary Records of Scotland, 1240–1571*, was ready for publication. This volume represented 2476 of the 5558 MS. pages of transcript prepared by William Robertson and his sons Alexander and William.[2]

The first doubts about the quality of this volume were expressed in a letter from Robert Dundas, Chief Baron of Exchequer and himself one of the Record Commissioners, to Lord Frederick Campbell, the Clerk Register, on 7 March 1804.[3] Dundas suggested that, as William Robertson was now dead, another qualified person should be appointed to supervise the work. On 20 March James Ferrier wrote to the Clerk Register to say that the Lord President and Lord Advocate joined in recommending 'a Barrister (*sic*) of ten years standing, named Thomas Thomson'.[4] At their meeting on 14 December the Commissioners considered a report by Thomson on the deficiencies of the volume, decided to suspend its publication, and appointed Thomson their sole Sub-Commissioner in Scotland. It is with the activities (or sometimes lack of activity) of Thomas Thomson that the rest of this article will be concerned.

Thomson's criticisms of the suppressed volume were undoubtedly justified. The Robertsons had merely transcribed faithfully the volumes called the 'Acts of the Parliaments' in the Register House. Thomson pointed out that only from 1466 were these the actual official records. Even after that date no attempt had been made to correct the haphazard way in which some of the volumes had been put together or to fill gaps from other sources, such as the printed version of 1566. It is more doubtful whether we would now agree with Thomson's criticism that the Robertsons had failed to distinguish between the legislative and judicial functions of the Scottish Parliament but had printed the whole record as it stood. This criticism is admittedly partly justified by the fact that the Parliamentary records contain some material exactly corresponding to that in a separate judicial record, the Acts of the Lords of Council.

However much the Robertsons were at fault in the selection and arrangement of their original material, there is much to be said for their method of publication. They did not use 'record' type. Perhaps they went a little too far in eschewing all editorial corrections or additions. But at least they made it clear from what point in the MS. original any passage came. Users of Thomson's later edition of the *Acts of the Parliaments of Scotland* will know that the same cannot be said of that monumental work. In Thomson's *Acts of the Lords of Council*, printed from the two sources mentioned in the previous paragraph, an example can be found of four consecutive entries coming alternately from different sources without any adequate indication of the fact.

The Commissioners were soon pressing Thomson for his detailed proposals for the revised

---

[2] Scottish Record Office [hereafter S.R.O.], Copies of Record Commission Correspondence etc., vol. I, p. 210.
[3] *Ibid.*, vol. I, p. 1.
[4] *Ibid.*, vol. I, p. 9.

publication of the Parliamentary records and also for a publication of the Retours of Services of Heirs on the analogy of the English index to the Inquisitions Post Mortem. The time that he could devote to their work was limited by his ordinary business as an advocate, but during 1805 he sent proposals for the publication of the Retours and reported on the difficulties that would be involved in selecting material for publication in the early Parliamentary records. Lord Glenbervie visited Edinburgh during the year and had many consultations with him, and Thomson himself visited London during October and November to search for Scottish material there.[5] The Commissioners realised that his full-time services were required and at their meeting on 21 January 1806 they recommended his appointment to a new post of Deputy Clerk Register. The Royal Warrant for payment of his salary is dated 19 June and his commission from Lord Frederick Campbell 30 June 1806.[6]

Thomson's first concern was to review the whole field of his new responsibilities. His commission had instructed him to report annually to the Clerk Register, which he did regularly from 1807 to 1821. These reports were printed by the direction of the Commissioners. On 2 April 1807 he submitted a full report to them under the various heads of the recommendations of the Select Committee.[7] At their meetings of 25 and 30 July they considered his report. A number of its recommendations were referred to the law officers or presiding judges concerned. Thomson was directed to carry out some of his proposals himself and to report further on others. He was also instructed to report quarterly to the Commissioners. These reports were printed in the appendixes to his annual reports and from them can be traced the course of his various undertakings. His quarterly reports from 1822 to 1831 were later printed by the Record Commission.[8]

At this point it is convenient to refer to some other results of the Select Committee's recommendations and those of the Commissioners on the basis of Thomson's report of 1807. A new building for the Court of Exchequer was provided in terms of an Act of 1806.[9] Various improvements were made in the methods of compiling a number of registers by Acts of Sederunt of the Court of Session of 1808 and 1811 and by an Act of Parliament of 1809.[10] The records chiefly affected were the Register of the Great Seal, the Register of Deeds, the Registers of Sasines (titles to land), the Registers of Hornings and Inhibitions, the Register of Abbreviates of Adjudication and the Sheriff Court Registers of Deeds. (All other local Registers of Deeds were abolished.) In general it was provided that registers should be kept in volumes marked and issued blank by the Register House and should in many cases be returned within three months from the completion of each volume. The pages of these volumes were ruled with 30 lines and compilers were required to maintain an average of 200 words per page, or 157 words of Latin. Thomson had commented unfavourably on previous practice. He wrote that either 'the pages are crowded with words, in a minute or slender character' or 'for the sake of swelling the amount of the fees of Registration, the pages must be filled, or must appear to be filled, with a small number of words, written in large characters of awkward and most unseemly form'.[11] The Sheriffs and Stewarts Depute in the various counties were to report annually on their records to the Commissioners of Justiciary, who were to transmit the reports to the Clerk Register.[12]

It is not always clear which parts of Thomson's work were carried out directly for the Record Commissioners and which parts came under his normal duties as Deputy Clerk Register

[5] Cosmo Innes, *Memoir of Thomas Thomson*, Bannatyne Club 1854, p. 60.

[6] *First Annual Report of the Deputy Clerk Register*, Appx., pp. 5–8.

[7] *First Annual Report*, Appx., pp. 13–52.

[8] Appendix to *The Case of Robert Pitcairn, Esq.*, 1835.

[9] 46 George III, cap. 154.

[10] 49 George III, cap. 42.

[11] *Second Annual Report*, p. 10.

[12] For the later history of this system see John Imrie and Grant G. Simpson, 'The Local and Private Archives of Scotland', *Archives*, vol. III, no. 19, pp. 137–9.

and were financed from the ordinary resources of the Register House. However, the subjects on which he regularly reported to the Commissioners were the repair and re-binding of 'decayed records', the compiling of repertories, the transfer of records to the Register House, the transcription or calendaring of records either for publication or as finding aids in the repository, and the preparation of indexes.

Thomson started his repair programme with the Acts of the Lords of Council. 'On examining these Books, which are in many Respects highly important and curious, many of them were found to be in great chronological Disorder, owing chiefly to the slovenly and ignorant Manner in which the smaller Fasciculi of which they consist had been joined together.'[13] He was to find the same disorder in other places. In 1815 he found in a volume of the Acts and Decreets of the Court of Session for 1582–3 proceedings of the Lords Auditors and Lords of Council for 1482–4 and 1483–5 respectively.[14] The method used for preserving the repaired paper folios was that of 'inlaying' in a broad frame of strong new paper. The work was closely supervised by Thomson, who had 2000 of the folios first repaired re-examined in 1808 and put into a better state. By 1816 he was able to report that the main part of the programme was complete and that the cost of future work could be transferred to the ordinary establishment of the Register House. He declared that most of the records on paper of a date before 1700 had required some repair and estimated that 33,000 folios had been inlaid and 6500 volumes rebound.[15]

The Select Committee had recommended the compilation of a general repertory of the volumes in the Register House. This work was completed by early in 1809. A press catalogue showing the locations both of the volumes and of the bundles of loose documents or 'warrants' was apparently completed in 1810, but of course had to be revised at intervals.

Apart from the regular transmissions of the main record groups to the Register House, special transfers of various groups were reported to the Commissioners. In 1808 the Register of Tailzies (Entails) was transmitted by its Keeper, James Ferrier, the former Sub-Commissioner.[16] Along with it came a small register bearing the prolix title of Register of Inventories of Heirs entering *cum beneficio Inventarii*. In 1809, on the other hand, the Barons of Exchequer refused to transmit their pre-Union records.[17] Such a transmission would probably have saved some of the records destroyed in the burning of the Exchequer building in 1811, though most of the pre-Union records were in the Exchequer rooms in the Register House.[18] Thomson acted specifically as Sub-Commissioner in obtaining, in 1811, the transfer of the Privy Council records from the Justiciary Office, as recommended by the Select Committee.[19]

Before his appointment as Deputy Clerk Register Thomson's attention had been chiefly concentrated on the transcription of the Acts of the Parliaments and the abridgment of the Retours for publication. The first of these publications made steady progress under his supervision. The second volume of the new series, covering the period 1424 to 1567, appeared in 1814. The subsequent volumes, also largely prepared from the official record and the minutes, were published in regular succession, the last appearing in 1824. Two years later the re-discovery in the State Paper Office in London of four missing volumes of the original records made obsolete the fifth and sixth volumes published, and Cosmo Innes eventually produced new editions of these between 1870 and

[13] *Second Annual Report*, Appx., p. 6.
[14] *Ninth Annual Report*, Appx., p. 7.
[15] *Tenth Annual Report*, Appx., pp. 11–14.
[16] *Second Annual Report*, Appx., p. 31.
[17] *Third Annual Report*, p. 9.
[18] See Athol L. Murray, 'The pre-Union records of the Scottish Exchequer', *Journal of the Society of Archivists*, vol. II, no. 3, p. 91; reprinted below, pp. 169–83, see particularly pp. 171–2.
[19] *Fifth Annual Report*, Appx., p. 20.

1872. Despite some criticisms which have already been made of the method of publication of Thomson's ten volumes, they are undoubtedly the chief publication achievement of the Record Commissions in Scotland. But Thomson never succeeded in finishing the first volume. There was, of course, only a small amount of official record available, and Thomson could never bring himself to make a final selection from the other sources and their various texts. Four years after the expiry of the last Record Commission the work was handed over to Cosmo Innes, who published in 1844. Thomson told Innes 'that it must be a forbidden subject between us'.[20]

It was Thomson's policy, as has been seen, to select 'judicial' matter from the Acts of the Parliaments and to publish it separately along with the separate record of the Acts of the Lords of Council. In this also there appeared the curious dilatoriness that he could combine with great activity. The text was printed by 1816, but Thomson was not yet satisfied with the indexes. Nothing more was done until 1833, when the Commissioners at their meeting of 9 March considered a letter from Thomson saying that he had postponed publication until the main work of the *Acts of the Parliaments* was completed, but promising to proceed immediately. Nevertheless the *Acta Dominorum Auditorum* and *Acta Dominorum Concilii* did not appear until 1839.

The other publication originally undertaken by Thomson, that of the Retours, went forward more smoothly. The two volumes of abridged text up to 1700 were published in 1811 and the index volume in 1816. The record consists of the returns of inquests, mostly on the subject of the right to succeed to landed property, and is mostly of seventeenth century date with some sixteenth century material. It is not one that would be likely to be chosen for publication today, but it has value for genealogical purposes and the study of place-names.

The Select Committee had suggested the printing of 'the earliest of the Royal Charters' and this was immediately undertaken by the Deputy Clerk Register. By 1810 the charters engrossed in the surviving rolls and the first volume of the Register of the Great Seal were printed to cover the period 1306–1424. At this point Thomson's fatal inability to accept a limited aim again intervened. In order to find original royal charters never registered and to fill the gaps in the record, he obtained the consent of the Commissioners to search in the archives of the royal burghs and among documents in private hands. He himself admitted that the second of these was 'a source which it is difficult to explore, without being lost in a bewildering detail'.[21] By 1812 the Commissioners were becoming alarmed at the number of Thomson's projects and the apparent unlikelihood that any one of them would ever be completed. The Secretary and the Clerk Register paid a visit to Edinburgh in October and November. They reported that they had 'endeavoured to impress on Mr Thomson's mind, and they hope successfully, the fact that, however curious and interesting the Charters and Muniments of private individuals, or even of corporate bodies, may be, they ought not to be sent forth into the world with an equal degree of authority to that which the Twelve Rolls and Book of Charters, otherwise denominated Registrum Magni Sigilli, ab A.D. 1306 ad A.D. 1424 entitle themselves to'.[22] Thomson was ordered to publish the part of the Register of the Great Seal already in print, to stop the copying of original charters and some other activities, and to concentrate on completing the *Retours* and producing more volumes of the *Acts of the Parliaments*. The Great Seal volume appeared in 1814.

Thomson was allowed to restart his copying of original royal charters in 1824 and by the time of his last quarterly report in 1831 more than 1500 dating from before Mary's reign had been transcribed.[23] It has been left to the committee of the *Regesta Regum Scottorum* in recent years to

[20] *Memoir of Thomas Thomson*, p. 228.
[21] *Fourth Annual Report*, Appx., p. 25.
[22] *Sixth Annual Report*, Appx., p. 33.
[23] *The Case of Robert Pitcairn, Esquire*, p. 108.

begin the actual publication of all the surviving acts of the medieval Scottish Kings. Their first two volumes were published in 1960 and 1971.[24]

In 1811 Thomson had started an abridgment of the Register of the Great Seal for the period after the end of the printed volume in 1424. This was also suspended in 1812 and resumed in 1824. Robert Pitcairn, author of *Ancient Criminal Trials in Scotland*, was then employed to prepare the abridgment. None of it was ever put into print by Thomson, but the copy prepared under his supervision was used when the publication of the *Registrum Magni Sigilli* was resumed in 1878.

Another of Thomson's publication projects that was stopped in 1812 was that of the Exchequer Rolls, which had been transcribed down to 1424. In this case he was clearly determined to evade the Commissioners' instructions. In 1816 he informed the Clerk Register[25] that this publication had been put to the press with a view to a limited edition. He described the work as 'not, in any respect, strictly official' and claimed that it had been 'so conducted as not to interfere with any other'. The printed copy was completed in 1817, but lay unused for at least 20 years. It was eventually published by Thomson, with some additions, as a presentation to the Bannatyne Club in three volumes. The first volume is something of a bibliographical curiosity, as its prelims bear four dates, 1817 (printing), 1837, 1841 and 1845 (preface).

One of these publication projects that never achieved printing, officially or unofficially, was that of the Privy Council Register. On 10 October 1808 Thomson wrote to the Secretary of the Commission that he had had transcripts made of some of the early volumes of the register, which begins in 1545. In a way similar to his selection of 'judicial' material from the Parliamentary records, he had selected and transcribed material relating to 'public affairs' from the Acts of the Lords of Council for the period before the beginning of the Privy Council Register. No further proceedings were authorised by the Record Commissioners, but publication of the register itself was begun later in the century and Thomson's earlier material (his 'curious prefix', as Cosmo Innes called it) was also eventually published, though in a different form.[26]

All the work of transcribing and abridging so far described was intended for publication. But other work carried out under Thomson's direction provided 'finding aids' for use within the Register House itself, whether in MS. or in print. In the case of the Retours he realised that full abridgment was unsuitable after 1700, but had a chronological list prepared, to which he intended to add an index. In the 1860s this list was transformed into an alphabetical arrangement which was printed and has been continued to the present day for the Services of Heirs, the legal successors of the Retours.

An abridgment of the Register of Tailzies (Entails) was completed by 1811. The Commissioners authorised the preparation of an index to the Register of Deeds from 1770, but from 1812 its compilation was taken over by the keeper of the register itself in terms of an Act of Sederunt of the previous year.[27] Some other indexing was reported to the Commission, but was actually carried out by the Register House staff as part of their normal duties.

In 1821 an Act of Parliament authorised the Court of Session to make Acts of Sederunt to regulate the indexes of a number of registers.[28] But work on one of the most important of them, the Register of Sasines (titles to land), was carried out under the Commissioners. Consultation of this register was made more difficult by the fact that it was kept in two forms, a General Register covering the whole country and Particular Registers for each county. With a view to eventual indexing Thomson decided to frame an abridgment from 1781 on a county basis, bringing together entries

[24] *Acts of Malcolm IV* and *Acts of William I*, ed. G. W. S. Barrow.

[25] *Tenth Annual Report*, p. 12.

[26] *Acts of the Lords of Council in Public Affairs, 1501–1554*, ed. R. K. Hannay, 1932.

[27] *Fourteenth Annual Report*, Appx., p. 10.

[28] 1 & 2 George IV, cap. 38, sec. 27.

from both types of register. This abridging was begun in 1822.[29] Despite the Act of 1821, when the new Deputy Clerk Register, W. P. Dundas, was reporting on the state of these abridgements and indexes in 1841 he could only write, 'The necessary funds have been provided by the Government; and I trust that the assistance which has hitherto been afforded will not now be withdrawn.'[30]

These abridgments of Sasines, together with those of the Register of the Great Seal, the transcription of original royal charters and the printing of the long-delayed first volume of the *Acts of the Parliaments*, constituted the work being carried out in Scotland at the time of the issue of the last Record Commission in 1831. (As has been seen, some other material already printed had not yet been published.) A frustrating correspondence ensued between Cooper, the new Secretary, and Thomson.[31] On 6 June 1831 Cooper wrote to ask for reports and estimates on the various works in progress, and on 24 June he directed that no further expense be incurred until the information had been supplied. During the remainder of the year Thomson wrote several times to apologise for his delay in replying, pleading ill health in his last letter. On 2 July 1832 Cooper wrote, 'I almost despair of ever hearing from you again', and informed Thomson that nearly all the Commissioners' works remained suspended to allow them to discharge the debt left by the former Commission.

Cooper's despair was almost justified. The next letter that he received from Edinburgh was dated 8 November 1834. It explained the 'most distressing situation' in which Thomson found himself when ordered not to incur any further expenditure. Thomson pointed out the experience and skill of the individuals employed and that nearly all of them had become mainly dependent on the work. He went on, 'I came to the resolution, for myself perhaps imprudently, of continuing in the mean time the principal works of compilation then in progress; . . . to such of [those concerned] as had been receiving from me monthly or quarterly advances to account of their annual remuneration, and who could not afford to go on otherwise, I undertook, in the mean time, from my own resources, or by means of my own personal credit, to continue to them their several allowances until a more proper arrangement should be obtained'.

Thomson's accounts, both public and private, were in fact in a state of complete confusion. The inquiry which was to make this clear was started by a letter from the Treasury to the Queen's and Lord Treasurer's Remembrancer in Scotland dated 2 January 1839.[32] The course of the inquiry, which led to Thomson's removal from office as Deputy Clerk Register in 1841, is described in general terms by Cosmo Innes.[33] As far as his unauthorised continuation of the works under the Record Commissioners is concerned, Thomson received £7781 7 1 to meet the cost of work on the Sasines from April 1831 to January 1838.[34] The Treasury authorised continuation of the payment of the salaries of those concerned up to 1 October 1841,[35] by which time Thomson had been replaced as Deputy Clerk Register. But his application for an allowance to himself as Sub-Commissioner since 1831 was refused.[36]

By the time of the expiry of the last of the Record Commissions most of the essential elements of modern record administration in Scotland were already in existence. Yet in 1733 a correspondent had written to William Maule, later Earl of Panmure, that he hoped that someone would be found 'that has at least so much of a publick spirit as not to allow the few remains of [our

[29] *The Case of Robert Pitcairn, Esquire*, p. 49.
[30] *Fifteenth Annual Report*, p. 7.
[31] *The Case of Robert Pitcairn, Esquire*, pp. i–vii and 1–21.
[32] S.R.O., Treasury Letter Book, Scotland (E.801), vol. 8, pp. 135–6. I am indebted to my colleague, Dr A. L. Murray, for pointing out this record as a source of information on Thomson's accounts.
[33] *Memoir of Thomas Thomson*, pp. 222–8.
[34] S.R.O., E.801/10, pp. 276–7.
[35] S.R.O., E.801/11, pp. 443–4.
[36] *Memoir of Thomas Thomson*, p. 227.

Registers and Records] to perish'.[37] A beginning of that work was made by the thirteenth Earl of Morton and Lord Frederick Campbell, who were largely responsible for the building of the Register House. Even when most of the records had been transferred there, however, they remained unrepaired, unlisted, unindexed and unpublished, while many abuses remained in the framing of new records. It was to remedy these defects that so much was achieved by the Record Commissioners through their gifted, enthusiastic, often dilatory and sometimes downright disobedient servant, Thomas Thomson.

PETER GOULDESBROUGH

---

[37] S.R.O., G.D. 45/14/427.

Diplomatic

The Origin
and Authenticity of the
Royal Anglo-Saxon
Diploma[1]

To say that much remains to be done in the field of English diplomatic is not a very original remark. Made by Stevenson in 1895, repeated by Tout in 1919, it still applies today in spite of all the time and effort which have been devoted to the study of English documents over the past fifty years.[2] Those fifty years have indeed been very productive in works on English royal diplomatic from the eleventh century onwards: they have seen the publication of such notable books as Dr Harmer's *Anglo-Saxon Writs*, Tout's *Chapters* and Maxwell-Lyte's *Great Seal*.[3] During the same fifty years have also appeared an impressive number of books and articles covering the first four centuries of English royal documents, from the introduction of documentary writing into this country, in the seventh century, to the birth of the writ, in the eleventh.[4] One title, however, is still wanting, that of a diplomatic survey of the royal charters issued during those four centuries, that is to say the diplomas or land-books. Several valuable essays, those contributed by Stevenson, Brunner, Levison, Drögereit, Miss Parsons and others, deal with particular aspects of the land-book or with well-defined periods of its history.[5] But the only general studies of the Anglo-Saxon diploma are to be found in Sir Frank Stenton's stimulating little book, *The Latin Charters of the Anglo-Saxon Period*, and in Professor Dorothy Whitelock's introduction to the 'Charters and Laws', neither of which claims to be a work on diplomatic.[6]

The explanation for this gap in our knowledge of English diplomatic is not hard to find. It was first put forward by Stevenson, again in 1895, and reiterated by Sir Frank Stenton after an

---

[1] I am very grateful to Professor V. H. Galbraith, Professor F. Wormald, Dr R. W. Hunt, Mr N. R. Ker and Mr N. P. Brooks for their assistance on a number of points. For what is controversial I alone am responsible.

[2] *The Crawford Collection of Early Charters and Documents now in the Bodleian Library*, ed. A. S. Napier and W. H. Stevenson (Oxford, 1895), p. viii; T. F. Tout, 'Mediaeval Forgers and Forgeries', *Bulletin of the John Rylands Library*, v (1918–20), pp. 224, 234. Recently, F. Barlow, *The English Church, 1000–1066* (London, 1963), p. 126, n. 1.

[3] F. E. Harmer, *Anglo-Saxon Writs* (Manchester Univ. Press, 1952); T. F. Tout, *Chapters in the Administrative History of Mediaeval England*, 6 vols. (*ibid.*, 1920–33); Sir H. C. Maxwell-Lyte, *Historical Notes on the Use of the Great Seal of England* (H.M.S.O., 1926). See also V. H. Galbraith, *Studies in the Public Records* (Nelson, 1948).

[4] See Professor D. Whitelock's bibliography, *English Historical Documents* [cited hereafter as *E.H.D.*], I (London, 1955), pp. 351–53; Tryggvi J. Oleson, *The Witenagemot in the Reign of Edward the Confessor* (Oxford Univ. Press, 1955); E. John, *Land Tenure in Early England* (Leicester Univ. Press, 1960); H. P. R. Finberg, *The Early Charters of Devon and Cornwall* (*ibid.*, 1954), *The Early Charters of the West Midlands* [hereafter *E.C.W.M.*] (*ibid.*, 1961), *The Early Charters of Wessex* [hereafter *E.C.W.*] (*ibid.*, 1964).

[5] See Professor D. Whitelock's bibliography, *E.H.D.*, I, p. 353; Mary Prescott Parsons, 'Some Scribal Memoranda for Anglo-Saxon Charters of the Eighth and Ninth Centuries', *Mitteilungen des Oesterreichischen Instituts für Geschichtsforschung*, XIV Erg.-Band (1939), pp. 13–32.

[6] F. M. Stenton, *The Latin Charters of the Anglo-Saxon Period* [hereafter *Latin Charters*] (Oxford, 1955); *E.H.D.*, I, pp. 337–49.

interval of sixty years: 'It cannot be said that the Old English charters have yet been edited'.[7] Without a critical and exhaustive edition of the Anglo-Saxon diplomas, no definitive study of their diplomatic can be contemplated.

It is true that Kemble's *Codex Diplomaticus*,[8] an edition which is both uncritical and incomplete, still remains, to date, the only comprehensive corpus of royal Anglo-Saxon land-books. Kemble's volumes, however, give us a text, unsatisfactory though it may be, of the majority of the surviving royal charters of the Anglo-Saxon period. One may wonder why this imperfect tool, supplemented as it is by the facsimile reproductions of most extant originals,[9] could not have proved adequate for working out at least an interim report on Anglo-Saxon diplomatic. Perhaps the failings of Kemble's edition do not lie so much in the inaccuracy or incompleteness of its text as in the mistaken arrangement of its contents. Kemble adopted a strict chronological order, as Birch did after him in his *Cartularium Saxonicum*.[10] Such an arrangement might reasonably be taken to imply that the whole corpus of royal Anglo-Saxon charters falls into one single group, whose components sprang from the same source, and whose evolution simply followed the passage of time, irrespective of topographical or other considerations. In other words, it would seem that Kemble presupposed the existence of a single royal Anglo-Saxon diplomatic, brushing aside any suggestion that we should perhaps think in terms of several, not necessarily royal, Anglo-Saxon 'diplomatics'.

That there was one single ultimate source for all Anglo-Saxon diplomas, as indeed for all European charters, is virtually certain, and that source is Rome, or rather Italy. It is generally believed that, until the last quarter of the seventh century, Anglo-Saxon grants of land were made orally, the use of words being probably accompanied by 'some sort of symbolic act of transfer, such as the placing of a sod on the altar'.[11] The credit for replacing or supplementing such oral declarations by written records is commonly attributed to Archbishop Theodore, who is thought to have brought along with him from Italy, in 669, the charter system to which he had been accustomed.[12]

The case in favour of the Italian origin of the Anglo-Saxon charter, as presented by Stevenson, Levison and others, is a strong one. The earliest known examples of charters drawn up in the south of England and particularly in Kent, in the late seventh and early eighth centuries, resemble in their structure and formulae the Italian private deeds of the period and of slightly earlier times; on the other hand, they differ considerably from their Frankish equivalents, either royal or private.[13] Such similarities and differences could hardly have been accidental.

The arguments invoked for crediting Theodore with the change over from oral to written grants are far less convincing. They are solely based on the fact that all the charters which purport to have been issued before the archbishop's arrival in England are clearly spurious, whereas several of those which claim to have been written during the decade 669–79 have survived in texts apparently irreproachable; the latter even include one original.[14] Perhaps the argument from silence, when applied to such early times, should have been used with greater caution, but it is only fair to

[7] *The Crawford Collection* . . ., p. viii; Stenton, *Latin Charters*, p. 9.

[8] *Codex Diplomaticus Ævi Saxonici* [hereafter *K.C.D.*], ed. J. M. Kemble, 6 vols. (London, 1839–48).

[9] *Facsimiles of Ancient Charters in the British Museum* [hereafter *B.M.F.*], 4 vols. (London, 1873–78); Ordnance Survey, *Facsimiles of Anglo-Saxon Manuscripts* [hereafter *O.S.F.*], 3 vols. (Southampton, 1878–84); *Chartae Latinae Antiquiores* [hereafter *Ch.L.A.*], ed. A. Bruckner and R. Marichal, III (Olten/Lausanne, 1963).

[10] *Cartularium Saxonicum* [hereafter *B.C.S.*], ed. W. de Gray Birch, 3 vols. (London, 1885–93).

[11] *E.H.D.*, I, p. 343.

[12] *Ibid., loc. cit.*; F. M. Stenton, *Anglo-Saxon England* (Oxford, 1947), p. 141.

[13] See, for example, *Urkunden und Akten*, ed. K. Brandi, 3rd edition (Berlin/Leipzig, 1932), no. 16; W. H. Stevenson, 'Trinoda necessitas', *English Hist. Review*, XXIX (1914), pp. 689–703, especially pp. 694–95 and notes and p. 702; W. Levison, *England and the Continent in the Eighth Century* (Oxford, 1946), pp. 228–33; G. M. Young, *The Origin of the West-Saxon Kingdom* (Oxford Univ. Press, 1934), pp. 21–26 (I owe this reference to the kindness of Mr James Campbell).

[14] *B.M.F.* I, I.

add that the advocates of the Theodore connexion have never claimed to provide anything better than a plausible reconstruction. They were well aware that no final pronouncement could ever be made unless a large enough group of formal records (as opposed to informal letters) issued in Theodore's name were one day to be discovered. Only one such record has so far come to light, the decree of the Council of Hertford (24 Sept. 672); we owe its preservation to Bede, who copied it in full in his *Historia Ecclesiastica*, leaving out, it seems, only the subscriptions.[15]

The Hertford document falls into the same diplomatic category as the *acta* of papal synods, on which it may have been modelled, but unlike them it contains the following formula amongst its final clauses:

Quam sententiam definitionis nostrae Titillo notario scribendam dictavi.

This *rogatio* clause seldom appears in genuine papal documents of any kind before the pontificate of Adrian I (772–95),[16] whereas it is regularly found in Italian private deeds of the sixth and seventh centuries. In Rome and Ravenna it occurs in the form *scribendum . . . dictavi*, while in Longobard charters alternative formulae such as *scribendum . . . rogavi* seem to have been preferred.[17] The following examples are worth quoting:

Quam largitatem . . . Severo forensi civitatis Rav' scribendam dictavi . . .[18]

Quam donationis meae paginam . . . Bono tabellioni hujus civitatis Rav' rogatario meo scribendam dictavi . . .[19]

Hanc autem suggestionem supplicationemque meam Æmiliano notario sanctae ecclesiae Romanae noto meo scribendam dictavi . . .[20]

If the subscriptions to the Hertford record had not been omitted by Bede, we might find that they included the subscription of the writer, Titillus, in a form similar to that used by the scribes of Italian deeds (*completio* clause).[21] Unfortunately we do not know who Titillus was, whether he came from a native stock or was brought from Italy by Theodore, but this does not make the Italian title of *notarius* which the Hertford document gives him any less interesting.[22] It shows that Theodore had at least one notary, who knew how to draw up a document in the true Italian fashion. On the other hand, the Anglo-Saxon charters which were drawn up in Kent during Theodore's pontificate and even during the next hundred years show no apparent trace of notarial influence. Not a single one of those among them which can be safely accepted as genuine contains a mention of the scribe who wrote them, and it is precisely the absence of the *rogatio* clause and of the scribe's *completio* which, according to Levison and others, mainly distinguishes the Anglo-Saxon charter from the Italian private deed.[23] If Theodore had been responsible for the introduction of written grants into England, is it likely that such an important feature of the charter as he knew it would have been deliberately omitted? One of the few early Anglo-Saxon formulae which stand reasonably close to the notarial *rogatio* clause occurs in a charter granted in 694 by King Wihtred of Kent to Æbbe, abbess of Minster in Thanet:

---

[15] Bede, *Opera Historica*, ed. C. Plummer, I (Oxford, 1896), pp. 214–17.

[16] See C. Paoli, *Diplomatica* (Florence, 1942 edition), pp. 172–75. For an example of the *rogatio* in a privilege of Paschal I, see *Exempla Scripturarum*, III (*Acta Pontificum*), ed. G. Battelli (Vatican, 1933), no. 1. For *acta* of papal synods, see *Mon. Germ. Hist.*, *Ep.*, *Gregorii I Papae Registrum Epistolarum*, I, pp. 362–67; II, pp. 275–77; Mansi, *Concilia*, x (1764), cols. 863 ff. See also Levison, *op. cit.*, p. 229.

[17] L. Schiaparelli, 'Note diplomatiche sulle carte longobarde', *Archivio Storico Italiano*, VII. xix (1933), p. 26.

[18] *I papiri diplomatici raccolti ed illustrati*, ed. G. Marini (Rome, 1805), no. 86.

[19] *Ibid.*, no. 93.

[20] *Mon. Germ. Hist.*, *Ep.*, II, p. 276.

[21] Paoli, *op. cit.*, pp. 175–77.

[22] M. Redin, *Studies on Uncompounded Personal Names in Old English* (Uppsala, 1919), p. 144.

[23] Levison, *op. cit.*, pp. 227–28. Compare n. 107 below.

Quam sepe dictam cartulam scribendam dictavi.[24]

But it does not name the writer (*rogatarius*), thus leaving out the most important element of the Italian *rogatio* clause. Does this not suggest that the Anglo-Saxon charter may already have been in existence for some time when Theodore arrived and that its form was settled by then? Theodore's notary – or notaries – may have come too late to make a durable impact on English diplomatic as a whole. Only the documents to which the archbishop himself was a party could be seriously affected by the presence in England of men like Titillus.

In 1839 Kemble wrote that he saw 'no reason to doubt that land was transferred by documentary forms, either with or without symbolic forms, from the very first introduction of Christianity among the Anglo-Saxons'.[25] In his opinion, the history of the Anglo-Saxon charter had begun in Augustine's time, in the last years of the sixth century. Although these views are no longer held, much can be said in their favour. We can be absolutely sure that Augustine and his companions brought along with them their writing habits, and that letter-writing formed part of their daily activity.[26] Not only could they write, they also had all the equipment required for training others to do the same, notably in the 'plurimos codices' which Pope Gregory had sent them.[27] We know with equal certainty that King Ethelbert of Kent granted them lands in Canterbury and Rochester.[28] Are we to suppose that men like Augustine, who were accustomed to documentary evidence and realised its importance, would have been satisfied with oral grants and symbolic gestures? Why should they have adopted the contemporary attitude of the Anglo-Saxons in such matters? There was nothing to prevent them from writing down themselves, in charter form, the grants of which they were the beneficiaries. Indeed this appears to have been common practice for grants made to the Church by later Anglo-Saxon kings. Then as always the charter system, an insurance against forgetfulness and treachery, was primarily designed to protect the beneficiary, not the grantor.

King Ethelbert himself seems to have soon appreciated the advantages of written records, since, in Augustine's time, that is before 604, he caused his dooms to be committed to writing 'juxta exempla Romanorum'. These dooms, so Bede tells us, were written in the vernacular, and their first article dealt with the question of compensation for thefts perpetrated to the detriment of the Church and of its ministers, both of which details exactly fit the text of the code attributed to Ethelbert in the *Textus Roffensis*.[29] Thus we have a genuine written record going back to the time of Augustine and involving the king personally. This is important in itself, but the subject-matter of the code's first article is even more significant: Ethelbert's first thought, in the first Anglo-Saxon code ever to be written, had been for the protection of church property. Whether it had been his own thought or that of his ecclesiastical advisers, one of whom – or a scribe trained by them – would have had to take charge of the actual writing of the code, need not concern us. What matters is that someone deemed it necessary to protect the worldly possessions of the Church in a written record. If we accept the authenticity of Ethelbert's laws, why should we reject any suggestion that his grants to the Church might have been written down in charter form? The laws protected the movable property of ecclesiastics, while the charters gave them security of tenure in their real estates.

It is true that all the extant texts which purport to be charters of Ethelbert have been proved to be spurious,[30] but these forgeries may have been made in order to replace genuine documents which perhaps had been lost or destroyed, or no longer fulfilled the needs of the grantees. One

---

[24] *B.C.S.*, no. 86; see also nos. 296, 373. For two typical forgeries, see nos. 32, 50.

[25] *K.C.D.*, I, p. vii.

[26] Bede, *Opera Historica*, ed. Plummer, I, pp. 87–88.

[27] *Ibid.*, I, p. 63.

[28] *Ibid.*, I, pp. 70, 85.

[29] *Ibid.*, I, p. 90; *E.H.D.*, I, pp. 357–59.

[30] Levison, *op. cit.*, pp. 174–233.

example of such practices in Kent is particularly illuminating. It concerns the earliest genuine Anglo-Saxon charter to have come down to us in the original. According to it King Hlothere of Kent granted lands in Thanet and Sturry to Abbot Beorhtwald and his monastery; the lands, with all their appurtenances, were to be possessed for ever by the abbot and his successors, in the same way as they had been held by the king until then. The grant is stated to have been made in the city of Reculver, in May, in the seventh indiction.[31] There is not the slightest doubt that Beorhtwald's monastery was in fact the abbey of Reculver and that the seventh indiction should be translated into the year of the Incarnation 679, but neither of these facts is specifically mentioned in the charter. In 949 the monastery of Reculver and its possessions were granted by King Edred to Christ Church, Canterbury,[32] and all the Reculver deeds, including Hlothere's charter, were presumably acquired by Christ Church at that time. Yet it was not the text of the original charter of Hlothere that the compilers of the cartularies of Christ Church used, but an entirely different version: this version begins with a note of the year of the Incarnation (correctly given as 679); the grantee's monastery is explicitly identified as Reculver; the Sturry land is said to extend to twelve hides and is granted 'liberam ut superiorem ab omni seculari servitio, exceptis istis tribus expeditione, pontis et arcis constructione'; even the anathema is different from that of the original.[33] Here we are confronted with a typical case of genuine charter which was transformed out of all recognition by a later scribe, not necessarily a conscious forger, but at least someone who had no scruples about adapting very freely his exemplar to the modern needs of his community: he abridged the text in some ways, expanded it in others; genuine early formulae were suppressed and methodically replaced by others of a later age, after a fashion with which the compiler of the *Liber Landavensis* was all too familiar.[34] Perhaps the extant spurious texts of Ethelbert's grants should also be regarded as representing later versions, drastically revised, of early genuine charters which have not been preserved.

Two passages in Eddi's *Life of Bishop Wilfrid* could be interpreted to mean that Northumbria, like Kent, may also have had some experience of written grants a decade or so before Theodore arrived in England. In the first passage, which mentions Alchfrith's grants of 'Stanford' and Ripon to Wilfrid (*c.* 660), the words used by Eddi, 'Alchfrithus dedit primum . . . *terram decem tributariorum æt Stanforda* et post paululum coenobium in Hrypis cum *terra triginta mansionum, pro animae suae remedio*, concessit ei', read like extracts from charters.[35] It may be to these problematic charters that the second of Eddi's texts (671 x 678) refers:

Stans itaque Sanctus Wilfrithus episcopus ante altare, conversus ad populum, coram regibus enumerans regiones, quas ante reges *pro animabus suis*, et tunc in illa die *cum consensu et subscriptione episcoporum et omnium principum* illi dederunt, lucide enuntiavit.[36]

In truth, one cannot positively state that the Anglo-Saxon charter was established as early as Augustine's time or even before Theodore's arrival, but the evidence for an early origin of the charter is at least as strong as the evidence against it. Besides, the primitive features of the charter, as displayed in its earliest extant examples and retained throughout its history, can in my opinion be explained more satisfactorily by an early origin: they seem to be more compatible with the rudimentary secretarial organization of early missionaries than with the apparently more sophisticated

[31] *B.M.F.* I. 1; *B.C.S.*, no. 45; E. A. Lowe, *English Uncial* (Oxford, 1960), plate XXI and p. 20.

[32] *O.S.F.* I. 15; *B.C.S.*, nos. 880–81. See also *English Hist. Review*, XXIX, p. 692, n. 18.

[33] *Monasticon Anglicanum*, I. 455; R. Twysden, *Hist. Anglicanae Scriptores decem* (London, 1652), col. 2207; *English Hist. Review*, XXIX, p. 696, n. 37. Compare J. Armitage Robinson, 'The Early Community at Christ Church, Canterbury', *Journal of Theological Studies*, XXVII (1926), p. 235.

[34] E. D. Jones, 'The Book of Llandaff', *The National Library of Wales Journal*, IV (1945–46), pp. 123–57.

[35] Eddius Stephanus, 'Vita Wilfridi Episcopi', *The Historians of the Church of York*, ed. J. Raine, I (Rolls Series, 1879), p. 12; *The Life of Bishop Wilfrid*, ed. B. Colgrave (Cambridge Univ. Press, 1927), p. 16.

[36] Raine, *op. cit.*, p. 25; Colgrave, *op. cit.*, p. 36. See *E.H.D.*, I, pp. 343, 693.

one of Theodore. Of all the royal diplomas it is the only one in Europe which was never provided with any outward marks of authenticity. It was never sealed, even in the reign of Edward the Confessor, although there was then an English royal seal. Anglo-Saxon charters end with a number of crosses and subscriptions, those of the grantor and of *testes* and *consentientes*, but the crosses and subscriptions, being non-autograph,[37] amount to nothing more than a list of witnesses. Such a list would have had a probative value if the charter had been attested by a notary or even by an identifiable monastic scribe, but even this attestation is lacking. Once the grantor and witnesses had died, nobody could prove the genuineness or otherwise of the document, at least by any of the secular methods which would fully satisfy a modern diplomatist.

What sort of authenticity can the land-book have had, which was obvious to contemporaries and is no longer evident to us? It was in my view a purely religious and ecclesiastical one. Throughout its history, the land-book remained essentially an ecclesiastical instrument, at least in form if not always in purpose. It begins with a pictorial or verbal invocation to God. The proem which follows sometimes consists of a banal statement that the probative value of written grants is superior to that of oral declarations of gift;[38] more often, it is a pious discourse on the brevity of life, on the need for man to expiate his sins on earth and think of eternal salvation.[39] The Anglo-Saxon diploma, unlike the majority of royal charters on the Continent, does not provide for any secular penalties against those who would presume to infringe the grant, but only for religious sanctions to be meted out on the Day of Judgment. To find such religious formulae in grants to the Church is not surprising, but their presence in grants to laymen is disconcerting. It is true that in Anglo-Saxon England charters in favour of laymen were often indirect grants to the Church, but all modern scholars agree that this was not always the case.[40] Even King Æthelwulf's grant to himself of twenty hides in the South Hams begins with an unexpected preamble on the theme 'Facite vobis amicos de mammona iniquitatis', and contains an anathema and blessing.[41]

To dismiss proems and curses as mere verbiage would be dangerous. They were essential elements in a complicated process of religious guarantees which surrounded the issue of land-books. Sometimes the original charter was placed on a church altar by the grantor;[42] sometimes it was copied into a gospel or some other sacred book,[43] a practice frequent in England and Wales from the ninth to the eleventh century, but apparently unusual on the Continent. Such originals and copies would, of course, be endowed with complete authenticity, since one had the right to assume that nobody would dare place on the altar anything which was not sincere, or copy a forged document into a holy book. Surviving gospel documents mostly consist of manumissions and of a few writs of the eleventh century, but a similar practice may have been used for landbooks earlier period.[44]

Let us consider for a moment the earliest original diploma to have been preserved, the charter granted by King Hlothere of Kent in 679 to Beorhtwald, abbot of Reculver.[45] Hlothere's

---

[37] I cannot agree with the editors of *Ch.L.A.* (III, nos. 190, 221) that some of the crosses may be autograph.

[38] *B.C.S.*, nos. 107, 111 (proems of the 'Quamvis solus sermo' type); V. H. Galbraith, 'Monastic Foundation Charters of the Eleventh and Twelfth Centuries', *Cambridge Hist. Journal*, IV (1932–34), pp. 205–22, especially p. 207. Proems are rare in early charters; when they occur, they are short.

[39] *B.C.S.*, nos. 164, 182, 187, 206 (proems of the 'Nihil intulimus' type). See also nos. 202–4, etc.

[40] Stenton, *Latin Charters*, pp. 59 ff.; John, *op. cit.*, pp. 77–79.

[41] *B.M.F.* II. 30; *B.C.S.*, no. 451.

[42] *Anglo-Saxon Wills*, ed. D. Whitelock (Cambridge Univ. Press, 1930), H. D. Hazeltine's preface, pp. xxxii–xxxiii and notes; John, *op. cit.*, pp. 168 ff.; Finberg, *E.C.W.*, pp. 159, 208.

[43] F. Wormald, 'The Sherborne "Chartulary"', *Fritz Saxl Essays*, ed. D. J. Gordon (Nelson, 1957), p. 106, n. 2; N. R. Ker, *Catalogue of Manuscripts containing Anglo-Saxon* (Oxford, 1957), p. 557: list of records in Old English preserved in gospel-books.

[44] For manumissions, see *E.H.D.*, I, pp. 348–49. For records of several types, see *The Text of the Book of Llan Dâv*, ed. J. G. Evans and J. Rhys (Oxford, 1893), pp. xliii–xlviii (from the Book of St Chad).

[45] *B.M.F.* I. 1; *B.C.S.*, no. 45; Lowe, *English Uncial*, plate XXI and p. 20; *Ch.L.A.*, III, no. 182.

charter displays a number of interesting features, one of which concerns its script. It is written in uncials, a type of script which on the Continent was used for books such as gospels, and occasionally for relic labels (*authentiques*), but apparently not for charters.[46] If we agree with Professor E. A. Lowe that the scribe of the charter was not Italian, but English,[47] we might perhaps suggest that the uncial script was the only one known to him. The argument would have some force if the Reculver charter was an isolated case of the use of uncials for documentary writings, but there are indications to the contrary. The post-Conquest scribe responsible for the forged charters of St Augustine's, Canterbury, was so convinced that early charters were normally written in uncials that he imitated this type of script in two of his fabrications.[48] Uncials were not only used in early Kentish charters, but also in Mercian documents as late as 736.[49] It would be strange if some sort of minuscule and cursive script had not been practised in England in Theodore's time, at least for the writing of letters and of such documents as the vernacular code of King Ethelbert and the record of the Council of Hertford of 672, the work of the notary Titillus. In the eyes of a seventh-century scribe uncials may have represented a superior kind of script, possibly even a sacred script, reserved for writings of unquestionable authenticity.

In Sir Robert Cotton's library the Reculver charter formed the last leaf, probably only a fly-leaf, of a volume which contained two other items, a psalter of the ninth century and a fragment of a gospel-book written not later than the beginning of the eighth century in the same scriptorium as the Codex Amiatinus.[50] Later, the volume went abroad, eventually to become MS. 32 of the Utrecht University Library, but without the charter, which remained in the Cottonian Library. Cotton's reputation for binding together manuscripts of diverse origins makes one hesitate to attribute any particular significance to the association in the same Cottonian volume of the gospel, psalter and charter.[51] As, however, there is no doubt that the psalter and the charter were both in Christ Church, Canterbury, in the twelfth century,[52] we may reasonably claim the same home for the gospel. It is difficult to say how early the connexion between the gospel and the charter may have been. The script of the gospel cannot be accurately dated, but it is roughly contemporary with that of the charter, and it is therefore not impossible for the two items to have been associated as early as 679. They may both have belonged to the abbey of Reculver before they went to Canterbury, the charter being inserted in the gospel as from the date of its issue. A charter kept in a book would be neither endorsed nor folded, both of which requirements are met in the case of the Reculver document: unlike most Christ Church deeds, it bears no endorsement of any kind, nor is it certain that it was folded for any length of time if ever.[53]

Another uncial charter, a grant of Æthelbald of Mercia dated 736, was in Cotton's time prefaced to a book, the Vespasian Psalter, but here the connexion between book and charter is a modern one: the charter was originally at Worcester whereas the psalter belonged to the library of St

[46] For 'authentiques', see *Ch.L.A.*, I, nos. 15–17. For an interesting case of the 'reverse process', a charter parchment being used after erasure as an additional leaf for a gospel-book, see *ibid.*, II, no. 175.

[47] E. A. Lowe, 'The Uncial Gospel Leaves attached to the Utrecht Psalter', *Art Bulletin*, XXXIV (1952), pp. 237–38.

[48] Levison, *op. cit.*, pp. 174–75 and notes.

[49] *B.M.F.* I. 7; *B.C.S.*, no. 154; *Ch.L.A.*, III, no. 183; Lowe, *English Uncial*, p. 21; *E.H.D.*, I, pp. 453–54.

[50] *Art Bulletin*, XXXIV, pp. 237–38.

[51] *Ibid., loc. cit.*

[52] *Codices Latini Antiquiores* [hereafter *C.L.A.*], ed. E. A. Lowe, x (Oxford, 1963), no. 1587. See *Medieval Libraries of Great Britain*, ed. N. R. Ker (Royal Hist. Soc., Guides and Handbooks, no. 3, 2nd edition, 1964), p. 39. Folio 92 of the Utrecht Psalter contains scribblings in a Canterbury script: see the facsimile in *Latin Psalter in the Univ. Library of Utrecht* (London, ? 1874).

[53] I am not sure that the 'five existing crosswise folds' mentioned by the editors of *Ch.L.A.* (III, no. 182) are in fact folds; the lines are very indistinct.

Augustine's, Canterbury.[54] Besides, the charter is endorsed and it was kept folded for a considerable period. Perhaps Cotton's librarian inserted it in the psalter after the Reculver diploma had been found in a similar book. The later copying of manumissions on blank leaves of gospels may have been the relic of a more ancient and more general practice consisting of placing original land-books in sacred volumes. Similar links between Anglo-Saxon charters and sacred objects are well known. One could quote the example of Edgar's famous charter of 966 for the New Minster, Winchester, which, as Professor Wormald has suggested, may have been kept on the altar.[55] Anglo-Saxon kings were also in the habit of housing in the royal sanctuary not only their relics, but also their land-books, thus providing for the latter a safe repository and at the same time conferring upon them a kind of *ex post facto* authenticity.[56] It was probably for the same reasons that ordinary laymen often chose to deposit in a monastery the charters of which they were the beneficiaries.[57]

The religious guarantees which surrounded the issue and custody of Anglo-Saxon charters largely explains the confidence placed in them by contemporaries. It is clear that the Anglo-Saxons attached as much importance to their land-books as the Franks did to their sealed royal charters. They do not appear even to have been aware that the authenticity of their books could be challenged. Whoever had a land-book in his possession was automatically presumed to have the title to the land granted in it.[58] The transfer of title to someone else was often effected by the mere handing-over of the original book, and it was only when the transfer of title did not extend to the whole of the original grant that difficulties seem to have arisen.[59] The loss of charters by accident, fire or theft was such a calamity that it often resulted in an application to the king for their renewal, 'ut alii . . . libri scriberentur eodem modo quo et priores scripti erant in quantum eos memoriter recordari potuisset'.[60] Not until we reach the reign of Cnut do we find any evidence of the depreciation of the Anglo-Saxon charter as a diplomatic form. This depreciation we gather from a remark which Archbishop Lyfing of Canterbury is supposed to have made to the king that 'he had charters of freedom in plenty if only they were good for anything'.[61] It is only a proof that the charter was by then becoming obsolescent; this was due to no other reason than the invention of a new and more effective diplomatic instrument, the writ.[62]

It was natural that in a credulous age any document which was kept in the company of sacred objects should have been presumed genuine. It has long been known, however, that even relics could be false, and one cannot help wondering whether both grantor and beneficiary of land-books, once the charter system had been well established, would not have insisted on more tangible guarantees of authenticity than those of a purely religious nature. In any case, some of the safeguards associated with religion probably lost much of their meaning as time went on. For example,

[54] Ker, *Catalogue of Manuscripts containing Anglo-Saxon*, no. 203 and note; *Medieval Libraries*, p. 43; *E.H.D.*, I, pp. 453–54.

[55] F. Wormald, 'Late Anglo-Saxon Art . . .', *Studies in Western Art* (*Acts of the 20th International Congress of the Hist. of Art*, Princeton, 1963), pp. 19–26, especially p. 25.

[56] *Anglo-Saxon Wills*, p. 151; *Anglo-Saxon Charters*, ed. A. J. Robertson (Cambridge Univ. Press, 2nd edition, 1956), no. lxxxv and p. 419.

[57] Some of the charters to laymen which are either found in the original in monastic archives or transcribed in monastic cartularies relate to lands which were never in the possession of the monasteries concerned. This seems to be true of *B.M.F.* IV. 18 and of *O.S.F.* II, Winchester Cath. ii.

[58] *Anglo-Saxon Wills*, p. xxxvi; John, *op. cit.*, p. 172.

[59] John, *op. cit., loc. cit.*; *E.H.D.*, I, p. 441.

[60] *O.S.F.* III. xxiii; *B.C.S.*, no. 603. See also *B.C.S.*, no. 410 (Finberg, *E.C.W.*, no. 565), no. 1186 (Finberg, *E.C.W.*, no. 607), etc.; Stenton, *Latin Charters*, pp. 14–15, 52–53; John, *op. cit.*, p. 174. Compare the continental *pancarta* (or *preceptum*) *de chartis perditis* (or *combustis*), A. Giry, *Manuel de diplomatique* (Paris, 1894), pp. 14–17; A. de Boüard, *Manuel de diplomatique française et pontificale*, I (Paris, 1929), p. 168; *Mon. Germ. Hist., Leg. Sect. V, Formulae*, ed. K. Zeumer (Hanover, 1886), pp. 63–64, 150–51, 302–3.

[61] Harmer, *Anglo-Saxon Writs*, no. 26.

[62] Stenton, *Latin Charters*, pp. 87–91.

the use of uncials as a charter script, which, as I have suggested, may have at one time been regarded as such a safeguard, had already been discontinued early in the eighth century. One way of protecting the interests of all concerned was to reserve the drafting and writing of the charters to a body of 'authentic' persons who could play among the Anglo-Saxons the same rôle as public notaries and royal secretariats did on the Continent.

It is generally agreed among modern scholars that until about the reign of Athelstan (924–39) Anglo-Saxon charters were drafted and written by or for the recipients. These conclusions have been based on a palaeographical study of the few extant originals and on a comparison of the formulae found in originals and copies.[63] On the actual identity of the draftsmen and scribes we can only speculate, since the charters themselves do not disclose it. Indeed, any Anglo-Saxon diploma which reveals the identity of its scribe is to day open to suspicion.[64] One exception has been made, however, in the case of a seventh-century Wessex charter (670–76), granted by Cenred, the father of King Ine of Wessex, to Bectun, the abbot of an unidentified monastery.[65] The land granted, extending to thirty hides (*manientes*), was situated south of the river Fontmell and north of the land of Bishop Leuthere 'of blessed memory' (*beate memorie*). One could argue that, since Leuthere witnesses the charter, he should not be referred to as 'of blessed memory', but Levison has shown that these words could be applied to living persons; in a later original, a writ of Henry I written by a royal scribe and dated 13 January 1130/31, Innocent II is also mentioned as 'domini et beate memorie Innocentii pape'.[66]

One of the curious features of Cenred's charter is that its anathema is followed by a clause of continental and probably Frankish origin, 'et hoc quod repetit vendicare non valeat'. This clause is so unusual in Anglo-Saxon charters that, so far as I have been able to discover, it only occurs in one other document, Edward the Confessor's alleged grant of Dawlish to his chaplain Leofric (A.D. 1044).[67] In King Edward's charter–an apparent original–the clause is found in a garbled form 'et quod indigne seu procaciter repetit non eum dicet', the scribe having misread the 'evindicet' of his model as 'eum dicet'.

Cenred's charter contains a second unusual feature, probably to be also attributed to continental influence: it concerns the last subscription, which reads 'Ego Wimbertus presbiter qui hanc cartulam rogantes [*sic*] supra effato abbate scripsi et subscripsi'. Levison, who identified the subscriber as Winberht, later abbot of Nursling, suggested that these continental formulae could be easily explained if one assumed that Bishop Leuthere of Winchester, who is mentioned in the text and also subscribes, had drafted the charter. Leuthere with his Frankish background–he was the nephew of Bishop Agilbert of Paris–was likely to introduce some continental clauses in the documents he drafted. This argument, however, does not explain why the charter should in some respects follow an Anglo-Saxon pattern and in others a Frankish one.

The charter displays yet another abnormal feature. In the form it has come down to us in the Shaftesbury cartulary, it is a transcript not of an original but of what is known as an 'insertion', a kind of early authentic copy, the ancestor of the *inspeximus* and *vidimus*.[68] This early copy is supposed to have been made in 759 on the occasion of the settlement of a dispute between the monastery

---

[63] Parsons, *op. cit.*, pp. 18, 20, 32 and notes; *Ch.L.A.*, III, *passim*.

[64] Levison, *op. cit.*, pp. 227 ff.; *E.H.D.*, I, p. 341.

[65] Levison, *op. cit.*, *loc. cit.*; *B.C.S.*, nos. 107 and 186; *E.H.D.*, I, pp. 441–43; Stenton, *Latin Charters*, pp. 23–24.

[66] T. A. M. Bishop, *Scriptores Regis* (Oxford, 1961), no. 675.

[67] *O.S.F..* II, Exeter xii. This charter is discussed in a paper on 'The Authenticity of the Royal Anglo-Saxon Diplomas of Exeter', *Bulletin of the Inst. of Hist. Research* XXXIX, no. 99 (May 1966). The formula occurs in Longobard charters, *e.g.* in the Farfa register; see *Il regesto di Farfa*, ed. I. Giorgi and U. Balzani, II (Rome, 1879), nos. xxxii, xxxviii, etc.

[68] H. Bresslau, *Handbuch der Urkundenlehre für Deutschland und Italien*, 3 vols. (Berlin/Leipzig, 1912–60), I, pp. 90–91; II, pp. 30, 301–8.

of Tisbury and the abbey over which Bectun had ruled. It is attested by Bishop Cyneheard of Winchester, who explains why the document was drawn up in that form.[69]

We cannot be certain that the insertion practice, current on the Continent as from the latter part of the eighth century, was not used in England as early as 759; if genuine, our example deserves to be quoted as one of the earliest to have survived in Europe. What is more disturbing is that some of the wording of Cenred's charter and of Cyneheard's attestation reappears respectively in a charter for St Augustine's, Canterbury, dated 686, and in another, also for St Augustine's, dated 762.[70] Winberht attests, as draftsman (*dictans*), a charter of King Ine for Malmesbury (A.D. 701) and, as scribe, a charter of the same king for Abingdon (wrongly dated 687), the second of which documents is undoubtedly spurious as it stands.[71]

In view of all its varied connexions, the Cenred charter is bound to raise doubts, and no great value should therefore be attached to its scribe's attestation. At least Winberht should certainly not be described as 'clericus regis', a title given to him by William of Malmesbury.[72] He can only have been what the charter claims for him, a scribe writing at the beneficiary's request.

The earliest royal scribe to have been credited in modern times with the drafting and writing of royal charters is Felix, 'secretary' to King Æthelwulf of Wessex. He was a Frank, like Lupus of Ferrières, who refers to him in a letter to Æthelwulf as 'qui epistolarum vestrarum officio fungebatur'.[73] This reference has been taken to mean that Felix was a Wessex chancery official, an interpretation which in my view cannot be accepted without further independent evidence, since letters and charters were not necessarily dealt with by the same scribes. Two famous original charters of Æthelwulf have been quoted as supporting evidence, the Chart diploma for the thegn Æthelmod (Mereworth, 28 May 843),[74] and the grant by Æthelwulf to himself of twenty hides in the South Hams (Dorchester, 26 December 846).[75]

In the charter of 843 Stevenson detected traces of Frankish influence, which he tentatively ascribed to Felix.[76] One of them, in the boundary clause, concerns the use of the word *theodoice* in the phrase 'unus . . . silva . . . quem nos theodoice snad nominamus'. The word, Stevenson suggested, should have read *theodisce*, a vernacular equivalent for such Latin expressions as *saxonice* or *in saxonica lingua*. Since it is true, of course, that *snad* is a correct translation for *silva*, Stevenson may be right. It is surprising, however, that in a boundary clause the name of the wood should not have been given more precisely, in a form similar to 'Biscopessnad'. To arrive at such a form, one would have to correct 'theodoice' to 'Theodo[r]ice[s]', an alternative reading which was rejected by Stevenson although the emendations required are not in fact more drastic than those suggested by him.[77]

As another sign of Frankish – and probably Felix's – influence Stevenson quoted the spellings

---

[69] *B.C.S.*, no. 186.

[70] *B.C.S.*, no. 67: 'quae supradicta terra conjuncta est terrae quam sanctae memoriae Lotharius quondam rex beato Petro pro remedio animae suae donasse cognoscitur'; compare *B.C.S.*, no. 107; 'ex meredie habet terram beatae memoriae Leotheri episcopi'. *B.C.S.*, no. 192: 'et ut nulla esset inposterum de hac contentio, hoc ipsum in libello primae donationis meae faciendum descripsi'; compare *B.C.S.*, no. 186: 'subtraxit tamen et donacionis primae litteras...;...terram de quam diu altercatio erat et praesens libellum ego discripsi atque excerpsi'. Compare also *donare decreverim* in *B.C.S.*, no. 107 (*cf.* no. 70), with *donare decrevi* in no. 103, *conferre . . . decrevi* in no. 65 and *impendere decrevi* in no. 71.

[71] *B.C.S.*, nos. 100, 103. See F. M. Stenton, *The Early History of the Abbey of Abingdon* (Oxford, 1913), pp. 11 ff.

[72] William of Malmesbury, *Gesta Pontificum*, ed. N. E. S. A. Hamilton (Rolls Series, 1870), p. 355.

[73] *Asser's Life of King Alfred*, ed. W. H. Stevenson (Oxford, 1959), p. 225; Parsons, *op. cit.*, p. 18, n. 29.

[74] *O.S.F.* III. xvii; *B.C.S.*, no. 442.

[75] *B.M.F.* II. 30; *B.C.S.*, no. 451.

[76] *Asser's Life of King Alfred*, pp. 202–4 and notes.

[77] Compare the form *ruienis* for *rurigenis* in *O.S.F.* II, Exeter vii, line 8.

Alahhere and *Walahhere* in the list of subscriptions found at the foot of the charter. These Old High German forms contrast with the normal Old English spellings *Alhhere* and *Wealhhere* given in a small schedule stitched to the charter. Since Stevenson's time Miss Parsons has proved beyond doubt that the charter, which incidentally comes from the archives of Christ Church, Canterbury, was drafted and written by a Canterbury scribe, and that the list of subscriptions at the foot of the charter was copied, and partly rearranged, by the same scribe from the attached schedule.[78] Thus it would seem that the Frankish spellings and any other peculiarities found in the charter should be attributed not to Felix but to a Canterbury scribe. In so far as the schedule is concerned, two scribes were involved, neither of whom can be identified with the writer of the charter. One of them, scribe A, wrote the column of witnesses headed by the king, while the other, scribe B, wrote the second column headed by the archbishop of Canterbury. Miss Parsons is probably right to argue that B belonged to the Canterbury scriptorium, but her suggestion that A was a royal scribe does not seem to be based on sufficient evidence.

Of all the charters of Æthelwulf none had better qualifications for being drafted and written by a royal scribe than the diploma of 846, a grant by the king to himself of twenty hides in the South Hams.[79] Indeed it is Miss Parsons' opinion that this document must be regarded as a chancery product.[80]

In the seventeenth century the charter was in Winchester Cathedral, as is proved by one of its endorsements (*Saxon'*) written in about 1640 by John Chase[81], notary public and registrar of Winchester Cathedral. It is possible, although by no means certain, that it was already there in Æthelwulf's time. The fact that its rare proem 'Siquidem sacris insertum voluminibus . . .' should have been found in only two other charters, one of which is a dubious document of Evesham provenance and the other a grant of Edgar for the Old Minster, Winchester, makes this possibility a very real one.[82] In other parts of its text, the charter of 846 resembles a number of other Wessex documents granted to various beneficiaries and coming from several archives, and its boundary clause is in a West-Saxon dialect.[83] It is therefore reasonably certain that the draftsman came from Wessex.

The script of the charter, a very distinctive one, reappears in one book, which in the fourteenth century belonged to the library of St Augustine's Canterbury.[84] It is also found in two original charters connected with Æthelwulf's first confirmation of the Council of Kingston, which confirmation, issued at Wilton in 838, is couched in what appears to be a Wessex formula. Both charters

---

[78] Parsons, *op. cit.*, pp. 15–19. Æthelwulf's charter of 843 (*O.S.F.* III, xvii. *B.C.S.*, no. 442) is written in the same hand as *B.M.F.* II. 6 (*B.C.S.*, no. 310), a record of the Council of 12 Oct. 803 which abolished the archbishopric of Lichfield and affirmed the primacy of Canterbury; this record is drawn up in the name of the archbishop of Canterbury and comes from the archives of Christ Church, Canterbury. There is therefore no doubt that the two documents were written by a Canterbury scribe, and that the record of the council cannot possibly be regarded as an original, but may be a copy made *c.* 843. There is a striking resemblance between the formulae of Æthelwulf's charter and those of a charter of Ceolnoth, archbishop of Canterbury, for the Canterbury *familia* (*B.C.S.*, no. 406).

[79] *B.M.F.* II. 30; *B.C.S.*, no. 451; *E.H.D.*, I, pp. 481–83; Finberg, *The Early Charters of Devon and Cornwall*, no. 10.

[80] Parsons, *op. cit.*, p. 18, n. 29; p. 32, n. 95.

[81] Compare the endorsements of Cotton Ch. VIII. 16A (*B.M.F.* III. 3; *B.C.S.*, no. 677), *O.S.F.* II, Winchester Cath. ii (*B.C.S.*, no. 1003), Cotton Ch. VIII. 12 (*B.M.F.* III. 21; *B.C.S.*, no. 926) and Cotton Ch. VIII. 9 (*B.M.F.* IV. 31; *K.C.D.*, no. 781). For a facsimile of a document written by John Chase, see *Documents relating to the History of the Cathedral Church of Winchester in the Seventeenth Century*, ed. W. R. W. Stephens and F. T. Madge (Hampshire Record Soc., 1897), plate opposite p. 57.

[82] *K.C.D.*, no. 797; Finberg, *E.C.W.M.*, no. 356. The Winchester charter of Edgar (*B.C.S.*, no. 1307; Finberg, *E.C.W.*, no. 122; from B.M., Add. MS. 15350, fo. 116 is corrupt in places: it contains two interesting misreadings in the proem, *unitatis* for *u*ᵣ*anitatis*, and *largitur* for *legitur*.

[83] *B.C.S.*, no. 410, 431; Finberg, *E.C.W.*, no. 567.

[84] Bodleian Library, MS. Bodley 426; *C.L.A.*, II, no. 234.

were in the archives of Christ Church, Canterbury, in the latter part of the twelfth century, but probably only one of them was already there in Æthelwulf's reign.[85] The other may have then belonged to a Kentish abbey, if we trust the following private note which is written on the dorse, in the hand of our scribe:

These are the agreements of Egbert and Æthelwulf with the archbishop and with their councillors [about] your election. If anyone should molest you for your election, then show this writing.[86]

The abbot whose election was in dispute may have been that of any of the monasteries which were later abandoned and whose title-deeds were acquired by the archbishop of Canterbury. The tone of the note and the way in which it refers to the kings and to the archbishop show that whoever dictated it was neither in the service of the king nor in that of the archbishop of Canterbury. He was undoubtedly a high ecclesiastic, either the bishop of Winchester or the bishop of Sherborne, the two Wessex bishops; both commonly witnessed Æthelwulf's charters. The actual scribe of the note, who, as we have seen, also wrote the charter of 846, was probably connected with one of the two bishops. A case can be made for Winchester: documents written at Winchester and Southampton have formulae in common with the scribe's works.[87] Arguments can also be adduced in favour of Sherborne: for example, Æthelwulf's first confirmation of the Council of Kingston took place at Wilton; Ealhstan, bishop of Sherborne, witnessed the charter of 846, whereas the bishop of Winchester did not. There would be a slightly stronger case for Winchester if one could be sure that the charter of 846 was already in the archives of Winchester during the reign of Æthelwulf. It is true that the period covered by the scribe's works (838–46) corresponds to the episcopate of only one bishop of Sherborne, Ealhstan, and of two bishops of Winchester, Eadhun and Helmstan, but this does not really affect the point at issue, because, if the bishop drafted the documents, he most probably did not write them himself. In so far as the formulae are concerned, they were probably handed down from one bishop to his successor, and we cannot be sure that formulae used by a bishop of Winchester always differed from those adopted at Sherborne.

If the drafting and writing of Æthelwulf's grant to himself was left to the care of an ecclesiastical scriptorium, we can hardly argue that there was then anything resembling a royal chancery. Was the composition and writing of Æthelwulf's charters left to chance or was it governed by a deliberate policy? Perhaps it was shared by several ecclesiastical scriptoria working either simultaneously on a territorial basis or successively on a rotating system similar to that followed in Alfred's court.[88] Such principles may have been adopted for charters concerning lands situated in Wessex proper or for charters issued there. They certainly did not apply to all the charters relating to persons or lands in recently-conquered Kent. There Æthelwulf's charters were sometimes drawn up according to a purely Kentish pattern which varied slightly from one beneficiary to another; this happened in the case of the Chart diploma of 843, which, as we have seen, was drafted and written by a Canterbury scribe. Sometimes Kentish formulae were used side by side with Wessex ones.[89] This suggests that the beneficiary could still play a considerable part in the drafting and writing of royal charters in Æthelwulf's reign.

To speak of Kentish, Mercian or Wessex formulae, before the reign of Athelstan, may give

---

[85] *B.M.F.* I. 17, dorse; *B.M.F.* II. 27, face; *B.C.S.*, no. 421. In both documents, the second confirmation (839) is written in a similar hand, but probably by a different scribe from the first confirmation.

[86] *B.M.F.* II. 27, dorse.

[87] *B.C.S.*, no. 431; Finberg, *E.C.W.*, pp. 206–8.

[88] *Asser's Life of King Alfred*, pp. 86–87; P. Hunter Blair, *An Introduction to Anglo-Saxon England* (Cambridge Univ. Press, 1962), p. 212.

[89] *B.C.S.*, nos. 438, 449, 459. The actual record of the Council of Kingston of 838 (*B.C.S.*, no. 421) follows a Canterbury pattern and is in *B.M.F.* I. 17 written in a Canterbury hand (compare the hand in *B.M.F.* II. 26, which has no royal confirmation).

the impression that from an early date each Anglo-Saxon kingdom had evolved a uniform and distinctive charter pattern. This is only partly true. In the first place, all Anglo-Saxon charters at one given time are roughly drawn up on the same lines, this being due partly to their common Italian origin, partly to the relations which continued to exist between the churches of the various kingdoms. Secondly, formulae could vary within a single kingdom, at least from diocese to diocese. For example, throughout Kent, early charters often made the king address the grantee in the second person, *tibi*. But some formulae were more common in Canterbury than in Rochester and vice versa. In Canterbury the granting words used both in royal and in archiepiscopal charters normally are *dabo et concedo*.[90] The same formula is also found in Rochester, but there the use of one single verb in the present tense is more common, *concedo* or *trado* or *perdono*.[91] In Wessex as a whole the granting verb is generally in the past tense, *largitus sum*, etc.

The fact that royal charters for Canterbury differ from those for Rochester and that royal charters for Canterbury resemble their archiepiscopal counterparts is an indication that, before the tenth century, the 'administrative unit' for the drawing up of royal charters in Kent was the diocese, and that the head of that unit was the bishop or archbishop, perhaps acting in collaboration with the beneficiary if the latter was a monastic community with a scriptorium. If we turn to Mercia, we also find that, in the eighth and ninth centuries, royal charters for grants within the diocese of Worcester have many points in common with the few extant charters of the bishops. Again the similarity applies to the granting words, *concedens donabo* or *donans donabo* or *tradens donabo*, and also to the dating clause, *conscripta est* or *gesta est*, and to the words introducing the grant, *cogitavi quod*, *precogitavi ut*, etc.[92] The same could be said of the anathema and blessing, *pax augentibus*, etc.[93]

If, as seems likely, the Anglo-Saxon bishops recruited the scribes of royal charters from among the personnel of near-by monastic communities, their task must have become well-nigh impossible by the reign of King Alfred, when most monasteries had either fallen into decay or been destroyed by the Danish invaders. The drafting of charters implied a reasonable knowledge of the Latin tongue, and this knowledge, we are told, was virtually non-existent when Alfred came to the throne.[94] Judging from the Latin of the Chart diploma of 843 and of Æthelwulf's grant to himself of 846, Latin scholarship was already very low in Æthelwulf's reign, in Kent as well as in Wessex. This, incidentally, had probably contributed to the gradual replacement of the short boundary-clause of Roman origin in Latin by a more detailed one in the vernacular, an evolution which had also taken place in parts of the Continent:[95] in many respects, the clause was the most important part of the charter and had to be understood by all. There is no evidence to show that the situation, in so far as learning and monastic life were concerned, had much improved generally by the time of Athelstan. Yet, during his reign, the flow of royal charters, which had virtually ceased fifteen years or so before his accession, started again with a renewed vigour.[96] The Latin of Athelstan's charters may be involved and full of hellenisms, but it certainly does not display a lack of learning. At the same time, the charters indicate that this learning was still confined to a privileged few. We no longer find, as before, that the majority of charters vary in form from diocese to diocese. There is now a striking tendency towards a uniformity of style which, instead of being restricted to isolated

---

[90] *B.C.S.*, nos. 342, 380, 406 (archiepiscopal charters); nos. 213–14, 328, 340, 346, 348, 370, 396, 400, 442, 496, etc. (royal charters).

[91] *B.C.S.*, nos. 194, 227–8, 242, 257, 260, 339, 502.

[92] *B.C.S.*, nos. 241, 283, 304, 455, 490 (abbatial and episcopal charters); nos. 117, 137–8, 164, 201–3, 216, 229–30, 246, 267, 450, 482, 488, 511, 513, 540, etc. It is not claimed that all the charters in this list are genuine.

[93] *B.C.S.*, nos. 304, 490, 534 (episcopal charters); nos. 295, 356–7, 360, 492, 509 (royal charters).

[94] *Asser's Life of King Alfred*, pp. 225, 303; Hunter Blair, *op. cit.*, p. 173.

[95] G. M. Young, *The Origin of the West-Saxon Kingdom*, p. 25.

[96] Stenton, *Latin Charters*, pp. 52–3.

formulae as in Æthelwulf's charters, extends in some cases to all the formal parts of the document. This applies to charters concerning a wide variety of beneficiaries (mostly laymen), granting lands distant from one another and issued in places as far apart as Buckingham, Winchester and Lifton, Devon.[97] Not only are the charters similar or identical in their formulae, but some of them are also written in the same hand. The practice of using the same draftsmen and scribes for a large number of charters which were connected with one another in no obvious way continued under Athelstan's successors and lasted apparently until some time in Edgar's reign.[98]

Since the only connexion between such royal charters appears to be the king as grantor, it is tempting to identify their draftsmen and scribes as officials of a royal chancery. Common draftsmen and scribes, however, can be explained without assuming the existence of a problematic chancery. If the state of learning in England at the beginning of the tenth century was such that most scriptoria had ceased to exist, it is obvious that the drawing up of royal charters would have had to be concentrated into the hands of the scribes of whatever scriptorium remained. Thus uniformity would have been achieved, not by royal design, but by accident. One such scriptorium continued to be active in the early part of the tenth century, the Winchester scriptorium, and it is with that scriptorium that at least six – and probably seven – out of eight so-called royal scribes found at work during the period 931–63 are associated.

Here is the list of the works of the eight scribes:[99]

Scribe (1): *B.M.F.* III. 3, 5 (*B.C.S.*, nos. 677, 702).

Scribe (2): *B.M.F.* III. 9, 10; *O.S.F.* III. xxv (*B.C.S.*, nos. 741, 753, 780).

Scribe (3): *B.M.F.* III. 12, 13, 16; *O.S.F.* III. xxvi, xxvii (*B.C.S.*, nos. 791, 813, 820, 869, 877).

Scribe (4): *B.M.F.* III. 21 (*B.C.S.*, no. 926).

Scribe (5): *B.M.F.* III. 20; *The Crawford Collection*, v (*B.C.S.*, nos. 961, 1347).

Scribe (6): *B.M.F.* III. 22, 23, 24, 25; *O.S.F.* III. xxx (*B.C.S.*, nos. 1055, 1066, 1082, 1083, 1101).

Scribe (7): *O.S.F.* II, Winchester Cath. II (*B.C.S.*, no. 1003).

Scribe (8): *O.S.F.* II, Winchester Coll. III (*B.C.S.*, no. 748).

Scribe (4) has been identified by Mr N. R. Ker as the probable writer of the 951 annal in the Parker Chronicle (Cambridge, Corpus Christi College 173) and is therefore a Winchester scribe.[100] Scribes (2), (3), (5), (7) and (8) write a hand of the same style as (4); (4), (5) and (7) use the same type of decorated chrismon, and so on. If we except (6) and possibly (1), the style of all the other scribes is so alike that one cannot even be sure that some of the works listed here under different hands were not in fact written by the same scribe.

The case of (1) and (6) is more difficult to solve. One of the two originals ascribed to (1), a grant of Ham, Wiltshire, to the thegn Wulfgar, was written (*perscripta*) at Lifton, Devon, on 12 November 931; the other, a grant to the thegn Ælfwold of land near Canterbury was written at Winchester on 28 May 934. The scribe cannot be identified with absolute certainty as a Winchester scribe, but his hand is in some ways similar to the script of a manuscript probably written at Winchester (Cambridge, Corpus Christi Coll. 183);[101] in addition, a document closely connected with the Ham charter, Wulfgar's will in which Ham is left to the Old Minster, Winchester, after the death of

---

[97] *B.C.S.*, nos. 677, 702, 704.

[98] R. Drögereit, 'Gab es eine angelsächsische Königskanzlei?', *Archiv für Urkundenforschung*, XIII (1935), pp. 335–436.

[99] *Ibid.*; T. A. M. Bishop, 'A Charter of King Edwy', *The Bodleian Library Record*, VI. i (Oct. 1957), pp. 369–73; Ker, *Catalogue of Manuscripts containing Anglo-Saxon*, p. lix.

[100] Ker, *op. cit., loc. cit.*

[101] *Ibid.*, no. 42; regarding the initials of this manuscript, see F. Wormald, 'Decorated Initials in English MSS. from A.D. 900 to 1100', *Archaeologia*, XCI (1945), pp. 115–16.

Wulfgar and his wife, is written in a hand resembling that of a passage in the Parker Chronicle.[102] It is therefore likely that (1) was also a Winchester scribe.

Scribe (6), the latest of the eight scribes, writes in a different style. Two of his works come from the archives of the abbey of Abingdon: one is a grant to the abbey itself (*B.C.S.*, no. 1066) and the other a grant to one of the abbey's benefactors, the thegn Wulfric (*B.C.S.*, no. 1055). This evidence is too slight to warrant a definite conclusion, but there is at least a possibility that the scribe may have been working at Abingdon during the abbacy of Æthelwold.[103]

From the end of Edgar's reign the situation seems to have reverted approximately to what it had been before the reign of Athelstan. This is true of the actual writing of the charters, which in a number of cases can be definitely related to the scriptorium of the immediate or eventual beneficiary, when the latter was an ecclesiastical community: for example, a charter of Æthelred for Bishop Ælfwold of Crediton (A.D. 997) is written in the same hand as the bishop's will;[104] other examples relating to Canterbury, Crediton and Winchester could also be quoted.[105] In so far as the drafting of the charters is concerned, it would seem that this part of the work was sometimes done under the direction or at the command of the bishop in whose diocese the lands granted were situated.[106] Occasionally, in the charters themselves either one bishop (not always the diocesan), or the abbot in whose favour the grant was made, claims in his subscription to have drafted (*dictavi, composui, perscribere jussi*, etc.) or even written the charter (*calamo scripsi*, etc.). Some of these charters are open to suspicion, but there are so many of them that their evidence cannot be entirely dismissed.[107] Since during the episcopate of Bishop Ælfeah of Winchester (934–951) royal charters were drafted and written at Winchester, the same procedure may have in turn been followed at Glastonbury and Abingdon under Dunstan and Æthelwold, both Ælfeah's pupils. Thus, after being concentrated into the hands of Winchester scribes for lack of any others, the drafting and writing of royal charters may have become more and more decentralized as new monastic and episcopal scriptoria were being set up or revived, following the monastic renaissance of Dunstan's time.

If, as I believe, the diplomas of all the Anglo-Saxon kings were drawn up by ecclesiastics, their authenticity may have depended on the degree of trust which was placed in bishops and abbots by grantors and grantees alike. Could we, at any rate, regard Anglo-Saxon bishops as *authentice persone* on the ground that their word was as good as the king's word, whether or not it was supported by an oath?[108] This is mere speculation, like so much else connected with Anglo-Saxon charters.

PIERRE CHAPLAIS

---

[102] *B.M.F.* III. 3B; *B.C.S.*, no. 678; Corpus Christi Coll., Cambridge, 173 (Ker, *op. cit.*, no. 39), fo. 25, lines 1–7. I owe this information to the kindness of Mr Ker.

[103] See T. A. M. Bishop, 'Notes on Cambridge Manuscripts, Part IV', *Trans. Cambridge Bibliog. Soc.*, II. 4 (1957), p. 333.

[104] *O.S.F.* III. xxxv; *The Crawford Collection*, X.

[105] Compare *O.S.F.* III. ii and xxxix; *B.M.F.* IV. 18 and *O.S.F.* II, Exeter xi; *B.M.F.* IV, 24 and 31.

[106] Harmer, *Anglo-Saxon Writs*, pp. 34–41.

[107] *B.C.S.*, nos. 724, 726, 816, 880, 889, 906, 920, 930, 935, 938, 941, 949, 956–57, 964–65, 967–68, 971, 978, 987, 1009, 1035, 1047, 1112, 1138, 1165, 1197, 1282, 1284; *K.C.D.*, nos. 621, 684, 736, 743–44, 787, 811, 817, 1289, 1292, 1296, 1305, 1308, 1316, 1332; *O.S.F.* II, Exeter viii, x–xii, xivd. See also *K.C.D.*, no. 754 (*O.S.F.* I. xxii), a charter of Archbishop Æthelnoth of Canterbury.

[108] *E.H.D.*, I, p. 363, art. 16.

The Anglo-Saxon Chancery:
From the Diploma to the Writ[1]

By the second half of the twelfth century most of those in England who belonged to the ranks of the 'lower nobility', and many peasant freeholders, had acquired a seal, once the privilege of kings and of their immediate entourage.[2] However regrettable it may have seemed to Richard de Lucy, Henry II's justiciar, that even a *militulus* such as Gilbert de Balliol should have possessed a seal, Gilbert was only one of many.[3] Owning a seal had become a necessity as much as a status symbol. At that time, royal intervention to stop the use of seals by lesser landowners, for instance by those below the comital rank, would have had the same effect, and caused as much resentment in lay and ecclesiastical circles, as measures forbidding them to make grants of land to the Church. Such grants were now normally made by sealed charters: to borrow someone else's seal for that purpose was hardly dignified,[4] and to impress one's own teeth on the wax as a substitute for a seal matrix required so much humility that even the promise of rich rewards in heaven might not have induced it easily.[5]

On the eve of the Norman Conquest the ancestors of those *militiuli* scorned by Richard de Lucy had scarcely been aware of the importance of seals, and possibly even of their existence. Duke William of Normandy himself had apparently never thought that it would enhance his ducal prestige to set a seal to his charters: he was quite content to draw a cross at the foot of the document, and in some cases he seems to have simply touched the parchment, leaving it to someone else to draw a cross on his behalf.[6] If he had a seal at all before he came to England, and there is no evidence that he had, he certainly did not use it for authenticating charters. Nor did he regard it as beneath his

---

[1] I am very grateful to Mr N. R. Ker for his comments on the script of some of the documents mentioned in this paper. Plates I and II are reproduced by courtesy of the Trustees of the British Museum.

[2] *Documents illustrative of the Social and Economic History of the Danelaw* [hereafter *Danelaw Charters*], ed. F. M. Stenton (Brit. Acad., 1920), p. xcii and n. 2. In the thirteenth century, unfree peasants also used seals; see *Carte nativorum*, ed. C. N. L. Brooke and M. M. Postan (Northants. Rec. Soc., xx, 1960), p. xlii and notes; R. H. Hilton, 'Gloucester Abbey Leases of the late thirteenth century', *Univ. of Birmingham Hist. Journal*, IV (1953–4), pp. 13–14.

[3] H. Jenkinson, *Guide to Seals in the Public Record Office* (London, H.M.S.O., 1954), p. 6 and n. 3.

[4] Stenton, *Danelaw Charters*, nos. 332, 350, 369, 371, 373; A. B. Tonnochy, *Cat. of British Seal-dies in the British Museum* (London, 1952), p. xli, n. 3.

[5] A. de Boüard, *Manuel de diplomatique française et pontificale*, I (Paris, 1929), p. 358, n. 3; British Museum, Harl. MS. 2110, fo. 18: 'Et ut magis rata sit donatio nostra et concessio, appendimus ceram huic cirographo loco sigilli et singuli illi cere dentes nostras impressimus'.

[6] *Recueil des actes des ducs de Normandie (911–1066)*, ed. M. Fauroux (*Mémoires de la Société des Antiquaires de Normandie*, XXXVI, 1961), p. 57.

dignity to leave the writing of his charters to scribes retained by the beneficiaries, i.e. monastic or episcopal scribes.[7]

William changed his ways, or so it would seem, soon after the Conquest. Possibly as early as 1066, and certainly not later than 1069, the Conqueror was using a splendid double-sided seal, which represented him as riding in battle on the obverse (Norman side) and sitting in majesty on the reverse (English side); the legend read, on the equestrian side: HOC NORMANNORUM WILLEL-MUM NOSCE PATRONUM SI, and continued, on the majesty side: HOC ANGLIS REGEM SIGNO FATEARIS EUNDEM.[8] Not later than 1069, and possibly from 1066, he had an official styled *cancellarius*, who can be assumed to have been the custodian of William's seal.[9] By the 1080s there was at least one royal scribe, whose hand has been identified in three of William's documents, a writ for the abbey of Westminster, a diploma for the abbey of Cluny (foundation charter of Lewes Priory) and a diploma for the abbey of Fécamp.[10] The identification of one single royal scribe scarcely justifies the view that the Conqueror had a fully organized chancery, but further research may possibly lead to other identifications. Even the most sceptical of scholars cannot fail to agree that the combination of a seal, a chancellor and one royal scribe formed the nucleus of a chancery organization, and this was far more than William had ever had in the duchy of Normandy before 1066.

That William the Conqueror regarded his kingdom of England and his duchy of Normandy as two separate entities is made abundantly clear in the design and legend of his seal. He was *rex* of the English in England and *patronus* of the Normans in Normandy. Whatever the obscure title of *patronus* may have been intended to convey, there is nowhere any hint that William had it in mind to subordinate one of his two dominions to the other or to impose the same system of government on both. Such charters of his as have survived in the original, admittedly only a handful, show how little impact the Conquest of England made on Norman diplomatic in the Conqueror's lifetime. As a rule, his grants of Norman lands to Norman beneficiaries continued to be made in the same traditional form as they had been before 1066, that of an unsealed diploma, authenticated by signa only and written by a scribe of the grantee. This is true in particular of the grants made to the two favourite abbeys of William and his wife, Saint-Etienne and La Trinité of Caen.[11] There is one apparent exception: the diploma of 1085 recording the grant of Steyning and Bury to the abbey of Fécamp is in the hand of a royal scribe and is authenticated with the royal seal.[12] It should be added, however, that this grant, unlike the other extant Norman originals, concerns lands situated in England. Although the charter unaccountably places William's title of *patronus Normannorum* before that of *rex Anglorum*, it was issued by him as king of England rather than as duke of Normandy. To that extent the Fécamp charter is no more Norman than the foundation charter of the priory of St Pancras, Lewes, written by the same royal scribe and also formerly sealed.[13] The sealed grant of Taynton to the abbey of Saint-Denis (1069), written by a scribe of the beneficiary, is also a

---

[7] *Ibid.*, p. 51. This question will be discussed in a forthcoming volume of facsimiles of Norman and Anglo-Norman charters.

[8] The most complete impression of William I's only authentic seal (the so-called second seal) is reproduced in *Facsimiles of English Royal Writs to A.D. 1100 presented to V. H. Galbraith*, ed. T. A. M. Bishop and P. Chaplais (Oxford, 1957), plate XXVIII.

[9] Ordnance Survey, *Facsimiles of Anglo-Saxon Manuscripts* [hereafter *O.S.F.*], 3 vols. (Southampton, 1878–84), II, Exeter xvi; D. C. Douglas, *William the Conqueror* (London, 1964), p. 293.

[10] P. Chaplais, 'Une charte originale de Guillaume le Conquérant pour l'abbaye de Fécamp: la donation de Steyning et de Bury (1085)', *L'abbaye bénédictine de Fécamp, Ouvrage scientifique du XIIIᵉ centenaire*, I (Fécamp, 1959), p. 94; *Facsimiles of English Royal Writs . . .*, plate XXV (a).

[11] British Museum, Add. Ch. 75503: Alençon, Arch. dép. Orne, H. 421/1; Caen, Arch. dép. Calvados, H. 1830/3-4.

[12] *L'abbaye bénédictine de Fécamp*, I, pp. 93–104 and plate I.

[13] *Early Yorkshire Charters*, VIII, ed. C. T. Clay, pp. 54–5, no. 2 and facsimile.

royal grant, not a ducal one.[14] Allowance must be made, of course, for the large number of originals which have been lost, but I doubt whether they would show, if they had survived, that William's seal and chancery played any significant part in the government of Normandy.

On the other hand, the English evidence suggests that William the Conqueror's seal was extensively used for English affairs. From 1066 to 1087 sealed royal documents are the rule. Two important exceptions are worthy of notice: one, the unsealed record of the Winchester 'council' of Easter 1072, probably drawn up under Lanfranc's supervision and possibly modelled on the records of earlier Norman councils, has autograph signa and autograph subscriptions;[15] the other, William's confirmation of a grant made by Bishop Leofric to the cathedral of Exeter (1069), follows in the main the pattern of the Anglo-Saxon land-books and ends like them with non-autograph signa and subscriptions.[16] The latter document has often been singled out for comment as a particularly striking link between Anglo-Norman diplomatic and its Anglo-Saxon predecessor. An even better proof of diplomatic continuity in England from the pre-Conquest to the post-Conquest period is the adoption and extended use by William the Conqueror of the Anglo-Saxon writ. This point has been made time and time again in recent years. We are constantly reminded that from 1066 to 1070 William issued writs in Old English, modelled to the smallest details on those of Edward the Confessor. It is only after 1070 that Latin, a language more readily intelligible to the Norman conquerors, at least to the literates among them, began to be used in writs and soon superseded English altogether. Whatever adaptations and improvements in the form of the documents this linguistic change made necessary or possible, they concern the later history of the Anglo-Norman writ and do not affect its origin and early history. As long as the writs continued to be issued in English, William had to leave their drafting and writing to scribes of English stock.[17] If now we add that the Conqueror's seal was double-sided, like Edward the Confessor's seal and unlike the seals of the contemporary rulers of France and Germany, we are faced, it might seem, with the inevitable conclusion that all the components of William's early chancery – documents, seal and scriptorium – had been taken over by him from his Anglo-Saxon predecessor, and that he did so exclusively, or almost exclusively, for the government of England: the silence of the sources on any extensive use of William's seal in the internal government of Normandy is matched by an equally significant lack of evidence regarding the regular use of writs, even the later ones couched in Latin, for Norman administration.[18] Are we not therefore entitled to regard the first chapter in the history of William the Conqueror's chancery as the epilogue to the history of Edward the Confessor's secretarial organization? How much organized was the Anglo-Saxon chancery which William inherited?

It is common knowledge that, if we leave the laws aside, all the documents issued in the name of Anglo-Saxon kings fall under two main categories, the diplomas, always unsealed, and the writs, of which sealed originals are extant for the reign of Edward the Confessor. In so far as the diplomas are concerned, it has been pointed out elsewhere that they were produced, not in a self-staffed royal

---

[14] *Facsimiles of English Royal Writs*, opposite plate XXVIII.

[15] *Palaeographical Society*, ed. E. A. Bond and E. M. Thompson, III (1873–83), plate 170.

[16] *O.S.F.* II, Exeter xvi.

[17] F. M. Stenton, *Anglo-Saxon England*, 2nd ed. (Oxford, 1947), pp. 633–4; R. R. Darlington, *The Norman Conquest* (*The Creighton Lecture in History 1962*, London, 1963), p. 5.

[18] The statement by C. H. Haskins, *Norman Institutions* (Cambridge, Mass., 1925), p. 54 and n. 258, that in William's reign 'writs fly in either direction across the Channel' is a gross exaggeration. Two documents which deal with Norman affairs may be described as writs: one, for the abbey of Jumièges, concerns a grant of lands in England (*Regesta regum Anglo-Normannorum*, i, no. 194; *Chartes de l'abbaye de Jumièges*, ed. J.-J. Vernier, I (Soc. de l'hist. de Norm., 1916), no. xli); the other, for the abbey of Marmoutier, concerns possessions of the abbey in Normandy, but its initial protocol is in a highly unusual form: 'Guillermus Dei gratia rex Anglorum, M. regine dilecte sue conjugi, perpetuam salutem' (*Regesta*, i, no. 161; *Revue catholique de Normandie*, x (1900), p. 348).

secretariat, but at all times in monastic or episcopal scriptoria.[19] It is with such scriptoria that even the interesting series of charters for which a royal chancery origin had previously been claimed should be associated. The series ranges in date from 931 to 963, a period which might be described as the formative years of the tenth-century monastic revival, following the black-out of learning and the disappearance of monastic life which characterized the reigns of Alfred and Edward the Elder. Among these charters the largest group, including the earliest, were written in the scriptorium of Winchester, one of the seven writers involved being the scribe who recorded the death of Bishop Ælfheah of Winchester (12 March 951) in the Parker Chronicle. Once the Winchester connexion had been established, one could not be surprised to find that most charters in the Winchester group had been issued during the episcopate of Ælfheah, the prime mover of the monastic renaissance, the teacher of St Dunstan and St Æthelwold. Nor could it be regarded as an unexpected development if the writing of royal charters, which had been concentrated at Winchester in the 940s, came to be done also at Glastonbury under Dunstan in the 950s and at Abingdon under Æthelwold in the 960s.

One further proof of the activity of the Winchester scriptorium as a centre for the writing of royal documents during Athelstan's reign has recently been found in the famous gospel-book presented by the king to Christ Church, Canterbury, Cotton MS. Tiberius A. ii. The book itself, written in a caroline minuscule of continental type, is supposed to have been originally given to Athelstan, some time between 936 and 939, by King Otto, who was later to become Emperor Otto I. This supposition is solely based on the fact that the two names *Odda rex* and *Mihthild mater regis*, each preceded by a cross, are found on folio 24[r] of the manuscript.[20] Whatever the early history of the book may have been, two separate inscriptions definitely state that it was eventually presented to Christ Church by Athelstan. The inscription on folio 15[r], a metrical one, after a eulogy on the king's achievements, records his gift to Christ Church and ends with an anathema against anyone who might steal the book.[21] The tone of the inscription suggests that it was written by a scribe of the beneficiary, Christ Church, while the appearance of the script, which is of the mid-tenth century, proves beyond doubt that the writer was of foreign origin, like the scribe of the main part of the book; he, too, writes in a caroline minuscule of continental type, his only concession to the insular alphabet being the use of the 'eth'–instead of th–in his transcription of the king's name.[22] He may have been of German extraction, like Frithegod, the Canterbury monk who wrote a Life of St Wilfrid during the pontificate of Archbishop Oda of Canterbury,[23] and like several priests who were living in various parts of England during the reign of Athelstan.[24]

The other inscription, on folio 15[v], is of a very different character.[25] The handwriting, strongly insular in appearance, is that of a Winchester scribe who wrote five royal charters granted to various beneficiaries and spread over the period 944–9.[26] The first part of the text explains, in the third person, that Athelstan *Anglorum basyleos et curagulus totius Bryttannię*–a style not uncommonly found in royal charters–[27] gave the gospel to Christ Church; the archbishop and the 'ministers' of the church were to ensure its safe custody. The last sentence, in the first person, is a request for

[19] *Journal of the Society of Archivists*, III, 2 (Oct. 1965), pp. 48–61. Reprinted above, pp. 28–42.

[20] *Cat. of Ancient Manuscripts in the British Museum*, II (London, 1884), pp. 36, 88.

[21] *Cartularium Saxonicum* [hereafter *B.C.S.*,] ed. W. de Gray Birch, no. 710.

[22] See F. Wormald in *Atti del X Congresso Internazionale, Roma 4–11 settembre 1955* (Rome, 1957), p. 163.

[23] *Vita Sancti Wilfridi auctore Fridegoda*, in *The Historians of the Church of York and its Archbishops*, ed. J. Raine, I (Rolls Series, 1879), pp. 105–59; see also *ibid.*, pp. xxxix–xlii. For the name Frithegod, see T. Forssner, *Continental-Germanic Personal Names in England* (Uppsala, 1916). p. 94.

[24] Stenton, *Anglo-Saxon England*, 2nd ed., p. 438.

[25] *B.C.S.*, no. 711. It is reproduced on Plate 1 (*left*), in reduced size.

[26] *Journal of the Society of Archivists*, III. 2 (Oct. 1965), p. 60, scribe 3. See above, p. 41.

[27] See, for example, *B.C.S.*, nos. 707, 714, 742.

prayers from Athelstan himself. There is no reason to suspect that this inscription, due to the Winchester scribe, was not written at the time of the gift, towards the end of Athelstan's life, whereas the Christ Church verses may have been inserted in the book at a slightly later date.

Winchester may have acquired the virtual monopoly of the writing of royal documents as a result of the decay of all the other episcopal and monastic scriptoria; it may have retained this monopoly as long as it remained the only native scriptorium in existence. The position was bound to change as soon as other monastic or episcopal scriptoria were set up or re-established. The first one to come to life again seems to have been at Glastonbury under Abbot Dunstan: during his rule, books and also royal charters for various beneficiaries were written in the abbey. Hatton MS. 30, now in the Bodleian Library, should be included among the books written in Glastonbury at the command of Dunstan, if we trust the following inscription which appears on the last folio: *Dunstan abbas hunc libellum scribere jussit.* The script of this book has the same general appearance, possibly characteristic of the Glastonbury scriptorium in the mid-tenth century, as that of an original charter of King Eadred granting twenty *cassati* in Pennard Minster, Somerset, to a nun of Wilton.[28] The charter was probably written by one of Dunstan's monks, and this could be easily explained by the comparative proximity to Glastonbury of both grantee and land granted. The short endorsement (*Pen()erd mynstres bóc*), written in the hand of the text, contrasts with the more elaborate ones found in most original diplomas of the period; typical Winchester endorsements read: 'This is the deed of x hides at N which A granted to B in perpetual inheritance'.[29] It should be noted that there is no subscription of Dunstan in the Pennard charter, whereas there is one in two diplomas closely connected with Glastonbury, both of which are claimed to have been written at the order of the abbot (*Ego . . . scribere jussi*, a phrase which reminds us of the inscription found on the last folio of Hatton MS. 30): both charters are indirect grants to the abbey of Glastonbury and they both concern Somerset.[30]

A more interesting case, if genuine, is that of King Eadred's grant of Reculver to Christ Church, Canterbury. The charter, an apparent original dated 949, is alleged to have been drafted and written by Dunstan himself. This claim is made in the last subscription to the charter:[31]

Ego Dunstan indignus abbas rege Eadredo inperante hanc domino meo hereditariam kartulam dictitando conposui et propriis digitorum articulis perscripsi.

Did Dunstan actually draft the charter himself and write it down with his own hand? W. H. Stevenson did not think so, and he rejected the document as spurious.[32] It is certainly true that its script has nothing in common with the hand D of the Bodleian Library MS. Auct. F. 4. 32 which Dr Hunt believes to be Dunstan's own hand.[33] It is equally certain, however, that the claims to autography which are often made in subscriptions, e.g. *manu propria*, should not be taken literally and were not meant to be so taken. In the case of the Reculver charter the wording of Dunstan's subscription may simply have been another way of saying that the document was written in the scriptorium of the abbey over which he ruled. This interpretation could be defended on the ground that the diploma shares several features with Glastonbury charters. In the anathema, for example, the

[28] *O.S.F.* II, Marquis of Bath ii; *B.C.S.*, no. 903; H. P. R. Finberg, *The Early Charters of Wessex* [hereafter *E.C.W.*] (Leicester Univ. Press, 1964), no. 469: A.D. 955.

[29] See, for example, *O.S.F.* II, Winchester Cath. ii; *O.S.F.* III. 25; *Facsimiles of Ancient Charters in the British Museum* [hereafter *B.M.F.*], 4 vols. (London, 1873–78), III. 9, 10.

[30] *B.C.S.*, nos. 816, 889; Finberg, *E.C.W.*, nos. 458, 466.

[31] *O.S.F.* I. 15. For a later 'facsimile' copy by a scribe whose latinity left much to be desired, see *B.M.F.* III. 15; *B.C.S.*, no. 880.

[32] W. H. Stevenson, 'Trinoda necessitas', *English Hist. Review*, XXIX (1914), p. 692, n. 18.

[33] *Saint Dunstan's Classbook from Glastonbury*, ed. R. W. Hunt (Umbrae Codicum Occidentalium, Amsterdam, 1961), pp. vi, xiv.

draftsman introduced the clause *vel passum pedis segregaverit*, a phrase to which no parallel has been found except in a Glastonbury charter of 944–6, which reads *vel unius pedis longitudinem . . . auferat*;[34] in both versions of the clause the word *vel* is redundant. In the Reculver charter the boundary clause is added on the dorse instead of being placed before the date and subscriptions. This unusual procedure may be compared with that followed in a Glastonbury charter of 946, which ends with the boundary clause.[35] Equally unusual at that date is the one-word endorsement (*Raculf*) due to the scribe of the charter, but a similarly short endorsement is also found on the Pennard charter for which a Glastonbury origin has been claimed above.[36]

Perhaps the arguments for connecting the Reculver diploma with the Glastonbury scriptorium have no great weight, but they cannot be entirely dismissed. Besides, the script of the face of the document seems to be contemporary and bears a faint resemblance to that of the words written on the book–and also along the rod–held by Christ on folio 1ʳ of the Bodleian Library MS. Auct. F. 4. 32; it is reasonably certain that these words were written by a Glastonbury monk in Dunstan's time.[37] The script of the boundary clause, on the dorse, is in a different hand, but, except for two obvious interpolations, it also appears to be contemporary.[38] In so far as the textual authenticity of the charter is concerned, no decisive argument against it can be advanced. The fact that the proem, apparently unique, uses a vocabulary reminiscent of Aldhelm's can hardly be regarded as a conclusive proof that the document was forged.[39] Nor does the utterly confused chronology of the period allow us to reject as impossible the attestation of *Osulf dux* on the ground that there is no evidence for Osulf's appointment as earl of Northumbria as early as 949.[40]

It may not be irrelevant to draw attention at this point to two well-known passages from the 'oldest Life' of Saint Dunstan, written between 995 and 1005. In one of them King Eadred is said to have committed to Dunstan's care, for safe custody in his monastery, *quamplures . . . rurales cartulas etiam veteres praecedentium regum thesauros necnon et diversas propriae adeptionis suae gazas.*[41] The other passage claims that a few years later Dunstan and all the others with whom similar deposits had been made were summoned to the king's death-bed and ordered to bring back Eadred's treasures.[42] If trustworthy, these passages imply that Eadred did not have a royal treasury proper, except perhaps for his relics which were kept by his priests,[43] but used instead as *ad hoc* repositories the monasteries in existence at that time, possibly those where his charters were written.

The latest of the so-called royal scribes of the mid-tenth century seems to have been an inmate of the abbey of Abingdon.[44] All the charters which he wrote are confined within the period

[34] *B.C.S.*, no. 817; Finberg, *E.C.W.*, no. 63.

[35] *B.C.S.*, no. 816; Finberg, *E.C.W.*, no. 458: one of the charters claimed to have been written on Dunstan's orders. See also *B.C.S.*, no. 1073; Finberg, *E.C.W.*, no. 485: a Somerset grant of Edgar to St Peter's, Bath; *O.S.F.* II, Exeter v; *B.C.S.*, no. 1056; Finberg, *The Early Charters of Devon and Cornwall* (Leicester Univ. Press, 1954), no. 83: a Cornish grant of Edgar to Eanulf *minister*.

[36] *O.S.F.* II, Marquis of Bath ii.   [37] See above, n. 33.

[38] In the description of the bounds the scribe uses *of* and *from* indifferently.

[39] Compare *Mon. Germ. Hist.*, *Auctores Antiquissimi*, XV (*Aldhelmi opera*), ed. R. Ehwald (Berlin, 1919), p. 268: 'praesago afflatus spiritu'; p. 368: 'tuba . . . reboat'; p. 442: 'virtutum meritis rutilans'; *O.S.F.* I. 15: 'sancti viri presago spiritu', 'tuba sanctae scripturae rebohans', 'meritis rutilantes'.

[40] *English Historical Documents* [hereafter *E.H.D.*], I, ed. D. Whitelock (London, 1955), p. 254 and n. 2.

[41] *Memorials of Saint Dunstan, Archbishop of Canterbury*, ed. W. Stubbs (Rolls Series, 1874), p. 29; *E.H.D.*, I, p. 829; V. H. Galbraith, *Studies in the Public Records* (Nelson, 1948), p. 39.

[42] *Memorials of Saint Dunstan*, ed. Stubbs, p. 31; *E.H.D.*, I, *loc. cit.*

[43] *Select English Historical Documents of the ninth and tenth centuries*, ed. F. E. Harmer (Cambridge Univ. Press, 1914), no. XXI (will of King Eadred): 'And ælcan minra mæssepreosta þe ic gesette hæbbe in to minum reliquium, fiftyg mancusa goldes . . .'. By the time of Æthelred II it seems that royal documents were kept in the king's sanctuary with his relics; see *Anglo-Saxon Wills*, ed. D. Whitelock (Cambridge Univ. Press, 1930), p. 151; *Anglo-Saxon Charters*, ed. A. J. Robertson (*ibid.*, 1956), p. 419.

[44] *Journal of the Society of Archivists*, III, 2 (Oct. 1965), p. 60, scribe 6, and no. 103. See above, pp. 41–2.

960–3, i.e. during the abbacy of Æthelwold, another former pupil of Bishop Ælfheah of Winchester. Before he was appointed abbot of Abingdon, Æthelwold had spent some time at Glastonbury as one of Dunstan's monks.[45] On the activity of the Abingdon scriptorium as a centre for the writing of royal charters, little can be added to what has already been said elsewhere. Two charters of King Eadred for the abbey of Abingdon are said to have been drafted by Æthelwold (*Ego . . . dictavi*), but their evidence is worthless since neither of them is authentic as it stands.[46] There are also two charters of Edgar, one for the abbey of Pershore and the other for the monks of Worcester, which Osgar, Æthelwold's successor as abbot of Abingdon, is alleged to have 'dictated' (*Ego Osgar abbas dict[avi]*).[47] The Worcester document was in all probability forged; in so far as the Pershore charter –an apparent original– is concerned, there is no doubt that it was tampered with, but the script is contemporary and it has a general appearance resembling that of authentic documents attributed to the scriptorium of Abingdon.[48] It may therefore have been drafted and written at Abingdon.

The twelfth-century author of the Liber Eliensis, in a famous passage, claims that from the end of Edgar's reign until the Norman Conquest the functions of royal chancellor (*in regis curia cancellarii . . . dignitatem*) were discharged in rotation by the abbots of St Augustine's, Canterbury, and of Ely and Glastonbury, each of them acting for four months at a time.[49] If the *cancellarii dignitas* which the Ely writer had in mind included the drafting and writing of royal diplomas, the evidence at present available suggests that the claim was unfounded; it may have been based on a wrong interpretation of what happened during the period 931–63 which we have just been considering. It may also be of some interest to note that the Ely story bears a remarkable resemblance to Asser's account of Alfred's court organization:[50]

in tribus . . . cohortibus praefati regis satellites prudentissime dividebantur, ita ut prima cohors uno mense in curto regio . . . commoraretur, menseque finito et adveniente alia cohorte, prima domum redibat, et ibi duobus . . . commorabatur mensibus. Secunda itaque cohors mense peracto, adveniente tertia, domum redibat, ut ibi duobus commoraretur mensibus. Sed et illa, finito unius mensis ministerio et adveniente prima cohorte, domum redibat, ibidem commoratura duobus mensibus. Et hoc ordine . . . in regali curto rotatur administratio.

There is not a shred of evidence to indicate that at any time between the seventh and the eleventh centuries Anglo-Saxon diplomas were drafted or written in what might be called, even loosely, a central royal secretariat, that is to say in a single organized department staffed with scribes who specialized in royal business.

Whereas we have a reasonably continuous series of original diplomas from 679 to 1066 (with a few well-known gaps), the earliest writs to have survived in the original belong to the reign of Edward the Confessor, and no copy, trustworthy or otherwise, has been traced for the period preceding the reign of Æthelred II (978–1016). This in itself does not prove anything regarding the respective antiquity of both types of document, since record survivals are often capricious. It is curious, however, that the appearance of the writs among the surviving records should coincide with a substantial decline in the number of extant diplomas, a fact which has been justifiably interpreted as a sign that the writ gradually replaced the diploma.[51]

---

[45] *E.H.D.*, I, p. 833.

[46] *B.C.S.*, nos. 906, 1047.

[47] *B.C.S.*, nos. 1282 (*B.M.F.* III. 30), 1284.

[48] Compare the script in *B.M.F.* III. 30 with that of *B.M.F.* III. 23, 25, etc. See also E. John, 'Some Latin Charters of the tenth century Reformation in England', *Revue bénédictine*, LXX (1960), p. 350.

[49] *Liber Eliensis*, ed. E. O. Blake (Camden third series, xcii, 1962), p. 146 and n.; Galbraith, *Studies in the Public Records*, pp. 39–40; F. Barlow, *The English Church, 1000–1066* (London, 1963), p. 125.

[50] *Asser's Life of King Alfred*, ed. W. H. Stevenson (Oxford, 1959), pp. 86–7.

[51] F. M. Stenton, *The Latin Charters of the Anglo-Saxon Period* [hereafter *Latin Charters*] (Oxford, 1955), pp. 87–91; *E.H.D.*, I, p. 346.

At first sight the writ and the diploma appear to have served different purposes and to have been complementary to one another.[52] The diploma seems to be a record, much embellished, of what took place when the grant was actually made; it describes one episode in the proceedings of a witenagemot attended by the king and by a number of royal councillors, ecclesiastical and lay, who represented the whole kingdom and as such witnessed and approved the grant.[53] The writ corresponds to a second stage in the history of the grant: it is a notification to the officials and suitors of the shire-court, that is to say to the relevant bishop and earl and to the thegns of the shire, that a grant in their shire has been made.[54] In all probability an oral declaration made by the king in a witenagemot formed the basis of every diploma. In the writ it is virtually certain that we have a record representing the substance of the words spoken on the king's behalf, and normally in his absence, to a shire-meeting: the writ is always in English, so that it could be understood by all; it consists of only a few sentences, devoid of rhetoric, which left no room for confusion or misinterpretation. The importance of the king's communication to the shire is evident, since it was before the shire-court that any disputes which might arise concerning the land granted would be brought and settled. For that reason it is probable that royal grants began to be notified to the shire-courts as soon as these courts were set up, long before the reign of Edward the Confessor.[55] That a notification of this kind should not only be delivered orally, but also be recorded in writing, and that the writing should be provided with an unimpeachable sign of authenticity may seem obvious to us, but how soon did it become obvious to the Anglo-Saxons?[56] If no appreciable decline of the diploma can be detected until the first half of the eleventh century, is it not precisely because at that time, and not before, declarations to the shire began to be recorded in writing? An oral declaration in the shire-court supplemented the diploma. The writ made it somewhat redundant. It is true that the diploma supplied details which were omitted from the writ; for example, it gave the detailed boundaries of the land granted, whereas the writ did not, but these boundaries were often 'well-known' as the earliest extant diplomas used to say.[57] The writ was delivered to the grantee to be kept by him with his other muniments; to that extent it was a title-deed, like the diploma, but a much superior one, because it bore the royal seal, a visible sign of authenticity which the diploma lacked. A better authenticity meant a better safeguard of the king's interests; it also meant a better security of tenure for the grantee.

The question of the origin of the writ has been discussed at length by Dr Harmer, who has collected all the available evidence in the introduction to her admirable edition of *Anglo-Saxon Writs*. In her estimation of the evidence, the writ, which she describes as 'a sealed letter used for administrative business', was already a familiar institution as far back as the reign of King Alfred and its origin 'is lost in obscurity'. W. H. Stevenson had already expressed similar views in 1912, but, as his arguments for pushing back to Alfred's reign the origin of the sealed writ were based on a misinterpretation of the famous Fonthill document, his conclusions, if right, could only be regarded as a happy guess.[58] Dr Harmer's thesis, on the other hand, based on two texts from Alfred's own works, is of the most compelling kind.

---

[52] See the remarks of Professor Barlow in *The English Church, 1000–1066*, p. 127 and n. 4.

[53] Stenton, *Latin Charters*, pp. 34–7; Tryggvi J. Oleson, *The Witenagemot in the Reign of Edward the Confessor* (Oxford Univ. Press, 1955), pp. 38 ff.

[54] F. E. Harmer, *Anglo-Saxon Writs* (Manchester Univ. Press, 1952), pp. 45–54.

[55] *Ibid.*, p. 46.

[56] After the Conquest the oral declaration followed the issue of the writ and consisted of the actual reading of the writ; see *ibid.*, p. 46 and n. 1.

[57] See, for example, *B.C.S.*, no. 45: 'juxta notissimos terminos'.

[58] W. H. Stevenson, 'Yorkshire Surveys and other eleventh-century Documents in the York Gospels', *English Hist. Review*, XXVII (1912), p. 5; Harmer, *Anglo-Saxon Writs*, pp. 11–12. The problem of the origin of the writ is also discussed in R. C. van Caenegem, *Royal Writs in England from the Conquest to Glanvill* (Selden Society, LXXVII, 1959), pp. 107–26.

In one of the passages apparently interpolated by Alfred himself in his vernacular translation of St Augustine's *Soliloquies*, Reason is made to say: 'Consider now, if your lord's letter and his seal (*ærendgewrit and hys insegel*) comes to you, whether you can say that you cannot understand him thereby or recognize his will therein'.[59] It may be true to say, as Professor Barraclough has done, that Alfred occasionally used the word *ærendgewrit* in a wider sense, to mean any kind of written message,[60] but in the passage under discussion 'letter' seems more likely to be the correct translation. It is the word *ærendgewrit* that, a century or so later, Ælfric used to render the Latin *epistola* in his glossary, whereas *gewrit* was his translation for *scriptura*.[61]

The Old-English word *insegel*, like our modern 'seal' and like the Latin *sigillum* in its normal usage,[62] could only mean either the matrix of a seal (in the shape of a signet-ring or of any other type of seal-die) or the impression made from it on wax, lead or some other soft material. It is clear from the context that Alfred meant by *insegel* an object which revealed to the recipient of the letter the identity of the sender. To use for that purpose a signet-ring or a seal-die of any kind, which by definition could only show a design and legend in reverse, would have been ludicrous.[63] Of course, the sender could have dispatched with his letter, not a signet-ring, but an ordinary finger-ring which perhaps had his name engraved on it, but, so far as I am aware, the Old-English word *insegel* was never used in that sense.[64] The Latin *anulus*, which corresponds to our 'finger-ring', is simply translated by *hring* in Ælfric's glossary.[65] Therefore the *insegel* to which Alfred referred could only have been the impression made, either on wax or possibly on lead, from a seal matrix.

From the preceding remarks it follows that Alfred's words *ðines hlafordes ærendgewrit and hys insegel* should be literally translated by 'your lord's letter and an impression of his seal'. Dr Harmer goes further and suggests that it was another way of saying 'your lord's sealed letter';[66] in other words, that the impression of the seal was attached to the letter. There is no doubt that the expression used by Alfred is very close to the *gewrite and insegle* of the Anglo-Saxon Chronicle and to the *brevis et sigillum* of Domesday Book, the first of which phrases possibly, and the second undoubtedly, refers to a sealed writ of Edward the Confessor.[67] Is it absolutely certain, though, that phrases such as these, which by the mid-eleventh century had acquired the technical meaning of 'sealed letter', had already done so two hundred years before? Bresslau believed that the expressions *epistola vel sigillum* and *sigillum et epistola* found in various continental laws and capitularies of the ninth and tenth centuries were synonymous, and that both should be rendered by 'sealed letter'.[68] But Bresslau's interpretation is open to doubt. German sigillographers have proved that seal impressions could be used loose, without being attached to any document. Such was the *sigillum*

---

[59] Dr Harmer's translation, *op. cit.*, p. 10.

[60] G. Barraclough, 'The Anglo-Saxon Writ', *History*, N.S. xxxix (1954), pp. 203-4.

[61] *Ælfrics Grammatik und Glossar*, ed. Julius Zupitza (Berlin, 1880), p. 304; Harmer, *op. cit.*, p. 1 and notes.

[62] The word *sigillum* is also sometimes used as a synonym of *signum*, i.e. the cross of a subscribing witness in a charter. The Old-English word for *signum* is *hondseten*, not *insegel*; see Harmer, *op. cit.*, p. 12; *Anglo-Saxon Charters*, ed. Robertson, nos. xxvii, xlvi, lv, lvi.

[63] Barraclough, *art. cit.*, p. 204.

[64] For surviving examples of such finger-rings of the mid-ninth century, see *Anglo-Saxon Ornamental Metalwork 700-1100 in the British Museum*, ed. D. M. Wilson (London, 1964), nos. 1 (ring of Queen Æthelswith, Alfred's sister), 31 (ring of King Æthelwulf); *Archaeological Journal*, xix (1862), fig. facing p. 326 (ring of Bishop Ealhstan of Sherborne).

[65] *Ælfrics Grammatik und Glossar*, ed. Zupitza, p. 303. The word *hring*, like *anulus*, could be used in the sense of 'signet-ring', but *insegel* or *sigillum* could not be used to mean a finger-ring which was not intended for sealing.

[66] Harmer, *op. cit.*, pp. 3, 10-13, and *passim*. She gives the same meaning to the *bréf ok innsigli* of Cnut mentioned in the Scandinavian sources (*ibid.* ,pp. 17-18).

[67] *Ibid.*, pp. 542-5, nos. 6, 10, 17, 18. Domesday Book makes it clear that in 1086 the word *sigillum* on its own could mean 'sealed writ' (*ibid.*, pp. 543-5, nos. 8, 9, 11, 13, 14, 16, 21). Compare H. Bresslau, *Handbuch der Urkundenlehre für Deutschland und Italien*, 1 (2nd ed., Leipzig, 1912), p. 684, n. 1.

[68] *Ibid.*, *loc. cit.*

citationis, used instead of a writing for court summonses in Hungary and elsewhere from the eleventh century until modern times.[69] It is this method of summons which the archbishop of Kalocsa rejected when he granted in 1268 that the people of Rimavölgy should be cited *nec per hominem nostrum nec per simplex sigillum sine litteris . . . nisi per litteras nostras speciales*.[70] In the Rhineland, loose seals have been found in reliquaries, where they had been placed – without having ever been attached to a document – to authenticate the translation of the relics: the owners of the seals had wanted to prove to posterity that they had either carried out the translation or at least witnessed it.[71] In Russia, loose seals were used as 'passports' before 944–5. In that year Prince Igor I of Kiev and the Byzantine emperors concluded a treaty which stated that until then the prince's agents going to Greece had carried gold seals and his merchants silver ones;[72] in future, the prince's agents and merchants were to be given a written certificate stating the number of ships which had been dispatched.[73] Regrettably, the text does not say whether a seal was to be attached to the document, or whether the writing replaced the loose seal or was to be carried in addition to it.

Nobody has ever considered that loose seals might also have been used in Anglo-Saxon England. Yet we have an unmistakable proof of it in the double-sided leaden seal of King Coenwulf of Mercia (796–821), now in the Department of British and Medieval Antiquities of the British Museum. No evidence has come to light on the early history of the seal. We simply know that after passing through several Italian collections it was eventually brought to England and acquired by the British Museum in 1847. In that year the following report appeared in *Archaeologia*:[74]

Nov. 18th, 1847. Sir Henry Ellis laid before the Society casts of the two sides of a leaden Seal or Bulla purchased at the sale of Walter Wilson Esq., July 26th, 1847 (Lot 445), English, and apparently of the Saxon period. The lead is somewhat decomposed, and the seal appears to have been attached to some Instrument, in the manner of the seals appended both in early and later times to the Papal Bulls . . .

Nine years later Sir Frederick Madden commented:[75]

. . . In the centre is a small cross moline, joined at the ends, as appears also on his [*i.e. Coenwulf's*] coins. This bulla was engraved in the *Archaeologia*, vol. xxxii, p. 449, but in the engraving the holes are not shown through which the cords passed to attach it to the charter, and the centre ornament is falsely represented as a quatrefoil . . .

In point of fact, the seal has no holes through which cords or any other means of attachment could have passed: what should have been said is that one side of the seal is slightly chipped near the rim, this being the result of a partial decomposition of the lead. A close examination of the seal shows quite clearly that it was never attached to a document. The fact that it was always loose makes its authenticity virtually certain. Besides, it cannot be a coincidence that, in its design and in the style

---

[69] Milan v. Sufflay, 'Sigillum citationis', *Mitteilungen des Inst. für Oesterreichische Geschichtsforschung*, XXVIII (1907), pp. 515–18; W. Ewald, *Siegelkunde*, in *Handbuch der mittelalterlichen und neueren Geschichte*, ed. G. v. Below and F. Meinecke, Part IV (Munich and Berlin, 1914), pp. 29–31 and notes; A. de Boüard, *Manuel de diplomatique française et pontificale*, I, p. 351 and n. 2.

[70] Bresslau, *op. cit., loc. cit.*; Ewald, *op. cit.*, p. 30.

[71] Ewald, *op. cit.*, p. 30 and n. 2. There is no connexion between such loose seals and the *sigillum osseum* (i.e. a bone matrix) which is alleged to have been found in St Nectan's tomb: 'Repertum est etiam iuxta sancti corpus sigillum osseum quod sancti martiris figuram, licet non totaliter, expressam, ex parte tamen digniori impressam, nominisque sui testimonio consignatam continet. Est autem distincta literarum impressio talis "Sigillum Nectani", ex qua videlicet duorum vocabulorum inscriptione colligitur quod proprium vocabulum martiris sigillo propter hoc imprimebatur, ut de propria eius persona non dubitaretur' (F. Wormald, 'The Seal of St Nectan', *Journal of the Warburg Institute*, II (1938–9), pp. 70–1). It would have been so convenient a find that the story, in any case, does not deserve much credit.

[72] The word used is *pyechaty*, that is to say a seal impression, not a finger-ring.

[73] *The Russian Primary Chronicle*, ed. S. Hazzard Cross and Olgerd P. Sherbowitz-Wetzor (Cambridge, Mass., 1953), p. 74; G. P. Bognetti, *Note per la storia del passaporto e del salvacondotto* (Pavia, 1933), pp. 174–5.

[74] *Archaeologia*, XXXII (1847), p. 449.   [75] *Archaeological Journal*, XIII (1856), p. 369.

of lettering of its legend, the seal should be, as noted by Madden, so similar to the coins of Coen-wulf.[76] As, unfortunately, we do not know the original home of the seal, it would be idle to specu-late on the use that was made of it.

If loose seals were commonly used in many countries, how can we be sure that the phrase *epistola vel sigillum* should never be translated, literally, by 'a letter *or* a seal'? It is not because, in expressions such as *nec per verbum nec per sigillum*, the word *sigillum* is used in the sense of 'sealed letter', as opposed to *verbum*, a verbal communication, that we should give it that meaning wherever it occurs.[77] Similarly, it is very likely that the phrase *sigillum et epistola* was originally used to des-cribe two separate objects carried together, a loose seal and a letter, and that it is only at a later date, when the seal was actually attached to the letter, that it acquired the meaning of 'sealed letter'. This hypothetical reconstruction is neither supported nor contradicted by the evidence now avail-able, but the two letters close of Carolingian kings which have survived in the original provide at least a useful link between the loose seal and the sealed letter: one is a mandate of Louis the Pious to Bishop Baderad of Paderborn (830–3),[78] the other a letter of Charles the Bald to the people of Barcelona (876).[79] Extant letters close of the twelfth and later centuries generally show some signs of their former sealing: sometimes they have one or several slits or holes made through the parch-ment for insertion of the fastening tie, sometimes a step and tear in the bottom left-hand corner of the document, and often an outline of the seal or traces of wax on the dorse when the seal was applied to the surface of the parchment.[80] There is nothing of the kind on either of the two Carolingian letters close. Indeed, if it were not for the address, which is written on the dorse, and for the peculiar arrangement of its wording, it would be difficult to tell them apart from contemporary copies. The mandate of Louis the Pious has the following address, written in one line:

ad Baderadum episcopum [*blank*] et missum nostrum.

In the letter of Charles the Bald it is written in two lines:

Omnibus Barchi [*blank*] nonensibus (*line 1*)
peculiaribus [*blank*] nostris (*line 2*).

Either the address was written before folding and fastening, and a blank space left where the tie was to be placed, or the address was written on either side of an already existing tie. In either case, we have to postulate the existence of a tie, which may have consisted of cords or of a parchment strip. It may be reasonable to assume that the ends of the tie were fastened together by means of a seal, but it seems that the seal did not actually adhere to the parchment of the document and that the sealed tie was simply wrapped around the folded letter after the fashion of our modern rubber-bands: the letter could have been opened and read by simply sliding it out of the wrapping tie; the seal was used for authenticating the document rather than for closing it.

In view of all this, it is difficult to regard as proved the contention that Alfred's words *ærendgewrit and hys insegel* should necessarily be interpreted as a reference to a 'sealed letter'. Even if it was a sealed letter, it is by no means certain that the sealing method which might have been

---

[76] See *Catalogue of English Coins in the British Museum*, ed. C. F. Keary and R. S. Poole, I (London, 1887), plate VIII. 10 and 17.
[77] Bresslau, *Urkundenlehre . . .*, p. 684, n. 1. Compare O. Redlich, *Die Privaturkunden des Mittelalters*, in *Handbuch der mittelalterlichen und neueren Geschichte*, ed. G. v. Below and F. Meinecke, IV. iii (Munich and Berlin, 1911), pp. 106–7.
[78] *Kaiserurkunden in Abbildungen*, I. 7a.
[79] Joseph Calmette, 'Une lettre originale de Charles le Chauve', *Mélanges d'archéologie et d'histoire*, XXII (French School of Rome, 1902), pp. 135–9 and plates IV–V.
[80] For facsimiles of letters close, see *Papsturkunden*, ed. A. Brackmann, in *Urkunden und Siegel* (Leipzig and Berlin, 1914), plate VI (a–b); A. de Boüard, *Manuel de diplomatique française et pontificale*, I (Paris, 1929), plates I. 2, II–III; C. Johnson and H. Jenkinson, *English Court Hand*, II (Plates), plate XII (c–d).

used in Alfred's time would have been the same as that adopted for writs in Edward the Confessor's reign.

The second text used by Dr Harmer in support of her argument that the writ was already common form in Alfred's time consists of the opening words of Alfred's preface to his Old-English translation of Gregory the Great's Pastoral Care:[81]

Ælfred kyning hateð gretan Wærferð biscep his wordum luflice ond freondlice, ond ðe cyðan hate ðæt . . .

In these opening words Dr Harmer sees the forerunners of the initial protocol and notification which are characteristic of Edward the Confessor's writs, for instance:[82]

Eadweard cyngc gret Leofwine b[isceop] and Eadwine eorl and ealle mine þegnas on Stæffordscire freondlice. And ic kyþe eow þ[æt] . . .

Of course, there are verbal differences between the two texts, as Professor Barraclough has pointed out,[83] but if one remembers that almost 200 years had elapsed between the writing of Alfred's preface and the issue of Edward the Confessor's writ, the discrepancies between them lose much of their significance. In my view, Dr Harmer is right when she claims that the initial protocol of the writ and its notification are close adaptations of the opening words used in vernacular letters as early as Alfred's time. But this does not mean that the letters to which Alfred referred had the same external appearance and served the same specialized purpose as the writs of Edward the Confessor. The only conclusion which we are entitled to draw from Alfred's writings is that during his reign a lord, that is to say someone with authority over men, could notify his commands to his inferiors by means of a letter (*ærendgewrit*) instead of always relying on the more primitive method of oral communications conveyed by envoys. This letter is likely to have contained an initial protocol (title, address and greeting) and a notification, both substantially the same as those found in Alfred's preface to the Pastoral Care and in Edward the Confessor's writs. It was accompanied by a seal, but we cannot tell whether the seal was carried loose or whether it was impressed on a loose tie or actually fastened to the letter itself. For all we know, Alfred's letters may have had the same external appearance and served the same purpose as the 'letters close' of Louis the Pious and Charles the Bald, in the same way as the writs of Edward the Confessor show some resemblance in appearance and object to the 'open' mandates of Philip I of France.[84]

What are the essential characteristics of all the extant writs of Edward the Confessor? They are not orders to one individual or to a group of people *to do* something; they simply are written notifications of royal grants to the appropriate assembly or assemblies, and there is no hint anywhere in them that the addressees were required to perform any particular duty; one of the regular features of the writ, on the other hand, is a general mandate to all *not to do* anything against the royal grant. It is not the notification itself which is characteristic of the writ, although it plays an important part in its structure; it is the matter notified, that is to say the grant. The writ is an administrative order only incidentally; this part of it will come to an end as soon as the oral declaration embodied in the writ has been made in the shire-court. Fundamentally the writ is a 'perpetuity', a title-deed, and that is why it is sealed 'open', in such a way that the seal will for ever testify to the authenticity of the grant to which it refers; that is also why the writ is delivered, not to the court, but to the grantee, so that it may be produced by him or by his successors at any time, should somebody else attempt to infringe the grant. Although all the extant writs of Edward the Confessor are in fact 'writ-charters', it is possible that he also issued in written form administrative orders of an ephemeral kind,

---

[81] Harmer, *Anglo-Saxon Writs*, p. 11.
[82] *Ibid.*, no. 96.
[83] *History*, N.S. xxxix, p. 203.
[84] G. Tessier, *Diplomatique royale française* (Paris, 1962), pp. 229–30.

but I very much doubt whether such 'writ-mandates', if they had survived, would show the same phraseology and method of sealing as the writ-charters.

That the writ-charter was not yet in existence in King Edgar's reign may be regarded as certain; otherwise, the two extant grants of Edgar to himself would most probably have been cast in the form of a writ, not in that of a diploma.[85] By the same token, it is possible to argue that the writ-charter was still an unknown diplomatic form by 1015, since the ætheling Æthelstan, son of King Æthelred II, stated in his will drawn up in that year that permission to grant his estates had been given to him by his father, not in a writ, but in an oral communication. The relevant passage from the will runs as follows:[86]

Now I thank my father in all humility, in the name of Almighty God, for the answer which he sent me on the Friday after the feast of Midsummer by Ælfgar, Æffa's son; which, as he told me in my father's words, was that I might, by God's leave and his, grant my estates and my possessions as seemed to me most advisable in fulfilment of my duties to God and men. And my brother Edmund and Bishop Ælfsige and Abbot Brihtmær and Ælfmær, Ælfric's son, are witnesses of this answer.

In the reign of Edward the Confessor, permissions of this kind were given by writ:[87]

And I inform you that it is with my full permission that Ailric has given the land at Greenford to Westminster, to Christ and to St Peter, in accordance with the agreement that the brethren and he have made.

It is true that two writ-charters are alleged to have been issued by Æthelred, one in favour of Winchester Cathedral, the other for St Paul's, London, but neither of them deserves much credit.[88] The Winchester writ claims to be the confirmation of a charter by which King Alfred renewed his predecessors' assessment of Chilcomb at one hide for taxation purposes.[89] The charter of Alfred is lost, but it probably was no more reliable than the extant charters of Æthelwulf, Edward the Elder, Athelstan and Edgar, all of which forgeries purport to be confirmations of the assessment of Chilcomb at one hide.[90] The charter of Edward the Elder (909), an apparent original, was written at Winchester not less than a hundred years after its alleged date;[91] it is in a hand which is similar to that of the last Winchester entries in the Parker Chronicle (973-1001) and may belong to the first or second quarter of the eleventh century.[92] To suggest that the forgeries were made in order to obtain Æthelred II's writ, and that the writ itself is genuine is wishful thinking. The textual similarities between the writ and two of the forged charters are so striking that the three texts are likely to be the works of the same forger:

And ic cyþe þe and eow eallum þæt	Her is geswutelod . . . hu
Ælfheah biscop sende to me þæs	Aþelwold bisceop begeat . . . þæt he . . .
landes boc æt Ciltancumbe . . .	geniwode Ciltancumbes freols . . .[93]
Þa licode me swyðe wel . . .	and heom eall þis swyþe wel licode . . .[94]
þe minne yldran on angunne	ealswa his yldran . . . on angynne
cristendomes into þere	cristendomes hit sealdan . . . into þære
halgan stowe gesetten . . .	halgan stowe . . .

---

[85] B.C.S., nos. 1118, 1127; Stenton, *Latin Charters*, p. 21.

[86] *Anglo-Saxon Wills*, ed. Whitelock, no. XX; cf. *ibid.*, no. XVI (2), p. 45.

[87] Harmer, *op. cit.*, no. 88; see also *ibid.*, nos. 2, 22.

[88] *Ibid.*, nos. 52, 107.

[89] *Ibid.*, no. 107.

[90] B.C.S., nos. 493, 620, 713, 1147-8; Finberg, *E.C.W.*, nos. 19, 40, 54, 110.

[91] *B.M.F.* IV. 10.

[92] *The Parker Chronicle and Laws* (facsimile), ed. R. Flower and H. Smith (1941), fos. 28ᵛ-30ʳ; N. R. Ker, *Catalogue of Manuscripts containing Anglo-Saxon* (Oxford, 1957), no. 39.

[93] B.C.S., no. 1148.

[94] B.C.S., no. 493.

Nu wille ic þæt hit man on eallum
þingon for ane hide werige swa swa
mine yldran hit ær gesetten and
gefreodan sy þer mare landes
sy þer lesse.[95]

and he geuðe þæt man þæt land on eallum
þingon for ane hide werode swa swa
his yldran hit ær gesetton and
gefreodon wære þær more landes
wære þær læsse . . .[96]

It is difficult to say when the pretended writ of Æthelred was forged, but a date in the second quarter of the eleventh century seems likely; at any rate, the forgery is certainly much earlier than 1086, since in Domesday Book Chilcomb is assessed at one hide as claimed in all the forgeries.[97]

The writ of Æthelred for the priests of St Paul's, London, is also open to doubt, but no decisive argument can be produced against its authenticity.[98] It looks as if the document might be nothing more than a shortened version of a later writ of Edward the Confessor for St Paul's. Dr Harmer has suggested that at some time the name of Æthelred might have been substituted for that of Edward; perhaps this was done after the Conquest in order to make the privileges of St Paul's appear more ancient than they actually were.

Although there is no trustworthy evidence that Æthelred II used the writ-charter to grant lands and liberties, it seems that, like Alfred, he occasionally issued administrative orders in writing, and that these written orders were accompanied by a seal. This is how one should probably interpret the *gewrit and his insegl* sent by the king to Archbishop Ælfric, ordering him and the thegns of East and West Kent to settle a dispute.[99] Was the seal loose or was it attached to the document? The question cannot be answered with any confidence. Another order to settle a dispute of a similar kind was given by Æthelred, this time to the shire-court of Berkshire:[100]

Then the king sent his *insegel* to the meeting at Cuckamsley by Abbot Ælfhere and greeted all the witan who were assembled there . . . and prayed and commanded them to settle the case . . .

In this second case I am confident that the order was delivered, not in writing, but orally, that the *insegel* was a loose seal carried by Abbot Ælfhere of Bath as a sign of credence, and that the royal greeting to the assembly was conveyed orally by the abbot. Throughout the medieval period, much of the royal business, internal and diplomatic, was conducted in this way; in the later Middle Ages, signs of credence such as tokens and loose seals had been replaced by letters of credence asking the recipient to believe what the bearer would say on behalf of the sender, but at all times the first task of an envoy entrusted with an oral message was to greet, on behalf of his principal, the person to whom he was sent. Thus Charlemagne's envoys to Adrian I were instructed to begin their mission by saying to the pope:[101]

Salutat vos dominus noster filius vester Carolus rex et filia vestra domna Fastrada regina . . .

Similarly the first article of a set of instructions to English ambassadors to France in 1324 reads: 'Primes, soit due salutacion faite . . .'[102]

In my view it is also to an oral message that the Anglo-Saxon Chronicle refers when it says

---

[95] Harmer, *op. cit.*, no. 107.   [96] *B.C.S.*, no. 1148.

[97] Finberg, *E.C.W.*, p. 231. As noted by Dr Harmer, *op. cit.*, p. 375, beneficial hidation was not uncommon in the eleventh century, but the authentic texts which have survived for the reign of Cnut and Edward the Confessor simply say that the assessment rate will be the same as before; they do not give the exact figure of the reduction (Harmer, *op. cit.*, nos. 29, 66). Sometimes the same scribe wrote genuine documents as well as forgeries; this might have happened in the case of Chilcomb, but it is on the whole unlikely. Compare also 'se wisa cing Ælfred' in the writ with 'þa godan cynegas and þa wisan' in *B.C.S.*, no. 1148.

[98] Harmer, *op. cit.*, no. 52.   [99] *Ibid.*, p. 541, no. 2.   [100] *Ibid.*, p. 541, no. 1.

[101] *Mon. Germ. Hist., Leg. Sect.* II, *Capitularia regum Francorum*, I (1883), p. 225.

[102] *The War of Saint-Sardos*, ed. P. Chaplais (Camden third series, LXXXVII, 1954), p. 184.

that in 1014 Æthelred sent to England from Normandy 'his son Edward with his messengers, and bade greet all his people, and said that he would be to them a gracious lord . . .'[103] In this instance, as in the case of Æthelred's order to the shire-court of Berkshire, the name of the envoy is given, a point which I believe to be of great significance. We have seen earlier that the ætheling Æthelstan also took great care to state in his will that it was Ælfgar, Æffa's son, who had brought him his father's oral permission to grant his estates as he saw fit.[104] In so far as oral messages were concerned, the trustworthiness and personality of the envoy was of primary importance, and his responsibility was fully engaged. That is why, in the records of the earlier and later Middle Ages, envoys of this type are normally mentioned by name, whereas mere couriers, bearers of written communications, seldom are.

There are indications that the officials of the shire-courts were accustomed to oral declarations. The record of a Herefordshire lawsuit of King Cnut's reign may serve as an example.[105] As a certain Edwin had come to the shire-meeting to sue his mother for a piece of land, the court sent three thegns to see the mother and hear her counterclaim. Edwin's mother told them that she had no land that belonged to her son. Then she

summoned to her her kinswoman, Leofflæd, Thurkil's wife, and in front of them said to her as follows: 'Here sits Leofflæd, my kinswoman, to whom, after my death, I grant my land . . . and all that I possess'. And then she said to the thegns: 'Act rightly and like thegns; announce my message to the meeting before all the worthy men, and tell them to whom I have granted my land and all my property, and not a thing to my own son, and ask them all to be witnesses of this'. And they did so; they rode to the meeting and informed all the worthy men of the charge that she had laid upon them. Then Thurkil the White stood up in the meeting and asked all the thegns to give his wife the lands unreservedly which her kinswoman had granted her, and they did so. Then Thurkil rode to St Æthelbert's minster, with the consent and cognisance of the whole assembly, and had it recorded in a gospel-book.

In this instance the whole case had been conducted orally from start to finish, and it had been left to the winning party to have the proceedings recorded in writing. This had been done in a gospel-book in order to give the record a greater authenticity and a better chance of preservation, a method of record-keeping of which other examples have survived for the reigns of Æthelred and Cnut.

Occasionally, depositions of important witnesses also appear to have been recorded in writing at the request of one of the parties and by a scribe acting on his behalf. Two records of this kind have survived for the reign of Æthelred II: one, an original, drawn up in the name of Archbishop [Dunstan], was formerly preserved among the archives of the bishop of Crediton and Cornwall; the other, in the name of Queen Ælfthryth, is copied in the Codex Wintoniensis. Dunstan's deposition, which concerns the history of the see of Cornwall, is in the form of a declaration written partly in the third person, partly in the first:[106]

Þis gewrit sendeþ se arcebisceop his hlaforde Æþelrede cynge. Hit gelamp þæt . . .

For Ælfthryth's deposition, which relates to the ownership of the manor of Taunton, an entirely different literary medium was used: it is cast in the form of a letter addressed to Archbishop Ælfric and Æthelweard the ealdorman:[107]

Alfðryð gret Ælfric arcebiscop and Eþelwerd ealdarman eadmodlice. And ic cyðe inc ðet ic eom to gewitnysse þæt . . .

---

[103] Harmer, op. cit., p. 541, no. 3. Compare the phrase 'and cwæð þæt he him hold hlaford beon wolde' with that used in Cnut's 'letter to the people of England': 'and ic cyðe eow þæt ic wylle beon hold hlaford' (F. Liebermann, Die Gesetze der Angelsachsen (Halle, 1903–16), I, p. 273).
[104] Anglo-Saxon Wills, ed. Whitelock, no. xx.
[105] Anglo-Saxon Charters, ed. Robertson, no. LXXVIII.
[106] The Crawford Collection . . ., ed. A. S. Napier and W. H. Stevenson (Oxford, 1895), no. VII.
[107] Harmer, op. cit., no. 108. This is not a writ-charter.

The authenticity of the statements made in the queen's name is not in doubt. This means that the words attributed to her in the 'letter' are substantially those which she spoke. It does not mean, however, that she was in any way responsible for the epistolary form in which her declaration was recorded or that the document was authenticated by her with a seal or in some other way. The bishop of Winchester, on whose behalf she testified, simply chose to have her deposition written down in letter form rather than in the form of a narrative statement in the third person. The phraseology of the 'letter' resembles that of a statement of approximately the same date ('Her cyð on ðysum gewrite hu . . .') concerning the settlement of a dispute between Bishop Godwine of Rochester and Leofwine, Ælfheah's son.[108] As this dispute was settled at Canterbury in the presence of Archbishop Ælfric, and as Ælfric is one of the addressees in Ælfthryth's 'letter', both documents may have been drafted by a Canterbury scribe acting on behalf of the beneficiary.

That the epistolary form could have been used as an alternative literary medium to that of a statement in the third person to record an oral declaration in writing is not as strange as it might at first appear. Approximate parallels can be found in the various forms used for wills. The will of a certain Æthelwold begins 'This is Æthelwold's will: first he prays his royal lord . . .' while the will of Wulfwaru is in the form of a notification to the king 'I, Wulfwaru, pray my dear lord King Æthelred, of his charity, that I may be entitled to make my will. I make known to you, Sire, . . .'[109] Wulfstan's *Sermo ad populum* in all manuscripts but one has the normal homiletic beginning 'Leofan men, understandað þæt . . .', the exception being MS. C where these words are preceded by an epistolary introduction:[110]

Wulfstan arcebisceop greteð freondlice þegnas on ðeode, gehadode and læwede . . . And ic bidde eow for Godes lufan þæt . . .

To explain the discrepancy between MS. C and the other manuscripts, it has been assumed that the sermon was not only preached but also circularized as a pastoral letter.[111] This assumption, however, seems unnecessary. Another famous document, the so-called 'letter of Cnut to the people of England' is also cast in epistolary form:[112]

Cnut cyning gret his arceb' and his leod biscopas and Þurcyl eorl and ealle his eorlas and ealne his þeodscype twelfhynde and twyhynde gehadode and læwede on Englalande freondlice. And ic cyðe eow þæt ic wylle . . .

Is it not significant that the only text of this document, written in a style characteristic of Wulfstan, should have been preserved in a manuscript associated with Wulfstan himself, a York gospel, and in a contemporary hand?[113] In my opinion, this suggests that Cnut never issued a sealed letter; he simply made an oral proclamation either in person on his return to England in the spring of 1020 or through envoys while he was still in Denmark; then, presumably with the king's permission, Wulfstan caused the proclamation to be written down in epistolary form, the words used being Wulfstan's, and not necessarily those spoken by the king. In any case, the initial protocol and notification of a letter cannot have been very different from the introductory phrases of a proclamation delivered orally.

Records in epistolary form which have not survived in the original should not automatically be regarded as representing letters actually dispatched, sealed or unsealed. When the records are

---

[108] *Anglo-Saxon Charters*, ed. Robertson, no. LXIX.

[109] *Anglo-Saxon Wills*, ed. Whitelock, nos. XII, XXI.

[110] D. Bethurum, *The Homilies of Wulfstan* (Oxford, 1957), no. XIII, p. 225.

[111] *Ibid.*, pp. 20, 339.

[112] Libermann, *Die Gesetze* . . ., I, p. 273.

[113] D. Whitelock, 'Wulfstan and the Laws of Cnut', *English Hist. Review*, LXIII (1948), p. 443; Ker, *Catalogue of Manuscripts containing Anglo-Saxon*, no. 402; see also *E.H.D.*, I, p. 414. Dr Albert Bruckner kindly informs me that, on the Continent, charters are also found in missals and similar books.

entered in a sacred book–gospel, pontifical, missal etc.–in a hand contemporary with the events recorded, it is likely that no original was ever issued. Cnut's 'letter to the people of England' falls under that category; so do six other documents of the reigns of Æthelred II and Cnut, one in a Sherborne pontifical, the other five in gospel-books of Christ Church, Canterbury. All of them are in the form of a letter, and all are in a contemporary handwriting.

The Sherborne document ('Æþelric biscop gret Æþelmær freondlice. And ic cyþe þæt . . .') is a statement by Bishop Æthelric of losses sustained by his bishopric.[114] The addressee is Æthelmær the ealdorman, that is to say the dignitary who normally presided with the bishop over the meetings of the shire. The information contained in the document is of the same kind as that given in Ælfthryth's testimony regarding Taunton, but here Æthelric testifies on his own behalf. There was no need for the bishop to send a letter to Æthelmær, since he had many opportunities to meet the ealdorman in the shire-court and could make his complaint orally, which he no doubt did before he had it recorded in the Sherborne pontifical.

The earliest of the five Christ Church documents is in the form of a letter addressed by Cnut to Archbishop Lyfing of Canterbury, Bishop Godwine of Rochester, Abbot Ælfmær of St Augustine's, Canterbury, Æthelwine the sheriff, Æthelric and all the king's thegns.[115] The king explains that the archbishop had complained of encroachments on the liberties of Christ Church and had declined his offer to let him draw up a new charter of freedom (i.e. a diploma): the archbishop had told the king that 'he had charters of freedom in plenty if only they were good for anything'. Cnut goes on to say:

Then I myself took the charters of freedom and laid them on Christ's own altar, with the cognisance of the archbishop and of Earl Thurkill and of many good men who were with me, in the same terms as King Æthelberht freed it and all my predecessors.

The document ends with a prohibition clause and an anathema.

It is obvious that this is no ordinary letter; it is the record of a ceremony which took place in Christ Church on the occasion of a visit of Cnut, some time between 1017 and 1020; Archbishop Lyfing was there, and so, presumably, were the abbot of St Augustine's and most of the other addressees. The document is copied in a Christ Church gospel-book now in the British Museum, MS. Royal 1 D. ix.[116] It is written in the hand of the scribe who wrote a diploma, apparently genuine, granted by Cnut to Archbishop Lyfing in 1018;[117] the same scribe was also responsible for the writing of two Canterbury forgeries, one of them an apparent original dated 716, the other a copy, in another gospel-book, of an alleged charter of Æthelred.[118] The scribe undoubtedly belonged to the Canterbury scriptorium during the reign of Cnut.

The second Christ Church document is copied in the famous Canterbury book known as the MacDurnan gospels in another contemporary, but unidentified, hand.[119] The form is that of a letter addressed by Archbishop Wulfstan of York to Cnut and his queen, informing them that he has consecrated Æthelnoth, Lyfing's successor as archbishop of Canterbury. This second document, like the first, was probably written by a Christ Church scribe.

The last three documents, probably all to be dated 1035, are in one hand, that of another

---

[114] Harmer, *op. cit.*, no. 63.

[115] *Ibid.*, no. 26.

[116] It is reproduced on Plate II, in reduced size.

[117] *O.S.F.* III. 39: the grant is made 'absque omni servitute terrena', and there is no mention of the three common burdens.

[118] *O.S.F.* III. 2 (*B.C.S.*, no. 91); Ker, *Catalogue of Manuscripts containing Anglo-Saxon*, no. 185, art. a.

[119] Harmer, *op. cit.*, no. 27.

contemporary scribe who entered them on two leaves of the MacDurnan gospels.[120] Their importance is considerable, because they are the only documents of virtually certain authenticity to have
survived in what may be regarded as a true writ-charter form before the reign of Edward the Confessor. If they were really written, as they seem to have been, at the time when the grants were
notified to the shire, there is every reason to think that no original, sealed or unsealed, was ever
drawn up, and that the copy in the gospel-book was the only record ever made of the royal notification
and indeed of the grant itself. It was a record made by the beneficiary of a royal proclamation delivered
orally to the shire-court. Perhaps oral declarations of this kind had been made ever since the setting-
up of the shire-courts themselves. If in Cnut's reign they began to be written down in one of the
beneficiary's gospel-books, it was because by then, as Archbishop Lyfing had told the king, the
diplomas had lost all their meaning. A royal declaration made in the shire by a royal representative,
and warning those who would presume to infringe the grant that they would incur the king's
wrath was more likely to protect the interests of the grantee than the apparently outmoded diploma.
Once the oral notification had been copied in a gospel-book, the grantee was provided with testimony more permanent than that of mortal witnesses, and some sort of religious protection was
assured as well.

     Copies in gospel-books were satisfactory for ecclesiastical grantees, but they were less so for
lay beneficiaries. Besides, the king and his advisers must have soon realised that unscrupulous
bishops or abbots could–and did–enter fraudulent documents in gospel-books. Sooner or later,
another system was bound to be devised for the better protection of both grantor and grantee. This
had been done by the time of Edward the Confessor, during whose reign the royal notifications to
the shire began to be issued in the form of original documents sealed with the royal seal.

     It is well known that all the extant writ-charters of Edward the Confessor were sealed with a
pendent seal attached to a tongue.[121] This sealing method required a seal of reasonable size; a
double-sided seal was also preferable. Was Edward the Confessor's seal modelled on a seal of Cnut
or was it the first English royal seal of its kind? Recent work on numismatics tends to show that the
latter is the more likely explanation and that Edward's seal was an adaptation of the German imperial
seal. It has been pointed out that the Confessor was the first English king to have had a coin on which
he was represented as seated on a throne. It has also been suggested that the same engraver, the
German Theoderic, might have been responsible for the 'majesty' coin of Edward the Confessor
and for his seal.[122]

     One might have assumed that, as soon as writ-charters began to be issued as sealed docu-
ments, their writing was automatically transferred from ecclesiastical scriptoria to a royal secretariat.
In fact, the evidence that such a change-over took place is lacking. It is reasonably certain that two
of the Confessor's writs, one for the abbey of Saint-Denis, the other for the abbey of Westminster,
were written by a scribe of the beneficiary.[123] For the other extant originals one can only say that
the evidence for relating their handwriting to the scriptorium of their respective grantees is at least
as strong as the evidence for connecting it with a royal department.[124] The same doubts apply to the
drafting of the writs: the stylistic similarities between all the extant writs of Edward the Confessor
were not necessarily due to the setting-up of a royal scriptorium; a long tradition of oral declarations

[120] *Ibid.*, nos. 28–30. See Ker, *op. cit.*, no. 284. Harmer, no. 29 is reproduced on Plate I (*right*), in reduced size.
[121] *Facsimiles of English Royal Writs*, plates III, XVIII, XXIII, XXVI.
[122] *Anglo-Saxon Coins (Studies presented to F. M. Stenton)*, ed. R. H. M. Dolley (London, 1961), pp. 215, 220.
See also Harmer, *op. cit.*, pp. 94–101.
[123] *Facsimiles of English Royal Writs*, plates XVIII, XXIII (b–c).
[124] This statement is based on comparisons between plates II and III of the *Facsimiles* and manuscripts known to
have been written at Bury and Canterbury.

made by the same royal representatives to the various shires might explain these similarities just as adequately.[125]

If it is true that all the royal diplomas of Edward the Confessor and some–if not all–of his writ-charters were written in ecclesiastical scriptoria, it would seem that the chancery organization which William the Conqueror is supposed to have inherited was far from being as highly developed as it has been hitherto imagined. Of this organization we only know for certain that it had a royal seal and that this seal was used to authenticate writ-charters and presumably royal mandates as well. Regarding the Anglo-Saxon chancery staff, we may assume that the Confessor had an official to look after his seal, perhaps the priest Regenbald.[126] We may also assume that he had a few royal scribes who wrote his private correspondence and his administrative orders.

It is not surprising, therefore, that we should find little evidence of a fully organized chancery in the first few years of William the Conqueror's reign. The fact that many writ-charters were issued in English between 1066 and 1070 is generally regarded as one of the proofs that the Conqueror took over the Anglo-Saxon chancery staff of Edward the Confessor.[127] Would it not be more correct to say that these vernacular documents continued to be issued between 1066 and 1070 because during that period the churches in whose favour they were granted were still in the hands of Anglo-Saxon bishops and abbots before their replacement by Normans, and because ecclesiastical scriptoria were still mostly staffed with Anglo-Saxon scribes? Out of six original writ-charters extant for the reign of the Conqueror, only one–which, perhaps significantly, belongs to the last year of his reign–has been definitely identified as the work of a royal scribe.[128] All the other five were not necessarily written in ecclesiastical scriptoria, but at least the authentic part of the Old-English writ for Christ Church is in the hand of the Canterbury scribe who wrote, among other things, the famous forged privilege of Boniface IV in Cotton MS. Claudius A. iii.[129] It is also likely, but not certain, that the Old-English writs for Deorman and for the citizens of London were written under the supervision of the bishop of London.[130] It is a peculiar feature of the writ for the citizens of London that, in the address and in the text of the grant itself, the king is made to speak to the beneficiaries:[131]

. . . And ic kyðe eow þæt ic wylle þæt get beon eallra þæra laga weorðe . . .

This feature, unusual in English charters of the writ type, was characteristic of the papal chancery and also of some other lay and ecclesiastical chanceries on the Continent. Perhaps its appearance in the London writ should be explained by the Norman origin of William, bishop of London, who had been brought over to England by Edward the Confessor.

Even by the end of William the Conqueror's reign, the royal chancery was still far from having acquired the monopoly of all the writings done in the king's name. Volume II of Domesday Book is unlikely to have been written by royal scribes; it is not certain that even Volume I can be regarded as a chancery product. If one day it is proved that the two books were written by ecclesiastical scribes, it will no doubt be suggested that even a well-staffed royal chancery would have

---

[125] No Anglo-Saxon formulary has survived, but this does not mean that there never was any.

[126] Harmer, *op. cit.*, p. 570 and references.

[127] Darlington, *The Norman Conquest*, p. 5.

[128] *Facsimiles of English Royal Writs*, plate xxv (a).

[129] *Ibid.*, Plates IV (a) and IV (b); Ker, *Catalogue of Manuscripts containing Anglo-Saxon*, no. 139, art. r; no. 185, art. f (part 2, lines 8–19 of fol. 6ᵛ) and fol. 7; R. W. Southern, 'The Canterbury Forgeries', *English Hist. Review*, LXXIII (1958), p. 217 and n. 2.

[130] *Facsimiles of English Royal Writs*, plates XIV–XV.

[131] *Ibid.*, plate XIV.

found it difficult to cope with such a vast undertaking without outside help. The king probably did not mind very much who did the work as long as it was well done. Before 1066 he had managed to rule successfully in Normandy without a chancery at all, and so had in England many generations of Anglo-Saxon kings.

PIERRE CHAPLAIS

Some Early
Anglo-Saxon Diplomas
on Single Sheets:
Originals or Copies?[1]

Sooner or later every student of Anglo-Saxon charters is faced with the problem of sorting the documents preserved on single sheets into originals, copies and forgeries. That the task is an arduous one comes home to him at an early stage, when, going through printed notices on individual charters, he finds that one particular item, the seventh-century charter of Œthelræd for the abbey of Barking, at one time regarded as an original, now generally thought to be a later copy, was also once in recent years classified as spurious.[2] To be sure this is an extreme case, but the fact that such diverging views on the same document could all have been defended by respected scholars and on seemingly valid grounds is, to say the least, discouraging.

By 'original charter' we normally understand a document drawn up in the name of the grantor and with his approval, written at approximately the same time as the oral grant was made, and provided with identifiable marks of authentication such as the grantor's seal or some autograph subscriptions or signa. In a copy the grantor's seal will be absent and the subscriptions and signa will not be autograph. Success in the detection of forgeries will largely depend on the forger's skill: if enough originals have survived, some forgeries will be recognizable at once by a comparison of their alleged marks of authentication with those found on the originals, while others will be eliminated after being subjected to a thorough palaeographical and diplomatic scrutiny.

Although a large number of Anglo-Saxon diplomas written on single sheets are extant, all of them – except the chirographic leases, which begin to appear in the middle of the ninth century[3] – lack identifiable marks of validation: they have no seal, and their subscriptions and signa are not autograph. For this reason, if we apply to them the classifying rules which have been summarized

---

[1] I am grateful to Dr R. W. Hunt, Mr N. R. Ker and Mr Francis W. Steer for their help and encouragement. The responsibility for the views expressed in this paper is, of course, entirely mine. Plates III and IV are reproduced by courtesy of the Trustees of the British Museum, and Plate V by courtesy of the Dean and Chapter of Chichester Cathedral.

[2] See C. R. Hart, *The Early Charters of Eastern England* (Leicester Univ. Press, 1966), pp. 133–5; *A Hand-Book to the Land-Charters, and other Saxonic Documents*, ed. John Earle (Oxford, 1888), pp. 8, 13.

[3] Birch, *Cartularium Saxonicum* (hereafter *B.C.S.*), no. 490, A.D. 855, apparently an original chirograph from Worcester, now lost. See H. Bresslau, *Handbuch der Urkundenlehre für Deutschland und Italien*, I (2nd ed., 1912), p. 670. Univ. of Edinburgh, Laing Charters, no. 18 (A.D. 854) is not an original, although the top halves of the letters of the word *CHIROGRAPHVM* appear at the foot of the parchment; its script may belong to the first half of the eleventh century, and the charter mentions the Old Minster, Winchester, although, at the time, the New Minster had not yet been founded; see *Anglo-Saxon Charters*, ed. A. J. Robertson (Cambridge Univ. Press, 1956), no. VIII and notes. The chirographic form may have occasionally been used for making 'authentic copies' of much older originals. The earliest original chirographs still extant belong to the early years of the tenth century (*Facsimiles of Ancient Charters in the British Museum* [hereafter *B.M.F.*], 4 vols. (London, 1873–78), III. 1–2).

above, we reach the surprising conclusion that no Anglo-Saxon diploma should be described as an original. Once we have disposed of the forgeries by diplomatic and other tests, the remaining charters can be safely divided into two groups only, the contemporary documents and the later copies, one group being distinguishable from the other by a study of their respective palaeographical and linguistic features.[4]

Nobody would wish to deny that among the Anglo-Saxon diplomas classed as contemporary texts there are bound to be some which were drawn up at the time of the grant recorded in them and whose dating clause represents the true date of writing: in this category should be placed, if they have survived, all the diplomas which are said to have been solemnly laid by their grantor on the altar of a church.[5] If such documents could be identified, they would deserve to be described as originals, although they had no visible marks of authentication. But how can they be identified with any certainty, since the exact time of writing cannot be determined by any known method? A hand-writing expert may be in a position to claim that a document dated 1000 could not have been written later than 1050 or even 1025, but he will never be able to prove that it was actually written in 1000. The script of an original written in 1000 and that of a copy made in the same scriptorium in 1025 are unlikely to have shown very different characteristics which could be precisely dated. It may be objected that a Chichester scribe of the fourteenth century could apparently differentiate an Anglo-Saxon 'original charter' from an 'ancient copy', if we trust his comments on the foundation charter of the monastery of Selsey attributed to King Ceadwalla of Wessex:[6]

tunc sequntur limites et bunde terrarum predictarum in lingua Saxonica videlicet in carta originali, sed in quadam alia copia veteri carte predicte sequntur bunde dicte terre sub hac forma.

The objection, however, is not very serious, because Ceadwalla's charter, in the form in which it appears in the scribe's copy, does not stand up to the most elementary tests of diplomatic criticism: among other errors, the diploma is subscribed by Archbishop Brihtwold of Canterbury, although Brihtwold did not become archbishop until after the death of King Ceadwalla; its dating clause, which states that the charter was written on 3 August 673, in the eleventh indiction, by all accounts an impossible date, seems to have been adapted from that of another Sussex foundation charter of the next century,[7] a practice common enough among forgers.[8] One would like to think that the text which the Chichester scribe, whose honesty is not in doubt, considered to be the original charter was in an older script than the 'ancient copy', but even that is by no means certain.

The difficulties involved in dating documents by their script alone–even within the comparatively wide limits of half a century–should not be underestimated. Two pieces of writing executed in the same year may in fact look one or two generations apart owing to such factors as their respective places of origin or the respective ages of their scribes: if it is likely that the evolution of one type of script proceeded at a slower pace in a remote monastery of Devon or Cornwall than in an active literary centre like Winchester, and that as a result a Cornish charter might seem to be older than a Winchester charter of the same age, it is equally probable that an old scribe would write a hand of an earlier type than his younger colleagues. The addition of marks of punctuation by a later corrector may have the opposite effect of giving to an early manuscript the appearance of a later work: for example, the punctuation of the charter in which King Eadred grants Reculver to Christ Church, Canterbury, is more likely to belong to the latter part of the tenth century than to the year 949 of its dating clause, but it is practically certain that the scribe of the charter only punctuated

[4] See, for example, *English Historical Documents* [hereafter *E.H.D.*], I, ed. D. Whitelock (London, 1955), p. 337.
[5] F. E. Harmer, *Anglo-Saxon Writs* (Manchester Univ. Press, 1952), pp. 170–1; H. Brunner, *Zur Rechtsgeschichte der römischen und germanischen Urkunde*, I (Berlin, 1880), pp. 155–6 (not all the examples given are genuine).
[6] Chichester, Diocesan Record Office, Ep. VI/1/2, fo. 4ᵛ (*B.C.S.*, no. 64).
[7] *B.C.S.*, no. 198, dated 3 August, indiction 3, A.D. 762 (for 765).
[8] Compare *B.C.S.*, nos. 86 and 296 (perhaps both forged), nos. 97 and 98.

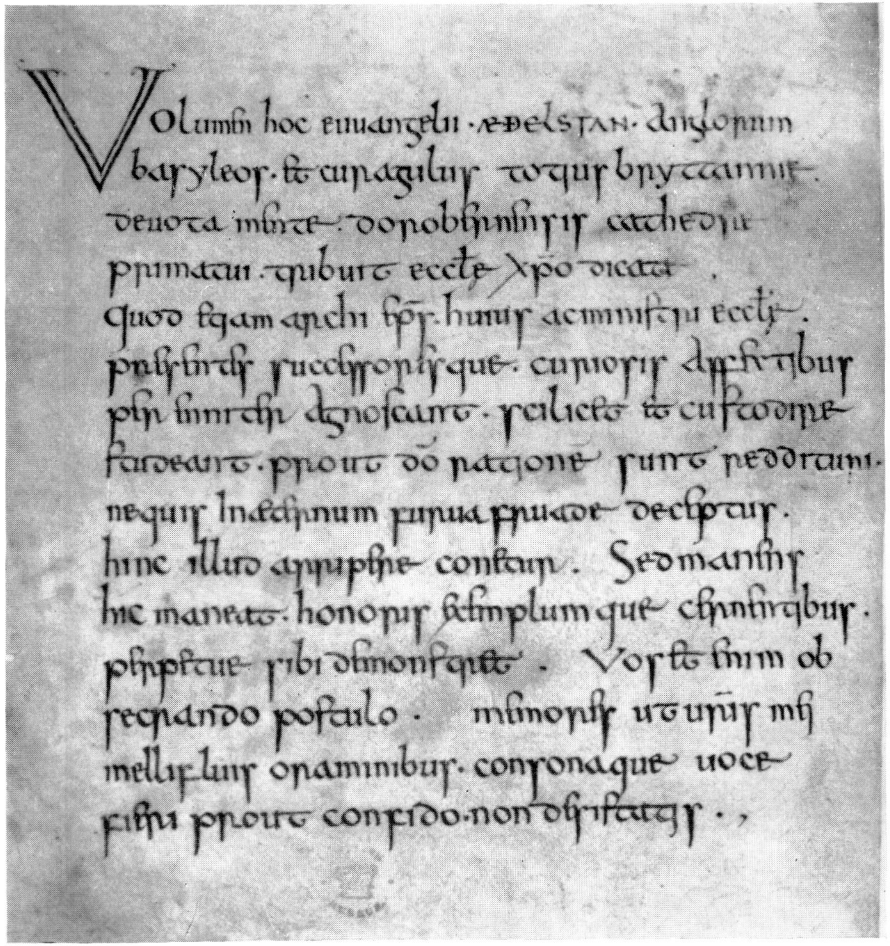

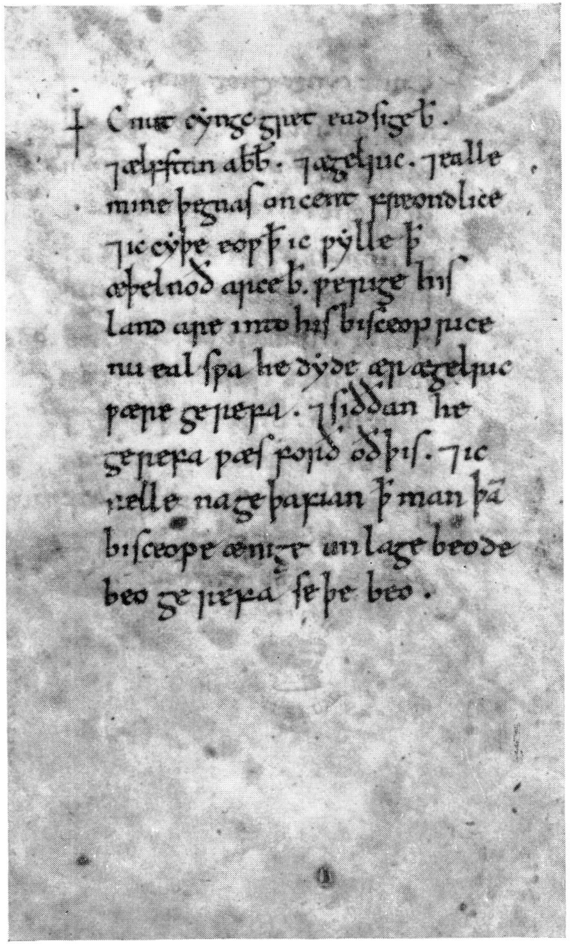

PLATE I

left Inscription recording the gift of a gospel-book by King Athelstan to Christ Church, Canterbury
(British Museum, Ms. Cotton Tiberius A. ii, fo. 15ᵛ)

right Writ of King Cnut for Æthelnoth, archbishop of Canterbury (British Museum, Ms. Cotton Tiberius B. iv, fo. 87ᵛ)

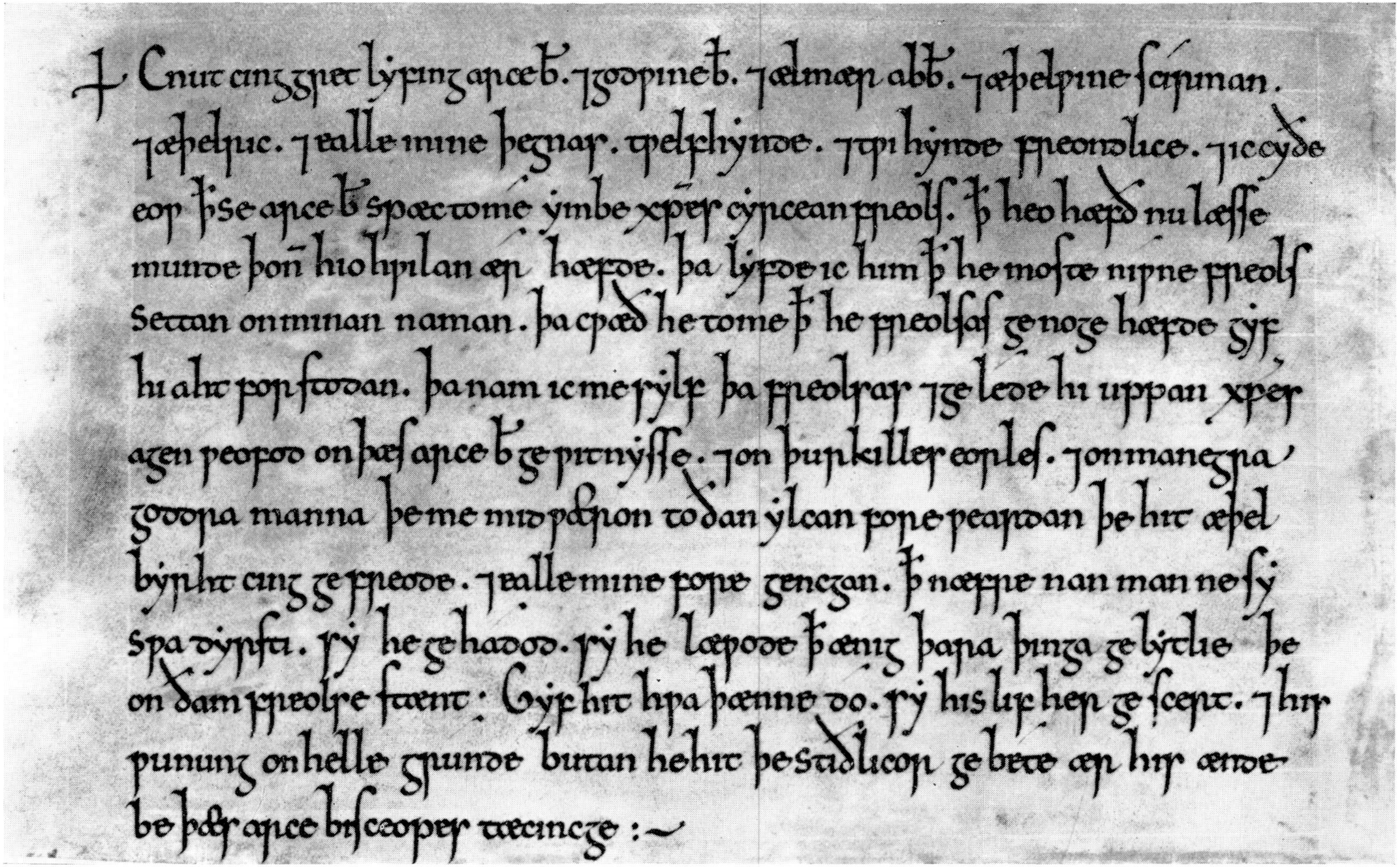

it with dots, all the other punctuation marks showing signs of having been inserted at a later date, possibly by Dunstan himself.[9]

To describe a document as contemporary is only slightly less unrealistic than to call it an original. If, on the sound principle that exaggerated caution can have a paralysing effect, we are prepared to presume a document genuine or contemporary unless or until it can be proved to be either a forgery or a later copy, we should also be ready to extend the same liberal attitude to the use of the term 'original'. There is adequate evidence that Anglo-Saxon diplomas were occasionally issued in more than one exemplar,[10] and cases of multiple originals may therefore occur; but it has yet to be established that it was common practice in Anglo-Saxon times to make single-sheet copies of an original soon after it was drawn up. If it is correct to assume that such an immediate need for copies is unlikely to have arisen very frequently, it follows that the risk of error in presuming all contemporary single sheets to be originals is very slight. Although we may not succeed in turning this presumption into a certainty, the search for clues with this objective in mind should not be abandoned. Each individual document should be examined and judged on its own merits, in the hope that at least in a few single sheets some exceptional features might be discovered which would identify them as originals beyond reasonable doubt.

John Earle believed that there were two–but only two–Anglo-Saxon diplomas of the seventh century whose 'originality' could not be doubted: one was the charter of King Hlothhere of Kent for Abbot Brihtwold of Reculver (May 679), the other the charter of Œthelræd for Abbess Æthelburh of Barking (March 687?).[11] In his view both were 'absolute originals'. This is indeed the view which many Anglo-Saxon scholars would like to share, but Earle's argument that, in so far as Hlothhere's charter is concerned, 'besides internal evidence, the originality of the document is attested by the uncial and doubtless contemporary penmanship' is hardly convincing.[12]

The text of Hlothhere's charter is rightly regarded as irreproachable. Its Latin may be faulty, but it is no more so than the barbarous Latin displayed in many Italian and Frankish charters of the sixth and seventh centuries.[13] Good Latin at the end of the seventh century would arouse suspicion rather than strengthen our confidence in the authenticity of the charter. The construction is awkward and repetitive, and the punctuation, often misplaced, is of little assistance to anyone who tries to separate the various clauses from one another. The scribe uses the accusative instead of the ablative after *pro* (*pro remedium animae meae*),[14] and what appears to be a dative form after *a* (*a . . . sanguini*);[15] he makes an accusative agree with an ablative (*cum omnibus ad se pertinentia*),[16] and replaces, perhaps under Greek influence, the ablative absolute by an accusative absolute (*manentem hanc donationis chartulam in sua nihilominus firmitate*).[17] In one clause, out of six words which should

---

[9] Compare the added punctuation marks in Ordnance Survey, *Facsimiles of Anglo-Saxon Manuscripts* (hereafter *O.S.F.*), 3 vols. (Southampton, 1878–84), I. 15, with those in *Saint Dunstan's Classbook from Glastonbury*, ed. R. W. Hunt (Umbrae Codicum Occidentalium, Amsterdam, 1961), fos. 27[r] and 27[v]. For Eadred's charter, see *Journal of the Society of Archivists*, III, 4 [pp. 43–62 above], p. 164 (where should be added, in note 34, a reference to another Glastonbury charter, *B.C.S.*, no. 169, which uses the words *vel gressum pedis . . . adimere* in its penalty clause). [See above, pp. 47–8.]

[10] *B.C.S.*, nos. 313, 421.

[11] *B.M.F.* I. 1–2; *B.C.S.*, nos. 45, 81; Earle, *op. cit.*, pp. 8, 13.

[12] *Ibid.*, p. 8.

[13] See Jeanne Vielliard, *Le latin des diplômes royaux et chartes privées de l'époque mérovingienne* (Biblioth. de l'École des Hautes Études, fasc. 251, Paris, 1927).

[14] *B.M.F.* I. 1, lines 2–3. Cf. *Archivio paleografico italiano*, ed. E. Monaci, I. 1–5 (G. Marini, *I papiri diplomatici*, no. 90), line 2: pro oblationem et remedium animae meae; Marini, *op. cit.*, no. 93, line 21: pro remedium animae meae.

[15] *B.M.F.* I. 1, line 20.

[16] *Ibid.*, lines 34–5. Cf. *Urkunden und Akten*, ed. K. Brandi (3rd ed., 1932), no. 16: cum omnia sua pertinentia.

[17] *B.M.F.* I. 1, lines 21–3; compare notes 91–2, below.

all be in the genitive, only four are actually in that case; of the remaining two one is in the dative or ablative and the other in the accusative (*cum consensu archiepiscopi Theodori et Ędrico filium fratris mei*).[18] The letter *i* is sometimes used for *ii* (*piscaris* for *piscariis*,[19] *Hlothari* for *Hlotharii*[20]), *o* for *u* (*cum consenso*, later corrected to *cum consensu*),[21] *u* for *o* (*demonstratus* for *demonstratos*),[22] and *b* for *u* (*antememorabimus* for *antememorauimus*):[23] the confusion between *b* and *u*, common on the Continent in the seventh and eighth centuries, is particularly unfortunate because it makes it impossible to distinguish some forms of the perfect indicative of a large number of verbs from the corresponding forms of the future. In one case a masculine past participle and a feminine adjective are used to qualify the same noun (*In ipsa antememorato die*).[24] The division of words at the ends of lines seems to have been governed by chance as often as by any logical principle (*nu-llo*;[25] *donatione-m*, the letter *m* having been later erased and replaced by an abbreviation mark above *e*;[26] *subscribere-nt*[27]), and is responsible for one case of dittography (*pertinen-tinentia*, later corrected by erasure to *perti-nentia*)[28] and one of quasi-haplography (*fon-nis* for *fonta-nis*).[29] The grantor is normally made to speak in the first person singular (e.g. *dono, expraessi*), but the plural occurs once (*conferimus*).[30] In two identical phrases of a prohibitive nature the verb is in the indicative, whereas it should have been in one instance in the subjunctive, and in the other possibly in the ablative absolute (*a nullo contradicitur*).[31] Other errors include the use of *ae* for *e* in *expraessi*,[32] *e* for *a* in *meriscis*,[33] *e* for *i* in *possedeas*,[34] *oa* for *o* in the curious form *proacuratoribus* of which there are two examples,[35] and the misspelling *cristianitata* for *cristianitate*.[36]

The latinity of the charter, which is characteristic of an age rather than typical of one particular people or scribe, does not yield any clue to the identity or even the place of origin of its draftsman. Nor is the diplomatic of the document of much help in that respect. One can only state once again the well-known fact that the formulae used in the charter are of Italian origin: those with

---

[18] *Ibid.*, lines 14–16. Cf. *Codice paleografico lombardo, saec. VIII*, ed. G. Bonelli (Milan, 1908), no. 2, lines 4–5: una cum consenso et volontate ipsius genitori suo.

[19] *B.M.F.* I. 1, line 7.

[20] *Ibid.*, line 41.

[21] *Ibid.*, line 14. Cf. *Codice pal. lombardo*, no. 1, line 6: mano sua propria; line 9: pro stato meo.

[22] *B.M.F.* I. 1, lines 10 and 30. Cf. *Chartae Latinae Antiquiores*, ed. A. Bruckner and R. Marichal (hereafter *Ch.L.A.*), no. 181, line 71: conparature (*for* comparatore); line 74: venditure (*for* venditore).

[23] *B.M.F.* I. 1, line 32. Cf. *Ch.L.A.*, no. 181, line 21: ribis; line 38: inliuatas; *Raccolta di documenti latini*, ed. L. Schiaparelli (Como, 1923), no. 66, p. 121: suscribsisse nobit.

[24] *B.M.F.* I. 1, lines 27–8.

[25] *Ibid.*, lines 13–14.

[26] *Ibid.*, lines 18–19.

[27] *Ibid.*, lines 25–6.

[28] *Ibid.*, lines 34–5.

[29] *Ibid.*, lines 6–7. This explanation for the unrecorded word *fonnis* seems more plausible than the assumption that it is a latinized form of the English word 'fen' (*Revised Medieval Word-List*, ed. R. E. Latham, *s.v.* 'fonnum'; *E.H.D.*, I, p. 443). *Fontanis* occurs in *B.C.S.*, nos. 36, 72, 86.

[30] *B.M.F.* I. 1, line 12: conferimus. Cf. Marini, *op. cit.*, no. 86, where the singular and plural are also used (conferimus, polliceor, etc.).

[31] *B.M.F.* I. 1, lines 13–14, and line 36. Cf. *M.G.H., Formulae*, ed. K. Zeumer, p. 539, line 10: nemine contradicente.

[32] *B.M.F.* I. 1, line 25. Cf. *Ch.L.A.*, no. 181, line 72: quimquae; Schiaparelli, *Raccolta di doc. lat.*, no. 66, p. 121: magnificae frater.

[33] *B.M.F.* I. 1, line 6.

[34] *Ibid.*, line 12. Cf. *Ch.L.A.*, no. 181, line 24: possedentur.

[35] *B.M.F.* I. 1, lines 10 and 30–1. Perhaps the scribe was influenced in his spelling by the word *proauctoribus* of an Italian model. See *M.G.H., Epistolae*, II, p. 438: auctoribus proauctoribusque meis . . . possessae sunt.

[36] *B.M.F.* I. 1, lines 19–20.

legal implications (mainly in the *dispositio*) can be traced back to the technical phrases which the notaries of the late Roman Empire had over the years evolved for private deeds, particularly for transfers of land by gift and sale, while the formulae with purely religious connotations (the *invocatio* and *sanctio*) were without doubt borrowed from ecclesiastical, probably papal, sources.

(*A*) *INVOCATIO.* Hlothhere's charter begins with a pictorial invocation in the shape of a cross, followed by a verbal invocation, *In n(omine) d(omini)*[37] *nostri saluatoris Ie(s)u Cr(ist)i*,[38] apparently a variant of *In nomine domini dei et* [sometimes without *et*] *saluatoris nostri Iesu Christi*; the latter form was used by Gregory I before and after his elevation to the papacy,[39] and adopted by Titillus, Archbishop Theodore's notary, in the record of the council of Hertford (24 Sept. 672);[40] a slightly different version, *In nomine domini dei saluatoris nostri Iesu Christi*, occurs in three models of the Liber Diurnus.[41]

(*B*) *DISPOSITIO.* There is no proem; the invocation is immediately followed by the dispositive clause:

Ego Hlotharius rex Cantuariorum pro remedium animae meae dono terram in Tenid quę appellatur Uuestanae[42] tibi Bercuald tuoque monasterio cum omnib(us) ad se pertinentibus campis pascuis meriscis siluis modicis fon[ta]nis piscaris omnibus ut dictum est ad eandem terram pertinentia, sicuti nunc usque possessa est, iuxta notissimos terminos a me demonstratus et proacuratoribus meis, eodem modo tibi tuoque monasterio conferimus, teneas possedeas tu posterique tui in perpetuum defendant, a nullo contradicitur, cum consensu archiepiscopi Theodori et Ędrico filium fratris mei necnon et omnium principum, sicuti tibi donata est ita tene et posteri tui.

The whole clause is in direct speech: the grantor, speaking in the present and in the first person, addresses the grantee in the second person, a feature also found in some Italian charters, for example in a Ravenna charter of 491,[43] in the well-known grant made in 587 by Gregory the Deacon (later to become Pope Gregory I) to his Roman monastery of Sant' Andrea al Clivo di Scauro,[44] in a charter of the bishop of Lucca dated 685,[45] and in a stone inscription of uncertain date.[46] The gift is made for the redemption of the donor's soul, *pro remedium animae meae*, the very words (with the same grammatical error) used in a sixth-century grant to the church of Ravenna;[47] the phrase *pro oblationem et remedium animae meae* also occurs in another Ravenna charter.[48] The object of the grant is the land called *Westanae* in Thanet: it is given to Abbot Brihtwold and his monastery in the same way as it has been possessed to the present day, with all its appurtenances, fields, pastures, marshes, small woods, wells and fisheries, and within the well-known boundaries which have been established by the king and his proctors. The Ravenna deeds of the sixth century use much the same terminology; for example, a deed of sale of 572 describes the estate sold as follows:

---

[37] L. Traube, *Nomina Sacra* (Munich, 1907), p. 146, rules out *d(ei)* as an alternative reading.

[38] In an English manuscript of this date *Cristi* seems to be more likely than *Christi*. *Cristo* is found unabbreviated in *Codices Latini Antiquiores* [hereafter *C.L.A.*], ed. E. A. Lowe, no. 280.

[39] *M.G.H., Epistolae*, II, pp. 275, 437; W. Levison, *England and the Continent in the Eighth Century* (Oxford, 1946), pp. 229–30.

[40] Bede, *Historia Ecclesiastica*, ed. C. Plummer, I (Oxford, 1896), p. 214.

[41] *Liber Diurnus Romanorum Pontificum*, ed. H. Foerster (Berne, 1958), pp. 132, 137, 145 (Codex Vat., nos. 74, 76, 83).

[42] Between *Uuestan* and *ae* there is a triangle of dots, the meaning of which is uncertain: perhaps it is meant as a transposition sign for the two letters *a* and *e* or as a word-division mark to emphasize that *Uuestan* and *ae* are two separate, vernacular, words (*westan* meaning 'west of', and *ae* meaning 'river').

[43] Marini, *op. cit.*, no. 84.

[44] *M.G.H., Epistolae*, II, p. 437. Cf. *Urkunden und Akten* (3rd ed., 1932), ed. Brandi, no. 12.

[45] *Codice diplomatico longobardo*, ed. L. Schiaparelli, I (Rome, 1929), no. 7.

[46] *Urkunden und Akten*, ed. Brandi, no. 16.

[47] Marini, op. cit., no. 93.   [48] *Ibid.*, no. 90; *Archivio paleografico italiano*, ed. Monaci, I. 1–5, line 2.

. . . id est fundi, cui vocavulum est Custinis, uncias quinque[49] . . . constitutum in territorio Ariminensi inter adfines fundum Varianum et fundum Titzianum atque fundum Quadrantula, . . . finibus, terminis, silvis, campis, pratis, pascuis, salectis, sationalibus,[50] . . . ribis, fontibus, aquis perennibus limitibusque earum et omnibus ad se pertinentibus, sicuti a suprascripto venditore et ab eiusque auctoribus bono, optimo et inconcusso iure possessae sunt et hucusque in hanc diem possedentur, ita et tradentur.[51]

Another estate given to the church of Ravenna in the sixth century is said to be granted with its lands and vines and all appurtenances,

. . . inter adfines circumcirca . . . sicuti a me meaque patrona, auctores et proauctores . . . possessum est atque nunc usque in hodiernam diem rite possedetur, ita et a me traditur a praesenti die suprascriptae sanctae ecclesiae Rav' . . .[52]

In one of the Albertini tablets, a Vandal deed of 493 from Roman North Africa, the field which is being sold is described in the following words:

inter adfines eiusdem agri a coro Martialis benditor et Ianuarius Fortuni, ab aquilo supradictus Martialis benditor, a meridie Quintianus, ab africo supradictus Quintianus et Victor, sibe quibus adfinibus cum quibus eos solbensisse [*for* soluisse] mostrarunt benditoribus [*for* uenditores] ex eredictate parentum cum transitis suis . . .[53]

This method of describing a land by reference to its northern, southern, eastern and western limits, common in Vandal deeds of the late-fifth century, was also often adopted in early Anglo-Saxon diplomas.[54] The boundaries of the land granted by Hlothhere, however, are not so given; instead they are described as *notissimos terminos a me demonstratus et proacuratoribus meis*, a phrase which is reminiscent of that used in the Vandal deed of 493, *adfinibus cum quibus eos solbensisse mostrarunt benditoribus*. The words *demonstratus* and *mostrarunt* may refer to an actual perambulation such as that described in a Ravenna document of the fifth century:

. . . Et cum hodie ambulassent et pervenissent ad singula praedia, adque introissent . . . et inquilinos sive servos et circuissent omnes fines, terminos, agros, arbos cultos vel incultos seu . . ., et traditio corporalis celebrata fuisset actoribus Pieri viri inlustris nullo contradicente . . .[55]

The purpose of Hlothhere's grant is to give Abbot Brihtwold and his successors the right to hold, possess and preserve the land of *Westanae* in perpetuity without interference from anyone. Here again we find the same expressions in Italian and Vandal charters of an earlier period. For example, the Vandal deed of sale of 493 already quoted gives the purchasers the right *ut abeant, teneant, possideant, utantur, fruantur ipsi eredesbe eorum in perpetum*.[56] In a Ravenna charter of the sixth century the donor, after reserving to himself a usufruct of ten days (*quia reservatio ususfructus, etiamsi stipulatio inserta non fuerit, pro traditione habeatur*[57]), defines the powers which the church of Ravenna is to have after expiry of the usufruct:

---

[49] Is *unculam* in B.C.S., no. 497 (*B.M.F.* II. 34) a diminutive of *unciam*, or should we regard *terre unculam* as one word, synonym of *terrulam* (*B.C.S.*, nos. 148, 199) and formed by analogy with *mansiunculam*?

[50] Compare *B.C.S.*, no. 67: omnes terras sationales.

[51] *Ch.L.A.*, no. 181.

[52] Marini, *op. cit.*, no. 93.

[53] *Tablettes Albertini*, ed. Courtois and others (Paris, 1952), no. 6; see also *ibid.*, nos. 3, 5, 9, 16, 19.

[54] *B.C.S.*, nos. 86, 163–4, 182, 187, etc. See W. H. Stevenson, 'Trinoda necessitas', *English Historical Review* [hereafter *E.H.R.*] XXIX (1914), p. 695, note 34.

[55] *Urkunden und Akten*, ed. Brandi, no. 8. By reserving a usufruct, the donor could dispense with the formality of the *traditio corporalis*; see below, note 57.

[56] *Tablettes Albertini*, no. 6; cf. *ibid.*, no. 3.

[57] *Codex Theodosianus*, VIII. 12. 9 (*Brev. Alar.*, VIII. 5. 2; *Interpretatio*); Ernst Levy, *West Roman Vulgar Law* (*Memoirs of the American Philosophical Soc. held at Philadelphia* . . ., XXIX, 1951), pp. 144–5; see also *Ch.L.A.*, no. 181, lines 54–7; *M.G.H.*, *Epistolae*, II, p. 438: quae retentio ipsius ususfructus praefato monasterio eiusque actoribus pro solenni et legitima traditione constare sanxerunt.

Post vero transactos dies usufructuarios meos memoratam portionem fundi suprascripti predicta ecclesia Rav' actoresque eius habeant, teneant, possedeant, iuri dominioque more quo voluerit imperpetuo vindicent atque defendant.[58]

In his grant of 587 to Sant' Andrea al Clivo di Scauro Gregory the Deacon reserves a usufruct of only five days and adds:

Transactum vero usumfructum meum superius designatum antefatum monasterium habeat, teneat, possideat, iure dominioque suo in perpetuum vendicet ac defendat.[59]

In Hlothhere's charter there is no mention of a usufruct, long or short, real or fictitious, to be retained by the king or anybody else, and the grant to Abbot Brihtwold was presumably to take full effect immediately, *a praesenti die et tempore*, as other Italian and Anglo-Saxon charters explicitly state.[60]

It is well to remember at this point that the rights transferred to the respective beneficiaries of the various documents cited above were not necessarily the same in practice. Wording similarities between deeds coming from different ages and lands suggest a common diplomatic ancestry; they do not imply identical effects in law.[61] It is evident, as Maitland suggested long ago, that Abbot Brihtwold and the other beneficiaries of royal Anglo-Saxon grants of the late seventh century cannot have acquired on the land given to them such absolute rights as did the purchasers of a North African field in a Vandal deed of the late fifth century.[62] Anglo-Saxon kings could only transfer to others the rights which they had themselves on the lands granted, and these lands cannot all have been waste lands in their own personal possession. The charter states that Hlothhere obtained the consent of Archbishop Theodore, Eadric and all the magnates. The agreement of the magnates in general may have been required simply because any grant of royal rights affected the kingdom as a whole.[63] This in itself is noteworthy, as it shows that the king could not dispose at will of the lands of his kingdom, but the mention of Theodore and Eadric by name suggests that their consent was more important than anybody else's and that it was needed for a special reason, obviously because they already had in Kent some rights of their own with which the grant of *Westanae* to Brihtwold might somehow interfere: Theodore was archbishop of Canterbury, and Eadric, who issued a legal code as joint king with Hlothhere, his uncle,[64] perhaps already enjoyed quasi-royal rights in Kent when the charter was issued.

(C) *SANCTIO*. In Italian private deeds of the sixth and seventh centuries the dispositive clause is often followed by what might be called a clause of warranty, consisting of a promise made by the donor or seller that neither he nor his heirs would infringe the terms of the grant or sale. The clause inserted in the grant of Gregory the Deacon is fairly typical:

In qua donationis pagina spondeo atque promitto nunquam me, haeredes successoresque meos nec per aliam quamlibet dolosam fictitiamque personam per cuiuslibet legis interventum contrariam inferre voluntatem; sed in huius me, haeredes successoresque meos promitto fidem chartulae duraturos.[65]

Another Italian charter, dated 553, expresses the same idea in a shorter form:

Contra quam donationem nullo tempore nullaque ratione me, posteros successoresque meos venturos esse polliceor invocato tremendi diem iudicii.[66]

---

[58] Marini, *op. cit.*, no. 93.   [59] *M.G.H., Epistolae*, II, p. 438.

[60] Marini, *op. cit.*, no. 86; *B.C.S.*, nos. 34, 67, 73, 86, 90, 148, etc.; cf. Pardessus, *Diplomata* (Paris, 1843–49), II, p. 426, no. 6.

[61] Levy, *op. cit.*, e.g. pp. 19–34.

[62] F. W. Maitland, *Domesday Book and Beyond* (Cambridge, 1907), pp. 230 ff.

[63] F. M. Stenton, *The Latin Charters of the Anglo-Saxon period* (Oxford, 1955), p. 35.

[64] *E.H.D.*, I, pp. 360–1.   [65] *M.G.H., Epistolae*, II, p. 438.

[66] Marini, *op. cit.*, no. 86, p. 133. Compare *Codex Theodosianus*, II. 9. 3 (*Brev. Alar.*, II. 9. 1): promissa ea, quae invocato dei omnipotentis nomine eo auctore solidaverit.

Similar clauses occur in several royal Anglo-Saxon diplomas of the last quarter of the seventh century, for example in a Kentish grant of 686:

Nunquam me hæredesque meos vel successores contra hanc donationis meæ cartulam ullo tempore esse venturos.[67]

In a Surrey charter the clause resembles a wish rather than a promise:

Numquam ego heredesque mei ullo tempore contra hanc donationis cartulam venire temptaverit.[68]

In Hlothhere's charter it is neither a promise nor a wish, but a general prohibition to everyone (*a nullo contradicitur*), inserted in the middle of the dispositive clause. In a postscript which states that, on the day on which the king granted *Westanae* to Brihtwold, he also gave him another land in Sturry, the prohibition is repeated, this time in a longer version:

A nullo contradicitur, quod absit, neque a me neque a parentibus meis neque ab aliis.

Here the word *parentibus* is used in the wide sense of 'kinsmen', that is to say the members of the grantor's *parentela* who, in a Worcester charter of the second half of the eighth century, are contrasted with the 'outsiders' (*externorum*).[69]

Originally the insertion of a promise of non-infringement in deeds of gift seems to have been the equivalent of a general renunciation by the grantor, not only of the use of force or treachery in order to recover what had been given, but also of all the legal loop-holes which the Theodosian and Barbaric Codes provided for the revocation of gifts.[70] Because gifts extorted by force, threats or trickery could be revoked,[71] Italian charters of the sixth and seventh centuries often state that the grant was made of the grantor's own free will, 'omni vi, dolo [*or* dolo malo], metu et circumscribtione cessante'.[72] This is specified, for instance, in a charter of the sixth century for the church of Ravenna, in which the grantor—a woman—adds that she renounces all the remedies provided by law for the revocation of gifts and in particular those open to women.[73] The promise that neither she nor her heirs or successors will infringe the terms of the grant was made, she says, because the laws stipulate that what has once been given to holy places cannot be taken back from them (*quoniam et legebus cautum est ut quod semel in loca venerabilia donatum vel quoquo modo cessum fuerit nullo modo revocetur*).[74]

---

[67] *B.C.S.*, no. 67; see also *ibid.*, nos. 34, 86.

[68] *Ibid.*, no. 72.

[69] *Ibid.*, no. 220. See *E.H.D.*, I, p. 453.

[70] See Marini, *op. cit.*, no. 90: excluso a me vel meos heredes omnium legum beneficia iuris et facti ignorantia fori loci militiaeque perscribtione seu quod de revocandis donationibus sunt per lege indulta donantibus.

[71] See the beginning of the Arcadian constitution (*Codex Theodosianus*, II. 9. 3; *Brev. Alar.*, II. 9. 1): Si quis maior annis adversum pacta vel transactiones nullo cogentis imperio, sed libero arbitrio et voluntate confecta putaverit esse veniendum . . . *M.G.H.*, *Legum Sectio* I. i (*Leges Visigothorum*), p. 18, fragm. 308: Res donata, si in praesenti traditur, nullo modo a donatore repetatur, nisi causis certis et probatis; *ibid.*, fragm. 309: Donatio que per vim et metum probatur extorta, nullam habeat firmitatem. Compare *Codex Theodosianus*, XV. 14. 9: Stent denique omnia, quae in placitum sunt deducta privatum, nisi aut circumscribtio subveniet aut vis aut terror ostenditur. See also *ibid.*, VIII. 13 (De revocandis donationibus), etc.

[72] Marini, *op. cit.*, nos. 92, 93.

[73] *Ibid.*, no 93: excluso erga me omnium legum beneficia quae de revocandis donationibus et de sexu femineo Belliianus [*recte* Velleianus] senatusconsultus mulieribus subvenire adsolet; quoniam ad hanc largitatem meam sponte et habeta deliberatione perveni, nullius cogentis imperio nec suadentis inpulso et haec irrevocabiliter me donasse profiteor: quam donationis meae paginam omni vi dolo metu et circumscribtione cessante . . .

[74] *Ibid.* See W. John, 'Formale Beziehungen der privaten Schenkungsurkunden Italiens . . .', *Archiv für Urkundenforschung*, XIV (1935–36), p. 17. See also *M.G.H.*, *Legum Sectio* I. i, p. 208: quecumque res sanctis Dei basilicis aut per principum aut per quorumlibet fidelium donationes conlate repperiuntur votive ac potentialiter, pro certo censetur, ut in earum iure irrevocabili modo legum eternitate firmentur. Compare *Codex Theodosianus*, XI. 24. 6: Quidquid autem . . . ecclesiae venerabiles . . . possedisse deteguntur, id pro intuitu religionis ab his praecipimus firmiter retineri . . . See also Nino Tamassia, 'La *defensio* nei documenti medievali italiani', *Archivio Giuridico Filippo Serafini*, LXXII. 3 (1904), p. 460.

It is evident that a promise of non-infringement, implying a renunciation of legal remedies, was hardly suitable in a royal charter. On the other hand, an order forbidding anybody to violate a royal grant was most appropriate and simply confirmed the accepted rule that royal gifts should remain in force, 'quia non oportet principum statuta convelli'.[75] Clauses of non-infringement of the prohibitive type are commonly found in papal grants of all kinds. In a document issued in 590 Gregory I, after stipulating that the lands which he had given three years earlier to the monastery of Sant' Andrea al Clivo di Scauro were not to be alienated by the abbot or his successors, added: *Et hoc constitutum nullus qualibet exquisitione vel nitatur arte dissolvere*.[76] Five years later, however, Gregory was using a promissory formula in a manumission:

Haec igitur quae per huius manumissionis cartulam constituimus atque concessimus, nos successoresque nostros sine aliqua scitote refragatione servare. Nam iustitiae ac rationis ordo suadet ut qui sua a successoribus desiderat mandata servari decessoris sui procul dubio voluntatem et statuta custodiat.[77]

In England neither the prohibitive clause, which still occasionally occurs in Kentish charters of the ninth century,[78] nor the promissory one ever became a regular feature of the royal diploma before the Norman Conquest.

Even promises solemnly given could be broken and strongly-worded prohibitions ignored. Grantees could not be expected to find much comfort in purely ethical rules such as those formulated by Gregory I that anybody who wished his successors to carry out his instructions should begin by showing the same respect for the wishes of his predecessor. One way of deterring possible transgressors was to insert a penalty clause in the text of the written grant. A constitution of Emperors Arcadius and Honorius (*Lex Arcadiana*, A.D. 395), incorporated in the section 'De pactis et transactionibus' of the Theodosian Code, had decreed that the party who broke an agreement would be declared infamous and would have to pay to the other party the penalty which had been laid down in the agreement.[79] Deeds of sale and other contracts could be regarded as covered by the provisions of the constitution, but unilateral gifts could not. Italian deeds of sale of the sixth and seventh centuries normally contain a clause imposing a money penalty on the party guilty of infringement;[80] on the other hand, Italian deeds of gift of the sixth and early seventh centuries have no penalty clause of any kind. This is true, for example, of Gregory the Deacon's grant of 587.[81] How soon were such clauses extended from bilateral contracts to unilateral grants, it is difficult to say. What is certain is that, as early as Gregory I's time, some papal confirmations of privileges granted to monasteries ended with a threat of excommunication against those guilty of infringement.[82] This religious sanction, obviously less effective than a pecuniary penalty, was the only one at the disposal of the Church: used first in purely ecclesiastical matters, it was gradually extended to the secular affairs of the Church. In the course of the seventh century it spread further to all sorts of private grants, although mainly to those intended for ecclesiastical uses; it is found, for example, in a charter of Bishop Felix of Lucca of 685.[83] Some Frankish private charters also stipulate religious penalties, but, from the early part of the seventh century, the normal penalty in Frankish charters is a secular one, providing for the payment either of double the value of the property involved or of a fixed sum of

---

[75] *M.G.H.*, *Legum Sectio* I. I, p. 210; see also p. 16.

[76] *M.G.H.*, *Epistolae*, I, p. 15.

[77] *Ibid.*, p. 391.

[78] *B.C.S.*, no. 313; see also *ibid.*, nos. 319, 442.

[79] *Codex Theodosianus*, II. 9. 3 (*Brev. Alar.*, II. 9. I, and *Interpretatio*). See Giorgio La Pira, 'La stipulatio Aquiliana nei papiri', *Atti del IV Congresso Internazionale di Papirologia 1935* (Milan, 1936), pp. 479–80; F. Brandileone, 'La *stipulatio* nelle carte italiane del medio evo', *Mélanges Fitting*, I (Montpellier, 1907), pp. 103–11.

[80] *Ch.L.A.*, no. 181; Marini, *op. cit.*, no. 120; *Urkunden und Akten*, ed. Brandi, no. 10.

[81] *M.G.H.*, *Epistolae*, II, pp. 437–9.

[82] *Ibid.*, I, p. 15; II, pp. 378, 380, 381.

[83] *Codice diplomatico longobardo*, ed. Schiaparelli, I, no. 7.

money, part of which is allocated to the fisc and part to the injured grantee.[84] By the end of the seventh century the system of pecuniary penalties had also infiltrated into Italian private charters, and soon it was universally accepted on the Continent, ecclesiastical penalties being sometimes added as a supplementary guarantee.[85] In Marculf's day, however, the draftsmen of charters still argued that in transfers of land by gift the insertion of a penalty clause was not necessary: *Licet in cessionibus poenam adnecti non sit necesse, sed nobis pro homni firmitate placuit inserendum.*[86]

No evolution of this kind took place in Anglo-Saxon England. From the seventh to the eleventh century the only penalty to be mentioned in Anglo-Saxon charters granting land in perpetuity is a religious one, threatening with excommunication or punishment in the next world those guilty of violating the terms of the grant.[87] Hlothhere's charter is no exception; its main penalty clause reads:

Quisquis contra hanc donatione(m) uenire temptauerit sit ab omni cr(ist)ianitata separatus et a corpore et sanguini d(omi)ni nostri Ie(s)u Cr(ist)i suspensus,

to which is added another, at the end of the Sturry postscript:

Si aliquis aliter fecerit, a d(e)o se damnatum sciat et in die iudicii rationem reddet d(e)o in anima sua.

The formulae used by Gregory I are considerably longer, but the punishment envisaged is the same:

Si quis vero . . . hanc constitutionis nostrae paginam agnoscens contra eam venire temptaverit, . . . a sacratissimo corpore ac sanguine dei domini redemptoris nostri Iesu Christi alienus fiat atque in aeterno examine districtae ultioni subiaceat.[88]

The main purpose behind all penalty clauses was to deter unscrupulous people from violating the terms of the grant in which the clauses were inserted. Even a money penalty was intended as a punishment for transgressors rather than a compensation for despoiled grantees. What the beneficiaries of charters particularly wanted was to be assured that, should an infringement take place, they would be restored to the *status quo ante*. For this reason the money-penalty clause of Italian and Frankish charters was normally followed by a phrase such as *sed presens cessio omni tempore inlibata permaneat*[89] or *et cartula ista . . . in sua permaneat nichilominus firmitate*.[90] In early Italian private charters the phrase is sometimes found in the accusative absolute, for instance in a Ravenna charter of *plenaria securitas* of 564 (*manente nihilominus hanc plenariam securitatem in sua firmitate*)[91] and in another Ravenna charter of 681 (*manentes hos libellos in sua nihilominus firmitate*).[92] It is this form in the accusative absolute which was adopted in Hlothhere's charter (*manentem hanc donationis chartulam in sua nihilominus firmitate*), a feature which is shared by a number of other Kentish diplomas of the seventh and eighth centuries.[93] It should be added that in Anglo-Saxon charters the formula is combined with the threat of a religious sanction, whereas in Italian and Frankish charters it seems to have been reserved for clauses stipulating a money penalty.[94]

---

[84] Pardessus, *Diplomata*, I, pp. 227–8; *Ch.L.A.*, nos. 40, 45, etc.

[85] *Monumenti Ravennati de' Secoli di Mezzo*, VI (Venice, 1804), pp. 263–4; *Codice diplomatico longobardo*, I, no. 12; *Ch.L.A.*, no. 44.

[86] *M.G.H., Formulae*, ed. Zeumer, p. 77; see also *ibid.*, pp. 19, 159, 175, 489. See also Fritz Boye, 'Über die Poenformeln in den Urkunden des früheren Mittelalters', *Archiv für Urkundenforschung*, VI (1916), pp. 77–148; Joachim Studtmann, 'Die Pönformel der mittelalterlichen Urkunden', *ibid.*, XII (1931–32), pp. 251–374.

[87] Sometimes the anathema (*sanctio negativa*) is followed by a blessing (*sanctio positiva*) as in papal documents.

[88] *M.G.H., Epistolae*, II, p. 378.

[89] *M.G.H., Formulae*, ed. Zeumer, p. 77.

[90] *Il regesto di Farfa*, ed. Giorgi and Balzani, II (Rome, 1879), no. 5; compare *Ch.L.A.*, no. 45, etc.

[91] Marini, *op. cit.*, no. 80.

[92] *Monumenti Ravennati de' Secoli di Mezzo*, VI, p. 263.

[93] *B.C.S.*, nos. 42 (doubtful), 159, 193, 196, 199, 228, etc.

[94] The phrase seems to make better sense at the end of a clause stipulating a money penalty.

(D) *CORROBORATIO*. The *sanctio* of Hlothhere's charter is followed by the announcement of the signs of validation: the king explains that he has 'confirmed' the charter by tracing the sign of the cross with his own hand and by asking witnesses to subscribe it:

Et pro confirmatione eius manu propria signum s(an)c(t)e crucis expraessi et testes ut subscriberent rogaui.

The words *Et pro confirmatione eius*, which give the clause its corroborating character, do not occur in Italian private charters, although they may have been used in papal and episcopal documents. In private charters written by Italian notaries the signs of validation (signa or subscriptions of the author and witnesses, and *completio* of the notary) are announced, not in a self-contained corroboration clause, but in the second part of the *rogatio*, the first part of which consists of a statement made by the author of the document that he has entrusted the writing of his charter to one particular notary whom he names. It is from the second part of the *rogatio* that most of the wording of the corroboration clause in Hlothhere's charter is derived. In a grant of 491 made to the church of Ravenna by a certain Maria, an illiterate woman, the *rogatio* reads:

. . . chartulam Iovino, noto meo, scribendam dictavi, cuique, quia ignoro litteras, signum feci, ad quod Castorium, virum clarissimum, carum meum, ut pro me suscriberet conrogavi, nobiles quoque viros qui suas suscribtiones dignanter adnectant pari supplicatione poposco, stipulantique tibi, vir beatissime pater et papa Iohannes, spopondi ego qui supra Maria, spectabilis femina.[95]

In a Ravenna deed of sale of 572 the notary states that he has written the document at the request of the seller,

. . . ipso praesente, adstante mihique dictante et consentiente et subter manu propria pro ignorantia litterarum signum faciente, et testes ut suscriberent conrogavit.[96]

When the author of the document can write, the subscriptions of witnesses are announced – in slightly different words – not only in the *rogatio*, but also in the author's own subscription. For example, Gregory the Deacon's subscription to his charter of 587 reads:

Ego Gregorius peccator, sanctae Romanae ecclesiae diaconus, huic donationi a me factae in praefato monasterio de supramemoratis fundis ad omnia suprascripta relegi, consensi et subscripsi et testes ut subscriberent rogavi.[97]

(E) *DATE*. The dating clause of Hlothhere's charter (*Actum in ciuitate Recuulf in mense maio*,[98] *indictione septima*) is also an adaptation of an Italian formula. Some Ravenna charters and two of Gregory I's manumissions have a dating clause which begins with the word *Actum*, followed by the place of issue.[99] The reference to the indictional year is undoubtedly of Italian origin: it is also in this way that the year is given in the record of the Council of Hertford of 24 September 672; towards the beginning of this record, the meeting is said to have been held *die xx°iiii° mensis Septembris*, *indictione prima, in loco qui dicitur Herutford*, and later on in the document, the dating clause is given as follows: *Actum in mense et indictione supra scripta*.[100] In this second date, as in the dating clause of Hlothhere's charter, the day of the month is not given. Other early Anglo-Saxon charters are also dated by the indictional year and the month only. Why this should have been so, it is impossible to say. Dating habits vary so much from one document to another that it would be futile to hazard an explanation.

---

[95] Marini, *op. cit.*, no. 84.
[96] *Ch.L.A.*, no. 181.
[97] *M.G.H.*, Epistolae, II, p. 438.
[98] A letter (?*d*) has been erased between *a* and *i*.
[99] *M.G.H.*, Epistolae, I, p. 391 (Actum in urbe Roma); II, p. 108 (Actum Romae).
[100] Bede, *Hist. Eccl.*, ed. Plummer, I, pp. 215, 217.

It is well known that in the second half of the seventh century at Canterbury, and presumably throughout Kent, the indictional year was reckoned from 1 September (Greek indiction). This is proved by the records of the councils of Hertford and Hatfield, which are respectively dated 24 September in the first indiction and 17 September in the eighth indiction: by using other dating elements Reginald Lane Poole has established beyond doubt that the two councils were held on 24 September 672 and 17 September 679, proving thereby that it was the Greek indiction which was in use in Canterbury in the time of Archbishop Theodore.[101] The view of modern scholars seems to be that the Greek indiction was in any case the only one known at the time and that the indiction calculated from 24 September was invented by Bede. If Bede really was responsible for this new reckoning, he must have known that, until he came on the scene, everybody calculated the indiction from 1 September. Yet in his *Ecclesiastical History* he wrongly converted the two Greek indictions of the councils into the years of the incarnation 673 (main text of the *History*) and 680 (*Recapitulatio*),[102] thus showing that he was unaware that the indiction could have begun on 1 September in Kent; worse still, he placed 24 September 673 in the first indiction, although in the system which he is supposed to have introduced this date should have been the first day of the second indiction. It has often been pointed out that Bede was not infallible in his chronology, but it seems rather odd that a man who gave in his *De Temporum Ratione* an easy way of calculating the indiction from the year of the incarnation[103] should have made three blunders, all connected with the reckoning of the indiction, in only two dating clauses. If, on the other hand, he did not invent the indiction of 24 September, but simply adopted it because it was already in use in Northumbria before his time, he might not have known that a different indiction, the Greek one, was current in Kent.

It has been suggested that either Bede made the year of the incarnation start on the same day as the indiction, in which case his dates 673 and 680 would not be errors at all, or he simply converted the indiction into the year of the incarnation by using the tables of Dionysius Exiguus and omitted to make the required corrections for dates falling between the beginning of the indiction and the beginning of the year of the incarnation.[104] Either of these two suggestions would explain Bede's dates of 673 and 680 for the two councils, but neither provides a satisfactory answer for a third date given by Bede, this time in his *Historia Abbatum*. Here Bede tells the story of Abbot Ceolfrid's arrival at Langres on Friday (*feria sexta*) 25 September 716 (*septimo kalendarum Octobrium die, anno ab incarnatione Domini septingentesimo sextodecimo*) at about 8 a.m. (*circa horam diei tertiam*), and his death there, on the same day, at about 3 p.m. (*decima ipsius diei hora; . . . post horam nonam*).[105] Bede's year of the incarnation, A.D. 716, in this instance is undoubtedly correct. Nor is there much doubt that Bede arrived at that year by calculating it from the indictional year given in the anonymous *Historia Abbatum*, on which Bede depends for much of his information:

Peruenit autem Lingonas Ceolfridus circa horam diei tertiam, septimo kal. Octob. ut diximus [*this day being described in an earlier chapter as* sexta sabbati, *i.e.* sexta feria], incipiente indictione XV.[106]

If Bede had used the Dionysian tables *without* making the necessary corrections or if he had made the year of the incarnation coincide with the indictional year, he would have given A.D. 717 as the

[101] R. L. Poole, *Studies in Chronology and History* (Oxford, 1934), pp. 9, 41, 44–9.

[102] Bede, *op. cit.*, ed. Plummer, I, pp. 217, 355.

[103] Bede, *Opera de temporibus*, ed. C. W. Jones (Med. Acad. of America Publ. no. 41, Cambridge, Mass., 1943), pp. 268–9.

[104] Poole, *op. cit.*, p. 41; C. W. Jones, *Saints' Lives and Chronicles in Early England* (Cornell Univ. Press, 1947), pp. 40–1, 171–2.

[105] Bede, *Hist. Eccl.*, ed. Plummer, I, pp. 385–6.

[106] *Ibid.*, pp. 400–2.

year of Ceolfrid's death. In my view this proves that Bede used a different beginning for the indiction and for the year of grace. In so far as the year of grace is concerned, Levison has shown that Bede made it start on Christmas Day,[107] and so probably did the anonymous *Historia Abbatum*, which refers to 12 January (*II id. Ian.*) as *anni sequentis exordiis*.[108] It also proves that Bede could make the necessary corrections for dates falling between September and 25 December. But on what day in September did Bede make the indiction begin? If it was 24 September, Bede should have dated the council of Hertford 24 September 672, and not 24 September 673 as he in fact did; on the other hand, Bede's years for the council of Hatfield and for Ceolfrid's death would fit in with an indiction beginning on 24 September. Assuming that Bede was using the same consistent system to arrive at the three years 673, 680 and 716, we must inevitably conclude that he placed the beginning of the indiction between what he regarded as the end of 24 September and the beginning of 25 September (not later than *hora prima* or 6 a.m.). In other words, the change in the number of the indiction took place between sunset on 24 September and sunrise on 25 September. If this interpretation is correct, it follows that the words *incipiente indictione XV* in the anonymous *Historia Abbatum* should be understood in the narrow sense of 'on the first day of the fifteenth indiction'. A tenth-century transcriber of the anonymous work seems to have been worried by the statement that the fifteenth indiction began on 25 September (*septimo kal. Octob.*) and he changed the word *septimo*, which was retained by Bede, into *VIII*.[109] If now we turn to Bede's *De Temporum Ratione*, we find that the author uses a particularly ambiguous phrase when he states on what day the indiction should change: *Incipiunt autem indictiones ab viii kal. octobres ibidemque terminantur*.[110] How could the old indiction end on 24 September and the new one start *from* that day also, unless again one makes the number of the indiction change between sunset on 24 September, that is to say at 6 p.m. since Bede thought that 24 September was the date of the autumn equinox, and sunrise on 25 September, i.e. 6 a.m.? This would mean in practice that a document issued on 24 September would still be placed in the old indiction and another issued on 25 September would fall in the new indiction. All the medieval calendars which have been studied in recent years are as vague as Bede in their references to the indiction: they note that the change took place on 24 September, one notable exception being an eleventh-century calendar wrongly attributed to Bede by Johannes Herwagen (*Hervagius*); if Herwagen can be trusted, the calendar which he used (probably a manuscript from a 'Swiss' monastery) had the following entry opposite 25 September: *Æquinoctium iuxta quosdam, et locus indictionum*.[111]

As we do not know whether the anonymous *Historia Abbatum* was written before or after the *De Temporum Ratione*, we cannot be certain that the indiction of 24/25 September was in use in Northumbria before Bede, but this seems likely; otherwise, he would probably have warned us that his computation was different from that used before his time and he would not have misdated the councils of Hertford and Hatfield. It may also be worth noting that one date in the anonymous work is given by reference to the year of the incarnation.[112]

In so far as Kent is concerned, the Bedan indiction had replaced the Greek indiction by A.D. 822;[113] in Worcester it was already in use by 780.[114]

(*F*) *POSTSCRIPT*. The dating clause is followed by a postscript in which Hlothhere states that

---

[107] W. Levison, *England and the Continent in the Eighth Century* (Oxford, 1946), pp. 265–79.
[108] Bede, *Hist. Eccl.*, ed. Plummer, I, p. 394; Levison, *op. cit.*, p. 269.
[109] Bede, *Hist. Eccl.*, ed. Plummer, I, p. 401, note 9.
[110] Ed. Jones, p. 268.
[111] *Opera Bedae*, ed. Iohannes Heruagius, I (Basel, 1563), p. 258.
[112] Bede, *Hist. Eccl.*, ed. Plummer, I, p. 390.
[113] *B.C.S.*, no. 370.
[114] *B.C.S.*, no. 236.

in ipsa antememorato die he made to Brihtwold an additional grant of land in Sturry. In form the postscript is a miniature charter, with a *dispositio* which is *mutatis mutandis* an abridged version of the dispositive clause of the *Westanae* grant, and with a prohibitive clause and an anathema which have already been quoted. The whole of the diploma is so clumsily drafted that one cannot be surprised by this addition or by the statement that the Sturry grant was made on the day 'aforesaid', although in reality the day of issue of the *Westanae* grant is not given in its dating clause.

(G) *SIGNS OF VALIDATION*. Italian private deeds of gift and sale were validated by the autograph signa or subscriptions of the author and witnesses, and by the autograph subscription (*completio*) of the notary who wrote the document. If the grantor or seller was literate, he wrote his own subscription himself, in the first person (e.g. *Ego . . . relegi, consensi et subscripsi . . .*).[115] If the author was illiterate, the notary wrote on his behalf a formula of the type *Signum* [or *Signum manus*] *Mariae spectabilis feminae suprascriptae donatricis*[116] or *Signum suprascripti Domnini viri honesti agellarii, venditoris*,[117] and the author traced with his own hand, next to the word *Signum*, a sign which normally was the sign of the cross.[118] Similarly, the witnesses who could write made their own subscription; those who could not write simply made a cross.

In so far as deeds of gift were concerned, this system of validation fitted in well with the publicity rules laid down in the Theodosian Code and in the *Interpretatio* of the Breviary of Alaric, and even better with the more precise regulations set out in the 'national' Barbaric Codes. The *Interpretatio*, after saying that every deed of gift should give the names of the donor and donee, and describe what was given, all this being done publicly, not in secret, added the following rule:

> Quam tamen donationem, si litteras novit donator, ipse subscribat; si vero ignorat, praesentibus plurimis eligat qui pro ipso subscribat.[119]

Some additional Visigothic laws are more specific:

> Si quis domum aut villam alio donaverit, hoc quod donavit per donationis cartulam firmet, ita ut in ea donatione ipse donator propria manu subscribat, et ipsa donatio non minus tribus testibus roboretur. Si autem ipse donator et testes litteras nesciunt, unusquisque signum propria manu faciat.[120]

All the Barbaric Codes have similar rulings, although the required number (*competens numerus*) of witnesses varies according to the Codes and sometimes according to the importance of the gifts; the minimum number is sometimes five, sometimes seven.[121] These witnesses, of course, had to be 'suitable' (*idonei*), an expression which the Visigothic laws interpreted as follows:

> In duobus autem idoneis testibus, quos prisca legum recipiendos sancit auctoritas, non solum considerandum est quam sint idonei genere, hoc est indubitanter ingenui, sed etiam si sint honestate mentis perspicui adque rerum plenitudine opulenti.[122]

According to the *Leges Burgundionum* a person without a stain on his character qualified as an *idoneus testis* (*quorum fama numquam maculata est*).[123]

Hlothhere's charter is attested by the king as grantor and by eleven witnesses. The king's attestation is in the form: *Signum manus Hlothari regis, donatoris*, and the attestation of each witness consists of the words *Signum manus* followed by his name in the genitive. All the attestations

---

[115] *M.G.H., Epistolae*, II, p. 438; Marini, *op. cit.*, p. 143, etc.

[116] Marini, *op. cit.*, no. 84.

[117] *Ch.L.A.*, no. 181.

[118] *Ibid.*

[119] *Codex Theodosianus*, VIII. 12. I (*Brev. Alar.*, VIII. 5. I).

[120] *M.G.H., Legum Sectio* I. i, p. 471.

[121] *Ibid.*, II (part I), p. 74; V (part I), p. 64; V (part 2), pp. 268–9.

[122] *Ibid.*, I, p. 96.

[123] *Ibid.*, II (part I), p. 113.

are written in the same hand, probably that of the scribe who wrote the rest of the document. In this respect the charter conforms to the practice normal in Italy and apparently everywhere in the sixth and seventh centuries: the *signum manus* was a non-autograph type of attestation which was written by the scribe of the charter and reserved for illiterate signatories. If, however, the charter had been written in Italy, the crosses which accompany the attestations would have been autograph. In fact Hlothhere's cross is in the same stylized form as the cross which is prefixed to the verbal invocation, and the crosses attached to the attestations of the witnesses, although less carefully drawn, are all undoubtedly in one hand and cannot therefore be autograph. As the king is made to state in the corroboration clause that he has drawn the sign of the cross with his own hand, it is clear that in England, as early as 679, the words *propria manu* had already lost their literal meaning: one might suggest that perhaps the king touched the charter with his hand to show his approval, a practice which became current in later times on the Continent;[124] each of the witnesses may have done the same. By the eighth century it was not unusual for Frankish charters to be wholly written in one hand, including the attestations and crosses; it was certainly the case at St Gallen, but there it was customary for the scribe of the charter to subscribe it and state that he was the writer. By contrast Hlothhere's charter–like all but a few Anglo-Saxon diplomas–does not even name its scribe.

Perhaps the latinity and diplomatic of the charter should have been examined and discussed in greater detail than has been done here, but I doubt whether this line of enquiry, however thoroughly it was pursued, would ever do more than strengthen our conviction that there is nothing in the document which can be regarded as inconsistent with its date, A.D. 679. If a proof that the charter is an original is to be found, it must be sought in its physical appearance and particularly in the appearance of its uncial script. Reservations have already been made on the value of palaeographical methods for determining the originality or otherwise of a document. In so far as Hlothhere's charter is concerned, we are even in a less favourable position than usual, because the charter, if it really is an original, is the earliest piece of English writing to have survived. The only comparative material of English origin available for the late-seventh and early-eighth centuries consists of a few books or fragments of books, the most famous of which is the Codex Amiatinus.[125] These are fine books, one of them a presentation copy, all written in Northumbria, miles away from Kent. How can we be sure that a Kentish scribe writing a charter, however important, would show the same loving care and the same degree of skill as a scribe of the Wearmouth-Jarrow school writing a gospel-book intended for presentation to the pope?

Here again the only safe statement that can be made about the script of the charter is that there is nothing in it which can be proved to be inconsistent with the year 679. There is one palaeographical feature of the charter, however, which in my view proves that the document cannot be anything but an original: it concerns the different appearance of the script in the attestations and in the text of the charter. From the beginning of the verbal invocation to the end of the Sturry postscript, the right-hand vertical stroke of the letter *N* has a triangular, 'wedge-shaped', finial; the same wedge-shaped finials also occur in the letters *C, E, G, L, S, T*; the letter *D* ends with a backward hook. On the other hand, there does not appear to be one single wedge-shaped finial in any of the attestations; instead, the letter *N*, for example, is topped by two horizontal serifs; the horizontal stroke of *E* consists of a short line of constant width; the letter *D* is not hooked at the end; in addition, the word *manus* in the third attestation has a *us* ligature, a feature which does not appear

---

[124] A. de Boüard, *Manuel de diplomatique française et pontificale*, II (Paris, 1948), p. 91. See *B.C.S.*, no. 293 (*O.S.F.* III. 7): et inspicis nomina principum qui hoc consensientes signum manus imposuerunt; *M.G.H., Legum Sectio* I. V (part 2), pp. 268–9: hoc per epistolam confirmet propria manu sua ipse et testes adhibeat vj vel amplius, si voluer it, inponant manus suas in epistula et nomina eorum notent ibi, quem ipse rogaverit.

[125] See E. A. Lowe, *English Uncial* (Oxford, 1960), Introduction.

in the text of the charter.[126] It may be argued that these palaeographical differences between the attestations and the text have no more meaning than those between the text-type of uncials and the capitular type, both found in the same books.[127] In the charter, however, the script differences are accompanied by other peculiarities which add to their significance: for example, the ink of the attestations is of a lighter colour than that used for the text of the charter; the lines of the text are roughly horizontal, whereas the lines of the attestations, although parallel to one another, slope slightly downwards from left to right. All these differences suggest that the attestations were written later than the text, although probably by the same scribe. In other words, the charter seems to have been written in two stages: the text of the grant, including the Sturry postscript, was prepared in advance, to be presented to the king for confirmation at a convenient time; the attestations were added when the king actually confirmed the grant, presumably at a solemn ceremony attended by witnesses. If this interpretation is correct, the conclusion that the charter is an original cannot be avoided.

The second single-sheet diploma to be considered is the charter of Œthelræd for the abbey of Barking in Essex (March 687?). Its Latin is closer to classical standards than the Latin of Hlothhere's charter, but it is not without examples of misuse of case, gender and number (e.g. *prouincia* perhaps for *prouinciae*;[128] *monasterii tui quae*;[129] *possideatis et quaecumque uolueris . . . habeatis*[130]). In so far as its formulae are concerned, the charter is also of undoubted Italian parentage. Unlike Hlothhere's charter it has no pictorial invocation, but the verbal invocation is the same in both except that the word *saluatoris* follows the words *Iesu Cristi* in Œthelræd's charter instead of preceding them as in the charter of Hlothhere.

A more important difference between the two documents is the presence of a proem in the charter of Œthelræd:

Quotiens s(an)c(t)is ac uenerabilib(us) locis uestris aliquid [o]fferre uidemur, uestra uobis reddimus, non nostra largi[mu]r.

This proem bears a striking resemblance to the preamble used by Gregory the Deacon in his charter of 587 to his Roman monastery:

Quotiens laudis vestrae usibus licet parva quaedam conferimus, vestra vobis reddimus, non nostra largimur, ut haec agentes non simus elati de munere, sed de solutione securi.[131]

Perhaps we should not attach too much importance to the resemblance, but it is worth noting that the proem is an uncommon one: the version found in the charter of Gregory the Deacon has been noticed in only one other Italian document, a decree of Pope Gregory II;[132] the version in Œthelræd's charter is apparently unique, but a third variant occurs in two Surrey charters, one of which records a grant of Frithuwold, sub-king of Surrey, to the abbey of Chertsey (A.D. 672–4) and the other a grant of King Ceadwalla of Wessex for the foundation of a monastery at Farnham (A.D. 688 possibly for 687):

Quotienscumque aliqua [*or* aliquid] pro opere pietatis membris Christi [*or* Christi membris] impendimus nostræ animæ prodesse [*or* fore prodesse] credimus, quia sua illi reddimus et nostra non [*or* reddimus, non nostra] largimur.[133]

---

[126] See Plate III (*top*).
[127] Lowe, *op. cit.*, Introduction.
[128] *B.M.F.* I. 2 (*Ch.L.A.*, no. 187), line 3.
[129] *Ibid.*, line 5.
[130] *Ibid.*, lines 10–11.
[131] *M.G.H., Epistolae*, II, p. 437; Levison, *op. cit.*, p. 230; W. H. Stevenson, 'Trinoda necessitas', *E.H.R.*, XXIX (1914), p. 702.
[132] *M.G.H., Epistolae*, II, p. 437, note 4.
[133] *B.C.S.*, nos. 34, 72.

It has been suggested, very plausibly in my view, that a common scriptorium would have accounted for the similarities between the three English charters. Eorcenwold, founder of the abbeys of Barking and Chertsey, became the first abbot of Chertsey and his sister Æthelburh the first abbess of Barking; when later he was appointed bishop of London, his authority as diocesan extended over Barking, Chertsey and Farnham. In one capacity or another he could therefore have had a hand in the drafting of the three charters.[134] The model available to him was probably Italian, although not necessarily the charter of Gregory the Deacon.

The study of the origin, adaptation and wanderings of proems from one country to another is one of the most fascinating aspects of international diplomatic. Far from being content always to resort to such common themes as *Nihil intulimus*[135] or *Omnia que videntur*,[136] possibly borrowed from formularies and based on quotations from the Pauline epistles, the draftsmen of early English charters occasionally drew on lesser-known sources: in a Worcester charter of the early eighth century the proem, *Tempora temporibus subeunt, abiit et venit ætas, sola sanctorum gloria durat in Christo*,[137] seems to be an adaptation in prose of the first four verses of *Carmen* XVI of St Paulinus of Nola:

> Tempora temporibus subeunt, abit et uenit aetas;
> cuncta dies trudendo diem fugit, et rotat orbem;
> omnia praetereunt, sanctorum gloria durat
> in Christo, qui cuncta nouat, dum permanet ipse.[138]

Two and a half centuries later, the draftsman of an Abingdon charter of 956 took his proem directly or indirectly from one of Marculf's formulae (II. 3) and interpolated in it another passage from an unidentified source. The passage borrowed from Marculf reads as follows:

Mundi terminum ruinis crebrescentibus adpropinquantibus etiam indicia manifesta et experimenta liquida declarant et ad discutiendum torpentes infidelium mentes illa dudum dicta oracula incumbere noscuntur ... opere precium reor futurorum temporum vicissitudinem preoccupans anticipari et incertum humane condicionis statum sagaci mentis intuitu providere quatinus ex his inflictis facinorum vulneribus indulta superne pietatis remedia merear adipisci.[139]

As Æthelwold, then abbot of Abingdon, is known to have had close connexions with the abbey of Saint Benoît-sur-Loire (Fleury),[140] a continental formula in a charter granted to his abbey would not be hard to explain. Unfortunately, the document belongs to a group of four, all concerned with Tadmarton in Oxfordshire, the authenticity of which has yet to be ascertained.

More interesting still is the proem found in two Kentish charters of the third quarter of the eighth century, one for the abbey of St Peter's (later St Augustine's), Canterbury (A.D. 761) and the other for Bishop Eardwulf of Rochester (A.D. 759-65):

Quamvis parva et exigua sint [*or* sunt] quæ pro admissis [*or* ammissis] peccatis offerimus, tamen pius dominus et redemptor noster [*or* pius omnipotens deus] non quantitatem muneris sed devotionem offerentium semper inspicit [*or* inquirit].[141]

Is it pure coincidence that during the same period, from 754 to 775, this should be the proem most commonly used in charters granted to the monastery of Fulda, a monastery founded in 744 by the

---

[134] Hart, *Early Charters of Eastern England*, p. 133 and references.

[135] *B.C.S.*, nos. 47, 59, 64, 114, 182, 206, 218, etc. (not all genuine).

[136] *B.C.S.*, nos. 62, 63, 70, 85, 1331, etc.

[137] *B.C.S.*, no. 122.

[138] *Corpus scriptorum ecclesiasticorum latinorum*, xxx (*Sancti Pontii Meropii Paulini Nolani Carmina*), ed. G. de Hartel (1894), p. 67.

[139] *B.C.S.*, no. 964. Compare *M.G.H.*, *Formulae*, ed. Zeumer, pp. 74-5.

[140] F. M. Stenton, *Anglo-Saxon England* (Oxford, 2nd ed., 1947), p. 442.

[141] *B.C.S.*, nos. 190, 194.

Anglo-Saxon Wynfrith (Boniface)? The proem of one of those charters (15 June 754) reads as follows:

Licet parva et exigua sunt, que pro immensis peccatis et debitis offero, tamen pius dominus noster Iesus Christus non quantitatem muneris perspicit sed devotionem offerentis.[142]

Is it also by accident that the proem reappears in the ninth century in charters for other continental monasteries also with close English connexions, for instance Echternach, founded by Willibrord, Hersfeld, founded by Lull, and Lorsch?[143]

The dispositive clause of Œthelræd's charter is, like its proem, derived from well-established Italian formulae:

Quapropter ego Ho[d]ilredus parens Sebbi prouin[c]ia East Sexanorum, cum ips[i]us consensu, propria u[o]luntate, sana mente int[e]groq(ue) consilio, tibi Hedilburge abbatissae ad augmentum monasterii tui quae dicitur Beddanhaam perp[e]tualiter trado et de meo [i]ure in tuo transscribo terram quae appellatur Ri[c]ingahaam Budinhaam Deccanhaam Angenlabeshaam et campo in silua quae dicitur Uuidmundesfelt, quae simul sunt coniuncta XL [*written over an erasure, probably of* LXXU] manen[ti]um usq(ue) ad terminos quae [ad] eum pertinent, cum omnib(us) ad se pertinentib(us), cum campis siluis pratis et marisco, ut tam tu quam posteri tui teneatis possideatis et quaecumq(ue) uolueris de eadem facere terra liberam habeatis potestatem.

The donor explains that he is making his gift of his own free will (*propria uoluntate*), that is to say without pressure of any kind from anyone; similar expressions are, as we have seen in connexion with the dispositive clause of Hlothhere's charter, usual in early Italian charters (e.g. *sine vi, metu . . . et circumventionis studio, sed deliberatione propria et voluntate prona*).[144] He is in full possession of all his faculties, *sana mente integroque consilio*: these words were at first used exclusively by testators, and they occur regularly in Italian wills of the fourth and fifth centuries,[145] but by the seventh century they had spread to the dispositive clause of ordinary grants *a praesenti*.[146] The dispositive words, *perpetualiter trado et de meo iure in tuo transscribo*, are very close to those used in Gregory the Deacon's charter of 587 (*dono cedo trado ac mancipo et ex meo iure in vestro iure dominioque transcribo*),[147] and in a Ravenna charter of the sixth century (*in potestatem perpetem transcribo cedo trado et mancipo*).[148]

The number of hides (*manentium*) granted to Abbess Æthelburh now appears as *XL*, but these numerals are clearly written by a different hand and over an erasure: the erased numerals seem to have been *LXXU*, but only the letters *L* and *U* are still visible.[149] In fact a charter of Bishop Eorcenwold claims that Œthelræd's grant to the abbey of Barking amounted to 75 hides:

Secunda quae ab Oedilredo tradita fuerat 75 manentium et appellatur Ricingahaam, Bydinhaam, Dæccanhaam, Angenlabeshaam cum campo qui dicitur Uuidmundes felth.[150]

Bishop Eorcenwold's charter may not be authentic in its entirety, but its diplomatic is unobjectionable. The title *seruorum dei seruus* used by the bishop was commonly adopted by bishops and archbishops in the seventh century, for example by Desiderius, bishop of Cahors, Eligius, bishop

---

[142] *Urkundenbuch des Klosters Fulda*, ed. E. E. Stengel, I (Marburg, 1913), no. 22. See also *ibid.*, nos. 23–33, etc.; *Archiv für Urkundenforschung*, XIV (1935–36), p. 51.

[143] *Archiv für Urkundenforschung, loc. cit.*; *Codex principis olim Laureshamensis abbatiae diplomaticus*, I (Mannheim, 1768), no. 265; II, no. 858.

[144] Marini, *op. cit.*, no. 85.

[145] *Raccolta di documenti latini*, ed. Schiaparelli, nos. 49, 65 (p. 116); Marini, *op. cit.*, no. 74; Levison, *op. cit.*, p. 186, note 3; *Archiv für Urkundenforschung*, XIV (1935–36), pp. 17–18.

[146] Levison, *op. cit.*, p. 186, note 3.

[147] *M.G.H., Epistolae*, II, p. 437.

[148] Marini, *op. cit.*, no. 93.

[149] See Plate IV (*top*).

[150] Hart, *Early Charters of Eastern England*, pp. 122–3.

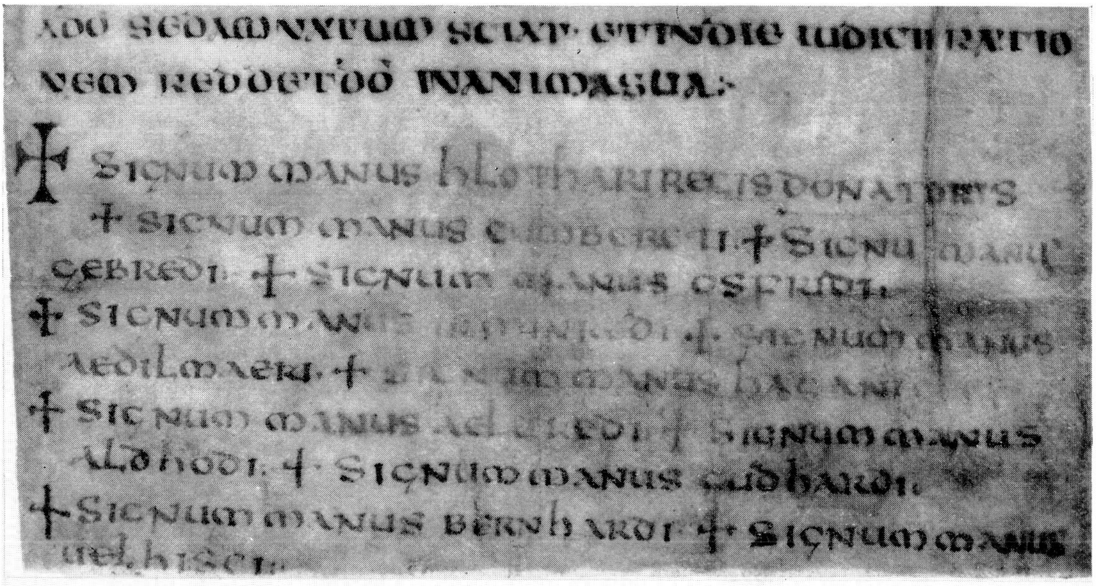

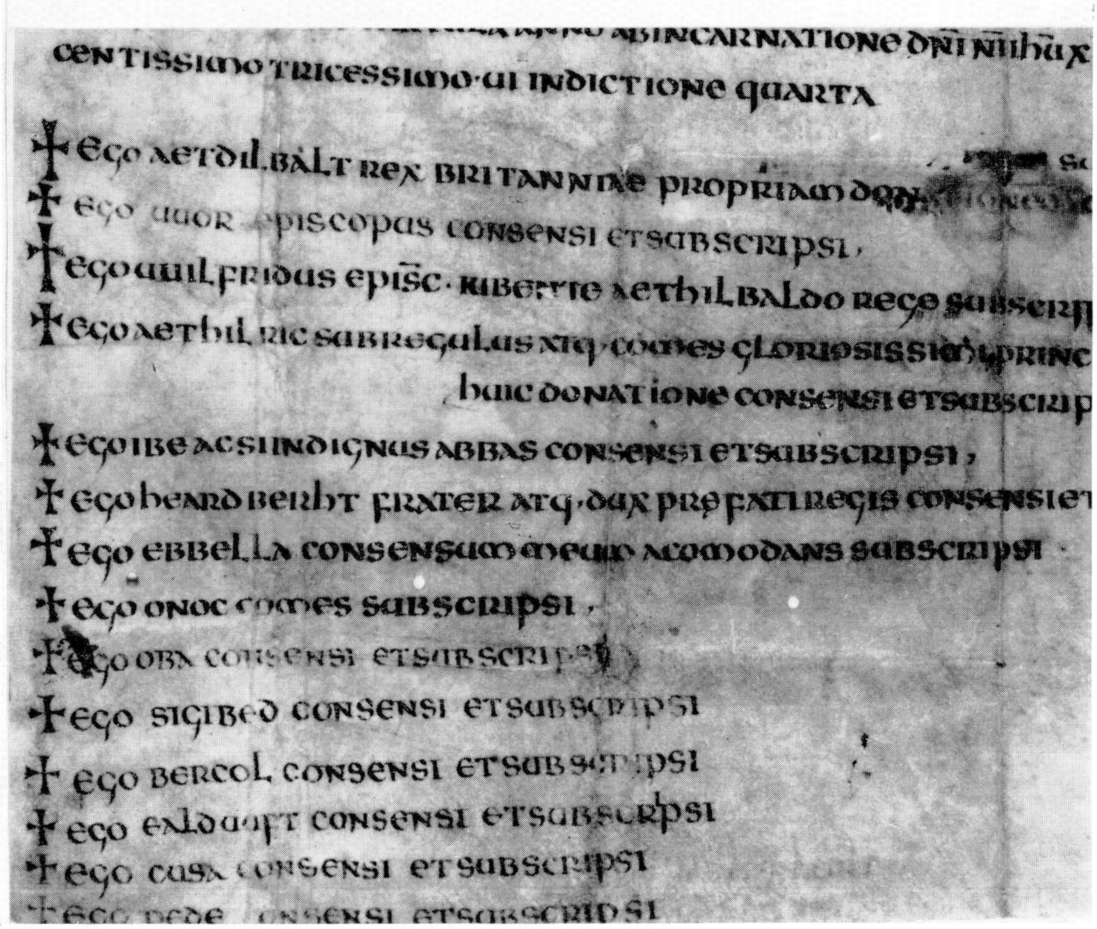

...oo seohm nxtuao scixt· ettnioie iuoicii ratio
veao reooetoo inanimasua:~

✠ signum manus hlothari regis donatorus
✠ signum manus gebred ii ✠ signu manus
gebredi ✠ signum manus osfriht·
✠ signum manus ...nabodi ✠ signum manus
aedilmaeri· ✠ ... manus bagani
✠ signum manus aelfredi ✠ signum manus
aldhodi· ✠ signum manus cudhardi·
✠ signum manus bernhardi ✠ signum manus
uel hisen...

...abincarnatione dni nihax
centissimo tricessimo· ui indictione quarta

✠ ego aetdilbalt rex britanniae propriam don...
✠ ego uuor episcopus consensi et subscripsi·
✠ ego uuilfridus episc· uberte aethilbaldo rege subscrip
✠ ego aethilric subregulus atq· comes gloriosissimi princ
huic donatione consensi et subscrip
✠ ego ibeacsiindignus abbas consensi et subscripsi·
✠ ego beardberht frater atq· dux prae fati regis consensi et
✠ ego ebbella consensum meum acomodans subscripsi·
✠ ego onoc comes subscripsi·
✠ ego oba consensi et subscripsi·
✠ ego sigibed consensi et subscripsi
✠ ego bercol consensi et subscripsi
✠ ego exldouft consensi et subscripsi
✠ ego cusa consensi et subscripsi
✠ ego bede consensi et subscripsi

PLATE III
top **Charter of King Hlothhere of Kent** (extract): May 679
bottom **Charter of King Æthelbald of Mercia** (extract): A.D. 736

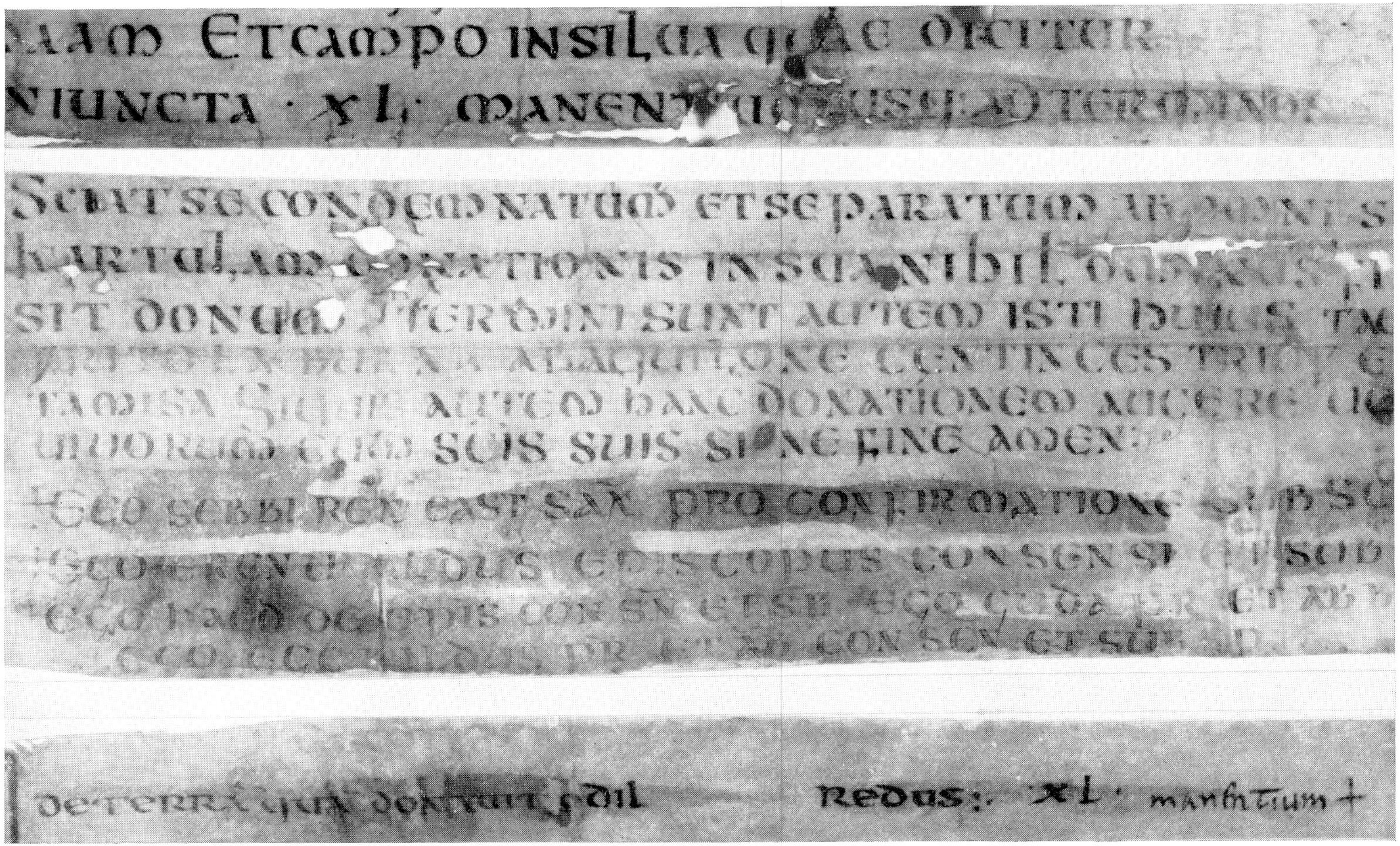

PLATE IV

Charter of Æthelræd for Barking Abbey: March 687?

top and middle Extracts from the face, *bottom* Extract from the dorse

of Noyon, by archbishops of Canterbury and York, and by St Boniface.[151] Gregory the Deacon also uses it in his charter of 587.[152] Nor is the clause concerning the monastery's freedom from episcopal interference, and guaranteeing a free election for its abbess, unusual in the latter part of the seventh century.[153] The dating clause is clumsily drafted and may have been interpolated in part. Its general meaning seems to be that, when Eorcenwold was in Rome ten years earlier, he was authorized by Pope Agatho to grant the charter. This alleged visit cannot have taken place before the summer of 678, since Agatho was consecrated in June 678; yet the charter gives the year of the incarnation as 677, in the first indiction. The mention of the year of the incarnation is probably a later interpolation. The first indiction, which ran from 1 September 687 to 31 August 688, probably refers, not to Eorcenwold's visit to Rome, but to the actual year in which the charter was issued. The date of the charter therefore appears to be June–August 688, but by that time Bishop Wilfrid, one of the subscribers, had already left for the North. In defence of the dating clause of the charter, it should be added that mistakes in the calculation of the indiction are not uncommon.

It is only too obvious that no forger would have changed the number of hides from a higher figure (75) to a lower one (40). One can only guess that, some time after Œthelræd's grant, the abbey of Barking lost some of its lands by exchange or gift and was required to alter the figure in the original charter. A similar procedure was used in 825 when the archbishop of Canterbury stipulated that the abbess of Minster should erase from her 'ancient privileges' the names of various lands which she had agreed to surrender to him.[154]

The description of the lands granted as *quae simul sunt coniuncta* recalls the formula which introduces the boundaries in Vandal deeds of the late-fifth century, e.g. *inter adfines eiusdem loci qui iungitur a meridie . . .*, etc.;[155] similar expressions occur in two Kentish charters of the seventh century.[156] The abbess and her successors (*posteri tui*, in the masculine) are given freedom to dispose of the land as they wish. This may have meant the power to give, exchange and sell the land, as other early Anglo-Saxon charters explicitly state (*a me habeatis licentiam donandi, commutandi, et in arbitrio vestro sit posita ;*[157] *possideas, dones, commutes, venundes vel quicquid exinde facere volueris liberam habeas potestatem*[158]). I doubt, however, whether this formula was meant to be taken literally; royal permission at least is likely to have been required before the land could be alienated. The formula was certainly not usual in grants of land such as those which were made to the church of Ravenna before the seventh century. It occurs, however, in a gift of a servant by Gregory I to the bishop of Porto (*et quicquid de eo facere volueris, quippe ut dominus, ex hac donatione iure perfecta libero potiaris arbitrio*).[159] On the other hand, in a charter to his monastery of Sant' Andrea al Clivo di Scauro, Gregory explicitly forbids the abbot and his successors to alienate any of the lands which he has given to the monastery.[160]

The dating clause of Œthelræd's charter (*Actum mense martio*) mentions neither the place of issue nor the indictional year. A *corroboratio* clause follows, announcing that the grantor has asked an adequate number of witnesses to subscribe (*et testes conpetenti numero ut subscriberent rogaui*). The phrase *conpetenti numero* also occurs in two Italian documents of the fifth and sixth centuries.[161]

The *sanctio* consists of a penalty clause of the religious type and it ends with the normal clause stating that infringements will not impair the validity of the charter (*m[anentem] hanc kartulam donationis in sua nihilominus firmitate*).

---

[151] *M.G.H., Epistolae*, III, pp. 195, 199, 200, 206, 282–3, 285–6, 398, 412, etc.   [152] *Ibid.*, II, p. 437.

[153] See *Codice diplomatico longobardo*, ed. Schiaparelli, I, no. 7.   [154] *B.C.S.*, no. 384; Levison, *op. cit.*, p. 252.

[155] *Tablettes Albertini*, no. 16; see also *ibid.*, no. 19.   [156] *B.C.S.*, nos. 67, 73.

[157] *B.C.S.*, no. 72.   [158] *B.C.S.*, no. 86 (doubtful).

[159] *Urkunden und Akten*, ed. Brandi, no. 12. See also *Marini, op. cit.*, no. 93: . . . quidquid ex eadem portionem iuris mei facere maluerint per quolibet contractu liberam et perpetem in omnibus habeant potestatem.

[160] *M.G.H., Epistolae*, I, p. 15.

[161] *Urkunden und Akten*, ed. Brandi, no. 11; *Raccolta di documenti latini*, ed. Schiaparelli, no. 65 (p. 116).

Then comes the phrase *Et ut firma et inconcussum sit donum*, which could be expected to introduce a clause such as *ego . . . pro confirmatione subscripsi*, but instead it introduces a boundary clause, which in turn is followed by a blessing of a religious kind promising divine rewards to those who would increase the donor's grant. The text of the charter ends with an appreciatio (*Amen*), and its validation signs consist of twelve subscriptions, nine of which are in the form *Ego . . . subscripsi* (some without a cross) and three in the form *Signum manus*; seven of them are on the face of the charter and five on the dorse. Neither the subscriptions nor the crosses are autograph.

Considerable doubts have been expressed on the originality of the charter. It has been said, for example, that the uncial script is 'somewhat artificial' and that 'the wide separation of words favours a date in the eighth century'.[162] It has also been argued that the use of *e* for unaccented Old-English *i* in the two names *Oedelraedus* and *Haedde* is a feature of the late-eighth century rather than of the late-seventh.[163] What needs emphasizing as well is that the script of the charter changes abruptly after the second word of the seventeenth line.[164] From the beginning of the verbal invocation to the end of the clause *Et ut firma et inconcussum sit donum* the charter (apart from the numerals *XL* in line 8) is in one single hand which I shall call Hand A. Then Hand B takes over, starting with the boundary clause (*Termini sunt autem . . .*), and is responsible for the rest of the document, including all the subscriptions on the dorse as well as on the face of the charter.

It is difficult to regard Hand A as inconsistent with the date of the charter (March 687?). The separation of words is not wider than–say–in the Stonyhurst Gospel, except in line 9, but there the gap seems to be due to an erasure for which the scribe of that part of the charter was responsible. Much of the apparent artificiality of the script is the result of partial retracing of some of the letters, particularly in lines 7–9. Hand A retains the unaccented *i* in *Hodilredus* and *Hedilburge*. The first part of the charter, written by Hand A, seems to be unobjectionable in every respect, and I am confident that this part, but this part only, should be regarded as an original.

The second part, written by Hand B, raises many difficult problems. Hand B, an ugly and unskilled hand, is undoubtedly imitative; it differs from Hand A in the shape of most letters and especially *A*, *C*, *D*, *M* and *U*. The part written by Hand B has a wider left-hand margin. It is only in that part that we find the later spellings *Oedelraedus* and *Haedde*, the runic wen instead of *uu* (twice in line 18) and the abbreviated form *accingit'* for *accingitur*. Hand B may belong to the second half of the eighth century.

It seems therefore that the original charter ended with the unfinished clause *Et ut firma et inconcussum sit donum*. As already stated, the clause should perhaps have continued *ego . . . pro confirmatione subscripsi*. It is possible that these last words were in fact written on a separate piece of vellum, on which all the subscriptions may also have been written, and that this piece of vellum, now missing, was once stitched as a schedule to the main charter. Although the charter was trimmed, presumably in Cotton's time, stitching holes are still visible along the lower edge. Perhaps what was written on the schedule was meant to be immediately copied on the main piece of vellum, as in Hlothhere's charter, but this was not done until the next century. As a result, we do not know how far the part written in Hand B can be trusted. Were the original spellings modernized to such forms as *Oedelraedus* and *Haedde*? Was the boundary clause, so incongruously introduced by a corroboration formula, already in the schedule, or was it added in the eighth century? Were all the subscriptions written in one hand and at the same time? None of these questions can be answered with any confidence. It is very puzzling to find King Sebbi subscribing twice, in one place in the form *Ego . . . subscripsi* and in the other in the form *Signum manus . . .*: it may be suggested

162 Lowe, *English Uncial*, p. 21, no. XXII.
163 W. H. Stevenson, 'Trinoda necessitas', *E.H.R.*, XXIX (1914), p. 702, note 66; K. Sisam, 'Cynewulf and his Poetry', *Proceedings of the British Academy*, XVIII, p. 325, note 5.
164 See Plate IV (*middle*).

that in the schedule Sebbi's alleged first subscription was not a subscription at all, but the continuation of the corroboration clause *Et ut firma et inconcussum sit donum*, and that his real subscription was the second one (*Signum manus Sebbi regis*). It is likely also that the last two subscriptions, those of Kings Sigeheard and Swæfred, were written in a different hand from the rest on the schedule, since they probably represent a later confirmation made by them as joint kings after the abdication or death of their father Sebbi.

An early endorsement, which may be contemporary, reads: *De terram quam donauit Odil–*[gap of almost one inch]–*redus*.[165] The early spelling *Odilredus* should be noted as well as the gap in the middle of the name; a similar gap is found on the dorse of two Carolingian 'letters close', in the middle of the address.[166] It seems that, in order to keep the charter folded for easy transport and storage, a loose thong was wrapped around it like a modern rubber-band, and the endorsement was written on either side of the thong. Gaps of the same kind occur in the endorsements of other Anglo-Saxon charters and of many St Gallen charters.[167] In England, at least from the latter part of the ninth century, a tongue partially cut from the lower edge of the charter in the same fashion as the wrapping-tie of the later writ, was occasionally used as an alternative to the loose thong. Such a tongue is still attached to a Canterbury private charter of the second half of the ninth century,[168] but this is an exceptional survival; normally the tongue has been torn off and a step in the bottom left-hand corner of the document is the only evidence we have of the former existence of the tongue.[169] Reginald Lane Poole drew attention to the surviving tongue and steps, but he wrongly interpreted them as evidence that some Anglo-Saxon diplomas were sealed.[170]

To the contemporary endorsement on Œthelræd's charter were later added the words *XL manentium*, in a cursive hand perhaps of the late-eighth century; the numerals *XL* appear to have been written over an erasure, but it is impossible to say whether the erased numerals were *LXXU* as on the face of the charter.

According to a late-medieval endorsement, the charter of Œthelræd was at one time regarded as the foundation charter of Barking Abbey: *Fundacio mon[asterii] de Bark[in]ge* (not *Karta de Con* . . . as usually printed).

Of all the arguments put forward in support of the view that the charters of Hlothhere and Œthelræd are both original, one *in toto* and the other in part only, those based on the script and physical appearance of the vellum are the most decisive. In both cases, it seems that the charter was drawn up in two successive stages, the second one being the addition of the signs of validation, that is to say the subscriptions. We have seen that some time elapsed between the writing of the text of Hlothhere's charter and the addition of the subscriptions, and that probably one single scribe was responsible for both stages of the operation. Over one hundred years later, a similar procedure was used for an important grant of King Cenwulf of Mercia to Christ Church, Canterbury.[171] The grant is said to have been made at Tamworth in Staffordshire in 799. Here again the charter is made up of two parts which differ from one another in the appearance of their script: the first part consists of the text of the grant, and the second begins with the dating clause, followed by the subscriptions. The same scribe wrote the text, date and subscriptions, but the script is smaller in the second part

---

[165] See Plate IV (*bottom*).

[166] *Journal of the Society of Archivists*, III, 4 (Oct. 1966), p. 169. See above, p. 53.

[167] *B.M.F.* I. 14, II. 33; *O.S.F.* II. Exeter 15; *Ch.L.A.*, nos. 109, 113, 116, etc.

[168] *O.S.F.* I. 9.

[169] *O.S.F.* I. 16 and 18; *O.S.F.* II. Exeter 15, Winchester Cath. 2, Earl of Ilchester 2; *O.S.F.* III. 42; British Museum, Add. MS. 7138. The following charters also have steps, but they are not original documents, and some of them are forgeries: *B.M.F.* III. 4; *ibid.*, IV. 9; *O.S.F.* II. Westminster 1 and 4, Earl of Ilchester 1.

[170] Poole, *Studies in Chronology and History*, p. 107, note 1 and plate.

[171] *O.S.F.* III. 7 (*Ch.L.A.*, no. 223; *B.C.S.*, no. 293; *E.H.D.*, I, pp. 470–1).

and the ink is of a different colour. There is no doubt that the charter is an original, and we may trust its contents without hesitation. The charter tells the story of the land which Cenwulf is restoring to Christ Church. It had first been given by King Egbert of Kent to his thegn Ealdhun, but the latter, before going overseas, had re-granted the estate to Christ Church. Then Offa seized it on the ground that it was wrong that a thegn should have presumed to transfer to someone else, without his lord's consent (*absque eius testimonio*, i.e. without his subscription), a land which his lord had given him. Does this mean that Christ Church had been unable to produce before Offa evidence that Ealdhun had obtained Egbert's consent before giving his estate away to their community? Another Canterbury charter, dated A.D. 811, claims that Offa had acted as if Egbert was not entitled to book land in hereditary right (*quasi non liceret Ecgberhto agros hereditario iure scribere*); in other words, Christ Church thought that in Offa's eyes it was not so much Ealdhun's re-grant which lacked validity as Egbert's original grant.[172] Whichever version is the correct one, the charter of 799 makes it clear that from at least Offa's reign a layman could not alienate his book-land without the king's permission.

The originality of two other Canterbury charters, both of the ninth century, is also beyond question (*B.M.F.* II. 9: *B.C.S.*, no. 326: A.D. 808; *O.S.F.* III. 17: *B.C.S.*, no. 442: A.D. 843). A schedule containing the list of subscribers is attached to each of them, and in both cases the schedule was used as a draft from which the subscriptions on the main parchment were compiled. In one of the two charters, the subscriptions were certainly written later than the text and by the same scribe;[173] in the other, the same procedure may have been adopted, but there is no obvious change, in the appearance of the script, from the text to the subscriptions.[174] If the views which I have expressed on the charter of Œthelræd for Barking Abbey are correct, the custom of attaching to the main charter a schedule containing the list of witnesses would go back to the latter part of the seventh century.

In another famous charter, which records the grant of some land at Stour in Ismere by King Æthelbald of Mercia for the foundation of a monastery, seven subscriptions were written at the same time as the text (nos. 1, 3–8), and seven were added later with a thinner pen (nos. 2, 9–14). As one of the added subscriptions was that of Bishop Wor of Lichfield, it could not be placed below that of a layman (no. 8), and for that reason, it was inserted between the subscriptions of the king and of Bishop Wilfrid of Worcester.[175] Since most of the witnesses have not been identified, it is impossible to say whether the division into two groups had a territorial basis or was purely accidental.

The charter owes its fame not only to the fact that it is written in uncials and on vellum like the charters of Hlothhere and Œthelræd, but also to the titles which it gives to King Æthelbald of Mercia: in the *dispositio* the king is described as *AEthilbalt d[omi]no donante rex non solum Marcersium sed et omnium prouinciarum quae generale nomine Sut Angli dicuntur*, and in the royal subscription as *AEtdilbalt rex Britanniae*. For this reason it was rightly given a prominent place in Sir Frank Stenton's discussion of the supremacy of the Mercian kings.[176] No doubt the titles given to the king in the charter reflect accurately Æthelbald's own claims to the supremacy over all the English pro-

---

[172] *B.M.F.* II. 11; *B.C.S.*, no. 332. See *E.H.D.*, I, note on no. 80.

[173] Mary Prescott Parsons, 'Some Scribal Memoranda for Anglo-Saxon Charters of the Eighth and Ninth Centuries', *Mitteilungen des Österreichischen Instituts für Geschichtsforschung*, XIV Erg.-Band (1939), pp. 15–19.

[174] *Ibid.*, pp. 21–2. I am not so sure as Miss Parsons, however, that the whole charter was written without a break.

[175] *B.M.F.* I. 7 (Lowe, *English Uncial*, plate XXIII; *Ch.L.A.*, no. 183; *B.C.S.*, no. 154; *E.H. D.*, I, pp. 453–4). The subscriptions are reproduced on Plate II (*bottom*). Note that each of the first eight subscriptions is followed by a punctuation mark; this is not so for the last six.

[176] F. M. Stenton, 'The Supremacy of the Mercian Kings', *E.H.R.*, XXXIII (1918), pp. 433–52, especially 438–9.

vinces south of the Humber, but it should be remembered that the charter, like all the other Anglo-Saxon diplomas, was drafted and written in an ecclesiastical scriptorium, possibly at Worcester, and not in a royal secretariat: its script resembles that of the famous Vespasian Psalter,[177] and the document probably comes from the archives of Worcester Cathedral, like another charter in which the king is called *Æthilbalth non solum Mercensium sed et universarum provinciarum quæ communi vocabulo dicuntur Suthengli divina largiente gratia rex.*[178] Like Hlothhere's charter of 679, the Stour charter of Æthelbald has a postscript explaining that the king made an additional grant to the beneficiary, but here the postscript is written on the dorse and in a different hand from the face of the document.[179]

Among the documents which can safely be regarded as originals, a well-known Sussex charter also deserves a place of honour: it is the charter by which Oslac, ealdorman of the South Saxons, granted to the church of St Paul a piece of land at Earnley in Sussex.[180] The grant is said to have been made at Selsey in 780 (*Factum est in loco que appellatur Siolesaei*), and the charter was probably written there. St Paul's church has so far defied identification, but perhaps it should be identified with the church of Selsey itself, although the dedication of the church of Selsey is thought to have always been to St Peter;[181] at any rate, the charter comes from the archives of Selsey. Oslac's grant is written on the face of the vellum, in an extraordinary type of script best described, in Sir Frank Stenton's words, as crude and unpractised.[182] Indeed, if it was not for its endorsements, the charter might well have been branded as suspect on account of its handwriting. Odd Latin forms include *concede* for *concedo* and the usual mistakes of case and gender. Probably written at Selsey, the charter was also presumably drafted there: its anathema is introduced by the curious phrase *Sic et regalis omnis dignitas dicit*; it seems that the phrase was also used in another Sussex charter of a slightly earlier date, but the original of this second charter has not survived and its transcriber probably copied the words inaccurately and incompletely (*Sic est regalis omnis dignitas*).[183]

Oslac's charter has several endorsements, the longest of which consists of a confirmation by King Offa of Mercia made in the next fifteen years.[184] This confirmation appears in the form of subscriptions, those of King Offa, Queen Cynethryth, his wife, King Egcfrith, their son (*Ego Egcfrið rex Merc' consensi et subscripsi*), Brorda, *prefectus*, and Bishop Unwona (of Leicester), followed by the statement that the ceremony took place at Irthlingborough in Northamptonshire. (*Hoc rite peractum in loco quæ nuncupatur Yrtlinga burg*). According to the words used by Offa in his subscription, it was at the request of Wihthun, bishop of the South Saxons, that the confirmation was made. The arrangement of the subscriptions shows that, when the document was presented to Offa, it had already been folded once vertically and once horizontally: the vertical fold forced the scribe to write the subscriptions in two columns on either side of the crease in the vellum, and the horizontal fold explains the abnormal gap between the subscriptions of Cynethryth and Egcfrith. When the confirmation was recorded, the charter already had one endorsement (*Earnaleah et Tielesora*), which prevented the scribe from writing Brorda's subscription opposite the king's subscription; he had to write it a little lower down.[185]

---

[177] *C.L.A.*, no. 193; Lowe, *English Uncial*, p. 21, no. XXVI and references.

[178] *B.C.S.*, no. 157.

[179] *Ch.L.A.*, no. 183.

[180] Chichester, Diocesan Record Office, Cap. I/17; *B.C.S.*, no. 1334; *E.H.D.*, I, pp. 464-5. Extracts are reproduced on Plate V.

[181] Levison, *op. cit.*, p. 261.

[182] Stenton, *Latin Charters*, p. 37. See Plate V (*inset*).

[183] *B.C.S.*, no. 145.

[184] Plate V.

[185] Stenton, *Latin Charters*, p. 37, and see Plate V.

Neither the subscriptions nor the crosses are autograph; they are in a single, good, contemporary hand, which contrasts sharply with the ugly script of Oslac's original grant. The writer of these subscriptions may have been a scribe attached to the service of Bishop Unwona of Leicester, one of the subscribers, or of the bishop of Worcester, who, however, does not subscribe. The formulae used suggest a Worcester draftsman: this applies for example to the words *deo donante rex*[186] and *peractum*,[187] and to the expression *conroborans subscribo*, which recalls such combinations as *concedens donabo*, *donans donabo* and *tradens donabo* so much in evidence in Worcester charters of the period.[188]

One interesting point which has so far passed unnoticed is that the half sheet of vellum from which the piece used for Oslac's charter was cut was originally meant for a psalter. If we place the charter face down and turn it upside down, the following words can be read just below the upper margin: *non amouit deprœcationem [meam] et misericordiam suam a me*, the last nine words of Psalm LXV; a little lower down, on the left: *Deus* (in an abbreviated form: a large uncial *D*; above it, an abbreviation mark; inside it, the letter *s*), the first word of Psalm LXVI. It seems that something went wrong with the writing of the leaf, and that it was discarded before completion of Psalm LXVI. Apart from the word *Deus*, the psalter fragment is written in an insular minuscule of the eighth century. If we were sure that the psalter was being written at the time of Oslac's grant, the fragment could be precisely dated 780. It is possible, however, that the psalter had been written some years before and the partially-blank leaf stored for some time before it was re-used. It seems reasonable to assume that it was written by a Selsey scribe; if so, he was certainly trained in a different scriptorium from that which produced the scribe of Oslac's charter.

The handful of charters which have been considered in this paper deserve to be regarded as originals. Their importance is therefore considerable, not only to the historian, but also to the diplomatist, who can use their formulae as a basis for the discussion of other charters whose text is known from cartulary copies only. The criticism of such copies, however, even with the help of originals, is always a hazardous venture. An alleged seventh-century charter copied in a cartulary may be spurious although all its formulae may appear to be as good as those of Hlothhere's diploma. What are we to think of *B.C.S.*, no. 86, a charter of King Wihtred of Kent for Abbess Æbba of Minster in Thanet, and of *B.C.S.*, no. 296, a charter of King Cenwulf of Mercia for Christ Church, Canterbury? Both charters share practically identical formulae, which can be traced back to reputable Italian precedents. It may be argued that by Cenwulf's time Anglo-Saxon diplomas no longer relied so heavily on Italian formulae and that Cenwulf's charter is spurious, the forger having used the charter of Wihtred, presumed genuine, as his model. There is no doubt that, in the form in which it has come down to us, Cenwulf's charter, a single-sheet document written perhaps in the eleventh century,[189] cannot possibly be regarded as genuine: the name of Cenwulf's wife is given as *Cenegitha*, a woman otherwise unknown; Archbishop Theodore of Canterbury (died 19 Sept. 690) and Abbot Adrian of SS. Peter and Paul, Canterbury (died *c.* 709), could not have witnessed a document together with Cenwulf (796–821) and his son Kenelm ('St Kenelm'). Cenwulf's charter is dated 16 kal. August [17 July], indiction 7, regnal year 3, all of which dating elements are remarkably consistent with one another, but we become suspicious when we realise that the feast of St Kenelm, one of the subscribers, was celebrated on 17 July.[190]

---

[186] *B.C.S.*, nos. 202–4, 240.
[187] *B.C.S.*, nos. 216, 356–7, and compare *ibid.*, nos. 187, 353.
[188] *B.C.S.*, nos. 137–8, 164, 201, 216, 230, 262, 267, 283, 304, etc.
[189] *B.M.F.* IV. 7.
[190] Levison, *op. cit.*, p. 249.

If we turn to Wihtred's charter, we find that there the king's wife is also called *Kinigitha*, although the name of Wihtred's wife seems to have been Æthelburh. Like the charter of Cenwulf, Wihtred's diploma is dated 16 kal. August, indiction 7, regnal year 3, and here again all the dating elements fit together in a remarkable fashion. But the date of 17 July is no less suspicious in this charter than in the other: the beneficiary of Wihtred's charter is Abbess Æbba of Minster in Thanet; in the first quarter of the ninth century, Cwenthryth, a woman of doubtful morals, was abbess of both Minster and Winchcombe, and it was at Winchcombe, during her rule, that St Kenelm was buried.[191] Was it also during her rule that Wihtred's charter was forged? The date of 17 July was certainly more likely to be remembered at Winchcombe than anywhere else.

If neither *B.C.S.*, no. 86, nor *B.C.S.*, no. 296 is genuine, what are we to think of the formula *cartulam scribendam dictavi*, an incomplete version of the Italian *rogatio* clause, found in both charters and in no other early Anglo-Saxon charter?[192] Was it in fact adopted from a formulary such as the *Liber Diurnus*? It seems possible that there was a copy of the *Liber Diurnus* at Winchcombe, and that it was from this book that two alleged papal privileges, whose authenticity was defended by Levison, were forged.[193] Levison argued that the privilege of Paschal I copied in the Winchcombe cartulary is genuine: the transcriber would have copied his text from the original papyrus, but this papyrus was then in a bad state of preservation; because the original was damaged, the copyist could not read the names of the lands and possessions confirmed by the pope; he also had difficulty in reading the script of the original and this led him to give a garbled version of the dating clause. By an extraordinary feat of editorial ingenuity, Levison reconstructed what he regarded as the likely dating clause of the original privilege. But Levison did not explain why it was only the dating clause which the transcriber could not read. He should have found the rest of the document just as difficult. Was it because the 'original' was damaged that the scribe had to leave out the names of the possessions granted by Paschal I, or was it simply because the *Liber Diurnus* model used by the forger (Codex Vat., no. 93.)[194] did not give names either? The text of the privilege of Paschal I ends with the words *sicuti inferius asscripta eadem loca atque agrorum prædia continere monstratur*; then comes the dating clause.[195] In the *Liber Diurnus*, the formula no. 93, which is for the most part reproduced in the privilege of Paschal I, also ends with the words: *sicuti inferius adscripta eadem loca atque agrorum predia continere monstratur scilicet*. I am convinced that the so-called privilege of Paschal I is a forgery: for the text the forger used the formula no. 93 of the *Liber Diurnus*, and for the date he used an original which he could not read. Since the formula of the *Liber Diurnus*, copied from a privilege of Pope Adrian I for King Offa of Mercia,[196] was the only one in the book which could be definitely connected with England, it was the obvious model for any forger to use.

PIERRE CHAPLAIS

---

[191] *Ibid.*, pp. 249–52, 257.

[192] *Journal of the Society of Archivists*, III, 2 (Oct. 1965), p. 50, see above, p. 30. The statement regarding the absence of the clause in papal documents requires further explanation: the clause is found in at least three documents of a special type issued by Gregory I; one of them is a manumission (*M.B.H.*, *Epistolae*, I, p. 391), and two are appointments of a *defensor ecclesiae* (*ibid.*, I, p. 307; II, p. 107).

[193] Levison, *op. cit.*, pp. 255–8.

[194] *Liber Diurnus Romanorum Pontificum*, ed. H. Foerster, pp. 172–3.

[195] See Levison, *op. cit.*, p. 256; *B.C.S.*, no. 363.

[196] Levison, *op. cit.*, p. 255. If *all* the Winchcombe charters perished in the fire of 1151 (*ibid.*, p. 253), the extant forgery is unlikely to have been made before the second half of the twelfth century. The majority of the charters mentioned in this paper are also discussed by Dr Albert Bruckner, 'Zur Diplomatik der älteren angelsächsischen Urkunde', *Archivalische Zeitschrift*, LXI (1965), pp. 11–45.

Who Introduced Charters
into England?
The Case For Augustine[1]

In an article first published in 1965 I suggested that a case could be made for crediting Augustine rather than Archbishop Theodore with the introduction of charters into England.[2] Some of the arguments put forward in support of this suggestion implied the tacit acceptance of the opinion shared by most Anglo-Saxon scholars from Bede to modern times that King Æthelberht I of Kent was converted to Christianity. Doubt has since been cast on the truth of that proposition,[3] thus – if well-founded – weakening our claim on Augustine's behalf. Since a pagan king was unlikely to make generous grants of land to the Christian Church, it is evident that, if we reject Bede's statement that Æthelberht became a Christian, we can hardly accept without hesitation his story of the king's benefactions to Augustine and his colleagues. To say that a charter presupposes a grant is to state the obvious.

That the birth and evolution of charters in Anglo-Saxon England was intimately bound up with the introduction and progress of literacy is another obvious point. Even if we succeed in proving that Æthelberht adopted the Christian faith, this will not entitle us to suppose that his grants of land to the Church were necessarily set down in writing; they could have been made by word of mouth only. It would therefore help Augustine's case if we could be reasonably certain that the king was interested in literacy, and that he understood and valued the advantages of the written word over oral declarations. It is true that Augustine might have kept a record of the king's grants as a matter of course, simply because in his Italian homeland grants of land were normally written down, but it cannot be denied that much of the incentive for doing so would have been lacking if he had known that the king had no use for writings. In the article already cited I suggested that Augustine, presumably at the king's bidding, might have been somehow connected with the writing and drafting of Æthelberht's legal code. This was at any rate how I interpreted the Code's first article, which gives a list of penalties for stealing the movable goods of ecclesiastics. The introduction of charters, which protected the landed property of the Church, was in my view a natural complement to the provisions of the Code's first article. Recently, however, it has been argued that the Code may have been written before Augustine's arrival and that its first article is an interpolation.[4]

---

[1] Professor T. J. Brown, Professor A. Campbell and Dr J. M. Wallace-Hadrill were kind enough to make valuable suggestions on some of the points discussed in this paper. I am deeply grateful to them, while not wishing to commit them to any of the views expressed here.

[2] *Journal of the Society of Archivists*, III, 2 (Oct. 1965), pp. 49–52, see above, pp. 29–33.

[3] H. G. Richardson and G. O. Sayles, *Law and Legislation from Æthelberht to Magna Carta* (Edinburgh Univ. Press, 1966), pp. 162–4. Doubts had already been expressed by Suso Brechter, *Die Quellen zur Angelsachsenmission Gregors des Grossen* (Münster in Westf., 1941), pp. 241 ff.

[4] Richardson and Sayles, *op. cit.*, pp. 7–12.

In view of these controversies it has seemed desirable to examine afresh and in more detail the question of the introduction of charters into England. In the following pages an attempt will be made to assess the results of Augustine's work in the fields of religion and literacy. Were those results conducive to the introduction of charters or at least compatible with it? If this question can be confidently answered in the affirmative, another point of decisive importance will still have to be resolved: does the form of the earliest Anglo-Saxon charters extant, those of the period immediately following Theodore's arrival in England, betray an early or a recent importation from Italy? If the pattern of these charters cannot be satisfactorily explained by reference to the conditions prevailing in Theodore's time, the case for Augustine will have been virtually won.

When Augustine and his companions left Rome for Britain in the late spring of 596, they probably knew very little about the people they were on their way to evangelize. That grave dangers might well lie ahead of them must have crossed their minds more than once as they advanced on their westward journey. When they reached south-eastern Gaul, they suddenly took fright—perhaps they had just heard some sinister tales about their intended flock—and they found themselves unable to proceed. 'Paralysed with fear' at the prospect of meeting a barbarous, cruel and heathen people 'whose language they did not even know', they all agreed that it would be safer to return home. Augustine retraced his steps to Rome to beg Pope Gregory I to release them from their hazardous mission. Gregory, although not unsympathetic, remained adamant: they were not to be deterred from their purpose by the hardships of the journey or by the wagging of evil tongues; the greater their toil, the richer would be their eternal rewards.[5] The pope acknowledged, rather belatedly, that language problems were bound to arise, and to allay Augustine's fears in this respect, he arranged for a group of Frankish priests to join the missionaries as interpreters.[6] Thus reassured, the party resumed its journey and eventually reached the island of Thanet in Kent early in 597.

Gregory and Augustine could have been misinformed about the state of learning and religion in Britain. In Wales and elsewhere in the neighbourhood of surviving British churches there may have been isolated pockets of christianity and semi-literacy. But there is no reason to doubt that the people of Kent as a whole were, at the time, as ignorant of the Latin tongue—apparently the only language known to Augustine[7]—as they were of the Christian religion. Their king, Æthelberht I, was at least aware of the existence of both, having some thirty-five years earlier married a Christian wife, Bertha, daughter of the Frankish king Charibert.[8] With her husband's permission and under

---

[5] Bede, *Hist. Eccl.* I. xxiii (ed. Plummer, I, pp. 42–3).

[6] *Ibid.* I. xxv (ed. Plummer, I, p. 45): 'Acceperunt autem, praecipiente beato papa Gregorio, de gente Francorum interpretes'; *Reg. Greg. I*, VI. 49 (*M.G.H., Epist.* I, p. 424): 'Quibus etiam iniunximus, ut aliquos secum e vicino debeant presbyteros ducere, cum quibus eorum possint mentes agnoscere et voluntates ammonitione sua, quantum Deus donauerit, adiuuare'. It is generally believed that the vernacular spoken by the Frankish priests would have been understood in England (Bede, *op. cit.*, ed. Plummer, II, p. 41). On the other hand, at the synod of Whitby (A.D. 664), Bishop Agilbert, a Frank by birth who had studied in Ireland for some time, declined to explain to King Oswiu of Northumbria the Roman usage concerning Easter and suggested that Wilfrid should do so in his place, adding: 'et ille melius ac manifestius ipsa lingua Anglorum, quam ego per interpretem, potest explanare, quae sentimus' (Bede, *op. cit.* III. xxv; ed. Plummer, I, p. 184). We gather from Bede that King Cenwalh of Wessex *qui Saxonum tantum linguam nouerat* regarded Agilbert's speech as barbarous and procured the appointment of another bishop in Wessex, Wine, who spoke his own language (Bede, *op. cit.* III. vii; ed. Plummer, I, p. 140). See Brechter, *op. cit.*, pp. 225–6 and notes.

[7] Like Gregory I he probably knew no Greek (*Reg. Greg. I*, XI. 55; *M.G.H., Epist.* II, p. 330).

[8] C. H. V. Sutherland, *Anglo-Saxon Gold Coinage in the light of the Crondall Hoard* (Oxford Univ. Press, 1948), p. 29, n. 1; Richardson and Sayles, *op. cit.*, pp. 164–5 and notes. The only solid argument for placing Æthelberht's marriage before his accession is based on the literal interpretation of the words used by Gregory of Tours to describe Bertha's husband, 'in Canthia regis cuiusdam filius' (*Hist. Francorum*, IX. 26; *M.G.H., Scriptores Rerum Meroving.* I, p. 382). Gregory's other reference to the marriage is unhelpful ('Porro Charibertus rex Ingobergam accepit uxorem, de qua filiam habuit, quae postea in Ganthia virum accipiens est deducta', *Hist. Francorum*, IV. 26; *M.G.H., op. cit.*, p. 160).

the spiritual guidance of Bishop Liudhard, her Frankish chaplain, Bertha had after her marriage continued to practise her religion, using for her devotions the ancient church of St Martin in Canterbury.[9] Not only was Bertha Christian, but Gregory I says of her that she was also *litteris docta*,[10] meaning presumably that, like Liudhard, she could read and write, and that she had a tolerable knowledge of Latin. Through the queen, her chaplain and their Frankish retinue, Æthelberht and his court came into direct and daily contact with Merovingian civilization, in some ways a more developed one than their own. In some respects they were influenced by it, notably in the matter of coinage. This at any rate appears to be true of the gold coins struck, apparently in Kent, by the moneyer Abbo.[11] It does not seem, however, that the influence of Bertha and Liudhard on the Kentish royal court had, before Augustine's arrival, extended to the fields of religion and Latin learning. By 597 Æthelberht and his court were still pagan and in all probability illiterate. The only language they knew was their native tongue, and there is no satisfactory evidence that they could either read or write.[12] Nor is there any indication that Bertha and Liudhard had made any serious attempt to convert the king and his immediate entourage to their Christian and literate way of life. In so far as religion was concerned, the policy on both sides seems to have been one of mutual tolerance.

For her failure to win her husband over to her faith Bertha may have deserved to be rebuked, as indeed she later was by Gregory I,[13] but in 597 she atoned for this sin of omission by smoothing the path of the Roman missionaries. Without her good offices the landing in Thanet might not have been effected as peacefully as it was. Instead of the hostile reception which Augustine and his forty[14] companions had anticipated, they met with nothing but courtesy. Understandably cautious at first, Æthelberht soon came to realize that he had nothing to fear from the Roman missionaries. He gave them shelter in his capital, Canterbury, and he granted them permission to preach the word of God. Before the end of the year a large number of conversions had already been made. On one single day, Christmas 597, more than ten thousand *Angli* had received baptism. Perhaps this figure, which is given by the pope in a letter sent to Bishop Eulogius of Alexandria in July 598,[15] was an exaggerated estimate, but there is no reason to doubt that Augustine's efforts had, as early as 597, been amply rewarded. To make mass conversions by preaching through second-rate interpreters was no mean achievement, and it is hard to believe that this could have been done without a more tangible support from the king than his almost legendary tolerance. According to Bede, Æthelberht himself had been baptized during Augustine's first year in Kent and it was after this momentous event had taken place that the number of converts had risen to the spectacular level mentioned in the pope's letter of July 598 to Bishop Eulogius.[16] By setting an example to his people, the king had struck a decisive blow for the future of Christianity in Kent.

Bede's story of Æthelberht's conversion and of its consequences makes sense, but, because it

---

[9] Bede, *Hist. Eccl.* I. xxv and xxvi (ed. Plummer, I, pp. 45, 47).

[10] *Reg. Greg. I*, XI. 35 (*M.G.H., Epist.* II, p. 304).

[11] Sutherland, *op. cit.*, pp. 31–2, 74–5.

[12] The arguments to the contrary put forward by Richardson and Sayles, *op. cit.*, pp. 158–62, are unconvincing· There can be little doubt that the Latin and runic alphabets were known to Bertha, Liudhard and their Frankish entourage, but the only inscription of English workmanship which can be ascribed to the period before 600, the Liudhard medalet, has some rune-like Latin letters which suggest that the engraver was copying from a model; he obviously knew the runic alphabet, but was not familiar with the Latin one. On the medalet, see P. Grierson, 'The Canterbury (St Martin's) Hoard of Frankish and Anglo-Saxon Coin-Ornaments', *British Numismatic Journal*, vol. 27 (1955), pp. 39–51, especially pp. 41–2.

[13] *Reg. Greg. I*, XI. 35 (*M.G.H., Epist.* II, p. 304): June 601.

[14] Bede, *Hist. Eccl.* I. xxv (ed. Plummer, I, p. 45): 'Augustinus, et socii eius, uiri, ut ferunt, ferme XL'.

[15] *Reg. Greg. I*, VIII. 29 (*M.G.H., Epist.* II, pp. 30–1).

[16] Bede, *Hist. Eccl.* I. xxvi (ed. Plummer, I, p. 47).

is not corroborated by the scanty sources of the early seventh century, it has been called in question. On the basis of two letters of Gregory I it has been argued that the king could not possibly have been baptized as early as 597 or even by June 601;[17] it has also been suggested that he might have died a pagan.[18] Of the two documents quoted by Bede's critics one is Gregory's letter of July 598 to Bishop Eulogius of Alexandria;[19] the other is his letter of June 601 to Queen Bertha.[20] How could the pope, it is asked, in a letter announcing to Eulogius the baptism of more than ten thousand *Angli*, have omitted to mention Æthelberht's own baptism, if this important event had already taken place? The answer may be that Gregory had every reason to suppose that the bishop would be far better pleased to hear of the conversion of a large number of pagans than of the baptism of one obscure king. In the eyes of the pope, Æthelberht's conversion was obviously a desirable end in itself, but it was above all the surest means of securing the evangelization of the whole Kentish nation. Gregory makes this point abundantly clear in his letter to Bertha:[21]

. . . Deum benediximus, qui conversionem gentis Anglorum mercedi vestrae dignatus est propitius reservare. Nam sicut per recordandae memoriae Helenam matrem piissimi Constantini imperatoris ad christianam fidem corda Romanorum accenderat, ita et per gloriae vestrae studium in Anglorum gentem eius misericordiam confidimus operari. Et quidem iam dudum gloriosi filii nostri coniugis vestri animos prudentiae vestrae bono, sicut revera christianae, debuistis inflectere, ut pro regni et animae suae salute fidem quam colitis sequeretur, quatenus de eo et per eum de totius gentis conversione digna vobis in caelestibus gaudiis retributio nasceretur. Nam postquam, sicut diximus, et recta fide gloria vestra munita et litteris docta est, hoc vobis nec tardum nec debuit esse difficile; et quoniam Deo volente aptum nunc tempus est, agite, ut divina gratia cooperante cum augmento possetis quod neglectum est reparare . . .

This passage does not prove, as it has been asserted, that Æthelberht had not been baptized by June 601. Nor does it prove conclusively that he had been baptized by then, but it suggests that, when Gregory wrote to Bertha, he had been informed that Æthelberht already believed in the true God and behaved like a Christian. What the pope deplored was that Bertha had not acted sooner in converting her husband; by her procrastination the queen had delayed the conversion of the Kentish people. Now, obviously because the king had become a Christian, the time was ripe for Bertha to act and 'repair what had been neglected'. She must strengthen her husband's mind in his love of the Christian faith (*in dilectione christianae fidei . . . roborate*), increase his love of God (*augmentum in Deum amoris infundat*) and urge him to work for the fullest conversion of his subjects. This is the sort of exhortation which the pope might be expected to make to the wife of a newly-converted king, but not to the wife of a pagan.

Our conviction that by June 601 at the latest King Æthelberht had embraced the Christian faith becomes even stronger as we read the letter which Gregory I wrote to him on the 22nd day of that month. There the pope presses the king to speed up the spread of the Christian faith among all his peoples (*christianam fidem in populis tibi subditis extendere festina*) and to instil into the kings and peoples subject to his rule the knowledge of one God the Father, the Son and the Holy Ghost (*vestra gloria cognitionem unius Dei patris et filii et spiritus sancti regibus ac populis sibimet subiectis festinet infundere*).[22] In his letter to Bertha the pope had referred to her husband as *gloriosi filii nostri*; in his letter to Æthelberht he addresses the king as *praecellentissimo filio* and *gloriose fili*, a choice of words which would have been hardly appropriate in a letter to a confirmed pagan. Although Gregory I

[17] Brechter, *op. cit.*, pp. 241 ff.
[18] Richardson and Sayles, *op. cit.*, pp. 162–4.
[19] *Reg. Greg. I*, VIII. 29 (*M.G.H., Epist.* II, pp. 30–1).
[20] *Ibid.* XI. 35 (*M.G.H., Epist.* II, p. 304).
[21] *Ibid., loc. cit.*
[22] Bede, *Hist. Eccl.* I. xxxii (ed. Plummer, I, pp. 67–70).

and other seventh-century popes sometimes applied the term *filius*, possibly for political considerations, to princes of such doubtful catholicity as the Arian kings of the Lombards Agilulfo and Rotair,[23] they do not appear to have used it for pagan kings. One could quote as evidence the letter written by Boniface V to King Edwin of Northumbria, who was still a pagan at the time: here the king is addressed simply as *viro glorioso Æduino regi Anglorum*,[24] whereas in a letter of approximately even date Boniface writes to Edwin's Christian wife, Æthelberg, daughter of King Æthelberht of Kent, as *dominae gloriosae filiae Ædilbergae reginae*.[25] After Edwin's conversion, the tone of the papal letters changed: he, too, now deserved to be addressed as *domino excellentissimo atque praecellentissimo filio Æduino regi Anglorum* and *excellentissime fili*.[26]

It would be pointless to repeat here other arguments of varying force which have been put forward in defence of Bede's account of Æthelberht's conversion.[27] What matters is that it has been established beyond reasonable doubt that Æthelberht became a Christian some time before June 601 and possibly as early as 597. From that time onwards the future of Christianity in Kent was assured, at least for Æthelberht's lifetime, and the way was open for the gradual infiltration of Roman literacy.

It may be broadly true to say that, through Augustine, Rome and her culture had returned to Britain in 597,[28] but the Rome of Pope Gregory was not the Rome of Caesar or even of Constantine the Great. In Gregory's vision of a world free from pagan idols there was as little room for the culture and literature of Ancient Rome as there was for the statues of her gods. He was an admirer of St Benedict, who had given up the study of the liberal arts to devote himself solely to the service of God:[29]

. . . Romae liberalibus litterarum studiis traditus fuerat, sed dum in eis multos ire per abrupta vitiorum cerneret, eum, quem quasi in ingressum mundi posuerat, retraxit pedem, ne si quid de scientia eius adtingerit, ipse quoque postmodum in inmane praecipitium totus iret. Dispectis itaque litterarum studiis, relicta domo rebusque patris, soli Deo placere desiderans, sanctae conversionis habitum quaesivit. Recessit igitur scienter nescius et sapienter indoctus.

Because one could not praise God and Jupiter in the same breath, Gregory held that to study the liberal arts, *at least for their own sake*, was frivolous and blasphemous, and that it was shameful for a

---

[23] *Reg. Greg. I*, XIV. 12 (*M.G.H., Epist.* II, p. 432): letter to Queen Teodelinda (Dec. 603), following a peace settlement with Agilulfo: 'petimus, ut excellentissimo filio nostro regi coniugi vestro pro nobis de facta pace gratias referatis'; in the same letter (p. 431) Gregory also calls Adoloaldo, son of Agilulfo and Teodelinda, 'excellentissimum filium nostrum Adulouualdum', but Adoloaldo had been baptized in the catholic faith ('catholicae cum fidei cognovimus sociatum'); compare *Reg. Greg. I*, IX. 66–7 (*M.G.H., Epist.* II, pp. 85–8); *Codice diplomatico del monastero di S. Colombano di Bobbio*, ed. C. Cipolla, I (Rome, 1918), no. xiii (4 May 643; a dubious privilege of Pope Theodore for Bobbio, alleged to have been granted at the request of Rotari and his catholic wife Gundeperga), p. 108: 'Dum igitur excellentissimus filius noster Rotharit rex et gloriosissima filia nostra Gundiberga regina gentis Langobardorum . . .', cited in O. Bertolini, 'I papi e le missioni fino alla metà del secolo VIII', *La conversione al cristianesimo nell' Europa dell' alto medioevo (Settimane di studio del Centro italiano di studi sull' alto medioevo*, XIV (Spoleto, 1967), p. 353, n. 71. For the alleged return of Agilulfo to the catholic faith, see Bertolini, *art. cit.* p. 345, note.

[24] Bede, *Hist. Eccl.* II. x (ed. Plummer, I, p. 100).

[25] *Ibid.* II. xi (ed. Plummer, I, p. 104).

[26] *Ibid.* II. xvii (ed. Plummer, I, pp. 118–19).

[27] R. A. Markus, 'The Chronology of the Gregorian Mission to England', *Journal of Eccl. Hist.*, XIV (1963), pp. 16–30.

[28] E. A. Lowe, *English Uncial* (Oxford, 1960), p. 6.

[29] *Gregorii Magni Dialogi*, ed. U. Moricca (*Fonti per la Storia d'Italia*, Rome, 1924), pp. 71–2. See P. F. Jones. 'The Gregorian Mission and English Education', *Speculum*, III (1928), p. 337. On education in the Merovingian period, see P. Riché, *Education et culture dans l'Occident barbare, VIe–VIIIe siècles* (*Patristica Sorbonensia*, vol. 4, Paris, 1962). For Gregory's attitude, see *ibid.* pp. 194–200.

bishop to indulge in singing or to teach grammar.[30] He had nothing but contempt for the grammatical rules regarding metacism or barbarism or the correct use of moods and cases, because it was intolerable that the words of the heavenly oracle should be confined within the rules of grammarians like Donatus.[31] There can be no doubt that Gregory would have made sure that his views on education were strictly put into practice in the abbey of Sant' Andrea al Clivo di Scauro, the monastery which he himself had founded on one of his own estates on the Coelian Mount.[32] There the Scriptures would be intensively read as well as the writings of the Fathers, but little else. It was from among the abbey's inmates, whose minds had not been polluted by any trace of pagan learning, that Gregory had chosen some of his missionaries to Britain. Who was better fitted to lead them than Augustine, the prior (*praepositus*) of Sant' Andrea, a man described by Gregory as full of the knowledge of the Holy Scriptures?[33] Unlike Christ's apostles, who had been sent into the world to preach *sine litteris*,[34] Augustine was literate–otherwise, in Gregory's time, he would not have been admitted to holy orders[35]–but his literacy could not be compared with that of Theodore, the last 'Roman' archbishop of Canterbury, who was versed in the profane as well as in the divine literature and who knew both Greek and Latin.[36]

Augustine does not seem to have been the kind of man who would have brought to England with him books of a secular nature.[37] Nor was Gregory likely to have included any other books than

---

[30] *Reg. Greg. I*, XI. 34 (*M.G.H., Epist.* II, p. 303): Gregory I to Desiderius, bishop of Vienne: '. . . . Sed post hoc pervenit ad nos, quod sine verecundia memorare non possumus, fraternitatem tuam grammaticam quibusdam exponere. Quam rem ita moleste suscepimus . . ., quia in uno se ore cum Iovis laudibus Christi laudes non capiunt. Et quam grave nefandumque sit episcopo canere, quod nec laico religioso conveniat, ipse considera . . . Unde si post hoc evidenter haec quae ad nos perlata sunt falsa esse claruerint neque vos nugis et saecularibus litteris studere constiterit, et Deo nostro gratias agimus, qui cor vestrum maculari blasfemis nefandorum laudibus non permisit . . .' In condemning the study of profane literature Gregory was following the example of Bishop Caesarius of Arles (F. Lot, C. Pfister and F. L. Ganshof, *Les destinées de l'Empire en Occident de 395 à 888*, I (Glotz, *Hist. du Moyen Age*, Paris, 1940), pp. 332, 374–5 and notes). See also Jones, *art. cit.* pp. 338–9. Regarding the attitude of the Church towards pagan culture in the fourth and fifth centuries, see J. Gaudemet, *L'Eglise dans l'Empire Romain (Hist. du Droit et des Institutions de l'Eglise en Occident*, ed. G. Le Bras, III, Paris, 1958), pp. 582–91.

[31] *Reg. Greg. I*, V. 53a (*M.G.H., Epist.* I, p. 357): '. . . Nam sicut huius quoque epistolae tenor enuntiat, non metacismi collisionem fugio, non barbarismi confusionem devito, situs modosque et praepositionum casus servare contemno, quia indignum vehementer existimo, ut verba caelestis oraculi restringam sub regulis Donati . . .' See Jones, *art. cit.*, p. 338. Cf. *Felix's Life of Saint Guthlac*, ed. B. Colgrave (Cambridge Univ. Press, 1956), p. 60. Another text of Gregory concedes that the teaching of the liberal arts may have some value: 'ad hoc quidem tantum liberales artes discendae sunt, ut per instructionem illarum divina eloquia subtilius intellegantur' (*M.G.H., Epist.* I, p. 357, n. 5) Gregory of Tours, unlike Pope Gregory, apologized for his insufficient knowledge of grammar: 'Sed prius veniam legentibus praecor, si aut in litteris aut in sillabis grammaticam artem excessero, de qua adplene non sum inbutus (*Hist. Francorum*, Pref. to Book I, *M.G.H., Scriptores Rerum Meroving.* I, p. 33).

[32] *Patrologia Latina*, ed. Migne, LXXV (Life of Gregory by John the Deacon), col. 65.

[33] *Reg. Greg. I*, IX. 222 (*M.G.H., Epist.* II, p. 213): '. . . per Augustinum, quondam monasterii mei praepositum . . .'; Bede, *Hist. Eccl.* I. xxxii (ed. Plummer, I, p. 68): '. . . Augustinus episcopus in monasterii regula edoctus, sacrae scripturae scientia repletus . . .'; *Patrol. Latina*, ed. Migne, LXXV, col. 99: '. . . Augustinum cum aliis domus suae monasterii monachis in Britanniam euangelizandi gratia destinauit'. A stone inscription on the façade of the church of Sant' Andrea listed among the former members of the abbey the first five archbishops of Canterbury (Augustine, Laurentius, Mellitus, Justus and Honorius), Bishop Paulinus of York (and later, of Rochester), and Abbot Peter of St Peter and St Paul, Canterbury (Count de Montalembert, *The Monks of the West*, ed. F. A. Gasquet, III (London, 1896), p. 183, n. 3).

[34] *Reg. Greg. I*, XI. 36 (*M.G.H., Epist.* II, pp. 305–6): Gregory I to Augustine: 'Qui [sc. Deus] ut mundum ostenderet non sapientia hominum, sed sua se virtute converteret, praedicatores suos, quos in mundum misit, sine litteris elegit, haec etiam modo faciens, quia in Anglorum gentem fortia dignatus est per infirmos operari'.

[35] *Ibid.* II. 37 (*M.G.H., Epist.* I, p. 133): 'Praecipimus autem, ne umquam inlicitas ordinationes facias, ne bigamum . . . aut ignorantem litteras . . . ad sacros ordines permittas accedere'.

[36] Bede, *Hist. Eccl.* IV. i (ed. Plummer, I, p. 202): 'Theodorus . . . uir et saeculari et diuina litteratura, et Grece instructus et Latine'.

[37] The same conclusion was reached by P. F. Jones in *Speculum*, III (1928), pp. 335–48.

religious ones among the many manuscripts which in June 601 he entrusted to Mellitus and the other members of the second Roman mission for delivery to Augustine: like the sacred vessels, altar coverings, church ornaments, sacerdotal vestments and relics which were despatched from Rome at the same time, the manuscripts formed part of what was regarded as essential to the administration of the cult and to the running of the Church;[38] they clearly were gospel-books, psalters, missals and similar books. These volumes have now perished, one possible exception being the famous sixth-century gospel-book, now MS. 286 in the Library of Corpus Christi College, Cambridge;[39] in the tenth century the manuscript belonged to the abbey of St Augustine, Canterbury, and it may have been there already in the seventh century, at a time when the abbey was dedicated to St Peter and St Paul. Although these books were meant primarily to serve a religious function, they could also be used, and were probably used, for teaching some of the new converts to read and write. Like Corpus Christi College MS. 286, most of them were probably written in uncials,[40] some perhaps in half-uncials, two scripts particularly easy to read. Most of them, again like the extant gospel-book of St Augustine, may have been copiously illustrated, which would have made the reading and understanding of the sacred texts easier for beginners.[41] In the same way as the paintings on the walls of churches were designed to provide those who could not read with an elementary religious instruction,[42] explanatory miniatures in early Christian manuscripts are likely to have served an educational end.

   Until 601 Augustine and his colleagues had been so occupied with their preaching and pastoral duties that, even if we suppose that they already had books at their disposal, they would have had little time to use them for teaching purposes. The harvest was so abundant and the workers so few that human reinforcements were required just as urgently as books. As soon as the second Roman mission, headed by Mellitus, Justus and Paulinus, had arrived in Kent, in the last quarter of 601, both these needs had been temporarily satisfied.[43] It would be wrong to assume, however, that the Roman missionaries had either the qualifications or the inclination to embark on a grandiose scheme for the education of the masses. They had come to England to spread the word of God, not to teach letters. If they decided to add teaching to their other numerous and onerous tasks, it was out of necessity rather than by choice. Their aim was to educate a small group of potential missionaries, not to transform the rugged English laity into a polished, lettered society, a goal which in any case was beyond the resources at their disposal. Without a steady growth in the number of churches and monasteries not only would the English Christian community cease to expand, but it might even relapse into its former pagan practices. More and more priests and monks would be needed, more and more bishops and abbots. The Roman missionaries themselves would not live for ever. Who would replace them at the head of the English Church after they had died? They could not rely on a constant and indefinite supply of monks from Rome. Besides, their own experience had taught them that Roman monks, handicapped by their ignorance of local customs and dialects, were not

---

   [38] Bede, *Hist. Eccl.* I. xxix (ed. Plummer, I, p. 63): '. . . generaliter uniuersa, quae ad cultum erant ac ministerium ecclesiae necessaria, uasa uidelicet sacra, et uestimenta altarium, ornamenta quoque ecclesiarum, et sacerdotalia uel clericilia indumenta, sanctorum etiam apostolorum ac martyrum reliquias, nec non et codices plurimos'.
   [39] *Codices Latini Antiquiores*, ed. E. A. Lowe, II, no. 126; N. R. Ker, *Catalogue of MSS. containing Anglo-Saxon* (Oxford, 1957), no. 55.
   [40] E. A. Lowe, *English Uncial*, pp. 5 ff.
   [41] On the illuminations of Corpus Christi College, Cambridge, MS. 286, see F. Wormald, *The Miniatures in the Gospels of St Augustine* (Cambridge Univ. Press, 1954).
   [42] *Reg. Greg. I*, IX. 208 (*M.G.H., Epist.* II, p. 195): 'Idcirco enim pictura in ecclesiis adhibetur, ut hi qui litteras nesciunt saltem in parietibus videndo legant, quae legere in codicibus non valent'; *ibid.* XI. 10 (*M.G.H., Epist.* II, p. 270): 'Nam quod legentibus scriptura, hoc idiotis praestat pictura cernentibus, quia in ipsa ignorantes vident, quod sequi debeant, in ipsa legunt qui litteras nesciunt; unde praecipue gentibus pro lectione pictura est'.
   [43] Bede, *Hist. Eccl.* I. xxix (ed. Plummer, I, p. 63).

the best persons to look after the English Church. Sooner or later, priests and monks would have to be recruited on the spot from among the native youths, but since literacy was one of the conditions laid down by Gregory I for admission to holy orders,[44] the local recuits would first have to be taught letters. Hence the need for some kind of school, however primitive, where the abbots and bishops of the future could be educated. That such a school existed and flourished in Kent in the early years of the seventh century may be inferred from a passage of Bede's *Ecclesiastical History* in which King Sigeberht is said to have set up, after his return from Gaul in about 630, a *scola* where East Anglian boys could be taught letters in the Kentish fashion.[45]

Augustine did not live long enough to see any of the English pupils at the Kentish school elevated to the episcopate. He died between 604 and 609, forty years earlier than the first recorded appointment of an English bishop. Not unexpectedly, this first English bishop was a native of Kent, Ithamar, appointed in 644 to the Kentish see of Rochester, which had become vacant on the death of Paulinus, one of the leaders of the second Roman mission. It was fitting that the privilege of conse-crating him should have been left to one of Gregory I's disciples, the last survivor of the group which had come to England and presumably the youngest, Archbishop Honorius, Augustine's fourth successor in the see of Canterbury.[46] Eleven years later, it was Ithamar's turn to consecrate another English bishop, this time a West Saxon, Deusdedit, who replaced Honorius as archbishop of Canterbury.[47] Unlike Ithamar, who had probably been taught by one of the original Roman mission-aries, Deusdedit may have owed his education to Birinus, the apostle of Wessex, sent to England by Pope Honorius I in about 634.[48] After Deusdedit's death, a Kentish priest, Wighard, who according to Bede had been 'adequately trained in all ecclesiastical matters by the Roman disciples of the blessed pope Gregory', was chosen to replace him, but he died in Rome before he had been conse-crated.[49]

Of the remaining English bishops of the mid-seventh century some, like Cedd, bishop of the East Saxons, were educated by Irish masters,[50] while others may have had a training which was partly Roman, partly Frankish. Among the latter should perhaps be placed Thomas, *de prouincia Gyruiorum*, deacon of the Burgundian-born Felix and his successor as bishop of the East Angles.[51] Thomas was himself succeeded by Beorhtgils, *de prouincia Cantuariorum*,[52] and Ithamar was re-placed at Rochester by Damian, a South Saxon.[53] For Beorhtgils and Damian a Kentish education can be reasonably claimed, but important centres of learning had also emerged in Northumbria by the last quarter of the seventh century: one of them was at Whitby, where no less than five English bishops received their education under Abbess Hild.[54]

Nobody would seriously suggest that King Æthelberht I of Kent was one of those who

---

[44] See above, note 35.

[45] Bede, *Hist. Eccl.* III. xviii (ed. Plummer, I, p. 162); *Speculum*, III (1928), p. 335.

[46] Bede, *Hist. Eccl.* III. xiv (ed. Plummer, I, p. 154): 'Ithamar, oriundum quidem de gente Cantuariorum, sed uita et eruditione antecessoribus suis aequandum'; *ibid.* v. xix (ed. Plummer, i, p. 323): 'Honorius, unus ex discipulis beati papae Gregorii, uir in rebus ecclesiasticis sublimiter institutus . . .'

[47] *Ibid.* III. xx (ed. Plummer, I, p. 169).

[48] *Ibid.* III. vii (ed. Plummer, I, p. 139).

[49] *Ibid.* III. xxix (ed. Plummer, I, p. 196); Bede, *Hist. Abb.*, c. 3 (*Hist. Eccl.*, ed. Plummer, I, p. 366).

[50] Bede, *Hist. Eccl.* III. xxi, xxii, xxv, xxvi (ed. Plummer, I, pp. 170, 172, 183, 189). The earliest bishops of Mercia (mid-seventh century) were either Irish (Diuma, Ceollach) or English with an Irish training (Trumhere); see Nora K. Chadwick, 'The Celtic Background of Early Anglo-Saxon England', *Celt and Saxon, Studies in the Early British Border* (Cambridge Univ. Press, 1963), p. 337.

[51] Bede, *Hist. Eccl.* III. xx (ed. Plummer, I, p. 169).

[52] *Ibid., loc. cit.*

[53] *Ibid., loc. cit.*

[54] *Ibid.* IV. xxiii (ed. Plummer, I, p. 254).

learned to read or write under Augustine and his colleagues. The fact that in June 601 one of Gregory I's letters was addressed to him cannot be adduced as evidence of his literacy, since the letter may have been read to him, in a vernacular translation, either by Queen Bertha or by one of Augustine's Frankish interpreters.[55] Nevertheless Æthelberht was not slow to appreciate the advantages of the written word over the spoken one. In an unknown year, but during his reign, and also, according to tradition, in Augustine's lifetime he caused a legal code to be committed to writing, the so-called 'Dooms of Æthelberht'. Bede mentions the fact as one among other salutary measures taken by the king for the benefit of the Kentish people. He also notes that these laws, in the form in which they had come down to his day, were written in English and that their first article fixed the tariff of the compositions to be paid for thefts perpetrated to the detriment of the Church, of a bishop and of the other ecclesiastical orders. In having his laws written down Æthelberht had followed the example of the Romans, or so Bede thought, and by imposing penalties on those who stole goods belonging to the Church and to its ministers he had shown his determination to protect those whose teaching he had received.[56] The laws of Æthelberht have been preserved in only one text, an early twelfth century copy made at Rochester (*Textus Roffensis*).[57] How far this copy represents an accurate transcript of the seventh-century original we shall probably never know, but we can at least be reasonably confident that, apart from the modernization of the form of some words,[58] it is close enough to the text examined by Bede or his informant. Like the text to which Bede refers,[59] the extant version of the Laws is in Old-English and its first article lists the penalties for stealing movable goods (*feoh*) belonging to the Church.[60]

---

[55] *Ibid.* I. xxxii (ed. Plummer, I, pp. 67–70). Bede also refers to a letter sent by Boniface IV to Æthelberht in 610: *ibid.* II. iv (ed. Plummer, I, p. 88): 'una cum epistulis, quas idem pontifex Deo dilecto archiepiscopo Laurentio et clero uniuerso similiter et Aedilbercto regi atque genti Anglorum direxit. Hic est Bonifatius, quartus . . .'.

[56] *Ibid.* II. v (ed. Plummer, I, p. 90): 'Qui [*sc.* rex Aedilberct] inter cetera bona, quae genti suae consulendo conferebat, etiam decreta illi iudiciorum, iuxta exempla Romanorum, cum consilio sapientium constituit; quae conscripta Anglorum sermone hactenus habentur, et obseruantur ab ea. In quibus primitus posuit, qualiter id emendare deberet, qui aliquid rerum uel ecclesiae, uel episcopi, uel reliquorum ordinum furto auferret; uolens scilicet tuitionem eis, quos et quorum doctrinam susceperat, praestare'.

[57] *Textus Roffensis*, ed. P. Sawyer, Part I (*Early English MSS. in Facsimile*, vol. VII, Copenhagen, 1957), fos· 1r–3v.

[58] It is impossible to say whether the scribe of the *Textus Roffensis* took his text of the Code from a seventh-century 'original' or from a later copy. His transcript does not pretend to be a facsimile; he uses the letter-forms of his own time, not those of his exemplar. Was the seventh-century original written in a majuscule or miniscule script, in an English, Merovingian or Roman hand? Was it all written in the Latin alphabet or were the sounds *th* and *w* and the conjunction 'and' represented by the runic 'eth', 'thorn' and 'wynn' and by the tironian *et*, as they are in the *Textus*? Two original Italian charters show that in the mid-sixth century the Ostrogoths of Italy used several runes, including the thorn and wynn, in their vernacular subscriptions (Marini, *Papiri diplomatici*, nos. 118–19; plates XV, XVII). The thorn and wynn were two of the runes which, according to Gregory of Tours, Chilperic I introduced into the Merovingian script (*Hist. Franc.* V. 44; *M.G.H., Scriptores Rerum Meroving.*, I, pp. 237–8). On English coins of the seventh century the thorn and other runes are found, sometimes mixed with Roman letters (Sutherland, *op. cit.*, p. 105, *s.v.* 'Runes'), but in English manuscripts the eth, thorn and wynn and the tironian *et* do not occur until the second half of the eighth century. In the few original Anglo-Saxon charters which have survived for the last quarter of the seventh century the sounds *th* and *w* are represented by the letters *d* (or *th*) and *uu* (or *u*) even in vernacular names (*Facsimiles of Ancient Charters in the British Museum* [hereafter B.M.F.], I. 1–2; Ordnance Survey, *Facsimiles of Anglo-Saxon Manuscripts* [hereafter O.S.F.], III. i (Birch, *Cartularium Saxonicum* [hereafter B.C.S.], nos. 45, 81, 97); the examples of wynn in B.M.F. I. 2 and O.S.F. III. i are later corrections or additions). As late as the second quarter of the ninth century the sounds *th* and *w* were still represented by *th* and *uu* as often as by the appropriate runes; see, for example, the note written in 839 on the dorse of B.M.F. II. 27 (printed in B.C.S., no. 421, p. 591, n. 13). In Anglo-Saxon charters the thorn seems to have been introduced later than the eth and wynn.

[59] Æthelberht's code may have been one of the Kentish documents copied on Bede's behalf by Abbot Albinus of St Peter and St Paul, Canterbury; see Bede's Preface to his *Hist. Eccl.*, ed. Plummer, I, p. 6.

[60] *English Historical Documents* [hereafter E.H.D.], I, p. 357 (transl. D. Whitelock).

PLATE V

Charter of Oslac, ealdorman of the South Saxons: A.D. 780

Extract from the dorse, *inset* Extract from the face

The property of God and the Church [is to be paid for] with a twelve-fold compensation; a bishop's property with an eleven-fold compensation; a priest's property with a nine-fold compensation; a deacon's property with a six-fold compensation; a cleric's property with a three-fold compensation; the peace of the Church with a two-fold compensation; the peace of a meeting with a two-fold compensation.

There is little doubt that Bede singled out this article for comment because he found it just as remarkable as we do. Out of the ninety articles of the Code it is the only one to make any specific reference to the Christian Church; the others do not show any sign of Christian influence and could have been issued by a pagan king. Even more remarkable is the comparative severity of the penalties laid down for the protection of church property. In its fourth article the Code stipulates a nine-fold composition for property stolen from the king, thus placing the latter on an equal footing with a priest, but below a bishop, who was entitled to an eleven-fold compensation. This we may find surprising, but not so incredible that we should feel impelled to brand the whole of the first article as a later interpolation.[61] On the contrary it could be argued that a king who had only recently been converted from paganism might easily have regarded the theft of church property as a more heinous crime than the theft of his own goods. At a time when Christians were outnumbered by pagans, stringent measures were needed if the safety of the missionaries and their belongings was to be assured.

Augustine and his colleagues could not fail to welcome Æthelberht's efforts to protect them against theft, but they may well have had serious reservations about the steps which had been taken to ensure their protection. Monks accustomed to a life of poverty and trained to despise worldly riches were bound to feel uneasy at the prospect of making handsome profits out of the sins of misguided pagans. To recover goods which had been stolen was legitimate, but to receive them back three to twelve times over was scarcely consistent with the monastic way of life. How far could Augustine come to terms with the pagan system of compositions? There were two main points at issue: one concerned the penalties to be meted out to the thieves, the other the compensation to be given to the aggrieved party. On those two points Gregory I, consulted by Augustine either before or after the 'publication' of Æthelberht's code, gave his ruling in the summer of 601. He was in no doubt that the culprits ought to be punished–even good fathers occasionally had to beat their own sons–but the punishment had to be inflicted with charity in mind, not in anger, and always within the bounds of reason. Before deciding on the nature and severity of the penalties, the motives for the crime and the circumstances of the criminal had to be considered. Some thieves were driven to stealing by penury, others by greed, and therefore sometimes leniency, sometimes severity ought to prevail. Now a pecuniary fine, now a beating would be an adequate punishment (*quidam damnis, quidam uero uerberibus*). In no circumstances, however, should the Church receive its earthly goods back with interest and seek gain out of such vanities.[62]

Gregory's verdict was in flagrant contradiction to the first article of Æthelberht's code in letter as well as in spirit, but both could be reconciled in practice. Gregory was not against compositions as such. He simply ruled that the Church should not take advantage of them in order to increase its wealth. He would therefore have condemned a bishop who kept for himself the full amount of an eleven-fold composition, while probably absolving another who only retained it to the value of the stolen goods and distributed the rest to the poor. The Penitential of Archbishop Theodore hints at a compromise of this kind when it stipulates in one article that money stolen from the Church should

[61] For the interpolation theory, see Richardson and Sayles, *Law and Legislation from Æthelberht to Magna Carta*, pp. 3–4. The composition rate for thefts of church property varies from one Barbaric code to another, but Æthelberht's laws seem to be unique in that they make that rate higher than for thefts of royal property. See, for example, *Lex Baiwariorum* I. 3 (*M.G.H., Legum Sectio* I, v. ii, pp. 270–72); IX. 1–2 (*ibid.* pp. 366–7); *Leges Alamannorum* VI (*M.G.H., Legum Sectio* I, v. i, p. 74), XXXI (*ibid.* pp. 89–90).

[62] Bede, *Hist. Eccl.* I. xxvii (ed. Plummer, I, pp. 49–50); *M.G.H., Epist.* II, p. 334.

be restored four-fold and in another that one third of the composition should be given to the poor.[63] Perhaps Augustine had used the same device to reconcile the views of the pope with those of Æthelberht. This is not to say that he would not have preferred some other method of dealing with the problem of theft of church property, or that he condoned the pagan customs which underlie other articles of the Code. He was wise enough, however, to realise that his missionary efforts would be doomed to failure if he tried to sweep away at once all pagan institutions and antagonized Æthelberht in the process. As Gregory I remarked to Mellitus in the summer of 601, the uprooting of heathenism could only be achieved in stages: 'anyone who tries to reach a high summit, climbs step by step, not by leaps and bounds'.[64] In any case the laws of Æthelberht were not unusually barbarous for the period. They were in some respects more humane than the later Kentish laws of Wihtred or the laws of Alfred. In the laws of Wihtred, death was one of the alternative penalties for stealing, if the thief, either a freeman or a slave, was caught in the act; it was for the king to decide whether or not the culprit was to be put to death.[65] In Æthelberht's code there was no room for choice: the penalty for stealing was in every case a money compensation, whereas in Alfred's laws a theft which had been committed in a church could be punished by mutilation.[66] Was the substitution by Æthelberht of compositions and fines for such corporal punishments as death and mutilation a direct result of Christian teaching and particularly of the doctrine of 'mercy which Christ taught', as the draftsman of Alfred's laws believed?[67] Or was it simply, as we may prefer to think, more or less freely adapted from some unidentified continental laws? At any rate the code of Æthelberht was an acceptable compromise between the pagan and the Christian views on crime and punishment. The opinion expressed by Bede over a hundred years later that the Code had been beneficial to the Kentish people[68] may also have been that of Augustine and his fellow-missionaries. None of its ninety articles could have been so distasteful to them that they would have felt it their duty to decline to play any part in setting it down in writing. Since they knew no English, they could not easily have written it themselves, although they may have collaborated in its drafting. The actual writing of the Code is more likely to have been left to Augustine's Frankish interpreters.[69]

Apart from Æthelberht's code and one Latin letter sent in 610 by Laurentius, Mellitus and Justus to the Irish bishops and abbots,[70] no record known to have been written in England, either in English or in Latin, has survived for the reign of Æthelberht or indeed for the whole period extending from Augustine's landing in Thanet to Archbishop Theodore's arrival in Canterbury in 669. A large number of letters and other types of records as well as books may in fact have been written in England during those seventy years, but with the two exceptions already noted they have all suffered the same fate as the *codices plurimi* sent by Gregory I to Augustine in June 601, all but one of which

[63] *Councils and Ecclesiastical Documents*, ed. Haddan and Stubbs, III, pp. 179–80: 'Pecunia ecclesiis furata sive rapta reddatur quadruplum; saecularibus dupliciter . . . Et cui furata det tertiam partem pauperibus . . .' Part of the composition may also have been reserved to the fisc, although no such provision is explicitly made either in Æthelberht's code or in Theodore's penitential.

[64] Bede, *Hist. Eccl.* I. xxx (ed. Plummer, I, p. 65): 'Nam duris mentibus simul omnia abscidere impossibile esse non dubium est, quia et is, qui summum locum ascendere nititur, gradibus uel passibus, non autem saltibus eleuatur'.

[65] *E.H.D.*, I, p. 364 (art. 26 and 27); *The Laws of the earliest English Kings*, ed. F. L. Attenborough (Cambridge Univ. Press, 1922), pp. 28–30.

[66] *E.H.D.*, I, p. 375 (art. 6); Attenborough, *op. cit.*, pp. 66–8. Like the laws of Æthelberht, those of Hlothhere and Eadric do not recognize death or mutilation as a punishment for any offence (Attenborough, *op. cit.*, pp. 18–23). See F. Liebermann, *Die Gesetze der Angelsachsen*, II, pp. 667–71, 'Strafe', and pp. 684–5, 'Todesstrafe'.

[67] *E.H.D.*, I, p. 373; Pollock and Maitland, *Hist. of English Law* (2nd ed.), I, pp. 48–9.

[68] Bede, *Hist. Eccl.* II. v (ed. Plummer, I, p. 90).

[69] If the Code was written in about 601, English scribes can be ruled out, since there probably was none available at the time. Several years may have been required for training a scribe.

[70] Bede, *Hist. Eccl.* II. iv (ed. Plummer, I, pp. 87–8).

have long since perished.[71] Pope Boniface V refers to a letter he had received from King Eadbald, Æthelberht's son and successor on the Kentish throne.[72] This letter, written–obviously in Latin– between 618 and 624, was presumably the work of one of the Roman missionaries or of one of their Kentish pupils. From a letter of Pope Vitalian we also gather that King Oswiu of Northumbria had written to him in 667.[73] Since Oswiu appears to have been unable to understand Latin,[74] his letter, like that of Eadbald, is unlikely to have been holograph. We also have a few mentions of letters written by the Roman missionaries, for example one sent by Laurentius, Mellitus and Justus to the British priests,[75] and another sent by Justus to Boniface V.[76] These casual references suggest that, once in England, the Roman missionaries corresponded by letter with the pope and with others, and that long before Theodore's arrival the kings of Kent and Northumbria had grown accustomed to sending messages in writing.

For anybody who could use a pen for writing letters or laws the writing of charters was not likely to present any particular problem, but their drafting required a specialized kind of competence and literacy which greatly exceeded the mere fluency in writing and even the skill involved in composing ordinary correspondence. The charters written in England in Theodore's time show that their draftsmen were familiar with a large number of traditional Italian formulae,[77] to which they presumably attached some legal significance even though they may not have been fully–if at all–acquainted with the legal texts on which the formulae were based. Since the Italian prototype of these formulae does not appear to have originated later than Augustine's time or to have become obsolete before Theodore's arrival in Canterbury, they could in theory have been brought to England at any time between 597 and 669 by anyone who had an intimate knowledge of Italian charters. A number of bishops and abbots of English descent, among them Wilfrid and Benedict Biscop, visited Italy, but they probably did not stay there long enough to have acquired that essential knowledge. Nor can we possibly regard as likely importers of Italian charters men like Felix, Agilbert and Leuthere, who, although they held English sees, were of Frankish origin and whose connexions were either purely Frankish or, in the case of Agilbert, partly Frankish and partly Irish.[78] Our choice therefore lies between two groups of men, Augustine and the other Roman missionaries of the early-seventh century, on the one hand, Theodore and his companion Hadrian, on the other.

If we relied exclusively on Bede's picture of Theodore and Augustine, the former being represented as a learned scholar, an energetic administrator and reformer, and the latter as a simple missionary and preacher, albeit a worthy and successful one, Theodore would be our obvious choice. We should remember, however, that Bede's informant on Canterbury matters was Albinus, Theodore's disciple and Hadrian's successor as abbot of St Peter and St Paul, Canterbury, a man whose

---

[71] See above, note 39. Bede refers to legislative measures taken by Eorcenberht, king of Kent (reigned 640–664), but no code of that king seems to have survived: 'Hic primus [*sc.* Earconberctus] regum Anglorum in toto regno suo idola relinqui ac destrui, simul et ieiunium XL dierum obseruari principali auctoritate praecepit. Quae ne facile a quopiam posset contemni, in transgressores dignas et conpetentes punitiones proposuit' (*Hist. Eccl.* III. viii, ed. Plummer, I, p. 142; see Richardson and Sayles, *op. cit.*, pp. 9–10).

[72] Bede, *Hist. Eccl.* II. viii (ed. Plummer, I, p. 96): 'Susceptis namque apicibus filii nostri Adulualdi regis, repperimus . . .'

[73] *Ibid.* III. xxix (ed. Plummer, I, p. 196): 'Desiderabiles litteras excellentiae uestrae suscepimus . . .'

[74] It was presumably for Oswiu's benefit that the proceedings of the synod of Whitby were conducted in the vernacular: *ibid.* III. xxv (ed. Plummer, I, p. 184).

[75] *Ibid.* II. iv (ed. Plummer, I, p. 88): 'Misit idem Laurentius cum coepiscopis suis etiam Brettonum sacerdotibusi litteras suo gradui condignas . . .'.

[76] *Ibid.* II. viii (ed. Plummer, I, p. 95): '. . . non solum epistulae a uobis directae tenor . . .'.

[77] *Journal of the Society of Archivists*, III, 7 (April 1968), pp. 317–31, reprinted above, pp. 65–81.

[78] Bede, *Hist. Eccl.* III. vii (ed. Plummer, I, p. 140): '. . . Agilberctus, natione quidem Gallus, sed tunc legendarum gratia scripturarum in Hibernia non paruo tempore demoratus'.

knowledge of Theodore was unrivalled but who perhaps was not so reliable and well-informed on the subject of Augustine.[79] We might also ask ourselves whether the Greek-trained Theodore was the most likely person to import Italian charters into England. Theodore's companion, the African-born Hadrian, who had been abbot of an Italian monastery, might be a more plausible choice.[80] But the real point at issue is not so much a question of personalities as one of periods. What we should like to find out is not whether the charter-system was introduced into England by Theodore rather than Hadrian, or Augustine rather than Abbot Peter of St Peter and St Paul, but whether this introduction took place in the first or in the third quarter of the seventh century.

The strongest argument in favour of the later period is, today as always, the undeniable fact that trustworthy charters have survived from the time of Theodore and from that time only. The two earliest Anglo-Saxon charters, extant in the original, date from the pontificate of Theodore (669–690): one is the famous charter of King Hlothhere of Kent for Abbot Brihtwold of Reculver (May 679), the other the charter of Œthelræd for Abbess Æthelburh of Barking in Essex (March 687 ?).[81] The next document to have survived on a single sheet, also probably an original, the charter of King Wihtred of Kent for the abbey of Lyminge (July 697), was issued within seven years of Theodore's death.[82] To these originals should be added a fair number of apparently reliable copies of charters granted to a wide variety of ecclesiastical beneficiaries not only by the kings of Kent, but also by the kings or sub-kings of Mercia, Surrey and Wessex.[83] That within two or three decades, under the influence of the ubiquitous Theodore, the habit of writing charters might have spread not only throughout Kent, but also from Kent to the neighbouring kingdoms need not surprise us unduly. But those years can hardly be said to have been propitious for the rapid dissemination of Italian formulae. By then the English Church was no longer run by monks sent from Rome, as it had been earlier in the century. Foreigners like Archbishop Theodore and Abbot Hadrian were now the exception; apart from them and from Leuthere, the Frankish bishop who held the see of Wessex from 670 to 676, all the leading churchmen in England in the 670s appear to have been of native stock. Therefore it was only through the agency of English bishops and abbots that in those years Italian formulae could have gained ground outside Canterbury. The most that could be expected of English draftsmen uninitiated in the art of composing charters was to copy as diligently as they could the models which had been provided for them, presumably from Canterbury. This should have resulted in diplomatic uniformity throughout the lands where the practice of writing charters was received. Only after some considerable time and experience were the local draftsmen likely to feel confident enough to depart from their models. In fact the charters of Theodore's time are anything but uniform. The only features which they have in common are first the presence in their text of one or more Italian formulae, which testifies to their descent from a common Italian ancestor, secondly the absence (except in one document whose authenticity is not absolutely certain[84]) of any

---

[79] *Ibid.*, Preface (ed. Plummer, I, p. 6): 'Albinus abba . . . qui in ecclesia Cantuariorum a beatae memoriae Theodoro archiepiscopo et Hadriano abbate . . . institutus, diligenter omnia, quae in ipsa Cantuariorum prouincia, uel etiam in contiguis eidem regionibus a discipulis beati papae Gregorii gesta fuere, uel monimentis litterarum, uel seniorum traditione cognouerat; et ea mihi . . . transmisit'.

[80] *Ibid.* IV. i (ed. Plummer, I, p. 202): 'Erat autem in monasterio Niridano [*Moore and Leningrad MSS.* Hiridano], quod est non longe a Neapoli Campaniae, abbas Hadrianus, uir natione Afir, sacris litteris diligenter inbutus, monasterialibus simul et ecclesiasticis disciplinis institutus, Grecae pariter et Latinae linguae peritissimus'.

[81] *B.M.F.* I. 1–2; *Chartae Latinae Antiquiores*, ed. A. Bruckner and R. Marichal [hereafter *Ch.L.A.*], nos. 182, 187; *B.C.S.*, nos. 45, 81. See *Journal of the Society of Archivists*, III, 7 (April 1968), pp. 317–32, reprinted above, pp. 65–83.

[82] *O.S.F.* III, 1; *Ch.L.A.*, no. 220; *B.C.S.*, no. 97.

[83] E.g. *B.C.S.*, nos. 34, 35, 36, 40, 41, 57, 67, 73, ?107, etc.

[84] *B.C.S.*, no. 107. See *Journal of the Society of Archivists*, III, 2 (Oct. 1965), pp. 55–6, reprinted above, pp. 36–7.

mention of the scribe's name, and this differentiates them from the Italian as well as from the Frankish charters. Examined in detail, the Anglo-Saxon charters of the period show appreciable differences, even within a group issued for the same beneficiary. Some have a proem, whereas others have none.[85] Some use the dating formula *Actum in mense . . ., indictione . . .* placed at the end of the text and before the subscriptions,[86] while in others the date occurs immediately or soon after the *intitulatio*, in the form *anno regni nostri . . ., indictione . . ., sub die . . .*[87] Sometimes the dispositive verb is in the present (*concedo*,[88] *concedimus et confirmamus*,[89] *conferimus*,[90] *dono*,[91] *trado et de meo iure in tuo transscribo*,[92] etc.), sometimes in the past (*contuli*,[93] *decreui dare . . . et . . bonum uisum est conferre*,[94] *iudicaui ut . . . impenderem*,[95] *placuit mihi . . . et subieci*,[96] etc.) and occasionally in the future (*dabo*[97]); sometimes a verb in the past tense is used together with another in the present (*donaui et dono*[98]).

It might be argued that differences of this sort are meaningless, since even the charters granted to the abbey of St Peter and St Paul, Canterbury, during Hadrian's abbacy, do not conform to a strict diplomatic pattern. If Hadrian was directly responsible for the introduction and spread of the charter in England, lack of uniformity in charters of his own monastery was bound to lead to diversity elsewhere. But why should the form of the charters for the abbey of St Peter and St Paul have varied in the first place? If we were sure that these variations could be classified into two main groups (e.g. the use of the past tense in the *dispositio* as opposed to the use of the present), each being the result of a distinct diplomatic trend, perhaps one group might be attributed to the influence of the Northumbrian Benedict Biscop, abbot of St Peter and St Paul in 669–70,[99] and the other to the influence of Benedict's successor, Hadrian himself. It might, no less plausibly, be suggested that what we witness in the abbey of St Peter and St Paul and elsewhere, in and outside Kent, is the juxtaposition of two diplomatic traditions, one Kentish and the other Northumbrian, both going back to the first half of the seventh century, both descended from the same Italian prototype but having over the years evolved in slightly different ways. Italian formulae could have reached Kent through Augustine and Northumbria through Paulinus, and it is conceivable that their evolution in the North could have been appreciably affected by Irish influence. Unfortunately the point is beyond testing, since no early Irish or Northumbrian charter has survived in a form diplomatically acceptable. The charter of King Ecgfrith of Northumbria for Bishop Cuthbert is so evidently spurious that any argument based on its phraseology will inevitably be treated with caution;[100] it is nevertheless interesting to find that one unusual formula in Ecgfrith's pretended charter *donavi villam . . . et tria miliaria in circuitu ipsius villæ*, bears a striking resemblance to the phrase *undique fines decernimus . . . ab omni parte per in circuitu miliaria quattuor* which occurs in early charters (none of

---

[85] Compare, for example, *B.M.F.* I. 1 and *B.M.F.* I. 2.

[86] Even the place of this particular dating formula varies slightly from charter to charter; compare *B.M.F.* I. 1–2, *O.S.F.* III. 1.

[87] *B.C.S.*, nos. 35, 36; compare no. 42 (perhaps not authentic *in toto*).

[88] *Ibid.*, no. 35.

[89] *Ibid.*, no. 36.

[90] *B.M.F.* I. 1.

[91] *Ibid.*, *loc. cit.*; *B.C.S.*, no. 57.

[92] *B.M.F.* I. 2; compare *B.C.S.*, no. 34.

[93] *B.C.S.*, no. 73.

[94] *O.S.F.* III. 1.

[95] *B.C.S.*, no. 41.

[96] *Ibid.*, no. 40.

[97] *Ibid.*, no. 85. No. 88 with *dabo et concedo*, which does not occur until the late eighth century, is not authentic.

[98] *Ibid.*, no. 67.

[99] Bede, *Hist. Abb.*, c. 3 (*Hist. Eccl.*, ed. Plummer, I, p. 367).

[100] *B.C.S.*, no. 66.

them genuine *in toto*) for the monastery of San Colombano founded at Bobbio by the Irishman Columbanus.[101] It is difficult to believe that the formula itself was forged or that a Northumbrian forger in quest of a model would have gone as far as Bobbio. The distance from Northumbria to Bobbio also rules out the possibility of a common forger. Perhaps the forger of Ecgfrith's charter accidentally preserved for posterity a genuine formula common to Irish and Northumbrian diplomatic, in the same way as the forged charters of Llandaff testify to the use of the verb *immolare* in the *dispositio* of genuine Welsh charters.[102]

The possibility of Northumbrian influence on southern charters is not so remote as one might think. It is not hard to imagine that the stay of Benedict Biscop in Canterbury and that of Wilfrid in Sussex and Wessex during the pontificate of Theodore might have had an impact on the diplomatic of those regions. Several decades earlier, connexions of a different kind had already been established between Kent and Northumbria. In 625 King Edwin of Northumbria had married Æthelberg, daughter of Æthelberht I of Kent. Following her husband's death at the battle of Hatfield (12 October 633), Æthelberg returned to her native Kent and settled at Lyminge, where, on the land given to her by her brother, King Eadbald, she founded a monastery.[103] Did this monastery become a refuge for other exiles from Northumbria and was its foundation the starting point of a lasting link between Lyminge and the North? At any rate, a charter granted by King Wihtred of Kent to the abbey of Lyminge more than sixty years after its foundation[104] hints at such a connexion. In date (July 697) the charter occupies the third place in the series of extant Anglo-Saxon originals: it was issued eighteen years later than the charter of King Hlothhere for the abbot of Reculver[105] and about ten years later than the charter of Œthelræd for the abbess of Barking.[106] Unlike its predecessors, both in uncials, the Lyminge charter is written in insular majuscule, a script which could not have come to Kent from anywhere else than Northumbria. Although the penmanship of the charter is far from equalling that of its contemporary, the Lindisfarne Gospels, there is no valid reason to think that its scribe was a Kentish pupil of a Northumbrian writing-master rather than a Northumbrian himself. His spelling of Christian names seems to point to a northern rather than a southern origin. Archbishop Brihtwold's name appears in the charter, in the form *Berichtualdus*, and that of the witness Egesbeorht in the form *Egisberichti* (in the genitive), both of which forms are apparently unattested in Kentish texts but have parallels in Northumbrian texts. Although the comparative material is too sparse to allow definite conclusions, it seems that the intrusion of the parasite vowel *i* in the form *bericht-* for *berct-* or *bercht-* is mainly a Northumbrian feature.[107] In Hlothhere's charter of 679 for Reculver, the scribe, presumably Kentish, gives Brihtwold's name as *Bercuald*. It is also worth noting that the scribe who, perhaps in the late eighth century, made an interpolated copy of the Lyminge charter adopted the spellings *Berhtuualdus* and *Egisberhti* instead of the forms *Berichtualdus* and *Egisberichti* of the original which he was imitating.[108]

The name of the land granted by Wihtred in the Lyminge charter has been the subject of much speculation. The scribe wrote it in the form *Pleghelmestun*. Perhaps in the first half of the

---

[101] *Codice diplomatico del monastero di San Colombano*, ed. C. Cipolla, nos. 3, 7, 9. Compare *B.C.S.*, no. 34: 'Omnia igitur in circuitu . . . pertinencia . . .'. The limits of the *sanctuarium* given by Athelstan to the church of Ripon are also supposed to have been *hinc inde ad unum milliare extra oppidum* (Dugdale, *Mon. Angl.*, II (1846), p. 132).

[102] *The Text of the Book of Llan Dâv*, ed. J. G. Evans (Oxford, 1893), pp. 76, 121, 159, 166, etc. Compare Asser, *Life of Alfred*, ed. W. H. Stevenson (Oxford, 1959), p. 9, lines 5–6: 'uni et trino Deo immolavit'.

[103] *Die Heiligen Englands*, ed. F. Liebermann (Hannover, 1889), p. 2; Bede, *Hist. Eccl.* II. xx (ed. Plummer, I, p. 125).

[104] *O.S.F.* III. 1; *Ch.L.A.*, no. 220; *B.C.S.*, no. 97.

[105] *B.M.F.* I. 1; *Ch.L.A.*, no. 182; *B.C.S.*, no. 45.

[106] *B.M.F.* I. 2; *Ch.L.A.*, no. 187; *B.C.S.*, no. 81.

[107] See A. Campbell, *Old English Grammar* (Oxford, 1959), para 360.

[108] *B.M.F.* I. 4; *Ch.L.A.*, no. 189; *B.C.S.*, no. 98.

eleventh century another scribe, probably a scribe of Christ Church, Canterbury,[109] altered the first two letters of the name: he changed *P* into a wynn and *l* into *i*, thus making the name *Wieghelmestun*; the same scribe explained in a dorsal note that the land granted was known in his own time (*nunc*) as *Wigelmignctun*. It has been explained that the amended form is the real one and that the original scribe was guilty of mistranscription, having in particular mistaken the initial wynn for *P*. This explanation presupposes that as early as the seventh century the runic wynn was already commonly used in written documents, as it was in carved inscriptions. In fact the evidence points in the opposite direction. The eth, thorn and wynn do not seem to have crept into the writing of charters until the latter part of the eighth century.[110] The scribe of Hlothhere's charter for Reculver and the scribe of the authentic part of Œthelræd's charter for Barking represent the sounds of the wynn and eth (or thorn) by the symbols *u* or *uu* and *d*.[111] For the same sounds the scribe of the Lyminge charter uses *u* and *d* (e.g. *meguines paed; bereueg*). If he was making his engrossment from a draft, it is likely that the draft also used *u* and *d* for those sounds. It follows that, if the name of the land granted was really derived from the personal name *Wighelm*, it would have been written *uighelmestun* in the draft, a form which even the most careless copyist could not possibly have confused with *pleghelmestun*. The scribe who a century or so later was responsible for the interpolated copy of the charter did not question the reading *Pleghelmestun* of the original. He incorporated it in his own text, thus showing that he presumably knew the place under that name. It may also be worth noting that this later scribe, unlike the scribe of the original charter, used a half-uncial *d* with a crossed ascender in the word *paed*.[112] How the place granted in the charter came to be known as *Wigelmignctun* in the eleventh century, or how it came, rightly or wrongly, to be identified as such by the Christ Church scribe who endorsed the original is a mystery. The name Pleghelm, from which *Pleghelmestun* is derived, is–unlike Wighelm–an uncommon one. Only four persons with the name Plechelm or Pleghelm are listed in Sweet's *Oldest English Texts* and in Searle's *Onomasticon*: the Irish saint Plechelm, who evangelized Guelderland in the late-seventh century, a clerk and a monk whose names are entered in the *Liber Vitae* of Durham, and a monk of Beverley,[113] all connected with either Ireland or Northumbria. Was the Pleghelm who gave his name to *Pleghelmestun* also of Northumbrian origin? This is, of course, a question which cannot be answered. The same could be said about the Mægwine whose name is at the origin of one of the boundaries in the charter, *meguines paed*; two clerks called *Meguini* occur in the *Liber Vitae* of Durham.[114]

Although, as I have remarked earlier, the charter is written in insular majuscule, the original scribe added, at the end of the text, two words in a neat minuscule script.[115] The two words, *uirum uenerabilem*, which are applied to Archbishop Brihtwold, had apparently been omitted through inadvertence, and it seems that they were inserted in a different and smaller script simply for shortage of space. The fact is worth noting because it shows that, whatever induced the scribe to write the charter in insular majuscule, it was not his ignorance of any other kind of script. He could also

---

[109] Lyminge was at the time a possession of Christ Church. For the theories on the name *Pleghelmestun*, see J. K. Wallenberg, *Kentish Place-names* (Uppsala, 1931), p. 26.

[110] See above, note 58.

[111] See *Journal of the Society of Archivists*, III, 7 (April 1968), p. 331, reprinted above, p. 82.

[112] I do not think that the uncial *d* in the original (*O.S.F.* III. 1; *Ch.L.A.*, no. 220) was ever crossed. For the same reason as Miss Parsons I believe that the added passage in *B.M.F.* I. 4 (*Ch.L.A.*, no. 189) is an interpolation; compare *B.C.S.*, nos. 148 (?doubtful), 190, 195, 199. See the editor's note in *Ch.L.A.*, no. 220.

[113] *The Oldest English Texts*, ed. H. Sweet (E.E.T.S.; Orig. Series No. 83), p. 520; W. G. Searle, *Onomasticon Anglo-Saxonicum* (Cambridge Univ. Press, 1897), p. 389.

[114] *Liber Vitae Ecclesiae Dunelmensis* (Facsimile), Surtees Soc. CXXXVI (1923), fos. 25v, 26r.

[115] I agree with the editors of *Ch.L.A.* that these two words appear to be by the same hand as the rest of the charter.

write a handsome minuscule. In several places he used the minuscule form of *a* at the end of a word.[116] In eight of the subscriptions the final *s* of the word *manus* assumes the half-uncial form. The scribe could also write uncials, since he uses the uncial form frequently for *R*, and less frequently for *G* (in an initial and medial position) and final *M*.

Diplomatically, the Lyminge charter has many features in common with the charter of Hlothhere for Reculver. The differences between them, some of which may be significant, only concern points of detail. The Lyminge charter begins with a pictorial invocation in the shape of a cross, followed by a verbal invocation, *In nomine d(omi)ni d(e)i nostri ie(s)u cr(ist)i*, which differs from the verbal invocation of Hlothhere's charter only in the order of the words and in the replacement of *saluatoris* by *dei*. There is no proem, the invocation being followed at once by the *dispositio*:

Ego Uihtredus rex Cantuariorum prouidens mihi in futuro decreui dare aliquid omnia mihi donanti et consilio accepto bonum uisum est conferre bassilicae beatae Mariae genitricis d(e)i quae sita est in loco qui dicitur Limingae terram iiii aratrorum quae dicitur Pleghelmestun cum omnibus ad eandem terram pertinentibus iuxta notissimos terminos id est Bereueg et Meguines paed et Stretleg.

Whereas in the Reculver charter Hlothhere says that he is making his grant for the salvation of his soul (*pro remedium animae meae*), Wihtred is more explicit: his motives are the consideration of his future (presumably in the next world) and his gratitude for God's gifts to him. The same idea is expressed in slightly different terms in other Kentish charters of the period, for example in charters of King Oswini and King Suaebhard of Kent for Abbess Æbba of Minster in Thanet (*ne ingratus beneficiis domini viderer;*[117] *miserationum domini memor quas erga me exercuit*[118]) and in a charter of Wihtred for Abbot Hadrian of St Peter and St Paul, Canterbury (*Beneficiis Dei et domini nostri Jhesu Christi nobis collatis non immemores*).[119] Wihtred makes his grant impersonally to the church of Lyminge, whereas the dispositive words placed in Hlothhere's mouth are addressed to Brihtwold, abbot of Reculver, in the second person (*tibi Bercuald*). Wihtred says that he is making his grant after taking the advice of others (*consilio accepto*), while Hlothhere refers, not to the advice, but to the consent of Archbishop Theodore, of Eadric and of all the other magnates (*cum consensu . . .*).[120] In both charters the land is granted as limited by its well-known boundaries (*iuxta notissimos terminos*), but it is only in the Lyminge charter that these boundaries are specifically given, although briefly. Another difference concerns the tense of the dispositive verbs: Hlothhere uses the present (*dono*) and Wihtred the past tense (*decreui dare . . . et . . . bonum uisum est conferre*).[121] A century later the use of the past had become a characteristic feature of the Wessex charters; in Canterbury the formula *dabo et concedo* was then preferred.

After the *dispositio* comes the *sanctio*, made up of two parts: first the king's undertaking that neither he, Wihtred, nor his heirs will infringe the terms of the grant (*quam donationem mea(m) uolo firmam esse in perpetuum ut nec ego seu heredes mei aliquid minuere praesumant*); secondly the threat of anathema against anyone who will dare to violate the grant (*quod si aliter temptatum fuerit a qualibet persona sub anathematis interdictione sciat se praeuaricari*). There is also a dual *sanctio* in the charter of Hlothhere, but the wording, although to the same effect, is very different.

The *corroboratio* which follows is introduced by the words *ad cuius confirmationem*, a close parallel to the phrase used in Hlothhere's charter, *et pro confirmatione eius*. Wihtred explains that,

---

[116] Some forms of the minuscule *a* in the main part of the charter are very similar to the *a* of *uenerabilem*, one of the two words added at the end of the text.

[117] *B.C.S.*, no. 40.

[118] *Ibid.*, no. 41.

[119] *Ibid.*, no. 90.

[120] *B.M.F.* I. I. See *B.C.S.*, no. 36: 'cum consilio . . . atque consensu . . .'

[121] *B.M.F.* I. I; *O.S.F.* III. I.

as he is illiterate, he has made the sign of the cross and asked suitable witnesses to subscribe, one of them being Archbishop Brihtwold of Canterbury:

ad cuius confirmationem pro ignorantia litterarum signu(m) s(an)c(t)ae crucis expressi et testes idoneos ut subscriberent rogaui id est Berichtualdum archiepiscopu(m) uiru(m) uenerabile(m).

Here the main difference with the charter of Hlothhere is that in the latter the king leaves out the reference to his illiteracy and claims that his cross was made *manu propria*; also, it is only in the Lyminge charter that the witnesses are described as *idoneos*.

The signs of validation consist of fourteen subscriptions, the first one, that of Archbishop Brihtwold, in the form reserved for literate persons (*Ego Berichtualdus episc(opus) rogatus consensi et subscribsi*[122]); the other thirteen subscriptions, among them those of the king as grantor and of his wife Æthelburh, are in the form *Signum manus* followed by the name of the alleged author of the cross. Each subscription is preceded by a non-autograph cross; there are two additional and unnecessary crosses, also non-autograph, one after the archbishop's subscription and the other in the *corroboratio*, between the words *litterarum* and *signum*. The scribe of the charter wrote all the subscriptions, including that of the archbishop, and drew all the crosses.

The last element in the Lyminge charter, the dating clause (*Actum in mense iulio, indictione x^{ma}*), is in the same form as that of Hlothhere's charter, but in the latter the place of issue (*in ciuitate Recuulf*) is added after the word *Actum*.

Studied in their various aspects, the three earliest Anglo-Saxon originals (respectively for Reculver, Barking and Lyminge) show a close relationship with one another and with other charters which have survived in trustworthy copies;[123] but their individual peculiarities are numerous enough, and in my view significant enough, to make us doubt whether they can all be fathered on the one or two Italian-trained ecclesiastics of Theodore's time. I firmly believe that, if the introduction of charters into England had been Theodore's work, the name of the scribe responsible for the writing of each document would have been duly recorded in its text, in the same way as the acts of the council of Hertford name the scribe who wrote them down at Theodore's bidding, the 'notary' Titillus;[124] the subscriptions of literate witnesses, such as that of Archbishop Brihtwold in the Lyminge charter, and the crosses prefixed to the subscriptions of illiterates would also have been autograph. One of the peculiar features of the Anglo-Saxon charter, its anonymity, suggests that there was an intermediate stage, which may have extended over a long period, between the first introduction into England of the Italian habit of recording land-grants in writing and the appearance of such single-sheet originals as the extant charters for Reculver, Barking and Lyminge. The intermediate stage may have consisted of recording the grants of land on blank leaves of a gospel-book belonging to the beneficiary. This would provide a plausible explanation both for the anonymity of the writing and for the absence of autograph features in the subscriptions.[125] When the recording in a gospel-book gave way to the drawing up of originals on single sheets, at a date which cannot be determined, the anonymity and non-autography remained. The fact that the earliest extant originals are written in a script used for gospel-books, either in uncials or, in the case of the Lyminge charter,

---

[122] Compare *Liber Diurnus Romanorum Pontificum*, ed. H. Foerster (Berne, 1958), p. 182 (Vat. 2): 'Ill. . . . consensi et subscripsi'; pp. 210-11 (Vat. 58): 'Ego . . . consentiens subscripsi'.

[123] Compare the formulae in *B.M.F.* I. 1-2, *O.S.F.* III. 1, with those in the documents mentioned above in note 83.

[124] See *Journal of the Society of Archivists*, III, 2 (Oct. 1965), pp. 49-50; *ibid.*, III, 7 (April 1968), p. 335, reprinted above, pp. 30-1 and 87.

[125] It may be worth adding, with the customary caution, that the earliest Anglo-Saxon original charters are written on vellum, like the early books written in England, while parchment was used on the Continent.

in insular majuscule, at a time when a minuscule script was known to English scribes,[126] is another indication that charters on single sheets may have been preceded by entries in gospel-books.[127] This, however, must remain a hypothesis, since only one gospel-book appears to have survived for the period preceding Theodore's arrival in England, namely the Gospels of St Augustine (Corpus Christi College, Cambridge, MS. 286) to which I have already referred.[128] Some records are indeed copied in this manuscript, but none earlier in date than the ninth century and none actually written in it before the tenth century.[129] It is unfortunate that the beginning of the gospel-book (at least twenty-two leaves) should be missing, as it is there, if anywhere, that one might have expected the early charters for the abbey of St Peter and St Paul to be copied.[130]

If it was not Theodore who brought to England the idea of keeping a written record of grants of land, who was it? It has already been suggested that it could only have been Augustine and his fellow-missionaries of the early seventh century. Since Augustine and those of his colleagues whose names are known to us (Honorius, Justus, Laurentius, Mellitus and Abbot Peter of St Peter and St Paul, Canterbury) were selected by Gregory I from the community of his abbey of Sant' Andrea al Clivo di Scauro,[131] the suggestion might appear less incredible if we found a connexion of some kind between the charters of Sant' Andrea and those of early Anglo-Saxon England. Such a connexion can in fact be established between one of the few early charters extant for Sant' Andrea, the famous grant made to the abbey in 587 by its founder, Gregory I, before he became pope,[132] and three Anglo-Saxon charters of the seventh century: one of these three charters is the original of Œthelræd's grant for Barking Abbey,[133] the second a copy of a grant of Frithuwold, sub-king of Surrey, for Chertsey Abbey,[134] and the third a copy of a grant made by King Ceadwalla of Wessex for the foundation of a monastery at Farnham in Surrey.[135] Not only the proem of the three English charters, but also the dispositive words of two of them are close adaptations of the corresponding parts of Gregory's charter.[136] These similarities are intriguing, to say the least. If it is true that the formulae originally came to England from Sant' Andrea, only Augustine and his colleagues could have brought them here. It may be objected that Wilfrid,[137] and perhaps other English ecclesiastics, visited Sant' Andrea in the late seventh century, but one can hardly imagine them searching through the archives of the monastery for some Gregorian formulae which they could use in their own charters. On the other hand, the Roman missionaries were likely, once in England, to use the formulae which they remembered, and those could only be the formulae which had been current in their former monastery in their own time.

We shall probably never find an incontrovertible proof that grants of land in England were written down as early as Augustine's time. Not once in the whole of his *Ecclesiastical History* does Bede mention charters as such either before or after 669. In his letter to Egbert he complains that

---

[126] Professor T. J. Brown has collected a great deal of evidence showing that minuscule was used in Northumbria from the middle of the seventh century onwards.

[127] See my comments in *Journal of the Society of Archivists*, III, 2 (Oct. 1965), pp. 53–4, reprinted above, pp. 33–4.

[128] See above, note 39.

[129] N. R. Ker, *Catalogue of MSS. containing Anglo-Saxon*, no. 55.

[130] F. Wormald, *The Miniatures in the Gospels of St Augustine*, pp. 4–5, 17.

[131] See above, note 33.

[132] *M.G.H., Epistolae*, II, pp. 437 ff.

[133] *B.M.F.* I. 2; *Ch.L.A.*, no. 187.

[134] *B.C.S.*, no. 34.

[135] *Ibid.*, no. 72.

[136] See also *Journal of the Society of Archivists*, III, 7 (April 1968), pp. 328–9, reprinted above, pp. 78–80.

[137] Eddius Stephanus, *Vita Wilfridi* (Historians of the Church of York, ed. J. Raine, R.S., vol. I), p. 8: 'et in oratorio Sancto Andreae Apostolo dedicato . . . genuflectens, adjuravit . . .'; (ed. B. Colgrave, p. 12).

in his own day laymen were using charters as a device for creating fraudulent monasteries, a practice which had begun some thirty years before, following the death of King Aldfrith of Northumbria (A.D. 704).[138] From this we can only infer that by 704 charters were in common use in Northumbria. Elsewhere in the works of Bede and in other narrative sources we find references to grants of land to the Church, but nowhere—except perhaps in one passage of Eddi's *Life of Bishop Wilfrid*[139]—can we find a clear hint that these grants were recorded in writing. When Bede, Eddi and the anonymous author of the *Historia Abbatum* say that a king gave land to an ecclesiastic for the foundation of a monastery (*ad construendum monasterium*[140]) and that he did so for the salvation of his own soul (*pro redemptione animae suae*[141] or *pro animae suae remedio*[142]), phrases which recur in countless Anglo-Saxon charters, they may have been quoting from actual documents, but this is not certain. Even when they give the extent of the land granted (e.g. *terram L familiarum*[143] or *terra triginta mansionum*[144]), this information may have been based either on oral tradition or on charters, although the latter alternative seems more likely.

If no conclusive proof can be found, we must be content with probabilities. Because the charter was a guarantee against forgetfulness and treachery, it protected both grantor and grantee. With the coming of Christianity to England a new type of land tenure was brought into being, a tenure *jure ecclesiastico*. The land was granted in perpetuity, it was to be held *tantum in Domino*,[145] in the service of God only, apparently with complete freedom from all secular burdens, at least until the first half of the eighth century. It was because this preferential treatment given to church lands was so advantageous that laymen tried in due course to convert their own lands into fraudulent monasteries. Augustine and his colleagues may have agreed with Gregory I that oral grants to the Church were perfectly valid in law, but they must have felt, as he did, that it was a wise precaution to record them in writing.[146] Even if Æthelberht I of Kent did not believe in the necessity of charters, there is no reason to suppose that he objected to them.

PIERRE CHAPLAIS

---

[138] Bede, *Hist. Eccl.*, ed. Plummer, I, pp. 416–17.

[139] *Journal of the Society of Archivists*, III, 2 (Oct. 1965), p. 52, reprinted above, p. 32.

[140] Bede, *Hist. Eccl.* IV. iii (ed. Plummer, I, p. 207): '. . . cui etiam rex Uulfheri donauit terram L familiarum ad construendum monasterium in loco, qui dicitur . . .'; *Two Lives of St. Cuthbert*, ed. B. Colgrave (Cambridge Univ. Press, 1940), p. 174. See also *Two of the Saxon Chronicles Parallel*, ed. C. Plummer, I (Oxford, 1892), p. 34: '669. Her Ecgbryht cyning salde Basse mæsse prioste Reculf mynster on to timbranne'.

[141] *Two Lives of St Cuthbert*, ed. Colgrave, p. 174; *Hist Abb. Anon.*, c. 11 (Bede, *Hist. Eccl.*, ed. Plummer, I, p. 391).

[142] Eddius Stephanus, *The Life of Bishop Wilfrid*, ed. B. Colgrave (Cambridge Univ. Press, 1927), p. 16.

[143] Bede, *Hist. Eccl.* IV. iii (ed. Plummer, I, p. 207; see also pp. 232, 237, etc.).

[144] *The Life of Bishop Wilfrid*, ed. Colgrave, p. 16; also 'terram decem tributariorum' (*ibid., loc. cit.*).

[145] *B.C.S.*, nos. 35, 42 (perhaps not authentic *in toto*), 293, etc. In no. 293 (an original) the reading is plainly 'in domino', and one cannot agree with Mr E. John's emendation to 'tantum in domin[i]o' (E. John, *Land Tenure in Early England* (Leicester Univ. Press, 1960), p. 4, n. 1; pp. 5, 48). The phrase 'tantum in Domino' is the equivalent of 'soli domino serviens' (*B.C.S.*, no. 275), 'tantum ut Deo . . . sit subiecta' (*ibid.*, no. 239), 'tantum ut Deo omnipotenti . . . æcclesiasticæ servitutis famulatum inpendat' (*ibid.*, no. 165).

[146] *Reg. Greg. I*, XIII. 5 (*M.G.H., Epist.* II, p. 370): '. . . et domos . . . verbo largitus es ipsaque donatio, licet possit iure subsistere, . . . ne quid futurum tempus oblivionis nubilo huic derogare quicquam valeat largitati, scripturae hoc desideras tradere monumentis . . .' (Sept. 602).

A Russian Royal Letter
of 1682

On 3 November 1682 Mr Nathaniel Symonds, Bailiff of Great Yarmouth, wrote to the Secretary of State, Sir Leoline Jenkins, announcing the arrival by packet boat from the Hague of a picturesque, if forlorn, figure.[1] The newcomer bore an impossible name, which sounded to the Bailiff's ear like 'Demetrius Seminitzky', and he claimed the impressive title of 'Secretary of State and Councillor to the high and Mighty Princes yᵉ Emperours of Russia'. He was also suffering badly from the rigours of the sea-passage and on being informed of the hasty arrangements put in hand for the completion of his journey to London by sea 'he was soe much concerned by reason of his great sicknesse and indisposition at sea and vomiting blood as he plainly declared he dar'd not adventure, being well assured he should not survive the voyage'. Nevertheless this Russian envoy, whose name was properly Dmitrii Simonovsky, impressed the Yarmouth authorities so forcibly with the importance of his mission and with his impatience to reach the capital that on 8 November they despatched him to London by coach, accompanied by a suitable retinue.

Simonovsky was not exaggerating. For he was the bearer of a letter addressed to King Charles II which contained momentous news. On 27 April the Tsar Feodor Alexeivich had died and after several weeks of intrigue and bloodshed the throne of Russia was now occupied jointly by two small boys. One of these boys, Ivan Alexeivich, half-blind, defective in speech and cretinous, would die obscurely in 1696. His ten year old half-brother Pyotr Alexeivich would achieve European and historical renown as Peter the Great, Emperor of All Russia, Father of the Fatherland.

This letter to Charles II is now preserved in the Public Record Office.[2] In calligraphy, decoration and diplomatic it is a remarkable document, the last of its kind to find its way into the collections of the former State Paper Office, a product of an administrative system which Peter was destined first to reform and, ultimately, to abolish. As one of the last documentary relics of pre-Petrine Russia preserved in English archives it is worthy of consideration not only for its intrinsic qualities but also as a reflection of the administrative machinery which produced it.

At the death of the Tsar Feodor Alexeivich the central administrative apparatus of the Muscovite state consisted of some forty *Prikazi* or Administrative Offices, each concerned with a particular aspect of government or with a particular province of the empire.[3] The date at which they

---

[1] Symonds to Secretary Jenkins, P.R.O., S.P.29/421, no. 61, 68.

[2] State Papers Foreign, Royal Letters, Russia, S.P.102/49, no. 47.

[3] The primary original source for the organization of the central administration is the treatise entitled *O Rossii v Tsarstvovaniye Alexeiya Mikhailovicha* (published, St Petersburg, 1884) by Grigory Kotoshikhin, a clerk in the Ambassadors' Office under Tsar Alexei Mikhailovich (1645–76). Kotoshikhin wrote this bitterly critical description of Russia whilst in exile in Sweden, where he fled to escape the hostility of his numerous and powerful enemies in Moscow. Useful information on the *Prikazi* can be found in L. V. Cherepnin, *Russkaya Paleografiya*, Moscow ,1956, and in *Ocherki po Istorii Arkhivnogo Dela v S.S.S.R.*, ed. I. L. Mayakovsky, Moscow, 1960.

were established cannot be fixed with any certainty but their origins are usually traced to the House-hold Administrations of feudal Russia, expanded and adapted to meet the needs of a growing and centralized autocracy. Each Office, or group of Offices, was nominally under the control of a *Boyarin*, or nobleman, and they appear to have developed upon the fairly standard pattern of a chancellery division, a separate financial administration and an archives department; each Office exercising, for the most part, judicial jurisdiction over its own personnel. Their functions were of a purely administrative nature, drafting and copying reports, despatches, legal schedules etc., and in general performing the secretarial work necessary for putting into effect the decrees of the Tsars and the orders of the Tsar's advisory, and to some degree executive, agency the *Boyarskaya Duma* or Council of Boyars. The number of Offices varied with a series of frequent and not altogether logical amalga-mations and subdivisions,[4] but throughout these changes the diplomatic correspondence of the state remained centred in the *Posolskiy Prikaz*, the Ambassadors' Office, in whose chancellery were prepared the letters, *Gramoti*, addressed to foreign sovereigns, the credentials and instructions of Russian representatives abroad and the general documentation necessary for the conduct of the Tsar's foreign relations.[5]

In the sixteenth century, when the diplomatic relations of Muscovy were limited to a small number of foreign states, the Ambassadors' Office had been of minor importance. Not until the reign of the first Romanov Tsar, Mikhail Feodorovich (1613–45), did it emerge as a government department of the first rank and not until the appointment of the enlightened and accomplished A. L. Ordin-Nashchokin as its director in 1667 did the empire possess anything which might colour-ably be described as a Minister for Foreign Affairs. Under Nashchokin the Ambassadors' Office at last began to organize an intelligence service for accumulating information about the countries with which it was dealing, a subject hitherto regarded with indifference or disdain, and so to prepare the foundations for a consistent and intelligent foreign policy. Nashchokin also seems to have been responsible for a noticeable increase in the number of foreigners employed as diplomats by Tsar Alexei Mikhailovich (1645–76) in preference to the incompetent and fantastically uncouth Russian nobles who had long excited the contempt of the Western European courts to which they were accredited. He was succeeded as head of the Ambassadors' Office in 1671 by Artemon Matvieyev, whose adopted daughter, Natalya Narishkina, became the mother of Peter the Great in 1672, and under Matvieyev the painful momentum of reform continued until his dismissal, on a charge of sorcery, at the accession of Tsar Feodor Alexeivich in 1676.

Despite these early attempts to 'westernize' the creaking administrative organization and procedure, the internal structure of the Ambassadors' Office remained substantially unchanged. The chancelleries of most of the *Prikazi* were divided into Departments (*Stoli*) which, in turn, were sub-divided into Sections (*Povitiya*), but that of the Ambassadors' Office, in common with certain

---

[4] For example between 1661 and 1663 the Siberian Office, detached from the Kazan Office in 1637, was temporarily merged with the Main Revenue Office. Similarly the different Judicial Offices exercising jurisdiction over the districts of Moscow, Ryazan, Vladimir and Dmitrov were integrated into the Moscow Judicial Office during Peter's minority in 1685. By contrast, the responsibility for military affairs was divided during the sixteen eighties between no less than eighteen different Offices. Peter himself carried out some reorganization; his most notable innovation, from the point of view of subsequent developments, being the establishment of the Secret Office of Pre-obrazhenskoe, exercising supervision over his new Preobrazhensky Guards regiment and, in particular, over the police duties which it took over from the disbanded Streltsi. In October 1702 the Office was formally granted jurisdiction in matters of treason and one of its departments controlled the earliest identifiable secret police organization in Russia. As such it was the direct precursor of the Tsarist *Okhrana* and the Soviet Cheka, G.P.U., N.K.V.D. and M.V.D.

[5] In the preparations for sending embassies abroad, the Ambassadors' Office collaborated closely with the Tsar's Private Office, which normally provided the secretaries sent with the ambassadors, not only to look after their papers and correspondence but also to watch and report upon their conduct and ensure that they did not depart from their instructions.

others, appears to have been divided by Sections only, each responsible for the conduct of relations with a group of foreign states. Three of the Sections were concerned with western Europe. Of these, the first handled relations with the Papacy, Spain,[6] the Reich, France and England; the second dealt with Poland, Sweden, the Porte, Moldavia, Holland and the Imperial Free Cities; and the third with Denmark, Courland and Brandenburg. Two Sections were concerned with Asiatic powers, Armenia, Georgia, Persia, Kalmyk, Bokhara and China. Besides purely secretarial duties, the Ambassadors' Office also had custody of two of the state Seals; the Great State Seal (*Bolshaya Gosudarstvennaya Pechat*), affixed to letters addressed abroad, and the more private seal used for correspondence with the ancient hereditary provinces of the empire and for letters to the Crimean Khans and the princes of Kalmyk. The various Sections of the Office maintained registers (*Knigi*) containing the texts of their correspondence which, in the case of English correspondence, frequently serve to provide the texts and Russian translations of documents no longer extant in the original.

The staffs of the *Prikazi* were of two basic grades. The Clerks (*Podyachi*) actually wrote the documents and, in many cases, prepared the initial drafts for submission to their seniors. Clerks were ranked as 'Middle' (*Sryedniye*) and 'Junior' (*Molodiye*) according to their qualifications and service. Above the Clerks were the Senior Clerks or Secretaries (*Diyaki*) who performed supervisory duties and countersigned the completed documents in accordance with established procedure. At the top of the secretarial hierarchy were a group of special Council Clerks (*Dumniye Diyaki*), never more than four in number, who attended sessions of the *Boyarskaya Duma* and transmitted its orders to their subordinates in the appropriate Offices for the necessary administrative action. Of these four Council Clerks, the most important in function (though not, apparently, in official status) was the *Posolskiy Dumny Diyak*, who presided not only over the Ambassadors' Office but also over the Seal Office (*Pechatny Prikaz*) and the Novgorod District Office (*Prikaz Novogorodskoy Chetverti*) acting as their link with the Tsar's Council.[7] Despite the pressure of its work, the Ambassadors' Office appears to have functioned with a relatively small secretarial establishment averaging two or three Secretaries and some fifteen Clerks. On the other hand its specialized staff of linguists was surprisingly large, numbering some fifty interpreters (*tolmachiki*) and translators (*perevodchiki*) skilled in Latin, Swedish, German, English, Greek, Polish, Tartar and other languages. Mostly foreigners, these experts enjoyed the relatively generous pay-scales of 100–50 roubles a year for interpreters and 40–15 roubles a year for translators.

The despatch of business was performed in accordance with a rigid procedure described in outline by Grigory Kotoshikhin, a clerk in the Ambassadors' Office under Tsar Alexei Mikhailovich (1645–76). 'When there is occasion to write letters to foreign states, directions are given to the *Posolskiy Dumny Diyak* and he gives directions to the Clerks (i.e. the *Podyachi*). He does not himself prepare the letters but merely corrects them, inserting or deleting passages as necessary. And when the letters are ready they are first presented to the *Boyarskaya Duma* and then to the Tsar in Council. All documents are ratified and dated by the Council Secretaries. The Tsar and the Council never set their signatures to any documents. This is the duty of the Council Secretaries. Documents of secondary importance are signed by the ordinary Secretaries (i.e. the *Diyaki*) and the Clerks (*Podyachi*) set their own names at the bottom'.[8] Kotoshikhin was speaking of the later seventeenth century but the system had not changed since the German *oprichnik*[9] Heinrich von Staden described

---

[6] Correspondence with the Courts of Spain, France and Portugal was very limited.

[7] The other Council Clerks were normally those attached to the *Razryadny Prikaz*, the Kazan Office (*Prikaz Kazanskogo Dvortsa*) and the Estates Office (*Pomyestny Prikaz*).

[8] G. Kotoshikhin *O Rossii v Tsarstvovaniye Alexeiya Mikhailovicha*, St Petersburg, 1884.

[9] A title applied to the personnel of the *Oprichnina*, or Reserved Lands, which, in 1565, Ivan IV brought under his direct personal control. They had their own Household, police, financial and administrative authorities, quite separate from the rest of the country, the *Zyemshchina*, where normal methods of administration continued. The *Oprichnina* ceased to bear this distinctive name in 1572.

the workings of the Moscow *Prikazi* under Ivan the Terrible nearly a hundred years before. 'The Clerks wrote out the letters in fair copy. The Secretary then took the document in his left hand and under the date wrote his own name in small characters. On the back of the document the Secretary then himself inscribed the titles of the Grand Duke in large characters'.[10] As in all administrations, great importance was attached to the correct procedure for signing documents, but the rules which Kotoshikhin and von Staden describe did not, apparently, apply to the *Gramoti* addressed to the Kings of England. After a copy of their texts had been entered in the 'English Registers' (*Angliskye Knigi*) these letters were folded and sent out with the State Seal as their only authentication as direct communications between the two sovereigns. The dating clauses are, however, often in hands markedly different from those in the body of the text, and were presumably written in by the Council Secretary in the regulation manner.

The regulations extended, as Kotoshikhin explains, not only to the writing of the documents but also to the type of paper employed and the quantity of gold decoration with which they were embellished. These varied in accordance with the rank and dignity of the recipients. To the Kaiser of the Holy Roman Empire 'The letters are written on the largest Alexandrian paper, with full floral decoration in gold. To the Kings of Sweden, Poland, England and Denmark, the letters are written on small or medium Alexandrian paper, according to the length of the letter; the gold decoration is of moderate extent. To the Electors of the Empire letters are written on small Alexandrian paper, with a floral heading in gold but with no decoration in the margins.' Characteristically the Russian government reserved its most resplendent creations for impressing the Infidel. Letters to the Sultan of the Ottoman Empire 'are written on the largest Alexandrian paper. Floral decorations extend from the top down to the middle of the paper, with decorations down the edges to the bottom and also at the foot. And at the top, amid the decorations, the Imperial titles and those of the Sultan are written all in gold; the message begins from the middle of the page.'[11]

Illumination was, of course, an important prestige ingredient in the Tsars' foreign correspondence, and for its execution the Ambassadors' Office employed the services of artists drawn from the master craftsmen of the *Oruzhenaya Palata*, the state Palace of Arms. Within the Palace of Arms were located the workshops not only of the master gunsmiths but also those of craftsmen employed in the manufacture of clothing, household utensils, ornaments and a host of other objects requiring skilled workmanship. By the middle of the seventeenth century it had become something of a repository for works of art and had attracted to its precincts some of the leading artists and illuminators of Russia. These were, in particular, the *Iconopistsi*, artists employed not only in the painting of icons but also in portraiture and the decoration of books and manuscripts. Division of labour, carried to a high degree, produced skilled specialized groups, notably the *Znamyenshchiki*, producing general artistic compositions, and the *Zolotopistsi*, the expert illuminators in gold. In the later seventeenth century the gold illuminators employed by the Ambassadors' Office, especially K. A. Zolotaryev and Grigory Blagushin, had attained great skill in document decoration, using styles which, though influenced by both western and oriental art, contrived to remain distinctively Russian.

As the influence of the Renaissance slowly permeated Eastern Europe in the course of the sixteenth century, the Russian artists had gradually abandoned the teratological style of ornamentation in favour of subjects drawn from nature. The result was the distinctive skein patterns of flowers, herbs and foliage traced upon the tops and margins of documents in the style known as *Fryazhsky*, a somewhat inappropriate adjective meaning 'French' or, in a general sense, 'foreign'. The pattern was irregular and customarily drawn in outline only. By the later seventeenth century this style was in turn giving way to another essentially native style, that of Russian Baroque, in

---

[10] H. von Staden, *O Moskvye Ivana Groznogo*, Leningrad, 1925, p. 83.
[11] The letters written to the Mogul Emperors were decorated in a similar style.

which the designs of flowers, foliage etc. were constructed with geometrical precision and thrown into relief by means of line shading and, occasionally, dark colouring. By the end of the century exponents of Russian Baroque had reached a high pitch of excellence using not only gold but also vermilion, black and white, later varied and reinforced with shades of yellow, red and green. Official correspondence remained, however, largely in the hands of the *Zolotopistsi*, and the ornamentation was executed almost exclusively in gold; only rarely relieved by the barest minimum of dark coloured shading. Decoration using gold leaf was exceptional and the artists employed by the Ambassadors' Office preferred the rather simpler method of gilding using a preparation of powdered gold suspended in gum arabic, or a similar adhesive, and applied with a pen for script and line work and with a fine brush for gilding surfaces. When lightly burnished the effect was impressive, though lacking the brilliance of illumination using gold leaf. Miniatures too were very rare on Russian official documents, and in the Ambassadors' Office appeared only upon the most important and most elaborately decorated of its records.[12]

Such was the Ambassadors' Office of the seventeenth century, with its clerks, secretaries and specialized staff of interpreters and artists conducting the Tsar's foreign correspondence in accordance with a strict procedure and with a fanatical devotion to protocol and the subtler points of diplomatic etiquette. But despite the resultant gloss of sophistication, its products reached the courts of western Europe like so many echoes from the Middle Ages. Its calendar began the Civil Year on 1 September and its dates were calculated, in accordance with the Mundane Era of Constantinople, from the Creation of the World; an event considered in Orthodox theology to have occurred upon 1 September 5508 B.C. For letters addressed to the heads of foreign states its clerks used a neat, clear diplomatic script, tracing the letters of the old Russian alphabet individually with frequent use of contractions and suspensions and employing a special brand of language, apparently concocted in imitation of the elegantly 'latinized' style of western European chancelleries and used in foreign correspondence regardless of the fact that, to most of the recipients, one Slavonic language was as unintelligible as another.

This was a variety of the *Dyelovoy Yazik*, the 'Business Language', a term applied to the basically Russian idiom employed in legal and administrative documents as distinct from Church Slavonic, which was used only for religious and literary writings. It is possible to distinguish three main varieties of the 'Business Language'. The most primitive form, characterised by the crudity of its syntax, was used largely for private writs and consisted simply of a number of formal phrases linked together by passages from the spoken language. The second grade, used for chancellery documents, remained cumbersome in character but was relieved by a somewhat more sophisticated phraseology. The most refined variety was the diplomatic language, an amalgam of spoken Russian, Church Slavonic and the composite language of White-Russian mingled with Ukrainian and Polish used in the chancelleries of the Polish–Lithuanian state; all blended together to produce a ponderous vehicle of expression, studded with colourful archaisms and defying adequate translation. As the Tatar grip on Russia slowly slackened at the end of the fourteenth century the Muscovite state had been able gradually to extend its relations with its western neighbours and establish contacts, in the first instance, with the Polish–Lithuanian state. Although the contacts were not particularly friendly they involved a considerable correspondence with the Lithuanians (direct exchanges with the Poles were infrequent in the early stages) and the composite language

---

[12] Notably upon the *Kniga Izbraniya i Vyenchaniya na Tsarstvo Mikhaila Feodorovicha*, or Book of the Election and Coronation of Mikhail Feodorovich, recording the accession of the first Romanov Tsar. Compiled in 1672, the *Kniga Izbraniya* was lavishly decorated by a number of the leading artists serving the Ambassadors' Office, including Grigory Blagushin, Ivan Maximov and Feodor Yuryev. Among its illustrations is a particularly striking prospect of the Red Square, St Basil's Cathedral and the wall and Spasskaya Tower of the Kremlin. The Book is now preserved in the State Palace of Arms in Moscow.

PLATE VI
Letter from Ivan and Peter Alexeivich to King Charles II, 9 June 1682
(Public Record Office, S.P. 102/49, no. 47)

Пресветлейшая идержавнейшая королепа намв любезнейшая сестра.

Понеже мы запотребно быти разсудили ва шему королепину величеству. Нашего комнатного иподполковника Отгвардіи інзя пукранина вныкоторыхв нужнейшихв дплехв послати. Того ради просимв Вше королепино величество дружебно братцки. Дабтогополите оном силонкю Аудиенцию дати, ичто оный онасв Поданномв ншемв указу предлагати Будетв. томy полнyю пербу Атти jоному приадоре пшего величества быть доншего емy указy позволити, Превываемв присемв,

Ошего величества силонный братв

Октявря 11 дня
Октявря 1709.

Петв

Гра Головинв

of the Lithuanian chancelleries soon began to filter into the diplomatic language of Russian administration. White-Russian was, indeed, never regarded as a foreign language in Moscow because the Tsars claimed most of the territory as their ancient patrimony, and it continued to be used for correspondence with Poland even by the reformed administration of Peter the Great. At least two important features of the Russian diplomatic language can be traced directly to Polish–Lithuanian origins. Throughout the seventeenth century the Tsars continued to employ the first person singular in their domestic correspondence but by the accession of Vasilii III, in 1505, the royal 'We' had become the standard usage in letters addressed abroad. Similarly, the formal second person plural slowly displaced the singular in documents addressed to the heads of foreign states, although, in this respect, the process was long and sporadic and the plural form did not become standard until the reign of the first Romanov Tsar, Mikhail Feodorovich (1613–45). Church Slavonic provided the opening address of letters addressed to the Kings of England, taken from the first chapter of St Luke, as well as a number of words and phrases designed to enhance the dignity of the text. Perhaps the most cumbersome feature of all was the Imperial 'Long Title', enumerating separately all the provinces of the Tsar's vast empire. When Ivan III had married Sofia Palaeologos, niece of the last of the Byzantine emperors, in 1472, he had evolved a title suitable to his new reflected Imperial glory which incorporated all the principalities over which he ruled. The array grew in the course of time into a bewildering catalogue of titles which the staffs of western governments attempted in vain to master and reproduce in their answering letters, sometimes with extraordinary results.

An English translation of our letter to Charles II can convey the general sense of the text, but cannot adequately reproduce the sonorous and clumsily repetitive quality of the original Russian. Somewhat amended, it is, none the less, impressive. The portions printed in italics are written in gold in the Russian original.

Through the tender mercy of Our God whereby the Dayspring from on high has visited Us to guide Our feet into the way of peace, by the grace of the same Our most Glorious God in Trinity We the mighty lords, Tsars and Grand Dukes Ioann[13] *Alexeivich [and] Pyotr Alexeivich, Autocrats of All the Great, Little and White Russias,* of Moscow, Kiev, Vladimir and Novgorod, Tsars of Kazan, Astrakhan and Siberia, Lords of Pskov and Grand Dukes of Smolensk, Tver, Yugorsk, Pyerm, Viatka, Bolghar and others, Lords and Grand Dukes of Novgorod in the Lower Country, of Chernigov, Ryazan, Rostov, Yaroslav, Beloozersk, Udorsk, Obdorsk, Kondinskoe and Sovereigns of all the Northern Parts, Lords of the Realm of Iversky and of the Princes of Kartaliniya and Georgia, of the Realm of Karbardin, of the Princes of Cherkask and Gorsk and of many other lands to the East, West and North Lords, Inheritors, Heirs and Sovereigns *to our Loving Brother the mighty lord Charles [Karlus] the Second, by the grace of God King* of England, Scotland, France and Ireland and of others [Our] brotherly and loving greeting.

With Our greeting We do report that the Almighty Lord God and Ruler of all things through whom Tsars hold dominion and monarchs do rule, by His Light and Just Will did determine upon the 27 day of the month of April in the year 7190 [from the Creation of the World] to translate Our brother, the mighty lord, Tsar and Grand Duke Feodor Alexeivich, Autocrat of All the Great, Little and White Russias, his Imperial Majesty, out of this earthly realm to the eternal bliss of His Heavenly Kingdom. And with the departure of His Imperial Majesty out of this world to everlasting felicity in the Heavenly Kingdom, We have succeeded to the hereditary throne of the mighty and most famous realm of Russia. And by the help of the same Almighty God, We, the mighty lords, Our Imperial Majesty, have jointly assumed the Imperial Crown and Throne and autocratic Sceptre and Sovereignty. And We, the mighty lords, Our Imperial Majesty, do certify this to you, Our

---

[13] This Germanic form of the Russian name Ivan was quite commonly used in documents addressed abroad

brother, mighty lord, to your Royal Majesty. And we do desire to be in brotherly amity and love with you Our brother, mighty lord, with your Royal Majesty. And with this letter from Our Imperial Majesty, We, the mighty lords, Our Imperial Majesty, have sent unto you, Our brother, great lord, to your Royal Majesty, Our Messenger, the clerk [*podyachi*] Dmitrii Simonovsky. And to you, Our brother, great lord, to your Royal Majesty, he will report, so that you may have unfailing friendship and love with Us, the mighty lords, with Our Imperial Majesty. And on receipt of the letters from Our Imperial Majesty, release him again to Us, mighty lords, to Our Imperial Majesty without hindrance. And having announced these things, We wish to you, mighty lord, to your Royal Majesty from the Lord God many years of prosperity. Written at Our Royal Court in the Imperial City of Moscow, the Year from the Creation of the World 7190, the month of June, the 9th day.

     Endorsed : To our loving brother, the mighty lord Charles the Second, by the Grace of God King of England, Scotland, France and Ireland and of others.

     This remarkable document presents several features of interest. The paper, measuring 15 by 18 inches, appears to be of oriental manufacture, slightly glossy on the surface and lacks the water mark found in papers produced in Europe. The ink is one of the carbon varieties made up of soot (lamp-black) suspended in gum, which remained popular in eastern Europe long after iron-based inks had replaced them in the west. The preference for this ink is not easy to explain. Iron inks were, of course, known in medieval Russia and there are many extant recipes for their preparation, varying from the simple process of boiling the bark of oak, alder and ash in water and adding rusted iron filings, to complicated formulae including cherry gum, tanner's ooze, sour honey and molasses as well as the basic iron and acid elements. Such inks as these were indeed sometimes employed for sixteenth and seventeenth century foreign correspondence but carbon inks remained favourites; an unfortunate choice from the archival point of view because of their extreme sensitivity to moisture. The gold decoration on the document comprises, in accordance with the Office regulations, a heading and marginal decorations extending three-quarters of the way down the sheet, made up of the customary floral and foliage designs, balanced, somewhat florid and line-shaded to produce the three dimensional effect of the Russian Baroque style, introduced on to Russian Royal Letters in the reign of Alexei Mikhailovich (1645–76). The opening formula and the first parts of the titles of the two sovereigns are also written in gold and the first word, *Milosyerdiya*, is written in the decorative lettering called (untranslatably) *Vyaz*, the characters being arranged in an oblong pattern and depicted with broad strokes executed, in all probability, with a brush. This is an unusual feature in Russian Royal Letters, which customarily begin with a decorative letter 'M' followed by a contracted rendering of the rest of the word written in the normal script.

     The hand is an elegant specimen of the diplomatic script, clearly formed, sparing in its use of contractions and suspensions and showing, in the case of certain letters, a marked development from earlier seventeenth century calligraphy towards the more familiar forms of modern usage. Although basically constructed in the 'Business Language', the grammar and syntax of this letter is less tortuous than that of many of its predecessors and the terminals are more in accordance with modern practice. The numerals of the dating clause are written, as usual, in the form of Cyrillic characters expressing numerical values of thousands, hundreds, tens and units. There is no signature of any kind but the letter was folded for despatch and sealed with a papered example of the enlarged State Seal which appears on Russian royal correspondence during the reign of Alexei Mikhailovich. Measuring five and a quarter inches in diameter, it is a beautiful product of the engraver's art, bearing the double-headed eagle, charged at the breast with a shield of arms of St George and the Dragon; the whole surmounted by three crowns and inscribed around the edge with the imperial titles.

     The letter which Simonovsky delivered to Charles II may therefore be classed as a specimen of the best work produced by the pre-Petrine administration. But this, as much else in Russia, would change under Peter's energetic direction to produce documentation of a radically different character, purged of most of its traditional features and prepared in close imitation of the documents passing between the Courts and governments of western Europe. When, twenty-seven years after the arrival of Simonovsky, Prince Boris Kurakin arrived in London as ambassador to Queen Anne, he presented as his credentials a short note addressed to the Queen which, in simple and direct terms, requested her to grant him audience.[14] The note was dated (in Arabic numerals) 11 October 1709, and was signed both by Peter himself and by his Chancellor, Count Gavril Golovkin. A translation of this letter of 1709 appears below and a glance at plates VI and VII readily conveys the visual contrasts between it and the letter of 1682; contrasts which themselves reflect a number of reforms carried through in Russia during the years which separate them. The Julian calendar was at last introduced into Russia in December 1699, and henceforth the New Year was reckoned from 1 January instead of from 1 September. The seventeenth-century 'business language' gave way to a literary style more closely akin to the spoken language and by 1709 a simplified form of script had been introduced into the administration. The alphabet itself had been pruned of a number of its more cumbersome signs and symbols in a process designed both to facilitate the spread of literacy and produce an alphabet capable of being cast into type with comparative ease.

Devoid both of verbal and visual decoration, Prince Kurakin's credentials are a specimen of what was to be the normal type of Russian royal letter throughout the eighteenth century. Gold decoration would, at times, re-appear in the middle decades of the century, but the colourful, anachronistic *Gramoti* of the seventeenth century pattern had disappeared for ever. In 1717–18 the Moscow *Prikazi* themselves would disappear, to be replaced by a new system of administrative Colleges, established on 'the Swedish model' and housed in a range of buildings gracing the eastern tip of the Vasilievsky Ostrov at the junction of the Great and Little Neva.[15] A new administration in a brand-new capital; 'Our Paradise, or Sankpiterburg'.

Translation of Prince Kurakin's credentials, 1709

Most Serene and Most Puissant Queen, Our most dear Sister: Whereas We have judged it necessary to send to your Royal Majesty Our Chamberlain and Lieutenant Colonel of Guards Prince Kurakin upon divers most urgent affairs, We ask your Royal Majesty in friendship to grant him an audience. And to give full credence to such things as he may propound, as We have instructed him, and to permit him access to your royal Palace as in accordance with Our orders to him.

> Your Majesty's devoted Brother
> *Pyotr*
> [Countersigned] *Graf Golovkin*

Thorn,[16] 11th day
of October, 1709.

NORMAN E. EVANS

---

[14] Public Record Office, State Papers Foreign, Letters from Foreign Ministers in England, S.P.100/51.

[15] Although Leibniz is often credited with suggesting the establishment of administrative Colleges on the Swedish model, there is no doubt that the idea had been simmering in Peter's mind for some time. In April 1715 the Russian representative in Copenhagen, Vasilii Dolgoruky, had been instructed to furnish full reports on the functions, powers and efficiency of the Danish Colleges, 'for We hear that the Swedes borrowed from them'. The new Russian Colleges functioned sluggishly and with a great deal of friction between the members of their various boards, both Russian and foreign. The College of Foreign Affairs, which succeeded the Ambassadors' Office, was for long virtually paralysed by the bitter rivalry between its President Golovkin and the Vice-President Shafirov. In 1722 Peter was compelled to dismiss most of the foreign members and the Colleges thereafter came to resemble the old *Prikazi*, operating under the direct and almost unchecked control of their respective Presidents.

[16] The letter was signed while Peter was conferring at Thorn with Augustus of Poland after the defeat of the Swedish army under Charles XII at Poltava on 27 June 1709.

Central Government and Parliament

The Formation
of the Archives of Parliament
1497–1691

'It was not one of the least glories of the reign of Queen Elizabeth, and for which posterity stand indebted to her, that the public records and muniments, which had long laid neglected, became the objects of her attention and were rescued from dust and oblivion by the effects of her patronage.'[1] As Professor R. B. Wernham has recently commented, Ayloffe in this encomium 'certainly gave Good Queen Bess quite as much credit as she deserved', but he concludes that we may accept Ayloffe's statement 'as a rough and ready approximation to the truth'.[2] What is true for the records of the executive government is in some sense true also for those of the legislature. The reign of Elizabeth I here as well marks a crucial turning point. Before then, as a seventeenth-century Clerk of the Parliaments observed, all the records lay 'in one confused mass';[3] by the beginning of the reign of James I orderly series of Journals, Bills and other records were beginning to be formed and it may be said that the Parliament Office was acquiring many of the characteristics of a record office.

The first century: 1497 to 1597
There is an important difference, however, between the archives of government and those of Parliament. Patent Rolls, Pipe Rolls and other key classes of governmental records stretch back in unbroken series to the twelfth or thirteenth centuries, whereas the archives of Parliament began to accumulate only at the end of the fifteenth century. In the earlier centuries there were, strictly speaking, no parliamentary archives at all.[4] At the end of a session the Clerk enrolled the 'substance of a Parliament',[5] the acts passed, certain petitions read, the sermons of the Chancellor, and similar

---

[1] Sir Joseph Ayloffe, *Calendars of Ancient Charters, etc.* (1774), p. xxvii, quoted by R. B. Wernham, 'The Public Records in the 16th and 17th Centuries', *English Historical Scholarship in the 16th and 17th Centuries* (1956), p. 16.

[2] *Ibid.*

[3] John Browne to John Walker, letter dated 21 May 1683, pasted in Vol. I, MS. Lords' Journal, (H[ouse of] L[ords] R[ecord] O[ffice]).

[4] The medieval clerks of the Parliament and their records have been the subject of a good deal of research since F. W. Maitland's epoch-making edition of *Memoranda de Parliamento* (1893). Cf. especially H. G. Richardson and G. Sayles, 'The King's Ministers in Parliament', *E[nglish] H[istorical] R[eview]*, Vol. 46 (1931), pp. 529–50 and Vol. 47 (1932), pp. 194–203, 377–97, and A. F. Pollard, 'The Clerical Organisation of Parliament', *op. cit.*, Vol. 57 (1942), pp. 31–58, and 'Receivers of Petitions and Clerks of Parliament', *op. cit.*, Vol. 57, pp. 202–26; also Pollard's 'Fifteenth-century Clerks of Parliament', *Bull[etin of the] Inst[itute of] Hist[orical] Res[earch]*, Vol. 15 (1938), pp. 137–61. For Clerks in the modern period, see 'Clerks of the Parliaments, 1509–1953', *E.H.R.*, Vol. 73 (1958), pp. 78–85, and 'The Office of Clerks of the Parliaments', *Parliamentary Affairs*, Vol. XII (1958–9), pp. 297–310, by the present writer.

[5] A. F. Pollard, *E.H.R.*, Vol. 57, p. 46.

matter, and took the enrolments back with him into Chancery, where they were preserved as Chancery records. The clerks of Parliament were recruited from the ranks of Chancery;[6] thus the medieval Parliament had no permanent 'Parliament Office' and no separate archives.

Then, at the end of the Parliament of 12 Henry VII, in March 1497, the Clerk, Master Richard Hatton, whilst duly making up the Parliament Rolls for that session, seems to have elected to preserve separately the complete series of sixteen original engrossments from which the enrolment had been made, and these sixteen manuscripts form the starting point of the archives of Parliament which have ever since been kept at Westminster in the custody of the Clerks of the Parliaments.[7] Richard Hatton's action was very likely part of a general administrative development. The Parliament Office was 'hiving off' from Chancery in a way well-known to medieval historians. Hatton's successor, Dr John Taylor, was not a Chancery clerk, although the Archbishop of Canterbury on 18 November 1509 was directed to admit him as a master in chancery in order that he 'should have recourse to the records of Chancery, which he may not be suffered to do, because he hath not the room of one of the masters of our Chancery.'[8] Taylor's more eminent successors as Clerk, Sir Brian Tuke, Sir Edward (Lord) North, Sir William (Lord) Paget and Sir John Mason were not clerics who had come up through a series of Chancery appointments, but laymen who had gained their earlier training in the Inns of Court or by serving the King in humble secretarial or diplomatic posts until they attained, along with the Clerkship of Parliament, eminent executive office. Tuke, for example, was Treasurer of the Household (as he appears in the well-known portrait by Holbein); Paget was the chief counsellor of Edward VI and the Comptroller of his Household.[9] Under men such as these the Parliament Office could certainly maintain its independence of Chancery.

Yet, although archivally this must have helped to preserve at Westminster those classes of record, such as the original Acts, which it was vital to keep, it does not seem to have assisted in the careful preservation of other classes, now no longer transferred to Chancery, such as petitions or engrossed bills. Apart from the Original Acts and the Subsidies of the Clergy there survive today in the Lords' Record Office from this period only some eight original petitions, dated 1531; the original Journals–with some gaps–from 1510; an engrossed Bill of 1542; some Amendment sheets and a number of Royal Commissions.[10] Otherwise, until 1558 all has vanished.

Some light is thrown on the confusion that must have prevailed in the Tudor Parliament Office by a letter of 6 November 1548 which has recently come to light.[11] This is from Protector Somerset to Sir Edward North, who had ceased to be Clerk of the Parliaments eight years before. It instructs him to hand over 'the acts and other muniments of Parliament' to Sir John Mason, who in fact was not then the Clerk, although he obtained appointment two years later, but must presumably have been acting previously as deputy Clerk. Sir John Mason's successors, Francis Spilman and his own adopted son, Anthony Mason, frequently came under the lash of Sir Simonds D'Ewes as that indefatigable scholar picked his way through the history of late sixteenth-century Parliaments.[12] Each was at different times said to have been 'very negligent' in the making and keeping of records, Mason being detected by D'Ewes not only in mistaking an Adjournment for a

---

[6] Pollard, *Bull. Inst. Hist. Res.*, *op. cit.*, p. 138.

[7] And now in the immediate care of H.L.R.O. (cf. Appendix, below).

[8] *Letters and Papers (Henry VIII)*, Vol. I, pt. i (1920), p. 257.

[9] For the careers of North and Paget, see G.E.C., *Complete Peerage*; for Mason's, the D[ictionary of] N[ational] B[iography].

[10] Cf. the records calendared in H[istorical] M[anuscripts] C[ommission], *3rd Report* (1872), Appendix, p. 4. and the entries, *passim*, in M. F. Bond, *Guide to the Records of Parliament* (1971).

[11] Photocopy in H.L.R.O. of MS. letter in Lord Mersey's Collection (H.L.R.O., F.229).

[12] Simonds, D'Ewes, *Journal of both the House of Lords and the House of Commons* (1693), pp. 103, 136, 204, etc.

Prorogation, but also the year 1587 for 1586.[13] 'All of which', concludes D'Ewes, 'may show how great inconvenience it may bring to take things upon trust from others without searching out the truth, seeing so many men in that which they were best skilled in, and had doubtless travelled in, yet should be so grossly mistaken.'[14]

Meanwhile, the keepers of the records in Chancery were becoming restive. Not only had no subsidiary records such as petitions or engrossed Bills been transmitted to Chancery, but the enrolments of Acts themselves had ceased to appear. An Order was made in Chancery in 1556 'that the Clerke of the Parliament for the time being should Certifie into his highnes Court of the Chauncery all and singuler Actes and Statutes of Parliament immediately after the Session wherein such Actes and Statutes were ordeyned and made untill nowe of late yeares, that is to say from 21° Henrici octavi . . .'[15] but nothing seems to have been done, and a more extensive order was made on 1 May 1567 which, if obeyed, would have extinguished the nascent archive at Westminster. Spilman was then ordered to transmit 'all rolls of Parliament, petitions, judgments, attainders and other records of Parliament' from 23 Edward IV to 1 Mary, then in his custody, to William Bowyer, Keeper of the Rolls in the Tower, 'to be kept there according to custom'.[16] But, in fact, apart from the Parliament Rolls, nothing seems to have been transmitted. As a result either of negligence or of a policy of stonewalling, the parliamentary records continued in independence (if also in some confusion) until later clerks, amongst them Bowyer's own son, were to give them at Westminster a greater substance and consistency.

The position in 1597, at the end of the Clerkship of Anthony Mason, was that whilst one class of record only was transferred, and many were neglected or lost, two classes were in fact preserved: from the time of Richard Hatton, the Original Acts, and, from that of Dr Taylor, the Journals of the House of Lords (not to mention at this point the Journals of the House of Commons which were beginning to be made and preserved, though in a different custody). The Acts were the engrossments on parchment made in the first House and later transmitted to the second House to receive amendments, provisos, etc., and ultimately the Royal Assent or Refusal. These texts, which still survive, enable the scholar on occasion to reconstruct the parliamentary history of a bill, as recently they enabled Sir John Neale to discover from the text of the Subscription Act of 1571 valuable indications of the relation of Queen and Commons in ecclesiastical matters.[17] The Private Acts in this series have the special significance, in the period with which we are concerned, that very few have been enrolled, and many were not printed; the text surviving at Westminster thus may be the sole surviving text as well as the master-text.

Of the Lords' Journals little need here be said. The researches of Professor A. F. Pollard,[18] Dr W. H. Dunham[19] and Professor A. R. Myers,[20] recently surveyed by Mr H. S. Cobb,[21] show

---

[13] *Ibid.*, pp. 382–3.
[14] *Ibid.*, p. 383.
[15] H.L.R.O., Office Copy of Order, Main Papers (Addit.), 1556.
[16] Public Record Office, C.66/1035 .Patent Roll. 9 Eliz. I, pt. VI, m. 22. This order was part of a wider campaign by Bowyer to have all outlying Chancery records transferred to his custody. Although this piece of 'empire-building' (in Professor Wernham's phrase) by Bowyer was supported by the Queen, it came to nothing. Cf. Wernham, *op. cit.*, pp. 17–18.
[17] *E.H.R.*, Vol. LXVII (1952), pp. 510–21. Cf. also S. T. Bindoff, 'The Making of the Statute of Artificers', in *Elizabethan Government and Society* (1961), pp. 56–94.
[18] 'The Authenticity of the "Lords" Journals', Tr[ansactions of the] R[oyal] H[istorical] S[ociety], 3rd Series, Vol. VIII (1914), pp. 17–39.
[19] *The Fane Fragment of the 1461 Lords' Journal* (1935).
[20] 'A Parliamentary Debate of the mid-fifteenth century', *Bulletin of the John Rylands Library*, Vol. 22 (1938), pp. 389–97.
[21] *The Journals, Minutes and Committee Books of the House of Lords*, H.L.R.O. Memorandum No. 13, revised ed. (1957).

that Journals were written before 1510, and that the series now surviving as the record copy seems to have been assembled from varied sources, perhaps during the reign of Elizabeth. A few parliamentary years are missing – one section has recently been found by Miss Brenda Howe in the British Museum[22] – but, on the whole, the Journals form a reliable and consecutive source for parliamentary history, with the particular advantage that each day's session is headed with a list of the peers that day present. D'Ewes may have found much negligence in the keeping of this record, but it compares favourably with those of other governmental bodies, and in its general format has been faithfully followed to the present day, allowing for a change from Latin to English for all but the headings and lists of peers present, which continue in Latin even today.

Acts and Journals form the basis for all parliamentary record and for research. But very much was still needed. The century from 1497 to 1597, from the clerkship of Hatton to that of Anthony Mason saw the foundations of a rational record system laid. It remained for the clerks of the following century from 1597 to 1691, to erect the superstructure.

The reforming clerks: 1597 to 1635

D'Ewes himself regarded 1597 as an important date, for then, he observes, the new clerk, Thomas Smith, became 'much more careful in observing and setting down the dayly passages thereof this Parliament'.[23] His successors even surpassed him, 'by the large and diligent digesting of the particular agitations of every day upon which the said House did sit'.[24] To Smith (clerk, 1597–1609) and his two successors (Robert Bowyer, 1609–21, Henry Elsynge, 1621–35)[25] great credit is due. They were clerks who, as a result of outlook and training, and of the needs of the moment, were recordkeepers, one might almost say, archivists, as much as heads of an administrative department.

Smith and Bowyer had been rivals for the Clerkship in 1597, Bowyer then gaining only the reversion in spite of the strong support of his patron, Lord Buckhurst, possibly (as his successful rival, Smith, pointed out) because he was not fit 'by reason of a great imperfection he hath in his speech'[26] – indeed a drawback in the days when the Clerk had literally to read all bills to the House three times. Whatever their reading capacities, however, they were a distinguished trio. Smith had the greatest range; he was in turn Public Orator at Oxford, Clerk of the Privy Council, M.P. for Cricklade and Tamworth, Latin Secretary to James I, and in the last year of his life, Master of Requests.[27] Robert Bowyer had been bred record-keeper; his father has already been noted applying for the transfer of the parliamentary records to the Tower of London, and Robert himself gained, by 1604, together with Henry Elsynge his nephew and colleague in the Temple, the post of Keeper of the Rolls of Chancery which his father had held.[28] Bowyer was also M.P. for Steyning in 1601, and for Evesham in 1605,[29] and has left us a valuable diary of Commons Proceedings for 1606–7.[30]

---

[22] H.L.R.O., photo-copy of British Museum, Harleian MSS. 158, ff. 141–4, containing entries for various days in 1512 and 1536. Cf. also Miss E. Jeffries Davis's 'Unpublished Manuscript of the Lords' Journals for April and May 1559' in *E.H.R.*, Vol. XXVIII (1913) and J. C. Sainty's text of *Further Materials from an Unpublished Manuscript of the Lords' Journals for Sessions 1559 and 1597 to 1598*, H.L.R.O. Memorandum No. 33 (1965).

[23] *Op. cit.*, p. 522. John Browne, looking back in 1683 over the intervening century, gave Smith credit for having put all the records 'into that order as they now are, and the same order hath been continued ever since'. MS. letter quoted in n. 3 above. In fact, as will be seen, there were many important new developments after Smith's time.

[24] *Ibid.*

[25] Varying dates have hitherto been assigned to these clerkships; cf. M. F. Bond, 'Clerks of the Parliaments, 1509–1953', *E.H.R.*, Vol. 78 (1958), pp. 78–85.

[26] *H.M.C., Hatfield MSS.*, Vol. VII (1899), p. 299.

[27] *D.N.B.*

[28] Cf. C[alendar of] S[tate] P[apers] D[omestic], 1603–10, p. 178 for confirmation of grant.

[29] *Return of Members of Parliament*, Pt. I (1879), pp. 440, 447.

[30] *The Parliamentary Diary of Robert Bowyer, 1606–7*, ed. D. H. Willson (1931). The original MSS. of books 1 and 3 of the Diary are now preserved in H.L.R.O. (Braye MSS. 59, 60).

He was followed as Clerk by his nephew Elsynge, who had already assisted him in the Parliament Office,[31] and who continued as Clerk until September 1635. Smith, Bowyer, Elsynge, together with their ultimate successor, John Browne, all belonged to that group described by Pollard: 'Secretaries of State, Clerks of Parliament, keepers of the Records, and private antiquaries [who] were bred in a common atmosphere and almost in a family circle.' 'The investigation of their family history,' he adds, 'would probably throw some light on the development of scientific records and record-keeping in England, and perhaps assist in tracing lost sources.'[32]

The Clerks' family history still for the greater part awaits investigation. Here it is only possible to enumerate some of the more important services rendered by this quartet of professional clerks, which, in the century between 1597 and Browne's death in 1691, transformed a thin and meagre parliamentary archive into the complex and rich series of records continued to this day.

The importance of the Clerk as maker and keeper of records in Parliament was emphasized when the first Oath was devised for the Clerks. Until the sixteenth century, as Chancery Clerks, the Clerks of the Parliaments took the oath specified for clerks of the Chancery in the Act 18 Edw. III, st. 5; and during the sixteenth century most of the eminent holders of the post were presumably controlled in their duties by the oaths taken by them as Privy Councillors. But, on 30 January 1610, Robert Bowyer on appointment was directed to take an oath specially devised for him, the central and most specific clause of which was 'ye shall also well and trulie serve his hignes in the office of Clerke of his Parliaments making true entries and Records of the things done and past in the same, Ye shall keepe secret all such matters as shalbe treated in his said parliaments and not disclose the same before they shalbe published but to such as it ought to be disclosed unto.'[33] This oath is substantially the same as that taken today: it marks the final emergence of the Clerkship as an independent office, separate from Chancery.

In the oath the 'making true entries' has prominence. From this period, 1597–1630, date the elaboration of the minuting system, and, in particular the establishment of the Journal as an official record. As has been seen, Journals, or rather lists of peers present daily, with brief though increasingly thorough lists of business transacted, had been made probably from the fifteenth century at least. On 10 November 1597 the House, for the first time, took active cognizance of its own records when the Lord Treasurer moved that 'for as much as the Journal Books kept heretofore, by the Clerks of the Parliament, seemed to have some error in them, in misplacing the Lords [in their true precedence in the lists of peers present], so as it was doubted how the same might be of true record, that it would please the Lords to take order, that the said books that henceforth should be kept by the Clerk of the Parliament, may be viewed and perused every Parliament, by certain Lords of the House to be appointed for that purpose; and the list of the Lords in their order to be subscribed by them; taking unto them for their better information, the King at Arms; and that this order might begin this present Parliament.'[34]

So it was in fact ordered, and from this time the Journal was kept with the greatest care. On 27 March 1621, to give the record still greater dignity and authority, it was ordered that the Journal should be engrossed on parchment,[35] and, for long, the signatures of peers are appended to its pages at irregular intervals to vouch for the accuracy of the record. The matter inscribed becomes increasingly full–petitions and reports of Joint Conferences, for example, may be entered in full, and even the critical D'Ewes remarks approvingly of the Journal of 1601, that it 'is plentifully stored not

---

[31] F. H. Relf, *Notes of the Debates in the House of Lords . . . 1621, 1625, 1628* (1929), p. vi, n. 3.

[32] *Tr. R.H.S.* 3rd series, Vol. VIII (1914), p. 39.

[33] H.L.R.O. Main Papers, 21 March 1620/1; cf. *H.M.C., 3rd Report*, App., p. 20. A *Memorandum* on the *Oaths of the Clerk of the Parliaments* is available from H.L.R.O.

[34] *L[ords] J[ournals]*, Vol. II, p. 195.

[35] *Op. cit.*, Vol. III, p. 74.

only with the ordinary business of Reading Bills, with the Committing, Amending and expediting of them; but also with divers very useful and good Precedents touching the Liberties and Priviledges of the House itself.'[36]

Moreover, in order to obtain a thorough and complete record, Bowyer and Elsynge seem to have developed a system of preliminary minutes which were at least semi-official. Bowyer himself describes the procedure: 'The Clerke of the Parliament, doth every day (sitting in the House or Court) write into his rough and scribled Booke not onely the reading of Bills and other proceedings of the House, but as farr as he cann, whatsoever is spoken worthy of observation; Howbeit into the Journall booke which is the Record he doth in discretion forebeare to enter many things spoken, though memorable, yet not necessarie nor fitt to be registered and left to posterity of record.'[37] As a result a number of 'Scribbled Books' survive of great importance in the history of the early Stuart parliaments; and in 1660 Browne began a new series of Minute Books, with fewer notes of speeches, yet more ample than the Journals. It is a matter for regret that the eighteenth century clerks abandoned the noting of points in debate, and that historians have to depend in the main on the efforts of anonymous hacks until, in the nineteenth century, record of speeches was once more thought suitable to be undertaken (though then not by Parliament's own staff, but by a private firm).[38]

In addition to the Scribbled Books of the seventeenth century there were Draft Journals—sometimes several for a given period, each kept by a separate clerk or assistant. In them we see the Parliament Office staff taking the greatest care to obtain an accurate record. Thus, in a 1621 Draft Journal, the supervising peers ordered the clerk to get notes from the Chancellor. This he failed to do, and had to use his Scribbled Book.[39] Later Bowyer noted 'Mr Benbowe [a Clerk in the Crown Office] tooke this reporte, when I was otherwyse buisye'.[40] The Treasurer on this occasion spoke so well that Bowyer minuted that he must try to get his notes;[41] later, however, adding 'I cannot gett yt'.[42] Other comments such as 'looke for the names and insert them here',[43] 'examine this with original'[44], 'the Earl of Warwick for the rest'[45] show the diligence displayed in the Parliament Office and justify Hakewill's conclusion that the Lords set a high standard to the Commons in record matters. If the lower House would only imitate the upper, their Journals moreover, 'would not (as now they may) come to the hands of Executors or Administrators, and be removed to and fro in hazard of being lost, or corrupted and defaced, as is well known that some of them have been, and that in passages of the greatest moment, whereby the Commonwealth may receive great prejudice if it be not prevented.'[46]

Besides minuting proceedings more fully, the clerks of the early seventeenth century undertook for the first time the careful preservation of all papers laid on the Table of the House, endorsing them normally with the date of reading, and the course of action to be taken on them. Whilst for the

---

[36] D'Ewes, *op. cit.*, p. 597.

[37] This account from Inner Temple Library, Petyt MS. 537, is quoted from E. Jeffries Davis, 'Unpublished Manuscript of the Lords' Journals for April and May, 1559' *loc. cit.*, p. 533.

[38] It is a remarkable fact that 'Hansard,' although now entitled 'Official Record', does not even today form part of the records of Parliament. Cf. M. F. Bond, 'The Victoria Tower and its Records', *Parliamentary Affairs*, Vol. VIII (1955), pp. 487–8.

[39] H.L.R.O., Draft Journal, Braye MSS. 11, 12 March 1620/1.

[40] *Ibid.*, 26 March 1621.

[41] *Ibid.*

[42] *Ibid.*

[43] *Ibid.*, 16 March 1620/1.

[44] *Ibid*, 20 March 1620/1.

[45] *Ibid.*, 23 March 1620/1.

[46] William Hakewill, *The Manner how Statutes are inacted* (1659), preface, quoted by A. F. Pollard, in 'The Authenticity of the "Lords" Journals', *op. cit.*, p. 32, n. 3.

early years of Elizabeth I's reign there are practically no papers at all, for the reigns of James I and Charles I there are fairly large numbers. Thus, for a typical period, the month of May 1628, there survive about 125 papers which had been laid on the Table.[47] These include forty-four Petitions concerning every manner of grievance–the inhabitants of Clerkenwell claimed they had been defrauded of money collected for them in time of plague; the son of the late 'Lord Steward to the Emperor of Persia' being destitute prays for relief; Anne, Countess Dowager of Dorset claims the Baronies of Clifford, Westmoreland and Vescy (incidentally, the first of the long and important series of Peerage Claim Papers). In addition there are some twenty original Orders of the House, twelve Appeal Papers, ten papers from Committees, seven from Conferences with the Commons, four Messages from Charles I (connected with the dispute then raging about the passage of the Petition of Right) and five papers concerning Public Bills. The quantity of such 'Main Papers' grows until each day's sitting may produce a considerable file of papers, each of which has been docketed and carefully preserved. In all, a rich mine of political, social, economic and religious history.

This material has proved to be vital for the historian. To the Parliament Office, however, the making and preserving of treatises and books of memoranda and precedents has been of equal importance. The key work was that of Henry Elsynge, *The Manner of Holding Parliaments*, the first part of which was finished in manuscript on 3 May 1625. Its Latin title, *Modus tenendi Parliamentum apud Anglos*, showed Elsynge's ambition that it should replace the completely out-of-date *Modus* which had been written in the fourteenth century, but was still treated, at least in the sixteenth century, as authoritative. Elsynge's *Modus* was never completed, but the main section was published in 1660, and other sections have since appeared in print.[48] Cotton testified to the 'painful labour of Mr Elsings' and Professor Cam has recently hailed him as a modern Glanvill or Bracton, scholar and civil servant who 'writes as a man who knows governmental machinery from the inside'.[49] Immediately on his appointment he guided the House, with Selden's aid, through the lengthy investigations into procedure, which produced in March 1621 the first roll of Standing Orders of the House.[50] (A by-product of this inquiry was Selden's important *Privileges of the Baronage of England*).[51] Elsynge, Browne and an assistant Clerk, John Relfe, all contributed memoranda books and procedural notes to the records, with the result that after the haze in which the parliamentary procedure of the sixteenth century is shrouded even the Upper House emerges in the seventeenth into some sort of light.

Perhaps, however, the greatest achievement of the Clerk in this period, from the point of view of the archives, was the establishment of a definite 'Record Office' for Parliament. For too long records had been for all practical purposes the personal luggage of the Clerks: in 1621, the year of Selden and the Standing Orders, the records gained a permanent home. One floor of the Jewel Tower at Westminster, then long since abandoned by the royal jewels, was set aside for the preservation of the Acts, Journals and other official records.[52] The inner of two rooms on that floor (which can still be seen) was provided with a brick vault to make it fireproof, and for further protection, an iron door was installed on which the royal cipher I:R: and the date 1621 commemorate the opening

[47] Cf. *H.M.C., 4th Rept.*, App. pp. 15–17. This, however, leaves out of account a few papers, calendared in *Manuscripts of the House of Lords*, Vol. XI, *Addenda* (1962).

[48] e.g. *Expedicio Billarum Antiquitus, an unpublished chapter of the second book of the Manner of Holding Parliaments in England*, ed. C. S. Sims (1954).

[49] *Ibid.*, p. xii. See also Professor E. R. Foster's valuable monograph, 'The Painful Labour of Mr Elsyng'.

[50] Cf. *The Manuscripts of the House of Lords*, Vol. X (1953), ed. M. F. Bond, pp. xxxix–xliii.

[51] *Ibid.*, p. xli.

[52] The Jewel Tower was restored by the Ancient Monuments division of the then Ministry of Works, and is now open daily, free, to the public. The facts that follow in this paragraph concerning its history are based on the official guide by A. J. Taylor, *The Jewel Tower, Westminster* (2nd. ed., 1965), especially pp. 11–19.

of another stage in the history of the Jewel Tower. The eventual outcome of this deposit of the parliamentary records in the Jewel Tower was that when the Palace of Westminster was burnt down in 1834 the records in the Tower at its remote south-western corner escaped unharmed, to be ultimately transferred (a generation later) to the new and mighty Victoria Tower erected opposite to it.

Thus, by the time Charles I dismissed his third Parliament in 1629, a great administrative and archival development had taken place. The Standing Orders and the *Modus* had systematised procedure on a firm basis; scribbled books, journals and minute books were providing a far better historic memory for Parliament than ever before; a record office was established where all the records could be preserved and consulted by peers and officials of Parliament; and over all presided a small group of able and scholarly clerks.

John Browne, Clerk of the Parliaments, 1638 to 1691

Smith, Bowyer and Elsynge went about their clerical and archival business without being very closely involved in the disputes of the day. Their successor, John Browne, member of a rich City Merchant's family,[53] became very much more of a public figure. As did his predecessors, he belonged to the inner group of civil servants, both socially and professionally. In addition he became known as a firm adherent to the Parliamentary cause during the Civil War, needing the Army's protection from its enemies,[54] and becoming, as the Commons observed in 1649, 'a great sufferer in his estate for adhering to the Parliament'.[55] His 'sufferings' were still further increased at that time by his loss of the Clerkship, as the Upper House itself was abolished and the Parliament Office with it. The Council of State, however, found Browne employment in a variety of capacities, as Commissioner at home[56] and as Envoy abroad.[57] His ability must have been marked (the records at Westminster bear ample testimony to his assiduity and thoroughness), and in 1660 on making full protestation of his loyalty to Charles II[58] he was reinstated in his post as Clerk, and continued to serve until his death in 1691.

As maker and keeper of records, however, Browne did not attain modern standards. This was not always his own fault, as when, for example, on 8 June 1671 he received a direction on behalf of Charles II to conceal certain original Acts in his custody from strangers who were trying to frustrate the King's intention to get back Sir John Collidon his French estates.[59] But Browne's chief derelictions of duty concerned the dispersal of important sections of the records in his care.

First, at some time before 1682, Browne allowed Dr John Nalson, antiquary and Canon of Ely, to borrow official records for the purpose of compiling his *Collections*.[60] In 1684 Browne wrote to ask for a list of these; he does not appear to have received one. In 1686 Nalson died, and these alienated records of Parliament never returned to Westminster, eventually coming into the possession of the Dukes of Portland.[61] As they comprise invaluable State Papers of the Commonwealth period, many of them communications from other European powers with Parliament, their loss to the archives at Westminster is very great.

---

[53] Cf. the will of his grandfather, Thomas Browne, merchant taylor, made 1 July 1579. P.C.C. 33 Bakon.

[54] *L.J.*, Vol. VII, p. 187.

[55] *Commons' Journals*, Vol. VI, p. 209.

[56] C.S.P.D., 1650, pp. 4, 24, etc.

[57] *Op. cit.*, 1655, p. 47.

[58] H.L.R.O. *Braye MSS.*, 3. Original declaration, 30 May 1660.

[59] C.S.P.D., 1671, p. 305.

[60] Cf. the account given by F. H. Blackburne Daniell in *H.M.C.*, *13th Rept.*, App., Pt. I (*The MSS. of the Duke of Portland*, Vol. I), pp. iii–iv. This volume contains a useful calendar of the records borrowed by Nalson.

[61] They have been deposited by the present Duke of Portland in the Bodleian Library, Oxford. A complete set of photo-copies is, however, now kept in the House of Lords Record Office, which is also accessible to students.

Secondly, when Browne died, a great volume of original Papers, draft Journals and other records which should have returned to Westminster (or, indeed, should never have been taken from there) were left at his country home in Northamptonshire and descended to his daughter, Martha Cave, ancestress of the present Lord Braye.[62] Since 1945 these papers have been offered for sale at a variety of auctions and in other ways. The greater part of them it has been possible to purchase for the House of Lords,[63] but a few are lost, and those returning to Westminster have of course returned without their archive quality.

These losses are important – they are the only large gaps in the records known to have been caused by dispersal at any time – yet in other ways Browne's career as record-keeper was distinguished. He continued the careful preservation of records initiated by his predecessors, carrying it to remarkable lengths. In spite of his two great alienations, it might be said that Browne was an administrator whose first instinct was to keep everything. He was meticulous in preserving Orders and other originals, although they were largely formal in character, and usually inscribed in Journals and Minute Books. Drafts, notes, stray letters, were also filed, and a general background to the records was provided by him in the compilation of Commonplace Books and Precedent Books. But his greatest service was performed on his return to office in 1660 when he began three separate series of Minute Books which have been maintained ever since, and have contributed much important historical material to the Calendars published in the Historical Manuscripts Commission series. These consist firstly of the Manuscript Minute Books, Browne's standardisation of the varied Scribbled Books of the earlier period; secondly, the Committee Minute Books, in which all proceedings in Select Committees were recorded, other than those appearing in the third series, the Committee Books of the Committee for Privileges. Where Bowyer and Elsygne were, at least in part, the antiquarian collectors of impressive speeches, unusual precedents, or material relevant to the consolidation of the powers of the House, Browne was the methodical annotator of business done, whether in the full House, in Committee, or in the recesses of the Parliament Office in the Jewel Tower. Considerable as were the services of Smith, Bowyer and Elsynge, John Browne is worthy to rank with them, for under his direction the archives of Parliament came to maturity, assuming the form which, with minor variations, they have ever since preserved.

MAURICE F. BOND

---

[62] The Braye MSS. are calendared in *H.M.C., 10th Rept.*, App., pt. VI, pp. 104–252. Cf. H. C. Maxwell-Lyte's introduction *op. cit.*, pp. 104–6.

[63] The manuscripts are calendared in *The Manuscripts of the House of Lords*, Vol. XI (1962), ed. M. F. Bond. General descriptions of certain of them are provided in H.L.R.O. *Memoranda* 7 (1952) and 11 (1954), and in the brief *List of Braye MSS.* (1956).

APPENDIX

(Page references to the *Guide to the Records of Parliament* (H.M.S.O., 1971) are given in brackets after the symbol GRP)

I The principal classes of the Records of the House of Lords

ACTS OF PARLIAMENT, 1497–date. GRP 93–103

BILLS, PRIVATE, with deposited plans, reference books, transcripts of evidence, etc., 1572–date. GRP 70–92

BILLS, PUBLIC, with ancillary papers, 1558–date. GRP 59–68

COMMITTEE PROCEEDINGS, 1610–date. GRP 41–58

DEBATES, RECORDS OF (Lords and Commons). GRP 36–40

GARTER'S ROLLS, 1621–1964. GRP 170–1

JOURNALS OF THE HOUSE, 1510–date. GRP 26–32

JUDICIAL RECORDS, including those of appeal cases, impeachments and trials of peers, 1621–date. GRP 106–26

MAIN PAPERS (Sessional Papers), including petitions, subsidies of the Clergy, Test Rolls, etc., 1531–date. GRP 127–59, 172–3

ORDER AND ORDINANCE BOOKS, 1640–95. GRP 171

PARLIAMENT OFFICE PAPERS, 1609–date. GRP 180–94

PEERAGE CLAIMS, 1604–date. GRP 160–9

PROTEST BOOKS, 1641–date. GRP 173–4

PROXY BOOKS, 1625–1864. GRP 174–5

WRITS OF SUMMONS, 1559–date. GRP 179–80

II The principal classes of the Records of the House of Commons

The House of Lords has had charge of the records of Parliament as a whole, as well as of its own domestic records: this has left a somewhat smaller bulk of materials for preservation by the House of Commons. The records surviving in the House of Commons were summarised in 1800 by the Commons' Clerk of the Journals in a report to the Select Committee on Public Records. He noted in particular the following main classes:

> Journals of the House of Commons, 1547–1800
>
> Minute Books, 1685–1800
>
> Committee of the Whole House Minutes, 1689–1800
>
> Books of Evidence, 1736–1800
>
> Petitions and other Main Papers, 1607–1800
>
> Return Books of Elections, 1625–1800
>
> Test Rolls, 1698–1800
>
> Qualification Rolls, 1727–1800

With the main exception of the Journals, these records were destroyed in the fire of 1834 which burnt down practically the whole Palace of Westminster (apart from Westminster Hall, the Jewel Tower, St Stephen's crypt and the Cloisters). The present records of the House of Commons consist of the following classes:

BILLS, PRIVATE, with deposited plans and other subsidiary material, 1819–date. GRP 227–31

BILLS, PUBLIC, (preserved with the House of Lords Main Papers), 1563–1649. GRP 226–7

BILLS, PUBLIC, (printed), 1731–date. GRP 227

COMMISSIONERS FOR THE HOUSE OF COMMONS, MINUTE BOOKS OF, 1835–date. GRP 237
COMMITTEE PROCEEDINGS, various dates, 1621–1742, 1833–date. GRP 218–25
DEPOSITED PAPERS, 1832–date. GRP 238
DISPUTED ELECTION RECORDS, 1869–1906. GRP 238–9
HOUSE OF COMMONS OFFICE RECORDS, 1710–date. GRP 243–8
JOURNALS OF THE HOUSE, 1547–date. GRP 205–12
PRINTED SESSIONAL PAPERS, 1712–date. GRP 233–6
PUBLIC PETITIONS, 1951–date. GRP 240–1
RETURN BOOKS OF ELECTIONS, various, 1835–date. GRP 238
SERJEANT AT ARMS' RECORDS, 1788–date. GRP 247–8
UNPRINTED SESSIONAL PAPERS, 1850–date. GRP 232–3
VOTES AND PROCEEDINGS, 1680–date. GRP 213–17

III Other official records preserved in the House of Lords Record Office

CLERK OF THE CROWN RECORDS, 1837–date. GRP 259.
EXCHEQUER CHIEF USHER PAPERS, 1770–1841. GRP 266.
LORD GREAT CHAMBERLAIN'S RECORDS, 1558–date. GRP 251–5
SCOTTISH COMMISSIONS RECORDS, 1803–56. GRP 264.
SHAW-LEFEVRE, SIR JOHN GEORGE, PAPERS, 1575–1857. GRP 264–5
STATUTE LAW COMMITTEE PAPERS, 1835–1954. GRP 263–4

IV Historical collections

HISTORICAL COLLECTIONS OF THE HOUSE OF LORDS RECORD OFFICE, 1451–date. GRP 269–84
(These include the Braye Manuscripts, 1572–1748; the *Complete Peerage* materials, 1910–date; the Commons and Footpaths Preservation Society Papers, 1720–1931; and the papers of the 1st Viscount Samuel, 1st Lord Ashbourne, Major A. L. Renton, Mr Benn Levy, 1st Lord Stansgate and of other Members of the Houses of Parliament.)
HISTORICAL COLLECTIONS OF THE HOUSE OF LORDS LIBRARY, 1600–date. GRP 285–90
(These include the notebooks of Lord Chancellor Bathurst and Lord Truro.)
HISTORICAL COLLECTIONS OF THE HOUSE OF COMMONS LIBRARY, 1610–date. GRP 291–9
(These include Parliamentary Surveys, 1646–9, the papers of Speaker Brand, Lord Emmott and Sir Courtenay Ilbert.)

V Bibliography

(a) GUIDE. A guide to the MSS., printed works and other records available to students in the H.L.R.O. Search Room is provided in M. F. Bond, *Guide to the Records of Parliament* (1971).

(b) CALENDARS. The records of the House of Lords are calendared for the period 1497–1693 in the Appendices to the following *Reports of the Historical Manuscripts Commission*: 1st (reissue, 1874); 2nd (1871); 3rd (1872); 4th (1874); 5th (1876); 6th (1877); 7th (1879); 8th (reissue, 1881); 9th (1884); 11th (1887); 12th (1889); 13th (1892); 14th (1894).

The records of 1693 to 1714 are calendared in the 11 volumes of the *New Series* of calendars, published by the House of Lords: I (1900); II (1903); III (1905); IV (1908); V (1910); VI (1912); VII (1921); VIII (1922); IX (1949); X (1953). Vol XI (1962) contains Addenda for 1514–1714.

Note that MS. lists of records of later date than 1714 are available for consultation in the House of Lords Record Office.

(c) OTHER PUBLICATIONS. The House of Lords Record Office issues *gratis* various *Memoranda* on the records in its care and on its work. Cf. especially:

Memorandum   1: *List of Main Classes of Records* (1972)

9: *Catalogue of Display of Manuscripts* (1955)

13: *The Journals, Minutes and Committee Books of the House of Lords* (1957)

16: *Private Bill Records of the House of Lords* (1957)

20: *Guide to House of Lords Papers and Petitions* (1959)

26: *Hand List of Paintings, Drawings and Engravings, etc., of the House of Lords and House of Commons, 1523–1900* (1972)

31: *Leaders and Whips in the House of Lords* (1964)

35: *The Political Papers of Herbert, 1st Viscount Samuel* (1966)

39: *A List of Representative Peers for Scotland, 1707 to 1963, and for Ireland, 1800 to 1961* (1968)

41: *Literary and Scientific Papers of Herbert, 1st Viscount Samuel* (1969)

43: *Letters and Diaries of Speaker Brand, 1855–92* (1970)

45: *Officers of the House of Lords, 1485–1971* (1971)

The Archives and
Archival Problems of the
Elizabethan and
Early Stuart Star Chamber

The High Court of Star Chamber, for all its contemporary pre-eminence and posthumous notoriety, was just one of a half-dozen major central courts proceeding by 'English bill' existing between the mid-sixteenth and mid-seventeenth centuries. With the High Court of Chancery and its double, the equity jurisdiction of the Exchequer, the court of Requests, the court of Wards and Liveries, and the court of the Duchy of Lancaster it shared a common procedural form which entailed written pleadings and written proofs. These courts, both in composition and in procedure (though not so much in jurisdiction and substantive law as is sometimes supposed) differed greatly from the traditional common law courts. In two great waves of abolition and reform their unique composition was wiped out, their jurisdiction absorbed, and their procedure irrevocably lost. In the mid-seventeenth century, with the abolition of the Privy Council's judicial function, Star Chamber and Requests were destroyed; Wards and Liveries fell with fiscal feudalism. In 1841 the equity jurisdiction of Exchequer was transferred to Chancery, which by the Supreme Court of Judicature Act of 1873 was in turn absorbed in the new High Court as a division of the same. The Duchy court had for all practical purposes ceased to be a court in the early part of the century. The first wave of abolition and reform in the seventeenth century marked the triumph of judicial professionalism – the lay element represented by the Privy Councillors in Star Chamber, the Lord Privy Seal's presidency in Requests, the Lord Treasurer in Exchequer equity, and the Master of the Wards's presidency of Wards would never again be seen in such superior judicial capacity at first instance. The Chancellor of the Duchy of Lancaster was the sole domestic vestige of the tradition of the lay-councillor jurist to survive into the nineteenth century. The second wave of abolition and reform in the nineteenth century was the ultimate victory of the common law procedure over 'English bill' procedure. The Victorian judicature acts' procedural consequences merely buried the wraith of 'English bill' – bill procedure had expired earlier with the advent of the writ of summons endorsed with the plaintiff's statement of claim.

Initially, perhaps, there was no necessary connection between the written pleadings of 'English bill' and the method of written proofs which came to be so intimately linked with it that it would as an evidential method fall with the extensive and verbose bill, answer, replication, and rejoinder. But the connection that grew up between written pleadings and written proofs was already firmly established by the middle of the sixteenth century. In the main this development can be accounted for by the composition of the judicial bodies which used this procedure: they were without exception benches of non-professional judges otherwise primarily engaged in administrative and executive functions, usually of the highest order. The great attraction of written pleadings and written proofs to men as multifariously busy as Privy Councillors was that they enabled a cause to be prepared to the point of hearing argument by counsel without demanding the bench's presence. A considerable amount of judicial business could be got through in the Star Chamber during only thirty-four sitting days each year. For Privy Councillors meeting increasingly frequently not much more time than this could be spared for what was essentially a secondary commitment for counsellors of state.

The records of the 'English bill' courts preserved in the Public Record Office have during the past half-century drawn historians into masses of bills and answers, interrogatories and depositions in search of the abundant detail which they provide concerning economic activity, agricultural organization, social structure, land holding, and governmental policy. The literary historian has feasted more deeply in these materials than in others, and surely the most artificial class of the Public Records is Requests 4, a portfolio of three Jacobean cases entitled 'Documents of Shakespearean Interest'. The records have not always been handled with the discerning criticalness they deserve. Words of art have been taken too literally, perjury has not always been detected, and the limitations of the probative value of the evidence (perjury aside) has seldom been appreciated. The formidableness of the records' bulk has discouraged systematic investigation of the individual courts as judicial institutions or of the group of courts in terms of their substantive law and procedure. Most significantly, their relation to Tudor–Stuart litigation has not been sufficiently investigated. The over-hasty conclusions as to the natures and place in Tudor–Stuart judicature of these courts arrived at by the Victorians on the basis of a treatise or two, a collection of reports, a look at Coke's *Institutes*, and a too-intimate knowledge of the court of Chancery on the eve of its demise – all coloured by a monochromatic Whiggism – are still rather too much with us. The Chancellor's 'conscience' still does service for his brain. Coke as the intrepid head of a band of common lawyers attacking Roman-lawyer Masters of Chancery and a magical 'equity' supplying the deficiencies of a petrified common law remain lively images. Star Chamber yet sports its tag of 'summary', the 'over-mighty subject' is still the fallen colossus under the Stars, and the 'popular' Elizabethan court still shines white against the despotically black Stuart Star Chamber. Serious historians find it hard to banish the 'poor man' from Requests. Few would voice all or even most of these saws if pressed; few would fail to credit at least one or two of them.

The purpose of this paper is to provide some guide to the documentation of one of these courts, both the material which has survived and that which has disappeared, with some consideration of the archival problems facing the contemporary officials of the court. The latter may have a certain grim interest for archivists today, who will derive some satisfaction from the thought that inadequate provision for the expansion of records is not new. For those who have occasion to use Star Chamber records this guide may prove of some use by placing the existing materials in the bureaucratic framework which produced them and by indicating something of the extent of the documents lost. One warning must be tendered at the outset: despite the similarities in judicial procedure among all 'English bill' courts, argument by analogy in the description of records is dangerous. What is presented here may have little applicability to Chancery or Requests because of the different administrative procedures obtaining in those courts.

I

The bureaucratic structure of the Star Chamber is the key to the court's records, though until the reign of Elizabeth little can be discovered about it beyond the names of successive clerks of the Council. Between 1485 and 1530, three men appear to have served the office of clerk of the Council. In May 1530 Thomas Eden was sworn and admitted clerk of the Council, an office which he would hold until 1567. It was during his tenure that there took place the bifurcation of the early Henrician Council into its two components, the Star Chamber and the Council in its executive capacity, the latter after some contractions and expansions becoming the Privy Council. Eden first served solely as the clerk of the Council in the Star Chamber, as law clerk to a law court, and it was doubtless due to his assiduity that the administrative instrument to what was increasingly a court exercising a defined jurisdiction proved able to cope with mounting business of mounting complexity. From his death until forty years later when the first of an unbroken line of sinecurist clerks of the Council in the Star Chamber was admitted in 1608, two capable men of outstanding administrative capacity held the office in succession. Thomas Marshe was admitted to the clerkship in May 1567; upon his death in the autumn of 1587 he was succeeded by William Mill.[1] These two men fashioned a sophisticated infra-structure of clerks in the chief office of the court and established the lines of devolution of responsibility upon them which remained in existence until the court's abolition in 1641.

The clerkship of the Council in the Star Chamber was one of four offices connected with the court, one of three granted by letters patent under the great seal. The clerk of the Star Chamber was accorded a fixed annual stipend by warrant to the Exchequer of £26 13 4. The clerks of the process was also appointed by patent but without stipend, and was responsible for the writing of all writs and processes issuing from the court under the great seal, from the subpoena to appear to the writ of extent to levy damages awarded to the successful plaintiff. Three generations of one family, Thomas (uncle), Bartholomew (nephew), and Thomas (grandnephew and son, respectively) Cotton, served throughout the reigns of Elizabeth and James I. The usher of the Star Chamber also held by patent without stipend; he undertook the physical maintenance of the Star Chamber proper and the duties of court cryer. The attornies of the court were appointed by the Lord Chancellor or Lord Keeper in his capacity of president of the court and received no stipend. From midway in Elizabeth's reign until 1593 there were three attornies, after that date, four. An attorneyship was the school for the clerkship of the Star Chamber, William Mill having long served therein before his admission as clerk, a precedent followed by one of the deputy clerks (under sinecurist principals) in the early seventeenth century. The attornies held a monopoly of the functions implied by their title, in legally representing parties *pendente lite*, briefing (but not retaining) counsel, moving on their clients' behalf in interlocutory motions, and undertaking for their clients the initial copying of all instruments connected with the litigation.

With the exception of the usher, the major officers were referred to in contemporary parlance as 'clerks of office' and they were ranked hierarchically in the order set down above, the clerk of the Star Chamber being known as the 'chief officer'. Under each 'clerk of office' there stretched a hierarchy of 'clerks of ease', underclerks hired by and responsible to the 'clerk of office' who remunerated them for their services to him. Theoretically, they were not entitled to any fees from litigants for work done but were to take the due fees for their master. Theoretically, control of the clerical establishment was exercised by the Lord Chancellor and the other Lords of the Privy Council by surveillance of and sanctions applied to the 'clerks of office' alone. In fact, by the 1620s the underclerks collected a whole range of 'gratuities' for themselves as well as fees for their master and all of them were recognized as considerably independent though not autonomous clerks under the principal 'clerk of office'. Compared to the establishment of the clerk of the Star Chamber, the hierarchies under the clerk of the process and the attornies were rudimentary. The clerk of the process had a number of underclerks who undertook the engrossing of process and noting the issue of it in an entry book, upon two of whom he reposed special trust for the oversight of the office. Each attorney had eight or nine clerks, engaged in copying, messenger services, devilling in court, framing affidavits for clients, suing out process, and generally handling the routine of busy offices.

By 1620 the 'clerks of ease' under the clerk of the Council in the Star Chamber numbered seven principal underclerks in six offices of quite clearly defined responsibilities. Most had a number of clerks under them–underclerks to underclerks. The order in which they are set down here pre-

---

[1] B[ritish] M[useum], Hargrave MS. 216, fos. 104-104ᵛ, 127ᵛ.

serves the contemporary notion of their precedence. The fact that the two examiners and the register were sworn officers, that is, like the 'clerks of office' took an oath of office before the Lord Chancellor, indicates how slight indeed was their inferiority to the head officer of the court, a sworn deputy clerk to a sinecurist principal.[2]

Two examiners: responsible for administering interrogatories to defendants examined and witnesses deposing in the office and, by the hand of their underclerks, taking down the answers to the interrogatories.

Register: responsible for drafting, entering, and copying all orders and decrees of the court and orders of the Lord Chancellor in chambers, drafting and entering recognizances, passing exemplifications of decrees (i.e., verifying the accuracy of the copy), drafting warrants for process of extent, injunction, and payment of damages (these process could be authorized only by order).

Clerk of the affidavits and register of the rules of the clerk: often referred to as 'under register', he was responsible for entering and copying affidavits, drafting, entering, and copying rules made by the clerk of the court and by the consent of attornies (save consensual dismission, which was entered by the register), making and entering all warrants for process of attachment, commission (including rebellion, dedimus potestatem to examine defendants in the country, and to take depositions of witnesses in the country), supersedeas, certiorari, habeas corpus, and duces tecum, filing and entering these process upon their return, making bonds for such as appeared upon contempt process, engrossing indentures for written exhibits brought in by duces tecum, and passing exemplifications of pleadings, examinations, and depositions.

Clerk of the files and warrants: variously known by this title and as 'clerk of the appearances and certificates', he was responsible for making all warrants for process of subpoena, receiving and filing all pleadings brought into court by the parties (bills, answers, demurrers, replications, and rejoinders), filing interrogatories and examinations/depositions, recording the appearance of and tendering the oath to all defendants bringing in their answers, swearing witnesses coming in to depose, receiving all certificates returned by committees on order of reference (judges, law officers, King's counsel learned, the clerk of the court), and copying the same. An underclerk of this principal underclerk appears by the end of the 1620s to have been largely responsible for the appearances and certificates side and was sometimes loosely referred to as the 'clerk of the appearances and certificates'.

Keeper of the records: responsible for the custody of records after the completion of litigation upon the same and for producing the original pleadings and proofs at trial in the Star Chamber; he will be treated in more detail later.

Copying clerk: he did not have custody of any records, and probably served the other principal underclerks in the second copying of instruments, the attornies having of right the initial copying of the same.

With the exception of the examiners and the copying clerk these principal underclerks had custody of various of the proceedings and other formal records of the court. By virtue of this custody each officer kept a calendar indexing the records under his control. The calendars were not solely an administrative convenience. They were the means to the largest single sustaining source of profit to the whole rank of officialdom in the clerk's office and the attornies' establishment—search for and copying of documents for the litigant. Every litigant, save only the Attorney General suing *pro Rege*, those admitted *in forma pauperis* and clerks of the court, was obliged to pay a fee for search of records by the clerk-custodian of the same, ranging between 6d and 2/- the search (more in fact, thanks to tolerated extortion), and a further fee for the copying of the same. Search and copying was a staple of the profession, and the litigant was forced to take copies of most of the instruments submitted in litigation because he had no right to exhibit the originals in court—they were brought to court only for the verification of the litigant's copies. The commissioners for fees in the 1620s, like an earlier investigator of the fees structure in Star Chamber,[3] exposed the inordinate pressure upon litigants to take unnecessary copies as one of the more blatant forms of fee-racking. That the bills of

---

[2] This information is based upon returns to the commissioners for fees, etc., in the 1620s, in Bodl[eian], MS. Tanner 101, fos. 58–148.

[3] H.E.H[untington Library], Ellesmere MS. 2749, articles 14, 19.

taxed costs are among the lost records of the court prevents us from forming an opinion as to how blatant the practice was, but what costs materials survive indicate that copying fees (for copies necessary and unnecessary) amounted to about one-quarter of the total clerical costs of litigation. It was by assigning the fees for search and copying that the 'clerk of office' – the clerk of Star Chamber and the attornies – remunerated his principal underclerks. To almost all the principal underclerks of the clerk of the Star Chamber this statement was applicable: they 'have the charge and custody of those records and are to make and keepe true callenders for the ready fyndeing out of every matter and in respect of their paynes and care therein they have benefitt of searches when occasion is'.[4] In turn, the underclerks of the principal underclerks depended upon the opportunity afforded by search and copy to touch the litigant for a 'gratuity'. For instance, the register had personally the fee for search and exemplification from the order and decree books, which his underclerk collected for him; his underclerk had no recompense from him save 5/- a week, and his lodging. Thomas Ailway, the register's underclerk, related to the fees commissioners in 1631 an incident wherein he copied two decrees of twenty-three sheets each for a party, and 'in respect there was then a multitude of busines in hand, for which this examinate [Ailway] demanded nothinge but tould him that hee deserved to have 10s. and asked what hee would be pleased to give him for it leavinge it to his consideracion, whereuppon hee gave him 10s.'[5] By the same token that much of the index material to the court's records was called into being by need for quick reference in record search, so the archival divisions within the office of the clerk of the Star Chamber were determined in part by the dependency of the principal underclerks and their underclerks upon search and copying for the profits of office.

Any attempt to describe the records of Star Chamber demands restraint and tentativeness. Whole classes have disappeared. Every other 'English bill' court despite the varying vicissitudes surrounding the preservation of their records is represented today by a larger proportion of a greater variety of their records than is Star Chamber. Besides the surviving classes in the Public Record Office, fragments, exemplifications, the odd document in a repository three thousand miles away buried in congeries of manuscripts, extracts privately collected, and contemporary references to records sometimes confusing and contradictory are about all that there is to go on in the reconstruction of what was once a vast archive in the Star Chamber office.

Proceedings

These were the pleadings and the proofs, the stuff of Star Chamber litigation, hallowed in contemporary parlance as 'the record' of the court, in the narrow legal sense of the term. Sir Edward Coke would deny that the court of Star Chamber was a 'court of record' since its proceedings were not formally enrolled in Latin on parchment,[6] but to the Lords of the Privy Council and the common law judges on the Star Chamber bench (including Chief Justice Coke), lawyers, clerks, and litigants, the pleadings and proofs were the court's equivalent of the plea rolls. The pleadings comprised the bill (if the plaintiff was a private party) or information (if the Attorney General), the defendant's answer or his demurrer, the plaintiff's replication, and the defendant's rejoinder. The bill or information was in petitionary form addressed to the King, the plaintiff 'humbly complaining' (bill) or 'humbly informing' (information), setting forth the circumstances of the alleged crimes in prolix detail, enumerating the specific crimes, naming the defendants, and praying subpoena against them. It was endorsed with the date of filing and was signed by the clerk or his deputy; usually the due date of return of the subpoena was noted too. The answer might be a simple not guilty or a detailed rebuttal or admission of the charges. It generally contained a saving clause for an exception to the

---

[4] BM, Harg. MS. 216, f. 193.

[5] P[ublic] R[ecord] O[ffice], E.165/47, pp. 269–70.

[6] See S. E. Thorne, 'Courts of record and Sir Edward Coke', *Toronto Law Journal*, II (1937–8).

bill's sufficiency, a specific plea of guilty or not guilty to every crime specified in the bill, usually a saving traverse of anything not sufficiently answered to, etc., and invariably ended with a plea for dismissal, usually with costs. If the answer was brought into court by the defendant, the clerk of the court or his deputy signed it in the upper left hand corner with a note and date of the defendant's oath to the verity of the answer and that he would truly answer upon his examination. The defendant might demur rather than answer, demurring either to the jurisdiction of the court or to the sufficiency of the bill, demanding order of the court whether he be required to answer. Demurrers were referred to committee (usually a common law judge), and if overruled, the defendant paid the costs of the reference and was required to make answer. The defendant might also plead-in-bar, either claiming the benefit of a pardon (general or personal), or that the plaintiff was outlawed or excommunicated, or that the same matter had been previously decreed in the court or was still pending in the court undetermined. Combined 'answers and demurrers', even 'pleas, demurrers, and answers', were not uncommon but were discouraged. Replication was required of the plaintiff to the defendant's answer within a given period of time or the action would be dismissed, unless the answer of the defendant was simply not guilty in which case no replication was necessary for the parties had reached issue. Upon replication, the defendant rejoined. Both replication and rejoinder were largely formal, mere averment that what the party had said in his previous plea was true and would be maintained. All pleadings were signed by counsel (save some bills of King's Almoner which were not signed by his general deputy, i.e. his counsel, and some answers put in to commissioners in the country), relator actions by the Attorney General bearing his signature as well as that of the counsel retained by the relator who bore the charges of the prosecution. The pleadings were filed by the clerk of the files and warrants.

With the pleadings completed, the parties moved to proof. If the defendant was allowed by the favour of the Lord Chancellor to make answer and be examined by commissioners in the country under dedimus potestatem, accompanying the commission would be a copy of the bill and the interrogatories upon which he was to be examined. By a specified return date, the defendant's answer, his examination (engrossed on parchment), the copy bill and the interrogatories, and the commission would be delivered to the clerk of the affidavits. If the defendant had appeared personally and put in answer in the office, he was shortly afterwards examined on interrogatories before one of the court's examiners. With the 'books' of examinations taken in court, the first paper entered the proceedings, for all the pleadings were engrossed on parchment (by a professional scribe) as were the interrogatories. Examinations and interrogatories, whether taken in office or the country, were delivered by the examiner (office) or clerk of the affidavits (country) to the clerk of the files for keeping. Whether the examination was conducted by an examiner or commissioners, the defendant signed the examination. The next stage of proof was the taking of depositions of witnesses upon interrogatories. Again, this could be done before the examiners in the court's office, in paper 'books', or before commissioners in the country empowered to act by commission ad examinandum testes, in which case the depositions would be engrossed on parchment by the commissioners' clerk. The interrogatories and depositions taken by commissioners in the country were delivered to the clerk of the affidavits, the carrier swearing that he had not unsealed the bundle of parchment which was the interrogatories and depositions (his oath was noted on the enveloping parchment membrane). Whether taken in the office or the country, the interrogatories to and depositions of witnesses were kept under seal of secrecy by the clerk of the files until all witnesses on both sides had been examined and the parties had agreed to or been ordered to 'publication', the opening of all depositions for perusal by both sides preparatory to hearing.[7]

---

[7] The most readily obtainable explanation and description of Star Chamber procedure in detail is Hudson' treatise, in *Collectanea Juridica*, II, ed. F. Hargrave (London, 1792), pp. 1–240.

The clerk of the files filed the pleadings alphabetically by the last name of the plaintiff on separate files for 1. bills, 2. answers and demurrers, 3. replications, 4. rejoinders. The parchment membranes were strung on a leather thong in the upper left hand corner, the earliest filed being at the bottom against the toggle which bore the initial of the file. No particular time span was comprised in any one file, the clerk putting as many on the thong as it would hold. Thus, a file of plaintiff 'A' bills might cover no more than two years while a file of plaintiff 'L' bills might cover ten years–'Attornatus Regis' was a frequent plaintiff.

The examiners divided their work by alphabet, the initial letter of the plaintiff's name, but they did not file interrogatories and examinations. Rather, they affixed the interrogatories to the appropriate examination or deposition 'books'. The clerk of the files then bundled all examinations together and all depositions together arranged by term and year. Each set of proofs was endorsed on the enveloping wrapper (usually the interrogatories) with the names of the parties, though in the case of depositions, the defendant named might be only the one on whose behalf the depositions were taken.

The clerk of the affidavits arranged the proofs returned to him by commissioners in the same manner as the examiners arranged proofs taken by them. The documents relating to each commission were affixed together. Then the commissions under dedimus potestatem were bundled together by the clerk of the files by term and year and the commissions for the examination of witnesses were bundled together by term and year. Among the dedimus potestatem bundles were, of course, defendants' answers taken by commission.

As Star Chamber 'proceedings' now appear in the Public Record Office, those for Elizabeth's reign (Sta.Cha.5) alone preserve something of the original order, though in straining for alphabetical arrangement the terminal arrangement of proofs has been destroyed by the nineteenth century arrangers. The proceedings for the reign of James I (Sta.Cha.8) have been completely rearranged except for sixteen original files preserved, including a file of ten 'K' bills from 1–10 James I on a handsome toggle-and-thong forty-two inches long.[8] The present arrangement of the Jacobean materials, the gathering together of all pleadings and proofs relating to one case, may have done violence to archival canons but it has facilitated use, especially since the calendars which enabled the original archivist to lay his hand on materials with considerable rapidity have been lost.

Entry books and documents for entry
In common with all 'English bill' courts, Star Chamber's register kept a book in which were entered the orders and decrees of the court. The line between orders and decrees was somewhat sharper in Star Chamber than in Chancery. The Star Chamber decree recorded the final judgement of the whole court upon full hearing of a cause, both the verdict rendered and the sentence. It was the most solemn memorial of the court's decision making. The order was essentially an interlocutory command, either pre- or post-decree. It could be either the decision of the whole court or the decision of the Lord Chancellor alone in his capacity as president of the court sitting in chambers.[9] Within the range of the order's competence, the Lord Chancellor could when the court was not sitting make a decision on any matter raised before him by petition, affidavit and motion, or motion alone, as binding as a decision of the whole court. In many matters the Lord Chancellor regularly acted alone: admission *in forma pauperis*, taxation of costs, reference to committee to rule on the sufficiency of a defendant's answers at his examination. Regardless of origin or importance, all orders joined decrees for entry in 'the register book' as the order and decree book was known.

---

[8] PRO, Sta. Cha. 8/190/31–40. The author has prepared a complete index (by computer) for Sta. Cha. 8 which will be available in the PRO search rooms in 1974.

[9] HEH, Ellesmere MS. 2764, f. 3.

The order and decree books have disappeared. How many and how big they were can be estimated with reasonable accuracy for most of the latter half of the sixteenth century. The penchant of early seventeenth century lawyers to make copious extracts from records for use as precedents produced many leaves of abstracts from Star Chamber order and decree books. The most valuable is virtually a whole volume of short notes from the books for the period 1552-96.[10] Numbering over six hundred items, the extracts are arranged in roughly chronological order and cover the period with remarkable density. Happily, the compiler noted against each extract the folio reference to the order and decree book. Tabulation by date of these folio references indicates that between 1552 and 1595, eleven entire volumes of between 250 and 500 folios each recorded the orders and decrees of the court.[11] Beyond 1595 guesswork only can supply any guide to the missing volumes. Rushworth in the appendix to volume II of his *Historical Collections* reproduces virtually verbatim 159 decrees drawn from the order and decree books, Easter term 1625 to Easter term 1636. Computed against the fines for the period (a nearly complete run) and in knowledge that a fine was a necessary corollary of almost every conviction in Star Chamber, these decrees represent just over one-half of all the decrees of conviction and sentence in those eleven years. Nothing about the size of the books can be judged from the decrees, however, since orders formed by far the bulk of a volume. By the 1630s, Requests's order and decree books ran some three hundred folios and covered one year of four terms each. From Elizabeth's reign, Chancery required two series of registers, each providing a volume of eight hundred folios a year.[12] Variations existed in the contents of the order and decree books of all three courts, but a book comparable to Requests's–perhaps a little bigger– would be credible for the 1630s.

Decrees originated in the full hearing of a case, and orders made by the whole court were initiated by the motion of counsel. An order of the Lord Chancellor in chambers might be based upon motion or petition–in the latter case, the endorsement of the Lord Chancellor's pleasure and his signature serving to move the register to draw an order giving effect to the command.[13] The problem in fast moving verbal proceedings was how to capture the sense of the court. The fortuitous survival of an early seventeenth century manuscript in the Bodleian, which has masqueraded as just another manuscript of law reports, supplies the answer. Mr. Henry E. I. Phillipps first detected the official origins of MS. Rawlinson C.827 in the 1930s.[14] MS. Rawlinson C.827 is in fact the Star Chamber's register's rough minute book of hearings for all the sitting days in Easter term 1636 and Hilary term 1637 to Trinity term 1638 inclusive. It bears the marks of an official compilation: the presence (Lords sitting), the parties' names carefully entered in the margin, full notes of counsels' arguments, the verdict and sentence of every member of the bench in a judgment hearing, and absolute completeness. It is rough, fast drawn, spare, and the writer's mandatory tone is in direction to himself. A marginal 'X' against virtually all items is a reminder of something done, of an order drafted. It bears a marked resemblance to the earliest Chancery 'Registrar's Court or Minute Book'.[15] The Bodleian manuscript has a counterpart in British Museum, Harleian MS. 4022, which contains all decisions in Star Chamber for Easter and Trinity terms 1634. It is a pretty book– nothing rough about it–but it is patently of the same genre as the Bodleian manuscript and was

---

[10] BM Harleian MS. 2143.

[11] 1552-7 (250 fos.); 1557-63 (275 fos.); 1563-71 (350 fos.); 1571-8 (350 fos.); 1578-80 (250 fos.); 1581-4 (375 fos.); 1584-6 (300 fos.); 1586-8 (350 fos.); 1558-90 (300 fos.); 1590-3 (500 fos.); 1593-5 (425 fos.)–all totals of folios approximate.

[12] e.g. PRO, Req. 1/37; C.33/99-160.

[13] Among the Star Chamber miscellanea in the Public Record Office there are a number of these petitions, PRO, Sta. Cha. 10/9, no. 42; 18, nos. 32-8.

[14] *The High Court of the Star Chamber, 1603-1641* (unpublished London M.A. thesis, 1939), Appendix i, cited as 'Register book of Star Chamber'.

[15] PRO, C.37/1, Mich. 1639.

probably taken from the no longer extant register's rough minute book for the period. The notable omissions from both manuscripts are any entries for orders made by the Lord Chancellor in chambers. It is probable that a different rough minute book was used on these occasions, perhaps in order to expedite the drafting of orders and decrees by preventing one book from being continuously tied up in use. Lord Keeper Egerton had been adamant in his administrative reforms of 1597 that orders and decrees were to be drafted within 'convenient tyme to be coppied with expedicion for the sutor and shalbe duely entred and fayre written in the regester booke within convenient tyme after the ende of everye terme'.[16] Drafting of orders and decrees was a difficult and delicate task and time-consuming emendations and deletions went into the perfecting of the draft.[17]

By 1620 at the latest the Star Chamber order and decree book did not contain two types of decisions, albeit of an inferior nature, which were exceedingly common and essential to the effective functioning of the court: rules entered by consent of attornies and rules of the clerk of the Star Chamber as to the course of the court when opposing attornies could not be brought to agreement.[18] The progress of a case from procedural stage to stage within the framework of the 'course of the court'–established by practice and general orders of reforming Lord Chancellors–depended on consent or the clerk's ruling, and a formal record of it was no less necessary than the register of orders and decrees. This record no longer exists, though it was often enough referred to at the time as the 'entry book' or 'register' of the clerk of the affidavits and register of the rules of the clerk. That we know anything about it we owe to a calendar index to it for the period Easter term 1631 to Trinity term 1641 preserved in the Folger Shakespeare Library, Washington, D.C.[19] The connection between this calendar (which carries no indication of its nature or provenance) and a class of record at most alluded to and quite lost to view depends upon circumstantial evidence, though of a peculiarly convincing kind. The calendar is a vellum bound large quarto paper book of 270 folios, divided alphabetically (plaintiff's name) and under each initial sub-divided chronologically by term and regnal year and serially progressive folio reference. The entry of term and regnal year and folio reference is marginal, and is followed by the plaintiff (surname first) versus defendant with an entry in the far right margin of 'pro q' or 'pro d' to indicate whether the plaintiff (querens) or defendant moved for the entry. The majority of the entries have written immediately beneath this first entry a succession of entries of term/regnal year/folio reference in strict chronological progression. From the folio references it is evident that the calendar indexes two volumes, the first of 420 folios (Easter term 1631–Michaelmas term 1635) and the second of 354 folios (Hilary 1636–Trinity 1641). An initial suspicion that it might have been the calendar to the order and decree books was raised by a transcript of the famous orders of 22 December 1597 reforming dilatory proceedings on the last folios with a note in the same hand that had made the case entries that 'these orders are entered in the register booke' for Hilary term 7 Charles I by order of the court. However, comparison with Rawlinson C.827, Harleian MS. 4022, Rushworth's extracts of decrees, and the manuscript law reports of Star Chamber cases of the 1630s reveals insufficient connection with orders and decrees to support this suspicion, to say nothing of the fact that *ore tenus* proceedings, verbal prosecutions by the Attorney General upon confession, do not appear in the calendar though a decree was the inevitable result of such a prosecution. Obviously then the calendar refers to prosecutions brought by the ordinary course of pleadings and proofs; yet the entries do not correspond with the known dates of pleadings and proofs available from the few surviving Caroline proceedings,[20] and folio references would have no pertinence to the filing and bundling of these documents. Comparison

---

[16] Bodl, MS. Tanner 101, f. 69v, order 15.

[17] PRO, Sta. Cha. 10/18, nos. 6–13, 14–17, 20, 25, 47–8.

[18] Bodl. MS. Tanner 101, f. 76; HEH, Ellesmere MS. 2749, f. 10.

[19] Folger, V.a.278, manuscript in the collection of Lord Willoughby de Broke.

[20] PRO, Sta. Cha. 9/1/1–19; nos. 20–5 in this bundle are not Star Chamber but Requests bills.

with the 1631 entries in the last entry book of the clerk of the process[21] does not establish sufficient correlation to support an argument that the calendar's entry book was primarily concerned with process. By a process of elimination, the calendar's entry book appears to have contained warrants for process other than subpoenas, entries of some common document likely to be required all along the progress of a case, and entries of some kind of decisions made with fair frequency at various procedural stages. This fits the records within the responsibility of the clerk of the affidavits and register of rules of the clerk of the court: 1. warrants for process other than subpoenas, 2. affidavits, 3. rules upon consent of the attornies or by the clerk of the court, all of which a contemporary description of the clerk's office indicated were 'entered'.[22] The Folger volume, then, is the calendar to the 'under register's register'.

The commissioners for fees in the 1620s remarked that the office of clerk of the affidavits and register of rules of the clerk had been separated from the office of register by 'Lord Chancellor St Alban'.[23] This need not be taken literally to mean by Bacon during his Chancellorship, 1617–21, but refers rather to his tenure as clerk of the Star Chamber from 1608, to whose ordinance this more properly belonged. It was natural that in this separation there should be assigned to the new officer the drafting and entry of rules of the clerk and consensual rules, and it seems likely that the new entry book came into being with the new office. In the 1597 investigations of the court's fee structure, the investigator referred to the copying of rules taken before the clerk of the court as being of 'equall charge to the copies of the Lord Keepers orders and beinge so many more in number is a burden'.[24] It is evident from his reference that the register of the court was responsible for both orders and rules, and it was likely that both went in the same book. The order and decree books, growing in size and shrinking in period covered, would with the increasing pressure on the register and Bacon's penchant for Parkinsonian development dictate the creation of the new officer.

Among the documents surrounding the general orders for 'the reform of dilatory proceedings' promulgated by Lord Keeper Egerton on 22 December 1597 and in the orders themselves, there are references to a 'titling book'.[25] In it went certificates of committees upon reference and notes of admission to attorney of defendants after their examinations. What else might have been entered is unknown, but these two items have in common the fact that they came within the purview of the clerk of the files and warrants, otherwise clerk of the appearances and certificates. In a certificate of reference upon an order in November 1593, clerk William Mill stated that he had 'perused the booke of apparance' and found that a party had not recorded his appearance the previous term, which might indicate that the clerk of the files kept a separate book of appearances–doubtless similar to Requests's 'appearance book'–although it does not rule out the possibility that the 'titling book' was otherwise known as the 'appearance book'.[26] Requests also had a separate 'Liber Testium' recording appearance of witnesses deposing in the court's office.[27] The administering of the oath to witnesses in Star Chamber was the duty of the clerk of the files, and if he kept a general 'titling book' that too might contain entries of witnesses sworn. One piece of material evidence confuses the whole search for the nature of the 'titling book'. In the British Museum, Additional MS. 37045 is a fair-drawn volume of 69 folios containing transcripts of certificates from committees,

[21] PRO, 30/38/24.

[22] BM, Harg. MS. 216, fos. 193–4v.

[23] Bodl, MS. Tanner 101, f. 138.

[24] HEH, Ellesmere MS. 2749, f. 10.

[25] Bodl, MS. Tanner 101, fos. 71–71v; HEH, Ellesmere MS. 2754, nos. 6–8.

[26] BM, Add. MS. 37045, f. 3v; PRO, Req. 1/104–17. The Requests's appearance book also recorded admission to attorney, which would take place in that court on appearance, rather than on examination as in Star Chamber, because the defendant was usually not examined in Requests.

[27] PRO, Req. 1/198–206.

Michaelmas term 1593 to Trinity term 1595.[28] It gives only the certificates and not the orders of committal. It stands up to comparison with the few existing original certificates (though there are none for the period covered by the book), but it is not very convincing as an *official* document. The absence of the orders of committal jars with the requirement that orders and certificates be preserved together and the fact that all existing certificates, whether originals or exemplifications, are always either written upon or attached to the order. The volume reveals omissions of names of parties and even of committees, is all too much of a oneness, too preciously drawn to inspire confidence in its workaday origins. It might well be another Jacobean collection of extracts from Star Chamber records. Beyond this, nothing more can be said about the 'titling book', though if in fact it was a comprehensive entry book for the documents connected with the office of the clerk of the files, it rather neatly rounded off a triumvirate of superior entry books created by the three principal underclerks–register, clerk of the affidavits, clerk of the files–responsible for the preservation of memorials of decision-making in Star Chamber.[29]

The triumvirate (if such it was) had a respectable ancestry. The early registers of the functionally undifferentiated Council of Henry VII and Henry VIII contained entries of orders and decrees, affidavits, warrants for process, notes of appearances, admissions to attorney, and rules upon consent as well as the executive activity that was the other attribute of the Council's function.[30] Of course, at that time all the judicial business took place in the face of the Council (saving only examining and such matters as the Council referred to arbitration) and the register kept by the clerk of the Council recording the daily proceedings before the Council recorded virtually the whole of the Star Chamber's activity. When in 1590 Clerk William Mill stated in a memorial to the Lord Chancellor

I have learned in this court and therefore I have good warrant to speake it, that untill of very late tyme even untill the tyme of my last predicessor [Thomas Marshe, 1567–87] in a manner there was nothing done either in the courte publiquely or in the Inner Star Chamber privately but it passed under the handes of my predicessors and was entred in the bookes of entryes remayneing of recorde in the court in my custody as the officer thereof at this daye[31]

he was alluding to 'the register' of the court, the register of the Henrician Council which with the creation of the Privy Council and its own registers recording the executive activity of the new body became the order and decree book of a wholly judicial Council in the Star Chamber. When Mill wrote this, the order and decree book no longer bore witness to the whole of the court's activity, because so much of it had moved out of court into the routine of office administration, implemented by the attornies and the clerk within the restrictions of the 'course of the court' and subject to the order of the court or of the Lord Chancellor. Affidavits, for instance, were no longer made in court, but were presented ready drafted to the clerk of the affidavits who administered the oath to the deponent and retained the written instrument. Appearances, admissions to attorney, warrants for process of course, and rules were all out-of-court and in-the-office. The history of the Elizabethan Star Chamber is the history of the devolution of procedural routine upon the clerical establishment, thus relieving the Lords of the Privy Council of the impossibly time-consuming tasks involved. Elizabethan and early Stuart privy councillors in fact spent less time in adjudication in Star Chamber and handed down more judgments for a given period of time than did the councillors of the early Tudors. Mill's 'book of entries' underwent metamorphosis in Elizabeth's reign, becoming an order,

[28] Purchased by the BM from Jaggard of Liverpool, 1905.

[29] PRO, Sta. Cha. 10/18, nos. 50–72, 16, 22.

[30] See *Select Cases in the Council of Henry VII*, C. G. Bayne ed., Selden Soc. 75 (London, 1958). HEH, Ellesmere MSS. 2654, 2655, 2768, *Libri Intrationum*. For early decrees, *in extenso*, 31–37 Henry VIII, see Guildhall Library, MS. 1751, pp. 199–250.

[31] BM, Harg. MS. 216, f. 119v.

decree, and rule book when it threw off the matters entered in the 'titling book', which in turn became solely an order and decree book with the creation of the clerk of the affidavits's entry book about 1610. When the first stage of metamorphosis took place is difficult to say. As late as 1557, an apparently complete run of extracts from the register for Michaelmas term of that year contains affidavits, warrants for process, admission to attorney ('Edwardes and Ronabanes called at the instance of Waters and admitted to attorney [retaining] William Mills'), a recognizance taken in court, publication granted (rule-of-the-clerk jurisdiction later), a fine paid, and orders and decrees.[32] These extracts came from the first term in the second order book of the eleven for 1552–95 mentioned above. A shrewd guess from a perusal of the time span-size ratios of those eleven order and decree books would place the establishment of the 'titling book' about the time that the comprehensive register jumped from an average of 50 folios per annum to 100 folios under the sudden pressure of a rapidly increased amount of business–the volume for 1578–80. This is, however, surmise.

In the early seventeenth century at least three other books existed in the clerk's office. Two were the 'generall booke of hearing' and the 'comission booke of heareing', or 'lespecial lievre de hearinges', in one of which was entered a cause when ready for hearing.[33] Nothing remains of them, but two lists of causes to be heard covering whole terms are extant and might have been abstracts from the hearing books.[34] Since publication was the necessary prelude for entry in the hearing book and this was either consensual (general) or ruled by the clerk (special), it is likely that the register of rules of the clerk was charged with keeping the hearing books. The third book probably was not a book at all, but a file of paper leaves 8×10 inches on which the clerk of the files and warrants entered all warrants for process within his competence. Three of these sheets survive, all are late Elizabethan, and all are written down one side, then turned over lengthwise and written down the other.[35] Correlation of the entries of the warrants for subpoenas on these sheets with the process books of the clerk of the process reveals the closest resemblance between the two records. While the clerk of the affidavits probably entered his warrants for process of contempt and commissions in his entry book, the clerk of the files would have been hard put to enter the warrants for subpoena in the 'titling book' since there were so many of them, and their presence so cluttering and dominating.

Calendars

Of these documents much has already been said. The Folger calendar to the entry book of the clerk of the affidavits is the only surviving example of what was once a large corpus of indexes. William Mill, in complaining to Lord Keeper Egerton in 1597 of a recent order abridging his fees, said that 'of auncient tyme yt appeareth of recorde that all billes, aunsweres, and other pleadinges were entered of recorde in the Bookes of Entries and the fee due for every name is 4d.'[36] No trace survives of any such book as this, but its successor would be the calendar to the bundles of pleadings kept by the clerk of the files for search in which he claimed 6d as well as the 6d search of the files (this calendar paid a direct profit[37]). The clerk of the affidavits and his predecessor in the register's

---

[32] BM, Lansdowne MS. 639, fos. 49v–52v–this MS. volume was the notebook of William Hudson, attorney in Star Chamber, counsellor practising there, and author of the most complete treatise on the court. The attorney William Mill mentioned here, who died in 1564, was the father of the clerk of the court of the same name (1587–1608), who had also been an attorney of Star Chamber.

[33] BM, Harg. MS. 216, f. 191; PRO, E.163/24/9 (anon. treatise); Harvard Law School Library, L.MS. 1128, no. 244.

[34] PRO, S.P.16/247, no. 66; 291, no. 123.

[35] PRO, Sta.Cha.10/7 pt. 1, nos. 107, 372; 17, no. 531.

[36] HEH, Ellesmere MS. 2680, no. 2.

[37] HEH, Ellesmere MS. 2678, no. 1.

office kept a calendar to the bundles of examinations and depositions taken in the country by commissioners.[38] Both the examiners and the register kept calendars to their records.[39] The keeper of the records also made a calendar to records previously calendared by their respective temporary custodians (the other clerks) when, following the conclusion of the case, the proceedings came to him.[40]

At his death in 1608, Mill's personal representatives (two of his clerks) turned over to his successor, Sir Francis Bacon, six calendars, among them four 'kallenders of orders', 1485 to Trinity 1538, Michaelmas 1538 to Hilary 1563, Easter 1563 to Trinity 1588, and Michaelmas 1588 to Trinity 1590, the last being 'in lose papers'.[41] Those of the Elizabethan period begin and end precisely with the beginning and ending of various of the order and decree books noted above. These calendars were, of course, equivalents of the register's current calendar, except that they were in the personal possession of Mill and not apparently connected in any way with the register. It is likely that all four of these calendars were in fact very recent productions, made up from the old registers by and for Mill as a guide to precedent. This suspicion is strengthened by the nature of the other two calendars turned over to Bacon. The fifth was 'one other boke or alphabet kallender conteinying all such matters as were debated in the Starchamber' from Michaelmas 8 to Trinity 13 Henry VIII (1516–21). The sixth was 'an alphabet kallender to give light of divers especiall presidentes, under Mr. Mynates hand.' Mynatt was an examiner of the court from the 1590s until he became deputy clerk of the court under Bacon in 1609. His successor as deputy clerk prepared a brief of precedents for Lord Chancellor Ellesmere on the subject of means by which the court might levy damages to the benefit of the successful plaintiff. The precedents range from 1485 to 1600, are apparently short extracts from the early registers and the later order and decree books, and are in every instance referenced by such neat marginalia as 'See lettre A, 10 Henry 8'.[42] Mr Mynatt's alphabet calendar was in this case put to good use, for these precedents formed the basis for a decision by Ellesmere that introduced a new writ into the court's armory of process, the writ of extent to levy damages,[43] and incidentally launched the court on a course of favouritism to the plaintiff's interest over the King's which vitally affected its future as a punitive tribunal.

Obligations

The subpoena had long since lost its penal sting by Elizabeth's reign. The uniform £100 pain specified in the subpoena to appear was virtually unleviable and the subpoena was little more than a summons. However, it was an originating summons but one which, thanks to procedural slackness developing over the years, it was customary not to appear upon. It was common practice for defendants to come in only upon attachment, a process of contempt. The defendant in contempt entered bond in £20 to answer his contempt, and then proceeded in the suit. He was in fact never proceeded against for the contempt. The bonds were mass produced by the clerk of the affidavits on parchment strips, filled in when signed by the party, and supersigned by the clerk of the court. Among eighteen files of these bonds, mostly late Elizabethan, there are some without the regnal year entered.[44] Normally redelivered to the party when his contempt was purged (i.e. the main suit completed) these were not. The overriding value of these bonds was the fees brought the clerk.

---

[38] HEH, Ellesmere MS. 2680, no. 7.

[39] BM, Harg. MS. 216, fos. 193–4v.

[40] Bodl. MS. Tanner 101, f. 107.

[41] HEH, Ellesmere MS. 2725–signed by Bacon as received, 19 Aug. 1608.

[42] HEH, Ellesmere MS. 2757.

[43] Brereton's Case (Trinity 1614) in Sir Francis Moore's own MS. reports, Folger, V.a.133, fos. 32v–9v. See Hudson in *Collectanea Juridica*, II, pp. 226–7.

[44] PRO, Sta.Cha.10/18, nos. 142–776, 785, 872.

Recognizances were a far different kind and form of obligation and one with teeth. They were entered into on order of the court or the Lord Chancellor, the party being bound in his own recognizance with sureties, and were penal in character, being void only upon the performance of very real provisions. They were a powerful instrument to preserve good order *pendente lite* and were with fair frequency imposed upon parties with condition to abide the decree and sentence of the court. When forfeit for non-performance, they were estreated into the Exchequer and levied as a debt due to the King. The register drafted recognizances (since they were upon order) on paper folded letter-style, and when signed and sealed they were filed.[45] Ostensibly he was to 'enter' them, but in what kind of entry book is not clear.

Process

In this period the Star Chamber's process went out under the great seal. The old privy seal subpoena became thoroughly Latinized when it came out under the great seal, and all the rest of the process mirrored the structure and form of the writs of the common law courts. The process were written on parchment strips in the Chancery hand by the underclerks of the clerk of the process in the Star Chamber, sealed sur simple queue, and bore a label.[46] In the case of the subpoenas usually the label alone was served on the party. All non-subpoena process were to be returned endorsed. When the clerk of the process received the warrants from the office of the clerk of the court, his clerks filled in the particulars on the prepared forms, entered note of a number of the process under teste date in the 'entry book' of the clerk of the process, and carried the process in batches for sealing to the great seal. The entry in the 'entry book' was in the briefest possible form, though the clerk was careful to note writs renewed ('ren'), writs under the same warrant as writs already issued ('vet'), writs for which no fees were due ('nihil pro Rege', etc.). Thanks to the generosity of a descendant of the last clerk of the process, the process books of the court between Hilary term 1580 and Easter term 1632 were presented to the Public Record Office a quarter of a century ago.[47] They share with the Star Chamber proceedings in the Office the distinction of being the most considerable records of the court extant.

Exemplification, estreats, abstracts, and breviates

This category consists of those documents produced by the court or its officers from the records of the court for official or quasi-official purposes. Formal exemplifications of orders and decrees, subsigned by the clerk of the court and passed by the register, are sprinkled about in numerous repositories, but very few of the other documents which were commonly copies in furtherance of the litigation are extant. The most prominent and important type of document produced by the court for official purposes outside the court was the estreat of fines prepared by the register and directed to the Exchequer for levying on the King's behalf by writ of mittimus out of the process office. A number of the writs and estreats (annexed) are to be found in the so-called 'Brevia Baronibus' class in the Public Record Office, but the majority of the estreats (albeit with some few omissions) are to be found on the King's Remembrancer memoranda rolls. Enrolled are 122 estreats of fines for the period 1596–1641,[48] and spot checking of the agenda books to the rolls indicates enrolment from at least as early as the beginning of Elizabeth's reign. Their value cannot be overemphasized: in the

---

[45] PRO, E.208/26 (last bundle) for a number of original recognizances estreated into Exchequer. HEH, Ellesmere MS. 5958 is a recognizance for appearance and good behaviour entered into in 1610 before Lord Chancellor Ellesmere and crudely scribbled in his own hand – where was the register?

[46] PRO, Sta.Cha.10/20, sack of filed subpoenas with a very few other process.

[47] PRO, 30/38/1-27.

[48] PRO, E.159/410-81; originals, E.208/26 (last bundle). The author has presented a fully indexed transcript of the estreats for 1596-1641 to the PRO for the use of students, available in the Round Room.

absence of the order and decree books they alone provide the outcome of most cases which went to hearing in which the defendant was convicted or the plaintiff fined for bringing false suit.

In a special class by themselves were the cause-lists and the fines' review agenda. The cause-lists were prepared shortly before each sitting day by the clerk from the hearing book, three cases usually being put down for the day's hearing. The cause-list contained the names of the parties, a brief indication of the nature of the offences, and carried a note if the cause was set down at the request of the defendant. The lists were distributed to the Lords at the sitting, and the more assiduous of the bench such as Ellesmere and Sir Julius Caesar earlier, the Earl of Bridgewater and Secretary Windebanke later used them to take notes of the hearing.[49] The fines' review agenda was prepared by the register from the decrees against the post-term sitting day of Hilary and Trinity terms (and sometimes other terms as well) when the Lords reviewed fines imposed before directing estreating of them into the Exchequer.

The papers of Sir Thomas Egerton, Lord Ellesmere, Lord Keeper and afterwards Lord Chancellor from 1596 to 1617, preserved in the Ellesmere collection in the Huntington Library, San Marino, California, reveal the full extent of the clerk's activity in the preparation of precedents for the consideration of the Lord Chancellor. These ranged from extracts from Mr Mynatt's alphabet calendar to the elaborate extracts from the Henrician registers which pass under the misnomer *Liber Intrationum*, to abstracts of decrees and notes of penalties imposed. They are official documents both in provenance and purpose.

Among the Ellesmere manuscripts and the papers of Sir Julius Caesar at Alnwick Castle are a few breviates of evidence relating to specific cases before the court prepared by the clerk's office.[50] They are to be distinguished from briefs submitted by attorneys and briefs headed 'the state of the cause' prepared by the clerk for procedural review. In essence they are abstracts of the proofs of the case, each item carefully referenced to the original examination or deposition. They were presented to the bench at hearings to make the evidence more manageable, and in their preparation the clerk performed a function not dissimilar to that of the *rapporteur* in contemporary French penal courts. There are not a great many of these breviates, but they are without peer in enabling the researcher to get behind the verdict so solemnly declared by the Lords.

II

By the first decade of the seventeenth century the clerk of the Star Chamber was in the throes of the classical archival crisis—high document growth rate and small space availability. The clerk of the court was the victim of two circumstances which plagued all Tudor 'new courts' but the Star Chamber somewhat more than others. First, the court had expanded rapidly in jurisdiction and activity in an increasingly litigious age. As a court open to private litigants—indeed, a pawn to the demands of the private litigant—Star Chamber got more than its fair share of the business provided by the new gentry's headlong rush to law. Spurred on by a complex law of property married to an unparalleled amount of property available in the century following the dissolution of the monasteries and the chantries, the gentry wrung every ounce of advantage that a confused and easily confusible law of property afforded in the quest for realty. By Elizabeth's reign, though Star Chamber no longer concerned itself with title, the court was the prime vehicle for the litigant to mount a collateral action to a suit for property brought at equity or common law. As such, its chief advantage to the plaintiff was often the ease of control over the pace of litigation that its procedure allowed him. Here the first great shortcoming of 'English bill' procedure fed vexatious and dilatory

---

[49] Ellesmere's and Bridgewater's are in HEH, Ellesmere MSS., Caesar's in BM, Additional MSS. (various), and Alnwick Castle, MSS. 9–10, and Windebanke's in PRO, S.P.16/159–461.

[50] E.g. Alnwick Castle, MS. 9, fos. 99, 120, and HEH, Ellesmere MS. 2741.

proceedings, thus attracting more litigants. By moving proceedings out of the face of the court and into the office of the clerk of the court, 'English bill' procedure largely removed the litigant from the surveillance and control possible in common law procedure. From the time of Egerton–who with a lively awareness of the tremendous growth of dilatoriness in Star Chamber tackled the problem of litigant irresponsibility within three weeks of his appointment as Lord Keeper in 1596–until the court's abolition in 1641, successive Chancellors managed what can at best be termed an orderly retreat in the face of dilatoriness.[51] The second great shortcoming of 'English bill' procedure nurtured the bulk of documentation. Proof by depositions of witnesses examined secretly upon interrogatories precluded cross-examination in the sense in which it takes place in open court upon oral testimony. Until publication, that is until all the proofs had been taken, each side worked in the dark. It was impossible to know what proof was being adduced by the adversary party. One might examine the adversary's witnesses on one's own interrogatories, but in ignorance of their evidence-in-chief a grave risk was run of merely magnifying their testimony in aid of the adversary. Consequently, both sides sought blind comprehensiveness at the proof stages, putting into their interrogatories scores of questions in search of every shred of relevant evidence. The inadequacy of this system of proof put a premium on pleadings packed with detail–the plaintiff so that he might have the greatest scope to rake up the maximum of damning evidence (he could not go to proof on any matters not charged in the bill) and the defendant so that his sworn answer might be used evidentially to plaster over gaps in his proofs or puncture holes in the unseen walls of his adversary's case. More litigants submitting pleadings larded with detail and going to proof on masses of interrogatories creating yet larger masses of depositions were the sources of the clerk's archival problems.

The second circumstance plaguing the clerk of the court was his 'homelessness'. The Star Chamber physically was one room of the Palace of Westminster and a retiring room (the Inner Star Chamber) to the same which doubled as the Lord Chancellor's chamber in the exercise of his out-of-court jurisdiction and one of the most frequented meeting places of the Privy Council in its executive function. In the days of Henry VII and Henry VIII when the amount and complexity of litigation was not much greater than that at a country quarter sessions, a clerk like Robert Rydon and Richard and Thomas Eden could set up office wherever he could put down his paper, quill, standish and pen dust. By Elizabeth's time, with the increased litigation and bulk of documentation and with the putting out of court of virtually all procedural stages of litigation before the hearing, clerks Marshe and Mill needed an established centre for the six-day week the office worked in term and out with plenty of storage space. It was probably Mill who established the Star Chamber office in the Holborn court of Gray's Inn, of which society he was a member. In 1590 he was accused by two dissident attornies in the court of establishing an office in his chambers and attempting to force them to do their copying there. Mill confessed that 'to his greate charge hee hath made an office meaneinge indeed to draw them [the attornies] thither for the more ease of the subject and better service of the court in the custody and preservacions of the records with which hee standeth charged. . . .'[52] That he succeeded is testified to by the benchers of Gray's temporarily continuing attorney Walter Jones in chambers in the Inn in 1602 upon a letter from Lord Keeper Egerton.[53] Mill paid for these rooms in Gray's himself, and it was to these quarters that he moved all the earlier records of the court and kept the current records for reference. He had solved the problem of homelessness, but in the next two decades he would find it difficult, in the expansion of his office staff essential to the continued efficiency of his office, to provide the extra space needed for underclerks fast becoming principal clerks and still house the growing bulk of documents.

---

[51] T. G. Barnes, 'Due process and slow process in the late Elizabethan–early Stuart Star Chamber', *American Journal of Legal History*, VI (1962), pp. 221–49, 315–46.
[52] BM, Harg. MS. 216, f. 105v. The Requests office was in the Temple.
[53] *Pension Book of Gray's Inn*, I (1901), p. 157.

Mill hit upon the solution which his successors would follow. A few months before Mill's death in the summer of 1608, a joiner constructed in the Star Chamber itself four large presses of wainscot with three partitions each, with locks and hinges, each six feet long, three feet deep, and eight feet high. In the term following Mill's death, the same joiner constructed five new presses of the same dimensions, putting four of them on top of the existing four and the fifth over the door.[54] Thirteen hundred cubic feet of space would be more than sufficient to house all of the pleadings and proofs in existence at that date, and it is evident that into these cupboards went all the proceedings save those currently needed in the office. At least temporarily, the clerk had solved his archival crisis.

The appointment of a keeper of the records by Sir Francis Bacon between 1610 and 1620 was not connected with any particular archival need.[55] The new office was in effect split from the office of the clerk of the files, who had previously acted as the ultimate custodian of all proceedings after the completion of litigation. However, the new principal underclerk, William Molins, was responsible for the safekeeping of all proceedings otherwise in the custody of the other officers when they were carried out of the Gray's Inn office, either to committees on reference or to Westminster for the hearing. In attending at the hearing he brought up the pleadings (taken off the files) and the bundles of proofs pertaining to the cases to be heard that they might be ready to hand if the court wished to verify copies. He would also cancel any pleadings in the face of the court if ordered to do so. For all this, he had no right to fees since his office had been created since the settling of the fee structure in 1598, though he managed to get a 'gratuity' of 2/- a day for attendance from the litigants. Since he was the ultimate custodian of all proceedings, he had the search and copying of proceedings delivered him after the end of the action, though he ruefully noted that this brought him little profit.[56] Little sympathy need be wasted on Mr Molins, for as one of the attornies certified the commissioners for fees in 1627, Molins 'will laye the byll and answer in one place, the dedimus in another, and examinacion in a third and take 2s. for every of them where his master [the clerk of the court] should have but one 2s. yf it be above a yeare for all and nothing within the yeare.'[57] If Molins' thirst for fees was second to none in the office, it is possible that he brought some care to the preservation of the proceedings if for no other reason than that it affected his profits. Yet as we will note in a moment, he might have been the last officer of the court to have it within his power to save the mass of records which disappeared in the seventeenth century.

During the court's existence the ordinary natural threats to the records were not much in evidence. The proceedings appear to have been kept in fairly good condition. The files of pleadings and bundles of examinations in court were belted with straps of 'Hungary' leather, replaced when perished. Office depositions of witnesses and commission depositions alike were placed in buckram or canvas bags.[58] Disorder in the documents was doubtless all too common, and it grew from the divided responsibility for the records among the principal underclerks and the quite archaic method of filing and bundling. The frequent unfiling and unbundling during the course of litigation was bound to introduce confusion. Dead proceedings probably enjoyed little attention. It was after all a busy office staffed by a burgeoning bureaucracy becoming progressively more departmentalized and independent of much oversight. No deputy clerk under a sinecurist principal of the post-1608 period could hope to wield the authority that Mill or Marshe had exercised before, and clerk Francis

[54] PRO, E.407/55, fos. 165–8, S. C. usher's account, Mich. 1608.

[55] Bodl, MS. Tanner 101, f. 138.

[56] Bodl, MS. Tanner 101, fos. 89, 107, 108. Molins was admitted to Middle Temple from New Inn, 6 Aug. 1601, but was not called until 7 May 1619, although he had chambers in Middle Temple throughout the period–an indication he was in a clerical office at law. Following call, he had a fairly extensive practice in Star Chamber, to judge by his signature on pleadings, in PRO, Sta.Cha.8.

[57] Bodl, MS. Tanner 101, f. 124v.

[58] PRO, E.407/55, fos. 165–8, 212.

Bacon's disturbing willingness to create new sub-offices made more tenuous the authority of the active deputy clerk. When in the late 1620s joint-clerkship by sinecurists became the fashion, one man would take the clerkship and the other the registership, and both offices would be exercised by deputies. These developments affected the total efficiency of the office, not least in its archival aspects. They indicated a retrogressive tendency contrary to a tradition of concern for the records begun by the Elizabethan clerks. Thomas Marshe had fought a hard battle against the attornies in the 1580s who carried off proceedings for copying; he kept the keys to the presses and had such success that the attornies had to break open the locks of the presses to get the documents, 'wherewith he was often offended'.[59] Mill won the victory over the attornies by drawing them into his office for copying. In this, he removed the greatest single potential danger of actual loss of the documents. It was not pure archival sentiment that moved him – the crux of the row between Mill on the one hand and the attornies on the other which raged through the 1590s was the 12d per sheet fee for copying by the attornies, of which Mill had the right to 6d but which he wished to ensure receiving by collecting the whole fee and then paying the attornies their moities. In the light of the virulence of this dispute between the clerk and the attornies, one must allow for exaggeration in Mill's charges that the 'losse and disorder' of the records came from the attornies having 'custodie of the recordes in their bagges, studies, and chambers'.[60] There is no proof that many records were lost, but disorder there certainly was. Mill had just cause to boast that commission depositions once 'kepte confusedlie in a cupboarde without kallender' were since his accession kept in bags by terms with a calendar to the same.[61] Mill's administration of the office marked a large advance in concern for the care and ordering of records. In this, William Mill reflected his age's new-found 'record consciousness' which pervaded government and in a more refined form was destined to pervert the constitution.

III

The fate of the records following the court's abolition by the Long Parliament in 1641 is an enigma. The 1732 report of the committee of the House of Commons appointed to investigate the fire damage done to Cotton's library and the state of the nation's records generally included the certificate of the Keeper of the Records in the Chapter House that 'bills, answers, interrogatories, depositions, and commissions of the Court of Star Chamber' were in his custody; table E of the same report stated that the dates of the Star Chamber documents in the Chapter House covered the period from 1487 to the reign of Charles I.[62] The select committee on the public records reporting in 1800 included a certificate to the same effect, dating the span as 'from Henry VII when the court was erected to 16 Charles I when the Proceedings in it ended'.[63] No credence need be given to the exactness of the dates, which reflected surmise from history rather than inspections of the records, for in fact the records in the Chapter House both in 1732 and 1800 were the records which are now comprised in the Public Record Office's classes Sta.Cha.1–9, proceedings which patently end with the beginning of the reign of Charles I.

The inescapable conclusion is that the records in the Chapter House at Westminster were the records moved there from the Star Chamber at Westminster. And what of the rest, the proceedings for 1625–41 and the order and decree books, entry books, 'titling books', calendars and the rest of the documents described above? They were the records which were not kept in Mr Mill's

---

[59] HEH, Ellesmere MS. 3007.

[60] HEH, Ellesmere MS. 2677.

[61] HEH, Ellesmere MS. 2680, no. 7. Clerks' notes on the dorse of some Jacobean proceedings in PRO, Sta.Cha. 8, allude to some instruments lost or not delivered from attornies, but such instances are rare.

[62] Reports from the Committees of the House of Commons I (1732), pp. 509, 528.

[63] Reports from Select Committees, Public Records (1800), p. 39.

wainscot presses in the Star Chamber but in the court's office in Gray's Inn. They had a definite use in the daily routine of the office no matter how ancient they were, for they were the records searched for precedents. The beginning of the reign would be a logical date from which to retain the Caroline proceedings in the office, many of which would be current and a number of which would be relevant to current actions. This is the explanation for the type and time span of the records of the Star Chamber preserved in the Public Record Office. It is not quite so romantic as that of our grandfathers who thought that the Caroline records were surely destroyed by the Constitutionalists wreaking vengeance on the most despotic instruments of the Stuart Tyrant.

As for the records in the Gray's Inn office, three years after the abolition of Star Chamber the benchers of Gray's were endeavouring to get Mr Molins to hand over the keys to the Star Chamber office. Mr Molins was still record keeper and he still had records. In April 1646, records of the court of Star Chamber yet remained in that part of the office that had not been reoccupied by the Inn, and the benchers assigned the residue of the chambers to Sir Henry Croke who was to 'take care of disposeinge the records ther in a fittinge way and hee is to call for the keys from Mrs Mollins'.[64] On 10 February 1647, the pension of Gray's ordered the Inn's members who were also Members of Parliament 'to move the House of Commons to dispose of the records and evidences in the Star Chamber office in some such place as they shall thinke fitt for their safetie'; on 6 July 1647 the pension reduced Croke's rent for the old Star Chamber office from £16 to £14 for the time being 'in regard ther are some small roomes thereof deteyned being fild with records and other writings'.[65] Sir Henry Croke was ostensibly something of an 'archivist' himself: from 1615 until his death in 1659 he was Clerk of the Pipe in Exchequer (first jointly, afterwards solely). Ironically, he had been prosecuted in Star Chamber in the later 1630s by the Attorney General on relation of the Commissioners for Fees, for exacting fees, and had to buy his pardon for a composition of £4,300.[66] What Croke did with the records (if he did anything at all) we do not know. Rushworth had access to the order and decree books for the reign of Charles I when he undertook the compilation of his *Historical Collections* in the 1650s. In 1705 the Deputy Chamberlains of the Exchequer stated in a paper delivered to the House of Lords that the last notice which could be had of the order and decree books was that they were in a house in St Bartholomew's Close, London.[67]

Perhaps the order and decree books or some of the materials in the office at the time of the abolition of the court will one day turn up as did the process books for 1580–1632, given to the nation by Sir Giles Sebright, Bt, in 1936. The process books came into the Sebright family by marriage of the third baronet to the daughter and heiress of Thomas Saunders, the sinecurist last clerk of the process from 1632 to 1641. What happened to the process books of his tenure is also a mystery. The process books were never kept in the Gray's Inn office. The clerk of the process had a separate office, curiously enough, in a house in Little St Bartholomew, London, in the well-yard of St Bartholomew's Hospital.[68]

Is it possible that the report of the Deputy Chamberlains of the Exchequer in 1705 touching the order and decree books being in a house in St Bartholomew's Close referred in fact to the process books in the former process office in the well-yard of St Bartholomew's Hospital? Or was it possible that in fact Croke or someone else had moved the Star Chamber office records, including the order and decree books, from Gray's to the old process office? If the latter was the case, there is

[64] *Pension Book of Gray's Inn*, I (1901), pp. 351, 352, 354, 356, 358.
[65] Gray's Inn: MS. Pension Book, fos. 459 and 462.
[66] G. E. Aylmer, *The King's Servants*, London, 1961, pp. 187, 196–200, 390–1; Folger, V.a.278, A.G. v. Sir Henry Cooke[*sic*], Trin. 1637.
[67] *Reports from Select Committees, Public Records* (1800), p. 39.
[68] PRO: Sta.Cha.8/93/8 and 126/10; Norman Moore, *The History of St Bartholomew's Hospital*, II, London, 1918, plan of hospital, 1617, facing p. 260; H. A. Harben, *A Dictionary of London*, London, 1918, p. 351.

still hope that the Gray's office records have survived. The disappearance of the process books for Saunders's tenure as process clerk in the 1630s indicates that the old process books that survived were not kept in the St Bartholomew's office but in Saunders's house, and hence escaped the fate of the current, in-use, process books in the process office. The fate of all the Star Chamber's in-use records was probably the same: destruction.

THOMAS G. BARNES

Records of the
Court of Augmentations

Historians have long been aware of the rich store of original materials to be found among the Augmentations documents of the Public Record Office, but few scholars have undertaken any systematic exploration of their contents. From time to time various series in the collection have been tapped, individual items consulted, or particular manuscripts, previously buried among masses of unrelated materials, discovered and cited; but for the most part research workers have wisely avoided an uncharted course through a maze of records most of which are neither calendared nor itemised, ending as often as not in a fruitless search. In point of fact, however, the serious student may be tempted to bypass a profitable field of inquiry, if only because he is baffled by the sheer bulk of unfamiliar sources confronting him. For all those not historically acquainted with the contents of the Augmentation Office, any description or interpretation of its manifold records is exceedingly helpful.

Consisting originally of only the records of the Court of Augmentations which flourished during the period 1536–54, this vast collection now represents many widely scattered areas of legal, administrative, and judicial documents as well as the more restricted series of Dissolution records and accounts of Crown lands. Among them, also, are included not only most of the record materials of the General Surveyors of Crown Lands but also many isolated manuscripts pertaining to the other revenue institutions of the early Tudors. Indeed, some understanding of the evolution of these important archives is fundamental to the study of administrative history for the entire sixteenth century. Moreover, an analysis of Augmentations records is particularly desirable when it is remembered that nothing has been written concerning either the administrative significance of the Court or the nature and extent of that vast collection of land and revenue records which eventually found lodgement within the Augmentation Office of the Exchequer. Since the two institutions, Court and Office, were distinctly separate, though historically related, it is important to note at the very beginning that a large part of the multitudinous records and manuscripts now classified by the Public Record Office as 'Augmentation Office' documents has no direct relation to the earlier Court. Indeed a great many of them antedate the sixteenth century while others cover the subsequent years down to the Restoration, with even a few items in certain series as late as the Georgian period. This peculiar classification is meaningful to the specialist, familiar enough with the chequered history of inter-related governmental institutions, but completely mystifying to the searcher, who logically expects the label of a document to indicate the nature of its source. In fact this unique collection of miscellaneous records is only rendered intelligible in the light of the various circumstances attendant upon the origin and development of the Augmentation Office.

When the second Court of Augmentations was annexed to the Exchequer in 1554, all its court records and numerous land and revenue documents were likewise transferred to that department. Even then the Augmentations archives were very comprehensive, embracing not only the combined records of the Court of Augmentations and the earlier office and Court of General Surveyors, which had been joined to it in 1547, but also surveys, monastic records, and numerous categories of documents and manuscripts relating to the Dissolution and to the various units of Crown lands formerly under the jurisdiction of the two courts.[1] Within the latter class are found the records of such larger divisions of property as monastic possessions, chantry lands, the ancient Crown demesne, attainted lands, purchased and exchanged lands, and the extended estates of the principality of Wales and the duchy of Cornwall.[2] The records of these Crown possessions, as well as all the miscellaneous documents and materials acquired by the Augmentations prior to its abolition, also came to the Exchequer. In order to accommodate such a large collection a new division of Exchequer records was created, which became known as the Augmentation Office. As such the office remained the official repository of a large section of Exchequer records until its abolition in 1834.

From time to time other documents were deposited in the Augmentation Office when they appeared to be related to the various series of records already retained in that depository. Such was the acquisition in 1620 of a register book of the monastery of Pershore, consisting of entries of deeds and other legal instruments all prior to the thirteenth century. When discovered, the book was sent to the Chancellor of the Exchequer, who immediately turned it over to the Keeper of the Records in the Augmentation Office.[3] Documents in that office were also occasionally transferred to other departments or storage centres, but more frequently Augmentations records 'escaped' into other hands and were lost by the Exchequer as a result of carelessness or inadequate supervision. It was a common practice for manuscripts or documents from the Augmentation Office to be requisitioned by auditors and other officials having need of them or to be exhibited as evidence in the law courts. Many of them, of course, were not returned to their original home. Similarly, deeds, evidences, accounts, court rolls, and various types of muniments related to crown property were often sent to purchasers of crown lands. Needless to say, a great number were never recovered. Many were destroyed, some remained in private hands, while still others strayed into foreign collections or were eventually acquired by public libraries.[4] The *Reports* of the Historical Manuscripts Commission have revealed numerous instances of isolated manuscripts which can be traced back to Augmentation origins.

The Augmentation Office repository was placed under the general administration of the Pipe Office in the Exchequer, but more specifically it was controlled by a clerk or keeper, who was

---

[1] Article 35 of the schedule attached to the patent of annexation provided 'that all Recordes late beyng in thesaid Courtes dissolued and belongyng to thesame Courtes shalbe Recordes in thesaide Courte of thexchequier and of thesame force and strength as they were in thesaid late Courtes dissolued'. Since many of the Augmentations documents were originally nothing more than personal notes or letters of officials, many a private manuscript or memorandum was thus raised to the dignity of a public record. Close Rolls, 1 Mary, pt. 7, mems. 3–6.

[2] The records of the duchy of Cornwall and the duchy of Lancaster were transferred from the Augmentation Office to the respective duchy offices in July 1800. At the same time over 4,000 rolls of Ministers' Accounts in the Offices of the Auditors of the Land Revenue were brought into the Augmentation Office. However, there are still scattered accounts for the duchy of Cornwall and a few records for the duchy of Lancaster remaining in the Augmentation Office. *Report from the Commissioners appointed to execute the Measures Recommended by a Select Committee of the House of Commons respecting the Public Records of the Kingdom* (London, 1812), 17, 19, 45.

[3] *Reports from a Select Committee of the House of Commons respecting the Public Records, 1800–1819* (London, 1820), Appendix V, 518.

[4] Warrants, lists, and memoranda concerning the delivery of records from the Augmentation Office. Exch., K.R., Miscellanea 12/9; Augm. Office, Misc. Books 472, f. 78; Augm. Office (E. 324), warrants for the delivery of records.

appointed by the Clerk of the Pipe.[5] Originally the records were housed in an 'ancient and inconvenient' brick building in St Margaret's Lane, near New Palace Yard, Westminster, adjacent to the Exchequer. Upon its demolition in 1793, however, they were removed to a more substantial structure known as the Stone Tower near Westminster Hall, where they were arranged in five large rooms, just over the records of the King's Bench Treasury; there they remained until the fire disaster of 16 October 1834, which destroyed both Houses of Parliament and imperilled all the nearby buildings. In the confusion that ensued frantic attempts were made to protect the threatened Augmentation records from any possible damage. The extent to which the archives were endangered remains a moot question, though the building in which they were stored actually adjoined the old House of Commons. The fact remains that their keeper, Sir Henry Cole, thought that they were in great jeopardy and had all of them carried to the safety of an adjacent church. These exciting events are recorded in his own words:

> The fire broke out about 7 p.m.: it was caused by the over-heating of flues, in burning the wooden tallies of many centuries belonging to the Exchequer, when, as Jack Cade says, 'our forefathers had no other books than the score and the tally'. I was fetched by Peter Paul, a workman engaged in the repair of the records, who was attached to the Augmentation Office, and I found that the office was threatened by the fire. With the aid of the Guards and policemen, I moved the whole of the Records into St Margaret's Church during the night, and in a few months they were sorted, re-arranged, and placed in safer circumstances than they had been before in the memory of man.[6]

Nevertheless, over-zealous hands can be responsible sometimes for what otherwise would pass for wanton destruction. During that hurried removal to the choir loft of St Margaret's Church nearby, some documents were lost or destroyed, while others were torn, water-marked, or even trodden under foot in the excitement of the moment. It was reported in Parliament that the records 'were all thrown out of the windows, to be preserved from the ravages of fire by the mire of Palace-yard, and soaked by water from the fire-mains'.[7] Still, the damage was not irreparable; after weeks of drying, cleaning, and repairing of the damaged documents, the Augmentation Office was restored to its normal order. Prior to that time, however, when the office of Clerk of the Pipe was abolished in 1833,[8] the records of the sub-department had been put under the jurisdiction of the Office of the King's Remembrancer. With the death of the last keeper, John Caley, in April 1834, the Augmentation Office was officially declared defunct.[9] Henceforth the keepership was under the appointment of the King's Remembrancer, being in fact exercised by a deputy-keeper. The office remained unchanged in status until its final absorption into the Public Record Office in the 1850s.

Meanwhile, on 8 February 1843, the Master of the Rolls ordered the Augmentation records to be removed from their previous quarters in St Margaret's Church, where they had been in temporary storage since the fire of 1834. During the following spring the complete transfer to a new home at Carlton Ride was accomplished under the careful supervision of Joseph Hunter, who as an

---

[5] Sometimes the Clerk of the Pipe Office retained the keepership of the Augmentation Office in his own hands. Beginning in 1554 with Christopher Smyth, the Office had a long list of keepers of whom Thomas Madox, John Caley, and Sir Henry Cole were the most prominent.

[6] Henry Cole, *Fifty Years of Public Work*, 2 vols. (London, 1884), I, 8.

[7] The speech of Charles Buller in the House of Commons on the condition of the public records, 1836. Buller went on to remark that records made admirable rat-traps. 'It was astonishing the quantity of remains of rats which were found amongst the records,' he explained. 'On one occasion the skeleton of a cat had been found amongst them.' *Ibid.*, II, 85.

[8] [29 August 1833.] 'An Act for facilitating the Appointment of Sheriffs, and the more effectual Audit and passing of their Accounts; . . . and to abolish certain Offices in the Court of Exchequer.' 3 and 4 William IV, c. 99, secs. xli and xlv, *Statutes at Large*, XIII, 505–12. This act became effective in October 1833.

[9] *Report of the Select Committee of the House of Commons on the Record Commission* (London, 1836), 29, 447. On the controversy over the control of the Augmentation records after the death of Caley, see below.

Assistant Keeper at the Public Record Office had been officially in charge of those records since November of 1841.[10] Carlton Ride, which had formerly been a riding academy attached to Carlton House, had nothing to recommend it as a storage building, save its spaciousness, and the possible fact that it was already half empty.[11] Nevertheless, this huge shell was soon converted into a temporary repository where various batches of records were collected into what was really a makeshift clearing-house, pending the erection of a permanent archives building. Thus it was that Carlton Ride became at once a storage depot and repair shop, where special blocks of records were mended, classified, and bound, preparatory to transfer to a future home. Actually, the parliamentary provision that all public records should be brought together at some definite place under the jurisdiction of the Master of the Rolls had been passed already, in August 1838, but various delays had postponed the implementation of the act.[12] Finally, work on the new repository began in 1851, though the first unit of the structure was not completed until 1856. Nominally under the Master of the Rolls, the Public Record Office was directed by a Deputy Keeper of the Records and a number of Assistant Keepers, each of whom was given special responsibility for certain categories of records. Among the many scattered divisions of the records then centralized in the new national archives building was the Augmentation Office series, which was kept intact as a distinct collection. They finally left Carlton Ride in 1856 and 1857 and were taken to the new repository in Chancery Lane.[13] With the abandonment of its old premises the Office henceforth continued in name only as one of the several important categories of Exchequer documents.

The circumstances attending the death of the last keeper of the Office in April 1834 gave rise to a bitter altercation between the Record Commissioners and the King's Remembrancer of the Exchequer, Henry William Vincent. When the keepership was thus vacated, the question of the future status of the Office immediately arose, since there was no longer a Clerk of the Pipe to appoint a successor.[14] C. P. Cooper, the Secretary to the Board of Commissioners then engaged in the investigation of the public records, took upon himself to appoint Henry Cole as overseer of the Augmentation Office, though the appointment proved to be of short duration. An ensuing quarrel between the two men led to Cole's dismissal, at which time the keys to the office were turned over to the King's Remembrancer. Vincent, in turn, had designated Thomas Adlington as the new keeper on the grounds that the Augmentation Office records had the same status as the other documents of the Pipe. The Board refused to yield its claim, however, until it was officially ruled that the custody of the Office lay in the Remembrancer's Division of the Exchequer.[15]

---

[10] *Third Report of the Deputy Keeper of the Public Records*, pt. I, 4; pt. II, 6; *Fourth Report*, 11–12; *Fifth Report*, 2. At that time the group of records known as 'Topographica' were transferred from the Augmentation Office to the Queen's Remembrancer's Office. This removal to Carlton Ride, in effect, marked the termination of the Augmentation Office as a separate repository. *Fifth Report*, Appendix I, 1. Upon receipt of the records in 1841, Hunter reported them to be 'generally in very good condition'.

[11] The building was used for the storage of old furniture from Carlton House which was subsequently put in the loft, together with an old stove, constituting the only heat in the place. Eventually the furniture was taken away, but only after protest had been lodged against the quite obvious fire hazards. Cf. Cole, *Fifty Years of Public Work*, I, 19–22.

[12] 'An Act for keeping safely the Public Records', 1 and 2 Victoria, c. 94, *Statutes at Large*, XIV, pt. III, 883–6. The act was subsequently amended by 40 and 41 Victoria, c. 55 and 61 and 62 Victoria, c. 12.

[13] *First Report of the Deputy Keeper of the Public Records*, I, 27b, 107a. A list of Augmentation records removed from Carlton Ride and Stone Tower to the new repository, showing their place of deposit on 31 December 1858, is presented in the *Twentieth Report*, Appendix, 77–92.

[14] The control of the Augmentation Office by the Clerk of the Pipe had ended the previous year with the abolition of that office, but the parliamentary act failed to mention specifically either the keepership or the records of the Augmentation Office. Consequently, these records were not immediately absorbed by the King's Remembrancer's Office as were those of the Pipe and other Exchequer departments abolished by the act, but were left under Caley's direction pending a legal clarification of their future custodianship.

[15] *Report of the Select Committee of the House of Commons on the Record Commission* (presented in August 1836), XVII, 10, 29, 30, 133–5.

In spite of the vicissitudes of three centuries of abuse, the Augmentations records were surprisingly well preserved when acquired by the Public Record Office.[16] Indeed they had fared far better than many of the other great archive groups, though this was due as much to sheer luck as to any preconceived design.[17] Reporting in 1836, Charles Buller's select committee of the House of Commons found the conditions in the old Augmentation Office building considerably worse than they had been during the previous century. Reliable witnesses testified that the rooms were dark and dirty, subject to ridiculous fire hazards, and inadequately secured. In the absence of any required attendance of the custodians, no one lived near the repository nor was any particular interest shown in the preservation of its valuable contents. That searchers were not permitted personally to enter the premises to inspect documents, for which privilege they had already liberally paid, is quite understandable for an archives 'as dirty as a chimney-sweeper's room'. One reputable informant pointed out that the Office 'had long been in a filthy state; it is possible that when the operation of cleansing the Records commenced, the rooms may have been so encumbered as to render order and neatness scarcely attainable; but it has long been unnecessary to leave the Records on the floor, or to permit the workmen to tread them underfoot when engaged in picking out those which might merit repair; and it was slovenly to leave heaps of dirt in the chimnies, to be blown over the bound books and cleansed Records every time the doors were opened'.[18]

Completely trusted and left to his own devices, John Caley probably contributed more to that deplorable neglect of the Augmentation Office than did all of his predecessors put together. During his tenure of office the records were in complete disorder, being in such a confused arrangement that hours were wasted in the locating of a desired document. As a result of his inefficiency manuscripts were bound together without regard to date or contents, inaccurately labelled, and separated from their seals, which were otherwise employed for wax reproductions to enhance a private collection.[19] Still more reprehensible was Caley's assumption that the records entrusted to his care could be used as private property, to be exploited for his own personal gain. Since his clerk performed the work of the office he seldom put in an appearance there, preferring instead the profitable use of the records in his own home at Spa Fields. The occasion for this peculiar arrangement was the mischievous practice, prevalent at the time, of requiring regular fees for the examination or transcription of all public documents, irrespective of the reliability of the investigator or the nature of the search. Considering the excessive costs of private research it is not at all surprising that original sources were seldom consulted except by corporations, public departments, and the legal profession. Modern scholars, accustomed to the courtesies of public officials and to the gene-

[16] The excellent condition of the Augmentation records was in part the result of the earlier care given them by conscientious custodians like the legalist and antiquarian, Thomas Madox, and Henry Cole – especially the latter – who gave special attention to the mending, sorting, and classification of those records. Madox himself bears testimony to the condition of the office in 1718: 'The most useful Records of this Office are in tolerable Order, but there are many others which were never yet Digested and Methodized. Several small Necessaries are wanting, to wit, Parchment Covers for many of the Records; Canvas to make New Bags instead of the Old ones, most of which are rotted: New Bindings of several Parchment Books of Enrollments, Wooden Boxes, and other small Things.' Report of Thomas Madox, presented 14 February 1718. *The Report of the Lords Committee appointed to View the Public Records* (London, 1719), 56.

[17] During the previous century when considerable attention had been given to the cleaning, sorting, and arranging of the records of the department of receipt in the Exchequer, the Augmentation Office records seem to have been ignored completely. See *Calendar of Treasury Books and Papers, 1729–1730*, I, 348, 401–2, 458. The several reports of John Lawson and Richard Morley, successively appointed to digest and classify the Exchequer documents, are presented in this and later volumes.

[18] *Report of the Select Committee of the House of Commons on the Record Commission*, VIII, XVI, XVII.

[19] In addition to accumulating a large library, Caley also acquired a valuable collection of casts of seals. The original seals detached from conventual leases and other Augmentation documents were retained by him for convenience in copying and making casts. Gordon Goodwin, 'John Caley', in *D.N.B.*

rous regulations established by national archives, would be appalled by the obstacles imposed upon the early nineteenth century student. For such a person the fees were excessive and the difficulties encountered were sometimes all but insurmountable. Having applied for permission to examine a particular Augmentation Office document, the petitioner would then have to await the convenience of the keeper, who meantime would have ordered all the volumes, rolls, and bags most likely to contain the requested manuscript to be brought to his house for purposes of reference. This was, in fact, not only a convenience to him but a real necessity, since all indexes and other research aids were retained at Spa Fields in Caley's own library. Other difficulties might arise and usually did, as when an untrained porter fetched the wrong lot of records and had to go back for another, which entailed still further delay before the search could begin. Finally, the reference located, the applicant had to content himself with the keeper's findings, for he had played no personal part in the quest; nor was he usually permitted to do more than examine the originals. If abstracts or transcriptions were required they were furnished by the keeper for what amounted to practically discretionary charges.[20]

Although the cleansing and repair work on the records was halted for a short period after Caley's death, most of the glaring abuses in the office were speedily eradicated under a new régime. With the capable supervision of Public Record Office officials the exploitation of what had become virtually a sinecurial office ceased,[21] and the indexing and calendaring of Augmentations materials proceeded anew. No longer were calendars considered to be the personal property of their custodians, nor departmental time consumed in personal undertakings.[22] Fees for the use of original materials, once a major concern of custodians of records, came to be less important than the preservation and accessibility of the documents themselves. In this, as in other respects, the Augmentation records profited from the general policy of the Public Record Office. A few changes in the earlier regulations were introduced before the end of the century, but the free and unrestricted access to the records did not come until 1909, when the present system of issuing 'student tickets' or research permits to readers, was inaugurated.[23] The public response was manifest almost im-

---

[20] There had always been charges for the examination or copying of records in the Augmentation Office, based on the schedule of rates allowable in the chancery, but Caley charged fees *ad libitum*, beyond all reason. The scale was a variable one, ranging from 1/6 per folio of seventy-two words for a copy or extract from the records up to £1 1 for any one day, but not less than 8/8 was charged for any one search regardless of the time consumed. For the examination or re-examination of a document, as certified by the keeper, the charges fluctuated from 2/- to 13/4. When the applicant was permitted to look at a document the fee was still 8/8. In some instances the fees for cases concerning peerages were quite unreasonable; later, on good authority, it was reported that a single fee was not infrequently a guinea or two, irrespective of the time wasted during the transaction. Nevertheless, despite the excessive fees, Caley took in an average of £199 9 5½ for a three-year period shortly before his death. *General Report to the King in Council from the Honourable Board of Commissioners on the Public Records* (London, 1831), Appendix, 209–10; *Report of the Select Committee of the House of Commons on the Record Commission*, 59.

[21] Ostensibly Caley had received no regular salary for the Augmentation Office keepership beyond the normal profits derived from fees nor for the custodianship of the records in the ancient treasury at Westminster (formerly the Chapter House records), which he had enjoyed since 1818. Moreover, in addition to these two lucrative positions he was also given a special assignment, as sub-commissioner, of superintending the repair and binding of the records. His fixed salary was only £200 per year, but there was an understanding with the commission that it should be made up in one way or another to not less than 500 guineas. *Ibid.*, 33.

[22] Caley refused to release the Augmentation calendars on the grounds that they were the personal property of the keeper. The Board of Commissioners negotiated with him for the purchase of the volumes but failed to reach a satisfactory agreement. When his library was finally liquidated, the twenty-five volumes of manuscript indexes sold for £225; his special collection of approximately 1,500 drawings of seals of English, Welsh, Scottish, and Norman monasteries brought £290. The impressions of those seals, made from Augmentation originals, were sold separately. 'The Obituary of John Caley, Esq.', in *Gentleman's Magazine*, new series, II (July–December, 1834), 320–1.

[23] *Seventy-first Report of the Deputy Keeper of the Public Records* (London, 1910), 2. Free research for literary purposes was tried in 1860, with 'cards of admission', but soon discontinued. Again, in 1866, fees were abolished for certain classes of documents but were reinstated in 1887. Fees are no longer payable in the public Search Rooms.

mediately. The new policy went into effect on 1 March; within ten months 733 student tickets had been issued. By 1949 the total number of 'Literary students' working at the Public Record Office had mounted to over 12,700.[24]

There is no record of the number of researchers using the Augmentation records during the earlier periods, but they were probably as much in demand as the other categories of government records. Actually, the testimony of those in a position to know the facts varies appreciably. Caley reported in 1800 that the Office was used by the public only occasionally, whereas some thirty years later the Deputy Keeper of the records in the Tower could observe quite differently on the use of the Augmentation documents. In the light of his own experience with public records he wrote: 'there is no Record Office, excepting the Rolls Chapel, to which such continual resort is had for Searches and Copies of Records; and these on subjects of the greatest importance, as connected with Tithe Suits, and where Parties derive their Titles, through the Crown, to possessions parcel of a dissolved religious House or an attainted Person'[25] Whatever the truth regarding the use of these records, the total amount of fees collected for any given year gives some indication of their popularity. In spite of the fact that it was in a most disgraceful condition, 'dirty and dark, and anything but what it should be', the profits from the Office increased from an average of £130 a year in 1778 to more than £199 in 1830.[26] The larger part of such fees came from the legal profession, by whom Augmentation materials were used as evidence in court or in the determination of land abstracts and titles. It was not until more modern times when popular interest in the Reformation stimulated intensive researches in the Dissolution activities that the records of the Augmentation Office became commonly known to students of history.

During the course of long years of peregrination, the contents of the Office have been subjected from time to time to numerous changes, and in the arrangement and re-classification at the hands of many custodians, individual items or indeed entire categories of documents have been added to or withdrawn from the original nucleus of records bequeathed to the Exchequer in 1554. However, the acquisitions were much more numerous than the losses, for most of the land and revenue records pertaining to the Crown demesne, formerly administered by the Augmentations, were retained by it as long as the reconstituted department of the Exchequer of receipt continued to function 'augmentation-wise'.[27] Thereafter, new materials, often foreign to the true nature of the collection, were added continually; such additions were accepted either through inadvertence or carelessness, or because they formed a logical and legitimate part of a larger series already acquired. Nevertheless, curious examples of inconsistency occasionally occur, and isolated cases of completely irrelevant or unrelated matter may be found.

---

[24] *Guide to the Public Records*, Part 1 (London, 1949), 48–50. The original distinction between 'literary' and 'non-literary' search has become purely fictional.

[25] *Privately Printed Tracts on the Record Commission*, of which the first is a tract by William Illingworth, Deputy Keeper of the Public Records in the Tower, written in May 1831: 'Observations on the Public Records of the Four Courts at Westminster . . .', 1–67. On the Augmentation Office, see pp. 55–61, espc. 58. Caley was apparently trying to minimize the extent of his profits derived from searches among the Augmentation records. His report in September 1832, showed that for attendance with a document at the Exchequer he received £1 1 per day. For a search of over three hours in the Augmentation Office, a similar fee was charged. *General Report to the King in Council from the Honourable Board of Commissioners on the Public Records*, Appendix G.19, 207–10.

[26] *Ibid.*, 210–12.

[27] Many of the Augmentation Office records were later transferred to the Office of Land Revenue, while others, especially the series of Ministers' Accounts, eventually were incorporated among the Special Collections of the Public Record Office. M. S. Giuseppi, *A Guide to the Manuscripts Preserved in the Public Record Office* (London, 1923), 1, 168–9, 343–4. [Revised *Guide to the Contents of the Public Record Office* (H.M. Stationery Office, London, 1963), 1, 89–90, 191–2. Ed.]

Of the thirty classes of the Public Record Office manuscripts and documents now classified as records of the Augmentation Office,[28] only a few series strictly appertain to the actual work of the original Court. Those categories most closely related to the history of the Court are the forty-six bundles of the Proceedings in the Court of Augmentations (E. 321), the Treasurers' Rolls of Accounts (E. 323), the mass of uncalendared and unclassified materials known as Miscellanea (forty-two bundles or boxes, E. 314),[29] and the series of bound volumes now labelled Miscellaneous Books (E. 315). Likewise, a number are directly concerned with the varied activities of the Court, such as Accounts of Wood Sales (E. 325), Deeds of Surrender of religious houses and chantries (E. 322; 278 vols.), Particulars for Grants of Lands and Offices (E. 316),[30] Enrolments and Particulars for Leases (E. 309 and E. 310), Conveyances of Crown Lands (E. 304), and Particulars for Grants (E. 318 and E. 319), and so on. However, these series constitute only a small portion of the total extant records of that institution which preserved its muniments most faithfully. Augmentation warrants, commissions, administrative orders and directives, ministers' accounts, surveys, indentures, recognizances, receipts, decrees, interrogatories, depositions, memoranda, and other items of court procedure are widely scattered among many separate collections of documents, often entirely unrelated to the chequered history of the Court itself. Such important items as commission returns, special surveys, letters of officials, or even accounts of the treasurer may turn up in the most unexpected places.[31] Whereas one would expect to find all the accounts of the collectors and receivers of the Augmentations among the Miscellaneous Books where some of them are preserved, many are found in the general series of Ministers' Accounts (S.C. 6) and in the third series of the Exchequer, L.R., Receivers' Accounts (L.R. 12).

More significant for the history of the Court than all of these, however, is the series of bound volumes classified as the Augmentation Office, Miscellaneous Books. Classification and binding in book form of related materials in the Augmentation Office was begun early in the nineteenth century under the direction of the Record Commission of the House of Commons.[32] Nevertheless, the first attempts in that direction by John Caley, as former keeper of the office, were not altogether successful since miscellaneous documents and manuscripts were sometimes brought

---

[28] (P.R.O.) *Class List of Records of the Court of Augmentations* (unpublished), E. 301 to E. 330. The calendars and indexes for the group comprise forty-three large manuscript volumes, some of which individually extend into several books or 'Parts'.

[29] Like most of the other classes, the Miscellanea contain many sections unrelated to the history of the Court. Unfortunately the material in the last two boxes of this series, entirely Augmentations documents, is so decayed and pulverised as to be of little value. In one of these boxes, 314/38, there are a number of privy seals for the Court of Wards and Liveries.

[30] This series is mislabelled as Particulars for Grants of Offices, though many of the earlier ones are particulars for leases. Covering the period from Henry VIII to Charles II, in 23 boxes, they still remain unindexed and unclassified. Those rolls for the reigns of Henry VIII, Edward VI, and Mary are leases by the Court of Augmentations.

[31] Among the Miscellaneous Enrolled Accounts of the Lord Treasurer's Remembrancer of the Exchequer is a long account of the treasurer of the Augmentations for the end of Edward VI's reign (E. 358/22). Similarly, the State Paper Office occasionally acquired the treasurer's Declarations of Account (S.P. 10/18, no. 14 and S.P. 11/1, no. 13).

[32] This commission was renewed six times and sat continuously from 1800 to 1831. It reported over fifty species of records in the Augmentation Office in 1800, arranged only alphabetically, for which about twenty volumes of indexes had already been made at governmental expense, in addition to the private indexes retained by Caley for his own use. In some 200 bags, miscellaneous records of many different kinds were thrown together without any pretence at logical arrangement. Once under way, reparation and binding proceeded apace after 1819; as many as 397 volumes of bound documents were available by 1832, principally charters, surveys, rentals, court rolls, inventories, certificates, and ministers' accounts, including approximately 5,000 ancient charters and deeds. *Reports from the Select Committee Appointed to Inquire into the State of the Public Records of the Kingdom* (4 July 1800), Appendix (G. 19a), 210–12; a report on the Augmentation Office submitted by John Caley on 15 September 1832, in the *General Report to the King in Council from the Honourable Board of Commissioners on the Public Records*, Appendix (G. 19), 207–10.

together without reference to date or character; but in the expert hands of trained Public Record Office officials many of the original errors in indexing and classifying were in time corrected. Presently the 524 volumes of Miscellaneous Books constitute the largest and most important single collection of all the Augmentation records.[33]

A number of these volumes have been indexed and calendared, which has made certain classes of documents much more serviceable to the research student. Thus, useful indexes are now available for Enrolments of Letters Patent and Indentures, Monastic Pensions, Inventories of Church Goods, Rentals and Surveys, Particulars for the Sale of Colleges and Chantries, and *Cartae Miscellaneae*.[34] A great many, such as Inventories, Leases, Pensions, Surveys, Wood Sales, Rentals, Warrants, and Ministers' Accounts, illustrate the official activities of the Court, while other volumes deal more specifically with internal Augmentations problems and court procedure. The Enrolment Books of leases, bills, indentures, and grants of offices, pensions, and annuities (Volumes 209–25, 232–6, and 238–43), Recognizances and Obligations (Volumes 252, 327), the Books of Payments (Volumes 249–62), and the nine volumes of Miscellaneous Letters and Papers (Volumes 472–80)[35] all relate directly to administrative or financial matters. The voluminous judicial Proceedings of the Augmentations are mostly records of the Court's orders and decrees, commissions, interrogatories, complaints, answers, and depositions (Volumes 20, 23, 91–105, 108–34, 165, 328, 436, and 516–22) which are intermixed with numerous legal instruments of a similar nature for the Court of General Surveyors. Finally, a few additional volumes yield further information on isolated aspects of Augmentations activities.[36]

Owing to the close relation between the Court of General Surveyors and the Court of Augmentations, the records of the two institutions have been hopelessly mixed up by official custodians who had little knowledge of the original jurisdiction of the two courts. Nor was the confusion due as much to carelessness as to the striking similarity of their records, since frequently the only possible differentiation between the respective documents must depend upon a minute acquaintance with the revenues and personnel of each court, or with some minor difference in administrative technique. Obviously, the various steps in the procedure of hearing cases was practically identical in both courts, so that comparable records are all but indistinguishable. Isolated documents of the Court of General Surveyors turn up repeatedly among the records of the Augmen-

[33] A complete list of the Miscellaneous Books, inadequately described and often mislabelled, is given in Giuseppi, *A Guide to the Manuscripts Preserved in the Public Record Office*, I, 144–59, but a revised and corrected typescript list is available in the Public Record Office Search Rooms and can be found in many libraries as List and Index Society volume no. 16 (1967). Volumes 209–18, 232–6, 248–55, 331, 442, and 456 are calendared in the *Letters and Papers, Foreign and Domestic, of the Reign of Henry VIII, 1509–1547*.

[34] Misc. Books 29–54 form part of a large collection within the Augmentation Office, earlier classified as *Cartae Antiquae*, *Cartae Miscellaneae*, and *Cartae Selectae*. These deeds were formerly scattered in several repositories before they were acquired by the Augmentation Office, many of them being originally records of the Court of Augmentations. They are chiefly conveyances of land, some dating back to the Norman period, but the collection also includes agreements, wills, bonds, acquittances, and other instruments related to private transactions from the twelfth to the sixteenth centuries. Most of these deeds concern either monastic possessions or the ancient estates of the crown, though many represent claims presented in the Augmentations and other courts of law as evidences of title. The volumes of this series are listed and analysed in Calendars and Descriptive Catalogues.

[35] These miscellaneous papers are chiefly reports of auditors and other officials in the Augmentations and Exchequer, together with original warrants, bills, receipts, and memoranda covering the reigns of Henry VIII, Edward VI, Mary, and Elizabeth. Volume 476 contains documents as late as 1698.

[36] Especially the Auditors' Patent Books (Volumes 4–7), Recognizances (Volume 352), Bills of Acquittances (Volume 1), an Appearance Book (Volume 3), and copies of acts of parliament relating to the work of the Court (Volume 2). A copy of the letters patent creating the second Court of Augmentations in 1547 is contained in Volume 17. Privy Seals of the Court are collected in Volume 331, and Volumes 336–49 contain the Ledgers of Receipts of the Treasurer of the Augmentations.

tations, and most of the extant records of the former court are found within the Augmentation Office classification. Besides innumerable other classes of documents pertaining to that institution, twenty odd of the Miscellaneous Books are materials which at one time belonged to the Court of General Surveyors.[37]

As in other series of Augmentation Office records a large number of Miscellaneous Books are but remotely connected with the main theme of the class, namely accounts of Crown lands and revenues and subsidiary documents relating thereto. However, such items as Household Books, Chamber Payments, Army and Navy Accounts, and Presentments of Concealed Lands are found there probably because of the earlier links between those institutions and the Court of General Surveyors or the Court of Augmentations. Less explicable in relation to the whole are accounts of the stannary courts in Devon and Cornwall, customs accounts, declarations of the revenues of Queen Anne of Denmark, certificates of musters, royal charters, and miscellaneous Exchequer documents for the late sixteenth and seventeenth centuries. Not illogically the Parliamentary Surveys for the period of the Restoration were transferred to this Office by the Clerk of the Pipe, where they were calendared in 1764. Likewise, some peculiar manuscripts have found their way into this series, including the interesting fifteenth-century treatise on conveyancing and an inquiry into the fees and allowances of English courts in 1634.[38] Since the Augmentations acquired the muniments as well as the estates of the dissolved monasteries, valuable collections of title deeds and other records of many houses were preserved virtually intact. Notable among such unique collections is that of the famous Syon abbey in Middlesex, suppressed by Cromwell in 1540.[39]

As already indicated the combined land and revenue records of the Court of General Surveyors and the Court of Augmentations bridge much of that wide expanse of time known as the Middle Ages, especially in the complete series of monastic cartularies, title deeds, court rolls, and accounts of land and land revenues under the survey of the Crown. However, just as the Augmentation Office became a convenient catch-all for miscellaneous documents of a much later period dealing with similar matters, so many portions of what were once properly Augmentations archives have been widely dispersed in all directions. Large sections of Exchequer records, Ministers' Accounts, Ancient Deeds, and various classes of records now classified as belonging to the Office of the Land Revenue are examples in point of fact, to mention only a few.[40] Equally important for the sixteenth century are the invaluable series of Enrolments of Leases, Particulars for Grants of Crown Lands, Accounts of Attainted Lands, Particulars for the Sale of Colleges and Chantries, Accounts of Wood Sales, and Grants of Pensions and Annuities. Even within the scope of the Court's jurisdiction the large collections of land surveys, surveys of woods, and commission returns by Augmentations ministers present a full cross-sectional view of the extended Tudor demense.

---

[37] Proceedings and decrees in the Court of General Surveyors, Misc. Books 19, 21-2, 106, 516-22; leases, *ibid.* 230; and records of attainted lands, *ibid.* 7-13, 248, 288, 298-9, 304, 307, and 384. Two Minute Books of the Court have survived in *ibid.* 313A and 313B. Many of the E. 321 series, which are classified as Proceedings in the Court of Augmentations, and the Augmentation Office Miscellanea (E. 314) are in reality documents relating to the Office or Court of General Surveyors.

[38] Augm. Office, Misc. Books 329 and 330.

[39] The Augmentation Office records of the abbey were noted in Thomas Tanner, *Notitia Monastica* and in Sir William Dugdale, *Monasticon Anglicanum*. Accounts of Syon lands and property prior to the Dissolution are found among the Ministers' Accounts (S.C. 6/7177-7236). See also Auditors of Land Revenue, Misc. Books 112; Exch. of Receipt, Misc. Books 152; and Augm. Office, Misc. Books 436.

[40] For the particulars of such categories of dispersed Augmentation Office records, see E. A. Lewis and J. Conway Davies, eds., *Records of the Court of Augmentations Relating to Wales and Monmouthshire* (Cardiff, 1954), Introduction, x-xi.

Although the surviving Augmentations records are largely centralized in one office, a number of Augmentation Office volumes and many individual documents and manuscripts have strayed into other national and private collections.[41] Most of these are records of the Office rather than of the Court, yet a few are closely related to various aspects of Augmentations development. In the Exchequer, Accounts Various,[42] Miscellaneous Books (K.R.), Miscellanea (K.R.), and Duchy of Lancaster Division, all have materials pertinent to the Court, while other odd volumes have been acquired by the British Museum. Among the latter should be mentioned especially Harleian Manuscripts (Volumes 433, 605–8, and 1509–11), Additional Manuscripts (Volumes 5063–5103, 21481, and 32469),[43] Royal Manuscripts (Volume 14 B.XI), and scores of isolated manuscripts found within the Stowe, Arundel, Lansdowne, and Cottonian collections.[44] Indeed, a few manuscripts have strayed rather far afield, one to Wales[45] and two across the Atlantic to find a permanent abode in American libraries. The Widener Library acquired by purchase an isolated Augmentations manuscript from a private collection relating to the plunder of Abingdon abbey, which probably represents an account originally delivered from the Augmentation Office to a purchaser of monastic lands.[46] Of more interest but greater uncertainty as to origin is the Augmentation item found among the early sixteenth-century manuscripts of the Folger Shakespeare Library in Washington, D.C. Prior to its acquisition by the late H. C. Folger in 1923, there seems to be no trace of the earlier history of the document. It is a bound manuscript copy, made near the end of Elizabeth's reign, of the original letters patent erecting the second Augmentations in January 1547.[47]

Far more widely scattered and much too numerous to list are the occasional references to court procedure and court personnel hidden away in unsuspected places. Land surveys and wood sales of both the Court of General Surveyors and the Court of Augmentations are dispersed generally among the various series of Exchequer records; likewise, stray warrants and receipts of the Court

---

[41] Among the valuable Manchester Manuscripts, three or four thousand in number, acquired by the Public Record Office in 1880, are 112 items relating to the first Court of Augmentations, covering the years 1536 to 1539. These particular manuscripts, originally in the private possession of Sir Richard Rich (first Baron Rich of Leighs), the first chancellor of the Augmentations, were retained by the Rich family and passed on to the Dukes of Manchester through subsequent marriage. The documents are of a varied nature, being principally warrants and orders of the Court, declarations of monastic plate delivered to the mint for coinage, charges for surveys of woods, receipts, miscellaneous accounts, copies of court decrees, and itemised expense accounts of Augmentations ministers. The latter are of especial interest, since they contain an abundance of material on sixteenth century prices. The entire collection has been fully described in the *Eighth Report of the Royal Commission on Historical Manuscripts* (London, 1881; reissued 1910), Appendix, Part II, espc. pp. 20a–27a. [The Manchester MSS. were withdrawn from the Public Record Office in 1969 and dispersed in the sale room. Ed.]

[42] Originally part of the 'Ancient Miscellanea' of the King's Remembrancer's Office, the Accounts Various were sorted and reclassified during the period 1886–94. Large sections of them are really Augmentation Office documents, as those relating to pensions, payments and transcripts of accounts of the treasurer of the Augmentations, warrants, receipts, and accounts of woodwards and wood sales. For these and innumerable other items, see *Lists and Indexes*, XXXV.

[43] This rare volume is an evaluation of Crown lands and revenues for 1541–2 under the survey of the Court of General Surveyors.

[44] Among the Additional Manuscripts are the Scudamore Papers (19 volumes), of which Add. MS. 11041, consisting of the correspondence of John Scudamore, receiver in the Court of Augmentations, is particularly revealing. Most of these letters from Augmentations officials relate to the sale and exportation of the 'king's lead'.

[45] A register of fees due to the Crown for leases and patents out of the Court of Augmentations. (National Library of Wales, Aberystwyth) Peniarth MS. 34. Likewise the notebooks and memoranda books of the Floyd Collection contain some materials relating to Wales extracted from the Augmentation Office records.

[46] (Harvard Univ.) MS. Lat. 101. *Compotus Edmundi Powel*; paper, 26 folios, 1538.

[47] The Folger Shakespeare Library, 1174.4 (58 folios). See Seymour de Ricci, *Census of Medieval and Renaissance Manuscripts in the United States and Canada*, 3 vols. (N.Y., 1935–40) I, 378. There are also several items in the Folger Library relating to various officers of the Court.

or excerpts from original accounts may turn up in any of a number of unrelated collections.[48] The Patent Rolls and Close Rolls contain scores of grants and commissions pertaining to the Court, while odd rent rolls, ministers' accounts, and isolated receipts are discoverable in almost all the land and revenue record series for the period. Moreover, collective data on Augmentations personnel are inexhaustible. Excluding purely local and minor officials, many of the dozen or so leading officers of the Court were influential ministers, active in other governmental service or in court life. With them the problem is one of an over-abundance rather than a paucity of material. In fact, it is sometimes difficult to determine in just what capacity the individual minister was officiating, so varied were his many activities. Ample evidence on the work and careers of most of the principal officials is available in the Acts and Proceedings of the Privy Council, Ministers' Accounts, the State Papers, and among the several collections of manuscripts of the British Museum. With the exception of the treasurer, Sir Thomas Pope, biographies of none of the officials of the Augmentations have been written,[49] though men like Sir Richard Rich, Sir Edward North, Sir Richard Sackville, and Sir Walter Mildmay ranked among the leading administrators of the period. Of the countless lesser figures concerned with the history of the Court, years of faithful service to the Crown in one of the major financial institutions of the day will ever remain for them their only claim to rescue from utter obscurity.

A full section on the Augmentation Office records in the revised *Guide to the Public Records*,[50] was prepared by Professor J. Conway Davies, who included as Augmentation Office materials several important classes of documents incorrectly classified in Giuseppi's *Guide*. Among other additions a large number of records of a miscellaneous character, heretofore unknown to the public, have been added to the present collection. As to the value of the Augmentations records for economic, constitutional, and administrative history, these archives speak for themselves. Any effort to render them more easily accessible to the searcher would be commendable. It is to be hoped that eventually some of the more important parts of the series will be published.[51]

WALTER C. RICHARDSON

---

[48] An Elizabethan list of officers in the Augmentations is held by the Library of the Society of Antiquaries of London, 205/7, and in addition to several general documents concerning the Court, the Bodleian Library, Oxford, has three interesting Augmentation items, viz.: extracts from ministers' accounts, extracts from deeds in the Court, and pensions payable out of the Augmentation Office 'to the late Incumbents of Religious Houses', 1553. Bodleian Library, Misc. MSS., 30694c., f. 60; 5005, f. 78d.; and 27657. Likewise, the Cambridge University Library has a manuscript copy of the articles of annexation of the Augmentations to the Exchequer in Mary's patent of 24 January 1554. MS. G.g. II. 7. A few isolated Augmentation items are also found among the Cecil Manuscripts preserved at Hatfield House.

[49] Thomas Warton, *The Life of Thomas Pope, Founder of Trinity College, Oxford* (London, 1772). An inaccurate and highly coloured biography but withal a comprehensive account of his career, based on original sources. Cf. Herbert E. D. Blakiston, 'Thomas Warton and Machyn's Diary', *E.H.R.* (April, 1896), XI, 282–300.

[50] Revised *Guide to the Contents of the Public Record Office* (H.M. Stationery Office, London, 1963), I.

[51] A comprehensive history of the Court by Professor Richardson is now available: *History of the Court of Augmentations, 1536–1554* (Baton Rouge, La.: Louisiana University Press, 1961). [Ed.]

The
Master of the Royal Tents
and his Records

In the mid-twentieth century tents are associated with fêtes and fairs, cricket-grounds and camps, beaches and the 'big top'. A number of people still spend their holidays under canvas, but hardly anybody lives under it for good, compared with the several thousand British families that were permanent tent-dwellers when the census of the population was taken in 1851. For all their pleasurable uses tents have rather come down in the world and it is, perhaps, not surprising that the master of the royal tents and his predecessors have been left in the margin of history.[1]

For five and a half centuries the kings and queens of England maintained officials solely concerned with the custody of the royal tents. As far back as the reign of Henry I there was a keeper of the tents (*cortinarius*) attached to the royal household.[2] As the king progressed about his realm the tent-keeper would erect the tents he carried with him on his sumpter mules as required. The king himself did not often sleep under canvas, but many of the lowlier officials of the itinerant court regularly had to put up with such makeshift accommodation. The royal pavilioner, as he became called in the fourteenth century, grew in importance with the popularity of the tournament in England; and at the tournament grounds at Tickhill and Brackley he would supervise the building of stands from which ladies could safely view the displays of chivalry. When the king took the field with his army, whether in the Welsh Marches or in France, the pavilioner would be in attendance to pitch the royal headquarters; the royal pavilion had not the cosiness of a modern field marshal's caravan, but it served the same purpose. As armies grew in size more and more soldiers had to be accommodated in tents. In the Marsh of Calais in 1346 arose whole streets and squares of tents for the troops and the army of court officials so that a Westminster chronicler imagined that London had been transported across the Channel.[3] The man responsible for this operation was John Yaxley, the first pavilioner we know by name, who served Edward II in his last years and continued in office down to 1357; the last of the line was John Wright who served at the end of Charles II's reign and had no successor.[4] By the end of the seventeenth century the office had become redundant

---

[1] T. F. Tout does no more than list the King's pavilioners of the fourteenth century (*Chapters in Administrative History*, IV, Manchester 1928, p. 390). J. H. Johnson makes no mention of the office in his seemingly exhaustive study of the royal household for the first decade of Edward III's reign in *The English Government at Work, 1327–1336* (ed. J. F. Willard & W. A. Morris, *Publications of the Medieval Academy of America*, 1940), I; and historians who have discussed the households of later kings and queens have passed over the office.

[2] 'Constitutio Domus Regis' in *Dialogus de Scaccario* (ed. Charles Johnson, *Nelson's Medieval Texts*, Edinburgh 1950), p. 135.

[3] John Reading; see Tout, *loc. cit.*, III, p. 169.

[4] Audit Office, Declared Accounts (A.O.1)/2297/40. These and all the manuscripts to which reference is made in this article are in the Public Record Office; the records quoted in which Crown Copyright is reserved are printed by permission of the Controller of Her Majesty's Stationery Office.

and such duties as remained in connexion with the provision of tents were transferred to other officials.

The main reason why his office has been passed over is that until the Tudor period few independent records of his department have survived. The pavilioner remained to the end an official of the Wardrobe and certain of his purchases of canvas, ropes and other materials in the medieval period can be traced in the Wardrobe Accounts among the records of the Exchequer; but since the records of the royal household proper have not come down to us for these centuries it is to the Chancery Enrolments and the Exchequer Accounts that one must turn for clues to his office.[5] One of the few particulars of account to have survived from the fourteenth century is concerned with the funeral of Piers Gaveston. In January 1315 Edward II was at last in a position to bury his favourite with full honours and he caused his body, which had lain for two years in the house of the Friars Preachers at Oxford, to be borne in state to King's Langley. Three pavilions were despatched to the Hertfordshire royal manor from the Tower of London for these obsequies at a cost of £4 13 1.[6]

However difficult and dangerous the journeys might be as the medieval kings progressed about their realm, the presence of the serjeant of the tents in the entourage guarded against their being stranded for the night. By the end of the middle ages each sub-department of the royal household had come to have its own tent or hale, just as it had always had its own sumpter mules. The wardrobe of beds and the wardrobe of robes had a large hale apiece while smaller hales sufficed for the larder, the buttery, the kitchen, the scullery, the spicery, the chandlery and the pitcher-house. The 'King's Lodging' comprised a thirty-foot pavilion for the guard, three hales of more than average size, a 'house of timber with the bents laced to the same and covered with canvas' and – surely a Renaissance touch here – a 'house called the house of Naples'; of the two last one formed the privy chamber, the other a bedroom.[7]

During the earlier part of Henry VIII's reign Richard Gibson was both pavilionary or serjeant of the king's tents, and serjeant of the revels, the court entertainment officer. He officiated in both capacities for instance at the jousts held to celebrate the marriage of the earl of Devon with Gertrude Blount in October 1519, when he provided gorgeous trappings for the horses suitably 'lozenged and cross-lozenged with cloth of gold, every lozenge embroidered with trueloves'.[8] As stage-manager of pageantry the arrangements for the Field of Cloth of Gold in 1520, for which he was largely responsible, were Gibson's tour de force. The summit meeting of the Kings of England and France was fixed for high summer, but the serjeant of the tents was reluctant to start work until spring weather had arrived. In early April Nicholas Vaux, the captain of Guisnes, wrote to Wolsey that the banqueting-house was far from complete and that Gibson 'who should cover the rofes with seared canvas, is not yet commen, and it is high time his works were in hand, for it must be painted on the outside, and after curiously garnished under with knots and batons gilt and other devices'.[9] After a late start Gibson and his team of workmen busied themselves with commendable zeal. The transport of all the materials from England across the Channel was quite a feat in itself – canvas, timber, ironwork, cloth and paint. Apart from the works at Guisnes a special pavilion, covered with cloth of gold, was erected at Gravelines for the meeting between King Henry and the Emperor Charles V. Elaborate galleries were constructed round the lists for the ladies and two great triumphal arches. For the English court and its great following nigh 400 tents of varying size were put up. There was friendly rivalry between Gibson's party and the French

---

[5] This point is forcefully made by V. H. Galbraith, *An Introduction to the Use of the Public Records* (1952 edn.), p .44.

[6] Exchequer, Queen's Remembrancer, Various Accounts (E.101)/375/15.

[7] E.101/414/7.

[8] *Letters & Papers of Henry VIII*, III, p. 1551.

[9] *Ibid.*, pp. 239, 259.

officials who were erecting the pavilions for the entourage of Francis I in the camp outside Ardres; each side strove to outdo the other in the splendour of their tents. When all was finished a French correspondent comparing the two camps considered the English tents were hardly fewer than the French and in fine order. Another witness of the scene at Guisnes grew rapturous at the beauty of Gibson's pavilions which, he thought, 'exceeded the pyramids of Egypt' in wonder.[10] But the most remarkable construction of all was Henry VIII's banqueting-house, 'the most sumptuous ever'. It rested on stone foundations and had brick walls, but the rest of the structure was of wood and canvas. The whole was covered outside by cloth painted to resemble brickwork *à l'antique*. Inside was tapestry of cloth of gold and silver, interlaced with the king's personal colours of white and green. The house contained four great *corps de maison* and eight *salons*. The chapel was painted blue and gold with hangings of gold and silver, and rich cupboards of plate. The gates were like those of a great castle. At one door were two gilt pillars, bearing statues of Cupid and Bacchus, from which flowed streams of malmsey and claret into silver cups for any who wished to drink. The whole scene seemed to the beholder to be very much attuned to the days of the knights errant.[11] The Field of Cloth of Gold, with the festivities lasting for a full twenty days in a cloudless June, rivals the Congress of Vienna as one of the most colourful spectacles of European history. It is as well that the man behind all this pomp should not be forgotten. At the end of the financial year it was discovered that the bill for the jousts and the king's jousting clothes alone topped £3,000; but Richard Gibson was rewarded for all his work during that year with no more than his usual £10.[12]

The court offices concerned with the royal tents and with the revels remained closely associated until 1560. Although after Gibson's death the revels became an independent office for a few years, they were once again amalgamated with the tents on the appointment of Sir Thomas Cawarden in 1545 to be both Master of the Tents and Master of the Revels, even if this was done by two separate patents.[13] There were not, after all, such great differences in the tasks which Cawarden had to perform in his two capacities. Erecting the stage and seating for a masque in Westminster Hall required the same skills and much the same equipment as erecting pavilions for the jousts; while the business of 'airing, repairing, laying abroad, turning, sewing, mending, tacking, sponging, wiping, brushing, making clean, folding and laying-up of the masques' garments' could all be done by the same staff that looked after the 'repairing, amending, airing and laying-up of the tents'. Under Cawarden the department was moved from Warwick Lane to Blackfriars. The greater part of the Dominican Friary was granted to Cawarden at the Dissolution, yet not content with this lavish grant he pulled down the parish church of St Anne on the plea that he needed the site as a storehouse; in fact he built private tennis courts there and turned the cemetery into a carpenter's yard. The enraged parishioners appealed to Henry VIII who instructed the master of the tents to provide a room for public worship in his house. Left a legacy under the terms of Henry VIII's will, Cawarden succeeded in keeping his post through all the political changes of the mid-sixteenth century.[14] He was clearly a man of some energy. One day he would be supervising the making of a hale for Cuthbert Vaughan who was leading 300 soldiers in the north, the next providing tents to store the victuals of the army in France and a week later putting on a masque at court.[15]

---

[10] *Ibid.*, pp. 280, 305–6.

[11] *Ibid.*, no. 869.

[12] *Ibid.*, pp. 305, 1544.

[13] See E. K. Chambers, *Notes on the History of the Revels Office under the Tudors* (1906), pp. 7–9.

[14] *Ibid.*, pp. 7–18 and also Chambers, *Elizabethan Stage* (1951 edn.), I, pp. 72–4; T. Craib, 'Sir Thomas Cawarden' in *Surrey Archaeological Collections*, XXVIII (1915), pp. 7–28. A. J. Kempe in *The Loseley Manuscripts* (1853) prints draft accounts and other documents of Cawarden but none of them concerns the tents. Cawarden was also Keeper of Nonsuch Palace during the reigns of Edward VI and Mary.

[15] Exchequer, Pipe Office, Declared Accounts (E.351)/2935.

It was during Cawarden's mastership that detailed accounts were kept for the first time. These begin in June 1555 and the series continues without a break until Michaelmas 1640; at the Restoration the series recommences and accounts have survived down to February 1676. These are all in the form of Declared Accounts and are to be found in both the Pipe Office (E.351) and the Audit Office series (A.O.1) in the Public Record Office. As is well known accounting-officers delivered two copies of their accounts for declaration: one, on parchment, which became the Pipe Office copy, the other on paper for the Audit Office. Complete sets of the accounts of the master of the tents have not survived in the records of each department, yet every year is documented from one series or the other: there are 25 rolls in the Pipe Office series while the Audit Office has 40 rolls.[16]

These detailed records not only shed light on the administration of the royal household and provide a footnote to some of the more interesting events in the court calendar of the Tudor and Stuart periods; they are also a source for wage-rates of skilled artisans and for prices of a considerable range of commodities. Between 1555 and 1559 when Sir Thomas Cawarden was both master of the tents and master of the revels these accounts are of even greater interest; no separate 'revels' accounts for those years have survived for Cawarden kept a combined account as master of the tents which furnishes details of some interest to the student of drama. Characters emerge such as Richard Bossome who was rewarded with 52/8 in 1555 'for devising of patterns for maskes': was he a wardrobe master, a painter of scenery or a choreographer? Two years later there was considerable expense in preparation for 'a great maske of Almaignes, Pylgrymes and Ireshemen' which was performed at court on the night of St Mark's Day. The art of theatrical make-up was not unknown to Cawarden for at one performance he spent 53/4 'in making of arms and legs stained flesh coloure'.

No one was busier than old Cawarden in the first year of Elizabeth's reign. Apart from the coronation, which involved him in furnishing awnings for Westminster Abbey and new pavilions for the Whitehall tiltyard, he was required to stage a brilliant series of court masques. In May 1559, for instance, he produced as master of the revels the 'Masque of Astronomers' at Whitehall in a new banqueting-house which he had constructed as master of the tents, with large windows made of basket-work. Later that summer, a few weeks before his death, he supervised the erection of another banqueting-house at Horsley in Surrey where a 'Masque of Shipmen and Maids of the Country' was acted before the queen on progress. All the gear went up river from Blackfriars to Hampton Court by barge and thence by land to Horsley.[17]

After Cawarden's death his various offices were distributed. Henry Sackford became the new master of the tents with a fee of £30 and served the Queen to the end of the reign. Sir Thomas Benger became master of the revels and was also placed in charge of the royal banqueting-houses. Cawarden had also acted for a number of years as master of the toils or hunting-nets, a post now granted to John Tamworth. The headquarters of all three offices were before long moved from Blackfriars to buildings in Clerkenwell, once part of the Hospital of St John of Jerusalem. The old chapel of the Hospital became a store-room for the tents.[18] The staff of the queen's tents now comprised a master, a clerk-controller, a clerk, a yeoman, a groom to look after the horses and a porter. This establishment with the allowances as laid down in 1560 remained in force for over a century. The officials were paid diet and wages according to the number of days they actually worked – an average of eighty days a year.[19] Tailors, painters, carpenters and other workmen were engaged as

---

[16] E.351/2935–2959; A.O.1/2292/1–2297/40. See *Public Record Office, List & Index*, II (1893), preface, and pp. 73, 277–8.

[17] E.351/2935 *passim*.

[18] Chambers, *Revels*, p. 20. In one account mention is made of payments for lead and solder 'to mend the church where the store of the office lieth' (E.351/2937).

[19] The master had 4/- a day diet and wages, the groom 18d, the porter 1/- and the other three officials 3/- apiece.

required and paid at piece rates. The very full accounts of Sackford's mastership provide us with
abundant details about the costs of materials: canvas, sackcloth, 'ropes of divers sorts for triangles,
crowsfeet and ground-tackle', leather, ironwork for pins, hoops and joints, timber for poles and
tubs for the poles to rest in, thread, tape, buttons and paint. The furnace 'to air the storehouse to
avoid mould and mustiness' consumed £40 of fuel a year; even with such care canvas tents did not
have a very long life once they had been thoroughly soaked by rain.

Queen Elizabeth's habit of progressing about her realm in full triumph to show herself to
her people involved Henry Sackford in a great deal of work. Each year various new tents and round-
houses were furnished 'against Her Majesty's progress'. His staff not only made and repaired the
tents but attended the queen on progress. Most of the tents and hales taken on progress were used
as stabling for the horses and coaches and lodgings for the grooms and the officials of the avenary.
Carts were hired to carry all the gear at the rate of 2d a mile. Between 1571 and 1601 Sackford made
32 hales, 12 round-houses, 2 square-houses and 2 chambers solely for the progresses; and by the
end of the century this had become an important item in the budget of the royal household.[20]

Each year there would be special functions at court demanding Sackford's ingenuity, for
whenever state pageantry was required out-of-doors there we find the master of the tents. Throughout the reign of Elizabeth I we keep coming across references to the construction of temporary
banqueting-houses by the master of the tents at several of the chief royal residences. Whitehall
Palace appears to have had no permanent banqueting-house until 1607,[21] when the forerunner of
Inigo Jones's building began its short and fateful life; at Nonsuch which had taken shape as a
glorified hunting-lodge the banqueting-house was an afterthought, and even at Greenwich there was
no room sufficiently spacious for entertaining large numbers of guests. Usually the structures of
wood and canvas devised by the master of the tents were little more elaborate than marquees at a
commemoration ball, but on occasion an exceptionally splendid banqueting-house was called for,
such as that erected at Whitehall in the spring of 1581 to impress the embassy arriving from France
to negotiate a marriage between Elizabeth and the Duke of Alençon. It was 'in manner and fourme of
a long square, 332 foot in measure about', consisting of uprights covered with canvas. The outside
was painted to resemble stone; the inside was decked out with spangled greenery and greengrocery
like a harvest festival; 'strang fruits as pomegarnetts, orrengs, pompions [pumpkins], cowcombers,
grapes, carretts, pease' hung from the roof and the rest of the interior was 'most cuninglie painted,
the cloudes with the starres, the sunne and sunne beames . . . most richlie garnished with gould'.
There were no fewer than 292 glass windows. Sackford's banqueting-house cost £1,744 19 2 and
was completed in twenty-four days, the three Liziarde brothers setting the pace for a team of
painters.[22]

Since James I was little less energetic than Elizabeth I in progressing about the kingdom the
master of the tents was kept fully occupied. At the beginning of the reign 11 hales and 5 round-
houses were made for the king's progress. In 1610 a great hale, a round-house and two tents were
provided for this purpose and seven years later 4 new tents were ordered for the king's return visit to
his Scottish realm. In 1619 Charles, Prince of Wales, became entitled to a tent of his own. Three old
hales that had remained in the storehouse on Queen Elizabeth's death saved the day when King
James announced at very short notice that he would take up residence for a few days in the Tower
of London. It was quicker to patch up the hales than repair the leaky roof in the White Tower. In
1607 James granted the buildings in St John's, Clerkenwell to Lord Aubigny. The clerk-controller
who had since 1560 lived on the premises was given £15 a year compensation and this allowance

[20] E.351/2936–7; A.O.1/2293/3.
[21] G. S. Dugdale, *Whitehall Through the Centuries*, London 1950, pp. 19, 33.
[22] E.351/2937; *L.C.C.*, *Survey of London*, XIII (1930), p. 117.

was paid to his successors down to the end of the Civil War. Under the first Stuart the expenses of the royal tents rarely exceeded £1,000 a year and sometimes were only a quarter of that sum.[23] Under Charles I, however, the tents, hales and pavilions swallowed up a great deal of public money.

A new reign demanded new tents and pavilions. Amongst other innovations was the making of a large gallery for the royal hunt. With the king's marriage painters were busy adding hatchments with the queen's arms to all the pavilions. We see the military importance of tents in the arrangements during the Bishops' Wars. The king's own pavilion needed extensive repairs; a new tent was provided for the Council of War, another for the heralds and a third for the royal chaplains, while a large hale was made for the king's bodyguard. The removing wardrobe, the cellar, the buttery, the larder, the kitchen and all the other 'below-stairs' departments of the household accompanied the king on his campaigns; Charles did not intend to rough it in the field. The expenses of pitching the royal camp at Goswick and elsewhere were not small as workmen had to be engaged to level the ground. The First Bishops' War involved the master of the tents in spending £5,779. Because of the outbreak of the Civil War he was unable to pass his account through the Exchequer until the end of 1649.[24]

With the Restoration tents and pavilions came into their own again. Everybody who was anybody was issued with one – General Monck, the Duke of Ormonde, Mr Secretary Nicholas, Colonel Russell of the Grenadier Guards, the Lord Privy Seal and the Keeper of the Privy Purse. The Duke of York had three tents for his use at Tonbridge. Before long the king's barber had one and the king's bargemaster and even the king's coffeeman. At last the master of the tents was permitted to issue himself with a tent. On his marriage Charles II ordered a wonderful new pavilion with four turrets and numerous pyramids to be set up at Hampton Court as a headquarters for honeymoon picnics. Catherine of Braganza's host of attendants all became entitled to tents before the honeymoon was out – ladies-in-waiting, chaplains and even shoemakers. Special awnings were made for Queen Catherine's use on her way to Mass. Barbara Villiers, Duchess of Cleveland, for some reason had to wait until 1675 before she was granted a tent of her very own. In 1662 the first aid tent arrived on the scene – 'two large tents with lodgings to attend the court for sick persons, if need should require' were made by order of the Lord Chamberlain. At a party held in Windsor Great Park in 1675, the royal musicians played from what appears to have been a canvas bandstand. Later in the reign, with the growing popularity of horse-racing, tents were erected as grandstands at the courses at Newmarket and Tonbridge where, from time to time, many were 'sorely wounded and torn by winds and foul weather'. Perhaps it was horse-racing that prodded the invention of horse-tents with 'built-in' mangers. Tents were increasingly used to house stores of one kind and another, notably in the dockyards, and were put to much the same uses as the Nissen huts of a later age. With all this activity the master of the royal tents, hales and pavilions was spending little under £10,000 in each year of the sixteen-seventies. Retrenchment was very necessary.[25]

Once the court had become permanently settled in Westminster there was little need for a master of the royal tents and the office remained unfilled after the Revolution. Royal progresses, no less than tournaments, had come to an end and when next a British sovereign travelled the realm it would be in the royal train. Under Queen Anne and the early Hanoverians the tents in the palace gardens at St James's, Kensington and Hampton Court and in Windsor Great Park gave way to classical temples, grottoes and summer-houses. If a king of England led his army in the field, as did William III and George II, suitable accommodation was provided by the military; while at

[23] E.351/2939; A.O.1/2292/4; A.O.1/2293/9, 11.
[24] A.O.1/2293/13; A.O.1/2295/23.
[25] A.O.1/2295/24–7; A.O.1/2297/38.

coronations and other state occasions temporary structures could be built by the officers of the king's works. Today whenever Her Majesty holds a garden party in the grounds of Buckingham Palace it is the Department of the Environment which erects the tea tent and the crimson *Shamiana*, with the dais beneath it, brought home by George V from the Delhi Durbar.

NEVILLE WILLIAMS

The
pre-Union Records of the
Scottish Exchequer

The records of the Scottish Exchequer do not form a continuous series. Since the structure of the financial administration was altered several times, any account of the records must be based on a study of its development. As the most complete change took place just after the Union of 1707, the present article is confined to the records prior to that date. It will give an account of their vicissitudes since the Union, a note on record publications and a brief examination of the records in reference to the development of the Exchequer and financial departments.

The Act of Parliament, 6 Anne c. 26, which came into force in May 1708, implemented the provision of article 19 of the Treaty of Union 'that there be a Court of Exchequer in Scotland after the Union for deciding questions concerning the revenue of Customs and Excises there, having the same power and authority in such cases as the Court of Exchequer has in England'. This re-organization affected the fiscal and administrative as well as the judicial functions of the Exchequer, all of which had to conform as closely as circumstances would allow to the English model. The Act not only gave the Scottish Exchequer its Chief Baron and Barons, but also divided its work among the four main offices of King's Remembrancer, Lord Treasurer's Remembrancer, Auditor and the Pipe, each office having its own staff of clerks. Nothing was said of the Clerk-Register, whose commission constituted him Clerk of Exchequer and who had hitherto appointed the subordinate clerks in that department. But when the Duke of Montrose presented his commission as Clerk-Register for recording in Exchequer on 25 July 1716, it appeared to the Barons that 'clauses are inserted which are in some measure contrary to and inconsistent with the Act of Parliament that constitutes the Court of Exchequer here', and accordingly it was recorded 'without any prejudice to any of the officers or clerks belonging to the Court of Exchequer'.[1] It was clear, therefore, that the Clerk-Register had no powers or functions in respect of the new Court of Exchequer and its records. The position of the pre-Union records was quite obscure. Most, but not all, of those dating from before 1660 were in the Clerk-Register's custody, while the post-Restoration records and some pre-Restoration records were kept by the King's Remembrancer, Lord Treasurer's Remembrancer and Auditor respectively, according to the use which could be made of them. If anything, they were an embarrassment, for as the Deputy Auditor wrote of the medieval Exchequer rolls in his custody, 'to put them in any kind of order would be attended with much expence, time and trouble, which it is humbly

---

[1] K.R. Office. Orders, Vol. 1, (E.306) III; Treasury Min. Bk., (E.305) Vol. 1, 236. Except where stated otherwise all MSS. referred to are in the Scottish Record Office.

presumed may be saved as they are of no sort of use now whatever unless to such as are curious in antiquity'.[2]

Throughout the eighteenth century the Clerk-Register lacked equally any interest in acquiring these records and room to house them. Accommodation became available with the building of Register House, in which the Treasury in 1792 allotted rooms for Exchequer records. Some were moved there, but as yet they were not in the Clerk-Register's custody. Thomas Thomson, appointed Deputy Clerk-Register in 1806, conceiving 'that the duties of superintendance and controul attached to the Office of Deputy Clerk Register, must be held to extend to this Department of the Publick Records of Scotland, although now withdrawn more than formerly from the direct interference of the Lord Clerk Register', undertook to 'embrace the earliest opportunities of making myself acquainted with whatever concerns their formation, custody and preservation'. He drew the Clerk-Register's attention to the records of the old Exchequer. 'I have reason to believe, that on an Application to the Barons of Exchequer, in your Lordship's Name, an Order will be granted for the immediate Transmission of all these Records. Some of them I know to be of great Importance to the Illustration of Scottish Constitutional History; and their Value in that respect cannot fail to be encreased, by restoring them to their proper place among the Publick Records of the Kingdom',[3] Accordingly in June 1808, a memorial to that effect was presented to the Barons, but the officers of Exchequer were reluctant to part with their records, although the Deputy-Auditor commented that in 32 years service he 'never once had occasion to have recourse to them' and that he conceived it 'immaterial whether they lie in the Exchequer or in the general Register'. Accordingly, on the Barons' instructions, the Deputy King's Remembrancer notified the Clerk-Register of the rejection of the memorial, on the grounds that 'it would be attended with the greatest inconvenience if the Records, however ancient, were placed in the custody of any person except the existing officers of this Court'.[4] This attitude was not wholly obscurantist since some of the Exchequer officials, notably the Lord Treasurer's Remembrancer, had to search through early records for information and precedents, but in the circumstances it was perhaps a little offensive to point out that the records could equally well be re-united by the Clerk-Register transferring those in his custody to the Exchequer rooms in Register House, in which case the Barons might make arrangements for sorting and indexing.[5] The Exchequer was soon to move into new quarters in Parliament Square where the records would be 'equally well secured from all risque of fire as if they were deposited in the General Register House'.

A little over two years elapsed after the rejection of Thomson's scheme. Then, early in the morning of Sunday, 10 November 1811, fire broke out in the new Exchequer buildings 'in a dark closet near the Lord Treasurer's Remembrancer's and Auditor's offices'; the cause apparently was 'the carelessness of a maidservant leaving an iron bucket full of burning coals on the preceding evening on a timber floor'. It was confined to the back part of the building, where the two upper storeys were burnt out. By the time it had been extinguished at 7 a.m., it had destroyed the Lord Treasurer's Remembrancer's Office and the rooms above 'in which were kept some papers' and damaged the Auditor's Office and the Treasury Chambers. The Deputy King's Remembrancer and other officials were able to remove most of their records to safety in the aisle of St Giles Kirk, while the records and papers of the Auditor's Office were also rescued from the flames. All were later

[2] Draft return to Committee on Public Records, 1800.
[3] *First Annual Report of the Deputy Clerk Register of Scotland, 1807*, 8, App. 45.
[4] K. R. Off. Letter Bk. (E.310), Vol. 8, 195–221.
[5] Thomson commented that until the officers of Exchequer produced an inventory 'It will be impossible to state on what terms, and by what reciprocal concessions, a reasonable and expedient arrangement can be made'. *Third Annual Report*, 9.

removed to temporary storage in the premises of the Bank of Scotland until the building was repaired.[6]

The Barons met on 11 November to consider the effects of the fire and notified the Treasury that 'we have the satisfaction to state that the most important records and papers are saved'. But Adam Longmore, an Exchequer official, wrote in quite different terms to Thomas Thomson, 'to acquaint him that he early this morning collected the few remains of the books and papers that were yesterday saved from the flames and sent them over to the apartment in the Register House which is alloted to the Auditor of this Court. Mr Longmore will now be happy to have the assistance of the people usually employed by Mr Thomson which he yesterday so politely offered and he has no doubt that every thing possible will be preserved. Mr Longmore has taken special care to have the whole rubbish which was cast down from the upper rooms examined and every piece of paper and parchment that has or can be laid hold of will be sent over.'[7]

It is quite impossible to guess at the extent of the loss and damage caused by the fire of 1811. 'A considerable number of Volumes, partly burnt, and all of them drenched with water, were brought to the apartments in the General Register House, and carefully dried and examined, preparatory to their being repaired and rebound.'[8] It seems likely that the Exchequer Registers for the years 1661-1708 perished, along with many rolls of sheriffs accounts which were in the custody of the Lord Treasurer's Remembrancer. Fortunately the Exchequer escaped the great fire of 15-16 November 1824, which destroyed all the buildings from the Tron Kirk to Parliament Square, but certain records were removed from the King's Remembrancer's Office as a precaution.[9]

Between 1830 and 1856 the Exchequer was re-organized once more under various statutes, resulting in the loss of its judicial functions and of many of its financial and administrative powers and the concentration of the remainder in one office, that of the Queen's and Lord Treasurer's Remembrancer. In consequence, there was no further need for the pre-Union records as well as for many post-Union records. Most of the remaining Exchequer rolls were transmitted to Register House in 1846[10] and there were several subsequent transmissions of all types of records, which the staff of Register House were then able to arrange and catalogue. The section 'Crown Patrimony and Revenue, Exchequer and Treasury' occupies nearly one quarter of Livingstone's *Guide to the Public Records of Scotland* (1905). This work, though valuable, suffers from the defective classification employed at the time, whereby, to take one example, records relating to the crown revenue from former church lands were described as 'ecclesiastical'. A more serious drawback, however, has proved to be that nearly all classes of records were incomplete. There were two reasons for this, the first being that successive transmissions still failed to exhaust the supply of pre-Union records remaining in the Exchequer and the second, that pre-Union and post-Union records transmitted were inextricably mixed together, presenting a problem of sorting with which the small staff at Register House could not cope. Piecemeal attempts to deal with the problem having succeeded only in adding to the confusion, it was decided to attack the whole mass and in the summer of 1958 both types of records were sorted into their main classes. As the removal of the Queen's and Lord Treasurer's Remembrancer from the old Exchequer buildings in Parliament Square was then imminent, the opportunity was taken to make a thorough search for all records remaining in his custody of date earlier than 1860. Among those transmitted to the Scottish Record Office in December 1958 were a number of pre-Union items. One may hope therefore that, at last, the records of the old Scottish Exchequer are now safely gathered into Register House.

---

[6] Treasury Min. Bk., Vol. 14, 344; Letter Bk., Vol. 12, 176.

[7] *Ibid.*, 123, 124.

[8] *Fifth Annual Report*, App. 18.

[9] Treasury Min. Bk., Vol. 23, 447.

[10] *Sixteenth Report of Deputy Clerk Register*, 3.

Since this article was first written in 1959 further material has come to light, none, however, in more curious circumstances than the papers, mostly in small fragments, which were found by workmen re-wiring St Giles's Cathedral, Edinburgh, in July 1961. These proved to include some seventeenth and eighteenth-century Exchequer documents, which may have been relics of the migration after the fire of 1811, though there were also unrelated items of later date. No one has been able to furnish a satisfactory explanation of how they came to be torn up and mixed with twigs and other rubbish in the roof-space above the Preston Aisle. Other items have turned up in private hands, though by far the most have been found during the course of sorting post-Union Exchequer material or in re-classifying other record groups in the Scottish Record Office. A large number, which still remain outside official custody, are presumed to form part of the records lost or dispersed after the fire. These, with some later items, were rescued from destruction by David Laing LL.D (1793–1878), the antiquarian, and were bequeathed by him to Edinburgh University Library in his huge collection of Laing MSS. The Exchequer material includes documents of the period 1479–1848, the most important of which are customs records for the fifteen years or so preceding the Union (La.II–490–1). In 1968 the present writer identified and listed the Exchequer material in the collection for the National Register of Archives (Scotland).[11]

II

Thomas Thomson found the early Exchequer rolls 'in a state of great disorder, and independently of more irreparable injuries, sometimes almost illegible from the dust with which they were encrusted'.[12] But he saw their unique value as a record of medieval Scotland. As early as 1810, he was drawing attention to the need for printing at least a selection of material from them, and by 1817 the text of three volumes of *The Accounts of Great Chamberlains of Scotland* was in print. Partly owing to lack of official support, the sheets of these volumes lay for over twenty years. In 1841 the first two volumes were issued to the members of the Bannatyne Club, followed in 1845 by an augmented third volume. A short introduction to the publication mentioned that 'within the last few years there has been found among the neglected treasures of the old Exchequer a large additional mass of public accounts'. In consequence this edition was later superseded by the full official publication, beginning in 1878, of the *Exchequer Rolls of Scotland*. Fortunately Thomson's beloved record type had fallen out of fashion and the editors provided a clear text, generally accurate and with repetitive matter carefully abridged. George Burnet, Lyon King of Arms, joint-editor of Volume 1, published another eleven volumes before his death in 1890 and left volumes 13 and 14 well advanced. G. P. McNeill, an advocate, had completed volumes 15 to 20 by 1899, but thereafter publication flagged and with volume 23 in 1908, bringing the series down to 1600, it lapsed altogether. The scheme of publication also included the printing of the Crown rentals (*Rentalia Domini Regis*) and the Responde Books (*Libri Responsionum*) as appendices to volumes 9–23.[13] It is unlikely, and probably undesirable, that the later rolls, which are very formal, should be printed, but additional early rolls which have come to light in recent years and copies taken from lost records will provide material for a projected supplementary volume.

The first volume of the *Accounts of the Lord High Treasurer of Scotland* (1473–98), edited by Dr Thomas Dickson, Curator of the Historical Department of Register House, appeared in 1877 but had no successor until 1900, when the series was resumed with Sir James Balfour Paul, Lyon King of Arms, as editor. By 1916 when publication was stopped by the war, eleven volumes had

---

[11] National Register of Archives (Scotland) Survey 0401. Historical MSS. Commission 72, *Laing MSS*, contains some of the more important items but the descriptions are not always accurate.

[12] *Fifth Annual Report*, App. p. 10.

[13] The nature of these records is described later in this article.

appeared, bringing the record down to 1566. Publication was resumed in 1970, with Dr C. T. McInnes, formerly Curator of Historical Records, as editor, and the series will be carried up to 1603 or later. The opportunity was taken to introduce certain improvements in volume XII, notably the calendaring or abridgement of formal or repetitive matter instead of haphazard omission of passages. The introduction describes the workings of the Treasury administration and the title of the series has been changed to the more correct *Accounts of the Treasurer of Scotland*.

Though scholars have every reason to be grateful to Thomas Thomson and the later editors, it is unfortunate that few of them made any serious attempt to study the organization of the Exchequer and the workings of royal finance. It is usual to refer to Dickson's preface to the first volume of the *Accounts of the Lord High Treasurer* as authoritative, but it owes this less to any intrinsic merit of its own than to the absence of anything else bearing on the subject. In fact, out of 270 pages, Dickson devoted only 24 to dealing with the Exchequer and related topics, the development of the office of Treasurer and list of its holders up to 1512 and a description of the MS. Treasurer's accounts. The editors of the Exchequer rolls sometimes gave up short sections of their introductions to various aspects of financial administration, but not in any systematic or satisfactory manner.

The fault, of course, lay not in the editors' scholarship but in their approach to the records, which was best expressed by Thomas Thomson: 'In truth it is chiefly in these Records that we must seek for all that can be known with certainty of the territorial produce, the domestic industry, the trade, the public revenue, the civil and military establishments, the modes of life, the food, the dress, and even the amusements of the people of Scotland, in the fourteenth, fifteenth, and sixteenth centuries; and, in a more indirect and incidental manner, they would be found no less useful in ascertaining and verifying innumerable details in the political history of the Kingdom, which remain at present vague and uncertain, or as to which the received statements are confused and inaccurate'.[14] Thus, while occasionally digressing into absolute trivialities, the editors were mainly concerned with illustrating general history from the financial records. In this they were no better and no worse than their English contemporaries, but a study of the administrative system and the manner of framing the accounts should have been a preliminary to any such use of the material.

The editors themselves lacked any source of information, other than the records, on the organization of the Scottish Exchequer. In 1681 Sir William Purves of Woodhouselee, Charles II's Solicitor General, drew up a complete rental of the crown lands and other hereditary sources of income in Scotland, prefacing it with some observations on the royal revenues.[15] The only published work on the Exchequer itself, Clerk and Scrope's *Historical View of the forms and powers of the Court of Exchequer in Scotland*,[16] was written some fifteen or twenty years after the establishment of the new court in 1708. Baron Sir John Clerk of Penicuik and his collaborator, Baron Scrope, were both judges of that court and their main interest lay in its procedure and practice. Clerk's chapter on the pre-Union Exchequer consists of citations of statutes with a brief linking narrative.

He did not realise that for the greater part of its existence the old Exchequer was not a permanent body or institution. Thus he could assert that 'A Court of Exchequer in Scotland may in some respects be said to be as ancient as the Crown itself; for as the Crown could not subsist without proper revenues, so these could not be managed without certain overseers who in time came to be

---

[14] *Fourth Annual Report*, p. 38.
[15] There are several MS. copies of Purves's rentals of 1667 and 1681 in the Scottish Record Office and the National Library of Scotland. A MS. of the 1681 rental in the British Museum was printed in 1897. *Revenue of the Scottish Crown, 1681*, ed. D. Murray Rose.
[16] Printed in 1820 from a MS. copy in the King's Remembrancer's Office (now in the Scottish Record Office). The book was written almost entirely by Sir John Clerk, whose original MS. forms part of the Clerk of Penicuik Muniments in the Scottish Record Office (No. 2850).

called the Lords Auditors of Checker'.[17] This statement is only true in the most general terms and certainly not in the sense in which Clerk intended it, for even until James VI's reign the Auditors of Exchequer were an *ad hoc* body, specially commissioned by the King to audit the accounts of his revenue. The Treasury accounts continued to be audited by such bodies until they were brought finally to an end by the Union. Once the audit had been completed, the commission expired and the Exchequer simply ceased to exist until the next audit.

Unlike Clerk, Thomson and later editors understood the impermanent nature of the Exchequer. They did not, however, appreciate all its consequences, particularly with regard to the records. Because the Exchequer was not a permanent institution, the Clerk-Register kept its records, not because he was Clerk of Exchequer, but because from one audit to the next the 'Register' provided the only possible storage for them. Up to the beginning of the sixteenth century the Exchequer was often itinerant, moving from Edinburgh to Linlithgow, Stirling and elsewhere during the course of the audit, accompanied on its travels by cart-loads of old rolls.[18] At the conclusion of the Exchequer its temporary staff of clerks returned to their normal duties in chancery and other offices and the rolls were restored to their usual repository in Edinburgh Castle. When at last the Exchequer became a permanent body, with a full-time staff, its clerks were still subject to the control of the Clerk-Register, who appointed them as his deputies.[19] They kept its current records, as well as such of the older rolls and registers as they required for frequent consultation, but he remained the legal custodian of all its archives. Thus a royal letter of 1664, commending William Law, a former clerk, narrated that 'while hee lived, he was at great paines and charges in preserving from the violence of the late usurpers the publict registers, ancient and late, of our Exchequer of our said kingdome of Scotland; and that since his death, by the faithfull care of Mr William Sharp, now husband to the executrix of the said William Law, they have beine so still preserved and now delivered in good condition to our Clerk of Register'.[20] Presumably the Clerk-Register added these volumes to the Exchequer archives in his own custody. In any case, this was the last transmission of records to him, and those remaining in the hands of the clerks were taken over by the officers of the new Exchequer in 1708, thus perpetuating a division in the records which was to last for another 250 years.

III

In discussing the records of the Exchequer, it is convenient to make a division between the seventeenth century records and those of an earlier date. Any account of the latter must take into consideration the work of Sir John Skene, who held office as Clerk-Register from 1594 to 1612. His legal dictionary, *De Verborum Significatione*, printed in 1597, contains references to the Exchequer and related topics. A few years later he drew up for James I and VI some 'Proposals anent the order of the Checker', in which he suggested procedural reforms.[21] His most important work, however, completed within the first year in which he held office, was the preparation of a complete inventory of the Exchequer records, 'Ane tabill and repertour of the Cheker rollis extant in the Register collectit and put in ordour conforme to the numer and ordour of the kingis in quhais tyme thai wer maid and of the yeiris of ilkane of the kingis forsaidis'.[22] A summary list showed the contents of each of the fifteen 'coffers of the Register' on 30 April 1595, while details were given of each class of the 'Kingis rollis and comptis'.

---

[17] *loc. cit.*, 96.
[18] See 'The procedure of the Scottish Exchequer in the early sixteenth century', *Scottish Historical Review*, XL (1961), 89–117.
[19] K.R. Off., Index to Exchequer Register, 1661–74 (E.337/7), p. 51.
[20] Warrants of Exchequer Reg. (E.8/14), 17 June 1664.
[21] Printed in *Miscellany One* by various authors (Stair Society, 1971), 147–55.
[22] The author has referred to a contemporary copy in the Scottish Record Office. The original MS. is *penes* the Earl of Haddington.

Although the 'tabill' also embraced account books, rentals and other records, the Exchequer rolls themselves formed the largest, oldest and most important group, filling seven out of the fifteen coffers. Altogether there were 894 rolls, covering the period 1264–1594, of which 572[23] survive at the present day. The total number, down to 1708, stands at about 850, but from 1673 onwards the rolls are actually large parchment books, in consequence of an Act of Parliament of 1672, which ordered 'that the present way of making the compts of Exchequer in rolls be altered, and that the same be maid heiraftir in bookes of parchment'.[24] Curiously, the Exchequer accounts of 1471 are also in this form, which appears to have been authorized by an Act of 1469.[25] The rolls proper are made of parchment membranes some 11 or 12 inches wide and up to 24 or 26 inches long, sewn together, head to tail, to the required length. For most years there are several rolls, each containing the accounts of a particular branch of crown revenue or of a different class of official.

Before proceeding to examine the Exchequer rolls in detail, it is necessary to draw attention to their importance as records. In Skene's time and earlier they were consulted frequently for information and precedents. Thus in reference to a case of 1483, involving the tenure of certain lands, the Clerk-Register was 'to pas and seik the ald Chekker rolls to se geif ony declaratioun can be had to schaw mare clerely how the sammyn landis ar halden'.[26] The Exchequer officials, too, might consult the old rolls, for instance to determine when a burgh had last rendered an account.[27] Skene himself searched through them to produce a list of crown lands which had been alienated and to establish the rates of customs paid in former times.[28]

As we have seen, about 300 rolls have been lost since 1595. Even at that date less than half a dozen thirteenth century rolls were in existence, all of which were subsequently lost or destroyed. Their contents are known from short extracts made for the first Earl of Haddington, in which it is noted of the roll of 1289, that 'the first comptis are revin, blekked and can not be red'.[29] The greatest loss, however, that of nearly all the sheriffs' rolls up to 1630, may be attributed to the fire of 1811. A return of the records in the custody of the Lord Treasurer's Remembrancer in 1800 mentioned that these rolls were 'tolerably complete' from about 1400. Nine only have survived, two of which (1489 and 1601) were discovered among unsorted records in 1957,[30] and there are also three rolls containing single accounts and copies of some of the accounts of 1535 and 1545[31]. The contents of the lost rolls after 1513 are partly known from the 'Responde Books' (E. 1), by which Chancery notified the Exchequer of the amounts for which each sheriff had to answer on infefting (*Anglice* infeoffing) the heirs of crown vassals. There is also an old index covering '*responsiones*' from 1437 to 1618.[32]

In contrast the burgh or custumars' rolls are almost complete from 1326. They are known by these alternative titles because one side of the roll contained the accounts of the bailies of the royal burghs of their burgh ferms and other payments due to the King and, until 1629, the other

---

[23] Some of which appear to be omitted from Skene's lists.
[24] *Acts of the Parliament of Scotland* (*APS*), VIII, 88.
[25] Exchequer Roll E.38/263; see *APS*, II, 97. The missing accounts of 1470 and 1472 were probably also in book form, but were lost before Skene's time.
[26] *Acts of the Lords of Council in Civil Causes*, CXX.
[27] *Exchequer Rolls*, XI, 384.
[28] 'Tabill', pp. 1a, 3–40.
[29] Printed in *Exchequer Rolls*, I, 1–51. All the rolls down to 1600 are printed in the 23 volumes of *Exchequer Rolls* with the exceptions referred to in notes 30, 31 and 40 below.
[30] E.38/294A and 536A (unprinted). The accounts for 1471 are in the parchment volume mentioned above.
[31] E.38/403A (fragmentary) and 425A.
[32] E.1/14. Strictly speaking, this is only an index to the Responde Books from 1492, the earlier '*responsiones*' being taken from the sheriffs' rolls. The index and the Responde Books themselves are printed as appendices to the volumes of *Exchequer Rolls*.

contained the accounts of the custumars of the great customs. The latter should be taken in conjunction with the series of customs books (E. 71) beginning in 1498 and ending in 1640. These books, now arranged under 29 ports, are detailed statements of each consignment of goods customed, in some cases mentioning the vessels on which they were shipped and their destinations. The largest and most complete group (78) is that for Edinburgh but there are 188 altogether. Skene had enough cockets, that is certificates of payment of customs,[33] to fill the whole of one coffer and part of another. Less than four dozen of these have survived.

The accounts of the *ballivi ad extra*, the chamberlains and receivers of the King's property and ward lands, were the latest to develop. The first roll, that of 1434, was short and contained only four accounts, but the forfeitures of powerful vassals, notably the Douglases, increased the crown lands to such an extent that for the last few years of James V's reign two rolls were required annually to record the accounts. The roll, also known as the property roll,[34] was closely related to the crown rentals or *Rentalia domini regis*, of which nine volumes survive for the period 1476-1588. Although Skene records eighteen volumes, it seems that the reduced number is the result of later rebinding and not of any losses. The *rentalia* differ from the seventeenth-century rentals, such as those drawn up by Purves, in that they are the actual record of the leasing of the crown lands by the King's commissioners, entry in the rental (rentalling) constituting and recording the tenant's right.[35] As a result of the extensive feuing of the crown lands in the sixteenth century the rentals ceased to be kept in the old form and at the same time the character of the property rolls changed, as the accountants became predominantly feuars rendering accounts of their feu duties. The property rolls and burgh rolls continued in an almost unaltered form after 1708, being kept by the Auditor and King's Remembrancer respectively.

Certain minor accounts appear in the fourteenth and fifteenth-century Exchequer rolls, for taxations, the mint and others described by Skene as 'auld rollis quhilk hes nocht daitis and ar of litill consequence'. Between 1461 and 1463 there are also rolls of the Queen dowager's Exchequer.[36] The enrolment of minor accounts had ceased by the sixteenth century when they were preserved in small books, of which Skene listed a number. Those surviving at the present day include an account of the revenues of the bishopric of Moray *sede vacante*, 1538, and an account of James VI's annuity from England, 1594-6.[37] There are several larger volumes of accounts, notably Cardinal Beaton's accounts of his receipts of the dowries of James V's queens and of his expenditure for the King in France.[38] The most important of the minor accounts are those of the Masters of Works (E. 36) for building and repair of the royal castles and palaces, 1529-1679, in 32 volumes, which are being printed in three volumes, one of which has been published.[39] It should be noted that these accounts do not cover all expenditure on royal buildings, for at various times the Treasurer made payments of a similar nature.

A number of references have been made to the Treasurer's accounts, so it is now necessary to consider the chief financial officers of the crown. In the fourteenth century there was one only, the Great Chamberlain, who drew upon all branches of the King's revenue and who met all classes

---

[33] The customs books have not been printed, although they would be of considerable value to economic historians. A Scottish cocket of 1456 is printed in *Bronnen tot de Geschiedenis van den Handel met Engeland, Schotland en Ierland, 1150-1485*, II, No. 1448.

[34] Skene compiled an index of the principal lands in the property rolls from 1440-1594. 'Tabill' pp. 135-63.

[35] The rentals are printed as appendices to the *Exchequer Rolls*, vols. VII-XXIII. They are of considerable value for social and economic history.

[36] *Exchequer Rolls*, VII.

[37] Various Accounts: E.30/7, printed in 'The revenues of the bishopric of Moray in 1538', *Innes Review*, XIX (1968), 40-56; E.30/14.

[38] *Accounts of the Lord High Treasurer*, VII, 1-64 (E.30/5).

[39] *Accounts of the Master of Works*, vol. I, 1529-1615.

of expenditure. Under his control were the Clerk of the Wardrobe and the Clerk of Liverance, the latter being responsible for the provisions of the King's household.[40] Soon after James I's return from captivity in England in 1424 two subordinate officers, designated 'thesaurarius' and 'contra-rotulator', were acting alongside him. By 1426, however, these subordinates had completely ousted him[41] and thenceforward his financial responsibilities were confined to accounting for the issues of the Chamberlain Ayre. Although it appears that a Chamberlain's account was rendered so late as 1515,[42] the last surviving one dates from 1435 and Skene knew of none later than 1456.

This altered state of affairs led to a change in the title of one of the new officials, from 'contrarotulator' to 'compotorum rotulator' or comptroller. The derivation of his new title is obscure but reflects the fact that his accounts had ceased to be connected with those of the Chamberlain and the Treasurer.[43] As nearly all their accounts up to James IV's reign are lost, the study of the development of the duties of the Treasurer and Comptroller is rather difficult, but the division of revenue and expenditure between them shown in an account of Scottish administration drawn up in 1559,[44] appears to have been settled almost a century before that date.

The Comptroller received the revenues of the royal 'property', comprising land rents, burgh ferms, the great customs, and certain annual payments, such as blench ferms and castlewards collected by the Sheriffs. Occasionally his title altered to that of 'Receiver-General', apparently as a means of making more effective his control over the subordinate receivers or chamberlains of crown lands. The fifteenth and sixteenth-century Receiver-general (i.e. Comptroller) should not be con-fused with the similarly-named seventeenth-century official, who was subordinate to the Treasurer. He paid certain pensions and minor charges, but his main responsibility was the provisioning of the royal Household. His accounts, however, only give his total expenditure for the Household under general headings, which are based on detailed day-by-day accounts. The 'Libri Emptorum' (E. 32), of which there are 13 volumes, 1511–12, 1531–8, 1542–3, and 1546–53, contain the purchases made by the 'catours'. The 'Libri Domicilii Regis' (E. 31) contain not only these purchases, but also all other deliveries of provisions to the household, in addition to current accounts of the stock in hand. Twelve volumes have survived, forming an imperfect series for the years 1525 to 1551, from which the Bannatyne Club printed a very valuable collection of extracts covering the period 1525–33.[45] From 1538 to 1565, with some gaps, another series, 'Despences de la Maison Royale' (E. 33), records the household expenses of Mary of Guise, wife of James V and later Regent, and of her daughter Mary, Queen of Scots. As their title suggests these volumes were written in French. Records of the household of James VI are very scanty and after 1603, of course, he and his suc-cessors only paid brief visits to Scotland. The minutes of the Board of Green Cloth for Charles II's household in Scotland, 1650–1 (E. 31/19) were recovered from private custody in 1968.

Because of their brevity and simplicity the Comptroller's accounts kept to the same standard form from year to year and were written in Latin until about 1588.[46] They were enrolled until 1567 although, curiously, the earliest separate accounts are portions of 'ane lytill buik in 4° contenand sum comptrollar comptis in King James the thridis tyme and of other comptrollaris in the tyme of King James the fourt'. The James IV accounts are now in two small volumes, one of which strayed

[40] The accounts of the Chamberlains, Clerks of Liverance and Clerks of the Wardrobe are printed in the *Exchequer Rolls*, vol. I–IV, except for one account of an acting Clerk of Liverance, 1387, Exchequer Roll No. 101B.
[41] *Exchequer Rolls*, IV, p. xciv.
[42] *Acts of the Lords of Council in Public Affairs*, 31; 'The last Chamberlain Ayre', *Scottish Historical Review*, XXXIX, 85.
[43] 'The Comptroller, 1425–1488', *Scottish Historical Review*, LII, 1–29.
[44] *Discours Particulier D'Escosse, Bannatyne Club*, 1824, 3–10..
[45] *Excerpta e Libris Domicilii Domini Jacobi Quinti Regis Scotorum*, 1836.
[46] *Exchequer Rolls*, XXII, pp. lxii–viii.

out of official custody in the nineteenth century and was restored to the Scottish Record Office in 1954.[47] It appears that the practice was to enrol accounts which had been made up and audited in book form.[48]

Although Sir William Purves wrote many years after the disappearance, except in name, of the office of Comptroller, he had a clear idea of its importance. 'He was esteemed in greater accompt then the Thesaurer, he haveing the management of the whole propertie, the placing of all Receavers, Challmerlaines, and uther officers, the taking of a cautione for thair fidelitie, the censureing and punishing them for abuses and disposing them of thair offices, passing of all infeftments of the propertie and the managing of the haill affairs pertaining and belonging theirto'.[49] Nevertheless the office was extremely burdensome to its holders and changed hands no less than twenty-three times between 1464 and 1492. The revenues from the property, hardly adequate to meet the charges of the Household, were further diminished by the King's misplaced generosity, of which Robert Barton complained in 1525, that 'quhatever mycht happin tocum thairthrow in tyme tocum suld nocht be laid to his charge, sen he has done his exact diligence, spendit his awn geir and may sustene na forrar'.[50] His successor, James Colville, stated more bluntly: 'Suppos the king wantit, thar suld na reproche be input to him tharthrow'.[51]

The office of Treasurer, therefore, was generally more attractive to magnates and prelates, although in 1599 the Earl of Cassillis absconded soon after his appointment, fearing that it would prove ruinous to him.[52] The 'casualty' or branch of revenue which the Treasurer administered came to consist largely of compositions paid in lieu of duties and penalties owing to the King, such as the casualties of ward, non-entry, relief and marriage, the 'unlaws' and escheats of the Justice Ayre[53] and other courts and other payments for gifts and charters from the crown. In doing this he negotiated directly with the persons concerned, the effect of which was to curtail considerably the sheriffs' functions as collectors of revenue. Thus the Treasurer's accounts contain a 'charge' in which receipts from the sheriffs form a small part, the bulk of the receipts being from compositions of various kinds.[54] He also received money levied by taxation, which was granted by the Estates for special purposes and not as a regular part of the royal income.[55] If then, the Treasurer's 'charge' was much longer and more detailed than the Comptroller's, his 'discharge'[56] exceeded the latter's in these respects to such an extent that it completely exhausted the clerks' Latinity. From the earliest full account in existence, that of 1473–4, the accounts uniformly employ Scots. The account of 1473–4 extends to 53 folios, the next, that of 1488–92, to 138 folios, much too lengthy for enrolment. All the Treasurer's accounts known to Skene were in book form, but he listed none earlier

---

[47] Printed in *Miscellany of the Scottish History Society*, Vol. IX, 59–75. The remaining Comptroller's accounts (E.24) are printed in the *Exchequer Rolls* up to 1600. A new series of publications is in preparation, which will contain the later Comptrollers' Accounts from 1600 to 1635. Accounts for 1450, and 1453, were entered on the Custumars' roll. *Exchequer Rolls*, V, 390, 604. A separate roll of 1456 contains a special account, not, in fact, rendered by the Comptroller, *ibid*, VI, 289.

[48] *Exchequer Rolls*, XX, p. liii.

[49] *Revenue of the Scottish Crown*, 22.

[50] *APS*, II, 296.

[51] *Acts of the Lords of Council in Public Affairs*, 250.

[52] *Register of Privy Council*, V, p. cx.

[53] The Treasurer and 'Lords Componitours' or 'Lords Compositours' accompanied the Justiciar on ayre to compound, with those who were amerced, the amounts that were to be paid.

[54] All the Treasurer's accounts (E.21) down to 1574 are printed in *Accounts of the Treasurer of Scotland*, with the exception of those mentioned in note 57 below and some fragments of an account covering June–August 1557.

[55] Early taxation accounts in the Exchequer rolls have been noticed above. The separate series of taxation records and accounts dates only from the end of the sixteenth century. (E.59–68).

[56] It must be stressed that 'charge' and 'discharge' are not equivalent to receipts and expenditure.

than 1469.[57] The form of the Treasurer's 'discharge' varied, although it tended to be a detailed list of items in each category of expenditure on a monthly basis; pensions and salaries, liveries, alms, the wardrobe, arms and artillery, buildings, etc. The management of the *Bursa regis*, the King's purse, passed during James V's reign to the 'pursmaister' of whom very little is known, apart from fragments of two of his accounts.[58]

In 1539–40 the Treasurer received about £28,200, while the Comptroller drew £17,900 from the property. The total amount, £46,000 Scots, was equivalent to £13,150 sterling.[59] James V left £26,000 in his coffers at his death[60] in spite of quite lavish expenditure. He had been able to supplement his income by drawing upon the wealth of the Church by means of taxes and 'voluntary' contributions[61] and by nominating his infant illegitimate sons to some of the greater benefices. Expedients such as these, however, did not require any innovations in the financial administration. No special department dealing specifically with church revenues existed before 1562, when the 'Collectory' was set up. It should be explained that the religious changes of 1559–61 had given the protestant religion *de facto* recognition, but no share in the endowments of the Church.

In February 1561–2 the Privy Council determined to levy one-third of the fruits of all benefices, to be applied partly to the payment of stipends of ministers of the Reformed Church and partly to the royal Household and the Queen's guard. Within a few years Knox had to comment that 'the gaird and the effairis of the kytcheing wer so gryping that the mynisteris stipendis could nocht be payit'.[62] But after the protestant revolution of 1567 the stipends became a prior charge upon the Thirds and the Crown took only the 'superplus' or unassigned portion. Rentals of the benefices were entered in the Books of Assumption (E. 48/1), while the sums due to the ministers were set down in the Register of Stipends (E. 48/2). The Thirds were received by twelve deputy collectors, over whom was a Collector General. The series of Collector Generals' accounts (E. 45) is almost complete for the years 1561–97 and there are large numbers of sub-collectors' accounts (E. 46) dated 1563–73. By a curious process Livingstone classified all these records as 'ecclesiastical'.[63]

The Scottish Reformation differed from that in England in that it was not accompanied by any dissolution of the religious houses. Even before the overthrow of the old Church, its endowments and wealth were passing steadily into lay hands. In 1587 most of the remaining temporalities were annexed to the Crown by an Act which was partially repealed in 1606 in so far as it related to the temporalities of bishoprics.[64] It was not until 1592, however, that proper provision was made for the King to receive this 'new augmentation' of his revenues.[65] Apart from a volume of accounts beginning on 1 November 1592 and ending in 1595, and rentals of the kirklands north and south of the Forth, there are very few records of the Treasury of the New Augmentation (E. 49). Its organization has yet to be studied.

Thus by the end of the sixteenth century there were four principal financial officers of the Crown: the Comptroller, Treasurer, Collector-General of the Thirds of Benefices, and Treasurer

---

[57] There is a short Treasurer's account for 1438 (charge only), *Exchequer Rolls*, v, 49, and an account of a receiver-general '*sub thesaurario*' for 1434, *ibid.*, IV, 497.

[58] Various Accounts, E.30/9. Printed in *Miscellany* x (Scottish Hist. Soc. 1965), 11–51.

[59] These figures, for net revenue from sources within Scotland, are based on the Comptroller's and Treasurer's accounts.

[60] *Registrum Secreti Sigilli*, III, No. 383.

[61] *See* R. K. Hannay, *The College of Justice* (1933), chap. IV.

[62] *Works*, ed. Laing, II, 417.

[63] The earlier accounts have been printed. G. Donaldson, 'Thirds of Benefices, 1561–1572,' *Scottish History Society*, 1949; see also G. Donaldson, 'Sources for the study of Scottish Ecclesiastical Organization and Personnel, 1560–1600', *Bulletin of Institute of Historical Research*, XIX, 188–203.

[64] *APS*, III, 455; IV, 282.

[65] *APS*, III, 564.

of the New Augmentation. It was the duty of each to protect the branch of revenue under his charge by seeing that it was not diminished by any ill-considered royal grants. As early as 1528 it was enacted that all signatures (warrants signed by the King) affecting the property and casualty must be signed by the Comptroller and Treasurer respectively and by three 'compositors'.[66] A register was kept to record the signatures and compositions payable on them. Having placed it in his *Guide* under 'Crown Grants and Titles to Lands, Dignities and Offices', Livingstone explained: 'This contains a record of all the signatures and warrants affecting the revenue under the charge of the Treasurer, as well as that administered by the Comptroller. As such, it might more strictly be placed with their accounts . . . But as the original signatures preserved go no further back than 1607, and this register is a continuous record from 1561, it is convenient, for purposes of reference, to insert it here as the earliest record of warrants for Crown grants'.[67] While perhaps logical in adhering to his own principles, Livingstone does not make it clear that the Register (E. 2) also served the Collectory and the Treasury of the New Augmentation. It ends in 1658, but another Register of Signatures, begun after the Restoration, is extant from 1703 in the form of copies of signatures, preserved in bundles up to 1715, and in volumes thereafter down to 1847 (E. 315–17). It is one of the few records linking the financial administration before and after 1708.

IV

During Skene's lifetime changes took place in the organization of the Exchequer, which were to have considerable effects upon its records. In the early sixteenth century it could carry out many of the administrative and judicial functions of the King's Council, of which it was an offshoot,[68] and its Auditors had special powers by royal commission for auditing the King's accounts and a statutory duty by Act of Parliament of 1535 of examining and supervising the accounts of the 'common good' of burghs.[69] A burgh's 'common good' consisted of the rents and profits of its lands, its petty customs and other items, and was liable, after payment of the burgh ferm to the King, for the maintenance of its administration. Over 300 accounts (E. 82), covering the years 1557–1684, are preserved for 55 burghs.[70] But because the Exchequer only sat for a month or so each year, no registers were kept of the administrative and judicial business with which it dealt. Until 1628 it was the practice to enter orders and minutes on blank pages in the Responde Books,[71] while at an earlier date judicial and other business was recorded in the Registers of Council.[72] Certain administrative changes took place in 1584[73] reflected in the earliest surviving Exchequer Act Book (E.4/1), which begins in that year.[74] For the first time the Exchequer became a permanent body.

The permanent Exchequer set up in 1584 did not fulfil the hopes entertained of it. 'Thair is not quhyte[75] nor beir,[76] silver nor uthir rent, to serve his Hienes sufficientlie in breid and drink nor uthirwayes',[77] or as James himself complained: 'In schort na trayst or dayet is keeped. Quhat is

---

[66] *APS*, II, 204; cf. *ibid.*, 328; III, 378, 560.

[67] *loc. cit.*, p. 107.

[68] 'Exchequer and Council in the reign of James V,' *Juridical Review*, new series V (1961), 209–25.

[69] *APS*, II, 349.

[70] With these are other accounts by the burghs of the small impost on wines, 1615–34.

[71] The function of the Responde Books has been explained. The minutes are printed as appendices to the *Exchequer Rolls* up to 1600.

[72] Acta Dominorum Concilii and Acta Dominorum Concilii et Sessionis, printed in full 1478–1501, and in part, 1501–54. See 'The Sources and Literature of Scots' Law,' *Stair Soc.*, pp. 16–24.

[73] *Register of Privy Council*, III, 626–7; *APS*, III, 309.

[74] There may have been an Act Book in 1569. *Exchequer Rolls*, XX, 399.

[75] Wheat.

[76] Barley.

[77] *Register of Privy Council*, V, 255.

spokin this nicht is forgot the morne. In the morninge I see nathing menid but to gurne'.[78] On 5 January 1595/6 a new commission of Exchequer was appointed consisting of eight members, known from that circumstance as the 'Octavians', among whom was Skene. Their greater efficiency was matched by unpopularity leading to their fall a year later, after which an Act of Parliament forbade any further permanent commissions of Exchequer. After James's accession to the English throne control of financial administration was vested for a time in a conciliar body, known as the Commissioners of Rents, which has left very few records.[79] In Charles I's reign, however, a permanent Exchequer was established once more.[80] Cromwell appointed judges for a Court of Exchequer in Scotland,[81] but after the Restoration the former Commissioners of Exchequer were replaced. The Exchequer Act Book or Register (E. 4) is preserved, with gaps, from 1584 to 1650 and contains orders and registered deeds as well as judicial decrees of the Auditors or Commissioners. The loss of the whole of the post-Restoration register is largely offset by the preservation of nearly all the original papers or warrants (E. 8) from which it was compiled. From 1630 to 1708 a Minute Book (E. 5) was kept, four volumes of which survive, including the minutes of Cromwell's Exchequer, 1655-9. Other judicial and administrative business is to be found in the series of Petitions and Processes (E. 10) of the Exchequer and Treasury, 1567-1708, of which about 95 per cent are post-Restoration.

The seventeenth century also saw the emergence of the Treasury as the controlling financial department. The need for this development is clearly shown by the provision of an Act of 1592, that the Treasurer, Comptroller, Collector and Secretary were 'to aggrie among thame selffis quhat dewlie and properlie appertenis to everie ane of thair offices'.[82] After 1610 the offices of Treasurer, Comptroller, Collector-General and Treasurer of the New Augmentation were united in one person, although the accounts of these offices were kept distinct until 1635 and they continued to exist, in name only, until 1708.[83] As the office of Treasurer became more exalted, many of its responsibilities passed to the Treasurer-depute. The Treasury was in commission from 1641 to 1644, from 1667 to 1682 and from 1686 to 1708. A Treasury Register (E. 6) and a Sederunt Book (E. 7) were commenced in 1667, both being complete down to the abolition of the Scottish Treasury in 1708, except for the first volume of the Register. A large series of warrants (E. 9), including royal letters, accompanies the Register.

As the Treasurer and the Commissioners of the Treasury became increasingly concerned with administration and policy, the actual receipt and payment of money was committed to a subordinate, known at first as the Receiver and after the Restoration as the Receiver General and Cashkeeper. The 'Articles anent abuses of Excheker' presented to Charles I in 1634 stated that 'because the office of receaveris, who are thrie, is fund to be a charge to your Majestie and that your Majesties service may be done without thame by the diligence of your Majesties Treasurer and deputy Treasurer, therefore wee doe conceave the samen not to be necessare'.[84] Nevertheless the office continued to grow in importance. The accounts of Sir Adam Blair of Carberry and Sir William Lockhart of Carstairs, who held office under several Treasurers between 1642 and 1651 (E. 27), were so involved that the audit was not completed until 1681. A mass of vouchers (Precepts and Receipts) and draft accounts record their activities. After 1661, the Receivers General or Cash-

[78] Murray Rose, *op. cit.*, xxxviii; 'menid', complained; 'gurne', grumble.
[79] Some proceedings of the Commissioners of Rents are to be found in the printed *Register of the Privy Council*.
[80] *APS*, v, 35.
[81] *APS*, vi, pt. ii, 751, 760, 892.
[82] *APS*, iii, 563.
[83] 'The Scottish Treasury 1667-1708', *Scottish Historical Review*, xlv (1966), 89-104.
[84] Exchequer Act Bk. (E.4/5) 1634-9, f. 22v.

keepers paid salaries, pensions and other sums, according to precepts drawn on them by the Treasury (E. 28), most of which are preserved.[85]

The financial confusion of the decade in which Blair and Lockhart held office resulted not only from the overlapping of the duties of Receiver and Treasurer, but also from Parliament's attempt to take over some of the functions of the Exchequer through the Committee for the Common Burdens of the Kingdom and the Committees for Moneys, Excise and Prosecution of Malignants. The registers and papers of these bodies form part of the records of Parliament.[86] Several volumes of accounts and papers relating to military expenditure during the Civil War are preserved among the Parliamentary records, while the maintenance of the standing army after 1660 has left a far larger series of accounts of various sorts (E. 91–99), as well as numerous muster rolls (E. 100) which were lodged with the Treasury.[87]

The Civil War and its aftermath had a permanent effect on the financial administration, even though the Scots government did not equal Cromwell's success in exacting revenue from Scotland.[88] The old hereditary revenue was of less consequence. Purves's rental of 1681 shows that it amounted to £89,821 Scots gross and only £47,445 net (£3,787 sterling). At the Union the whole revenue was estimated in sterling at £100,000 for customs and excise, £8,500 for crown rents and casualties, £2,000 from the post office, £1,500 from the coinage and £48,000 for land tax, £160,000 in all.[89] The levying of excise duties was a direct consequence of the Civil War, for they were first imposed in 1644 for the maintenance of the army, continued in 1660 and permanently annexed to the Crown in 1685. The 'inland excise' and the 'foreign excise' were collected and accounted for separately, the latter being assimilated to the customs. Apart from accounts of the general and local collectors of the inland excise (E. 79), the Record Office also possesses minutes of the Commissioners of Excise for Selkirkshire (CO. 10/1–2). It may be noted here that Commissioners of Assessment and Commissioners of Supply were also established in every sheriffdom as part of the re-organized system of taxation. The customs and foreign excise were under managers or tacksmen, whose sederunt books (E. 77) are extant for 1692–9 and 1704–5. Import and export books (E. 72) are preserved for the principal Scottish ports.

The Revolution of 1688 was followed by the forfeiture of James VII's principal adherents, including Viscount Dundee and the Earl of Dunfermline, the accounts of whose estates form a sequel to those of the Covenanters and others under the previous régime (E. 57). It also led to the final abolition of episcopacy and the assumption by the Crown of the revenues of the bishoprics and archbishoprics. The accounts of Bishops' Rents (E. 54), with related papers, extend beyond 1708, as do those of the Vacant Stipends (E. 56), that is the ministers' stipends of churches during vacancies, which were collected and administered by the Treasury.

Military operations in Scotland and other necessities led William III's ministers to seek for further sources of revenue. A hearth-tax was imposed in 1690 and a poll-tax in 1693, 1695, and 1698.[90] As the tacksmen or farmers of the first poll-tax found their bargain unprofitable they were freed of their liability to pay more than they had collected, and a Parliamentary Committee was appointed

---

[85] The series of Precepts and Receipts of the Treasury (E.23) and Comptrollery (E.25) begins in 1511 but the bulk of them are seventeenth century. After 1667 treasury precepts were recorded in the Treasury Register but it appears that no record was kept in earlier times. Warrants under the Privy Seal (principally for pensions) are to be found in the Register of the Privy Seal (printed 1488–1580).

[86] 'The financing of the cause of the Covenants', *Scottish Historical Review*, LI, 89–123.

[87] C. S. Terry, 'Papers relating to the Army of the Solemn League and Covenant', *Scottish History Society*, 1917, 2 vol.; C. Dalton, *The Scots Army, 1661–1668*, 1909.

[88] The report by Thomas Tucker on the settlement of the revenues of Excise and Customs in Scotland, 1656 (*Miscellany of the Scottish Burgh Records Society*, 1881) is of considerable value and interest.

[89] Murray Rose, *op. cit.*, xlviii–ix.

[90] Reports on the collection of these taxes were presented to Parliament in 1701. *APS*, XI, 170–3, 185–7.

to deal with the arrears. The papers of this committee have been preserved, along with a number of hearth-tax (E. 69) and poll-tax (E. 70) accounts for the years 1693–8, which are, of course, of considerable interest to genealogists.[91]

Of necessity much has had to be omitted from this brief survey of the records of the old Exchequer of Scotland. It has tried to place the main groups in their historical and administrative context and to give some idea of their purpose and value. These records form easily the largest and most important government archive of the pre-Union kingdom and while the historian and the archivist may regret what has been lost, what remains can still afford a fruitful ground for the labours and studies of both.

ATHOL L. MURRAY

[91] Some hearth tax and poll tax records have been printed, though these have been mainly taken from copies in local or private muniments, e.g. 'The Hearth Tax', Dumfriesshire and Galloway Natural History and Antiquarian Society *Transactions*, XLVII (1970), 147–77; *List of Pollable Persons within the shire of Aberdeen* (1844); *Edinburgh Poll Tax Returns for 1694* (Scottish Record Society, 1951); see also 'Hearth Tax and Poll Tax', *Scottish Genealogist*, XI (3), 8–12.

The Administrative Background to the Presentation to Parliament of Parliamentary Papers on Foreign Affairs in the Mid-Nineteenth Century

The ever-growing series of British Parliamentary Papers[1] with all its accompanying problems of accommodation for the archivist is too often treated as a rather dull, if useful, source of information on almost all subjects and as very little more. Statistics of population, industry and trade, evidence of housing conditions and health, reports on the state of the armed services and annual government accounts are but a minor part of the mass of material available to the researcher interested in nineteenth and twentieth century subjects: one has only to master the rather confusing series of indexes to the Papers before being able to find almost anything one could want. While the accuracy of the data to be found in Parliamentary Papers may occasionally be questioned, there is generally a lack of interest in the background to the presentation of these papers to Parliament in the first place, with all the attendant political tensions and squabbles, not to mention constitutional adjustments, frequently involved. This lack of interest is largely encouraged by an acceptance of the papers as an automatic means by which the government of the day supplies Parliament and therefore the public with information. The present practice of producing Parliamentaty Papers is one of laying them before Parliament on the instance of the government, and cases of parliamentary pressure for information are now so rare as to be almost non-existent. Such a situation was not always so. The procedure for the production of facts for Parliament has often resulted in friction between Parliament and government, between one government department and another, and between the parliamentary and permanent heads of government departments. Although fascinating examples may be found in the history of all departments of such disputes and of the development of a formalized procedure, there is no department of state where the production of Parliamentary Papers has produced such varied and complex problems as the Foreign Office.[2] And there is no period when the production of diplomatic correspondence, the reports of consuls and secretaries of legations and other information on foreign subjects for Parliament has generated so much excitement as in the fifties and sixties of the nineteenth century.

The conduct of foreign affairs lies within the prerogative of the Crown – that is the monarch advised by her ministers.[3] That prerogative enables her to appoint and recall diplomatic represen-

---

[1] This description includes everything published by and for Parliament and numbered in the official series, *i.e.* reports of select committees, reports of commissioners, accounts and papers. Recently a new series of reprints of papers from the official series has been published by the Irish University Press. This new series organized under subject headings should not be confused with the original publication.

[2] See Select Documents XLVI in the *Bulletin of the Institute of Historical Research*. XXIII. 1950. S. Lambert: 'The presentation of Parliamentary Papers by the Foreign Office'.

[3] A. D. McNair: *The Law of Treaties*. Oxford. 1938. p. 7. Also see Sir William R. Anson: *The Law and Custom of the Constitution*. 2 vols. Oxford. 1886–92. II. p. 273 ff.

tatives, to negotiate, sign and ratify treaties with foreign powers, and to make war or peace. Never has there been any constitutional tradition of parliamentary interference in these functions except in so far as Parliament's legislative or financial powers might be involved. Should any treaty signed by the British government affect the right of the subject within the kingdom as in the case of extradition or naturalization agreements,[4] or incur any financial commitment as in the case of a commercial treaty[5] or arbitration settlement,[6] then Parliament must be consulted before the ratification of the relevant articles of any such treaty. Although Parliament is thus so limited by the prerogative in the actual conduct of foreign relations, the existence of ministerial responsibility, in particular to the House of Commons, ensures that a government must, to a certain extent, keep in line with current parliamentary opinion. No cabinet can face with equanimity the possibility of a successful vote of censure. Nor are the officials at the Foreign Office any less conscious of the sensitivities of the Commons. But the appearance and growth of rigid party organization since the 1870s has limited the already rare opportunities of the Commons to have any real effect on a government's foreign policy. In the middle years of the nineteenth century the situation was very different. The split in Peel's Conservative party over the repeal of the Corn Laws left the Commons with no clear party alignments or cohesion and thus permitted the re-appearance of the independent member as a force to be contended with in English politics. If governments could only rely on very narrow guaranteed support, a handful of members could easily dictate the results of divisions in the Commons. This political fragmentation inevitably resulted in weak governments and negative policies. Contemporaries, concerned about the fragility of one administration after another, could foresee little relief for their frustrations and could have in no way imagined the results of the work of Gorst and Schnadhorst twenty years later. In the no-confidence debate of 1859, Sidney Herbert warned the Commons on the prospect of a new government:[7]

I do not think we shall get from it what may be called a strong government; many lament that; they say parties are broken up, and that is lamented also, without recognising the causes. Though some political questions may bring masses in the House together, yet the tendency on both sides is to break up the old lines of party. You will never get a strong government in the sense the country did formerly. Then society was weak, and a strong government was necessary to repress and guide it; now society is strong and dominates the government set over it.

In these circumstances a group of members of Parliament could have much more influence on a government than later when their allegiances became more strictly confined.

Coinciding with this period of unusual independence on the part of individual members was an upsurge of eager interest in foreign affairs which tended to concentrate members' attention on a government's activities abroad rather than at home. Both of these factors resulted in greatly increased publication of Parliamentary Papers on foreign affairs by the Foreign Office.[8] On the one hand it was possible for members to press for information which a government might wish to withhold and succeed in getting a motion for papers through against the expressed view of that government; and the increased interest in foreign affairs produced demands for information of a type which later would have held little attention in the Commons. On the other hand, governments were concerned to present their policies in the best possible light, and, in view of the increased efficiency

---

[4] e.g. the passing of the Extradition Treaties Act Amendment Bill in 1866. *Hansard*, 3rd series. CLXXXIV. See a question asked by M'Cullagh Torrens and answered by Stanley on 26 July 1866. *Ibid.* 1533.

[5] e.g. the commercial treaty with France in 1860. See *Hansard* CLVII–CLX for details of procedure.

[6] e.g. the passing of the Treaty of Washington Bill in 1872. See *Hansard* CCXII for procedure and many questions on the bill and the arbitration settlement.

[7] *Hansard* CLIV. 334. 10 June 1859.

[8] H. W. V. Temperley and L. M. Penson: *A Century of Diplomatic Blue Books, 1814–1914.* Cambridge. 1938.

of newspaper reporting, realised the value of issuing authoritative accounts of diplomatic negotiations. At this period, Parliamentary Papers were presented to the Commons in two ways, either by Command or in response to Address, the latter method in general indicating that the paper was pressed for by the Commons.[9] While it might seem in theory easy to distinguish between the two methods, as concerning the Foreign Office they were in practice by no means distinct or exclusive. Since the conduct of foreign affairs lay within the prerogative of the Crown, the Foreign Office had the right to present all papers to Parliament 'by Command' and that is the phrase printed on the cover of each one. On some there may be an indication of the real origin of the paper with the description 'Presented by Command in response to Address'[10] but on others there may be no reference to the Address which originally inspired the presentation.[11] This official origin may be discovered by a scrutiny of the *Journals* of the Commons and the Lords. On a less official level, real Command Papers, or papers presented on the initiative of the Foreign Office, could have been prompted by informal hints from Members of Parliament of a parliamentary desire for information. Such a presentation evinced a wish to 'get in first' with the publication of documents which might appear less embarrassing if produced voluntarily. The Blue Book on Central America presented by Command in August 1860 concealed all references to Sir Charles Wyke's agreement on behalf of the British Government to contribute to the building of a road from the capital of Guatemala to the Atlantic coast near Izabal, an agreement made without the British Government's knowledge and which was to prove a great embarrassment to them.[12] It was often a politic move to step in first to avoid the indignity of being forced to produce information.[13] If the Commons were given an apparently adequate set of papers before they had had time to feel aggrieved at their ignorance of events, they might be less likely to peruse foreign newspapers with that avidity which was so often revealed.[14] There were after all many instances of parliamentary questions as a result of careful reading of Blue Books and members were not slow to point out any slip in proof-reading which indicated 'pruning' of despatches by the Foreign Office.[15] There were however many quite straightforward cases when Foreign Office papers laid in response to an Address were prepared directly as a result of that Address, such as that of an Address for papers on consuls and their salaries in 1859.[16] But

---

[9] There were in fact two other means by which information might be demanded by Parliament. A department might have to produce returns in accordance with an Act of Parliament as was the case with the returns on the Russian, Dutch, Sardinian and Greek loans. Or it might have to respond to an order of the House of Commons. This latter situation was rare in the Foreign Office.

[10] e.g. A&P. (1857–8) HC. LX. [2356] 135. The address was for, 'Copies of correspondence between Her Majesty's Government and that of the Emperor of the French on the late alterations in the Passport system. Of the several Regulations respecting Passports issued by the Foreign Office since 1815 with fees charged on their delivery: and copies or extracts received at the Foreign Office since 1 January 1856 relative to the inconvenience sustained by British workmen, who had arrived in France with passports given by French consular agents in Great Britain.'

[11] e.g. A&P. (1864) HC. LXVI. [3361] 595 and [3307] 607.

[12] A&P. (1860). HC. LXVIII. [2748] 653. *Cf.* Public Record Office, F.O. 15/102–14.

[13] See *Hansard* CLVIII. 1549. 21 May 1860. In answer to a question by Dalglish about the protection of Italian refugees by British warships, Russell was able to say he had just laid the relevant instructions on the table of the House of Commons.

[14] On occasions, Members of Parliament showed a quite amazing detailed knowledge of the Foreign Office's activities; e.g. *Hansard* CLIX. 332. 12 June 1860, when Mr O. Stanley questioned Palmerston closely on minor Foreign Office appointments.

[15] *Hansard* CLIX. 1938–9. 16 July 1860. Normanby pointed out that in the papers recently presented on the subject of Savoy there was a despatch from Cowley of 5 February which was stated to have arrived on the 8th. This seemed an unusually long delay for so important a despatch. He also pointed out that Granville had been able to give the contents of the despatch in an answer in the Lords on 7 February. This was explained on the part of the government by the hint of a possible telegram and Wodehouse's unconvincing remark that Cowley frequently antedated his despatches.

[16] Public Record Office, F.O. 83/207. HC address, 19 July 1859.

often when an Address was unopposed by the government, and members always carefully en-
quired beforehand whether this was so,[17] the return was usually ready at the time the Address was
moved.[18] Occasionally an Address was moved for papers well on the way to completion at the
Foreign Office for presentation by Command and they would then be laid in response to Address.[19]
There is even a hint that when correspondence for which an Address was moved did not exist, it
was begun so that it could be produced.[20] Thus the real origin of Blue Books was frequently concealed in the final mode of presentation.

The laying of despatches and treaties before Parliament on the conclusion of a series of
diplomatic negotiations was usual, automatic and courteous. This presentation was, however, in
effect a publication of details concerning the government's activities, and that publication would
reach a much wider public at home and abroad than just the members of both Houses of Parliament.
In the preparation of Parliamentary Papers, therefore, there was always an element of propaganda
involved. This might take the form of self-justification in the face of rumour and criticism, as in the
case of Malmesbury's Italian Blue Books,[21] or of a certain pride in results achieved. As a means of
publication, Parliamentary Papers had their limitations, the chief of which was the brevity of the
parliamentary session.[22] In times of recess the obvious alternative was publication of information
in the more important London newspapers. The Commons were however very sensitive on this
point, especially as the Foreign Office came to extend this practice into the parliamentary session if
the Foreign Secretary felt the situation demanded it. This publication might take the form of a
special communiqué, as when editors were directly supplied with news.[23] Austen Henry Layard,
when Parliamentary Under Secretary at the Foreign Office, wrote from Florence to his Permanent
colleague on 2 November 1865:[24]

. . . I am glad to hear that Lord Russell is going to publish a résumé of our actions in the Abyssinian
business. There has been so much misrepresentation that it is well to have an authentic statement before the
public. I suppose it will be in the *Times*—if not please send me a copy. . . .

Otherwise, Blue Books were directly supplied to the press on completion. The urgency of this is
reflected in a memorandum for the Librarian from a clerk in the Permanent Under Secretary's
office.[25] 'Mr Hammond desires that *all* Parliamentary Papers should be sent to the Daily Papers as
soon as possible'. Convention required that these Blue Books should be laid before Parliament
first, in advance of the Press. Palmerston as Foreign Secretary acknowledged this principle in 1848:[26]

No copies should be sent to any newspaper till Monday, that is to say, till *after* the copies have been
delivered to members.

---

[17] *Ibid.* F.O. 96/25–27 contain many instances of this.

[18] *Ibid.* F.O. 83/207. HC address, 14 July 1859.

[19] *Ibid.* F.O. 96/27. A memorandum by Hammond on the Japanese papers, 11 May 1860.

[20] British Museum. Layard Papers. Add. MSS. 38,988. f. 73.

[21] Malmesbury had been accused by the Opposition of backing Austria against Italy in the crisis months of early
1859. These attacks on him were quite unjustified as the Blue Books showed. A&P. (1859–II) HC. XXXII. [2524] and
[2527] 1 and 443.

[22] The parliamentary session generally lasted from February to July or late August. There was only very rarely
an autumn sitting and then it would only be called for some specific purpose. It was called in late 1867 to vote money
for the Abyssinian campaign.

[23] British Museum. Layard Papers. Add. MSS. 38,959. f. 106. Layard, then Parliamentary Under Secretary,
wrote to Hammond, Permanent Under Secretary: 'I am to inform Delane tomorrow of Bulwer's demission.' This was
clearly urgent news and of obvious importance for the editor of *The Times*.

[24] *Ibid.* f. 194.

[25] Public Record Office. F.O. 83/329. Memorandum by Staveley, 6 February 1863. The papers listed were *The
Times, Daily News, Morning Herald, Morning Post, Standard, Daily Telegraph, Express, Sun, Globe, Morning Ad-
vertiser, Morning Star,* and *Observer*.

[26] *Ibid.* F.O. 96/22. Minute by Palmerston, 27 May 1848.

Although the House of Commons was very sensitive on this point, it became more and more difficult to observe the principle in practice. The press usually received their copies at the same time as
the paper was laid in the Commons, and that time was not necessarily the same time as members
were supplied with theirs. And, in the parliamentary recess, it was hardly likely that a government
would wait from perhaps July to February to publish information of great importance, convention
or no convention. But the special publication of politically significant information on the foreign
relations of the government must not be exaggerated in the full picture of official publication.

The production of information for Parliament had become a major task for the Foreign
Office by the middle of the nineteenth century. In June 1829, Louis Hertslet as Librarian appealed to
Backhouse[27] for some new annual allowance for 'the extraordinary length of time consumed by me,
in the preparation of the several large masses of Papers for Parliament during the Session just
terminated,' and which 'laborious and not unimportant duty' normally involved extra hours of his
time, and he quoted the Slave Trade papers, his particular responsibility, as averaging 350 pages
each session.[28] Preparing papers for Parliament necessitated the checking and rechecking of vast
quantities of manuscript and printed proofs at all levels within the Office: when ill at home in 1862,
Hammond informed the Parliamentary Under Secretary:[29]

I daresay tomorrow I shall be able to take up the only pressing business which I must attend to, i.e.
Parliamentary Papers; but they are as straight as possible, and so far advanced that two or three days are all
that are required to finish them.

and, two days later:[30]

I shall be at work after breakfast with the papers for Parliament and I hope to make good progress.

Every presentation required approval by the Secretary of State.[31] A clerical machinery existed
throughout the Office for the collection and selection of material for printing. Hammond passed
his experience on to one of his clerks:[32]

I wish you would commence *immediately* with printing, and if you will adopt the method I always did, you
can carry it on with very little disarrangement of your ordinary business; but you must set to work practically
and not theoretically. I mean that you must not wait to get the papers given to you from other divisions
(which theoretically you have a right to expect), but get them yourself, and in this way.

Do not waste your time in looking through the Registers, and making a list of the papers you want; but
go at once to the Presses: you will find the papers tied up in bundles and you have only to look at the Dockets
on each bundle and drag out the papers you want; keep them in order as you do this: the first date upper-
most: and keep the drafts and despatches separate: the same with official communications from Foreign
Ministers. It would not take you an hour thus to collect a month's papers from the several departments.
When you have got the bundles together before you, then reverse the game of Patience at cards, and take
from each bundle in succession according to their receipts of dates of despatches the papers: and you will
very quickly get them all in order and tied up in common bundles. Having done this, get some ruled paper
and take a list of the papers which you are giving to the printer. You need only take the name, number and
date and leave two lines blank between each paper so recorded. I am convinced that by adopting this plan,
and solely depending on yourself to get the papers from the different divisions, you could put the whole of
the papers from the commencement to the present time in order for printing in a single day; and you will
spare yourself much labour, much worry and much loss of temper which would be severely tried if you
depend on others to do what you can best do for yourself. . . .

---

[27] John Backhouse was then Permanent Under Secretary in the Foreign Office.

[28] Foreign Office Library, Vol. I. *Librarian's Department, 1801–54*. Draft. 26 June 1829.

[29] British Museum, Layard Papers. Add. MSS. 38,951. f. 5. 29 January 1862.

[30] *Ibid.* f. 7. 31 January 1862.

[31] See Public Record Office. F.O. 83/207 and 329 for the sanction of successive Secretaries of State.

[32] *Ibid.* F.O. 96/25. Hammond to Forster, private, 19 October 1856. H. F. Forster had been appointed to a Senior
Clerkship, 10 April 1854. This method would apply equally well to the organization of manuscript for the production
of confidential print.

. . . Afterwards, when you go through the papers, the preparatory list which I have mentioned will be of the greatest use to you. You have the framework of your index; and you may fill it up either by going through the register or what is best by entering afresh in the list the several papers as you read them over. . . .

The work of the clerks in the preparation of Parliamentary Papers varied little in that they collected relevant documents for the heads of departments in the same way whether the subject was a purely routine one as in the case of quarantine regulations in New Granada[33] or one of real political and diplomatic importance as were the publications on Italy in 1859 and on the American Civil War in the sixties.

A careful study of the Foreign Office records at the Public Record Office and comparison of them with the Blue Books reveals many omissions, paraphrases, and alterations of the original documents in the published versions. That the official documents were carefully selected and 'extracted' or 'weeded' for publication was not in general criticised either in the House of Commons or the press during the 50s and 60s, since a certain code of conventions respecting the publication was accepted by both legislature and executive. Officials and members of the diplomatic service recognized that normal despatches between the Foreign Office and ambassadors or ministers were of their nature available for publication: hence the Parliamentary Under Secretary's advice to the Secretary of State:[34]

My doubt is whether it be prudent to insist upon your line of argument in a despatch which may hereafter be published.

And, unless Parliament moved specifically for 'copies or extracts' of despatches, the Foreign Office felt obliged to publish them in full; if, for various reasons, it could not publish *in extenso*, it would ask the mover of the Address to change its form from asking for 'copies' to 'copies or extracts.' Thus Parliament would at least know that it was not getting the full story. On 5 May 1864, Russell wrote to his Parliamentary Under Secretary:[35]

I understood from you that Gibson meant to refuse the return, at which I was rather surprised.
No doubt the right course is to agree to Copies or Extracts and if Forster will move the address in that shape there ought to be no difficulty.

This type of request was often made and Members of Parliament generally accepted that information which it was 'not in the Public interest' to publish might be withheld from them. Occasionally, however, they felt the government was taking advantage of their forbearance. Frequently changing administrations produced in both Houses a body of men of various political complexions who had previously held office and who could raise questions or provide information embarrassing to the existing cabinet. A large group of ex-Foreign Secretaries, Under Secretaries and ambassadors made debates in the House of Lords events of some consequence for the Foreign Office and government. From his recent experience as Foreign Secretary, Lord Malmesbury asserted in the face of strong arguments by Granville who, as Lord President of the Council, was defending the government's policy in the Lords, that the House had a right to much more information on the subject of Savoy and Nice than they had as yet been given. He protested that the government 'had imparted to us not information, at least only bits and scraps; . . . and out of this confused mass we have to try and extract something like the truth.'[36] Such complaints generally inspired considerably fuller collections of published despatches at a rather later date when the topic had lost some of its urgency.

---

[33] *Ibid.* F.O. 83/207. HC address, 18 July 1853.
[34] British Museum. Layard Papers. Add. MSS. 38,990. f. 319. Layard to Russell, undated.
[35] *Ibid.* f. 216. Also see f. 206. Russell to Layard, undated: 'If Ayrton will move for copies or extracts etc. of correspondence which took place at Athens in 1860 respecting the loan——, I shall have no objection.'
[36] *Hansard* CLVI. 1017. 14 February 1860.

The vital question is to discover who decided which of these 'bits and scraps' to present, what should be said in Parliament and how much news should be given to the press. The answer is far from easy to find, but in the mass of official diplomatic correspondence and interdepartmental memoranda are hidden those minutes from which emerges an outline of the people and practices involved.

No accepted routine existed for the making of these decisions concerning the publication of information as it did for the composition of draft despatches and diplomatic instructions. Too much depended on international events, the British political situation, the attitude of Parliament, the temper of the press, and the special needs of commercial and industrial interests at a particular moment for any uniform practice to have developed. No facile analysis is possible. If anything, the most interesting impression created by the many notes and memoranda is that in this sphere of Foreign Office activity, as much if not possibly more than in any other, the subtle interplay of personalities, irrespective of official position, dominated the initiation of publication and the final decision before presentation. It is difficult to distinguish a clear-cut relationship between the two Under Secretaries, the Foreign Secretary, the Prime Minister and other members of the cabinet in the selection of papers, except in so far as the Under Secretaries regularly prepared material relating to the political departments under their care, then submitted it to the Secretary of State for approval, and afterwards passed it on to the other Under Secretary for his views. It is important to note that the Parliamentary Under Secretary, despite his title, only dealt with the Blue Books of the departments under his control. The political departments of the Office were divided geographically, and at this period the Permanent Under Secretary controlled the more important section. It was however quite usual for the two Under Secretaries to consult together to advise the Secretary of State on the question of Blue Books. Hammond, while Permanent Under Secretary, submitted many collections of papers for publication to the various Secretaries of State, just as his predecessor, Addington, had done before him,[37] usually noting any features which required special attention. In March 1861 he noted for Russell:[38]

The correspondence with Lord Cowley in this and partly in the preceding portion will require great attention. I have marked it to the best of my judgment, and when Your Lordship has decided on it, a revise must be sent to Cowley.

Wodehouse, Layard and Seymour Fitzgerald, as Parliamentary Under Secretaries, provided papers for their Foreign Secretaries' consideration.[39] Hertslet too, as Librarian and Keeper of the Foreign Office records, compiled sets of papers and his opinions were often accepted in view of his long experience.[40] But the control of publication lay with the person deciding in the first place to print, if the papers were to be laid by Command, or what to print, if an Address was received from either House.

The person taking the initiative in printing for Parliament, as far as the Office was concerned, was the Secretary of State: but although he was influenced by a consideration for the interests of the Office, he was controlled in some cases by other members of the cabinet, mostly by the Prime Minister. Malmesbury found his Chancellor of the Exchequer, Disraeli, a far more limiting force than Derby, his Prime Minister. In 1859, the Foreign Secretary grandly ordered, 'All Italian Papers to be printed',[41] and these were very fully prepared. When finally published, these Italian Blue

---

[37] Public Record Office. F.O. 83/207. Many examples.

[38] *Ibid*. F.O. 96/26, 28 March 1861.

[39] *Ibid*. and British Museum. Layard Papers. Add. MSS. 38,991, f. 331.

[40] See S. Hall's unpublished M.A. thesis in the University of London, 'Sir Edward Hertslet and his work as Librarian and Keeper of the papers of the Foreign Office from 1857 to 1896.' London, 1958.

[41] Public Record Office. F.O. 96/26. Undated.

Books were highly praised by Clarendon and the Duke of Bedford,[42] neither of whom were supporters of Derby's government; but the publication came just too late to help prevent the defeat of that government. In his memoirs, Malmesbury blamed Disraeli for delaying the publication, asserting that had they been produced in time, the government would not have fallen.[43] Disraeli later insisted that the papers were not ready in time, but in fact Malmesbury had written to Hammond on 10 June, 'I must have a dummy of the second set of Italian Papers to lay tonight . . .'[44] which suggests that on that date the first and vital set was already in print. But even more conclusive was the fact that before that date, he had made frantic appeals to Disraeli to present the papers and he used strong political argument:[45]

In the event of an *adverse* division how are the Italian papers to be presented at all? We cannot do so after we have tendered our resignation. My successor will then publish the *originals* unrevised and very likely our *intended* proofs side by side.

This was however a hollow threat as Malmesbury well knew the Foreign Office convention of showing papers originating in the administration of a previous Foreign Secretary to him for approval. Also, Malmesbury knew that the next administration would find little that would stand to his discredit in those Italian papers. What he wanted was to see that what credit they reflected on Derby's government should be brought to light when it might work to save it rather than after its fall.

In the next administration the Foreign Secretary, Russell, had always to consider his Prime Minister's views, because Palmerston, unlike his predecessor Derby, had a great interest in the publication of documents and information on foreign affairs. As Foreign Secretary he had published much, and could hardly have been expected to leave Russell to control the government's publicity in matters of political importance. Poland inevitably attracted his attention, and in March 1863 he suggested to Russell:[46]

I wish you would consider by tomorrow whether you would think it objectionable or advisable to lay before Parliament before the adjournment any papers about Poland; our despatch to Napier and his answer giving the explanations of Gortchakoff might perhaps be given.

Having once taken the initiative, he was by June clearly in charge of publication: Hammond informed Layard:[47]

I have got with me the duplicate of the Polish Papers before Lord Palmerston, and have been waiting to look at them till we heard his decision. . . .

The Prime Minister kept a close watch on the answers given to parliamentary questions and on the composition of statements given to the two Houses, although by these statements he himself would sometimes involve the Foreign Office in publication.[48] There were also signs that the possible publication of information to Parliament was no small consideration in his foreign policy. His correspondence with Russell reveals constant anxiety as to the possibility of publication:[49]

The Japan despatches are unpleasant. Surely we ought to make some demands and take measures to enforce them for indemnity for the past, and security for the future. We should have some difficulty in

---

[42] *Ibid.* F.O. 519/179. Clarendon to Cowley, 12 June 1859 and Clarendon MSS. C.561. 20 June 1859.
[43] Malmesbury: *Memoirs of an Ex-Minister.* 2 vols. London. 1884. II. pp. 188-9.
[44] Public Record Office. F.O. 83/207. 10 June 1859.
[45] Disraeli MSS. XIII. Letters from Malmesbury, 7 June 1859.
[46] Public Record Office. PRO 30/22/14. Palmerston to Russell, 26 March 1863.
[47] British Museum. Layard Papers. Add. MSS. 38,952. f. 37. Hammond to Layard, 26 June 1863.
[48] *Ibid.* Add. MSS. 38,990. f. 263 and Clarendon MSS. C.88. ff. 98-9, and 110-11.
[49] Public Record Office. PRO 30/22/14. Palmerston to Russell, 20 October 1862.

justifying to Parliament and the country our sitting with our arms folded and neither extorting atonement for past outrages nor security against similar outrage in future.

This was a recommendation in October 1862, and two months later he was writing:[50]

I think you have taken this matter of the arms too easily. There is no use in talking to Brunnow about it. He is a sly fox and puts us off with the sort of evasions which you record in this draft, and by which he endeavours to baffle us. The matter is serious, and if the correspondence should be laid before Parliament we shall be blamed for apathy and be told that we were afraid of speaking out at Petersburg.

On the other hand, the alternative to changing one's policy to suit the Blue Book was the avoidance of writing anything in a public despatch which was likely to be politically embarrassing: Palmerston advised Russell in 1861:[51]

Your amendment would do very well, or what would be better would perhaps be to let the matter rest upon what has been said in debate, and not to put any prospective declaration on record to be inserted in a Blue Book.

thereby getting round his own view of Parliament's right to information:[52]

Let the House have what it chooses. It has a good right to have whatever it thinks useful for its deliberations.

This occasionally involved the writing of despatches especially for Blue Books.[53]

Palmerston's decisive influence on the publication of diplomatic correspondence had certain disadvantages as far as the Foreign Office was concerned. Hammond constantly complained of delays in the preparation of papers since Palmerston was slow in going through them. On 23 March 1861, he told Layard:[54]

As to the old papers, I have received nothing from Lord Palmerston, but will in a day or two write to him for them. If we get on well with the new ones, the press will be clear for the old ones. . . .

and on the 24th:

On Saturday, I will stir Lord Palmerston up about the old papers. If Lord Russell returns me the marked copy this evening, as I have begged him to do, the overseeing may be completed tomorrow. . . .

and on the 26th, when he was taken ill, he asked Layard to look after the papers when Palmerston eventually returned them. Pressure of business obviously delayed Palmerston in his scrutiny of Blue Books and inevitably prevented him from overseeing all of them. Less important collections of papers were left entirely to the supervision of the Foreign Secretary.

Russell himself, as Foreign Secretary, was severely criticized by Clarendon, then out of office, for a tendency to mould his foreign policy too much with reference to the publication of Blue Books, especially with relation to the Italian question. He was very free in his publications and initiated the majority of the Blue Books during his term of office, often supervising detailed omissions from the official documents:[55]

I wish to have American Papers prepared, to be laid before Parliament. That is to say any dispatches to Lord Lyons relating any interviews with Mr Dallas and Mr Adams on the subject of the American mission. One or two dispatches of Lord Lyons might likewise be given etc. Some of my dispatches to Lord Lyons relating the correspondence with our ambassador and chargé d'affaires at Paris. . . .

---

[50] *Ibid.* 31 December 1862.
[51] *Ibid.* 24 April 1861.
[52] PRO 30/22/15. Palmerston to Russell, 15 April 1864.
[53] e.g. British Museum. Palmerston Papers. Add. MSS. 48,582. Palmerston to Russell, copy, 9 September 1861.
[54] Layard Papers. Add. MSS. 38,952. ff. 131, 133, 136 and 137.
[55] Public Record Office. F.O. 96/26. Memorandum by Russell, 28 June, undated.

Mary Anderson, in her thesis on Hammond as Permanent Under Secretary, has shown how Russell frequently overruled his slender collections of documents, desiring a wider picture of British policy to be presented.[56] Two interesting features of Russell's term of office were his development of the use of communications to the press in place of Blue Books as the chief organ of government publication, and his gradual leaning on his Parliamentary Under Secretary, Layard, for advice on the selection of material for Parliamentary Papers. The extensive use of the press on an official level was new and unpopular with some contemporaries.[57] Earl Cowley, the British ambassador in Paris, disapproved of the novel practice:[58]

I do not admire the plan which has sprung up of publishing dispatches in the Gazette. It ought to my opinion never to be done except in cases such as that of the 'Trent'. What can it signify whether what has happened with regard to Denmark is published now or when Parliament meets. . . .

and commented:[59]

The publication of the Hudson correspondence will do the Earl no good, and in my opinion he made a great mistake in going out of his way to publish them in the Gazette. After waiting so long he might at least have let Parliament take the initiative in producing them.

Although it was a practice begun during the parliamentary recess so that news could be published quickly, its use was greatly extended by Russell: from time to time he instructed Elliot to give facts on foreign affairs to the *Globe*.[60] In these communications to the press, the *London Gazette* had priority because of its impartiality,[61] though other papers were often used when speed was necessary, as information placed in the *Gazette* did not always appear quickly enough.[62]

This wide use of the press coincided with Russell's dependence on Layard, who reported to his Secretary of State in September 1865:[63]

I saw the editor of the Daily News today and set him right about Cameron and Rassam. I think a little letter or paragraph ought to be sent to the papers giving a short account of what Rassam is about to do.

This dependence of the Secretary of State on his Parliamentary Under Secretary was naturally determined by the personalities of the people concerned and their personal relationship, which in the case of Russell and Layard developed slowly. Layard's predecessors, Wodehouse and Seymour Fitzgerald, had played rather insignificant roles in the selection of documents, but as Layard gained experience in the Office and his contacts in the House of Commons and throughout Europe aided his judgement, his suggestions submitted with papers to the Secretary of State came to be altered or cancelled but rarely. Just as pressure of work limited the practical possibility of the Prime Minister keeping a close watch on Foreign Office publication, so it prevented the Secretary of State checking as much as he would have liked the various collections of papers. In January 1865, when Layard asked 'Will you look at these papers printed for Parliament—on Mr Lindsay's motion?', Russell replied, 'I shall never get through this mass of papers. I leave it entirely to your discretion'.[64] But despite his frequent use of Layard, Russell was very much his own master when he could find

---

[56] M. A. Anderson: 'Edmund Hammond, Permanent Under Secretary of State for Foreign Affairs, 1854–1873'. Unpublished Ph.D. thesis in the University of London, 1956.

[57] The press had been used unofficially for a long time particularly by Palmerston who had considerable interests in several papers. The Palmerston Papers from Broadlands contain long series of letters with their editors.

[58] Public Record Office. F.O. 391/5. Cowley to Hammond, 4 December 1862.

[59] Clarendon MSS. C.88. f. 149. Cowley to Clarendon, 2 November 1863.

[60] British Museum. Layard Papers. Add. MSS. 38,990. f. 80. Russell to Layard, undated.

[61] *Ibid*. Add. MSS. 38,989. ff. 31,309 and 335 and Add. MSS. 38,991. f. 345.

[62] *Ibid*. Add. MSS. 38,991. f. 344–5.

[63] *Ibid*. Add. MSS. 38,959. f. 153.

[64] *Ibid*. Add. MSS. 38,991. f. 15.

time to glance rapidly over suggested selections. Layard submitted the Brazilian papers to him in February 1863 and received the reply:[65]

> I think you should leave in most of the passages you propose to omit, and most of Mr Stevens's letters. I have no time to look over the papers, but I shall make a short statement tonight in answer to Lord Derby.

and even in the face of a firm refusal by Palmerston to his request to publish a despatch from Thouvenel, the French Foreign Minister, Russell printed it.[66] Thus it is clear that during the years of Palmerston's administration, 1859–65, the control of the selection of Foreign Office papers for publication was very much in the hands of the Prime Minister and Russell, the latter assisted by the Parliamentary Under Secretary, Layard, as much if not more than the Permanent Under Secretary. When Layard acted as the government's spokesman in the Commons, his judgement concerning parliamentary statements was generally approved in retrospect by his political chiefs.

Layard continued as Parliamentary Under Secretary when Clarendon took over the Foreign Office. He had offered to resign when Russell became Prime Minister, protesting that his appointment as Under Secretary was a very personal one and that a new Secretary of State would be perfectly justified in expecting his resignation. The offer was not accepted. Clarendon generally followed his advice on publication.[67] With his selection of Abyssinian papers Layard submitted a long memorandum to which the Secretary of State replied:[68]

> I have looked through these papers and with the exception of the passages marked, I see no objection to their being published. . . . It will be better to give all that can be given without fear of injury to the prisoners than to wait till they are asked for.

Clarendon also continued the practice of communications to the press.[69]

Few memoranda and minutes exist in the Foreign Office records for the ensuing Conservative administration, and it is therefore difficult to judge whether Stanley pursued any new line in the publication of official documents. It is doubtful whether any change was made in the methods used by the Office in the preparation of Blue Books, although it must be noted that the Prime Minister, Derby, took little practical interest in the selection of material. Such then was the control exercised in practice by the Prime Minister and Foreign Secretary over the production of information, and it was clearly extended or limited by the personalities and abilities of the persons concerned as well as by the exigencies of the political situation. As far as the rest of the cabinet was involved, certain other members might influence decisions, particularly those relating to military or naval matters, but it does not seem likely from the evidence available that the cabinet as a whole in any of the administrations of the middle years of the nineteenth century considered the question, nor does the Queen appear to have taken more than a general interest.[70]

The officials of the Foreign Office possessed a subtle influence on the compilation of their material once the initial decision to publish had been taken. Hammond had his own theory to follow:[71]

> My principle is to keep steadily in view continuity of history – to give what is required to maintain an unbroken narrative, and to strike out all beyond this. Hence the difference between Lord Russell and myself:

[65] *Ibid.* Add. MSS. 38,989. f. 57.

[66] Public Record Office. F.O. 519/178. Clarendon to Cowley, 21 and 24 March 1860. This was in fact very rare because of the Foreign Office convention concerning despatches of other states. See below, p. 197.

[67] British Museum. Layard Papers. Add. MSS. 38,992. ff. 230, 231.

[68] *Ibid.* ff. 158–76.

[69] e.g. *Ibid.* f. 307.

[70] There were isolated instances of the Queen taking an interest as during the Schleswig Holstein crisis, but these tended to be where her family connections were involved.

[71] British Museum. Layard Papers. Add. MSS. 38,952. ff. 1–2. 28 January 1863.

he dislikes Extracts as giving rise to suspicion of quibbling – my conscience being quite clear!! On that point, I am strongly in favour of saying no more than is absolutely necessary to save one from the charge, as made out from the papers themselves, of having left anything unsaid.

and his desire 'to convey the information within the narrowest compass'[72] inevitably had its effect. Sir Robert Morier certainly feared that Hammond would manage to curtail the papers relating to the commercial negotiations with Austria.[73] Sometimes however Hammond himself took the initiative in producing papers:[74]

I send you a collection of papers which I have had picked out in order to see whether it was worthwhile laying any of them. The collection contains all that I could pick out of Lyons' correspondence which seemed capable of being laid. . . .

only to be crushed by Russell:

I doubt whether any good will be done by producing these papers. My instructions as to protection of vessels trading to Matamoras are not given. Let them be added, and the papers kept to be produced if necessary.

On the other hand, Hammond's suggestions for the publication on the Japanese executions were approved.[75] Many of the collections of papers which he assembled on Russell's instructions were accepted, and since he was in charge of all the details of preparation, he had then to co-ordinate the various objections, if they existed, of British ambassadors abroad to the contents of a publication, and it was his duty, if the Blue Book contained correspondence with other government departments, to contact those departments to get their permission to use it. Much depended on his tact in these transactions. After the several alterations had been made to the printed proof, a revise was printed which would again be submitted to the Secretary of State:[76]

I send Your Lordship the revise for Parliament of the first portion of the Syrian papers, in which I have adopted Cowley's and Bulwer's alterations.
The only questions I have to submit to Your Lordship are on the pages mentioned overleaf. As soon as you can return me this part, I will have it finally corrected. I am only waiting for Cowley to send you the remainder. . . .

This was approved by Russell as the final revise usually was. Hammond's next task was to supervise the details of production. He instructed Alston, one of his clerks:[77]

You will see that Lord Russell approves of three of the revises. A paper to be added to one of them. They may therefore be struck off. Let me however see a proof of the new paper.

Layard and the other Parliamentary Under Secretaries of this period similarly supervised the production of the Blue Books associated with the work of their departments, and close cooperation existed between the two Under Secretaries in this as in other aspects of Office business. Hammond and Layard in particular often consulted together on the details of publication.

Irrespective of the main policy decisions, it was the duty of the Under Secretaries to watch that the conventions of Blue Book making were observed: Hammond summarised some of them for Layard:[78]

We do not refrain from giving as much of any despatch as we like, though it may be marked 'confidential', but we strike out the word. It is hard to lay down any general rule – we ought not to give what is reported to

---

[72] *Ibid.* Add. MSS. 38,951. f. 81.
[73] *Ibid.* Add. MSS. 38,995. f. 191.
[74] Public Record Office. F.O. 96/27. Memorandum by Hammond, 19 April, undated.
[75] *Ibid.* 5 March, undated.
[76] *Ibid.* Hammond to Russell, 4 April 1861.
[77] *Ibid.* Hammond to Alston, 1 February, undated. Alston had been since 1857 a senior clerk.
[78] British Museum. Layard Papers. Add. MSS. 38,952. f. 1. 28 January 1863.

have been said by a third person; or what has been said by the Sovereign – or what is given as personal opinion – or what may compromise any party. But still keeping these points in view, there is much in confidential despatches which it is necessary to give to complete the story; yet of course one looks more closely to the terms of such a despatch in marking extracts. . . .

These conventions had chiefly developed as common sense precautions in much the same way as the House of Commons had appointed a Printing Committee to keep a watch on Parliamentary Papers in order to avoid the publication of possibly libellous matter.

    The major class of conventional omissions was that of references to foreign governments and their policies, which references often consisted of frank criticism of those governments by British ambassadors in their despatches. Proofs of Parliamentary Papers were normally sent to the British representatives concerned for their approval, and in some cases the references to foreign governments were shown to the respective foreign ministers. This was an accepted practice in the 1840s, and was after all a sensible precaution. The man on the spot might well see in the proof copy some passages which would prove offensive to the government to which he was accredited, and which would seem unobjectionable to the officials in England. In May 1848 Palmerston was most anxious on this point:[79]

    I should like Sir Henry Bulwer to look over these sheets to see if I have left in anything which he would wish to have omitted. I will send the others by and by for the same purpose.

In the fifties and sixties ambassadors generally approved the projected Blue Books,[80] but this fact did not diminish the importance of getting their sanction; the use of the telegraph enabled the correspondence to be conducted with great speed. On the subject of the Danish papers in 1864, Hammond advised Layard:[81]

    I have told Buchanan, Paget, and Bloomfield, that the papers will be brought down to the 21st and that if they are nervous about any of their despatches between those in the revise and that date, they must telegraph. Buchanan is to send home the revise by Monday morning: but Bloomfield and Paget can only telegraph their wishes. . . .

and the next day:[82]

Keep at all events the marked Blue Paper copy, although indeed this is no occasion for sending over the revise in a hurry, for we shall not hear from Germany and Denmark before Monday . . .

Ambassadors and other representatives occasionally objected to phrases as well as to the inclusion of specific despatches. Cowley at Paris was particularly sensitive to the effect that Blue Books might have in France, even suggesting at one time that his official despatches should be considered as less official than those of other ambassadors and ministers at other courts.[83] When he returned the Italian papers in 1860, he commented:[84]

    I think that it would be as well to leave out in No. 22 the words 'by the intrigues of Sardinian agents' as Thouvenel might not like its being known that he had spoken in that way to me. . . .

and protested in 1862 that he had not seen certain papers before they were laid.[85] Rarely were errors of judgement made, but when they were, profuse apologies followed:[86]

[79] Public Record Office. F.O. 96/22. 25 May 1848.
[80] e.g. British Museum. Layard Papers. Add. MSS. 38,951. f. 15.
[81] *Ibid.* Add. MSS. 38,952. f. 131. 23 March 1864.
[82] *Ibid.* f. 135. 24 March 1864.
[83] Public Record Office. F.O. 391/5. Cowley to Hammond, 9 March 1860.
[84] *Ibid.* 7 March 1860.
[85] *Ibid.* 10 June 1862.
[86] *Ibid.* F.O. 96/26. Russell to Bloomfield, draft, 12 April, No. 150, undated.

I much regret the disagreeable effects which have resulted from the publication of your dispatch to me marked 21 in Blue Book. The dispatch was not marked confidential. . . .

I am glad to find you are not accused of mis-representing the language of Baron [Schleinburg]. Her Majesty's Government regret the publication, as it has given pain to that estimable minister.

Russell supported Cowley's objections to the publication of reports of confidential conversations with foreign sovereigns and statesmen–'the practice of giving conversations frightens our interlocutors everywhere–I have struck out more than Cowley.'[87] Five years later Cowley explained his reasons:[88]

I entertain very strong objections to putting reports of confidential communications with the Emperor into Blue Books. It is not fair to him personally because, as in the present instance, he may entertain opinions at variance with the majority of his subjects, and it is not right that he should be shown up. Although therefore I have not marked the whole of No. 53 for omission I had much rather that it was not published, nor the extract from No. 59.

I have also marked for omission those dispatches which relate to conversations which I have at different times had with Rouher. He was not Minister for Foreign Affairs, and had no business to give me any information.

While necessary and desirable to have British ambassadorial consent to the inclusion of despatches, it was also imperative to secure the approbation of foreign ambassadors and representatives in England to the publication of any letters or despatches from their own governments shown by them to the British Secretary of State. Hammond admonished Layard:[89]

I desired Bidwell to remind you that in laying communications from Foreign Ministers you must be very careful to obtain their assent. This of course does not apply to papers officially addressed or given.

In many cases the British ambassador would be officially instructed to ask the Foreign Minister of the government to which he was accredited for formal permission to print despatches. All these precautions, if taken, provided against later protests by foreign governments as well as against unfortunate results in other countries. From this motive, reference to intrigue abroad was always omitted.

Correspondence between the Foreign Office and other government departments also produced difficulties. Russell's view was that it should rarely be given in Parliamentary Papers;[90] Hammond agreed:[91]

On principle I think it objectionable to publish the consultation between two departments on matters of public policy. They are necessarily confidential and many things might be mooted in them, many differences of opinion be disclosed, which it would be very inconvenient to make public.

This principle was generally followed. Great care was always taken that when such a publication was deemed necessary, permission to publish was given by the department concerned.[92] It was also desirable to remove references to private informants in order to avoid the danger of such sources of information drying up.[93]

Apart from this question of permission to print certain types of despatches and letters, the Foreign Office had its own reservations on the publication of its despatches.[94] Public despatches in the numbered series were generally printed in full; confidential despatches on the other hand were

---

[87] *Ibid.* F.O. 391/5. Russell's minute on Cowley to Hammond, 9 March 1860.

[88] *Ibid.* only dated '1865', in Cowley's hand.

[89] British Museum. Layard Papers. Add. MSS. 38,952. f. 8. 30 January 1863.

[90] *Ibid.* Add. MSS. 38,990. f. 195. Minute by Russell, 26 April 1864.

[91] *Ibid.* Add. MSS. 38,952. f. 145. Hammond to Layard, 26 April 1864.

[92] e.g. Public Record Office. F.O. 96/26. Dufferin to Forster, 10 July 1861.

[93] British Museum. Layard Papers. Add. MSS. 38,952. f. 40.

[94] Some of which are mentioned above pp. 195–7.

often printed, but generally with omissions, and marked 'extract' in the print. Even 'separate' despatches might be printed in full. The numbers of despatches and the headings 'confidential' or 'separate' were always omitted in the print, except when a clerk forgot and, in checking, the number and description passed unnoticed. Where telegrams were printed, because Parliament generally criticised the use of the electric telegraph in negotiations, and objected to any reliance on it as a means of diplomatic correspondence, they were often presented as if they formed a small section of a long public despatch and were marked 'extract', although in fact they were given in full. Later this practice disappeared and the telegrams were acknowledged in the print, but their texts were then altered to avoid the incidental disclosure of cyphers to foreign governments. The Law Officers' reports on questions of international law were by custom omitted on the ground that the possibility of future publication might inhibit the lawyers in their decisions and expositions. There were however exceptions when a report as in the case of the *Cagliari* was included in a Blue Book.[95]

Thus for various reasons many omissions were made from the official documents in the compilation of Parliamentary Papers, and their existence inevitably demanded careful checking of the selections which were to be published for any tell-tale reference to them. Russell often repeated to his staff the need for care:[96]

These papers require infinite care in order to avoid immediate requests for papers omitted.
The various dispatches of 31 December will make some confusion, unless the original numbers are looked to.
Mr Bergne might be of use in comparing the printed dispatches with the originals. . .

Punctuation, spelling, and syntax were often corrected so that the despatches should read well. Some British diplomatic representatives would be most concerned to alter phrases when they realised they were to be published. Forster, when asked if he would like any omissions from his report on Turkish finance, replied:[97]

The only one which I recollect is I think in the part relating to the Accounts, where in speaking of the facility with which documents can be altered owing to the use of Indian Ink and highly glazed paper, I make use of the expression 'a *lick* of the tongue answers better than an eraser', or some such words – 'an *application* of the tongue etc.' would be a more elegant word for a Parliamentary Paper.

Documents often had to be rewritten in a correct form for publication: Hammond telegraphed to Longworth to send another, proper, copy of the protest of the consuls about the bombardment of Belgrade for the Blue Book.[98]

Private letters were occasionally inserted in Parliamentary Papers as was Sir Charles Wyke's letter to Hammond reporting his negotiations in Central America, but would be presented as if they were despatches. The House of Commons objected to any suggestion of the use of private letters between the Secretary of State and British representatives abroad in diplomacy:[99]

There has been a deal of talk in and out of Parliament about the private letters from you to Lord John which are alluded to in your despatch – They were never shown to the cabinet and when asked for by some of its members in consequence of Derby's observations, it was said they were burnt and could not be produced!!!

So Clarendon wrote to Cowley, who had been forced to refer to his private letters as he had not written formal despatches on Walewski's statements. If the reference to these letters had been omitted, Parliament would have moved for despatches which did not exist.[100] Hammond however had not been happy about the reference,[101] although it was generally accepted in cabinet circles that such

---

95 A&P. (1857–8) HC. LIX. [2361] 399. 'Further correspondence respecting the *Cagliari*. (Opinions of the Law Officers of the Crown, dated April 12, 13 and 17, 1858).'
96 British Museum. Layard Papers. Add. MSS. 38,990. f. 127. Russell to Layard, undated.
97 Public Record Office. F.O. 96/27. 23 April 1862.
98 *Ibid*. Hammond, 15 May, undated.   99 *Ibid*. F.O. 519/178. Clarendon to Cowley, 14 March 1860.
100 Clarendon MSS. C.558. Cowley to Clarendon, copy, 10 February 1860.
101 Public Record Office. F.O. 391/5. Hammond to Cowley, copy, 11 February 1860.

letters were vital for the efficient conduct of diplomacy.[102] Despite this incident Clarendon denied to the 1861 Select Committee on the Diplomatic Service that anything of importance existed in private letters which was not in despatches,[103] but he himself was careful to avoid criticism for his own use of private letters:[104]

As some of the snobs in the House of Commons object to the Foreign Secretary ever writing private letters to Foreign Ministers, I am desirous that my communication to Napier should not be so called and shall be obliged by your cutting it out of his dispatches together with his apology for sending it to Malmesbury.

The use of private letters for the communication of material which was on the whole unsuitable for publication only reflected the general acceptance in the Foreign Office that if Parliament were to move for despatches, those despatches would have to be produced. The Office scrupulously observed the conventions of Parliamentary procedure, always presenting a document mentioned in debate or read to the house.

Closely supervised by the Secretary of State and the Under Secretaries, the final Blue Books contained few clerical errors or contradictions, except for the rare index reference to an omitted document. Every publication was finally sanctioned by the Secretary of State, but his control of the selection of documents was in practice limited by his inability to read through all the relevant papers in the time available. Both Malmesbury and Russell published fully and managed to keep a close watch on their subordinates, but quite naturally in the circumstances took a greater interest in the publication of documents of political significance. This increasing pressure of work increased the influence of the Under Secretaries in that, although the Secretary of State might initiate a publication, it was their duty to provide the first selection of documents for him, and draw his attention to salient points. But it must always be remembered that in the last resort, as Palmerston himself said, it was he as Prime Minister who was responsible for all information provided for Parliament, and it was the duty of the Foreign Secretary to know what was thus provided. This then is just an indication of the official background to one type of Parliamentary Paper, and a hint of the general questions which its publication raises. Perhaps it is possible to go some little way towards meeting the attack made by the member for County Cork in a Commons debate of 1865 on the civil service estimates:[105]

Parliamentary papers pour into members' houses to such an extent that they become an absolute nuisance. Why not have a small epitome of what papers are to come out and will be ready for perusal at the Library with the votes? I object to having tons of papers which are never opened sent to my lodgings. I have been out of town for a few weeks, and on my return, instead of being able to go to the Derby I had to wade through a mass of parliamentary papers. I put away 1 lb and threw away about 2 cwt. I could not sell the residue; I could not exchange them for books for that would be selling them; I could not burn them, for that would be voted a nuisance. Why should these tons of paper be thrust on unwilling members?

The answer was that in the main the members wanted them. Once the demand diminished, so did the supply.[106]

VALERIE CROMWELL

---

[102] Disraeli MSS. Letters from Earle. Earle to Disraeli, 8 March 1860.

[103] A&P. (1861) HC. VI. 459. p. 106. Questions and answers 988–92.

[104] Public Record Office. F.O. 391/3. Clarendon to Hammond, 26 August 1860.

[105] *Hansard* CLXXIX. 1140. 1 June 1865. The vote was for £265,410 for printing and stationery.

[106] I should like to thank the following for their kind permission to consult and quote from manuscript collections in their charge: the Controller of Her Majesty's Stationery Office for material in the Public Record Office, the National Trust for the Disraeli papers at Hughenden Manor, the Librarian of the Foreign Office, and the Earl of Clarendon for the Clarendon papers in the Bodleian Library.

Customs and Commerce

The
Archival History of the
Customs Records

Historically H.M. Customs and Excise is an amalgamation of a number of revenue-collecting services, some of them dating from very early times. The Customs is much the senior partner. The excises were not introduced until the time of the Long Parliament, but although their descent has been chequered it has until quite recent times been one entirely independent of the Customs. The descent of the Customs has not only been much longer than the Excise but also more complicated, and this complication is reflected naturally enough in the greater complication of the surviving archive. It is not surprising, therefore, if more than one scholar seems to have 'lost his way for the moment amid the famously complicated paths of these records'. Where one class of record will begin or end quite abruptly, another will do so as a gradual process. The survival or non-survival of one class, or the place of present custody of another, may seem quite fortuitous–if not capricious. It is intended, therefore, in this present paper to attempt to relate these and other apparent vagaries of the Customs archives to the associated facts of administrative reform, constitutional development, physical casualty, or other relative circumstance.

The national or 'great' customs (*magna et antiqua custuma*), as distinct from any local or 'petty' customs (*minuti consuetudines*), is usually stated to have originated either in a commuted form of toll-in-kind which was originally allowed as a payment in return for a royal protection, or else in a vague right of the crown to a prerogative purveyance pre-emption or prisage. In any case their early history,[1] at least up to the twelfth century, is very indistinct. Already before the middle of the eighth century–according to Richard James's (fragmentary) extracts from the Saxon charters of St Paul's–Ethelbald, king of Mercia, had granted to the then bishop of London *unius navis vectigal atque tributum*, adding–with whatever significance–*quae mihi antea iure competebant.*[2] From the time of the heptarchy, then, the kings were taking customary tolls from trade; this, however, was certainly not on any uniform or national plan, but possibly merely in the royal ports and demesnes, and only in accordance with the customary rights of the place. It is significant, perhaps, that at the same time the magnates also were taking a sort of custom within their own franchises, out of their own tenurial rights.

Chancery records
The Winchester assize of 1203–4 has been referred to as 'the Customs of the Realm of England', and Gras[3] accepts it as a deliberate effort on the part of the crown to replace an older system that had

---

[1] The best account of the early Customs is N. S. B. Gras, *Early English Customs System* (Harvard, 1918).
[2] M. Gibbs, *Early Charters of the Cathedral Church of St Paul* (Camden, Third Series, LVIII, 1939), p. 6.
[3] Gras, *op. cit.*, p. 53.

lapsed into localism by a central system centrally administered. Certainly it was the earliest completely national customs in this country, and hence the first to produce anything like a systematic archive. The tax of one-fifteenth *ad valorem* was chargeable only upon oversea trade (whether import or export), but certain coastwise traffic–although not itself liable to customs duty–had to be brought under official control in order to prevent foreign (dutiable) trade being coloured as coastwise and free.

The administration of this duty, its assessment, collection and account, remained always (so far as is known) in the hands of the crown, and was never infeudated or granted out, either to any of the lords or to the harbour-towns. In every port-town half a dozen or so of the wisest and most substantial men, learned in the law (*sex vel septem vel plures de sapientioribus et legalioribus et ditioribus et valentioribus hominibus portus*) were 'picked out' to keep the assize.[4] This is not the place to discuss whether this formula of 1203 was the origin of the later *profitables et sachaunz* (or *profitables plus sachants*)–the 'commendable worthy and knowing men'–of the petty customs or *minuti consuetudines* (for example, of the Southampton Oak Book of *c*. 1300),[5] nor to discuss the precise implications of *eligere*[6] in this context; but the administrative machine of 1203 seems, like Aphrodite, to have arisen fully fashioned from the waves. Not only was the Winchester assize, in one sense, the foundation of all medieval customs administration, but it contained furthermore all the characteristic elements of the modern assessing, collecting and accounting system. In the result, all sea-borne trade, both foreign and coastwise, was properly recorded, with a sufficient description of the goods, the date of shipment, and the name of the merchant concerned. Particulars of coastwise shipments were required to be enrolled, the merchandise valued, and bonds taken from the shippers, to secure that any goods cleared coastwise from a port were in fact landed at some other place within the realm. Transactions in the foreign trade were required to be enrolled, the merchandise valued, the *quindecima* assessed and the duty collected in cash. The duty due was to be paid to the local collectors or bailiffs, who were to keep the proceeds under lock and key (*in una salva arca* under *tres claves vel quatuor*) until returned to the 'head collectors' (*donec redatur capitalibus custodibus per cirographa contra baillivos*). Other officials were appointed to be the more direct officers of the crown, comptrollers, who should keep a counter-roll (*rotulos contra eos facient*), an independent record of all moneys received, but should not themselves receive any. Geoffrey Chaucer[7] was such a comptroller for the port of London when Richard Bembre and John Philpot ('of Philpot Lane') were the *electi* collectors.[8] The particular significance of this form of organization was that the sea-ports were, at least for this purpose, taken out of the body of the shire, and they accounted to the Exchequer direct, without the intervention of the sheriff.

The text of the Winchester assize of customs, dated 14 June 1203, was enrolled as a letter patent[9] and, incidentally, the mere position of this item in the roll itself misled Faber into assigning it to the wrong year.[10] Summary accounts of the yield, from its inception until the end of November 1205, for example, in respect of the ports from Newcastle 'south-about' as far as Fowey, are entered on the relative pipe roll.[11] It is not clear either when or why this tax succumbed, but the *Carta Mercatoria* of 1266 seems to imply the decay of the Winchester assize. The later impost, although

---

[4] *Rotuli Litterarum Patentium*, I. 42–3.

[5] *Southampton Record Society*, X (1910), 44–5.

[6] See 'The Collectors of Customs', H. M. Mills, in W. A. Morris and J. R. Strayer, *English Government at work, 1327–1336* (Mediaeval Academy of America, 1947), II. 171.

[7] Patent Roll, C.66/290 (48 Edw. III) mem. 13, and C.66/296 (51 Edw. III), mem. 14.

[8] L.T.R: Enrolled A/Cs, Customs: E.356/14, mem. 16(2).

[9] *Rotuli Litterarum Patentium*, I. 42–3.

[10] R. Faber, *Die Entstehung des Agrarschutzes in England* (Strasburg, 1888), 62–4.

[11] Pipe roll [6 John] Mich. 1204: rot. 17, dorse, mem. 1. (Pipe Roll Society (1940) p. 218.)

sometimes referred to as an 'aid' (*auxilium* or *novum auxilium*),[12] was sometimes recorded as a 'customs' (*custuma* or *consuetudino*).[13]

In 1275, with the introduction of the *nova custuma*[14] of Edward I (which later came to be known as the *antiqua custuma* or *magna et antiqua custuma*), the institutional history of the Customs entered a new stage. In each harbour-town collectors and comptrollers of the customs were appointed by direct authority of the crown, and the fact of their appointment to the place by patent, and the fact that the cocquet seal[15] was placed in their custody (for the treasurer of the Exchequer sent down *sub pede sigilli Scaccarij in quadam bursa illa sigilla quae deputantur pro Coketto*[16]), itself gave to the harbour-town what Matthew Hale, the constitutional lawyer of the Restoration, called 'the super-induction of a civil signature',[17] that is to say, gave such harbour-town the franchise of a 'port'. According to Blackstone,[18] it had always been held that the king was lord of the whole shore, and particularly was guardian of the ports and havens which are, as Coke had it, *portae regni*, the gate-ways of the realm.[19] By the feudal law, all navigable rivers and havens were computed among the *regalia majora et minora*, or prerogatives of the crown.[20] Hence, in order to safeguard and assure his maritime revenue, the king had a prerogative power to appoint and assign the harbours or places where alone vessels in the dutiable trade could lade and unlade—*ibi, et non alibi*—that is, he could 'appoint' ports and 'assign' quays. It was for this reason that Coke placed the grant or appointment of ports among the franchises or liberties, and that from early times no haven could be erected into a 'port' except by lawful process; any pretended liberty was seizable *quo warranto*.[21] Already by the fifteenth year of John's reign the pipe roll provides an example of the arrest of a vessel *quae applicuit alibi quam in portu*.[22] The particular instrument, then, by which a 'port' was so appointed was the letter patent of the collector of customs for the crown.

From the year 1275, in every such 'appointed' port two men were chosen, mostly from the burgesses or freemen of the place, to be (joint) collectors, and 'to keep one piece of a seal' (or matrix), and another man was appointed by the king to be his comptroller, to represent the king's special interests, 'and have another piece.' This clearly follows the pattern of the Winchester assize of 1203. It now became the practice for the crown to appoint commissioners who required the sheriff to select and summon certain *probi et legales homines*; and it was these who 'picked out' the most sufficient and proper men to be the collectors, who were in due course appointed by letter patent, warranted by writ of privy seal.[23] The patent, however, was entered in the fine roll, on account of the customary fee, until the reign of Charles I, when that series of chancery enrolments was discontinued. Thereafter it was entered on the appropriate patent roll until 1725, after which year it appears on the so-called 'Bishops' patent roll'. The comptroller was appointed by letter patent (likewise by writ of privy seal) but was entered on the patent roll throughout.

---

[12] *Cal. Pat. Rolls, Hen. III* (1264–73), 129.

[13] *Ibid.*, 129, and *De Antiquis Legibus Liber*, 109.

[14] *Parliamentary Writs*, I, 1, and *Cal. Fine Rolls*, I (1272–1307), 47. (Its exact date is determined by its position on the rolls.)

[15] Or matrix, rather. 'Cocquet' with its variants is derived from *quo quietus est*.

[16] Memoranda roll, 26 Edw. I, rot. 71, 25–6.

[17] '*Treatise in three Parts: Pars Secunda*,' cap. ii (in F. Hargrave, *Collection of Tracts* (1787), 46).

[18] *Commentaries*, Bk. I, cap. vii.

[19] 4 *Institutions*, XXIV.

[20] Blackstone, *op. cit.* Bk. I. cap vii (citing 2 Feud. t. 56), and Hale, *De Portibus Maris: Pars Secunda*, cap. viii.

[21] See for example *Cal. Pat. Rolls, Hen. III* (1232–47), 292–3, where Henry III in 1242 caused inquisition to be made as to which ports in Wales 'are and ought to be the King's Ports, and who have made any ports to the nuisance of the King and by what warrant'.

[22] Pipe Roll, 15 John, rot. 15b.

[23] *Cal. Fine Rolls*, I (1272–1307), 47. A Steel, 'The Collectors of Customs at Newcastle upon Tyne in the reign of Richard II', in *Studies presented to Sir Hilary Jenkinson* (1957), 390–413, is an informative essay.

Exchequer records

At the Customs the comptroller's account was related to the collector's much as at the Exchequer the chancellor's roll was related to the pipe roll. The collector's roll of 'particulars of account' (*particule compoti*) was returned into and declared at the Exchequer, where the exchequer clerks prepared an account for enrolment (*compotus collectorum custume lanarum coriorum et pellium lanutarum in portu . . .*).

Although the separate duties in the Exchequer of the king's remembrancer and the lord treasurer's remembrancer respectively were not defined by ordinance until 1323, yet the bundles of local particular accounts, the (earlier) 'port-books' or small rolls with their associated subsidiary documents, will be found among the records of the king's remembrancer, and the enrolled accounts in the lord treasurer's remembrancer's, both from the time of Edward I. The particular accounts, the work of the local collectors and comptrollers of customs, will demonstrate all the vagaries of calligraphy, language and methods of account. In contrast, the enrolled accounts, the work of the exchequer clerks, will demonstrate a uniformity in handwriting, terminology and method, with the detail well digested, summarized and balanced.

The particular accounts show in detail the description, quantity and value of the merchandise, the date and place of shipment, the name and owner of the vessel, and the name and nationality of the shipper. Associated with these particular accounts in the Exchequer are such ancillary records as the files of cockets[24] and landing certificates, coast-bonds, tronage (or weighing) accounts, searchers' and other subsidiary accounts, ledgers and receipts, certificate-books, returns, commissions, bonds, inquisitions and so forth.[25] These particulars of account and their associated records remain an exchequer class until the administrative reforms in the Customs of the Lord Treasurer, Winchester, in 1565, after which date, although the associated documents continue in the class,[26] the particulars of account are superseded by the Exchequer port-books.[27]

The practice of enrolling and declaring customs accounts (in common, of course, with other classes of account) was an Exchequer and (later) Treasury practice, rather than of the Customs; hence the enrolled and declared customs accounts are not properly any part of the Customs' archive. At the time of the final audit, certain so-called 'foreign accounts' were made up, either on account of their volume or their special character; among these the customs rolls run from Edward I until the time of the 'Great farm' (Christmas Day 1604),[28] but thereafter certain related documents only continue in this exchequer class. Except for the periods during which the customs had been let to farm the totals, both of the customs and the subsidies in respect of each port,[29] are to be found in the lord treasurer's remembrancer's enrolled accounts.

The customs declared account took two forms, 'the general account' and the 'cash account', prepared upon separate rolls. The general account is a statement of the actual receipt in every port distinguishing each separate heading of duty; it thus relates directly to the overseas and other dutiable trade. The cash account, in contrast, is a statement of the net sums paid into the Exchequer after deduction of the salaries and other expenses of the establishment, bounties, tallies and 'drawbacks';[30] this account, therefore, is a financial statement rather than a trade account.[31] The practice

---

[24] The word had by now come to be applied to the documents bearing the seal as well as to the seal itself.

[25] See also P.R.O., E.209.   [26] E. 122.   [27] E. 190, but see below.

[28] See A. P. Newton: 'The Establishment of the Great Farm of the English Customs', in *Transactions of the Royal Historical Society*, 4th ser. I (1918), 129–55.

[29] The word 'port' in this context is a technical term–a delimited length of the coast under the superintendence of the designated port-town, designated from 1558 by commission returned into the court of Exchequer, and earlier by prescription. See R. C. Jarvis, 'The Appointment of Ports', *Economic History Review*, 2nd ser. XI (1959), 455–66.

[30] Moneys 'drawn back' (or refunded) in respect of the import duty (or later Excise duty) paid on goods subsequently re-exported or exported.

[31] The difference in the two classes of account is well illustrated in the introductions to the *Calendars of Treasury Books*.

of declaring accounts at the Treasury, although fully established in the seventeenth century, seems to have been introduced somewhat earlier. Two copies of the account were prepared in the Audit Office, one on paper and the other on parchment, and forwarded to the Treasury, to be declared and signed. The paper copies were then returned to the Audit Office where they remain on record, those of the receiver-general of the new impost from 1604 to 1649,[32] and those of the farmers (and later the Commissioners) and their collectors and comptrollers, from 1602 onwards.[33] The parchment copy was sent through the king's remembrancer and the lord treasurer's remembrancer to the clerk of the pipe, in each of which offices it was again in some form enrolled. For this reason, therefore, the parchment copies remained Exchequer archives and survive there from 1545 to the end of farming and the administrative reforms of 1671.[34] Where the Pipe Office series and the Audit Office series fully duplicated each other, those after 1714 in the former series were transferred to the Bodleian Library, Oxford.[35]

By 1821 it had 'been found by experience' that 'the ancient course of practice of the Exchequer' occasioned 'great inconvenience and much unnecessary labour expense and delay'.[36] It was therefore provided that for the future one account only should be made out and declared, and that that should be 'written on paper in the English language in common characters'.[37] The parchment copy in the Exchequer therefore ceased. With the ensuing administrative reforms in the Audit Office, a new method was adopted in the 1820s, of preparing and declaring the accounts. Instead of each appearing on a separate roll, they were written out on sheets of paper of uniform size, convenient to be later gathered and bound into volumes. From 1827, therefore, the customs declared accounts (both of the receiver-general and the comptrollers) are found, in common of course with other Departmental and other series, in a separate archive class–'Declared Accounts in Books, various'[38] as distinct from the 'Declared Accounts in Rolls.'[39]

The Exchequer port-books

To revert to the later medieval period, a variety of factors had caused trade at the ports to develop in a form not fully congruent with the Plantagenet pattern. The practice of restricting overseas trade to London and particular (anciently) privileged outports, somewhat after the procedure of the staple, seemed inconsistent with commercial and maritime development. Notwithstanding the clear text of the law, extra-statutory trade in certain forms, in particular of the outports–although not specifically permitted or authorized by the Customs–was not suppressed: it was 'suffered' to continue. A notable compromise in the control of these outports by the central administration was achieved in 1558 by an administrative reform of Lord Treasurer Winchester, a reform that created an important new body of record, the exchequer port-books.[40]

In the interests of developing commerce, a new act[41] conceded for the future a clear statutory authority for the overseas trade which the Customs had in the past only extra-statutorily 'suffered' to take place. On the other hand, in the interests of the crown, all overseas trade was brought under closer central control; for the future shipment and unshipment should be confined to certain hours on certain days, at certain 'assigned' places (called 'legal quays') within certain 'appointed' harbours

[32] A.O.1/bundles 72 to 78, rolls 772–91.
[33] A.O.1/commencing at bundle 594, roll 1.
[34] E. 351/607–66.
[35] Under Rules made under the provisions of the Public Record Office Act, 1877 (40–1 Vic. cap. 55).
[36] 1–2 Geo. IV, cap. 121, preamble.
[37] Ibid., sec. 7.
[38] A.O. 2/1–34.
[39] A.O. 1.
[40] E. 190.
[41] 1. Eliz. I, cap. 11.

(called 'ports'), assigned and appointed by virtue of a commission out of the Court of Exchequer. A scheme of account, originally devised quite possibly in response to particular frauds resulting from an indulgence granted in 1428,[42] was reformed and developed by the lord treasurer. New orders were made in 1564, 'particularly entered written and expressed in a Booke, conteyning in nombre fyfteen Leaves, written on both sides, and signed in the Begynning and endyng with our signe Manual'.[43] For the future there should be sent down out of the Exchequer 'to every Porte Haven and Creeke in this oure Realme,' every Trinity and Hilary term, a parchment book 'in a Tynne Box with the Leaves nombred of Recorde'. It is these parchment books–'with Leaves nombred of Recorde'–that constitute the remarkable series of exchequer port-books, the most comprehensive record of the commerce of the late sixteenth and seventeenth centuries to be found in this or any other country. For example, Dr Neville Williams says that in comparison with these the Sound Toll registers of the Baltic trade are slight and uninformative.[44]

Of the fourteen or fifteen thousand books that are contained in the bundles in this class, about half relate to the overseas trade and about half to the coastwise. They now vary greatly in their physical condition if only because of the vicissitudes of their earlier custody. Although some of the books returned from the creeks are in English from the beginning, the entries until the end of the sixteenth century are mostly in Latin, but generally in what Dr Williams calls 'a *patois* known rarely outside the customs house'.

Departmental records: trade statistics

For the gradual decay and eventual discontinuance of this form of exchequer record, one must look not so much to the history of the Exchequer as to the history of the Customs. The Long Parliament, after its breach with the crown, regulated the collection of the revenue–the ancient customs and the newly instituted excise[45]–by means of parliamentary committees, and therefore Customs commissioners were appointed by a parliamentary ordinance of 21 January 1643.[46] Nevertheless, later farms were in fact negotiated, but as from Michaelmas 1671 the practice of farming was finally discontinued, and what has come to be known as 'the first Board of Customs' was then established by patent.[47] Thereafter, the ports (including the port of London) accounted not to a syndicate of farmers but to the Board of Commissioners, who in their turn accounted to the Treasury. This arrangement of a continuous commission, in contrast to a series of intermittent farms, had a number of effects, not the least of which was the creation of a Departmental archive and a consequent improvement in the methods of preparing and keeping records and accounts. For example, already during the time of the Commonwealth the need was felt for more exact records of overseas trade– that is to say that customs accounts should record trade as well as taxation. At the Restoration however, when the customs were put in farm again, those who farmed the taxes did not collect additionally the statistics of trade. It was only with the establishment of the commission in 1671 that this became possible, and it is significant perhaps that this change took place at just the time when great interest was developing in mercantilist economics and 'political arithmetic'.

---

[42] *Proceedings and Ordinances of the Privy Council* (ed. Sir H. Nicolas. Rec. Com.) III, 1422–9, 316 (16 November 1428).

[43] Memoranda Roll, 7 Eliz. I, Hilary, rot. 319; and *Modern Practice of the Court of Exchequer* (1730), 431 ff.

[44] See, for example, N. E. Bang, *Tabeller over Skibsfart og Varetransport gennen Ørsund, 1497–1660* (Copenhagen and Leipzig, 1906–22); and N. E. Bang and K. Korst, *Ibid.,* 1661–1783 (1930–53).

[45] Ordinance 22 July 1643 (art. iii), C. H. Firth and R. S. Rait, *Acts and Ordinances of the Interregnum, 1642–60,* I, 203.

[46] *Lords' Journals,* V, 567.

[47] Patent roll, 23 Car. II, p. 2 no. 1, dorsa, 27 September 1671; and T.51/15A, p. 219. For a detailed account of the administration of the Department, see E. E. Hoon, *The Organisation of the English Customs System, 1696–1786* (New York, 1938, Newton Abbot, 1968).

Before the close of the century, however, the Board of Customs represented to the Treasury that if any 'distinct accompt of the Importation and Exportation of all commodities into and out of this Kingdom' were required to be prepared in order 'to make a balance of the trade between this kingdom and any part of the world', no such accurate account, on the basis of the past or even the current records, could be compiled.[48] When in consequence of such representations an office was instituted in 1696 within the Customs, and an officer was appointed as inspector-general of imports and exports, to 'make up the accounts of imports and exports',[49] trade statistics in the sense in which we know them today could be said to be properly instituted. It is for this reason that from the end of the seventeenth century the Departmental records of the inspector-general tend to displace–and eventually do in fact entirely displace–such continuing records of the Exchequer as the older port books. The administration was even yet not fully 'out of court', and this is an interesting example in administrative history of a new Department *not* being vested with any authority over the older court procedures within its own structure. The Department, therefore, busied itself with making good the 'want of method' in the old, by devising a new procedure of its own, with its own accounts and its own archive. The new authority, having no means to kill the old, therefore let it die. Hence, while the newer Departmental forms of record built themselves up into greater reliability and accuracy, the older exchequer forms of record tended first to falter and then to wither away. Although some ports continued to return their port-books into the Exchequer, for example New-castle until 1798, Lynn until 1794, Chester until 1789 and Bristol and Exeter until 1788, parallel with the new statistical procedure, other ports appear to have discontinued over half a century earlier–at least no port-books have survived in respect of Chichester later than 1731, Ipswich and Cardiff later than 1736, and Carlisle later than 1743. Naturally, these now redundant forms of exchequer record attracted a certain amount of contemporary criticism, for example from the Commission to Examine Take and State the Public Accounts in 1783[50] and from a Select Committee in 1797. Eventually they were discontinued in England by Treasury order dated 14 March 1799.

It would be tedious to trace the office of the inspector-general of imports and exports through all the vagaries of its history to the present Statistical Office of H.M. Customs and Excise, which prepares and publishes the *Annual Statements of the Trade of the United Kingdom*. Statistics survive, however, under their various titles–accounts, ledgers, abstracts, abstract-summaries, or statements –from 1696 until today.

Headquarters archive

From the time of their establishment by patent in 1671, the Commissioners of Customs made their headquarters in the London Custom House, and commenced to acquire a Departmental archive both at their headquarters and in the outports. Because the Elizabethan Custom House had been lost in the Great Fire of 1666, Wren had been commissioned to rebuild it. The plan finally sub-mitted by 'Dr Chr. Wren' (after proper consultations) in the March of 1671–the farmers would be discontinued that Michaelmas–provided for 'the Farmers to have the West end of the Custom House to themselves. The Great Long Room[51] to be in common. The East end [to be] for the accommodation of the King's Officers.'[52] It was here, therefore, that 'the King's Officers' com-menced to accumulate the records of the Customs of England, later of Great Britain, later still of the United Kingdom, and eventually of the Excise of the United Kingdom as well as the Customs.

---

[48] Treasury Board Papers, 15 July 1696 (P.R.O., T.1/38, 302).

[49] Treasury Minute Book, 1695–6 (P.R.O., T.29/8, 358–9).

[50] Fourteenth Report of the Commissioners Appointed to Examine Take and State the Public Accounts', in [J. Lane] *Reports of the Commissioners* . . . III (1788) pp. 103. and 563 ff.

[51] The term 'Long Room' used in a highly technical sense has spread round the ports of the world.

[52] *Cal. Treasury Books, III* (1669–72), II, 797.

The place became the headquarters of the overseas administration also and hence the Board accumulated archives relative to their superintendence of certain of the oversea territories.

The headquarters records suffered seriously in a disastrous fire in 1715[53] and another in 1814[54]. In the former, 'the Long Room and the Eastern part of the building' was so far preserved 'that the officers were able to go on with their business', but 'at the West end the Commissioners' Room, the Secretary's Office, the Comptroller-General's, the Receiver-General's, the Solicitor's and several other offices' were 'very badly damaged'.[55] In 1814 Ripley's rebuilt Custom House was practically destroyed.

In the meantime, the customs of Scotland had remained in farm until the time of the Union, but in 1707 a Board of Commissioners was set up in Scotland[56] for the first time. The Scottish Board was established in general after the pattern of the English except that (a) the net produce of Scottish customs was required to be paid, not to the Treasury, but to the receiver-general of the English customs; (b) the Scottish Board had no hand in the plantation business in America nor in the Four-and-a-Half-Per-Centum duties in the West Indies;[57] and (c) the Scottish Board of Customs collected also the Excise duties upon salt in Scotland, but remitted the yield to the English Salt Commissioners. In 1723, however, an act provided that the English and Scottish customs might be placed under the management of a single commission for the whole United Kingdom (of Great Britain);[58] the current patents were therefore cancelled and a single board was set up accordingly.[59] Nevertheless, in 1742 the existing joint patent was cancelled by royal warrant,[60] and separate boards were re-instituted in respect of England and Scotland.[61] The situation was still further complicated in the last century, when in 1823 an act was passed to extinguish the two Customs boards and the two Excise boards of England and of Scotland respectively, and the single revenue board for Ireland, and to establish in their place two boards only, one of customs and one of excise, both for the whole of the United Kingdom.[62] Then, in 1849, the Board of Excise, the Stamps Office, and the Assessed Taxes, were amalgamated to become the Inland Revenue,[63] but in 1909 the Excise branch was withdrawn from the Inland Revenue to be amalgamated with H.M. Customs, to become thus H.M. Customs and Excise.[64] As might be expected, the complications of so involved a descent have left their complications in the archive also – complications enough to add a fifth to Agarde's well-known four-fold hurts that 'bringe wracke to records'.

A considerable number of volumes of the records of the then existing or extinguished commissions appear to have been deposited at some time with the Treasury. In 1835, however, that is to say before the Select Committee of the House of Commons was appointed in 1836 to enquire into 'the present state of the Records of the United Kingdom', over 560 volumes were transferred from the Treasury to the London Custom House. In 1848, after the passage of the Public Record Office Act (of 1838),[65] 438 of these were sent from the Custom House to the Rolls House, on the site now

---

[53] See *Daily Courant*, 15 January 1715. (The occurrence is usually misdated, 1714.)
[54] Board's minute, 12 February 1814.
[55] P.R.O., T.1/87 no. 28. (It is not an accurate précis at *Cal. Treasury Papers*, 1714-19, p. 73.)
[56] Patent roll, 6 Anne, p. 6, no. 16 (5 June 1707).
[57] See below.
[58] 9 Geo. I, cap. 21.
[59] Pat. roll, 9 Geo. I, p. 2, no. 12 (27 June 1723).
[60] Warrant under royal sign manual, 25 August 1742.
[61] Pat. roll, 15 Geo. II (*sic*, presumably 16 Geo. II). p. 5, nos. 3 and 4 (9 September 1742).
[62] 4 Geo. IV, cap. 23.
[63] 12 Vic. cap. 1.
[64] 8 Edw. VII, cap. 16, sec. 4.
[65] 1-2 Vic. cap. 94.

occupied by the Public Record Office Museum. In 1846 and 1847 many other volumes were transferred thence from Treasury Chambers, and in 1851 a further 127 from the Custom House. In 1853 and 1854 further rearrangements took place, both from Treasury Chambers to Rolls House and from Rolls House to the Custom House. More recently, those records that were created by the now extinguished Scottish Board, but which have hitherto been held in the custody of the United Kingdom Board (physically in England), have been forwarded for custody to the Register House in Scotland. There have also been so transferred certain other record items which, although relating solely to Scotland, were created by the Board of the United Kingdom. When records themselves (as distinct from microfilm or other forms of photocopies) are fragmented from that other and major part of the archive of which they are an integral part (presumably for purposes of user convenience) it may or may not offend against the best principles of archive keeping, but it certainly adds another complication to their already confused archival history. As a result, therefore, first of involved administrative and constitutional changes, and secondly of unsystematic physical migrations, the precise location of some of those items may now seem somewhat arbitrary.

The whole body of the Departmental archive, including that remaining in the physical custody of the Board of Customs, lately legally under the charge and superintendence of the Master of the Rolls, was transferred on 1 January 1959 by the Public Records Act to the Lord Chancellor. Under section 5(2) of the act, however, the records remain in the custody of the Department for 100 years. Notwithstanding the great concern of the Department regarding any possible 'breach of good faith', as the act expresses it, relating to any 'information which was obtained from members of the public' under conditions of confidentiality (or implied confidentiality), the Department will be found very liberal in so far as its responsibilities allow in opening its archive to disinterested research.

Apart from the minutes of the Irish Board,[66] the Departmental records now physically in the Public Record Office are mostly registers and ledgers, mainly[67] of a statistical character, in 26 classes.[68] The main body of the Departmental records still remaining in its custody (with the exception of the outport ship registers as to which see below) is housed in the official repository in the London Custom House under the control of the Librarian (King's Beam House, Mark Lane, E.C.3, nearby) through whom any access to them is arranged.

Board's minutes, letter-books, etc.
Certain runs of minute books escaped the fire of 1814, for example the receiver-general's minutes 1716–84,[69] general business minutes 1734–1813,[70] bench minutes 1768–1812,[71] port of London searcher's minutes 1671–1781,[72] and surveyor's minutes 1712–1812.[73] The English Board's earliest minute books, however, have not survived in their originals. A collection of 'notes and digests' of the Board's minutes from 1696 was however prepared–to all appearances from the originals–for Sir William Musgrave, a commissioner from 1763 to 1785.[74] Incidentally, Musgrave was a noted scholar and antiquary (a fellow of the Royal Society and of the Society of Antiquaries) and hence, at least potentially, yet another 'hurt' that 'bringe wracke to records'. It was through him that some

---

[66] P.R.O., Customs 1.

[67] As to the establishment registers, see below.

[68] Customs 2–27.

[69] Customs 42/1–8.

[70] Customs Library accession no. (cited as 'CL' below) 887–96. (Thus cited where the items await 'Customs' classification under the new arrangements.)

[71] CL 1279–86.

[72] CL 11893.

[73] CL 1287 and 10575–92.

[74] Customs 29/1–15.

of the Board's records[75] (as well as some of the Board's printed books) found their way out of the Department's custody, and – at least some of them – into the British Museum. Apart from the chance surviving minute books and the 'notes and extracts' referred to above, the original minutes of the English Board (later the United Kingdom Board) survive only from 1814.[76] Minute books relating to the Irish business survive from 1696 to 1830,[77] and those relating to the Scottish business (however the Board was constituted) are unbroken from 1723 to 1828,[78] with general orders from the date of the Union.[79]

The earliest Board's letters to the outports, where they survive at all, survive only in the form of in-letters at the ports themselves; here they are sometimes in the form of the original letters bound into volumes, and sometimes contemporary transcriptions into local letter-books. When in the former state, they bear of course the signatures of such commissioners, for example, as George Downing ('of Downing Street') in England, and Adam Smith in Scotland. The office copies of the 'general letters' of the Scottish Board to the Scottish outports are located in the Custom House, Leith, the last seat of the Scottish Board. The later English and the United Kingdom out-letter books are in the library repository, in various series at different periods, for example, 'Northern ports', 'Western ports', 'Scottish and Irish ports', 'Other Public Office', and so forth.

On the side of legal business, 31 volumes of 'Opinions of Counsel', 1701–1841, contain interesting discussions and decisions, not only in the narrowly fiscal field, but also on wider juridical and constitutional issues.[80] They help to document the development of policy relating to the operation of the navigation laws, flag discrimination, the nationality and 'freedom' of ships, and, for example, the precise status at particular times of the revolting or late revolted colonists. There are also other records of Exchequer, King's Bench, Assize, and other proceedings.

It is perhaps the special character of the patronage system, and particularly of the eighteenth century – about which, incidentally, much has been written that is mistaken and ill-informed[81] – that has made the staffing records of the Customs (and the Excise also for that matter) of particular interest to genealogists, biographers, social historians and others. There are tolerably complete quarterly salary lists arranged by ports, and other subsidiary establishment material, in respect of England and the United Kingdom from 1675 almost to present times,[82] of Scotland from 1712 to 1824,[83] and of Ireland from 1692 to 1885.[84]

Outport records

The records in the outports have commencing dates varying with the exigencies of the particular ports, but in no port do they pre-date the Restoration.[85] Such records survive in respect of no less than 200 ports or places in England and Scotland, apart from those in Ireland, the Isle of Man and the Channel Isles.[86] The letter-books of Great Yarmouth, for example, survive from 1662, those of Dartmouth from 1675, Stockton also from 1675, Exeter from 1676, Sunderland also from 1676, Weymouth from 1694, Harwich from 1699, Lynn from 1700, Cowes from 1701, Swansea from 1709 and Southampton from 1714.

[75] BM: Add. MSS. 11255-6.
[76] Customs 28/11.
[77] CL 850-1 and 872, and P.R.O.: Customs 1.
[78] CL 1480-1542 and 1621. (As to Scottish locations, see above.)
[79] CL 1553, 9456, 21243. (As to Scottish locations, see above.)
[80] Customs 41/1-11 and CL 1547-9 and 21618-38.
[81] Hoon, *op. cit*, 1968 ed., pp. xii-xix.
[82] P.R.O. Customs 18-9, Customs 40, T.42/1-9, 10-47 and T.43/1-4.
[83] CL 1633, 754, 7572-90 (as to Scottish locations, see above) and P.R.O., T.43/5-14.
[84] CL 7640-94 and P.R.O. Customs 20.
[85] The gap at the interregnum will be noticed also in the Exchequer port books (P.R.O., E.190).
[86] For a summary list, see E. Carson, *The Ancient and Rightful Customs* (1972), pp. 273-7.

In the headquarters Library selective transcripts of letter-books, reasonably representative of the main ports[87] (and some of the lesser ports – over 50 in all) have been prepared, typed and bound into volume form, and are available to accredited researchers. The statutory registry of British merchant ships remains located at the respective ports;[88] it is particularly to be noted that this is not a record of the movement of ships (not their report and clearance – that is to say, not their arrival and sailing) but the substantive title-deeds under the current Merchant Shipping Acts to the property-title in British ships or shares in ships.

Shipping records

Another office instituted at about the same time as the inspector-general of imports and exports was the register-general of shipping. The archives of this office have had a very chequered history. It is usual to see the origin of the office in the tightening of the administration of the navigation laws at the end of the seventeenth century, and the urge at about the same period to collect more detailed information about the movement of ships; in both of these respects the administration seemed ahead of the legislature.[89]

The earlier records about the nationality (or 'freedom') of ships are to be found undifferentiated among the chancery or exchequer records or state papers. The more modern series of navigation laws are usually held to derive from an ordinance of the Commonwealth, as re-enacted at the Restoration.[90] By them all plantation and coastwise trade was reserved (under stipulated penalties) to vessels English-built and English-owned; foreign goods were required to be imported in such English vessels or vessels of the country of the goods' origin (or their place of usual shipment). The operation of these provisions naturally brought into existence a body of record dealing with the nationality of ships – it is to be noted, incidentally, before the doctrine of the nationality of ships had been properly developed. At the commencement of the Departmental archive in 1671, records of this character appear undifferentiated among the other routine records of the Department, much as they had earlier appeared undifferentiated among the chancery and exchequer records or the state papers. Copies of certificates of freedom, for example, prize condemnations, plantation registries, prerogative licences (exempting particular English-owned vessels from the provisions of the Act of Frauds), declarations of nationality and ownership, instructions to collectors of customs (as registrars of English ships), 'forms of entry' from the English outports to the registrar-general in London, Mediterranean passes and other licences; all these are found entered, not in a reserved form of record (which might have given rise to a separate archive class), but undifferentiated and entered merely at the appropriate date or opening of the relative port records.

Central responsibility for the maintenance of the general register, at least by 1701,[91] was laid by patent to a commissioner by name,[92] but the office was placed on a more formal basis in 1707[93], when an article in the Act of Union directed that all Scottish vessels should (in proper procedure) be 'entered in the General Register of all Trading ships belonging to Great Britain'.[94] It is particularly to be noticed that from 1707 the law recognized only one register of British merchant

---

[87] For the general character of these selective transcripts, see Chetham Society, Third Series, vol. VI, 1954, (R. C. Jarvis, *Customs Letter-Books of the Port of Liverpool, 1711–1813*).

[88] See below.

[89] For the archival history of these records, see R. C. Jarvis, 'Ship Registry – to 1707', *Maritime History*, vol. I (1971), 'Ship Registry – 1707 to 1786', *ibid.*, vol. II (1972), and 'Ship Registry – 1787', *ibid.*, vol. III (forthcoming).

[90] Ordinance, 8TH October 1651 (Frith and Rait, II, 559–62), and statute 12. Car. II, cap. 18; and 14 Car. II, cap. II, sec. 6.

[91] P.R.O., T.27/16, 391.

[92] Pat. roll, 13 Will. III, p. 3, no. 1 (18 December 1701).

[93] P.R.O., T.1/103, 94.

[94] 6 Anne, cap. II, art. V.

ships, and this embraced all ships, whether registered in England, Scotland or the plantations. The Board of Customs in London therefore commenced to build up an archive relating to British merchant ships, whether built, owned or trading in any part of the world, and this archive early became separable from other Departmental records. In the home ports also, particularly in the larger ports, registry of shipping business came to be of sufficient importance to create a new type of record relating exclusively to registry matters, for example, at Liverpool under the Plantation Act of Frauds of 1695 and the Wool Act of 1739, and at Campbeltown before the Act of General Registry in 1786.

The act of 1786[95] required the official registry of every British vessel (with certain negligible exceptions), whether built or owned at home or in the plantations, and in effect the re-registry of every such vessel then afloat. This gave rise to an entirely new body of record, both centrally and locally, and constituted a statutory registry. It is this registry which is the source of the 'states of navigation' accounts,[96] tonnage statistics,[97] and all similar compilations.[98]

After the general repeal of the navigation laws in 1849,[99] a variety of considerations led to the transfer of the general superintendence of this work to the Board of Trade,[100] although the Customs remained the executant registrars in all ports in the British Isles. The Customs therefore transferred the whole of the surviving (and separable) headquarters archive of ship registry, together with all surviving muster-rolls and oversea transcripts, to the Board of Trade who later transferred them to the Ministry of Transport. The archival history of this body of record is very complicated.

Plantation records

Although an act of 1672[101] authorized the English Commissioners of Customs to control the collection of the duty upon enumerated goods shipped in the plantations but not brought to England, the authority for the English Board of Customs to control the plantation customs generally was never apparently explicitly stated, either in the statutes or in any of the relative patents. It is perhaps typical of English method in constitution-building (or the lack of method) that when collectors of customs were first appointed in America and the West Indies, they came under the direct control of the English Board of Customs–a practice no one seems to have questioned. In England the outports were divided, for purposes of administrative convenience, into two groups: the 'Northern ports', being those from the Thames 'north-about' to Beaumaris (Barmouth) and the 'Western ports', being those from the Thames 'south-about' to Aberystwyth (Barmouth). When the English Board first assumed responsibility for the plantations, the plantation ports were laid to the 'Western Department', but later a special Plantation Department was established. In 1767, a separate board of American commissioners was created[102] with headquarters at Boston in Massachusetts, and this Board took the 'collections' of Newfoundland and those of the continental seaboard down to Pensacola in Florida beyond the Strait, and also Bermuda, leaving the 'collections' of Barbados, Dominica, Grenada, Jamaica, St Christopher and the ports of Montserrat and other Leeward Islands with the English Board. As later the plantations and settlements in the other territories were established–in Australia, New Zealand, Ceylon, Cape of Good Hope, Sierra Leone, Mauritius, St Helena, Curaçao, and so on–these also were managed by the English

---

[95] 26 Geo. III, cap. 60.
[96] P.R.O., Customs 17.
[97] P.R.O., B.T.6/185.
[98] P.R.O., B.T.6/191.
[99] 12–13 Vic, cap. 28.
[100] 17–18 Vic. cap. 104.
[101] 25 Car. II, cap. 7.
[102] Pat. Roll, 7 Geo. III, p. 5, no. 11 (8 September 1767).

Commission, as were likewise (after 1783) the remaining North American territories other than the (now) United States, that is to say, the Canadas, Cape Breton, Montreal, New Brunswick, Newfoundland, Nova Scotia, Prince Edward Island, Quebec and Montreal. Over 800 volumes or bundles of plantation records survive in the Customs Library repository–some of them 'selected' and some 'promiscuous'–including 179 Canadian, 297 West Indian, 32 African, 62 Australian, and 132 other territories, and 127 volumes relating solely to general establishment matters and the head office administration.[103] A number of these have been microfilmed for the benefit of oversea universities and governmental agencies.

The English Board ceased to administer plantation (or colonial) customs, for in due course its responsibilities in that regard were transferred to the respective colonial legislatures, on dates varying with the different territories–Tobago in 1844, Gambia in 1845, South Australia in 1848, Newfoundland in 1849, Honduras in 1850, and so on. By 1853–seventy-nine years after the Boston tea party–it could finally be said that the imposition of imperial customs in the territories abroad had been abolished; therefore no colonial records accumulated to the home Customs thereafter. The collection of local colonial imposts was now regulated by acts and ordinances of their local legislatures, subject only to the approval and confirmation of the home government and to the comprehensive provision that they are not repugnant to any imperial act.

Another curious responsibility of the English Board, which also resulted in the creation of other records of peculiar overseas reference, was as 'Husband of the Four-and-a-Half-per-Centum Duties'. In 1663 the local legislature of Barbados (followed the next year by the legislatures of Nevis, Antigua, Montserrat and St Christopher) granted to the Crown 4½ per cent of 'all dead commodities, of the growth or produce of the Island, exported'. Initially the collection was put in farm, but in 1686 the crown placed it under the English Board of Customs.[104] The proceeds were a non-parliamentary source of income to the crown, and were used by the crown for pensions and various other purposes, outside the scope of Parliament. In the reform year of 1832 there was a movement to reform the duties,[105] and upon the accession of Victoria the various payments were charged against the Consolidated Fund,[106] and the duty was repealed by act of the United Kingdom Parliament.[107] If the Board of Customs were 'husbands' by patent even after this statutory divorce, it was only to have authority to collect the arrears of duty–if any. The whole procedure remains an interesting example of a Department of State, borne on a Parliamentary vote, continuing to perform a prerogative function direct for the crown and independent of parliamentary control, by virtue only of a patent authority.

In the above essay no reference has been made to the special constitutional status of particular islands in relation to the crown or the home government, and hence not to the records specially arising from that relationship. The fact that the Channel Islands are not part of England, but were deemed to be for the purpose of certain privileges under the navigation acts; that the Isle of Man was part of the Crown but not of the Realm of England until 1765, when it was revested in the Crown after purchase by the Customs with customs money, but still enacts its own insular customs; that the Isles of Scilly have always been administered by the Customs as part of England, but by Excise as though they were not–and hence by the Customs and Excise today as though they are part of England for certain purposes and *not* part of England for certain others; these, and a number of others, are special features–may we never come to regard them as anomalies!–that may very well never meet their *gleichschaltung*.

RUPERT C. JARVIS

[103] Customs 34. For a summary list, see Carson, *op. cit.*, pp. 267–70.
[104] Patent roll, 2 Jac. II, p. 9, no. 6 dorsa (25 June 1686).
[105] Board's minutes (notes and extracts), IX (1832–8), p. 158.
[106] 1–2 Vic, cap. 2.   [107] 1–2 Vic, cap. 92.

Local Port Customs Accounts
Prior to 1550

'There were anciently very many duties due in ports which were usually called *consuetudines* and customs, which belonged to the king either as incident to his customs or as perquisites to his ports, as also to other lords and owners of ports by prescription or charter.'[1] This description of local port customs, taken from Sir Matthew Hale's seventeenth-century treatise on ports and customs, is largely confirmed by the evidence of documents of the twelfth and later centuries. Fifty years ago, Professor N. S. B. Gras drew attention to the large number of documents relating to local customs which survive in both local and central archives.[2] Gras was concerned with local customs only in so far as they were prototypes of the national customs, but he expressed a hope that a comparative study of local customs would be undertaken at some future time.[3] This article is an attempt to survey the surviving examples of one type of local customs record – the detailed accounts of the collection of such customs – with brief descriptions of the varying administrative systems which produced these accounts.

The main characteristic of local customs or *custuma ville* was that they were levied on all goods brought into or taken out of a town, irrespective of their provenance or destination.[4] Other local or national duties were, in contrast, restricted in their incidence either to particular commodities or to overseas trade. References to local port customs occur as early as the eleventh century[5] and their origins remain largely a matter of conjecture. The differences between the rates of local customs levied at various ports, which are apparent by the thirteenth century, suggest that they had no common origin.[6]

In addition to the customs, a number of special tolls were levied at most ports in the later

---

[1] M. Hale, 'A Treatise in Three Parts. De Jure Maris et Brachiorum eiusdem; De Portibus Maris; Concerning the Custom of Goods imported and exported', *A Collection of Tracts relative to the Law of England*, 1, edited by F. Hargrave (London, 1787), 131.

[2] N. S. B. Gras, *The Early English Customs System* (Cambridge, Mass., 1918), 25.

[3] Such a study has still to be written and Hale and Gras remain the chief authorities on the subject.

[4] There are a few exceptions to this, e.g. at Exeter local customs were levied only on imports.

[5] There is an eleventh-century list of tolls levied on ships and goods at Billingsgate, printed in Gras, *op. cit.*, 153–5. Also cf. the claim of the monks of Christ Church, Canterbury, to levy tolls at Sandwich by virtue of a charter of King Cnut.

[6] With the possible exception of the local custom on wine which was levied at the rate of 4d per tun at Berwick, Exeter, Sandwich, Southampton and Torksey, amongst other places (Gras, *op. cit.*, 157, 165, 197; Southampton Corporation MS. Port Books; Exeter Corporation MS. Customs Rolls). This custom may have derived from the 'semi-national' custom of pence on wine (Gras, *op. cit.*, 28).

Middle Ages. The most common of these were anchorage and keelage on ships, frequently claimed as a prescriptive right by the owners of ports,[7] and murage, wharfage, quayage, pesage, measurage, tronage and cranage, on goods, which usually originated in a grant from the Crown. The collection of these tolls is frequently recorded in local customs accounts.

The administration of local customs

Local and national customs were separately administered at the ports, each system having its own body of officials.[8] As we have seen, Hale distinguished between those ports where the local customs belonged to the king and those where they were in the hands of other lords. The 'king's ports' fall into two main groups so far as the local customs are concerned: first, those ports where the Crown retained some control over local customs administration by the appointment of royal bailiffs, and secondly, those where the control passed to local officials when the ports in question were granted their fee farms. The first group includes Sandwich, Winchelsea, Rye, Dartmouth and Bristol, whilst London, Southampton, Exeter, Yarmouth, Ipswich and Chester are to be found in the second.

At Sandwich, in the twelfth and thirteenth centuries, the port customs and other tolls were collected by officials of the priory of Christ Church, Canterbury, which claimed to have received these and other rights in Sandwich from King Cnut in a charter of 1023.[9] Accounts survive from 1220 onwards of annual receipts of customs and other tolls from the port. Until 1244 the accounts were rendered by a succession of monks acting as treasurers, but from then until 1261 the account-ant was a certain Laurence the Clerk who received £4 5 annually for his services. The annual audit of the accounts was held at the Priory at Michaelmas. There was a break in the series of accounts during the troubled period of the Barons' Wars and their aftermath, and when they were resumed in 1276 the official who rendered them was the portreeve. These accounts continue until 1289 and at least one (that for 1276) contains details of the commodities upon which the customs were levied.[10]

In 1290 the priory surrendered the port and its customs to Queen Eleanor for life and, after her decease, to the Crown in perpetuity, receiving other lands in Kent in compensation.[11] Adam de Lyminge acted as portreeve during the period of transition in the ownership of the port and in 1291 he was appointed keeper of the town and port of Sandwich during the king's pleasure. Until 1299 the revenues from the port went to the executors of Queen Eleanor for the payment of her debts. In the latter year Hugh de Helpestone was appointed royal bailiff of Sandwich and instructed to

---

[7] Hale, *op. cit.*, 74.

[8] Occasionally, however, the same man might be a collector of both local and national customs as was Richard Imberd at Southampton in 1342. Even in this case, however, the two types of customs were accounted for separately at the Exchequer (P.R.O. Exchequer K.R. Customs Accts. 137/12; *Calendar of Fine Rolls* [hereafter *C.F.R.*], *1337–47*, 208, 321).

[9] The authenticity of this charter has been questioned because of certain of the privileges granted in it which are unique for the pre-Conquest period. These include, 'the haven of Sandwich and all the landing places and the water dues from both sides of the river . . . and toll of every ship that comes to the said haven' (*Anglo-Saxon Charters*, edited by A. J. Robertson (Cambridge, 1939), 158–61). Professor Stenton has suggested that the granting of such exceptional privileges may have been occasioned by an especially important event, namely the translation of the martyred St Ælfheah from London to Canterbury under Cnut's protection (F. M. Stenton, *The Latin Charters of the Anglo-Saxon Period* (Oxford, 1955), 17).

[10] D. Gardiner, *Historic Haven: the Story of Sandwich* (Derby, 1954), 41–4; Christ Church Canterbury, *Chartae Antiquae*, S266–282; Register H. fos. 161–85. In his old age Laurence the Clerk dictated a table of the customs of the port of Sandwich (Register H. fos. 161–3).

[11] Gardiner, *op. cit.*, 37–40. The reign of Edward I was notable for the number of ports which were taken into the King's hands or refounded by him, cf. Winchelsea, Dartmouth and Hull, below.

render account at the Exchequer for all the issues of the bailiwick. He was to receive the considerable wage of 1/- per day for his services.[12] The detailed accounts which Helpestone rendered for the local custom and other town revenues survive for the years 1299 to 1304.[13]

The duties of the royal bailiff of Sandwich at this time are described by Adam Champeneys, the Town Clerk, in his *Consuetudines et Usus Ville Sandwici*, written in 1301[14]. The bailiff, after being admitted to office, was to appoint a deputy or sergeant and the king's dues were to be collected by these officials or by a collector appointed for that purpose.[15] Relations between the royal bailiffs and the townspeople of Sandwich and other Cinque Ports were often uneasy.[16] Champeneys reveals the suspicion with which the bailiff was regarded when he says that if the latter 'produces letters close, or even if he has letters patent and will not be sworn as is aforesaid' (to faithfully execute his office and maintain the estate of the king with due regard to the liberty of Sandwich), 'he is not looked upon as bailiff until he has complied with all forms'. Furthermore, the mayor and jurats of the town were to remonstrate with the bailiff if he exacted higher duties from merchant strangers than were customary and, if he persisted in these malpractices, the merchants were to be advised to seek redress in the king's courts. Champeneys did, however, suggest that it was good for the mayor and the bailiff to be on amicable terms, 'because each in his office might derive advantage from the other's friendship and advice'.[17]

Helpestone's successors in the early fourteenth century held office on the same terms as he had done.[18] In 1315, however, the castle and bailiwick were committed to Nicholas le Archer of Dover for an annual rent of 100 marks.[19] The bailiwick and its revenues were farmed out on several other occasions during the fourteenth century and this probably accounts for some of the gaps which occur in the series of bailiff's accounts at this time.[20] Several of the bailiffs were men of Sandwich, one of whom received, in 1340, a grant of the bailiwick for himself and his heirs.[21]

In the fifteenth century there was a reversion to the earlier practice of granting the bailiff a fixed wage.[22] There was also a return to the system of regular accounting at the Exchequer for the receipts of the town and port, and a full series of bailiff's accounts survives from *c.* 1410 to the latter part of the century.[23]

The early sixteenth century witnessed the progressive decline of Sandwich as a port[24] and this was for a time reflected in the bailiff's accounts which became more summary as the customs receipts dwindled. The accounts for 1524–30, rendered at the Exchequer by the then bailiff, Sir

---

[12] Gardiner, *op. cit.*, 39–40; W. Boys, *Collections for an History of Sandwich in Kent* (Canterbury, 1792), 441; *C.F.R.*, *1272–1307*, 290.

[13] P.R.O., Exchequer K.R. Customs Accts. 124/5, 6, 12, 14. The final, summary account is in Ministers Accts. 894/22.

[14] With later additions. Printed in Boys, *op. cit.*, 428–581.

[15] *Ibid.*, 434–5, 442.

[16] K. M. E. Murray, *The Constitutional History of the Cinque Ports* (Manchester, 1935), 6.

[17] Boys, *op. cit.*, 434–5.

[18] *C.F.R.*, *1272–1307*, 500–1; *ibid.*, *1307–19*, 8.

[19] *Ibid.*, *1307–19*, 236.

[20] No accounts have survived for 34 Edw. I to 15 Edw. III, 27 to 42 Edw. III and 49 Edw. III to 1 Hen. V. Those surviving are in P.R.O., Ministers Accts. 894–5.

[21] John, son of William Condy, who received the grant, 'for good service and in recompense of the ransom of John de Eyle whom he took in a naval battle off the port of Swyne', (battle of Sluis). In 1346 arrangements were made for deputies to keep the bailiwick during the minority of John's heir (*Calendar of Patent Rolls* [hereafter *C.P.R.*] *1340–3*, 18; *C.F.R.*, *1337–47*, 450–3). The bailiwick passed out of the family's hands in 1355 (*C.P.R.*, *1354–8*, 300). For a period after 1357 the bailiff again received 1/- per day (*C.F.R.*, *1358–68*, 58).

[22] £24 p.a. in 1438 (*C.P.R.*, *1434–41*, 153). The fifteenth-century bailiffs were mostly officials of the royal household and grants were usually for life (*C.P.R.*, *1441–6*, 160; *ibid.*, *1467–77*, 108; *ibid.*, *1485–94*, 275, 469).

[23] P.R.O., Ministers Accts. 895–6.

[24] Largely due to sandbanks forming in the harbour (Murray, *op. cit.*, 208–10).

Edward Ryngeley, record only the commodities on which local custom was charged and omit the names of merchants and the other details which are to be found in earlier accounts.[25] Accounts are lacking between 1531 and 1537 and when they re-appear in 1538 they are even more summary in form. During the period 1531 to 1542 the bailiwick was farmed by Ryngeley to the corporation which appointed deputies to act as bailiffs.[26] Fully detailed accounts are to be found again from 1546 onwards.[27]

The port of Winchelsea was, like Sandwich, in monastic hands until the thirteenth century. The Norman abbey of Fécamp held the port and its tolls by virtue, so it was claimed, of a charter of Cnut.[28] In the twelfth century an agreement was made between Henry I and the abbot of Fécamp to share the tolls on ships at Winchelsea.[29] In 1247 both Winchelsea and Rye were surrendered to the Crown by the abbey, on the grounds that the latter could not fortify the ports adequately in time of war.[30] Two years later both towns were farmed to their respective barons and burgesses, but this arrangement was not lasting and the farms were granted to a number of individuals for short periods in the years immediately following.[31] In 1265 the custody of both towns was committed to Stephen de Pencestre who was deputed by Prince Edward to keep them on his behalf.[32] This was probably the reason why an account was rendered by the bailiff of Winchelsea at the Exchequer for its issues (including local customs), in 1267.[33] This is the earliest detailed account for local customs to survive. Such accounts were rendered until 1275 and two years later Winchelsea was farmed out for 40 marks annually.[34] At this time the port was being threatened by coastal erosion and its ruin was completed by a storm in February 1288. In the following June the barons of the town were confirmed in their possession of a new site for the town at Iham.[35] A few years later the bailiff of New Winchelsea was accounting at the Exchequer for the local customs and other town revenues in the same manner as had been done for the old town.[36]

In the fourteenth century, as at Sandwich, the profits of the bailiwick were sometimes farmed and sometimes accounted for at the Exchequer, with the result that there are gaps in the series of accounts.[37] The bailiffs at this time were usually men of Winchelsea and held their office during pleasure.[38] Between 1360 and 1380 Winchelsea suffered greatly from French attacks, culminating in the sacking of the town in the latter year.[39] The last extant bailiff's account is for 1371-2 and in 1374 the local customs and tolls, including 'shares, anchorage and bulgage' on ships and boats, and

[25] P.R.O., Exchequer K.R. Various Accts. 518/45, partly printed in Gras., *op. cit.*, 194-8. In the late fifteenth and sixteenth centuries the custom seems to have been levied almost entirely on the goods of alien merchants and in 1530 is called 'le bailage from alien merchants'. For the grant of the bailiwick to Ryngeley see *Letters and Papers, Hen. VIII*, IV, pt. 1, 86 (28).
[26] Boys, *op. cit.*, 424.
[27] P.R.O., Exchequer K.R. Various Accts. 518/45. In 1547 the bailiff received 1/- per day as had his predecessor in 1299 (P.R.O., Exchequer K.R. Customs Accts. 130/17, 218/35).
[28] Cnut's charter grants to the abbey 'the land called Rammesleah with the port and all things pertaining to it'. 'Rammesleah' included Winchelsea and Rye. The text of the charter, which survives in a cartulary of the abbey, also contains a grant of 'two parts of the toll in the port which is called Winchenesel' but this is probably a later interpolation (C. H. Haskins, 'A Charter of Canute for Fécamp', *English Historical Review* (1918), 343-4).
[29] *V.C.H. Sussex*, IX, 62.
[30] *Ibid.*, 50.
[31] *Ibid.*, 51; *Calendar of Close Rolls*[hereafter C.C.R.], *1253-4*, 197; *ibid.*, *1261-4*, 315.
[32] *C.P.R., 1258-66*, 507.
[33] Bailiff's accounts survive for 1267-75 (P.R.O., Ministers Accts. 1031/19-24).
[34] *C.F.R., 1272-1307*, 79.
[35] Murray, *op. cit.*, 208; *V.C.H. Sussex*, IX, 63.
[36] Bailiff's accounts, 1293-1307 (P.R.O., Ministers Accts. 1031/25-6, 1032/1).
[37] The accounts are extant for 1342-6, 1350-8, 1365-72 (P.R.O., Ministers Accts. 1032/2-13).
[38] *C.F.R., 1272-1307*, 545; *ibid.*, *1307-19*, 104, 215, 322; *ibid.*, *1319-27*, 18, 23, 379; *ibid.*, *1337-47*, 212, 244, 331; *ibid.*, *1347-56*, 144, 277, 293, 393.
[39] *V.C.H., Sussex*, IX, 66-7.

other 'petty customs' were leased for four years to the parson of St. Thomas, Winchelsea for a rent of only 43/9 annually, an indication of the extent to which the trade of the port had declined.[40] From the late fourteenth century onwards the bailiwick of the town was usually granted to royal officials. In 1506 the Crown finally resigned its rights in Winchelsea by a grant of the bailiwick and all the customs to Sir Richard Guldeford in tail male.[41]

Rye, as we have seen, was taken into the hands of the Crown in the same year (1247) as Winchelsea. The two ports were held in joint custody until 1275 when the farm of Rye was granted to Queen Eleanor.[42] The earliest surviving Rye bailiff's accounts, for 1272–4, record receipts from 'petty customs', such as are to be found in the Winchelsea accounts of the same period.[43] In 1289 the bailiwick of Rye was committed to Robert Paulyn of Winchelsea, who also held the bailiwick of Winchelsea and Iham from 1317 onwards.[44] The bailiwicks were held jointly from this time until 1358.[45] The few surviving Rye bailiff's accounts for this period record receipts for the custom of 'shares' on fishing boats, but not for any general customs on commodities of trade.[46]

In 1358 the bailiff of Winchelsea was ordered to surrender the office of bailiff of Rye to William Taillour of that town, who was to answer for its issues at the Exchequer.[47] Taillour's accounts for 1362–4 record receipts of 'shares, anchorage, and bulcage' on ships, and 'petty customs' on a number of commodities.[48] These accounts suggest that Rye was in a rather more prosperous state than Winchelsea at this time, and the decay of Winchelsea appears to have brought a further increase of trade to Rye in the fifteenth century.[49] Between 1374 and 1379 the bailiwick was leased out to various individuals at from £18 to £20 annually and in 1382 it was leased to the town for the latter amount, for thirteen years.[50]

The office of bailiff of Rye, which had never been as important as that of Winchelsea, eventually became the perquisite of local magnates.[51] The town, however, collected some of the local tolls, and occasional receipts from these are entered in the town 'Chamberlain's Account Books' which are extant from 1448.[52]

At Dartmouth, unlike the Cinque Ports, the evidence for local customs does not appear to go back beyond the late thirteenth century. In 1275 a jury there testified that 'the port of Dertemouth and the water channel were free from all customs to all men coming to and passing that port up to the death of King Henry (III) . . . and then came William de Cantelowe, lord of Totton (Totnes) and Eva his wife and appropriated the said water channel and there the aforesaid William and Eva levied many different customs on account of that water, throughout the whole port'–here the rates of custom are specified–'by what warrant they know not'.[53] Seven years later the succeeding owner of the 'waterway of Dertemue', Milisent de Monte Alto, was also challenged as to her right to levy customs there and she replied that she held them as part of the inheritance of Cantilupe (or

[40] The grant was renewed for ten years in 1378 (C.F.R., 1369–77, 261; ibid., 1377–83, 108).

[41] V.C.H., Sussex, IX, 68.

[42] C.P.R., 1272–81, 91, 104–6.

[43] P.R.O., Ministers Accts. 1028/8–9. The Rye accounts are, however, less detailed than those of Winchelsea.

[44] C.F.R., 1272–1307, 258; ibid., 1307–19, 322.

[45] C.F.R., 1319–27, 18, 23, 376, 379; ibid., 1337–47, 212, 244, 331; ibid., 1347–56, 144, 277, 393.

[46] The accounts are for 1342–5 (P.R.O., Ministers Accts. 1028/11–13).

[47] C.F.R., 1356–68, 71.

[48] P.R.O., Ministers Accts. 1028/15.

[49] V.C.H. Sussex, IX, 54.

[50] C.F.R., 1369–77, 262–3, 298; ibid., 1377–83, 67, 125, 133, 290.

[51] V.C.H. Sussex, IX, 50.

[52] H.M.C. 5th Rept., Appendix, 490–3. It would appear that in the sixteenth century local custom was again being levied on behalf of the Crown (R. F. Dell (ed.), Rye Shipping Records 1566–1590 (Sussex Record Society, vol. LXIV, xxxiii).

[53] Hundred Rolls 4 Edw. I, printed in H. R. Watkin, Dartmouth, vol. I., Pre-Reformation (The Devonshire Association, 1935), 353.

Cantilowe).[54] In 1306 William la Zusche, the then lord of the manor of Totnes, granted his lord-ship of the port of Dartmouth and the water of the Dart to Nicholas de Tewkesbury, a clerk of the royal household. Nicholas in his turn conveyed the port and water rights to the king in 1327.[55]

The water of the Dart and its profits were granted in 1333 to John, earl of Cornwall and they remained continuously in the possession of the Duchy of Cornwall from this time.[56] In 1345 the Crown (as holder of the Duchy) appointed John Shroop to the office of water bailiff in the ports of Sutton and Dartmouth, to hold the same for life, receiving 'the fees and profits customary.'[57] The subsequent water bailiffs, in the fourteenth and fifteenth centuries, were mostly royal ser-vants who held office on the same terms as Shroop.[58] There is no evidence that they accounted for their receipts of local customs and other revenues at the Exchequer and, indeed, the terms of their patents did not require them to do so.[59]

The corporation of Dartmouth did not acquire possession of the bailiff's office until 1505, when it was surrendered to the Crown by the then bailiff William Symondes, who was a clerk of the royal scullery. The mayor and burgesses were to pay 12 marks a year for the office during Symondes' lifetime, and afterwards 22 marks a year, payable to the Receiver General of the Duchy at Lost-withiel.[60] The first surviving water bailiff's account dates from 1508 and is preserved in the Duchy of Cornwall Office.[61] In 1510 the grant of the office of bailiff to the corporation was made per-petual and, although the validity of this grant was later disputed, the corporation retained the office until 1860 by a series of leases from the Duchy.[62] Some light is thrown on the administration of the Dartmouth local customs by a letter under the Privy Seal of 1521, which authorized the mayor and his deputies to search all ships entering the port and its creeks and to examine the national customs books, so that the town should not be defrauded of its rightful dues.[63] The series of water bailiff's accounts continues with few gaps from 1537 onwards.[64]

The early history of the local customs of Bristol is much more obscure than that of the ports already mentioned. The farm of Bristol and its issues was held by the men of the town from 1227 to 1261, but the nature of these issues was not specified.[65] In 1313 the office of 'sergeant of the water' of Bristol was granted to William Vyvyan for good service to the Crown,[66] and when, in 1320, Hugh le Despenser the younger received a grant of the custody of Bristol, he was ordered to pay the 'keeper of the water' 26/8 annually.[67] During the remainder of the fourteenth and the early fifteenth century (except for short periods), the farm and bailiwick of town and port were held by successive Queens of England.[68] The office of 'sergeanty of the sea water' or 'water bailiff' was

[54] *Ibid.*, 11.

[55] *Ibid.*, 19, 28. It has been suggested that the eventual acquisition of the port by the king had been intended from the time when it was granted to Nicholas de Tewkesbury (P. Russell, *Dartmouth* (London, 1950), 7).

[56] Russell, *op. cit.*, 7; Watkin, *op. cit.*, 355.

[57] Watkin, *op. cit.*, 45.

[58] *Ibid.*, 369, 372, 374, 391, 394, 399, 401, 407–8, 411.

[59] In 1468, however, it was alleged that recent bailiffs had failed to account at the Exchequer for the 'issues and profits of the water, fishery, wreck and haven' although required to do so (Watkin, *op. cit.*, 402–3).

[60] *Ibid.*, 411.

[61] The account is for 1508–11 (*Ibid.*, 412). Seventy volumes of these accounts, dating between 1508 and 1860, were handed over by the corporation to the Duchy office in 1866, as the corporation had ceased to hold the bailiwick after 1860 (Russell, *op. cit.*, 56).

[62] Watkin, *op. cit.*, 412; Russell, *op. cit.*, 56–7.

[63] It was said that such searches had been made by sub-bailiffs when the office of bailiff had been in private hands in the previous reign (Watkin, *op. cit.*, 412–4).

[64] There is a gap between 1511 and 1537 (*Ibid.*, 412).

[65] *C.P.R.*, *1225–32*, 107; *ibid.*, *1232–4*, 47; *ibid.*, *1247–58*, 570.

[66] *Ibid.*, *1307–13*, 569.

[67] *Ibid.*, *1317–21*, 514.

[68] H. Bush, *Bristol Town Duties* (Bristol, 1828), 5–8.

granted during this period by the queen to royal servants, usually for life, and the grants were confirmed by the Crown by letters patent.[69] Thomas 'Wesenham', a sergeant of the pantry, who became water bailiff in 1434, was to discharge his office in person or by deputy and was to receive the usual 'fees, wages and profits'.[70]

On the death of Queen Joan in 1437, the issues of the town escheated to the Crown and the only surviving Bristol local customs account dates from this time. This account, for 1437–8, was rendered at the Exchequer by Clement Bagot, who was mayor and escheator of the town. It shows that a wide range of local customs was being levied in the port at that time.[71] In January 1439 the office of water bailiff was re-granted to Thomas 'Wesingham', who was to take 'dues in the said water . . . as other "waterbailiffs" have in lesser ports . . . such as Plymouth, Dartmouth and Sandwich.'[72] Later in the same year the town, with its 'local tolls . . . fairs, markets, waters, rivers' and other issues, was committed to the mayor and community.[73] It is not clear whether the local customs were shared at this time between the town and the water bailiffs, who continued to be appointed by the Crown.[74] In 1519 all tolls on ships and merchandise were granted to the sheriffs of the town, who held them until 1640.[75]

Turning to the second group of 'king's ports', those which were granted their local customs with their fee farms, we find four, Southampton, Exeter, Yarmouth and Chester, where long series of local customs accounts have survived *in situ*. Southampton received the grant of its fee farm and local customs in 1199.[76] In the fourteenth century it was claimed that these customs had been levied in the town during the whole time in which it had been in royal hands prior to 1199.[77] The administration of the local customs remained in the control of the town and its officials throughout the later Middle Ages, except for a few short periods when the town was taken into the hands of the Crown for alleged misdemeanours.[78]

Considerable light is thrown on the early administration of its local customs by the Southampton Oak Book Ordinances of *c*. 1300. The collection of the customs was entrusted to two bailiffs, chosen annually from the most 'profitables et sachaunz' men of the town.[79] The method of accounting was laid down as follows: 'every entry of a ship and of customable goods and every outgoing (of goods) from the town and of customable goods going out by sea, shall be enrolled, so that at the end of the week the amount (of the customs) of the town may be known . . . and then that amount shall be enrolled in a double roll, so that the chief alderman shall have one roll and the bailiffs another'.[80] The ordinances forbade the lending of money by the bailiffs from the customs receipts and the taking of pledges for payment of custom.[81] Despite these prohibitions, which were

[69] *C.P.R.*, *1327–30*, 443; *ibid.*, *1334–8*, 226; *ibid.*, *1354–8*, 13; *ibid.*, *1399–1401*, 67.

[70] *C.P.R.*, *1429–36*, 332.

[71] The account is printed in Bush, *op. cit.*, 9–25.

[72] *C.P.R.*, *1436–41*, 229.

[73] *C.F.R.*, *1437–45*, 85–90. This grant was made perpetual in 1462 (*C.P.R. 1461–7*, 170).

[74] John Berewe was appointed bailiff in 1456 on the same terms as Wesingham (*C.P.R.*, *1452–61*, 350).

[75] Bush, *op. cit.*, 48, 75.

[76] H. W. Gidden (ed.), *The Charters of the Borough of Southampton* (Southampton Record Society, 1909) I, 12. The charter, like those for other ports, speaks vaguely of the 'liberties and free customs' of the town, but in disputes with other towns over the payment of local customs it was accepted that Southampton received them by this charter, cf. dispute between Southampton and Marlborough in 1239 (*Calendar of Charter Rolls, 1226–57*, 244).

[77] e.g. testimony of a jury in a dispute with Lymington in 1328 (T. Madox, *Firma Burgi*, (London, 1726), 220–2).

[78] As in 1276, 1285 and 1338 (J. S. Davies, *History of Southampton* (Southampton, 1883), 33, 35; A. A. Ruddock, *Italian Merchants and Shipping in Southampton* (Southampton Record Series, 1951), 32–3.

[79] 'Profitable and witty' in a translation of 1473 (P. Studer (ed.), *The Oak Book of Southampton* (Southampton Record Society, 1910–11), I, 44, 91).

[80] *Ibid.*, I, 46.

[81] *Ibid.*, I, 47, 127.

repeated in later sets of ordinances, the bailiffs frequently entered pledges for custom in the fifteenth century accounts and many of them were probably guilty of lending customs money, as is suggested by the number of accounts which remain permanently in arrears.

None of the weekly enrolled accounts, as described in the ordinance, has survived, but annual accounts are extant for the years 1339 to 1342. In October 1338, the government of the town was taken out of the hands of the mayor and burgesses because of their failure to defend it against an attack made by the French and Genoese earlier in the same year.[82] The town was recommitted to the mayor and burgesses in March 1339, on condition that they answered at the Exchequer for 'the issues and all other profits thereof and the liberty thereof',[83] hence the survival of these accounts amongst the Exchequer records.[84] The accounts, rendered by the mayor and one bailiff, record the local custom, which was collected both at Southampton and its member ports which included Portsmouth and Lymington.[85] In December 1342 the town and its revenues were granted to Queen Isabella for life, and the accounts cease after that date.[86]

The next extant Southampton local account is the first of the (misleadingly) named 'Port Books', dated 1426-7, and there is a series of such books surviving from this time onwards.[87] The Port Books are mostly final accounts, compiled from rough preliminary returns and presented for audit at the end of the bailiff's year of office. By the fifteenth century the collection of port customs had become the responsibility of one of the bailiffs only, and he received an annual wage of £6 13 4.[88] From at least 1438 the bailiff was assisted by a clerk, who at first received part of the wage but, by 1450, was being paid the full £6 13 4 and by then seems to have been carrying out most of the bailiff's functions.[89] An ordinance of 1505 deprived the bailiff of one of the last of his practical duties, laying down that henceforth 'the water bayle shall resseive no money growinge yn his office but his clerke to find suerte to the Town, and he to ressave the money and weekly to accompt before the meyer'.[90] Presumably the clerk, or 'petty customer' as he was now called, was more amenable to the control of the town authorities than the bailiff, who was usually one of the leading men of the town.

The fifteenth-century Southampton local customs system was more highly developed, both in its administration and the range of its customs duties and special tolls, than any other local customs system for which evidence has survived. Custom was levied at both specific and *ad valorem* rates and the tolls included anchorage and keelage on ships, and cranage, wharfage, pontage, and ostilege on imported and exported goods. The Port Books are the earliest of such local accounts in book form and are far more detailed in their content than the contemporary customs rolls of other ports.[91]

The mayor and citizens of Exeter claimed the right to levy 'petty customs' on imported

[82] Ruddock, *Italian Merchants, op. cit.*, 32-3.

[83] *C.F.R., 1337-47*, 124.

[84] P.R.O., Exchequer K. R. Customs Accts. 137/8, 10-12; 193/10.

[85] The limits of the port were specified in 1328 as being from Hurst in the west to Langstone in the east (Madox *op. cit.*, 220-2).

[86] *C.P.R., 1340-3*, 572.

[87] There are books for some twenty years of the remainder of the fifteenth century (Southampton Corporation MSS). There is no early warrant for the title 'Port Books' and they were probably so-called in the nineteenth century because of their resemblance to sixteenth-century Exchequer 'Port Books'.

[88] P. Studer (ed.), *The Port Books of Southampton, 1427-30* (really 1426-30), (Southampton Record Society, 1913), 119.

[89] See the audit pages of the MS. Port Books, 1438 onwards.

[90] A. B. Wallis-Chapman (ed.), *The Black Book of Southampton* (Southampton Record Society, 1912-15), II, 61.

[91] The origins and administration of the local custom and special tolls of Southampton are discussed more fully in the present writer's edition of *The Local Port Book of Southampton for 1439-40* (Southampton Record Series, vol. v, 1961).

goods, by virtue of the grant to the town of the fee farm and the port and its members by Edward III.[92] Since, however, the earliest extant Exeter local Customs Rolls date from the reign of Edward I, it seems probable that, in the thirteenth century, these customs were collected as part of a grant of the fee farm made to the town by Richard, earl of Cornwall in 1259.[93]

In the latter part of the thirteenth century, the river below Exeter was narrowed to a channel some 20 feet wide by the weirs constructed there by order of Isabella de Fortibus, countess of Devon. Hugh Courtenay, Isabella's successor, had even this channel blocked and after this, Topsham, some three miles down river, became Exeter's port.[94] The port of Topsham belonged by prescription to the earls of Devon,[95] and Hugh Courtenay was said to have built a quay with a crane there and to have compelled all merchants to load and discharge their merchandise upon it. In spite of this, Exeter had a bailiff at Topsham from the early fourteenth century onwards, to collect 'the towne custome for all kynde of wares and marchandyses dyscharged within the porte or Ryver or the members thereof'.[96] The bailiff accounted for the custom to the receiver of Exeter, whose name appears at the head of the fifteenth-century Customs Rolls. The series of these rolls extends from the reign Edward I to 1610, with a few gaps.[97]

A sixteenth-century description of the duties of the bailiff at Topsham shows him to have had wide powers there. He was to have the custody of the quay and river and 'to gather and recover and collecte all manner of issues, profits and duties whatsoever doth apperteyn to the Queenes Majestie, or the mayor, bayliffe and commonaltie of the citie of Exon now farmors to the same, and yerely at the tyme of the yere apoynted he to give a trewe, iuste and proper accompt of the same'. The bailiff was also to hold courts of piepowder and admiralty and to act as coroner upon the quay and within its liberties.[98]

At Yarmouth the burgesses dated their right to levy local customs from the grant of the fee farm in 1208.[99] The earliest record of receipts from these customs is contained in the 'Pix', or 'Treasury', Roll of 1312. The local Customs Rolls begin in 1331 and continue in a regular series until 1605.[100] They have the appearance of being final accounts, probably written up at the end of the year and their membranes are attached to those of the Court, Recognizance and other borough rolls for the year, in Exchequer style. From 1352 the Customs Rolls are headed, 'Memoranda Rolls of the Customs and other issues of the water'. By the sixteenth century the customs rolls were being compiled from draft accounts which were entered in the Chamberlain's Books.

The fourteenth-century rolls are headed with the names of four bailiffs, who presumably shared the work of collecting and recording the customs and tolls. In the fifteenth century two bailiffs and two chamberlains jointly rendered each account. A town ordinance of 1491 laid down that the chamberlains were to choose a water bailiff who was to receive an annual wage of 33/4 and

---

[92] Hale, op. cit., 138.

[93] After litigation lasting from 1324 to 1332, this grant was declared invalid, on the grounds that the earl had never possessed a status in the city which would entitle him to grant such privileges. It was then stated that in the time of Henry III and earlier, the city was of Ancient Demesne and was answered for at the Exchequer by the sheriff of Devon. The city and its farm were therefore taken into the king's hands, but subsequently the farm was regranted to the mayor and citizens for £20 rent annually (Calendar of Charter Rolls, 1327–41, 259–60).

[94] W. J. Harte, J. W. Schopp, H. Tapley-Soper (eds.), The Description of the Citie of Excester by John Vowell alias Hoker (Devon and Cornwall Record Society, 1919), II, 32–4.

[95] Hale, op. cit., 56.

[96] Harte, Schopp and Tapley-Soper, op. cit., 32–4.

[97] Exeter Corporation MSS. The membranes of the earliest rolls are rather confused in order, comprising accounts of Edward I and II.

[98] The commonplace Book of John Vowell c. 1580–92. (Exeter Corporation MS. Book 51), fos. 54–5.

[99] Hale, op. cit., 61; A. Ballard, British Borough Charters 1042–1216, 230.

[100] They are described and listed in P. Rutledge, Handlist of the Archives of Great Yarmouth Corporation of date before 1835 preserved in the Town Clerk's Department (list reproduced by the Historical Manuscripts Commission, 1965), 10–11, 21–64.

a gown. The chamberlains were to collect, with the bailiff's assistance, 'all manner of rentys . . . customes by water and land and all murages'.[101]

Chester, as a palatinate port, differed in status from the royal ports already mentioned, but since it became a crown fief in 1237 it would seem reasonable to consider its local customs system together with theirs. Between 1274 and 1280, when the receipts of the earldom belonged to the king as earl, the Pipe Roll accounts for Cheshire show that 'small tolls and custom of ships and boats' comprised part of the issues of the city. In 1300 the citizens obtained the fee-farm of the city in perpetuity with all 'appurtenances, liberties and free customs' which would undoubtedly have included the right to levy tolls and customs in the port. Further evidence is lacking as to the nature of Chester's local customs system until 1398, the date of the first surviving local customs account. This shows that the sheriffs of the city were responsible for the collection of local customs which they entered in the Sheriffs' and Mayors' Books together with proceedings in the civic courts, recognizances, fines and other matters. During the early sixteenth century most of the non-commercial entries disappeared from the Sheriffs' Books so that by the reign of Henry VIII they can be regarded virtually as local port books. The fifteenth and early sixteenth-century accounts are fair copies written up annually from original returns, but from late in the reign of Henry VIII the entries are in a rough hand and are probably a day-to-day record of the customs levied.[102]

Local customs accounts are unfortunately lacking for the other 'king's ports'. The most important of these is London, which had been granted its sheriffdom with 'all things and customs which pertain to (it) . . . by land and water', in 1199.[103] The sheriffs and their officials were responsible for raising the farm of £300 annually from the profits of the courts, the customs and other taxes. The form of the oath administered to the under-sheriffs in the early fourteenth century shows that they were allowed to farm the customs and it would appear that this was the regular practice, hence the absence of accounts for the customs collected.[104]

Hull was founded in the late twelfth century by the abbey of Meaux and it would appear that the abbey's bailiffs administered the town during the first century of its existence. In 1293 Hull was acquired from Meaux Abbey by Edward I (who probably needed an adequate supply port in the north) and it was governed on the king's behalf by a royal keeper who was sometimes styled 'bailiff'. The town was freed from the authority of the royal keeper by a charter of 1331 which granted the fee farm to the mayor and bailiffs for £70 per annum. In 1382 a further royal charter extended the town's jurisdiction to the haven of the river Hull. During the fourteenth century Hull received a number of royal grants of tolls for 'pavage and murage' on goods coming to the town for sale, by sea as well as by land, and it appears that these tolls may have developed into local customs as they continued to be collected after the expiration of the last grant in 1406. In 1423–4 the chamberlains, who recorded annual receipts of 'pavage and murage', substituted the words 'tolls and measures in the water' for them in their accounts. An officer known as a 'brogger' was responsible for collecting the 'tolls in the water' during the fifteenth century and towards the end of that century he began to be known as the 'water-bailiff'. Although receipts from these tolls were recorded by the chamberlains in the corporation records throughout the fifteenth century,

[101] H. Manship, *The History of Great Yarmouth*, edited by C. J. Palmer (Yarmouth, 1854–6), I, 358; II, 51. There had been a subsidiary official much earlier, who was known as the 'water bailiff' from 1405.

[102] The Chester local customs system is very fully described in K. P. Wilson (ed.), *Chester Customs Accounts, 1301–1566* (The Record Society of Lancashire and Cheshire, vol. CXI, 1969), 8–17. In the sixteenth century the sheriffs were assisted by a water-bailiff who acted as searcher for the city with power to arrest ships, merchandise and individuals in the Dee estuary (*Ibid.*, 10).

[103] Ballard, *op. cit.*, 220.

[104] S. L. Thrupp, *The Merchant Class of Medieval London* [1300–1500] (Chicago, 1948), 86–7. According to Hale 'tolls by water in London have been usually demised to their water-bailiff in farm' (Hale, *op. cit.*, 137).

detailed accounts of their collection do not appear to have survived and the rates of local custom were not set down until 1575.[105]

Ipswich received the grant of its fee farm in 1200[106] and a list of 'the custumys longyng to the ferme of the kyng of the toun of Gippeswych', compiled in about 1290, is preserved in the town's custumal.[107] In spite of this, no local customs accounts have survived, nor are they mentioned in a list of the town's records which was compiled c. 1330.[108]

No detailed local customs accounts have as yet come to light for those ports which, in the Middle Ages, were in the hands of private lords. Such a port was Lynn, which was held by the bishop of Norwich until 1536, when it and the bishop's other temporalities were vested in the Crown. In 1525 the 'ancient tolls and customs of the port' had been specified and confirmed to the bishop by patent. The burgesses of Lynn were granted the fee farm in 1557 and the earliest extant rolls of petty tolls date from the reign of Elizabeth.[109]

South coast ports in seignorial hands included Romney, Hythe and Lydd, which were subject to the control of the bailiffs of the Archbishop of Canterbury, as was Faversham to the bailiff of its abbot.[110] Weymouth belonged in the mid-thirteenth century to the church and convent of St Swithun, Winchester, who took customs there. An inquisition of 1367, however, revealed that the water of the Wey from the middle of the channel to Melcombe on the north bank then belonged to the king and the burgesses of the town, who took keelage and other customs there, whilst the southern half of the water and Weymouth belonged to the duke of Clarence, who had quayage of ships there and customs on goods.[111] There is no record of local customs at the ports of the Duchy of Cornwall, other than those levied at Dartmouth.[112]

Local customs records are equally lacking for the northern 'seignorial ports'. Thus Hartlepool belonged from the early fourteenth century to the bishop of Durham who had prisage of wine there, and the fifteenth-century accounts of the sheriff of Durham contain summary returns for this prise and for wreck and the farm of fisheries, but not for customs.[113]

The form and content of the accounts

The earliest detailed accounts for local customs, those of the bailiff of Winchelsea (from 1267 onwards), record the customs, tolls and other town revenues. The entries are arranged in weekly sections, each dated by the Saturday of the week and they contain the names of the shipmasters and of their home ports, the names of merchants and their towns, and the quantities of the commodities bought and sold in the town by each merchant. The tolls recorded include 'sede navis' and 'shares' levied on ships.[114] The mid-fourteenth-century Winchelsea rolls are rather less detailed, the

---

[105] V.C.H. Yorkshire East Riding, I (ed. K. J. Allison), 11–22, 26–8, 45–8. There are a few detailed accounts of the 'pavage and murage' collected in the fourteenth century (ibid., 46).

[106] Ballard, op. cit., 226.

[107] One version of which is printed in T. Twiss (ed.), The Black Book of the Admiralty (Rolls Series, 1873), II, 185–97.

[108] G. H. Martin, The Early Court Rolls of the Borough of Ipswich (Leicester Department of English Local History, Occasional Papers no. 5), 30. I am indebted to Mr D. Charman for ascertaining that no customs rolls have survived.

[109] H.M.C. 11th Report, Appendix, pt. III, 206–8, 212. The tolls were on goods coming to or from the town by water or by land, and were collected by the water bailiffs.

[110] Murray, op. cit., 5.

[111] H.M.C. 5th Report, Appendix, 575; Calendar of Inquisitions Miscellaneous, 1348–77, 246. The earliest extant Weymouth local customs accounts are for the late sixteenth century (H. J. Moule, Descriptive Catalogue of the Charters, etc. of the Borough of Weymouth (Weymouth, 1883), 150, 170–6).

[112] The Haveners' Accounts for the Duchy ports are for national customs, and for such receipts as profits of courts, prize of wine and wreck, e.g. accounts for 1404 (P.R.O., Ministers Accounts 818/13–14).

[113] Hale, op. cit., 55; P.R.O., Durham 20, 2–6.

[114] P.R.O., Ministers Accts. 1031/19–21. Two fragments of accounts printed by Gras, op. cit., 177–191, which he attributes to Sandwich, are identical in form with these and almost certainly relate to late thirteenth or early fourteenth-century Winchelsea.

entries being arranged in months and the home ports of the shipmasters are often omitted. The tolls at this time include anchorage, 'bulkage' and 'shares' on ships and there is also an *ad valorem* custom of 2d in the £1 on a few commodities.[115]

The Rye accounts for 1272–4 record weekly totals for 'petty customs', but omit details of the merchants and their goods. The accounts of the 1340s are also summary in form, giving only the names of those paying the custom of 'shares' on fishing boats, apart from certain tolls levied in the town, such as stallage. The account of 1362–4 is, however, more detailed and contains the names and ports of shipmasters paying anchorage and bulkage, and the quantities of the commodities on which custom was paid.[116]

The earliest Sandwich accounts are mostly confined to totals of customs collected, although one (for 1276) contains details of commodities.[117] The accounts of 1299–1304, however, supply details of shipmasters, merchants and commodities, and each entry is dated. Apart from custom, the accounts contain payments for anchorage and passage ('transverso') on ships.[118] The Sandwich accounts from the mid-fourteenth century onwards are less detailed, the entries being arranged by months and the names of shipmasters being omitted. A few commodities are valued for *ad valorem* custom of 2d in the £1. The account for 1469–72 is entered in a parchment book, the first to be in this form, and between 1488 and 1494 the bailiff entered the customs in a book which was rather in the nature of a diary.[119] The early sixteenth-century accounts are in general rather summary, that for 1524–30 recording only the amount of each commodity on which custom was charged, whilst the 1538–44 accounts merely give totals for the anchorage, lastage and petty custom received in the year.[120]

The Dartmouth accounts of 1508 onwards specify the name and date of entry of each ship, the names of the shipmasters and merchants and the goods customed.[121] The sole Bristol account, of 1437–8, gives full details of trade with the exception that the entries are not dated. This account also records consignments of goods which were free of custom.[122]

The earliest Southampton accounts (1339–42) are extremely summary and record only the amount of each commodity paying custom (weekly in 1339–40 and annually for 1340–2). They also contain entries for keelage and for custom collected at the member ports.[123] The fifteenth-century local 'Port Books' are detailed accounts, resembling in form the Exchequer 'particulars of customs'

[115] Namely iron, millstones and fish (P.R.O., Ministers Accounts 1032/11).

[116] P.R.O., Ministers Accounts 1028/8–9, 11–13, 15.

[117] Christ Church Canterbury, Chartae Antiquae S.266–282.

[118] P.R.O., Exchequer K.R. Customs Accts. 124/5, 6, 12, 14. The account for Michaelmas to December 1304 is printed in Gras, *op. cit.*, 167–72.

[119] P.R.O., Ministers Accounts 896/13; *ibid.*, Henry VII, 341–2. Between 1488 and 1494 separate accounts were rendered for the 'port' and the 'town'. In other years, although some accounts are headed 'port and town' and others 'town' only, the port customs would usually appear to be entered in both.

[120] P.R.O., Exchequer K.R. Various Accts. 518/45, partly printed in Gras, *op. cit.*, 194–9. The accounts are more detailed again, however, from 1546 onwards (K.R. Customs Accts. 130/17).

[121] Watkin, *op. cit.*, 412.

[122] Bush, *op. cit.*, 9–25.

[123] P.R.O. Exchequer K.R. Customs Accts. 137/8, 10–12; 193/10. The latter of these accounts is printed in Gras, *op. cit.*, 174–6. Extracts from the fourteenth-century Southampton, Winchelsea and Sandwich accounts are contained in a return made by the Treasurers and Barons of the Exchequer in 1391, as to 'what ancient customs were paid for each last of herring, pitch, tar, ashes and for boards called Eastland boards, together with the names of the merchants bringing the same merchandise into the kingdom of England in the time of Edward I and afterwards . . . and what kind of men were accustomed to be quit of such customs'. The return survives in Letters Patent of Exemplification of 1408, made for a Southampton burgess (H. W. Gidden (ed.), *The Sign Manuals and the Letters Patent of Southampton to 1422*, (Southampton Record Society, 1916), I, 74–89). The enquiry probably arose from a petition of Hanse merchants in 1391, complaining that the men of Southampton and Sandwich had 'newly and unlawfully' compelled them to pay certain tolls on herring, pitch, etc. 'over and above the ancient custom' and 'contrary to the charters and liberties granted to them by former kings' (*C.C.R. 1389–92*, 250).

of the same period. The 'Port Books' record the dates of entry and exit of each ship, the names of shipmasters and merchants and their ports or towns of origin, the quantities of commodities (and their value if they were subject to *ad valorem* custom), and a number of special tolls on ships and goods.[124] The books are divided into separate sections for the 'Northern' and 'Mediterranean' trades and are also notable for their detailed audit pages which show the payments made by the bailiffs and clerks, from their receipts, to the steward and other town officials and the allowances claimed by the bailiffs and clerks for their wages and for expenses incurred whilst in office.[125] The books record a proportion of the goods of merchants who were exempt from local custom and the entries also occasionally indicate the direction of trade.

The Exeter local customs rolls retain practically the same form from the late thirteenth to the sixteenth century. The entry of each ship is recorded, with details of the master, merchants and imported commodities. Custom is the only duty recorded and exports, being free of custom, are omitted from the rolls. The goods of 'free' merchants are frequently entered, but the direction of trade is not given.

The fourteenth-century Yarmouth customs rolls contain full details of the dates of entry and names of ships, the names of the masters and merchants and the quantities of imported and exported commodities. Besides custom, the rolls record 'segeagium' and anchorage on ships, and measurage, murage, cranage, and tronage on goods.[126] The form of the rolls deteriorates in the fifteenth century in that the entries are usually not dated and the merchants and their goods are not entered under the ships in which they were carried, the ships often being recorded together at the head of the roll. The direction of the trade is rarely recorded on the rolls and the goods of 'free' merchants are not entered, except on the few occasions when they were subject to the payment of special tolls such as cranage.

The earliest surviving Chester local customs accounts, for 1398 to 1420, rarely record ships arriving in the port but they contain details of merchants and commodities. From 1420 onwards the accounts record the name, home port and master of each ship and the date of its arrival, followed by the names of the merchants and the quantity of merchandise carried (expressed in horseloads or cartloads). Goods coming to the town by land for export are similarly recorded. After 1514 exports cease to be entered and the Chester local customs accounts are concerned solely with merchandise shipped into the port. The practice of describing imports by the horseload or cartload gives way at this time to a detailed itemization of commodities. Merchants exempt from custom are not fully recorded in the accounts until the reign of Henry VIII.[127]

The value of the accounts to the historian

Apart from the light which these accounts throw on the local administration of ports, they are also very valuable for their evidence of seaborne trade. The earliest Winchelsea local accounts of 1267 onwards pre-date the first detailed national customs accounts by a number of years. The earliest of such national accounts, those for the 'Ancient Custom' imposed in 1275, relate only to the export

[124] See page 222 above.

[125] Certain of the books have been printed: P. Studer (ed.), *The Port Books of Southampton 1426–30* (Southampton Record Society, 1913); B. Foster (ed.), *The Local Port Book of Southampton of 1435–36* (Southampton Record Series, VII, 1963); H. S. Cobb (ed.), *The Local Port Book of Southampton for 1439–40* (Southampton Record Series, V, 1961); D. B. Quinn, *The Port Books of Southampton for the reign of Edward IV (1469–81)*, (Southampton Record Society, 1937–8).

[126] Cranage and tronage were, in some years of the fifteenth century, entered on separate rolls (P. Rutledge, *op. cit.*, 21–64). Entries from the fourteenth to the sixteenth-century Yarmouth rolls, relating to Anglo-Dutch trade, are printed in H. J. Smit (ed.), *Bronnen Tot de Geschiedenis van den Handel met Engeland, Schotland en Ierland 1150–1485, 1485–1585* (The Hague, 1928–50).

[127] K. P. Wilson, *op. cit.*, 9–13. The accounts for 1404–5, 1467–8 and 1525–6 are printed in this volume (*Ibid.*, 103–142).

of wool, woolfells and hides.[128] The 'New Custom' of 1303 imposed an *ad valorem* duty ('petty custom') on all the goods (except those already customed) of alien merchants, and Exchequer accounts are extant for this custom from this time.[129] It was not, however, until the imposition of the subsidy of tunnage and poundage in 1350 that the national duties were levied on all the commodities of trade of both alien and denizen merchants and that, in consequence, the national customs accounts began to record as wide a range of trade as had the local accounts from their inception.[130]

The Exchequer Enrolled Accounts, which begin in 1279 for most ports, provide from that time onwards an almost unbroken record of the total amounts collected at each port for the various types of national customs. In the Enrolled Accounts separate figures are given for those commodities (wool, cloths, wine, hides and wax), on which specific duties were paid, but the other commodities are lumped together under the total amounts collected for petty custom and poundage.[131] The Exchequer 'particulars of customs', upon which the Enrolled Customs totals were based, have only survived in part and thus, even after 1350, the local customs accounts are a valuable source for details of the overseas trade of many ports.[132]

An especially valuable contribution which the local customs accounts make to the history of trade is the information which they give concerning medieval coastal trade. Unlike the national duties, local customs were usually levied upon both coastal and overseas trade without distinction. In the national customs system from the early fourteenth century onwards, traders were usually required to put themselves under bonds, to ensure against the exportation of English goods overseas under colour of coastal trade. They were released from these bonds on presentation of a certificate showing that the goods had been duly landed at an English port.[133] It was not until 1549 that these bonds and other such documents were regularly entered in 'certificate-books', which from that time onwards are the main source of evidence for the coastal trade.[134] Prior to 1549 the local customs accounts are the only records to provide an overall picture of the coastal trade of a particular port in any given year. The limitations of the local accounts must, however, be emphasized. Firstly, that series of accounts survives for only a few ports and even these contain many gaps. Secondly, the accounts seldom state the direction of the trade and indeed it is often difficult to distinguish the coastal trade from the overseas trade which is also recorded in them.[135] And lastly the accounts omit a great deal of denizen trade which was subject to many exemptions from local customs.[136] Nevertheless the local customs accounts constitute a valuable source for the history of both overseas and coastal trade in the later Middle Ages.

HENRY S. COBB

---

128 Gras, *op. cit.*, 62, 224–56.   129 *Ibid.*, 66, 265–413.   130 *Ibid.*, 85–8.

131 P.R.O. Exchequer L. T. R. Enrolled Customs Accts. Between 1279 and 1304 many of the accounts are on the L.T.R., Pipe and Chancellor's Rolls. Being compiled from the particulars of customs, the enrolled accounts omit the bulk of denizen trade until 1350.

132 Thus Exchequer 'particulars of customs' for Yarmouth survive for only thirty years of the fifteenth century, whilst Yarmouth local accounts survive for the majority of years of that century.

133 Gras, *op. cit.*, 145. Many of these bonds survive amongst the Exchequer records but they are not open to inspection.

134 A few earlier books survive, e.g. for Lynn from 1531 (Gras, *op. cit.*, 145).

135 The distinction can be made with some certainty when a local account and an Exchequer particular account survive for a port in the same year, e.g. as they do for Southampton in 1426–7, 1433–4, 1438–9 etc. Only the Southampton and Yarmouth local accounts contain any explicit indication of the direction of trade and even these do so only rarely.

136 The merchants of many towns claimed exemption on the ground that they had royal charters of general exemption from tolls which pre-dated the charters by which the ports were empowered to levy local customs. Merchants who were tenants, of Ancient Demesne, of many ecclesiastical estates and of Honours and other franchises, also claimed exemption. Only the Exeter, Southampton and Bristol accounts record such exempt merchants and their goods as a regular practice.

The Merchant Adventurers
and their Records

In 1933 Professor E. M. Carus-Wilson discovered in the first book of the Acts of Court of the Mercers' Company the only surviving medieval records of the Merchant Adventurers and in the same year she published an article in the *Economic History Review* entitled 'The Origin and Early Development of the Merchant Adventurers' Organisation in London as shown in their own medieval records'. Three years later the first book of the Acts of Court, which covers the period 1453–1527, was edited and published by Laetitia Lyell and Frank D. Watney, then Clerk to the Mercers' Company, and in the *Economic History Review*, vol. v, 1934/5, Miss Lyell published an article on 'The Problem of the Records of the Merchant Adventurers'.

In this article Miss Lyell put forward suggestions to account for the abrupt termination of the Merchant Adventurers' records in 1526. As she pointed out, the second book of the Mercers' Acts of Court contains no minutes of meetings of Adventurers and, basing her conclusions on an entry in that second book of Acts relating to the appointment of John Coke as Clerk to the Mercers' Company in 1527, she went on to suggest that by 1527, and perhaps earlier, the headquarters of the Merchant Adventurers had moved from London to the continent. Miss Lyell also referred to an inventory of 1547 in the British Museum[1] which describes itself as an inventory 'of all suche pryveleages grauntes and other munymentes as remayne in a cheste of woode bounden wt. yron bilonginge to the said fellawshipp of marchauntes Adventurers and standinge in the Inner Treasoury in the mercers halle wt. in the forsaid Cytie of london' and suggested that this too indicated that by 1547 the Merchant Adventurers no longer had their headquarters in London.

I have had occasion to make extensive use of the early books of the Acts of Court of the Mercers' Company and I have come across a number of additional entries relating to the Merchant Adventurers and their records. I have also made some study of the members of the Company and particularly of those who held office in the Company in the sixteenth century and the evidence thus acquired, together with other evidence gathered from records outside Mercers' Hall, has enabled me to supplement the information gleaned by Professor Carus-Wilson and Miss Lyell about the Merchant Adventurers and their records.

To start, as Miss Lyell did, with the appointment of John Coke as Clerk to the Mercers' Company, there are two entries in the Acts of Court relating to this matter. The first of these occurs on 17 July 1527,[2] and reads as follows:

---

[1] B. M. Sloane MS. 2103, f. 2. Printed by G. Schanz in *Englische Handelspolitik gegen Ende des Mittelalters*, Leipzig, 1881, vol. II, p. 574.

[2] Acts of Court of the Mercers' Company, 1527–60, f. 2. [Referred to henceforth as A. C.]

John Coke mercer and late Secretary to the Marchantes Aduenturers by consent of the right worshipfull Wardeyns Aldermen Assistentes and generaltie aforsaid for certeyn consideracions them mouyng Is admytted to the Rome of Clerke to the feliship of the Mercery wt. suche fees profites and aduantaiges as alwais hertofore hath apperteyned to the said office in as ample and Large maner as the fornamed John Eston Roberd Gedge or any other have enjoied and posseded the said Rome who Immediatly receyued thoth therto belongyng And admytted by semblable auctoritie into the Lyuerey of this Feliship.

The second occurs on 31 December 1527,[3] and reads:

For so moche as the fee profites aduantaiges and aduayles of the feliship of Marchantes Aduenturers Lately perceyued and had not oonly by John Eston sumtyme Clarke of this feliship of the Mercery but also by Robert Gedge and other hertofore enjoying the said office is wt. drawen and taken from the same Rome by meanes wherof the greatest partye of the lyvyng of the said office is decaied and mynysshed Wherfore it is ordeyned and agreed by the right Worshipfull Wardeyns and Assistentes at this present Courte assembled that John Coke nowe Clarke of this company to thentent he shuld aswell geue his attendance at the hall from tyme to tyme as nede requyreth As also applye hymself to the redusyng and bryngyng into good ordre sondry bokes belonging to this feliship shall haue and percyue yerely of the gifte of the forsaid company over and beside the wages and profites alwais accustumed and belongyng to his said office of Clarke to the mercery duryng his contynuance in the said office the somme of tenne poundes st. To be paid yerely by the seconde Wardeyn alwais for the tyme beyng. Prouyded alwais that if the said John Coke wt. his owne money can fynde the meanes to bye thoffice of waier of silke or oon of the meters of lynen cloth or otherwise can come to any of the said offices or any other by fauor and gifte of the company Or if it shall fortune the Marchantes Aduenturers hereafter to kepe here their assembles and courtes in like maner as hertofore they haue been used and accustumed by meanes wherof the same John may haue perceyue and enjoye the fee profites and aduantages afore rehersed That then this present annuytie to surcease and to be had of noon effect.

Two points of particular interest emerge from these two entries:
1. John Coke is described in the first entry as late Secretary to the Merchant Adventurers;
2. the fees and profits which previous Clerks to the Mercers' Company had received from the Merchant Adventurers evidently arose from courts and assemblies held at Mercers' Hall since it was specifically stated that, if these were resumed, then Coke's annuity of £10 was to cease.

The Acts of Court from 1453 to 1527 show that Coke was Clerk to the Merchant Adventurers at least as early as 1521 for at the Quarter Day on the 19th June in that year[4] '. . . . was redd a Supplycacion brought yn by John Coke Clerke unto the Marchauntes adventurers, theffect therof was desyryng to be a brother of this felyshipp, the whiche was to hym graunted, he paying for his entre as other doth'. Coke appears to have been a member of the Merchant Taylors' Company originally[5] and apparently thought it necessary to become a member of the Mercers' Company when he became Clerk to the Merchant Adventurers. From 1521 to 1527, therefore, the Merchant Adventurers had their own Clerk and the office was not combined with that of Clerk to the Mercers' Company for between 1516 and 1527 this latter office was held by John Eston.[6] Furthermore this is not the only period when the Merchant Adventurers had a Clerk of their own. In 1487 the Adventurers were reproved by the Lord Chancellor on behalf of the King because they had chosen John Colet '. . . . here reputed and called the Kynges rebell for that he to his Power there supported, maynteyned & set further the Kynges rebelles and traytours of late oute & from thoos parties' to be Clerk of their Fellowship.[7] The Adventurers were pardoned, however, and Colet remained their Clerk until 1497 at least.[8] During this period the Clerkship of the Mercers' Company was held by

---

[3] A.C., 1527–60, f. 8.

[4] *Acts of Court of the Mercers' Company, 1453–1527*, edited by Laetitia Lyell and Frank D. Watney, Cambridge University Press, 1936, p. 532. [Referred to henceforth as *L. & W.*]

[5] *L. & W.*, p. 457.

[6] *Ibid.*, pp. 437–44, 756.

[7] *Ibid.*, p. 300.

[8] *Ibid.*, p. 633.

John Pereson.[9] It seems reasonable to suppose that the appointment of a separate Clerk by the Merchant Adventurers followed the Act of Common Council passed on 22 March 1486/7,[10] and apparently amended on 6 April following,[11] which established the organization of the London Adventurers and which was dealt with fully by Professor Carus-Wilson in her article.

Between 1497 and 1521 it has not proved possible to identify a separate Clerk to the Merchant Adventurers and it may be that during this period the office was held jointly with that of Clerk to the Mercers' Company. Certainly the entry in the Acts of Court for 31 December 1527, quoted above, states that Robert Gedge, who was Clerk to the Mercers' Company between 1511 and 1516,[12] received fees from the Merchant Adventurers. But if the two offices had been held by one man then it would seem reasonable that some adjustment should have been made in John Eston's salary when John Coke was appointed Clerk to the Adventurers and there is no evidence that this was done. If John Eston went on receiving fees from the Adventurers between 1521 and 1527, during the time that Coke was their Clerk, what duties was he performing for them and why did they cease in 1527?

It is at this point that the form of the first Book of the Acts of Court of the Mercers' Company is worth some study. As Miss Lyell pointed out, this book does not contain the original Acts of Court but is a compilation from a number of books no longer in existence, made by William Newbold who was appointed Registrar to the Company in February 1522/3.[13] It is impossible, therefore, to say with any degree of certainty how the original Acts were made up but we are afforded some clues by the insertion, also mentioned by Miss Lyell, on two occasions of Acts for a period earlier than that with which Newbold was dealing at the time. Following the entry for the Quarter Day held on 18 March 1506/7,[14] Newbold wrote: 'Here Seessith thorder of this boke to vj olde bokes be past, whiche were found whan this boke was written hitherto and cowde neuer be herde of afore, whiche be of the yeres of oure lorde xiiij^{c}lxv, xiiij^{c}lxvj, xiiij^{c}lxxxj, xiiij^{c}lxxxv, xiiij^{c}lxxxvj & xiiij^{c}lxxxvij, and than ye shall fynde the boke of xv^{c}vij and so furth folowyng in order &c.' and following the entry for the Quarter Day held on 19 June 1523,[15] he wrote: 'Here sessyth the course of this boke unto vj olde bokes be past whiche were founde the xiiijth daye of June Anno xv^{c}xxv^o and coude neuer afore be found nor harde of afore whyche tyme thys boke was written hytherto. And they be of theis yeres Anno xiiij^{c}iiij^{xx}xiij^o, xiiij^{c}iiij^{xx}xv^o, xiiij^{c}iiij^{xx}xvj^o, xiiij^{c}iiij^{xx}xvij^o, xiiij^{c}iiij^{xx}xviij^o and xiiij^{c}iiij^{xx}xix^o'. In each case, that is to say, six books were found, each of which appears to have contained the Acts of Court for one year. If we look at these Acts, however, we find that they include Acts relating to the Merchant Adventurers as well as to the Mercers' Company. In other words, in each of these annual volumes the Acts of the Merchant Adventurers and of the Mercers' Company were recorded indiscriminately.

There is no reason to suppose that this state of affairs was any different in 1526/7, the last year for which we have any Acts of the Merchant Adventurers. The Courts of the Merchant Adventurers and of the Mercers' Company are recorded throughout that year, with one small exception, in strict chronological order, and no attempt has been made to group the Acts of the two Companies. The inference must surely be that the Acts were recorded by one Clerk and yet we know that in 1526/7 the Merchant Adventurers had their own Clerk. Is it not reasonable to conclude, therefore, that the minutes of the Merchant Adventurers were kept by the Clerk to the Mercers' Company down to 1526/7, as long as the Merchant Adventurers met at Mercers' Hall,

9 *Ibid.*, pp. 658–60.
10 Corporation of London Records Office, Journal 9, f. 101.
11 *Ibid.*, f. 102.
12 *L. & W.*, pp. 386, 441.
13 *Ibid.*, p. 556.
14 *Ibid.*, p. 277.
15 *Ibid.*, p. 572.

for which service he received fees from the Merchant Adventurers, and that the keeping of the minutes was not one of the duties performed by the Clerk to the Merchant Adventurers?

If we look at the duties which were performed by John Coke while he was Clerk to the Merchant Adventurers as recorded in the Acts of Court this contention does seem to be acceptable. On 10 January 1521/2,[16] the Adventurers decided to send a letter to their Treasurer overseas forbidding the sailing of ships for lack of safe conduct and giving authority to the Treasurer and to 'John Coke your Clerke there' to see that the order was carried out. On 27 February 1525/6,[17] John Coke was ordered to assist John Pakyngton, solicitor, and others appointed to examine the Intercourse between England and the Empire in order to settle a dispute about the types of cloth which were being exported to Bruges. On 5 March 1525/6,[18] it was decided that new ordinances should be drawn up for the Merchant Adventurers. Seven persons were appointed to draft these ordinances and it was also ordered 'that a boke therof may be drawne by John Coke Clerke unto the marchauntes adventurers ayens the next Courte of marchauntes adventurers when Maister Wardens shall thynke convenyent'. The new ordinances were read and approved at a General Court of the Adventurers held on 18 April 1526.[19] The Court also 'willed Maister Wardens that the Copie therof myght be sent over unto this Synxson Marte and by theym there to be perused and there at their Courte to be redde whanne it shalbe thought most convenyent and to put all suche thyng of theym in strength as shalbe by theym agreed uppon, the whiche Articles were delyvered unto John Cooke their Clerke'. From these entries it would appear that, as Clerk to the Merchant Adventurers, John Coke was largely concerned with legal and constitutional matters concerning the Merchant Adventurers and, moreover, that he frequently travelled abroad in the course of those duties.

Unfortunately the Acts of Court do not provide nearly so much information about the duties of John Colet when he was Clerk to the Merchant Adventurers but we do know that he was abroad on at least one occasion. On 15 September 1497,[20] the General Court of the Merchant Adventurers received 'iij lettres togeder closed to us brought fro John Etwell (then Governor) & John Colet, recityng of certen scottysshippes of warr in Seeland &c.'

The second of the entries relating to the appointment of John Coke as Clerk to the Mercers' Company seems to prove beyond doubt that by 1527 the Merchant Adventurers were no longer meeting at Mercers' Hall and Miss Lyell concluded that the headquarters of the Company had moved overseas. It is worth asking, however, whether this was the reason why the Merchant Adventurers left Mercers' Hall in 1527. On 3 September 1527,[21] it was reported to the Mayor and Aldermen that there was great controversy and variance grown among the Merchant Adventurers whereby the common fame was that the King's peace was likely to be broken and disturbed. It had already been agreed that the two parties should be called before the Court of Aldermen so that the 'Grugge' might be known and a good peace and a charitable and loving end set between them. On this day there accordingly appeared Mr Withipoll, Mr Perpoynt, Mr Shether, Mr Thomson, Mr Coke, Mr Cleymond and Mr Hampton. They disclosed their 'Grugge' and it was decided to send for the other party who appeared on the following day. It consisted of Richard Gresham, Benjamin Digby, Mr Barnard, Mr Botrey, Mr Bromewell, Mr Hynde, Mr Kemp, Mr Waren, Mr Reynold and Mr Kitson. The entry concludes with a memorandum that in effect all this variance was whether the election of Richard Gresham to be Governor was good or not and it was ordered by the Court that both parties should bring in what grants and privileges they had so that the Council

[16] Ibid., p. 535.
[17] Ibid., p. 715.
[18] Ibid., p. 716.
[19] Ibid., p. 723.
[20] Ibid., p. 633.
[21] Corporation of London Records Office, Repertory 7, f. 213b.

of the City might see them. The Lord Mayor also ordered that neither party was to hold any assembly within the City until the Lord Cardinal had returned to the realm.

Unfortunately, the Repertory of the Court of Aldermen does not inform us of the outcome of this dispute but if we take a look at the composition of the two parties an interesting situation is revealed. The members of the first party can be identified as follows:

Paul Withipoll: Merchant Taylor.[22] Elected one of the two Governors of the Merchant Adventurers
    on 5 July 1526, according to the new ordinances made in that year.[23]
Thomas Perpoynt: Draper.[24]
Robert Shether: Merchant Taylor.[25]
William Thomson: Draper.[26]
John Coke: presumably the Clerk to the Merchant Adventurers, appointed Clerk to the Mercers'
    Company in 1527. If this is indeed John Coke his presence here is strange since, as will be
    seen, this party appears to have been in opposition to the Mercers' Company. In origin, of
    course, John Coke was a Merchant Taylor.
Oliver Cleymond[27] alias Clement.[28]
William Hampton.[29]
It has not been possible to identify the parent Companies of the last two members of this party but they were not Mercers.

The members of the second party were all Mercers. They were:[30]

Richard Gresham:	admitted 1507	Thomas Hynde:	admitted 1490
Benjamin Digby:	1494	Edmund Kempe:	1503
John Barnard:	1487	Ralph Warren:	1507
William Botrey:	1486	Richard Reynold:	1504
William Bromewell:	1490	Thomas Kitson:	1507

Moreover they were all important members of the Mercers' Company, in 1527 forming a considerable section of the Court of Assistants.[31]

The cause of the dispute, the election of Richard Gresham as Governor, probably stemmed from the ordinances made in April 1526, to which reference has already been made. The first of these ordinances read:[32] 'First it is thought right propice and necessarye for the felyship of marchauntes adventerers to Electe nomynate and Chose two discrete and expert Marchauntes every pasche marte to exercise the Rome of Gouernours joyntly and seuerally the space of two Martes, that is to saye from the begynyng of euery suche Pasche Marte unto thende of Synxson Marte than next folwyng. And at the Synxson Marte than next folowyng to electe and chose two other discrete Marchauntes to contynue from the Balmes Marte than next and Immedyatly folowyng unto thende of the cold Marte than ensuyng. So always that oon of the said Gouernours chosen from tyme to tyme as ys aforsaid be always resident and contynuyng in those parties durying the tyme of the said ij Martes. Acertenyng to the said Gouernours a resonable fee for their Paynes taken

[22] L. & W., p. 560.
[23] Ibid., p. 731.
[24] Ibid., p. 560.
[25] Ibid.
[26] Ibid., p. 702.
[27] Ibid., p. 352.
[28] Ibid., pp. 457, 463, 548, 558, 715.
[29] Ibid., pp. 433, 435.
[30] The dates of admission have been taken from 'Names of all the Freemen of the Mercers' Company from 1347'.
[31] L. & W., p. 762.
[32] Ibid., p. 723.

in that partie. Provided that there shalbe no Marchaunt of the Compeny contynuyng alwayes in thoos parties elected nor chosen to the said Rome of Gouernour in any wyse'. At a General Court of the Merchant Adventurers held on 23 July 1526,[33] a letter was read from the Company at Antwerp reporting that on 5 July last '. . . we held Generall Courte, where amonges other thynges folowyng your discrete advise and our auctorities we haue elected two Gouernours for the Balmas & Colde Martes next that is to say the worsshipfull John a Parke and Poule Wethipoll, and haue ordeyned bothe of theym to be at Dover by the xxiiijth day of September next comyng, takyng there the next fayre passage after the said daye to thende they may be here in the begynyng of the said Bamas Marte and to continue unto Colde marte folowyng either of theym uppon payn of xx li. sterlinge'. Paul Withipoll we have already met. John Parke was a Mercer, admitted in 1505,[34] but he never took up the office of Governor of the Merchant Adventurers. At a General Court of the Merchant Adventurers held on 22 November 1526,[35] John Parke begged to be excused from holding office on the grounds of ill-health ('. . . he coulde not streyn his body in goyng of borde of the ship nor in the Shipp by reason of wederyng but it shulde put hym in Joperdye of his lyfe'). On 5 December, therefore, the Wardens of the Mercery wrote to the Company at Antwerp asking them to excuse John Parke from holding the office of Governor and to discharge him from any penalty thus incurred. Perhaps the Mercers' Company attempted to have Richard Gresham elected Governor in Parke's place and Paul Withipoll and his party objected. This may have been the moment when any smouldering resentment at the continued domination of the Merchant Adventurers by the Mercers' Company finally came to the surface. It may be of some significance that the proposal to make new ordinances for the Merchant Adventurers in 1526 seems to have been discussed first at a Court of Assistants of the Mercers' Company and the persons appointed to draft the new ordinances, including the ordinance for the election of two Governors, were all Mercers.[36] There can be little doubt that the dispute about the election of the Governor had split the Merchant Adventurers into two camps, one favouring the Mercers' Company and the other opposed to it. It also seems likely that this was why the Merchant Adventurers ceased to meet at Mercers' Hall.

Whether the headquarters of the Merchant Adventurers then moved overseas is another problem. All the evidence indicates that during the sixteenth century control of the Merchant Adventurers passed from London to the continent. In addition to the evidence cited by Miss Lyell, support can be given to this view by certain evidence relating to admissions to the freedom of the Merchant Adventurers.

Down to 1525 it seems to have been quite usual for the formal admission to the freedom of the Company to take place in London. Thus on 9 March 1517/18[37] the Acts of Court record that 'John Pakyngton Citizyn and mercer of London was admytted fre of the felyshipp of merchauntes adventerers franke & fre gyven unto hym by acte of Courte in the cold marte last past, and toke his othe in the presence of Maister John Hewster, Gouernor, the ixth daye of marche' and that 'John Champeneys, Citizin and Skynner of London was admytted fre of the merchauntes adventerers and toke his othe in the presens of Maister John Hewster, Governor, the ixth daye of Marche . . .' Similarly on 12 and 21 October 1525,[38] 'William Huckysley of London grocer was admytted and sworne fre of the felyship of Marchauntes adventerers the xijth daye of October in the presentes of Maister John Hewster gouernor and Robert Smyth mercer &c.' and 'John Caunton Citizyn and haberdissher of London & Alderman of the same Citie was admytted & sworne fre of the said

33 *Ibid.*, p. 731.
34 'Names of all the Freemen of the Mercers' Company from 1347'.
35 *L. & W.*, pp. 742, 743.
36 *Ibid.*, pp. 716, 717.
37 *Ibid.*, p. 453.
38 *Ibid.*, p. 703.

felishipp of marchauntes adventerers the xxj[th] daye of October & toke his othe in the presens of Maister John Hewster Governor'.

We do not know whether any of these particular Adventurers qualified for membership of the Company by apprenticeship, but as early as 1529 it seems that the procedure for admission by apprenticeship described in Wheeler's Ordinances of 1608[39] had already been adopted. On 14 July 1529, the following entry occurs in the Acts of Court of the Mercers' Company:[40] 'For somoche as Robert Sturgis apprentise to John Aphowell mercer by reaport of the said John hath craftely and deceitfully used and handeled hymself aswell in these parties as beyonde the see in biyng and sellyng to his owne use wt.out his licence consent or knowleige And also hath not truly serued the said John his maister accordyng to the tenor of his endenture beyng evidently approued in presence of the said Robert wherfore it is ordeyned that the said Sturgis shall not be accepted or admytted to the liberties of this feliship nor also the Wardeyns nowe beyng nor noon other herafter shall write for his admyssion unto the liberties of Marchauntes Aduenturers in the parties of Brabant unto suche tyme as it be sufficiently approued and justified bifore the Wardeyns for the tyme beyng that he hath justly truly and diligently serued out his yeres of apprentishod yet to come accordyng to the custume and maner of the Citie of London and tenure of his indenture aforsaid'. There is further evidence, moreover, from the records of other Companies that this was the normal method of admission by apprenticeship to the Merchant Adventurers throughout the later sixteenth century. Charles M. Clode in his *Early History of the Merchant Taylors' Company*[41] printed a letter from Richard Hilles to Thomas Cromwell, dated 26 January 1532/3, in which he stated that he was apprenticed to Nicholas Cosyn on London Bridge and that his master 'sent me over six days before Christmas last to be made free in Flanders' and in his *History of the Worshipful Company of Drapers*[42] A. H. Johnson printed a list of Drapers' apprentices who were admitted to the freedom of the Merchant Adventurers during the reign of Elizabeth, and many of the entries in the Repertories of the Acts of Court of the Drapers' Company to which he referred relate to the certificates which were supplied by the Wardens of the Company to apprentices seeking admission to the Merchant Adventurers. By 1555 the control of apprentices was clearly in the hands of the Adventurers overseas for on 18 December in that year the Mercers' Company entered the following order in their Acts of Court:[43] 'Also at this Courte it is agreed that this wordes Ac Mercatores adventurarij shalbe expressed in the prentices Indentors of our companye that entende to enioye theire freedome by yonde the see, accordinge to an order newelye established & made in the yengelyshe house be yeonde the see for the same and suche as ar not mynded to make theire prentices free by yeonde the see nor be not free theire theym selfes the same wordes abouesayde maye be omitted and leafte oute of the indentors of prentices and then he shalle have bute his freedome of London onlye but yf the partyes be mynded to make theire prentices free by yonde expresse the wordes aboue sayde in any wyse or elles the parte shalbe in ioberde of his freedome thorrowe the follye of the maker of thendentures'.

It seems possible, however, that the headquarters of the Merchant Adventurers was not suddenly and deliberately transferred overseas in 1527. What seems more likely is that the control of the Company was acquired gradually by the Court abroad, perhaps partly as a result of the dissension among the London Adventurers which manifested itself in 1527. Reference has already been made to the inventory of 1547 in the British Museum[44] of the records remaining at Mercers'

---

[39] B.M. Add MS. 18913. Printed by W. E. Lingelbach in *The Merchant Adventurers of England*, University of Pennsylvania Press, 1902.

[40] A.C., 1527–60, f. 22.

[41] Charles M. Clode, *Early History of the Merchant Taylors' Company*, London, 1888, Part II, Appendix 2, p. 351.

[42] A. H. Johnson, *History of the Worshipful Company of Drapers*, 1915, Vol. II, Appendix xxxa, p. 457.

[43] A.C., 1527–60, f. 277.

[44] B.M. Sloane MS. 2103, f. 2.

Hall at that time. This inventory is interesting for a variety of reasons but there are two points which
are of special relevance here.

First, the inventory was compiled in the presence of 'Mr Emanuell Lucar marchant taillour
deputie unto the right wurshipfull fellawshipp of marchauntes adventurers in the Citie of London of
me Thomas Nycolls and of Leveriche Foster, under Clarke unto the mercers'. Emmanuel Lucar
was Master of the Merchant Taylors' Company in 1560. In 1553 he was first implicated in the attempt
to establish Lady Jane Grey on the throne and later imprisoned in the Tower as one of the jury who
failed to find Sir Nicholas Throgmorton guilty of treason.[45] Leverich Forster, who was son-in-law
and apprentice to William Newbold, was appointed Under-Clerk to the Mercers' Company on 26
July 1541,[46] and his duties seem to have consisted largely in registering earlier records of the Company. He became Clerk to the Company on 18 September 1555,[47] but was dismissed in 1567 for
absenting himself without leave[48] and for being in debt to the Company for the sum of £105 15 8.[49]
We know much less about Thomas Nicholls, who seems to have been the actual compiler of the
inventory, but from three items printed in Smit's *Bronnen tot de geschiedenis van den handel met
Engeland, Schotland en Ierland*[50] it appears that he was Secretary and Notary to the Merchant
Adventurers. One of the documents printed by Smit describes him as Secretary of the London
Residence of the Merchant Adventurers in 1555.[51] The reason why this inventory should have been
compiled by these three persons at this particular time is not apparent. There is no indication that
any order for its compilation came from overseas and a footnote to the inventory informs us that a
copy of it was to be retained by 'maister deputie', presumably by Emmanuel Lucar himself.

Secondly, the documents named in the inventory are nearly all grants and privileges of
various kinds, including Letters Patent of Henry IV, Henry V, Edward IV, Richard III, Henry VII,
Henry VIII, the grant of arms dated 1498, the appointment of Commissioners to conclude a peace
treaty with Flanders in 1459, a decree and an agreement concerning relations between the Merchant
Adventurers and the Merchants of the Staple in 1504 and 1516, grants of privileges by the Dukes of
Brabant, the Earls of Holland and Zeeland, the towns of Middlesbrough, Barrow, Antwerp (including the gift of the English house there) and Bruges and the discharge of William Overy from the
office of Governor in 1462. There is no mention of any minute or order books or accounts and the
nearest approach to purely administrative records of any kind are the safe conducts, the 'placards'
for the export of cloth and supplications concerning divers suits which are listed in general terms at
the end of the inventory. We must assume, therefore, that the records concerned with the day to day
business of the Company had been removed from Mercers' Hall and that only those documents which
may be said to affect the constitution of the Company were left behind. This certainly supports the
view that Mercers' Hall was no longer the place where the main business of the Merchant Adventurers was transacted but if there had been a wholesale translation abroad in 1527 surely these records too would have disappeared from Mercers' Hall. In fact we have some evidence that, in the
eyes of the Mercers' Company at least, the rightful place for these records was in London. At the
Quarter Day on 17 June 1534,[52] it was '. . . agreed by this worsshipfull assemble that the prive-
ledge of Andwarpe sued for to be sente ouer shall not be delyuered nor sende ouer in noo wyse
wt.oute a specyall lettor hadde from the Compenye be yeonde the see for the dyscharge of this

[45] For further details of Emmanuel Lucar's career see Clode, *l.c., passim.*
[46] A.C., 1527–60, f. 138.
[47] *Ibid.*, f. 278.
[48] A.C., 1560–95, f. 90.
[49] *Ibid.*, f. 101.
[50] H. J. Smit, *Bronnen tot de geschiedenis van den handel met Engeland Schotland en Ierland, 1485–1558*, vol. II, S'Gravenhage. Martinus Nijhoff, 1950, items 911 and 1279 and p. 467, n. i.
[51] Item 911: B.M. Cotton MS. Galba B XI, f. 165.
[52] A.C., 1527–60, f. 70.

fellyshippe' and on 16 December following[53] it was reported that '. . . where as the Prevyleage of Andwarpe was sente over see to maister William Wylkynson than beynge Gouernor of the Felly-shipe of marchauntes adventurers there by force of a letter from the holle Compenye there, to Mayster wardeins derected whiche pryvelage was shewed for certeyn causes therin debated The sayde Mr Wylkynson oppenly in this Courte delyuered the sayde pryvvylage ayen to Mr wardeins & to be putte in the chyste ayen there to be hadde in saue Custodye as it was afore'. Later still, on 26 September 1552,[54] the Acts of Court record that 'As consernynge the delyuere of a certayne Iron cheste belonginge to the Merchauntes Adventurers and whiche nowe is delyverede to Emanewell Luker deputye to the saide merchauntes adventurers It is agreede at this Courte that thacte made by yonde the see wherof a copeye is sente hydder therof for the dyscharge of the delyvere of the same by the wholle Commen assemble of the said merchauntes adventurers shalbe subscrybede wt. the hande of the saide Emanewell Lucker and the same savelye to be kepte to be shewede yf nede shalbe herafter'. Unfortunately we do not know what this iron chest contained but it was perhaps the chest of iron with three locks ordered to be bought at a General Court of the Merchant Adventurers on 11 March 1517/18,[55] to house the Company's treasure. It may even have been the chest of wood bound with iron referred to in the inventory of 1547. This time the initiative had clearly come from abroad, but it is interesting that even at this date what must have been one of the important belongings of the Merchant Adventurers still remained in London.

Why, when and how the headquarters of the Merchant Adventurers moved abroad must, unless fresh evidence comes to light, remain a matter for conjecture. Even if the general rule and government of the Adventurers was exercised from the Low Countries by the middle of the sixteenth century, the London Adventurers must have continued to meet from time to time. Gross, in *The Gild Merchant*,[56] stated that '. . . the Mercers' Hall was the headquarters of the Merchant Adventurers until the fire of 1666' but it can now be shown that this was true to only a limited extent. The Adventurers made use of Mercers' Hall for the accommodation of some, at least, of their records but that would seem to be their only connection with the Hall after 1526/7.

Our knowledge of the later connections between the Merchant Adventurers and Mercers' Hall begins on 3 April 1568,[57] when it was '. . . graunted to the merchauntes aduenturers upon the sewte of Mr Marshe there gouvernor and others made to this felliship that they shall haue libertie to make a hansome presse aboue in the wardrope wt.in our haulle where the gentill womens maides usually do sitt, to lay and sorte there privileges and writinges in at there pleasure, the same to be sett upp at there owne costes and charges in an Anglle hard adioyninge to the ladies Chambre there payinge yerely the some of vj li. xiij s. iiij d. provided alway that the company euery quarterday and feaste day haue the use therof for them and there officers at their libertie and plesure wt.out lett or contradiccon'. The Renterwardens' accounts[58] indicate that the rent of £6 13 3 was first paid by the Merchant Adventurers in the year 1570/1 but it was stated that this rent was for the Silk Weigh House under the Hall and not for the Wardrobe above as in the Acts of Court. Some account of this room beneath the Hall occurs in the Acts of Court for 10 November 1525,[59] when it was first insti-tuted. It was then '. . . shewed unto the said assemble that in tyme past great trybulacion and vexacion hathe bene for the beme Scales and Weyghtes belongyng to this felyshipp for waying of Sylkes. Wheruppon it ys nowe by the said assemble concluded & agreed as foloweth that ys to saye

---

[53] *Ibid.*, f. 76.
[54] A.C., 1527–60, f. 258.
[55] *L. & W.*, p. 453.
[56] Charles Gross, *The Gild Merchant*, Oxford, 1906, vol. I, p. 149.
[57] A.C., 1560–95, f. 131.
[58] Mercers' Company: Renterwardens' Accounts, 1538–77, f. 333.
[59] *L. & W.*, p. 708.

that the said beme Scalys & Weyghtes from hensford shall Remayne in the lowe parlour belongyng to oure Hall at saint Thomas of acres'. The weighing of silk was always to take place in this room and the person who held the office of Weigher of Silk was to pay £4 rent annually for the use of the room.

The Merchant Adventurers retained this room until 1666. There was a suggestion made at one time that the Mercers' Company should also make use of the room for some of their records. At a General Court held on 16 March 1572/3,[60] a motion was proposed '. . . that the howse benethe wch. the merchauntes adventurers occupy shoulde be made a place to serue to ley the evidences of the Compauny in for towe chestes of Iron for to put them in, This matter is referred to some more conuenient tyme to be better considered on'. Evidently no more convenient time was ever found for the matter does not seem to have been discussed again.

Although the Merchant Adventurers originally acquired this room 'to lay and sorte there privileges and writinges in' not all the records they deposited at Mercers' Hall were housed there. On 23 November 1614,[61] '. . . Mr Bladwell and Mr Wm. Robinson presented from the Companie of Merchaunts aduenturers a white box to be kept here in safe Custodie with this inscription videlt. In this box is the counterpaine of an Indenture sealled by sondry Feoffees the 26th of October 1614 unto the companie of merchauntes aduenturers and maie be opened & shewed by your worships to any that shall shewe you sufficient reason for the viewinge of the same. This box is remayninge in the Chest withe the company's commen seale'. We know for a fact that the Mercers' Company's seal was destroyed in the fire of 1666[62] so we may hazard a guess as to the fate of this particular record of the Merchant Adventurers.

In March 1657/8,[63] the Clerk to the Mercers' Company was ordered to give legal warning to the Merchant Adventurers that at the end of six months from Lady Day next they were to leave their office or 'Assistent house' under Mercers' Hall. It appears that Benjamin Thomlinson, a grocer, had petitioned for a lease of the room[64] but the Secretary to the Merchant Adventurers declared that the Merchant Adventurers claimed a title to the room so the whole matter was referred to a special committee. This committee was slow to act but on 11 May 1660, it met at Mercers' Hall[65] and Mr Skynner, the Secretary to the Merchant Adventurers, appeared and stated that the Adventurers '. . . held the Company of Mercers to be domini fundi and that they onely desire according to the antient amity that hath bin betweene the two Societies that (if the Company of Mercers owne occasions will permit) the said Merchants Adventurers may still injoy the use of the said roome though it were wth. the increase of some rent'. The committee could still not view or value the room because (and this is an interesting sidelight on the politics of the Merchant Adventurers at this time) Mr Skynner's man '. . . who hath the Custody of the key was lately gone over to the kings Majesty But upon his returne promised that the key should be ready upon the summons of this Committee'. On 19 March 1660/1[66] Mr Dawnay moved that the business might not be allowed to fall into oblivion, and finally on 22 May 1661[67] the General Court, on the recommendation of the committee and of the Court of Assistants on 15 May,[68] 'in regard the said Merchants have long injoyed the said roome and are a Corporacon of greate antiquity and have had long affinity with this Company', were granted a lease of the premises for 21 years from Midsummer 1661, at a yearly rent of £15.

[60] A.C., 1560–95, f. 229.
[61] A.C., 1595–1629, f. 137.
[62] A.C., 1663–9, f. 75.
[63] A.C., 1657–63, f. 19.
[64] *Ibid.*, f. 32.
[65] *Ibid.*, f. 106.
[66] *Ibid.*, f. 144.
[67] *Ibid.*, f. 150.
[68] *Ibid.*, f. 149.

They were to be bound by covenants in the lease 'not to lett nor sett the premises nor any wayes to alienate the same to any other person or persons whatsoever; nor to make or cause to be made any other doore or way into the said roome or office, nor to have any other way of ingresse egresse or regresse into or from the premisses then what now is or hath bin comonly used or accustomed in times past, and that at seasonable howers in the day time'.

At one point in the negotiations for the renewal of the lease of this room at Mercers' Hall, on 11 April 1660[69] the committee appointed to deal with the matter '. . . having considered of some particulars concerning the roome under the hall now in the occupacon of the Company of Merchants Adventurers they left the further consideration of that matter until Fryday next at which time they appoynted to meete againe, And ordered that Mr Basset the Beadle should attend the Court of the said Merchants Adventurers which are to sitt this Afternoone at Founders Hall and to acquaint them with this appoyntment to the end they may give this Committee a meeting at the same time'. This led to an examination of the records of the Founders' Company which have been deposited in the Guildhall Library and the Wardens' accounts[70] disclosed that the Merchant Adventurers were meeting regularly at Founders' Hall from 1555 to 1666. In the account for 1555/6 the Wardens recorded the receipt of £3 rent from the Merchant Adventurers for the three quarters ending at Lady Day, Midsummer and Michaelmas. They continued to pay rent for the use of Founders' Hall at the rate of £4 a year down to 1611 when a note occurs in the accounts to the effect that it had been agreed that the rent should be increased to £8 a year. The last payment for rent was for the half year ending at Michaelmas 1666.

It appears too that the City authorities provided the Merchant Adventurers with a meeting place for a time. At the Court of Aldermen held on 28 July 1553[71] two requests from the Merchant Adventurers were dealt with. The second of these '. . . for the graunting of the Guyldhall Chappel to them to assemble in after the deliberate debating thereof the Court agreed that it should be lawful for them from time to time until our Lady Day in Lent next coming at their pleasure to meet and assemble in the said chapel so that they do it at such convenient times that they do not interrupt or let the Lord Mayor Aldermen and Commons when they shall have occasion to assemble and meet there. And also that they do reasonable see unto the officer keeper of the said chapel for attendance to be given there upon them'.

Regrettably, this still leaves us with a gap in our knowledge for the period from 1526 to 1553. It is by no means the only question concerning the Merchant Adventurers which remains unanswered but patient research or lucky chance could still provide the solutions to some of these problems.

JEAN M. IMRAY

---

[69] *Ibid.*, f. 103.
[70] Guildhall Library, MSS. 6330/1 and 2: Wardens' Accounts of the Founders' Company, 1497–1687.
[71] Corporation of London Records Office: Repertory 12, No. 2, f. 511.

Ecclesiastical Administration

The Records of the
Church Commissioners

The Church Commissioners for England have existed as such since 1 April 1948 when the amalgamation of the Governors of Queen Anne's Bounty for the Augmentation of the Maintenance of the Poor Clergy (Queen Anne's Bounty from now on) and the Ecclesiastical Commissioners for England (hereafter the Ecclesiastical Commissioners) took effect under the provisions of the Church Commissioners Measure, 1947.

The records discussed in this paper are those of the Commissioners' two predecessors and also those of the Commissioners for Building and Promoting the Building of Additional Churches in Populous Parishes (for convenience the Church Building Commissioners) whose powers, duties, and papers the Ecclesiastical Commissioners inherited in 1856.[1]

All these three bodies were statutory corporations, Queen Anne's Bounty having been founded by Act of Parliament supplemented by Royal Charter whilst the Church Building Commissioners and the Ecclesiastical Commissioners were both established by Act of Parliament alone; and on all three bodies Parliament and the Crown conferred throughout their lifetimes additional duties and powers, which produced the records which are the subject of this paper. Each of these bodies is unique in its way, and it seems best therefore to summarize their histories and their powers whilst discussing their records.[2]

Queen Anne's Bounty

An Act of Parliament, 2 & 3 Anne c.11, enabled the Queen to establish a corporation to take over the Crown revenues from the First Fruits and Tenths of the Clergy and to apply them in the augmentation of the incomes of the poor clergy. By charter under the Great Seal dated 3 November 1704 the Governors of Queen Anne's Bounty were incorporated and rules for their governance laid down.

The early years of the Bounty must have been frustrating both to the Governors themselves and more so to the poor clergy who looked to them for some alleviation of their poverty. The Governors discovered that their revenues were encumbered by some thirteen pensions and salaries and that they were responsible for the payment of the beneficiaries during their life-times unless they

---

[1] 19 & 20 Vic., c. 55.
[2] For a full-scale history of both the Ecclesiastical Commissioners and Queen Anne's Bounty, see G. F. A. Best, *Temporal Pillars*, Cambridge, 1964. For the first years of Queen Anne's Bounty, see A. Savidge, *The Foundation and Early Years of Queen Anne's Bounty*, London, 1955. For an account of the Church Building Commissioners, see M. H. Port, *600 New Churches*, London, 1961.

could buy them out. Some payments were in arrear to the extent that more than one year's income of the Governors was owing. Although it was widely known that many of the beneficed clergy were living in extreme poverty the only available statistics of benefice incomes were those in the *Valor Ecclesiasticus* of Henry VIII.

The charter directed the Governors to ascertain what benefices in England and Wales were of an annual value of less than £80. This they did, and discovered that no fewer than 5,082 of the approximately 10,000 benefices were worth less than £80 per annum, of which more than 3,000 were under £40 per annum and 471 under £10 per annum. £80 per annum was regarded as a reasonable income for an incumbent. This information was acquired for the Governors through diocesan bishops and through ordinaries of exempt jurisdictions, and was assembled between 1705 and 1707. At the end of 1707 the results were made into a book and presented to the Queen, presumably to show Her Majesty that they had not been idle even if they had not yet augmented a benefice. Under an Act of 1707, which authorized the discharge from First Fruits and Tenths of all livings under £50 per annum on production of a certificate of value to the Exchequer, the Governors' income was reduced by a further £3,000. After further delays described in detail by Savidge the Governors were ready to start their work of augmentation. Their second charter, dated 5 March 1714, laid down the procedure to be adopted in augmenting benefices. Their revenues of something over £13,000 a year were to be laid out in grants of £200 each, firstly by lot to all livings under £10 per annum, and secondly to meet benefactions offered for livings, initially for those under £35 per annum. The funds resulting from their augmentations were to be invested in the purchase of land, the rent of which would increase the revenues of the benefice. Until suitable land could be purchased (and this was often difficult), the Governors paid interest to incumbents. The 1714 charter laid down the general lines of this important part of the Governors' work which continued for over 200 years. The funds available for grants were increased for the period 1809 to 1820 by eleven grants of £100,000 each made by Parliament.

This side of the Governors' work produced, apart from the complete series of general minute books from 1704 to 1948, firstly, a series of certificates of values of livings; secondly, a series of files dealing with requests for grants; and, thirdly, a series of legal papers and title deeds for those benefices successful in obtaining grants.

The minute books, which, of course, cover all aspects of the Governors' work including augmentation, exist in duplicate, the original signed copies and drafts presumably written by a secretary either at or just after the meetings. The Governors felt it necessary to check the value of livings which became due for augmentation either by lot or by benefaction, and called for up-to-date certificates of value. Up to about 1760 these exist as separate documents, but later they took the form of an enquiry into the general circumstances of the living by a Bishop's commission, normally the clergy of adjoining livings, and are to be found in the files referred to above. These files contain the in-correspondence leading up to a grant and generally a rough draft of the replies. Apparently the practice was to keep a fair copy of out-letters in letter books, but unfortunately few of these survive. Once a grant had been made and suitable land for purchase had been found, a separate file for the legal correspondence leading up to the purchase was opened. Most of these survive, but a number were destroyed up to the beginning of the war when the estates purchased had been sold. The title demanded was long in accordance with eighteenth-century practice, and hence each purchase was normally supported by a considerable body of title deeds. Again, most of these survive, although a considerable number have been handed away on sale.

Under the Clergy Residences Repair Act of 1776[3] the Governors were empowered to lend not more than 3 years' income of all benefices, rich or poor, towards the cost of providing or repairing

---

[3] 17 Geo. III. c. 53, Gilbert's Act, after its promoter, Thomas Gilbert, also of Poor Law fame.

parsonage houses. This power was not much used at the beginning, and the only early records of its use are to be found in the Governors' minute books and in the brief particulars of works carried out to be found in the Gilbert Act minute books; but it is important in that it provided the Governors with their first contact with the parsonage house question which was later to become a large part of their work. In 1803 they were empowered by Act of Parliament to expend money for the endowment of benefices, not only on land in the usual way but also towards building or purchasing parsonage houses. Under the Parsonage Act, 1838, which gave an incumbent power to sell his parsonage with the consent of his bishop, patron and archbishop, the proceeds of sale were to be paid to the Governors who had the duty of providing another house either by purchase or building. Where building took place after 1803 the Governors acquired plans, specifications and estimates, and these papers survive from the earliest time up to 1948. It should be noted, however, that many parsonages were built by rich patrons or clergy without the Governors being concerned, and also that many parsonages were built under the powers both of the Church Building Commissioners and the Ecclesiastical Commissioners. Nevertheless between 1803 and 1948 the Governors were concerned either by building or purchase with some 4,500 houses, sometimes two or three for the same benefice. Many of these houses have long since ceased to be parsonage houses and probably quite a number no longer survive. Plans and other particulars of houses which are no longer parsonage houses have been deposited in the appropriate county record office, but those of houses which remain as the residence of the incumbent are available in the Commissioners' records. Since 1930 the Governors have been parties to the sale of all parsonage houses and have details of such sales, but prior to 1930 they knew only the fact of sale and the amount of the sale proceeds.

The Governors first became concerned with dilapidations on parsonage houses and glebe property under the Ecclesiastical Dilapidations Acts, 1871 and 1872. These Acts provided for a compulsory survey of all benefice buildings on each vacancy, and the payment of the amount of dilapidation money assessed to Governors who had to superintend its application. The files of correspondence dealing with this side of the Governors' work have perished, but the ledgers still remain as a memorial to what must have been a very unsatisfactory system, both to the incoming and outgoing incumbent.

In 1924 the Ecclesiastical Dilapidations Measure, 1923, replaced the 1871 and 1872 Acts. This Measure provided for quinquennial inspections of benefice building by a Diocesan Dilapidations Board and annual payments by the incumbents to the Governors for future repairs and insurance. The Governors disbursed this money when repairs had been completed against certificates issued by the Dilapidations Boards. The Governors made grants towards the annual payments for the poorer benefices. These grants took the place of the augmentation grants which had formerly been the Governors' method of helping poor livings.

Up to 1918 the Governors' only connection with tithe rent-charge was to receive and invest on behalf of benefices money received under an Act of 1846[4] for the redemption of tithe rent-charge. Redemption under that Act and amending Acts during the century proceeded slowly as the agreement of both the tithe owner and the tithe payer was required; but in 1918, when the level of the tithe rent-charge was high as a result of the war-time high prices for wheat, barley and oats, an Act[5] was passed providing for the redemption of tithe rent-charge on a fifty-year annuity basis without the consent of the tithe owner, and fixing the value of tithe at its then value for six years. This Act brought a flood of work to the Governors from landowners wishing to take advantage of these favourable terms, for the Act was administered by them. The end of the six-year period of stable value for tithe in 1925 was obviously destined to be a time of trouble, because the 1918 Act had pro-

---

[4] 9 & 10 Vic., c. 73.
[5] 8 & 9 Geo. V, c. 54.

posed that thereafter tithe rent-charge was to be assessed on a fifteen-year basis, which would have caused a rise in the value of tithe to about £131 per £100 par value from the stabilized value under the 1918 Act of about £109, and this in a period when agricultural prices were falling and rates were rising. The 1925 Tithe Act[6] fixed the value of tithe rent-charge in perpetuity at five per cent – about its par value – and provided for the redemption of the ecclesiastical part of it by the creation of a sinking fund into which an additional four and a half per cent of par value was to be paid to extinguish tithe rent-charge altogether after about eighty years. The most important provision as far as the Governors were concerned was the vesting in them of all ecclesiastical tithe rent-charge. Thus the Bounty received the duty of collecting the tithe rent-charge (and by its efficiency in so doing acquired no small notoriety in farming circles) until by the 1936 Tithe Act[7] the Governors were relieved of their responsibility by the redemption of tithe rent-charge by the payment of Government 3% stock to the tithe owners, and by the setting up of the Tithe Redemption Commission to collect the new tithe annuities created to reimburse the Government. The existing records of these very busy years of the Governors' history are disappointingly few. This is chiefly because for administrative convenience the Governors worked through fifteen area committees, whose agents and solicitors had most of the contact with the tithe payers, and partly because of the destruction of papers during the late war. Nevertheless there remains a considerable body of files and books awaiting detailed study. The information therein would be more relevant to a detailed study of the tithe question than to particular benefices or landowners.

In conclusion one should perhaps mention the material relating to Queen Anne's Bounty at the Public Record Office (*Guide to the Contents of the Public Record Office*, London, H.M.S.O., 1963, vol. I, pp. 86–8 and 188; vol. II, p. 118).

The Church Building Commissioners

The Commissioners were constituted in 1818;[8] twenty Acts of Parliament and thirty-eight years later they were dissolved, and their remaining powers and duties transferred to the Ecclesiastical Commissioners. Their most active period was the first fifteen years of their life, when they were engaged in spending the £1,500,000 put at their disposal by the Government in 1818 (£1,000,000) and 1825 (£500,000) in the erection of churches, almost entirely in places where the rise in population had rendered the existing church accommodation inadequate. Port's *600 New Churches* sets out in detail the churches so erected. Their powers were by no means confined to the erection of churches. They were empowered to accept the conveyance of sites for churches, burial grounds and parsonages, and to establish tables of pew rents for the churches towards the building of which they had contributed. This latter was an important factor in paying the clergy to serve the churches, and a source of considerable difficulty in later years when the pew rent paying classes moved elsewhere. They possessed and exercised the power to create new cures for the incumbents of the new churches by preparing schemes for ratification by Order in Council. Prior to 1818 new cures could be formed only by the promotion of a local Act of Parliament. On their dissolution in 1856 their papers passed to the Ecclesiastical Commissioners and most of them survive in the hands of the Church Commissioners. The legal work of the Church Building Commissioners was carried out by the Treasury Solicitor, who at some time after 1856 handed over to the Ecclesiastical Commissioners his legal papers, which were added to their files.

Files of in-letters exist for all the 1077 new cures with which the Commissioners were concerned during their lifetime. Out-letters seem to have been kept in letter books and these are no longer extant. In all earlier cases the files deal with the acquisition of church sites and also usually

---

[6] 15 & 16 Geo. V, c. 87.
[7] 26 Geo. V and 1 Ed. VIII, c. 43.
[8] 58 Geo. III, c. 45.

of parsonage sites, the erection of the churches, the constitution of separate cures, and the establishment of tables of pew rents. After the mid-1830s, when the bulk of their money was spent, the Commissioners ceased to contribute largely to the erection of churches, but continued to contribute a nominal five pounds so that they could exercise their power of fixing pew rents. Here again there is usually a wealth of useful information for local historical purposes. Unfortunately the original plans of the churches built, which were formerly in the possession of the Ecclesiastical Commissioners, have with a few exceptions disappeared. The Church Building Commissioners' general minute books numbered 1–67 (of which eight are missing) and those of their Building and Division sub-committees (again defective) are a useful source of information about their administration whilst the Surveyors' report books throw considerable light on the actual building of their churches.

The Ecclesiastical Commissioners

The Reform Bill received the Royal Assent on 7 June 1832, and on 23 June in the same year a Royal Commission was set up to enquire into the revenues and patronage belonging to the archiepiscopal and episcopal sees, all cathedral and collegiate churches, and all ecclesiastical benefices, with or without cure of souls, in England and Wales. The Church thus took its place as one of the first targets of the reform movement. This Commission, generally called the Ecclesiastical Revenues Commission, reported in 1835, and the original returns on which the report was based are to be found, as far as England only is concerned, in the Commissioners' records. The Report merely recorded the facts and seems to have convinced the Government at least, and probably a large part of the public, that the aggregate revenues of the Church were not excessive for providing for the spiritual needs of the nation, as had been asserted by the enemies of the Church. It was, of course, another question whether these revenues were rightly distributed, and this question was referred to another Royal Commission, generally known as the Church Inquiry Commission, which was to consider the state of the dioceses in England and Wales with reference to the amount of their revenues and to the more equal distribution of episcopal duties; they were also to consider the state of cathedral and collegiate churches with a view to suggesting such measures as might render them most conducive to the efficiency of the Established Church, and to devise the best mode of providing for the cure of souls with special reference to the residence of the clergy in their respective benefices. This Commission presented four reports (and prepared a fifth which was not presented because of the death of William IV), which formed the basis of three Acts of Parliament, from two of which the existence, resources and duties of the Ecclesiastical Commissioners have their origin.

The first of these Acts, the Ecclesiastical Commissioners Act of 1836,[9] set up and incorporated 'The Ecclesiastical Commissioners for England' and charged them to carry out the recommendations of the Church Inquiry Commission so far as they related to the re-arrangement of dioceses and the creation of the new sees of Manchester and Ripon, the reduction of income of some sees and the increase of income of others, the provision of fit residences for bishops and the abolition of peculiar jurisdictions within dioceses and archdeaconries. This was to be done by schemes prepared by the Commissioners and laid before the King in Council, and after approval ratified by Orders in Council. The Act gave legislative force to two additional recommendations of the Commission, firstly that no bishop should hold a benefice or office *in commendam*, and secondly that each archdeacon should have full jurisdiction within his archdeaconry. The rest of the recommendations were left to the Commissioners to vary, modify and enlarge if they felt fit in ways not repugnant to the original recommendations. Hence although the Commission had recommended the union of the dioceses of Gloucester and Bristol, Carlisle and Sodor and Man, and St Asaph and Bangor, only the first union was actually carried out. The results of the Commissioners' labours under the 1836 Act are to be

---

[9] 6 & 7 Will. IV, c. 77.

found in the Orders in Council published in the *London Gazette*, and the detailed work leading to these results survives in their minute books and files.

The second of these Acts arising from the work of the Church Inquiry Commission, the Pluralities Act of 1838,[10] is important in the general reform of the Church but touched the Commissioners hardly at all.

The third Act of the series, the Cathedral Act of 1840,[11] was probably the most important enactment affecting the Commissioners. It transformed them from a body appointed to deal with a limited reform affecting only the Church itself, and then only its hierarchy, to a continuing body whose work affected not only the Church and mass of church people but also a large section of the community outside the church.

The Act firstly fixed the number of residentiary canonries to be retained in each cathedral church of both Old and New Foundation and in collegiate churches. This meant the suspension of many canonries–for instance Canterbury, Westminster, Durham and Worcester lost six each–and the creation of one new one each at St Paul's and Lincoln. It also provided that the holders of prebends and offices in cathedrals of the Old Foundation, for example Chancellorships and Treasurerships, which were endowed with their own separate estates, should on the next vacancy forfeit these estates. It also provided for the suppression of all the sinecure rectories in the patronage of the Crown (thirty in number) or of any ecclesiastical corporation.

The profits arising from these various alienations and suspensions were transferred to the Ecclesiastical Commissioners. Thus the shares of the suspended canonries in the corporate revenues of cathedrals were receivable by them, also the separate estates of all deaneries and canonries including those not suspended, of all prebendaries and holders of cathedral offices, and of all suppressed sinecure rectories vested in the Commissioners. The Commissioners were directed to pay all the revenues from this property into a Common Fund out of which, or by the conveyance of the land vesting in them, additional provision should be made under the authority of schemes ratified by Order in Council 'for the cure of souls in parishes where such assistance is most required in such manner as shall by the like authority be deemed most conducive to the efficiency of the Established Church'. This still remains the general purpose or trust to which the Commissioners' disposable income must be devoted.

The transfer to the Commissioners of the prebendal and other separate estates of cathedral officers was subject always to the interest of the holder in 1840. Hence on the passing of the Cathedrals Act there were immediately vested in the Commissioners only the estates of those preferments which had been kept vacant since 1835 in anticipation of this legislation. The vesting of the remainder would have taken many years, bearing in mind the longevity of the clergy, who would normally hold these largely sinecure preferments until death did them part. The process was however shortened by the provisions of the Cathedral Act which enabled the Commissioners and the holders of these preferments to agree to exchange their estates for a fixed money payment. This proved popular where the estates were leased for lives, with a small annual rent and a large fine on renewal or the addition of a further life, but unpopular where the estate was situated in an area where agricultural land was becoming building land, for example the estate of the St Paul's prebend of Cantlowes, upon which most of Camden Town and Kentish Town and part of Highgate were built during the middle years of the century.

The 1840 Act did not vest the corporate estates of deans and chapters in the Commissioners, but gave them only a share in the corporate revenues where canonries had been suppressed. However, this Act and its amending Acts did give power to the Commissioners, with the agreement of

---

[10] 1 & 2 Vic., c. 106.
[11] 3 & 4 Vic., c. 113.

deans and chapters, to acquire their estates in exchange for money payments secured on the Commissioners' Common Fund and the surrender by the Commissioners of their share of the corporate incomes in respect of the suppressed canonries. Between 1852 and 1867 such arrangements were effected with eighteen Chapters. In 1867 it was discovered that because of a defect in the Acts under which these arrangements had been made their validity was doubtful and a special white-washing Act had to be passed, followed by a further Act laying down more complete provisions under which the corporate estates of all deans and chapters except three passed into the Commissioners' hands in exchange for money payments.

The transfer of the corporate estates to the Commissioners was not the final operation in the re-arrangement of cathedral endowments. Most chapters were subsequently re-endowed with other estates and tithe rent-charges to the value of the money payments, but freed from the restrictions of the old system of leases for lives. The re-endowments were mostly completed by 1875, but under the provisions of the Cathedrals Measure of 1931 these new estates again reverted to the Commissioners in exchange for new money payments, leaving the chapters generally with only the precincts of the Cathedrals in their possession. (Manchester and Durham are special cases.)

The bishops were left in possession of their estates following the 1836 and 1840 Acts, but the richer sees had to pay a part of their revenues to the Commissioners, and the poorer received an addition to their income from the Commissioners. From the point of view of the richer sees this was unsatisfactory because they had the responsibility of administering their whole estate only to receive a part. From the point of view of the Commissioners the situation was also unsatisfactory because they had to rely for a part of their income on a source over which they had no direct control. This situation remained until 1860, when by an Act of that year the ancient episcopal estates were vested in the Commissioners for the purposes of their Common Fund as from the next vacancy of the see after the Act, subject to the securing to each Bishop of the income fixed for him by the 1836 Act.

Provision was thus made by Act of Parliament or by commutation authorized by Act of Parliament for the estates of all ecclesiastical corporations, with the exception of the parochial incumbents, to vest in the Ecclesiastical Commissioners for the benefit of their Common Fund. Most of these estates when they vested in the Commissioners were subject to leases for terms of lives or years, granted, in accordance with the practice general in such estates, upon the payment of a large fine paid when the lease was granted and of small annual reserved rents, almost nominal and having no relation to the actual value of the property demised. It was calculated that the actual annual value of the estates (land and tithe rent-charge) of bishops, deans, chapters, and cathedral officers in 1840 was about £1,750,000, but that the average income received annually was £518,000, made up of £257,000 reserved rents and £261,000 from fines on renewal of leases. Thus the income received from their estates by ecclesiastical corporations was less than one third of their estimated annual value. The policy of the Ecclesiastical Commissioners was to free the lands vested in them as quickly as possible from the shackles of the old system of leasing, which was from the Church's point of view at least uneconomic, either by selling their freehold reversion to the lessees or by purchasing the leasehold interest from the lessees in suitable cases.

I have dealt with the subject of the Commissioners' estates in some detail partly because the acquisition of this property and the subsequent dealings in it were the foundation and prime source of the Commissioners' revenues, and also because from this side of their work sprang important records. Before an estate became vested in them the Commissioners had little idea of the terms of the lease under which it was held, the situation and extent of the property, and its general condition. Especially where some of the smaller prebendal estates were concerned they often had difficulty in discovering when the estate had become vested in them by death or vacation of the prebendary, and further difficulty in determining what, if any, estate documents existed. It was their invariable practice when an estate vested in them to call for a thorough survey by their outside surveyors, Messrs Clutton for the southern part of the country, and Messrs Pickering and Smith for the northern part. These surveys were normally arranged as follows:

Firstly, a general statement of the property vesting, the amount of tithe rent-charge, the acreage of the land and whether it was leasehold or copyhold tenure or in possession, the parish or parishes in which it was situated and brief particulars of the current lease if any, that is, name of the lessee and names and ages of the lives if appropriate.

Secondly, a summary of the current lease; and thirdly, full particulars of the fields and acreages, often with field names and the names of the occupiers under the lessee.

Fourthly, a valuation of the property; and fifthly, a note giving particulars of the ecclesiastical benefice or benefices in the parishes in which the estate was situated, giving an account of the condition of the parish church, whether there was a parsonage house and school and their condition, and a note of the benefice income, sometimes with its sources. Lastly, the surveyors made recommendations for the disposal or otherwise of the estate, often adding that such and such a field which adjoined the benefice glebe or parsonage should be annexed to the benefice. Each survey was accompanied by a map showing the property and often also the benefice glebe. These surveys and maps are extant in the Commissioners' office and are important in providing the first complete record of ecclesiastical property since the Cromwellian survey of 1649/50.

The records of the Commissioners' initial dealings with their inherited estates by leasehold enfranchisement as well as by purchase of leasehold interests are also available both in files of correspondence, which give details of the negotiations, and in copy and duplicate deeds, which record the final arrangement. Often it had been the custom of ecclesiastical corporations to charge their estates with the payment of stipends to parochial clergy, and frequently the impropriate tithe rent-charge which came into the Commissioners' ownership was subject to the liability to repair chancels and parish churches. The Commissioners were careful to pass on these liabilities when they enfranchised an estate but they retain to this day the liability as lay rectors for the repair in part or in entirety of the chancels of many parish churches. Incidentally, their knowledge of ancient parish churches is confined to those for the chancels of which they are liable.

It was also the Commissioners' practice, where they acquired the freehold of an estate, to purchase adjoining land to improve that estate. These freehold purchases were dealt with in the same way as the property inherited from ecclesiastical corporations, that is, a full report was prepared by their surveyors.

The Commissioners acquired considerable property which became ripe for development by housing. They had no power to develop themselves, and it was their practice to grant building agreements for the erection of houses within the estate and to grant direct leases when the houses were built. The files and deeds for these grants throw considerable light on urban housing development in the latter part of the nineteenth century. Perhaps the most interesting example of this side of the Commissioners' records is their Paddington estate. This estate belonged to the Bishop of London and had been leased by him to trustees, who obtained an Act of Parliament in 1795[12] to enable them to develop the estate for housing by the grant of long-term leases. Two thirds of the income arising from the estate was retained by the estate trustees and the remaining third paid to the bishop. This latter share passed to the Commissioners when the bishop's estates passed to them, and they thus became consenting parties to the development after 1868. In 1953 they acquired the entire interest in the estate by buying out the remaining interest of the trustees, and thereby acquired the records of the trustees, which date from the commencement of the development.

There were many cases where the Commissioners and the lessees of the ecclesiastical

---

[12] 35 Geo. III, c. 83.

corporations were unable to agree on terms for the enfranchisement of property, either by purchase of the freehold interest by the lessee, or by the sale by the lessee of his leasehold interest. In these cases the Commissioners had to wait until the lease fell in, usually on the death of the last life, before the property came into their possession. Some of the property acquired in this way was an embarrassment to the Commissioners, but was instrumental in enabling them to carve a niche in nineteenth-century social history. In 1881 the lease fell in of property in Southwark, the worst type of Victorian slum, heavily overpopulated. Had they retained it they would have acquired the reputation of being slum landlords; had they demolished and rebuilt, many people would have been rendered homeless. The solution lay in the employment of Miss Octavia Hill, who was able on this estate, and also on a similar estate in Walworth which fell in years later, to develop her ideas of estate management on a much larger scale than she had been able to do heretofore. The Commissioners' files contain many of her characteristic letters, but unfortunately her official position as a sub-collector of rents to the Commissioners' agents, Messrs Clutton, means that much material which otherwise might have been in the Commissioners' records is absent.

The Commissioners' corporate property fed their Common Fund which they had been directed to devote towards making additional provision for the cure of souls where such assistance was most required, which meant in the parishes both already existing, and to be created.

Firstly, it was the Commissioners' duty to give primary consideration to the needs of parishes within which the estates of the ecclesiastical corporations were situated, that is, those parishes which had a 'local claim'. This they did by raising the incomes of the benefices by the annexation to the living either of land or tithe rent-charge, provided, of course, the property which they had inherited in the parish was sufficient to permit such augmentation, and also provided the value of the cure merited it. Much of this augmentation was done by annexing tithe rent-charge, which gave rise to an interesting sideline in the Commissioners' activities. By the District Churches Tithes Act of 1865[13] they were permitted to erect either into rectories or vicarages, as might be appropriate, all livings being perpetual curacies which could be shown then to possess either all the rectorial or vicarial tithe or their equivalent arising in the parish. This they did by Instrument under their seal published in the *London Gazette*. This Act was repealed in 1868 and was replaced in the same year by the Incumbents Act[14] which permitted all perpetual curates, the usual status of incumbents of all new cures and not a few ancient ones, to be styled 'vicar' for purposes of tithe only. Livings having a local claim also received where necessary a capital grant of up to £1,500 towards the cost of providing a suitable parsonage house.

The normal ways in which the Commissioners carried out their duty of making additional provision for the cure of souls were by providing:
1. the endowment of newly-formed cures
2. augmentations of existing cures
3. grants towards the provision or improvement of parsonage houses
4. grants of either a permanent or temporary nature towards the stipends of assistant curates
5. pension grants to retiring incumbents

Details of all these are to be found in the files for the benefice concerned, and in the Commissioners' Annual Reports to Parliament. There seems no need to detail the precise methods adopted, but it should be noted that the applications for assistance from incumbents often give a complete account of the pastoral activity of the clergy in the parishes. Many, of course, merely filled in the necessary form and left it at that.

Early in their career, in 1843,[15] the New Parishes Act laid upon the Commissioners the duty

---

[13] 28 & 29 Vic., c. 42.
[14] 31 & 32 Vic., c. 117.
[15] 6 & 7 Vic., c. 37.

of forming and endowing new parishes; in 1856 they inherited the powers of the Church Building Commissioners under the Church Building Acts for forming parishes. Thus they became concerned with the acquisition of church and parsonage sites and the approval of churches and parsonages built on the sites. The files dealing with these matters are generally not as interesting as they might be, because it seems that the disputes which must have arisen over boundaries when a new cure was formed were normally settled locally before the Commissioners were approached. Similarly, although the Commissioners had the duty of approving a church as a suitable building to become a parish church, and usually the plans were sent to them for comment by their architect, no plans remain with the Commissioners, as it was their practice to return them, when approved, to the person who had sent them, with instructions to produce them when the completed building was ready for inspection. Again, details of the finance of new churches are generally missing from the files, as these were the concern of the local building committee only. Where the Commissioners' solicitor acted for them in the acquisition of sites for churches, parsonage houses and burial grounds, the legal papers survive, together with abstracts of title and copies of the deeds of conveyance.

The Commissioners have been concerned not only with the expanding church by the formation of new parishes, but also with the contracting church by the union of benefices. This process started under the Union of Benefices Act 1860[16] which authorized the union of certain parishes in the City of London and demolition of churches and disposal of their sites, and has continued up to date under the provisions of the Union of Benefices Measure 1923 and subsequent legislation. Most of these unions involved no demolition of churches or disposal of church sites, but the movement of population from the centres of cities and large towns, and the destruction of the last war, have increased the number of redundant churches which have perished. Their fate is dealt with in the Commissioners' files.

The Commissioners became concerned quite early with first the leasing and then the sale of benefice glebe, but the glebe records are incomplete, firstly because they never had complete details of glebe owned by the benefices, and secondly because, although the majority of glebe sales took place under the provisions of the Ecclesiastical Leasing Acts administered by the Commissioners, it was also possible to sell glebe under the Glebe Lands Act of 1888,[17] which was administered by the Board of Agriculture, and the Commissioners have no knowledge of what was sold. Also, of course, exchanges of glebe lands took place under the Inclosure Acts, and further sales were carried out under the compulsory powers acquired by statutory undertakers, such as railway companies.

In all, the Commissioners have about three shelf miles of files and some 400,000 deeds, most of which they are prepared to produce for bona fide students. The students, however, must realize that the Commissioners' office is a business office and not a record office, and that their records are administrative records akin somewhat to the County Council element in a County Record Office.

E. J. ROBINSON

---

[16] 23 & 24 Vic., c. 142.
[17] 51 & 52 Vic., c. 20.

The Records of the
Tithe Redemption Commission

As with all records, some knowledge of the historical background is necessary in order to understand the nature and purpose of the records in the custody of the Tithe Redemption Commission. Again, as in the case of so many English institutions and series of records, the starting point is the twelfth century. It is from that period that the parochial organization was established which subsisted with little change until the nineteenth century, while at the same time the payment of tithes to the rector of the parish had become universal. Tithes were of two kinds, personal and predial, that is, agrarian, and all we are concerned with in the present connection is the latter – the tenth sheaf, the tenth fleece, the tenth lamb and so forth, the tenth part of the yearly increase which the cultivator could not claim for himself but must give to the Church. In principle, tithes were payable in kind; but from very early times arrangements were made which substituted a money payment for a render of the actual produce of the land. The tendency to substitute payment in money for payment in kind was stimulated by the progress of inclosure and particularly by the Parliamentary inclosures of the eighteenth century. The object of these inclosures was the improvement of the land, and had they proceeded without some arrangement regarding tithes, the result would have been that rectors and vicars would have received an increased income without any contribution on their part. Of course, the same result happened if cultivation was improved without preliminary inclosure, and to this point we shall come. But one object of the local Inclosure Acts of the eighteenth and early nineteenth centuries was to get rid of the obligation of paying tithes. This was done in two ways: by the allotment of land in lieu of tithes or by the substitution of a money payment, which might either be fixed or might vary with the price of corn (hence the name of corn-rents applied to payments in lieu of tithes). The limits of the land allotted or of the lands charged with a money payment were, as a general rule, delineated on a map attached to the Inclosure Award.

Statutory inclosure was a purely local affair, promoted by local landowners, and though much of the country was covered, yet by 1836 tithes were still payable in the great majority of parishes in England and Wales. By that time the government of the day had decided upon the commutation of tithes throughout the country.[1] The reasons for this general commutation were, in the words of Lord John Russell, then Home Secretary, when he introduced the Bill, that tithe was generally held to be 'a discouragement to industry, a penalty on skill, a heavy mulct on those who expended the most capital and displayed the greatest skill in the cultivation of the land'. The payment of tithes was, he said, one involving great evils, and it was in view of the growing discontent of agricultural interests and of the tithe payers on the one side, coupled with the universal disposition

---

[1] Scotland and Ireland have a different history: the Tithe Acts did not apply to them.

of the clergy to say that 'if any fair method of commutation could be devised no set of men would be more glad to get rid of this objectionable payment', that the measure was introduced. The Bill received the Royal Assent on 13 August 1836, three Tithe Commissioners were appointed, and the process of commutation commenced. Although the Tithe Act, 1836, is a long and complicated piece of legislation, the underlying principle was the simple one of substituting for the payment of tithes in kind corn-rents of the same sort as were already payable in many parishes under the authority of a local Inclosure Act. These new corn-rents, known as tithe rent-charges, were not subject to local variation, but varied according to the price of corn calculated on a septennial average for the whole country. Existing corn-rents were left unaffected: they continued to be paid according to the varied provisions of the local Acts which created them.

It must be remembered that in 1836 there were no large-scale Ordnance Survey maps. Parish boundaries were a matter of repute, and it was only recently that there had been compiled (for the purpose of the decennial Census) a complete statement of the parishes and non-parochial places into which the country was divided. The Tithe Commissioners appointed under the Act therefore started upon their task of commuting the tithes of England and Wales with the advantage that they had an accurate index of every administrative unit in the country and with the disadvantage that it was a matter of chance whether or not there was a reliable large-scale map of that unit. In the great majority of cases there was no such map.

The first task of the Commissioners was to ascertain to what extent commutation had already taken place, and enquiries to that end were directed to every parish or township listed in the Census returns. The results of these enquiries are to be found in Tithe files which cover the whole of England and Wales and not only those parishes and townships where tithes remained uncommuted. There were a good many districts in which, although the tithes were commuted under the provisions of the Act of 1836, there was no Apportionment. This was either because the amount involved was negligible or because the landowners were themselves the tithe-owners and the agreement or award of a gross tithe rentcharge was followed by the redemption or merger of the tithe rent-charges. By this means the expense of a formal apportionment and of the preparation of a map was avoided. In such cases the result of the proceedings will be recorded in a formal Agreement or instrument of Merger.

In the normal way, however, for those parishes where uncommuted tithes were found to exist there ultimately resulted a Tithe Apportionment. The steps by which this result was reached can be followed in the legal textbooks of the day which reproduce the various forms drawn up by Tithe Commissioners for the guidance of landowners and tithe-owners and the officials–the Assistant Commissioners and Surveyors–who did the actual work.[2] These books are still essential for those who would fully understand the documents they may wish to consult. Later textbooks, dealing with the Tithe Acts, are naturally not greatly concerned with the machinery by which the Tithe Apportionments came into being. This complicated machinery it is unnecessary to describe here, and most enquirers who consult tithe documents for particular purposes have no need to master it. Suffice it to say that a tithe district generally comprised the district for which overseers of the poor were separately appointed, but the Tithe Commissioners could direct a separate district to be constituted in any particular case (Tithe Act, 1836, S.12). A list of tithe districts is contained in a House of Commons Return (No. 214 of 6 July 1887), which shows in respect of each district the amount of the tithe rentcharge awarded, and the character of the tithe-owner–spiritual rector, appropriator, impropriator or vicar.[3]

---

[2] L. Shelford, *The Acts for the Commutation of Tithes* (London, 1848); G. H. Whalley, *The Tithe Act* (London, 1838).

[3] Spiritual rectors and vicars are the incumbents in charge of parishes. Appropriators and impropriators are other owners of tithes: the former term is applied to ecclesiastical, and the latter to lay, persons and bodies.

Tithe apportionments

These generalities may suffice as an introduction to a more detailed description of the several classes of tithe documents. The most important in bulk and content, not only for historical purposes but for day-to-day administration, are the Tithe Apportionments, and these will be first described. Legally the Apportionment and Map constitute one document but they are best dealt with separately. Moreover in a majority of cases (over 8,300) the Apportionment and Map differ considerably in size and they have consequently been separated to ensure the better preservation of the Maps (Tithe Act, 1860, S.26). Thus, in only about 3,500 cases are the Apportionment and Map still combined, and these are, generally speaking, of the smaller tithe districts.

Most Apportionments follow the general pattern which was set out in the instructions issued at the time of general commutation. In the main, they are prepared on parchment sheets of a standard size ($21\frac{1}{2}$ by $18\frac{3}{4}$ inches) engrossed in manuscript, but there are exceptionally a few cases in which the Apportionment has been printed. The standard form of Apportionment – used in most cases – contains columns for the names of the landowners, the occupiers (since until the passing of the Tithe Act, 1891, payment of tithe rentcharge was the occupier's liability), the number of the tithe area, the name or description of the lands, the state of cultivation, the quantity in statute measure, the amount of rentcharge payable and the name or names of the tithe-owners. The Apportionment opens with a preamble reciting the names of the tithe-owners, the circumstances in which they owned the tithes, and whether the amount of rentcharge to be apportioned was the subject of an agreement between the landowners and the tithe-owners, for in default of such agreement a compulsory award was made by the Tithe Commissioners. The preamble usually contains, too, statistics as to the area and state of cultivation of the lands in the tithe district; the extent of the land subject to tithes and, if such be the case, of any lands exempt on various grounds from payment of tithes; and the amount of commons, roads, etc. It concludes with a statement showing the respective numbers of bushels of wheat, barley and oats which would have been obtained if one-third of the aggregate amount of rentcharge had been invested in the purchase of each of those commodities (Tithe Act, 1836, S.57) at the prices prescribed by the Tithe Act, 1837, S.7, namely $7/0\frac{1}{4}$ per Imperial bushel of wheat, $3/11\frac{1}{2}$ for barley, and $2/9$ for oats. The detailed apportionment of the aggregate tithe rentcharge then follows. A rentcharge is set out against each unit of charge, which may be a single close or a number of closes, termed a tithe farm. The amount of the charge is the par value, not the amount actually paid, which varied from year to year. The annual value of tithe rentcharge was ascertained and published yearly (Tithe Act, 1836, S.56), and tables were issued from 1837 onwards which enabled the precise payment due to be calculated for the par value of any amount of rentcharge.

Neither in the method adopted for apportioning the aggregate tithe rentcharge nor in the amount of detail given in the instrument of Apportionment was there any uniformity. In cases where the sum awarded was the subject of agreement it was unnecessary to set out a separate rentcharge on each inclosure and since this method was the cheaper, apportionment on farms instead of closes was encouraged. But by 1840 farm apportionment had been found so inconvenient that it was enacted that a field-to-field basis of apportionment was to be adopted unless a majority of the landowners requested otherwise (Tithe Act, 1840, S.21). One Apportionment may contain instances of both types of apportionment. Speaking generally field-to-field apportionments are more instructive (since they give more details of land utilization) as well as more convenient administratively.

A brief explanation of some seeming anomalies may be inserted at this point. If tithes had already been commuted for a modus or composition real, this payment, always of relatively small amount, was converted into an equivalent rentcharge. A corn-rent, also usually relatively low, might be similarly treated. The rentcharge awarded was not necessarily apportioned over all the lands at any uniform rate per acre, nor did the sum placed on any close or holding bear any relation to the actual amount of tithes paid when the land had been cultivated in the manner described in the Apportionment. The apportionment, in the majority of cases, was the subject of agreement between the tithe-owners and the landowners and occupiers of the lands, who naturally served their own convenience. Only in default of agreement was the apportionment the result of an award by the Tithe Commissioners. Land subject to tithes was frequently set out in the Apportionment free of rentcharge: this was possible if a landowner had other lands which afforded adequate security for the rentcharge. Conversely, small areas are sometimes charged with what seems a very high charge. It may often be found in such cases that the high rate of charge represents the yield of tithes from a particular type of property, e.g. a corn mill, which has long since disappeared.

The Tithe Acts provided for the making of an original and two copies of every confirmed instrument of Apportionment. All were sealed and signed by the Commissioners. The originals were retained in the custody of the Commissioners and their successors. The copies were deposited (i) with the Registrar of the diocese, (ii) with the Incumbent and Churchwardens of the parish (Tithe Act, 1836, S.64). Similarly, statutory copies of every subsequent Altered Apportionment and Certificate of Redemption were likewise made and sent to the respective custodians of the statutory copies. These local copies have been the subject of a good deal of legislation and their legal custodians have not infrequently been changed over the years. By the Tithe Act, 1936, S.36(2), they were placed in the charge and superintendence of the Master of the Rolls under whose directions many have been transferred to County Muniment Rooms or Record Offices. The documents which remained in the custody of the Tithe Redemption Commission were the originals. They are complete and have been maintained in good order: every subsequent change has been annotated upon them (or documents which have been substituted for them), and consequently all changes made by legal authority can be traced without difficulty. On the other hand the local statutory copies have in many cases suffered from neglect and accidental loss or destruction. They are rarely complete, and do not record any changes since 1936. This is a necessary warning. Nevertheless for many purposes the local copies may be found as serviceable as the originals. Great trouble has been taken by some county archivists to supply gaps in the series in their charge by photographic copies: in such cases there is rarely any purpose to be served in consulting the originals.

Altered apportionments

From the nature of things, the property divisions recorded in the original Tithe Apportionments speedily changed. In some few parishes, properties have passed undivided from generation to generation, but such instances are increasingly rare. Over much of the country changes in ownership have been great and repeated and have accelerated in the present century. These changes are reflected in the tithe documents, and notably in the Altered Apportionments. Historically the interest of these documents is not very great, especially since the formal document may follow an actual change in ownership only after a number of years, and a great many changes in ownership were not in practice followed by an Altered Apportionment at all. Nevertheless an interesting stage of urban development may be illustrated, and some striking examples of Victorian town-planning (which could be very good) are to be found among these documents. Their interest decreases with the publication of the large-scale Ordnance Survey maps. Prior to 1936 Altered Apportionments were laced up with the original Apportionment, unless their bulk necessitated a separate roll. Since 1936 these documents (Orders for Apportionment as they are termed by way of distinction) are filed separately: their interest is purely administrative.

Tithe maps

The Tithe Maps, of which there are approximately 11,800, are by no means as uniform as the

Apportionments: they vary greatly in scale and accuracy and, of course, in size, which may be from
1 ft to 14 ft in width, with corresponding length. The Tithe Commissioners had at the outset
endeavoured to secure a uniform standard. Their advice–and they could do no more than advise–
was that maps should be constructed on the scale of 3 chains to an inch (corresponding very closely
to the modern 25-inch scale). Unfortunately, however, in the absence in most cases of existing
maps which could be utilized for the purpose, there was no alternative to a new survey if a really
satisfactory map were to be produced. There were a good many highly skilled land surveyors whose
services were available, but the expense of any survey required fell to be defrayed by the landowners, and it soon became obvious that, where there was no suitable map already in existence, in-
sistence upon a high standard would retard the progress of commutation. Concessions therefore
had to be made, and when the 1836 Act was amended in the following year a provision was inserted
to the effect that, whilst every Tithe Map should be signed by the Commissioners, a map or plan
should not be deemed evidence of the quantity of the land or treated as accurate, unless it was
sealed, as well as signed, by the Commissioners (Tithe Act, 1837, S.1). Incidentally, in the case of
sealed Maps, the Poor Law Commissioners were empowered to pay out of the rates any portion of
the costs of making or providing such a map or plan for the purposes of the commutation proceedings: where this was done, the Guardians of the Poor had the right of free access to, and of making
copies or extracts of the Map (Tithe Act, 1842, S.13).

The scales to which the Tithe Maps were drawn vary from 1 to 12 chains to the inch,
although maps on the 3-, 4-, and 6-chain scales predominate, being utilized for, roughly, three-
fourths of the maps. They are not only of different sizes, due largely to the varying scales adopted,
but they vary widely in the degree of accuracy and finish. This explains why approximately 1,900
only of the Tithe Maps–about one-sixth of the whole–were sealed by the Tithe Commissioners, and
it is these alone–called first-class maps–which can be accepted as accurate. The unsealed (or second-
class) maps constitute a very mixed collection–indeed, some are little more than topographical
sketches. Many others contain discrepancies between Apportionment and Map which have in
subsequent years caused difficulties to the administration, although at the time of commutation,
when all the landowners concerned were intimately acquainted with the ground, accuracy of
mapping or refinements in the matter of acreage might appear to be matters of little significance.
Each landowner or occupier concerned knew his own land and its situation in relation to that of his
neighbours, so that the precise area of that land or its precise delineation on a map was of little interest. The matter assumes more importance nowadays, since it is when the boundaries of old tithe
enclosures have become obliterated by later developments that difficulties arise in present-day
administration. It is unnecessary to discuss in detail the problem of interpreting a Tithe Map; but
it is well to bear in mind that reliance cannot be placed upon the area of individual enclosures,
stated in an Apportionment or computed from the Tithe Map, unless the Map is sealed.

The numbers of the tithe areas on the Map correspond to those in the schedules to the
Apportionment. These numbers are not consecutive. In order to facilitate reference, most Tithe
Apportionments of any size have therefore been supplemented by a number list showing the page
of the apportionment upon which each tithe area appears. (These number lists are purely for convenience of reference and form no part of the original documents.) Even so, there are traps for the
unwary. The same series of tithe area numbers may be duplicated upon a tithe map, due, in most
cases, to the fact that more than one township is included in the same tithe district. But there are
some anomalies and duplications that are not easily explained. Again, different series of numbers
may be differentiated by letters or some other sign, either in the original Apportionment or subsequent Altered Apportionments as, for example, 22, 22A, 22^a, 22A^a, A22. Confusion may easily
result if care is not taken to observe the absolute correspondence of the number in the Apportionment with the number on the Map.

Awards and agreements

As stated above, the initial process in the commutation of tithes in a parish was an Agreement between the tithe-owners and landowners or, in default of agreement, an Award by the Tithe Commissioners. In the general case the next stage was apportionment, and the substance of the preceding Agreement or Award is then recited in the preamble of the instrument of Apportionment. Consequently a reference to the Award or Agreement will provide little more information than can be found in the Apportionment. Such interest as the preliminary documents afford lies only in such points as whether the parties acted by themselves or by attorney and the signatures of the parties: the kind of material, in fact, that may interest the family historian and has rarely any other significance. Where, for some reason or other, the commutation proceedings did not result in apportionment, these documents may be of greater interest, in conjunction with the correspondence on the relative Tithe file.

Deeds of Merger

Tithes (or tithe rentcharge) did not merge in the land merely by unity of possession, and the Tithe Acts provided for Mergers to be confirmed under the seal of the Tithe Commissioners. There are a large number of deeds of Merger executed under various provisions of the Acts in force until, by the Act of 1936, all tithe rentcharge was extinguished. Merger, either of tithes or tithe rentcharge, might take place before apportionment, and in such cases the Merger may have been effected by the original Agreement or Award and not by a separate deed. The instrument under which Merger was effected may be important to establish liability for chancel repairs.

Tithe files

The correspondence of the Tithe Commissioners is preserved in the Tithe files. These show the nature of the proceedings in the course of commutation. The files have been rather heavily 'weeded'. They contain, however, the reports of the Assistant Commissioner, who conducted the various meetings in the district in connection with commutation, and the draft of the Award where one was made. Some of the files also contain correspondence and drafts relating to later proceedings under the Tithe Acts, for example, the exchange of glebe land, the sale of tithe barns, the apportionment and redemption of tithe rentcharge. Where there was an Agreement between the parties, the files are not likely to contain very much of interest. The correspondence and reports of meetings leading up to a compulsory Award, on the other hand, are frequently instructive. Equally instructive are some of the files relating to the more uncertain payments in the nature of tithes which were ultimately ruled to be outside the scope of the Tithe Acts. The correspondence sheds a good deal of light upon the circumstances of some of the clergy in the early years of the nineteenth century and the attitude of their parishioners. Other files contain information on such matters as Inclosure and explain the limitations or the absence of an Apportionment.

Extraordinary tithe rentcharge

The Tithe Act, 1836, enacted (S.42) that the amount charged by any apportionment upon hop-grounds or market gardens should be divided into two parts, one called the ordinary and one the extraordinary charge, the latter to be at a rate per acre. This extraordinary charge ceased if the lands to which it was applied were no longer so cultivated after commutation. Conversely the extraordinary charge was payable in respect of grounds newly cultivated as hop-grounds or market gardens.

In 1886, however, the Extraordinary Tithe Redemption Act of that year provided for the cessation of this extraordinary charge and for its capital value to be ascertained and certified by the Tithe Commissioners. When the capital value had been ascertained, the land subject to the charge was thereafter charged with the payment of an annual rentcharge at the rate of 4 per cent per annum on the certified capital value, until the charge was redeemed. Under this Act Certificates of Capital Value were made in respect of some 500 districts in sixteen counties. A list was published as a House of Commons paper (109 of 1890).[4] In effect, this was a further process of commutation, providing for another set of tithe documents, consisting of the Certificate of Capital Value and the related Map. These documents differ from the original tithe documents both in size and form, the maps being prepared on 6 inch Ordnance Survey sheets, and dealing, in the main, with larger areas; the Act required the capital value to be certified in respect of 'each farm or, where not a farm, on each parcel of land in respect of which the charge is payable at the date of the passing of the Act'. Under the Tithe Act, 1936, payments made under the Extraordinary Tithe Redemption Act, 1886, were extinguished and replaced by terminable annuities of the same amount. In most cases these annuities have since been consolidated with other annuities charged on the same land.

Certificates of Redemption

Certificates of Redemption constitute one of the most numerous classes of documents. They record the redemption of tithe rentcharges under the various Tithe Acts. Until 1918 redemption could only be by payment of a lump sum, and the Certificates are of little interest. The Tithe Act, 1918, made provision for the redemption of tithe rentcharge by means of terminable annuity payments, initially for a period up to fifty years, but later extended by the Tithe Act, 1925, to sixty years. Consequently, since 1918 the Certificates are of two kinds, one class relating to outright redemption, and the other class (numbering about 5,000) relating to cases in which the tithe rentcharge was redeemed by means of a terminable charge,[5] which during its currency was itself liable to redemption or to further apportionment. Certificates of Redemption of the latter type are similar to Tithe Apportionments. They may be supplemented by the addition of later apportionments and they are annotated to show subsequent transactions. But it does not necessarily follow that all subsequent transactions are recorded since there is nothing to prevent the informal redemption of an annuity. Lands subject to such annuities can generally be identified by reference to the original Tithe Apportionment or, where the tithe areas have become divided in ownership, by the maps attached to later Altered Apportionments.

Corn-rents may similarly be redeemed either outright or by terminable annuities which are in all respects like the annuities for the redemption of tithe rentcharge. The lands charged are, however, identifiable either by reference to an Inclosure Award or to the map attached to an Order for Apportionment of Corn-rents.

Corn-rents

Under the Tithe Acts corn-rents may be apportioned and redeemed, and the Orders for Apportionment and Certificates of Redemption are among the records of the Commission. The original instruments creating the corn-rents are not, however, deposited with the Commission. These instruments are usually the Awards made under a local Inclosure Act, which are deposited with the custodians prescribed by the Act. Sealed copies of any Order for Apportionment or Certificate of Redemption under the Tithe Acts are sent to those custodians to be placed with the original instrument, while the original Order or Certificate is retained by the Commission and may be inspected like any other public document in its custody. It should be noted that an Inclosure Act may itself contain provisions for the apportionment or redemption of corn-rents, which are exercisable concurrently with the provisions of the Tithe Acts or have been exercised in the past. The records of the

---

[4] This list omits one case in the county of Dorset.
[5] Legally termed a corn-rent annuity, a term that also applies to an annuity for the redemption of a corn-rent.

Commission do not therefore cover all transactions relating to corn-rents carried out under legislative authority. It is known, moreover, that informal transactions are not infrequently carried out between the owners of corn-rents and landowners.

Records of Ascertainments

The duty of repairing the chancel of an ancient parish church fell on the owner of the rectorial property and was more particularly associated with the rectorial tithes, which, in so far as they had not already been commuted into corn-rents or allotments of land, were either merged or commuted into tithe rentcharge under the Tithe Act, 1836. So far as spiritual rectors were concerned their liability was for the most part transferred to Parochial Church Councils by the Ecclesiastical Dilapidations Measure, 1923. However, there still subsisted in 1936 a substantial amount of rectorial rentcharge in the ownership of ecclesiastical corporations, universities and colleges and other corporate bodies as well as private persons (commonly known as lay rectors). In other cases rectorial tithes and tithe rentcharge had been merged in land under the Tithe Acts and liability attached to the ownership of that land. The Tithe Act, 1936, extinguished all tithe rentcharge and it was necessary therefore to provide for liability for chancel repairs that had hitherto attached to the ownership of rectorial tithe rentcharge and any vicarial rentcharge that exceptionally fell into the same category. The proportionate liability of all these tithe-owners was ascertained and this is set out in a Record of Ascertainments. The liability continues in the case of ecclesiastical corporations, certain universities and colleges, the owners of merged land and the owners of land in which tithe rentcharge was constructively merged by the operation of Section 21 of the Tithe Act, 1936. In all other cases, where there was liability in respect of the ownership of tithe rentcharge, it was extinguished and compensation paid by the tithe-owner to the appropriate ecclesiastical authorities.[6]

Records of Ascertainments are bound in county volumes in alphabetical order of chancels. Where the ascertainment was to the effect that no such liability attached to tithe rentcharge or, if such liability existed at commutation, that it had ceased to exist, a Declaration was made accordingly. These Declarations, which sometimes embrace a number of chancels, will usually be found at the end of the respective county volume.[7] In interpreting these records, it will be appreciated that, since the liability is related to the ownership of tithe rentcharge, the identity of the lands in respect of which the liable rentcharge was payable will need to be ascertained by reference to the appropriate tithe documents, which may cover either an entire parish or a separate district prescribed within a parish. Where the rentcharges were merged before apportionment the lands will usually be described without reference to a map, and such information as is available regarding them is to be found in a deed of Merger or sometimes an Agreement.

A copy of the Record of Ascertainments should be among the parish papers and, if the Tithe Apportionment is also there, as well as all the subsequent Altered Apportionments up to 1936, the whole of the material necessary for the interpretation of a record exists locally, unless in that particular parish there was a merger of tithe rentcharge before apportionment. Where the whole of the liability falls upon one or other of the corporate bodies mentioned above, the record by itself gives all the information necessary in regard to liability formerly attaching to the ownership of tithe rentcharge, but not, it should be noted, in regard to liability attaching to other forms of rectorial property. The Commission has issued a leaflet[8] on this complicated and highly technical subject and to this the reader is referred for further information.

---

[6] This took the form of an issue of Stock, which was deducted from the amount which otherwise would have been issued to the tithe-owner.

[7] Some are bound in separate volumes.

[8] Form 1724, which may be obtained on application to the Commission.

Registers

When the Tithe Act, 1936, was passed it was contemplated that the Tithe Apportionments and Maps would be superseded by a new series of Registers (Tithe Act, 1936, S.9). Under post-war conditions, the expense of preparing and maintaining Registers to cover the whole country was found to be prohibitive, and, accordingly, by amending legislation Registers are prepared only where the Apportionment is no longer serviceable. Few Registers have, in fact, as yet been made and the great majority of Apportionments are consequently still in use for administrative purposes and are likely to continue to be used until 1996, after which redemption annuities (which have superseded tithe rentcharge) will cease to be payable.

Annotations on tithe documents

In order to enable the incidence of tithe rentcharge to be readily ascertained the original Tithe Apportionments have been annotated to record later official transactions for Altered Apportionment, Merger or Redemption. The same system has been extended to Certificates of Capital Value, Altered Apportionments of all kinds (tithe rentcharge, extraordinary tithe rentcharge, corn-rents, corn-rent annuities, redemption annuities) and Registers. The annotations form no part of the tithe document, but they afford an index to amending transactions and enable the present position to be ascertained with the minimum of trouble. The local copies of tithe documents do not bear official annotations.

The foregoing statement is subject to some obvious qualifications, which it is necessary to bear in mind. Where the Commission have made and sealed a Register under the Tithe Act, 1951, or have made a Declaration thereunder that no annuities subsist in the tithe district, then, for all purposes connected with current administration, the original tithe documents have been superseded. Again, the original tithe documents may be superseded by an Order (and Map) made under the Tithe Acts, 1936 and 1951. Where this has been done in any tithe district, the number-list in the relative Tithe Apportionment will be marked 'All annuities determined'. Wherever, therefore, any of these three types of document exist–Register, Declaration or Order determining all annuities– the original tithe documents cease to be annotated because they no longer disclose the current position. Nevertheless these documents will still be required for the purpose of identifying lands originally charged with tithe rentcharge in that district, e.g. in connection with chancel repairs.

Inspection of documents[9]

All the records included in the list in the Appendix are open to inspection free of charge.

Tithe Apportionments (and connected documents) bear a reference consisting of the county number and district number. Thus Bedfordshire bears the county number 1 and the districts in Bedfordshire are numbered serially 1/1 to 1/64.[10] Extraordinary tithe districts are in a separate county series beginning with number 56. Other series of records are not, however, classified in this way, but usually bear serial numbers within the class.

Enquirers should bear in mind that the location of every district is that of the time of commutation and not necessarily that of the present day. For example, no tithe districts are classified under the County of London, the Isle of Ely or the Soke of Peterborough. Tithe districts in what now

---

[9] Since this article was written there have been changes in the custody of the records referred to. In 1960 all of them passed into the custody of the Board of Inland Revenue but the Tithe Apportionments (and the altered Apportionments bound with them), Tithe Maps, Deeds of Merger and Tithe Files, and Awards and Agreements other than those referred to in the final sentence of the paragraph so headed, have since been transferred into the custody of the Public Record Office and the annotation of Tithe Apportionments and Altered Apportionments has been discontinued. Application to inspect documents in P.R.O. custody, or to be supplied with copies of them or extracts from them, should be made to that Office. Similar applications in respect of documents which remain in Inland Revenue custody should be made to the Tithe Redemption Office, Inland Revenue (H), Barrington Road, Worthing, Sussex.

[10] This system is also used, as a rule, for the current records of the Commission which are not open to inspection.

comprises the County of London (outside the City of London, for which there are no tithe documents in the custody of the Commission) are shown under Middlesex (21), Kent (17) or Surrey (34), as the case may be, those in the Isle of Ely under Cambridge (4), and those in the Soke of Peterborough under Northampton (24). Many parishes now in the county of Northumberland (25) appear (as formerly) under Durham (11), whilst many others appear in counties different from those of which they now form part. The name of the tithe district is also that at the time of commutation: many districts have been subsequently divided and many absorbed wholly or in part in modern administrative areas. Enquirers who experience difficulty in deciding which particular documents administrative areas.

H. G. RICHARDSON

APPENDIX

	Dates
Awards and Agreements	
(Tithe Acts 1836–60)	1836–66
Chancel Repairs	
Records of Ascertainments	1939–51
Corn-Rents	
Altered Apportionments	1862 onwards
Certificates of Redemption	1886 onwards
Extraordinary Tithe Rentcharge	
Certificates of Capital Value	1886–9
Redemption Annuities	
Orders for Apportionment (Tithe Act, 1936)	1937 onwards
Registers (Tithe Acts, 1936 and 1951)	1951 onwards
Tithe Files	
Correspondence of Tithe Commissioners and successors	1836–93
Tithes and Tithe Rentcharge	
Declarations of Merger	1837–1936
Tithe Rentcharge	
Apportionments and Maps	1836–86
Altered Apportionments	1843–1936
Certificates of Redemption	1847–1936

The Archives of the English Province of the Society of Jesus at Farm Street, London

By way of preliminary to a brief catalogue raisonné of the archive titled above, a short note on the organization of the Society of Jesus, as it affects the English Province, seems indispensable. The division of the Society for administrative purposes has not changed much in its main principles during the four hundred years or so of its existence. The General, at least until the time of writing (June 1965), has always been elected for life by a General Congregation specially summoned for the purpose at the death of his predecessor, in accordance with rules laid down in the Constitutions. All other superiors, including Provincials (heads of Provinces), hold office for a term only, six years being a norm for higher appointments, and for all practical purposes. The world-mission of the Society is divided into Assistancies, each consisting of one nation or group of nations, associated usually according to language or culture, and having an appointed representative in Rome to advise the General in governing the Assistancy. The Assistant is appointed from one of the constituent countries or Provinces of the Assistancy. So there is, for example, a French Assistancy, a German, Spanish, Italian, Indian, and an English-speaking Assistancy. Although of the same language, the United States form another Assistancy. The Assistant does not give orders: advises only. Each Assistancy is divided into Provinces headed by the Provincial appointed from Rome. The Provincial has authority to command and institute policy, albeit under the supervision of the Roman Curia of the Society. The offices of the latter are staffed by responsible Jesuits of appropriate nationality so that no unnecessary conflicts arise. Every Provincial has a Socius, or secretary, and a Procurator to deal with the financial side of provincial administration: also Consultors to advise. According to these various divisions by office and responsibility, the contents of the archive under review may be conveniently grouped; and the terminology given above will suffice to explain most, or at least much, in the labels.

The English Province, which included Wales from its beginnings, and Scotland from the beginning of the restored Society (1815), came into formal existence as such in 1623. From the coming of Edmund Campion and Robert Persons in 1580 until 1619, this area was a Mission with a local superior in England and a head in Rome. From 1619 until 1623 it was a Vice-Province dependent on Flanders. In 1623 it became an independent Province. The Province archives are mainly concentrated in two places. Stonyhurst College, Lancashire, has most of the extant early papers and transcripts running from about 1580 and covering the seventeenth century, but with many later papers as well. The Stonyhurst collection has been summarily surveyed in the second and third reports of the Historical Manuscripts Commission of 1870 and 1872 respectively. Farm Street has most of the later papers on general province affairs running from about 1700, especially those dealing with procuratorial matters. These have not previously been adequately summarized or calendared in any published report.

The logical point at which to begin this short survey would appear to be the correspondence with Rome. There are six volumes of photographic reproductions of the Generals' letters to Mission Superiors and Provincials. The originals, covering the same period, 1605–1769, are kept in Rome. Signed originals of similar letters for 1750–1892 occupy four more volumes, while for subsequent years the letters form a loose collection. These letters, written by hand by secretaries and signed by the General, are more confidential in nature, and were intended mainly for the attention of Provincials and their confidential advisers. In this they are opposed to circular letters sometimes addressed to the whole Society, sometimes to an Assistancy, or even a single Province. Provincials also issued their own circular letters to their Provinces from time to time. The Generals' circulars begin in the Farm Street collection at 3 April 1587 (a reprint of a letter detailing passages from the Old Testament to be omitted by the public readers during meals in the Society's refectories). The series is only continuous from about 1830. Letters from the Assistant are included in a bound volume, 'Foreign Correspondence, 1776–1859' (472 ff.), and also in a series of loose letters for 1877–88. Nineteenth-century transcripts from old catalogues in Rome give terse but essential details of birth, place of origin, time in the Society, health, studies and work of individual members of the Province between 1593 and the suppression in 1773. There are also printed catalogues of Jesuits in Russia for 1803/4, 1805, 1809/10, and although there are no recognizable British names among them, one is reminded of the curious and transient connection of the English Province with the Russian Empire. As is general knowledge, the 1773 Bull of suppression remained unpromulgated in Russia since Catherine the Great withheld her *placet*, an essential condition to its valid application. Thanks to the irony of circumstances, Protestant Britain likewise made no special move against the Society, and without continuing the title, the Jesuits in Britain virtually pursued a policy of business as usual. Indeed, on 27 May 1803, Pope Pius VII gave oral permission for the former British Jesuits to affiliate themselves to the unsuppressed Jesuits in Russia. From the universal restoration of the Society in 1815 until the present day, the series of printed catalogues is fairly complete, especially from about 1840.

From 1623, England and Wales were divided for provincial administrative purposes into 'Colleges' and 'Residences'. 'College' is here taken in its sense of a group or assembly, as used, e.g., in describing the College of Cardinals, and indicated an area of operation, certainly not a building. 'Residence' was used in much the same sense, and was used to refer to an area of lesser importance and usually smaller extent, where the superior had less power of individual action, theoretically, than the Rector, who ruled a College. In fact, the superior of a Residence could come to enjoy more freedom, perhaps, than the Rector himself since the latter was bound more specifically and expressly in his work by the written Constitution of the Society in a way the local superior, technically his subordinate, was not. As correspondence in the archives makes clear, in the Society as elsewhere, a great deal always depended on personalities. In the days of persecution, the Jesuits were scattered for the most part among the houses of Catholic gentlemen and nobles. With the eighteenth century, if not before, Jesuit communities and houses as such became more common, resembling the smaller houses of the contemporary Society. Even in the darkest days, however, there were a few houses where Jesuits could be reasonably secure from pursuit, and lie up for a brief while for rest, and go through the spiritual exercises of St Ignatius. All of which explains how it was possible to preserve records at all, but also why there are so many lacunae and inadequacies in these archives.

The bulk of the records described here are divided according to these 'Colleges' and 'Residences'. Many are still kept in files or deeds-envelopes, but they are gradually being guarded and bound in volumes, beginning, of course, with the oldest and most interesting: or one should perhaps say resuming, since many early papers were bound in the late nineteenth century.

The College of St Ignatius covered London and extended into Middlesex, Berkshire, Kent and Hertfordshire. It retained the title of 'novitiate' until 1773, although in fact no novices were trained here after the celebrated 'Clerkenwell search' of March 1628. The Jesuits were established in this 'College' at some twenty-nine places at different times in the seventeenth century. Included was the well-known 'White Webbs', associated with Father Henry Garnett sj from 1604 to 1606.Two colleges in an educational sense existed from 1687 to 1688 at the Savoy, and in Golden Square at the Bavarian Embassy. Of these no more need be said since there is no record of these earlier institutions at Farm Street beyond modern notes. The earliest original records of the London District begin at 1750 and are mainly financial, dealing with gifts and bequests to the mission made by Charles, Earl of Shrewsbury, Frances Rawe, Father John Poyntz, and others. There are details of a school or college which ran in London from 1824 to 1835, the earlier ancestor, in some sense, of the contemporary Jesuit schools at Stamford Hill and Edge Hill, Wimbledon, each of which has a deeds-envelope in the archive. From about 1834, when a church was established at St John's Wood, re-cords become more numerous. Records of the nineteenth century throw light on a church in Westminster which preceded the cathedral, Farm Street Church, opened in 1849, a residence at 9 Hill Street, about the same time, and the chapel of St Augustine at Tunbridge Wells. There are a number of early registers, account books and files also dealing with the Church of the Immaculate Conception, Farm Street, and a recently bound volume (315 ff.) illustrating the history of the church and its earliest origins from 1802 to 1865. More light on this project may be found in a box-file on Cardinal Manning which includes letters and papers also on a proposed Catholic University College (1880–8), and the foundation of a central school at Westminster. Concerning the latter is a 'Prospectus for establishing in London a great Catholic central middle-class school for boys, on the great commercial principle of the age, cooperation and limited liability'. There are also a few interesting papers, some printed, on the question of Catholic attendance at Protestant universities which was a live issue from 1869 to 1885.

The College of the Holy Apostles operated mainly over Suffolk and Norfolk, Cambridge and Essex. The most important papers for 1775–1840 have been bound (309 ff.). They deal principally with Norwich and Bury St Edmunds. A foolscap box-file contains later nineteenth-century material while the Bury *Historia Domus*, account books and other papers bring the story down to 1929 when the parish was handed over to the secular clergy.

Lancashire, Cheshire, Staffordshire and Westmorland formed, in 1623, the College of Blessed (afterwards Saint) Aloysius. This district included Stonyhurst College, the oldest surviving institution in the Province, and has left behind the largest group of documents in the collection for a single area. They fill some eighteen deeds-envelopes as well as a number of account-books, day-books and financial analyses drawn up in the mid-nineteenth century. From 1660, Staffordshire hived off to form the Residence of St Chad, becoming a College in 1671/2. For archive purposes, this distinction is practically ignored. Records for Lancashire begin about 1700 with a file on the costs of salaries and services for 1702–1836, and another on district affairs, 1725–65. Procurators' letters for the district run from 1744 to 1792. Portico, Prescott, Bedford, Leigh, Gilmoss, Croxteth, Fazakerley, Dunken-halgh, Formby, Croft, Westby Hall, Ince, Crosby (Little), Accrington, Blackpool, Chipping, Clitheroe, Clayton all have at least a few papers, commonly starting from about 1750. Preston, especially the three churches of St Wilfrid, St Ignatius and St Walbergh, has several files. Liverpool is also well represented. Separate files deal with the Mile End Chapel and its transfer to the secular clergy, 1822–4; the Edmund Street Chapel, and a dispute with the good Benedictines, 1743–1844; St Anthony's Chapel, 1819–40 and Sir Thomas's Buildings' Chapel, 1788. There are two modern files on the church, parish and school of St Francis Xavier's Salisbury Street, a mid-nineteenth-century foundation. Wigan and St Helens each has a file of modern papers. Two envelopes enclose the accounts of the curious West Leigh Corn Tithes, a source of income to the Society recorded here from 1656 to 1941, and not always yielding its modest harvest without controversy. Papers on Stony-hurst in London are source material from 1793 onwards: that is from the time of its transfer from the continent owing to disturbances created by the French Revolution. There is also much original material for its history while at Saint-Omers, which has been put to good use most recently by the Rev. H. Chadwick sj in his *Saint-Omers to Stonyhurst*, London, 1962. The college also made a relatively brief stay at Liège. Its history is contained in several volumes: 'Correspondence relating to Saint-Omers and North Wales, 1666–1781' (volume 1, 284 ff.), and 'Liège: Procurators' Correspondence, 1682–1739' (volume 2, 307 ff.); volume 12, (305 ff.), is devoted to Saint-Omers and Stonyhurst in the period 1763 to 1829 as well as with the restoration of the Society and the Paccanarists, which may be described as an interim substitute for the Society.

The Old College of St Francis Xavier, as opposed to the present homonymous institution in Liverpool and its dependencies, was founded for the West Country, including not only Devon and Cornwall but also Wales. Incidental references apart, records at Farm Street only begin with 1743 for this College as a whole. A volume of papers on Bristol and its environs begins at that date and ends in 1847. Unfortunately, many of these papers were damaged seriously at some time by damp. They have recently been 'sundexed', guarded and bound in black buckram. They form an interesting supplement to the papers held by the Bishop of Clifton. Another volume for 1746 to 1853 is made up of general and mainly financial documents on the mission (282 ff.) and at least touches on Bristol, Shepton Mallet, Hereford, Swansea and Glamorgan. Hereford also has a volume to itself for 1779–1855 (224 ff.). After 1666/7, North Wales ceased to be part of the College of St Francis Xavier, when it became the Residence of St Winefride. A volume noted above (vol. 2), dealing with Saint Omer, also embraces the St Winefride papers for 1666–1781. In addition, there is 'An abstract of writings relating to the Star Inn in Holywell' for 1639 to 1669 (2 ff.); also an 'Abstract of old writings relating to Llanvechan', 1620–1728 (8 ff.). There are two copies of this. A deeds-envelope of loose documents deals mainly with the shrine and the Society's interest at Holywell for 1743 to 1843, but the papers are not numerous.

Returning to the north of England, Durham, Cumberland and Northumberland comprised the Residence of St John the Evangelist. One rather inadequate volume (212 ff.) covers its history from 1717 to 1858. A Residence of St Dominic, also part of the primitive foundation, and dealing with Lincolnshire, was transformed in 1676 into the College of St Hugh. Its papers for 1723 to 1869 have been bound. Yorkshire formed the Residence of St Michael which served at different times or simultaneously some thirty-seven mission posts. Its headquarters was at York until 1685 when it transferred to Pontefract. In 1849 it was raised to the status of a 'College'. A bound volume (417 ff.) covers the period 1813 to 1860. Richmond, Pontefract, Wakefield, Skipton, Huddersfield, Selby, Brough Hall, and Leeds are the centres mainly covered.

Oxfordshire, Buckinghamshire, Bedfordshire and Northamptonshire formed the Residence of St Mary. A volume (358 ff.) having as its main subject Oxford itself runs from 1729 to 1876. It includes a number of holograph letters from Bishop Ullathorne and a short, hitherto unpublished (?) letter from Cardinal Newman to the Jesuit Provincial, dated 22 February 1871: 'My dear Father Provincial, Thank you for your letter. Nothing can be more natural than that the Society, which so lately has had the mission of Oxford, and for so long, should resume it. Yours [&c.]'. There are also several letters from the Marquess of Bute dated between 1871 and 1876.

Moving south brings us to the oldest series of papers on the English mission. They occupy a volume (321 ff.) for the period 1613 to 1839 and are the records of the Residence of St Thomas of Canterbury. This part of the mission included Sussex, Wiltshire, Hampshire and Dorset; and the main stations for the missioners were at Soberton, Bonham, Canford, Stapehill, Lulworth, and Wardour. The many names of donors and benefactors have among them the distinguished Arundell family of Wardour, the heads of which enjoyed the very rare distinction of being Counts of the Holy Roman Empire as well as barons of their titular seat. Next to this residence in time, though not of course in space, was another named after St George which covered Worcestershire and Warwickshire, the earliest papers of which fill a volume (238 ff.) beginning at 1635 and going up to 1695. Two more foolscap files contain eighteenth-century and later papers. Among other interesting items in the volume is a small account book for the two years preceding the Popish Plot of Titus Oates. It includes two pages in the hand of Anthony Turner, the Jesuit martyr, who was executed for alleged complicity in the plot. This diary has been published by Mrs A. M. Hodgson in a recent issue of the journal of the Worcestershire Catholic Historical Society. The volume also contains references to, and signatures of, the Winter/Wintour, Windesor and Talbott families among many others. The south-west of England was, for Jesuit purposes, the Residence of Blessed Stanislaus (Saint Stanislaus from 1701) and comprised Devon and Cornwall. A smallish volume (228 ff.) contains much of the Jesuit history of this area for 1655–1845. Ugbrooke and Chudleigh were the principal stations. The documents include a number of references to the family of the Lords Clifford, Barons of Chudleigh. The bulk of these letters date from the end of the eighteenth century. Here too there are references to the family of the Barons of Wardour. The Rev. Joseph Reeve, superior of the ex-Jesuit mission in the Napoleonic era, is well represented, and provides an example of the continuity of the work of the Society in England even after its formal suppression. In this part of the collection there are interesting letters from Lord Petre and Dr George Oliver, an old Stonyhurst boy, who made valuable historical collections for the history of the Society and the Catholic Church in the West Country generally (see below, p. 270).

With the achievement of Catholic emancipation in 1829, the 'Second Spring', and wider opportunities for expansion, the Society in England, with the approval and, indeed, orders of the Roman authorities, began to turn its attention to foreign missions. Even before this, from the 1630s in fact, English Jesuits were deployed in the Maryland mission. Letters from 23 January 1772 until 10 March 1835 make up volume 25 of these archives. They include original letters from the hand of Bishop Carroll of Baltimore, Bishop Neale his co-adjutor, and from a number of Jesuits. The British Guiana mission was entrusted to the English Province in 1857. A good series of letters and reports contained in two files covers the history of the mission from the foundation year until 1939. It contains, among other items, Bishop Etheridge's notes for a history of the mission up to 1877, although the relevant material for the period prior to the Jesuit take-over is missing, presumed destroyed. Letters for the Rhodesian, formerly known as the Zambesi, mission begin at 1878 and continue until 1934. There are many original letters, and most recently, by courtesy of the Rev. W. F. Rea SJ transcripts of letters still in Zambia itself have also been added. There are also tables of general statistics and a clip on colleges. An interesting relic is part of the diary of an early pioneer, Peter Prestage SJ for 1882–3, eaten by white ants through some of the pages but still preserving valuable information. The other half of this diary is still in Africa but a microfilm of it has been sent to London. Here also is the first register of the first school opened at Empadeni in 1887 by Father Prestage in the days of Lobengula. Admittedly, it is not a prepossessing relic, being a small notebook of the cheapest kind.

Until quite recently, the English Province had a direct hand in missionary endeavour in India. The Catholic mission at Calcutta was founded by the Prince Bishop of Paderborn in 1802. English Jesuits went to the mission from 1834. By that time it was clear that English-speaking missionaries would be indispensable if proper liaison were to be maintained with the paramount political, and growing cultural, influence. A clip on general history and lists of personnel includes a brief history, printed in India, consisting of three magazine articles with written notes at the end; also a copy of the 'Relatio . . . fundationis' of 1802; a report for 1832–41, and a list of Fathers and Brothers from 1834–47. Another clip of outgoing letters from India covers 1834–47, while nineteen letters addressed from Dublin, Rome, London, Clongowes, and Stonyhurst deal at least in part with this mission from 1833 to 1848. With the sale of St Francis Xavier's College to the Protestant Bishop of Calcutta, Dr D. Wilson, at the end of 1847, the connection of this Province with India seems to have ended for a time. Apart from a few miscellaneous and undated papers, there are general accounts and financial details for 1834–49. The English Jesuits' connection with India was re-established a few years later. Documents on the Bombay mission, including printed memorials, especially concerning the Portuguese question, go from 1861 to 1911, though very intermittently. There are also letters on Madras (1871), Karachi (1870–1), an address from Travancore of 1881, Poona letters of 1889–92, and one from Cannanore (24 January 1893).

A mission in Jamaica began in 1837 and consisted of one Jesuit. The mission was held by the English Province until 8 December 1893, when it was transferred to the Maryland and New York Province. Correspondence in this archive goes over the whole period of its association with the English Province and even beyond: until 1901 to be precise. Among the documents is an interesting diary for 1872 kept by one of the Fathers. It mentions many details of local life and illustrates a few of them with small sketches. The first move made to bring British Jesuits to Honduras seems to have been in 1821. The first superior of the English mission was appointed only in 1853, although until 1875 his charge was to some extent subordinate to Jamaica. In 1882, Salvador de Pietro became Superior, Prefect Apostolic in 1889, and received consecration as a bishop in 1893. On 8 December of that year, Honduras was transferred to the American Jesuit Province of Missouri. Correspondence at Farm Street runs from 1821 to 1897, and includes statistics and two sketch-maps; but is scanty being limited to some fifty-two pieces.

Malta, as is a matter of general knowledge, came under enduring British political influence at the close of the Napoleonic wars by the treaties associated with Vienna. With the early 1840s, English cultural pressures were considerable; and there was some fear of a Kulturkampf between the indigenous Catholic tradition of the island, with strong Italian influences, and the new factor being rather forcefully introduced by the Anglo-Saxons. The British Jesuits were called in, primarily by the authorities of the Catholic Church and the Society itself, but also by sheer destiny, perhaps, to avert, as far as they could, a serious clash. Their task was to preserve the essentially Catholic features of Maltese higher education, at the same time making it compatible with the northern tradition. In this they were at least tolerated by the English civil administration as the lesser of two evils, the worse one being unmitigated Italian and Mediterranean influence. Nevertheless, there were many cross-currents, as ever in this small but highly complex island, and the history of the colleges run at different times by the English Province was far from unchequered. Farm Street papers on the Maltese ventures fill three large deeds-envelopes. Among them are two small diaries kept by the Minister, or vice-Superior, between 1848 and 1858 when the first college–St Paul's as it became–was kept open. The staff was mainly Italian, although British Jesuits taught English and mathematics. The General of the Society leaned rather to Italian, it seems, than English culture, if only because the islanders themselves were more in sympathy with this at that time; and it then seemed a more obvious vehicle for Catholic education. The Archbishop of Valletta was not friendly to the anglicizing element, and even refused to give the college a church. Financial difficulties were present from the start. Finally, Father Beck, the General, deemed it prudent to yield to the views of the Archbishop, and on 21 May 1858 the college was suppressed. The need for higher education remained, however, and since, for political reasons, the government refused to countenance an Italian college as such, it was almost inevitable that the English Province should be called in to make a fresh attempt: this time with what had once been a Protestant school at St Julian's Bay. Father John Morris SJ, later editor of *The Month* and well-known for his writing, was appointed Rector on 26 July 1877, and the school opened in November. Its transactions mainly fill another deeds-envelope. On the whole this College of St Ignatius flourished for some years; but there were difficulties, this time with the University of Valletta, very much under the same enduring Italian influence. The college came to an end in 1907, although Joseph Dobson SJ remained behind to wind up its affairs, and only returned to England in the following year. Property rights in the college were not relinquished for some time: papers from 1908 till 1928, in fact, form the third section of this part of the archive.

Since the British civil administration took a lively interest in these colleges, the letters from the Governors of Malta and other officials concerned give the subject of Malta a wider appeal, perhaps, than other documents, or than many of them: hence the somewhat larger treatment given them here. A movement began to re-open a college run by British Jesuits soon after the first world war. Times had changed, and from 1921 to 1923 the British authorities, hesitant enough in the nineteenth century, fully favoured the re-entry of the English Province to the island in an educational way. Negotiations came to nothing, but they occupy another file. The failure was due, as much as anything, to pressure on the manpower of the Society in England and elsewhere. Special clips among these Maltese papers deal with one or two personal causes célèbres; also the question of mixed marriages between Catholics and non-Catholics, a problem which came to the fore between 1891 and 1896, and involved correspondence with the Archdiocese of Westminster as well as with the Governor. Not only the English Province but the Sicilian was concerned with Maltese higher education at one time; and representing as they did diverse ethnic cultures, something like rivalry developed between them, if not a serious difference, as is apparent from documents for 1888–98 when the problem of English versus Italian influences in education became rather acute. A few interesting transcripts of original documents on the island and elsewhere illuminate the expulsion of the Jesuits from Malta in 1768 and events leading up to it. A printed monograph of Dr Alfredo Mifsud, published in Malta in 1914, enlarges on the same topic.

The above collections, systematized according to place, consist in large part of letters and reports of individuals. Sometimes individual members of the Society and others left behind sufficient letters, or were important enough in their own right, to justify the classification of their correspondence, as it was thought, under their own names. The following are the more significant collections, perhaps, of this kind, but from the foregoing it will be evident, no doubt, that the fact that an individual is thus listed does not mean that some of his letters do not appear elsewhere under place, or other headings. The earliest collection of this kind fills volume 1, 'Notes and Fragments of Father Thorpe, 1585–1790'. John Thorpe SJ was at the English College, Rome, from 1757 till the suppression in 1773. He stayed on in Rome, acting as agent for his brethren until his death on 12 April 1792. He was professor, seemingly, of *literae humaniores* and English penitentiary at St Peter's. He was responsible for saving much and even most of the English Province records from loss or destruction at the time of the suppression. Thus he deserves special mention even in so short a paper. The best of what he saved or salvaged is now at Stonyhurst. The volume under review, as the name implies, is in the first part mainly a collection of torn letters and scraps, but there are a number of complete original letters and transcripts in the volume, and the whole is of considerable interest if only for some of its autographs and signatures. Among them may be found writings of Dr Barrett, President of Douai College–his is the first fragment, of 19 November 1585–Robert Persons, Richard Blount, Giles Schondonck, John Gerard, Ralph Bickley, all of the Society of Jesus, and, conjecturally, of Tobie Matthew. There is a good deal in the way of notes and transcripts on the English College, Rome, itself in the hands of Father Thorpe. Another volume is filled with his extracts for 1707–73, while transcripts of his own correspondence from Rome with Henry, eighth Baron Arundell of Wardour, between 1773 and 1791, fill another. Charles Brooke SJ likewise compiled interesting historical notes and transcripts for the seventeenth and eighteenth centuries which fill two small volumes.

As one would expect from the introduction to this brief survey, the more numerous, and probably more significant, letters kept at Farm Street date from the middle of the eighteenth century. A volume of letters (351 ff.) from bishops and cardinals for 1753–1853 includes correspondence from Cardinal Wiseman and Bishop Ullathorne of Birmingham. A companion volume (492 ff.) is made up of letters from non-Jesuits, mainly priests and Catholic laymen, for 1766–1857. Included are a number of letters of Dr George Oliver, the antiquarian and scholar, who published a valuable *Collectanea* on the Society in Britain (two editions, Exeter, 1838 and 1845). Dr John Lingard, a shining light of Ushaw, is represented in original correspondence, including his own letters, which fill a 260-folio volume and run from 1818 to 1860. Among his correspondents in this volume was Canon M. A. Tierney. Another two volumes of transcripts of Lingard's correspondence cover together 1818–51. Among other eighteenth and early nineteenth century collections, one must note a volume of original letters of Father Charles Plowden sj running from 1764 to 1821 (428 ff.); also transcripts of his and Father William Strickland's letters for 1779–91; letters of Marmaduke Stone (1788–1832) (124 ff.), of Nicholas Sewell (1776–1832) (124 ff.), and of James Connell (1792–1803) (67 ff.), all of the Society. These letters were taken to Rome in 1895 by John Hungerford Pollen sj at Father General's request, re-arranged in chronological order, and rebound in July 1898. Dr John Milner, Vicar-Apostolic of the Midland District, wrote fairly often to Charles Plowden and his brother Robert, also a Jesuit, and to others whose letters are bound together in two volumes for the period 1790 to 1826, the year of Milner's death. To complete a reasonably detailed picture of life for the Jesuits and ex-Jesuits in the years preceding, during, and following the suppression, i.e. at the restoration, there is also the volume of William Strickland's letters for 1756 to 1811 (244 ff.). Further information on the English scene at this time is contained in volume 10 (327 ff.), 'Scottish Mission: eighteenth and nineteenth Century'. Thomas Glover sj, sent to Rome in 1825, was secretary to the General from 1829 until 1849. During his stay he compiled three volumes of historical transcripts which went to Stonyhurst. The third volume was copied once again, and very legibly, by a Servite nun of South Tottenham in 1896. This copy was given to the Rev. J. H. Pollen. It bears the title, 'Re-establishment of the English Province, S.J., 1773–1829'. A further mine of information on this era of Province history is provided by Brother Henry Foley's five manuscript volumes on which his widely-known 'Records of the English Province . . .' are based. There is a fair amount of unpublished material here, although the ore takes a good deal of digging out from the inevitable informality and almost disordered array at times of what are essentially personal notes.

Penetrating more deeply into the nineteenth century, the Rev. Joseph Stevenson sj was, in his day, Rector of All Saint's (C. of E.) Church, Leighton Buzzard, part-editor of the Calendar of State Papers (P.R.O.), a scholar of eminence, and eventually a Jesuit. He maintained a wide correspondence, and Farm Street possesses a fair number of his received letters. Four loose-leaf books, home-made from contemporary (?) printed works, contain letters of 1831–2 from R. Wedall and J. Smith; of 1833 with R. Pitcairn, R. Wedall and I. Morton while the recipient was working in the Department of MSS. of the British Museum; of 1829–33, and of 1834 with largely the same correspondents. Other letters of Stevenson's include an interesting correspondence with J. Hosack, the writer on Mary, Queen of Scots, on precisely that subject; with various Catholic notables, bishops, fellow-Jesuits and scholars, including Sir J. Duffus Hardy and his colleagues in connection with the publications of the Rolls Series. Stevenson's interests ranged over a broad field of scholarship, and a considerable number of transcripts, mainly medieval, from his hand or by his commission, are kept at Farm Street. They fill fifteen foolscap files and are principally in French, Latin and English. They begin with Alcuin and end in the seventeenth century; include John de Trokelow's annals of Edward II (from a Cotton MS.), documents from the Vatican before 1500, from the Inquisition at Lisbon (demolished 1822), antiquities of Leighton Buzzard (Henry II–Richard II), a list of historians from the eleventh to the fourteenth centuries whose work at the time Stevenson wrote was either in print or manuscript, the Nuncio Grimani's correspondence with Cardinal Farnese of 1543, de Selve's dispatches to the King of France for 1547–8, Acts of the Privy Council for 1555 (Harleian MS. 353, ff. 146–79v.), Queen Christina of Sweden's *Draco Normannicus*, and many other documents including royal letters of 1438 to 1605. One may note in passing the extensive collection of Elizabethan and Jacobean transcripts at Farm Street, but these are, for the most part, in active and continual use by the historiographers of the Province and are not generally available.

Further collections of nineteenth-century letters include transcripts of Canon M. A. Tierney's (editor of Dodd's Church History) letters to ecclesiastics and scholars. The Rev. Henry Coleridge SJ, who wrote a life of Mary Ward, left behind a correspondence on the subject. There are also copies of letters sent to him by John Henry Newman. Richard Cooper's letters to Thomas Cooper, of 1842–4, deserve mention, but more important are those of Henry Schomberg Kerr SJ who has been honoured with a full-length biography. The archive has his letters from Cyprus of 1879, papers concerning the Kerr family at Dalkeith (1738–1896), his chaplaincy to Lord Ripon, Viceroy of India, a correspondence between Lady Kerr and E. Bellasis of 1850 and 1870, and H. S. Kerr's letters from the Zambesi mission together with his journals and diaries. Joseph Keating SJ a former editor of *The Month*, left a number of letters, among them two from A. Conan Doyle of 1894. Augustus Henry Law SJ, another pioneer of the Zambesi and Rhodesian mission, is well represented in letters, journals and diaries for the period 1845–80. Among the letters of J. H. Pollen SJ, historian (d. 1925), is a holograph from W. E. Gladstone of 15 May 1894. Edward Purbrick SJ, Provincial for the uniquely long period of eight years (1880–8), was probably responsible for a *Liber Responsorum* of 1864 to 1896 recording the answers of the Generals to various queries ranging from the time to be given to examinations in philosophy to whether *The Month* should discuss the question of the Papal temporal power. Another Purbrick notebook has for subject the Provincial, General and Procurators' Congregations between 1883 and 1906. This Jesuit was an ardent educationist, and a collection of his printed papers on higher Catholic education is useful for related topics from 1871 to 1895. Apart from what may be learned of him in his letters, there is an anonymous MS. account of him by one who knew him personally. A well-known writer in his day on spiritual matters was Joseph Rickaby SJ, whose diaries and correspondence, with a few other papers, run mainly from 1889 to 1926. William Amherst SJ, brother of a bishop, is recorded not only in letters to his mother and to the Poor Clares, but also in a rather valuable collection of documents, notes and transcripts, including some original correspondence and press-cuttings, for a history of the Catholic Church in England from 1748 to 1850, with notes for subsequent years also. A separate foolscap box-file holds the correspondence of his brother Francis Kerril Amherst, Bishop of Northampton from 1858 until his resignation in 1879. Among them are letters written when the bishop was present at the First Vatican Council describing its incidentals to family and friends. James Albany Christie SJ bequeathed to posterity an album of correspondence and press-cuttings with other papers which throw light on–*inter alia*–a case in Chancery in 1873 involving the Baroness Weld. Another court case which left behind a considerable amount of paper was associated with the Rev. W. H. Eyre SJ, while the Caddell–Jerningham case of 1888 involved Father Peter Gallwey, a well-known writer, in a charge of 'undue influence' in the making of a will. With the exception of Father J. Stevenson, and possibly Brother Foley, the largest number of papers and letters in the archives were left behind by Herbert Thurston SJ who wrote journalistically but very reliably on a vast number of topics. He reached depth in several of his researches especially in the field of psychic phenomena. Unfortunately, his handwriting is often very difficult to decipher. John Morris SJ, editor of *The Month* for a time, and author, also left behind a significant correspondence which includes original letters from Cardinal Manning. Many of the documents outlined above have already been used in various published works.

Every growing archive collects a certain number of documents which do not fit readily into any general scheme of classification, or which deserve mention in their own right. Among Farm Street papers of this kind one may note four short tracts or studies formerly among the Phillipps MSS., with their catalogue numbers in that collection: 'News from Spain, 1618' (7186) (cf. British

Museum, Stowe MS. 281, a pamphlet by Thomas Scott, printed in 1620 and suppressed, and re-printed in Somer's Tracts, vol. II, 1809); a 'Life of Pope Gregory the Great' (8694); 'Rome's Plea for her Popes' (9439); and 'England's Safety' (9454). All appear to be in an early seventeenth-century hand. An original letter, seemingly, of Michael Baius, the celebrated theologian of Louvain, to Father Polanco, Secretary of the Society, bears the date 17 March 1569. The oldest document in the collection is an indenture concerning the village of Hyndley in Lancashire, and is dated 25 March 1537 (28 Henry VIII). A devil's advocate view against raising Cardinal Robert Bellarmine to the altars is provided in 'Voto dell . . . Cardinale Domenico Passionei fatto e presentato a N. S. Papa Benedetto XIV nella causa di beatificazione del . . . Cardinale Roberto Bellarmino', a manu-script of 231 pages written in 1757 at Rome. A gift of Alexander Fullerton Esquire was the French MS. 'Tableau de l'Ordre Religieuse en France avant et depuis l'Edite de 1768'. It is possible that it came from the library of the Archbishop of Paris when the Archevêché was destroyed in 1831. It is a neatly drawn-up catalogue of 210 pages giving details on the principal French foundations of the various Orders and Congregations throughout France, viz their numbers, houses and incomes. The small quarto volume retains its original eighteenth (?) century binding in red morocco leather with embossed spine and gold tooling. It carries the following notice on p. 210, 'Délibéré et approuvé en l'assemblée générale du Clergé de France sous la présidence de Monseigneur l'Archevêque de Nar-bonne, Primat: session de . . . [1773] . . . 2° exemplaire'. A curious heraldic album with coats of arms in colour, 'Preuves de Noblesse des Dem [oiselles–cf. index] de St Cir', is another leather-bound small quarto volume of some 100 pages, each indicating the descent of a girl received at the college. Its conjectural provenance may be the same as for the last. From the other side of the world are thirty holograph oaths of obedience made in accordance with the Papal Bulls *Ex illa die* of 1715 and *Ex quo singulari* of 1742. Such oaths had to be taken by all Catholic missionaries to the Far East between 1742 and 1942. Signatures include the Bishop of Peking, of Nanking, of Macao and also for some Annamite priests for whom the oath had been translated according to an early form of the romanization of that language. Some of these missionaries were Jesuits, and all are of the eight-eenth century. For the other side of the world, there are notes and papers on the unsuccessful canonization cause of John Palafox (1600–59), Bishop successively of Angelopolis (near Mexico) and Osma. Original letters to the Rev. William Bliss from the Rev. John Keble, and from the latter to William Henry Bliss, son of the clergyman, have been stuck in an album. The letters are dated from 1812 to 1866. There are also a few from Dr Pusey to W. H. Bliss seemingly taken–torn, in fact, and clumsily enough in places–from another similar album. This volume is inscribed, 'The library of William Henry Bliss, Oxford, 1866' with 'from' inserted before Bliss's name. It is further inscribed on f. 1, 'Sent to the Revd H. J. Coleridge SJ 29 July 1870. Will. H. Bliss'–all in the latter's hand.

Artistically, the two most attractive documents, if historically among the less significant, are a communication of the spiritual privileges of the Society to the noble ladies Magdalen, Veronica and Anne Cecily, all of Hatstein: such communication was sometimes granted to notable benefactors of the Jesuits, and this document is signed by the General, Mutius Vitelleschi, given at Rome on 8 March 1628: also an authentication of a gift of relics of Saints Sulpicius and Aurelia to William Wolfgang, Duke of Neustadt, likewise signed by Vitelleschi, and dated from Rome, 15 March 1616. Both documents are illuminated on vellum, beautifully written in capitals in a Spanish (?) style in brown ink with gold initials. Although the illumination is not comparable in fineness of execution with the best work of this kind, it is competent enough, the same hand apparently producing both documents.

The Farm Street archive, to sum up, is a small, highly specialized collection, but having con-nections with subjects more generally pursued, and certainly indispensable for some aspects at least of the history of the Roman Catholic church in Britain.

FRANCIS O. EDWARDS SJ

Local Administration

Land Drainage Authorities
and their Records[1]

This article makes no claim to be an exhaustive survey of its subject. In the first place it does not attempt to deal with records of land drainage prior to the Statute of Sewers of 1531. Such of these as have survived, almost all among the Public Records, do not constitute a series, and no very satisfactory picture of the workings of medieval drainage administration can at present be drawn from them. Secondly, my examples are for the most part taken from those parts of the country, and those collections of drainage records, with which I am personally most familiar, so that the reader will detect a territorial bias in favour of the eastern half of England. Thirdly, very little is said here about those chartered corporations which administered drainage in Hatfield Chase, the Great Level of the Fens (the Bedford Level), and Romney Marsh, since, interesting and indeed important as these are for the historian of the subject, they cannot be called typical land drainage authorities.[2] My purpose in what follows is to give some account of the more usual types of drainage authority and of the records these produce, in the hope that it may prove of some interest and use to those who need to explore a class of records which, for both archivists and historians, is still largely *terra incognita*.

The literature of the subject is indeed scanty. No general history of land drainage in this country exists, save only Sir William Dugdale's classic *History of Imbanking and Draining* which first appeared in 1652[3] and is thus not merely out-of-date but concludes before many extant series of drainage records begin. This is not to belittle its value–which is very considerable–for the history of medieval drainage and the work of the seventeenth-century 'adventurers' in the Fenland, but it is essentially 'collections for a history' rather than a connected account. A more recent attempt to cover the ground is that of the Webbs, who in the fourth volume of their work on English local government included a chapter on the history of courts of sewers and other types of drainage

---

[1] Based on a paper read to a meeting of the Eastern Region of the Society of Archivists on 6 October 1962. Reports on many of the collections mentioned can be seen at the National Register of Archives. Not all even of those collections which are in record offices have been fully sorted and listed; partly for this reason, I have made no attempt to give precise references in the footnotes to individual documents quoted. I should like here to express my gratitude to all those officers of drainage authorities and to those archivists, who have allowed me access to documents in their charge or have in other ways assisted me. For the purpose of this reprint I have added references to a few publications of the last decade and made some essential corrections, in part the outcome of my own further research but mainly necessitated by the administrative changes resulting from the Water Resources Act of 1963.

[2] The records of the Hatfield Chase Corporation are now deposited in the Department of Manuscripts, Nottingham University; those of the Bedford Level Corporation in the Cambridgeshire Record Office; and those of the Lords, Bailiff and Jurats of Romney Marsh in the Kent Archives Office.

[3] 2nd edition, revised by C. Nalson Cole, 1772.

administration.[4] The usefulness of this is limited, first, by the authors' primary concern with the century and a half from 1689 to 1835, the treatment of earlier and later periods being rather summary; secondly, by their greater familiarity with the courts of sewers in and around London than with those in more rural parts, whose administrative vagaries they seem to have found somewhat bewildering. The metropolitan commissioners of sewers, preoccupied with the drainage problems of built-up areas and in particular with the disposal of urban sewage–with sewers, that is, in the modern sense[5]–were, however, not typical, the average land drainage authority being concerned first and foremost with the drainage of agricultural land and, in coastal areas, its protection from the sea. The student of land drainage will therefore do better to turn to some of the local studies that have appeared since the Webbs wrote.

No complete bibliography of the subject can be attempted here, but attention should be drawn to a few studies which deal particularly with its records and not merely with its history. For London itself, the work of the Webbs has been superseded by Miss Darlington's paper on the London Commissioners of Sewers' records.[6] An edition of the late sixteenth-century records of the commissioners of sewers for the Parts of Holland in Lincolnshire is being published; the first volume, edited by Miss Mary Kirkus, contains a useful introduction and bibliography of more than local interest.[7] Accounts of numerous other collections of drainage records in the county are to be found in the printed annual reports of the Lincolnshire Archives Office. Similar collections in Kent –locus classicus for the historian of land drainage–are described in the Guide to the Kent Archives Office; several other local record office guides include accounts of drainage records. The present writer has, in a brief article, described two large accumulations of records (mainly of statutory drainage commissions) relating to West Norfolk and has also discussed the usefulness of sewers records to the historian.[8] Other studies less directly concerned with the records, but throwing light on the administrative history, include an article by S. G. E. Lythe on drainage organization in the East Riding;[9] H. C. Darby's two volumes on the Fenland;[10] the work of Samuel Wells on the Bedford Level, published in 1830[11] but still indispensable for the administrative history of that district; M. Teichman-Derville's admirable survey of the history of the Lords, Bailiff and Jurats of Romney Marsh;[12] and Michael Williams's account of the Somerset Levels.[13]

At the present time (1972) there is a two-tier system of drainage administration in England and Wales. The upper tier consists of 27 river authorities and 2 catchment boards, the lower of some 360 internal drainage boards or similar bodies; the relationship between them may perhaps be compared with that between a county council and county district councils. This is the latest stage of an administrative tidying-up process which began in earnest only with the Land Drainage Act of

---

[4] S. and B. Webb, *English Local Government*, IV (1922), ch. I, 'The Court of Sewers'.

[5] 'Sewer' originally meant simply a watercourse, a channel for fresh water. The modern sense appears to have originated *c*. 1600 (see *O.E.D.*).

[6] Ida Darlington, 'The London Commissioners of Sewers and their Records', *Journal of the Society of Archivists* vol. II, no. 5, reprinted below pp. 282–98.

[7] *Records of the Commissioners of Sewers in the Parts of Holland 1547–1603*, I, ed. A. M. Kirkus (Lincoln Record Soc. 54, 1959); II, ed. A. E. B. Owen (Lincoln Record Soc. 63, 1968); a further volume is in preparation.

[8] 'Land Drainage Records of West Norfolk' (unsigned), *Bulletin* of the National Register of Archives, no. 10 (1959). 'Records of Commissions of Sewers' (Short Guides to Records no. 15), *History* LII (1967), pp. 35–8.

[9] 'The Court of Sewers for the East Parts of the East Riding', *Yorkshire Archaeol. Journal*, XXXIV (1939), p. 11. This volume also contains a further article by the same author (p. 282) on medieval drainage organization in the district.

[10] *The Medieval Fenland* and *The Draining of the Fens* (1940).

[11] *History of the Drainage of the Great Level of the Fens called Bedford Level*. 2 vols.

[12] *The Level and the Liberty of Romney Marsh* (1936). An appendix lists the records of the Lords, Bailiff and Jurats (then at New Hall, Dymchurch), and relevant material elsewhere.

[13] *The Draining of the Somerset Levels* (1970).

1930 and is still going on.[14] Before that Act the scene was a good deal more confused. So recently as 1927 the Royal Commission on Land Drainage in England and Wales found what Darby describes as 'a tangle of authorities with antiquated powers and inadequate resources'.[15] The number of drainage authorities had proliferated, especially in the nineteenth century, to such an extent that they were literally getting in each other's way. The authors of a standard work on land drainage law published in 1884[16] complained that there were then so many assorted authorities possessing jurisdiction under private Acts of Parliament that the successful application of public statutes of drainage was impossible. They instanced the position on the river Nene, between Peterborough and the sea, where no less than fourteen different sets of commissioners had jurisdiction over a distance of only thirty miles. Those imaginary authorities the Fen Drainage Board, the Wale Conservancy Board, and the East Level Waterways Commission, invented by Dorothy Sayers for her detective novel *The Nine Tailors*, which has a Fenland setting, were not much more litigious and irresponsible than many authentic ones.

The area administered by a river authority or catchment board is in general based on a single major river system such as the Thames, Severn, or Great Ouse, but in parts of the country with no very large rivers the boundaries of the area have some relation to county boundaries. Thus in Lincolnshire the Lincolnshire River Authority administers the county area *minus* those parts in the south within the catchment area of the Welland and Nene River Authority and those parts in the north-west within the area of the Trent River Authority. Within the catchment area of many, but not all, of these authorities are a varying number of internal drainage boards,[17] which are frequently the direct successors of older bodies – courts of sewers or statutory drainage trusts or commissions – and in such cases have usually inherited their records. For example, the West of Ouse Internal Drainage Board in Norfolk Marshland is the successor of the Norfolk Court of Sewers, which survived under that name down to 1949 and possessed records beginning in the late sixteenth century.[18] The Minsmere I.D.B. in East Suffolk is the successor of the Minsmere Level Drainage Trust set up under the Minsmere Level Act of 1810 and possesses the Trust's records. Some of the river authorities are likewise successors of older bodies. Thus the Great Ouse River Authority is heir to the Bedford Level Corporation. The Somerset River Authority succeeded the Somersetshire Drainage Commission set up under the Somersetshire Drainage Act of 1877, that body being itself the successor of the old commissioners of sewers for the county.

Although the statutory drainage commissions and trusts are of later origin than the courts of sewers, it will be convenient to discuss them first since their composition and records are relatively uniform and straightforward in character. These statutory bodies were often set up in districts

---

[14] Under the Water Resources Act 1963 the functions previously exercised by 32 river boards were, with effect from 1 April 1965, transferred to 27 river authorities, which at the same time took on new duties in respect of water resources. For a detailed account of the present-day constitution and workings of river authorities and drainage boards, see A. S. Wisdom, *The Law of Rivers and Watercourses* (2nd edition, 1970), especially ch. 11, 'Land Drainage'.

[15] *The Draining of the Fens*, p. 256. Some idea of the variety of bodies concerned with drainage which existed forty years ago may be had from the relevant pages of the *Local Government Directory*. The issue for 1932 names some 460 such bodies in England and Wales, including catchment boards, commissioners of sewers, drainage boards and a miscellany of other authorities. Almost all the commissioners of sewers have now been replaced by drainage boards and the number of miscellaneous authorities has been much reduced.

[16] G. G. Kennedy and J. S. Sandars, *The Law of Land Drainage and Sewers*, pp. 8–10.

[17] The *Year Book* of the Association of River Authorities for 1972 shows the Great Ouse River Authority with 79 I.D.B.s, Yorkshire Ouse and Hull 63, East Suffolk and Norfolk 39, Trent 27, Welland and Nene 21, Somerset 20 Essex 19, Lancashire 16, Lincolnshire 14, Gwynedd 12, Kent 11, Severn 8. Ten river authorities had between 1 and 6 I.D.B.s each, the remainder none. In some cases, however, the internal boards are directly administered by the river authority, e.g. all those in Essex, 15 out of 16 in Lancashire, and 11 out of 12 in Gwynedd.

[18] The records of the Norfolk Court of Sewers to approximately 1900 are now deposited in the Norfolk and Norwich Record Office.

where commissions of sewers already operated. This overlapping arose from the need to remedy a supposed defect in the law. Kennedy and Sandars[19] considered that it had probably been the intention of the authors of the Statute of Sewers of 23 Henry VIII – the statute on which all subsequent legislation was founded – that commissioners of sewers should have power to order the construction of new works of drainage 'where, in their discretion, it should be beneficial and necessary'. But the wording of the statute left room for uncertainty; the courts took a narrow view and held that commissioners of sewers had no power to construct new works but only to maintain or improve existing works. To overcome this difficulty, the practice arose of obtaining a private Act conferring the desired powers on a body of drainage commissioners or trustees for a particular district, and a large number of such bodies were created in the eighteenth and nineteenth centuries to execute new works of drainage or make radical improvements. An example is the River Adur Navigation Trust in Sussex, set up under an Act of 1807.[20] The trustees included the commissioners of sewers for the Rape of Bramber, and the Act obliged the trustees to obtain the consent of the commissioners before the proposed works for improving the navigation could be executed; financial responsibility was to be shared between the commissioners and the trustees. It seems clear that the trust was really a device to enable the commissioners of sewers to carry out new works which would otherwise have been ultra vires.

In the Great Level of the Fens the Bedford Level Corporation became, on its creation in the seventeenth century, the sole commission of sewers within the district. But its responsibility was limited to maintaining the main drains, and for various reasons these became increasingly inadequate to prevent flooding. As time went on, 'groups of landowners were forced to supplement the larger drainage scheme by local district enterprise'. Following a test case, a series of local drainage districts regulated by commissioners were created within the area by private Act from 1727 onwards.[21] The purpose of such a commission may be found explained in the preamble to the Act (a copy of which is often attached to the flyleaf of the commission's minute book) in some such words as 'for draining and preserving certain lands and fen grounds lying in the parishes of Outwell, Stow Bardolph, Wimbotsham and Downham' (Bardolph Fen Drainage Commission), 'for draining and improving certain fen lands, low grounds and marshes and other lands' in Wormegay and six other parishes (Wormegay Polver Drainage Commission), or 'for more effectually draining and preserving' lands in the Stoke Ferry district (Stoke Ferry Drainage Commission).

The records of these bodies comprise, besides the conventional minutes, accounts, correspondence, etc., of any organization, various classes produced by their specialized functions, e.g. engineers' reports, agreements with contractors, plans and sections of proposed drains, etc. There may be extensive records of rates or loans, since the drainage commissions financed themselves by levying rates on the land benefiting, or expected to benefit, from drainage schemes, or sometimes by a loan based on the security of future income from such rates; the earliest records of the Stoke Ferry Drainage Commission are a number of assignments of rates and taxes as security for loans from 1771 onwards. Particular mention should be made of the maps which may be found in records both of statutory commissions and courts of sewers from the late eighteenth century onwards. Notable examples of these are bound up with surveys and jury 'verdicts' relating to the coastal districts of East Lincolnshire among records of the Alford and Spilsby courts of sewers, such as a verdict of 1777 which includes a coloured map by John Hudson of lands in several parishes

---

[19] *Op. cit.*, p. 59 etc.

[20] *Descriptive Report on the Quarter Sessions, Other Official and Ecclesiastical Records in the Custody of the County Councils of East and West Sussex* (1954), pp. 193–4.

[21] The first private district Act within the Bedford Level, passed in 1727, was 'An Act for the effectual draining and preserving of Haddenham Level in the Isle of Ely'. This level comprised about 6,500 acres in four parishes. Darby, *Draining of the Fens*, pp. 118–21.

assessed towards a new sea bank at Sutton-le-Marsh, and a survey made in 1816 by Thomas Mager of lands in Sutton below high-water mark (i.e. the whole parish) with a large-scale map on which all fields are marked and numbered. In West Norfolk the records of one drainage board include a map of Stow Bardolph Fen made about 1798, with fields numbered and all roads and drains named. Such maps can form a most useful supplement to the usual estate, tithe and enclosure maps for the topographical enquirer.

Courts of sewers provide a good deal more variety than do statutory commissions. Local idiosyncrasies of administration and peculiar classes of record abound. Some of these local peculiarities may well have their roots far back in the Middle Ages, representing a survival of local forms of organization which evolved naturally from the peculiar needs of local drainage,[22] and which persisted despite official attempts to impose everywhere a system based on the custom of Romney Marsh.[23] Considerations of geography suggest that the Romney Marsh form of administration was not always best suited to the very different conditions in other parts of the country; and it is scarcely surprising that in the Somerset levels, for example, or in the great expanses of the Fenland and adjacent low-lying areas, vestiges of the older organization should have survived well into the nineteenth century, to baffle the Webbs and delight the connoisseur of administrative nonconformity.

In some parts of the country it was customary for all the commissioners of sewers–all, that is to say, who were prepared to attend–to meet as a single court of sewers administering the whole area within the commission. Thus the East Kent commissioners met regularly at Canterbury;[24] but this was a compact area with a meeting-place conveniently central. In Somerset and Lincolnshire, each covered by a single commission of sewers, the practice was altogether different. Here 'we see the commissioners dividing themselves into groups, according to the locality of their properties, and holding regularly several separate courts . . . each exercising jurisdiction only over a particular district . . . and each attended, in practice, only by its own set of commissioners'.[25] The Webbs felt obliged to castigate this system as 'extra-legal', but no legal objection seems ever to have been raised (the system was, after all, no different from that of the J.P.s deployed in petty sessions), though judicial exception was taken to another facet of local autonomy, the 'standing juries' of Somerset, early in the nineteenth century, as a result of which they were discontinued.[26] In Lincolnshire the sub-divisions of the commission corresponded roughly to those ancient county divisions the wapentakes, which were of a convenient size for administrative purposes. The organization was, however, flexible, so that for some two centuries after the Statute of Sewers of 1531 we find a considerable area of East Lindsey between the Humber and the Fens, large enough to be later divided amongst half-a-dozen autonomous courts, apparently being administered as a single unit.

The writer has devoted some study to the records of these East Lindsey courts.[27] It is difficult to judge how far their practice may or may not have been typical of courts of sewers generally, but some notes on them may at least help to unravel complexities of sewers administration in other parts of the country. In Lincolnshire, as elsewhere, the local administration centred on the clerk of sewers. Though not a permanent official in the modern sense, he was, as Miss Darlington remarks of

---

[22] An example of such survival is discussed in A. E. B. Owen, 'The Levy Book of the Sea: The Organization of the Lindsey Sea Defences in 1500', *Lincolnshire Archit. and Archaeol. Soc. Reports and Papers*, IX, pt. 1 (1961), pp. 35–48.

[23] From at least as early as 1427, when the first Act of Sewers was passed, commissioners of sewers were enjoined to proceed in accordance with 'the custom of Romney Marsh'; but a determined effort to impose it generally does not seem to have been made until the sixteenth century.

[24] S. and B. Webb, *op. cit.*, p. 46.

[25] *Ibid.*, p. 52.

[26] Kennedy and Sandars, p. 88. For further information on these 'standing juries', which also existed in Kent, see S. and B. Webb, pp. 41–51, and M. Williams, *op. cit.*, ch. 7.

[27] These records are deposited in the Lincolnshire Archives Office.

the London clerks, 'the kingpin of the organization in each of the levels'. In the early seventeenth century there may have been a single clerk for the whole of the Lindsey division of the county, since the first two minute books of the East Lindsey series, beginning in 1626, contain entries for all parts of it. But this must have been too large an area for efficient administration, especially when floods necessitated speedy action. From about the middle of the seventeenth century to the 1740s the six easternmost wapentakes of Lindsey–Ludborough, Loutheske, Calceworth, Candleshoe, Hill and the Soke of Bolingbroke–seem to have formed the effective unit of administration, the principal repository of records for the area being the sewers office over Louth church porch. In the 1730s Maurice Johnson refers to a clerk of sewers at Spilsby.[28] In 1742 Thomas Brackenbury was clerk not only for the six wapentakes just named but for the adjacent ones of Gartree and Horncastle as well; but there were already signs of administrative fission. Separate minute books began to be kept for the Alford court (Calceworth wapentake) in 1741, for the Horncastle court (Horncastle and Gartree) in 1743, and for the Spilsby court (Candleshoe, Hill and Bolingbroke) in about 1750; and this was followed by a division between the courts of the records hitherto kept at Louth.

The minutes record some of the stages in this division and are worth quotation for the light they throw, not only on the administrative history but on methods of local record-keeping. The minutes of the Alford court, 28 March 1751, state that it had been represented to the court by several of the commissioners attending it

that the records of sewers in Louth church porch for want of sufficient repairs thereof and other accidents are very much damaged and several of them destroyed. It is therefore ordered by this court that William Marshall esquire Richard Pilkington and Mr Lister Fitzwilliam with the Clerk of the Sewers do as soon as conveniently may be search for and take out of the said church porch all the records and papers concerning the sewers that belong to the wapentake of Calceworth and lodge the same carefully in a convenient place to be provided for that purpose in the parish of Alford within the said wapentake. And they are thereby ordered and empowered to provide a box or chest with three locks for the preservation of the said records.

This task had evidently been carried out by 10 May 1753, when the court ordered the clerk 'as soon as conveniently may be' to lodge all the sewers records for the wapentake now in his hands (presumably the more recent records) 'amongst the records of sewers in Alford church porch'. The Spilsby court followed suit. On 8 May 1753 the court ordered that the records in Louth church porch for Candleshoe, Hill and Bolingbroke be removed as soon as possible to 'some convenient place' in Spilsby. Once again, this proved to be the church. On 25 March 1755 the court ordered

that the building[29] erected in Spilsby church for lodging the records of sewers belonging to this division be forthwith painted and made convenient within for placing the said records. And that the Revd Mr William Shepherd Mr Joseph Brackenbury and Mr John Wright together with the Clerk of Sewers do sort the said records and place the same in order in the said building as soon as they conveniently can. And that the three keys provided for the said building be kept by the Reverend Mr Shepherd the Treasurer, the Revd Mr Joseph Brackenbury and Mr Thomas Brackenbury Clerk of Sewers.

It is now time to see what these records were. Courts of sewers produced not only the conventional records of administration and the technical records of drainage, such as have already been mentioned in connection with the statutory commissions, but certain classes of a judicial character. The earliest series of sewers records begin in the mid-sixteenth century. The main record of each court's business is comprised in the minute books, which deserve particular mention since they often survive from an earlier date than other classes of record. This main record may be found under a

---

[28] Owen, 'The Levy Book . . .', p. 35. Maurice Johnson, the Spalding antiquary (1688–1755), was himself a clerk of sewers for Holland and 'a very earnest searcher of the records in his custody' (Lincs. Archives Office, *Archivists' Report*, 1954-5, p. 43); my reference is taken from his own volume of collections on sewers, now in the possession of the Spalding Gentlemen's Society.

[29] The 'building' was presumably a large cupboard.

confusing variety of titles, e.g. 'order and decree books' (though separate registers of orders and decrees only were also compiled), 'court and order books' or 'presentment books', and the term 'minute book' may sometimes denote only the draft of this record. The earliest such records known to me are the 'order and decree books', actually original minutes, of the East Kent commissioners, which begin in 1562 and constitute a very good series.[30] The minutes of the Surrey and Kent commission covering most of what is now London south of the Thames, which begin in 1569, are the only published minutes of a commission of sewers.[31] Outside south-east England, the earliest minutes – again, a good series – known to me are those of the Gloucestershire commissioners which begin in 1585.[32] The minutes of the East Lindsey courts, as already mentioned, do not begin until 1626; in other respects, however, the records of these courts form one of the fullest and earliest collections existing, with classes such as dikereeves' accounts and 'laws of sewers' (see below) surviving in abundance from soon after 1560. Among characteristic classes in Lincolnshire sewers records are: the original commissions; 'verdicts' or presentments of the sewers juries, setting forth the state of the sewers and sea banks and indicating who was responsible for their upkeep; so-called 'laws of sewers', really orders or decrees of the court giving effect to the jury's findings; sets of 'general laws' or by-laws; and records of various officers such as the treasurer and surveyors. It may be noted that as the commissioners came to rely more and more on their technical officers, the surveyors or engineers, for information about the works needed, the jury verdicts became increasingly formal. The various London commissioners found that such presentments had outlived their administrative usefulness before the end of the eighteenth century, though they contined to be compiled down to 1847.[33] In Lincolnshire formal presentments were still being made by at least one court of sewers as late as the 1920s, though by that time the presentment was written out in advance and a jury of 'twelve old topers' was then rounded up by the clerk and given a shilling apiece for swearing to what was put before them.

The dikereeves, whose name explains their function, were local officers apparently peculiar to Lincolnshire, the Marshland district of Norfolk, and the northern parts of the Isle of Ely.[34] Elsewhere officers of sewers, such as marsh bailiffs, discharging similar duties were appointed directly by the commissioners.[35] But the dikereeves were elected parish officers, usually two in number, comparable in status with the highway surveyor or the constable, being under the orders of and responsible to the courts of sewers much as the surveyor and constable were responsible to quarter sessions. In Lincolnshire the dikereeves submitted their accounts annually to the courts of sewers. The original accounts survive in great numbers in the East Lindsey records from the 1560s

---

[30] I am indebted to Dr Felix Hull for drawing my attention to the East Kent series, which is in the Kent Archives Office, and to the true nature of the 'order and decree books'. That the series originally began even earlier is apparent from an entry in the first surviving book which refers to the need to search 'the last book of decrees'.

[31] *Court Minutes of the Surrey and Kent Sewer Commission*, vol. 1 (no more published) (London County Council, 1909). Covers the years 1569–79.

[32] The records of this commission and of its successor, the South Glos. Drainage Board, are in the Gloucestershire Records Office. I am indebted to Mr B. S. Smith for information about them.

[33] Darlington, *art. cit.*, p. 288.

[34] In the original version of this article I postulated that East Yorkshire also had dikereeves, on the basis of a statement by Lythe, *op. cit.*, p. 17, who refers to 'seadyke-graves' or 'syddy-graves' as collecting drainage rates in Holderness. But I could find no other reference to such officers in Yorkshire, and Mr N. Higson, the East Riding archivist, now tells me that he cannot recollect ever encountering officers with this title or the title of dikereeve in the East Riding. It must therefore be assumed that dikereeves were not, in fact, found north of the Humber.

[35] After the standing juries had been discontinued in Somerset, officers called dikereeves were appointed 'to inspect, oversee and take care of the several works heretofore within the view of such juries' (minutes of a court of sewers held at Bridgwater, 8 October 1824, quoted by S. and B. Webb, p. 53). The Act of 12 & 13 Vic. c. 50 (1849) deals in detail with the appointment of dikereeves for drainage districts. But these officers of nineteenth-century creation are not to be confused with the far more ancient Lincolnshire ones, for whose history and functions see A. M. Kirkus, *op. cit.*, pp. xxxii–xxxv.

onwards and are a mine of information on many topics besides drainage; similar accounts were kept in Holland (Lincs.), though only a very few earlier than 1600 survive. The practice in Norfolk Marshland has not been definitely established; some parishes kept dikereeves' account books for their own use (as was sometimes done in Lincolnshire), and returns were certainly made to the court of sewers, but no such series of original accounts as in Lincolnshire survives in the court's records.

Around the Wash, in Holland and in Norfolk Marshland, the upkeep of the sea banks called forth special classes of records known as joyce books and acre books. In this region every landholder in the coastal parishes was liable to maintain a length of the parish sea bank, so many feet of bank for each acre of land held, each man's length being marked out on the ground by stakes. This liability was entered in a 'joyce', or adjoistment (agistment) book, while the acre books recorded the amount of each man's holding as a basis for assessment. The curiously localized character of sewers practice is evident in the absence of these classes from the sewers records of nearby Lindsey, though they have something in common with the 'scot books' of Kent.

In the life of those communities to whom it was a matter of almost daily concern, the organization of drainage could hardly fail to have a place of importance. Consciously or not, the commissioners of sewers who in three Lincolnshire towns chose the parish church–traditional heart of the community–as the most appropriate place for their records expressed their own view of this. Efficient drainage and strong sea banks were more than a matter of dry feet and a better living for farmers–they might, in emergency, mean the difference between life and death for all. For historians, therefore, the records of land drainage can offer (as I myself know) a unique reflection of the life of communities themselves unique.[36]

A. E. B. OWEN

---

[36] For some sidelights on the economic history of the Lindsey Marsh (such as the problem of timber supplies for coast protection works in a treeless area) provided by the dikereeves' accounts, see A. E. B. Owen, 'The Upkeep of the Lindsey Sea Defences, 1550–1650', *Lincolnshire Historian*, II, no. 10 (1963), pp. 23–30.

The London
Commissioners of Sewers
and their Records

Out Sovereign Lord the King . . . considering the daily great Damages and Losses which have happened in many . . . Parts of this his said Realm, as well by the Reason of the outrageous Flowings, Surges, and Course, of the Sea, in and upon Marsh-grounds and other low Places heretofore . . . won and made profitable for the great Commonwealth of this Realm; as also by occasion of Land-Waters and other outrageous Springs . . . Hath . . . ordained . . . That Commissions of Sewers . . . shall be directed in all Parts within this Realm, from Time to Time, where and when Need shall require . . .

Statute of Sewers, 23 Hy. VIII c. 5 (1531)

'Outrageous flowings' of water are no respecters of man-made boundaries, and the appointment of *ad hoc* Commissioners to function over wide areas in times of emergency probably seemed to medieval administrators an excellent device for dealing with the problem. In 1427, a year of 'unseasonable weathering'[1] an Act of Parliament[2] ordained that during the ensuing ten years 'several commissions of sewers' should be made to 'divers persons . . . to be sent into all parts of the realm where shall be needful'. This Act was renewed in 1439[3] and again in 1444,[4] this time for 15 years. Similar Acts were passed in 1472[5] (for 15 years), in 1487[6] (for 25 years), and in 1514[7] (for 10 years). Nothing further seems to have been done until the 'gret wyndes and fluddes'[8] of 1530 stirred King and Parliament to action. In 1531 was passed the Act from the preamble of which the quotation given at the head of this article was taken. It gave general statutory authority for the issuing of Commissions of Sewers whenever they might be required throughout the country, and its provisions, with only slight modifications, governed the work of the Commissions of Sewers until the nineteenth century.

Under the Act Commissions could be appointed for periods of three years (extended to 5 years in 1549[9] and 10 years in 1570).[10] The Sheriffs were required to summon jurors to report on damage or disrepair in embankments and on impediments to the free passage of water in streams and sewers, together with the names of landowners or occupiers of lands responsible for the same. It was the duty of the Commissioners to force such owners or occupiers to carry out repairs or to tax them in order that such repairs could be carried out. The Commissioners were authorized to appoint

---

[1] Stow's *Chronicle*.
[2] Act 6 Hy. VI c. 5.
[3] Act 18 Hy. VI c. 9.
[4] Act 23 Hy. VI c. 9.
[5] Act 12 Edw. IV c. 6.
[6] Act 4 Hy. VII c. 1.
[7] Act 6 Hy. VIII c. 10.
[8] *Greyfriars Chronicle*.
[9] Act 3 and 4 Edw. VI c. 8.
[10] Act 13 Eliz. c. 9.

bailiffs, surveyors, collectors, expeditors, and other officers and a clerk 'for writing of Books and Process' and to pay the same out of the money collected. Although, therefore, the old form of administration by Commissions which had only a limited term of life was retained, and the areas they were required to administer remained quite fluid both in theory and in practice for many years, the Act made provision for a continuing administrative set-up, and for the keeping of books of record.

So far as I am aware no administrative records of the pre-1531 Commissions of Sewers have survived, but there are collections of records in various parts of the country of the Commissions set up under the 1531 Act. The seven Commissions of the London area which were in 1847 amalgamated into the Metropolitan Commission of Sewers[11] left a large body of records. In particular, the records of the Westminster Commission are very extensive. They are of considerable interest firstly because they illustrate the struggle to adapt a form of organization intended in the main for an open countryside to a rapidly expanding urban area, with its attendant problems of divided ownership, the disposal of house drainage, etc.; and secondly, because they show the development of modern administrative methods, especially on the financial side, within the straitjacket of the medieval procedure laid down by the 1531 Act.

The London Commissions and their powers

In one important respect the London Commissioners had wider terms of reference than those in other parts of the country. The 1531 Act, though imprecise in its language to a modern reader, seems to have been interpreted at the time as limiting the jurisdiction of Commissioners of Sewers to navigable watercourses or to those which flowed directly into the sea. With the extension of building round London at the end of the sixteenth century, the need for some control over the smaller watercourses and ditches became obvious, and in 1605 an Act[12] was passed giving Commissioners of Sewers powers over all 'Walls, Ditches, Banks, Gutters, Sewers, Gotes, Causeys, Bridges, Streams and Watercourses, navigable or not, within the Limits of Two Miles, of and from the City of London, which Waters have their Course and Fall into the River of Thames'. This power of dealing with unnavigable watercourses became increasingly important as the area became urbanized, and it was considerably strengthened in 1690 by an Act[13] which extended it to new sewers and drains constructed since 1660 within the Cities of London and Westminster and all places within the weekly Bills of Mortality.

None of the pre-eighteenth-century original Letters Patent appointing Commissions of Sewers in the London area has survived, and, since early in the reign of Elizabeth I the practice of enrolling them on the dorse of the Patent Rolls lapsed and the series of Crown Docquet Books begins only in the last years of her reign, it has not been possible to trace with certainty the beginning of the seven London Commissions. The only Commission of Sewers which has been found on the Patent Rolls was that issued in 1554[14] for the Surrey and Kent area, covering the whole of what is now London south of the Thames as far as the River Ravensbourne. The minutes start in 1570 and, with one or two gaps, are continuous to 1847. A Commission for Greenwich Marshes was issued in 1624[15] and the minutes start in the following year. The existence of earlier Commissions is however

---

[11] The City of London did not have a separate Commission until after the Great Fire. The City Commission remained separate in 1847, and its powers were vested in the Common Council of the City of London by the London Sewers Act of 1897 (60 & 61 Vic. c. 133 local). As related below, the Sewer Commissioners were superseded by the Metropolitan Board of Works in 1855, which was in turn superseded by the London County Council in 1889. The records of the Commissioners were therefore inherited by the Council and are now in the Greater London Record Office.

[12] Act 3 Jas. I c. 14.
[13] Act 2 Wm. & Mary (Sess. 2) c. 8.
[14] P.R.O., C 66/885 m. 9d.
[15] P.R.O., Ind. 4211.

indicated by the Act of 1545 which authorized Expenditors and Collectors to distrain on the goods of owners of land in Combe Marshes who refused to contribute towards repairs.[16]

North of the river Commissions for the area drained by the Turnmill Brook and the Fleet River (including the City of London) were issued from 1600 onward, and these were the predecessors of the Holborn and Finsbury Commission, though the 'Divisions of Holborn and Finsbury' are not specifically mentioned until 1699. The minutes start in 1683. In the meantime a separate Commission had been instituted for the City in 1682. No continuing Commission for the north-eastern area, later known as the Tower Hamlets, seems to have been established until 1686, and minutes are extant only from 1703. A Commission was, however, issued as early as 1598 'for her Mats . . . Chrashe milles in the parishes of St Botulphes without Algate . . . and St Marye Matfellon alias Whitechapple'. Commissions for the Poplar area (usually referred to as Stepney or Poplar Marsh) can be traced back to 1600, and the registers of orders start in 1629. The little Precinct of St Katherine's by the Tower had a separate Commission in 1646, though its earliest records, the presentments, have only survived from 1748. A Commission was issued for 'certen lymitts in and aboute Westm'' in 1596. A minute of the Court of the Westminster Commission of Sewers for 1662 refers to 'many and sundry ancyent Records of this Court now Remaining with Mr Wattson of Clements Inne', and Sir William Wheeler was authorized to collect them, but he either fell down on the task or he failed to hand them over to the clerk, for no administrative records of the Commission have survived in official custody prior to 1659.

The boundaries set out in the early Westminster Commissions show the widest variation; that for 1619 extends only 'from Chelsea to Westmr. and to Temple Barre'; those for the Commonwealth period repeat this description with the laconic addition 'and elsewhere'. There was undoubted over-lapping with the area under the jurisdiction of the Holborn and Finsbury Commission until a boundary was agreed in 1774. In the earliest surviving Letters Patent the area is described as 'extending from the parishes of Hampton, Teddington, Twitnam, Isleworth, Hanwell, Cranford, Acton, Eling, Hammersmith, Fulham, Kensington and Chelsey in the County of Middlesex and the City of Westminster and precincts of the same And so to Temple Bar . . . and from thence within the Parishes of St Giles in the Fields, Pancras, Marylebone, Hampstead, Wilsden, Paddington and to the River of Thames'.[17] In practice the Commission mainly confined its attention to Westminster and its immediate environs, but it was occasionally active in the outer areas.

In 1769 the Court received several presentments[18] concerning the bad state of the sewers in Acton, Chiswick and Hammersmith, the jurors stating that the watercourses there should be cleansed and repaired at the charge of the local landowners, and proposing that a rate should be levied. The rate was opposed by a Hammersmith man, and a test case in the Court of King's Bench was decided in his favour on the ground that Hammersmith was outside the two-mile limit within which the Commissioners had jurisdiction over unnavigable watercourses.[19] The Commissioners immediately appointed a Committee to consider an application to Parliament for the extension of this limit, and the matter seemed to be going forward prosperously, although a counter-petition was produced, but on 19 April 1771 abruptly and without explanation the Court dissolved the Committee[20] and the application was dropped.

In 1806 another Committee was appointed to apply for a new Act of Parliament, this time successfully. The Act of 1807[21] brought under the supervision of the Westminster Commissioners all the parishes north of the river and west of the City within what became the County of London,

[16] Act 37 Hy. VIII c. 11.
[17] P.R.O., Ind. 4211.
[18] Westminster Commission of Sewers records [hereafter W.C.S.] 332/297/1–5.
[19] W.C.S. 57, p. 58.   [20] W.C.S. 57, p. 153.   [21] Act 47 Geo. III c. 7.

with the exception of Fulham and Hammersmith, but including part of Willesden. This Act also conferred on the Commissioners power to widen, deepen and alter the existing sewers and to make new ones, and to control the construction of sewers by private and other builders. For the first time the initiative lay with the Commissioners. Two years later the Surrey and Kent Commission was given similar powers.[22]

The seven Commissions worked entirely independently. There are a few indications of local rivalries and jealousies, but on the whole there was little friction. The Westminster Commission was the most go-ahead, and on occasion the other Commissions borrowed its ideas, but all the Commissions were ham-strung by their antiquated constitution, and they had neither the knowledge, the powers, nor the flexibility to cope with the problems created by the enormous increase of population and building of the late eighteenth and early nineteenth centuries, by the introduction of the water closet and by the cholera epidemics. Most of the districts under their supervision had by the 1840s coalesced into one urban area for which the old piecemeal drainage systems were quite inadequate. Sewage accumulated in cesspools and open ditches and even on the surface of the ground, fouling the water supply. Cholera epidemics increased in frequency and intensity until the government was forced to take action. In 1847 the Royal Commission appointed to 'inquire whether any, and what special means might be requisite for the improvement of the health of the metropolis, with regard more especially to . . . better house, street and land drainage' reached the conclusion that it was essential that the drainage of the Metropolitan area should become the responsibility of one competent body. Action to this end was taken in advance of legislation by the simple expedient of summoning the same 23 Commissioners for all the seven districts. The Act of 1848 consolidating the Commissions swept away much of the old cumbersome procedure, but the new Metropolitan Commission still lacked the powers necessary for the colossal task of replanning the whole main drainage system of London. A body of technical and administrative staff could not be created overnight, and though both Commissioners and staff struggled on for ten years to do what was needed they succeeded in little more than building a few new sewers and getting some uniformity into their administrative routine. The task was transferred to the newly created Metropolitan Board of Works in 1855, and within ten years, largely due to the skill and energy of (Sir) Joseph Bazalgette, lines of intercepting main sewers were built across the Metropolitan area from west to east, and, with the pumping stations and outfall works, at last made adequate provision for the main drainage of London.

The Commissioners

The 1531 Act laid down that the Commissioners of Sewers were to be 'substantial and indifferent persons . . . named by the lord chancellor and lord treasurer of England, and the two chief justices . . . or by three of them'. The Commissions were similar in form to Commissions of the Peace and the Act specifically stated that the Commissioners were appointed 'to be our justices' with power 'to tax, assess, charge, distrain and punish' persons liable for the upkeep of sewers and walls, etc. The procedure of enquiry 'by the Oaths of the honest and lawful men of the Shire' was normal to a medieval court of law, and the Elizabethan and Jacobean minutes of the Surrey and Kent Commission consist largely of the presentments of the Jurors with notes of the decisions of the Court of Commissioners following the pattern of a manorial Court Leet roll or book. The Greenwich Commissioners, appointed to deal with the flooding of the Greenwich Marshes in the early years of Charles I's reign, decided that piecemeal repair of the river wall by individual landowners was quite inadequate, and tried to undertake a general repair, charging the cost on the landowners and pressing labourers for the purpose. In spite of their statutory authority they met with considerable resistance and on several occasions issued a warrant to their bailiff to distrain on the goods and chattels of

---

[22] Act 49 Geo. III c. 183 (local).

defaulters. In 1632 they ordered the Constable of the parish of East Greenwich to arrest three labourers for 'divers Willful Contempts' and punish them in the stocks 'for the space of one hower' and then convey them to 'his Majesties Goale at Maidstone'.

In all the London Commissions throughout their existence the majority of the Commissioners were local gentry and landowners but, particularly in the later years, there was often a sprinkling of architects and surveyors. Sir John Denham and Hugh May were both members of the Westminster Commission in 1662 and Sir Christopher Wren served in 1692. The last (1847) Westminster Commission included Thomas Leverton Donaldson, George Gutch, surveyor to the Bishop of London's Paddington Estate, and Henry Edward Kendall, all of whom were founder members of the District Surveyors' Association, as well as Frederick Crace and William Chadwell Mylne, architects.[23] George Gwilt was serving as a Commissioner for Surrey and Kent in the early 1800s at the same time that his son, Joseph Gwilt, held the office of surveyor to that Commission. Similar examples could be quoted from the other Commissions. In these circumstances it was almost inevitable that the suspicion should arise that Commissioners sometimes used their position to further their business or professional interests. The Commissioners were fully aware of this danger, and tried to provide against it. In 1813 the Westminster Commissioners resolved 'That no Person being a Commissioner of Sewers nor any Person related to a Commissioner . . . nor connected with a Commissioner by Copartnership in any Business or Concern shall hereafter be continued to hold any Office or Place of Profit or Emolument under . . . this Court, or be allowed to furnish any Article or do any Business . . . for which Money appertaining to Sewers is to be paid'.[24]

Section 13 of the 1531 Act stated that the Commissioners should have 4/- out of the rates 'for every Day that they shall take Pain in Execution of this Commission of Sewers'. With the decline in the value of money this became no more than a token payment, the only other official emoluments being refreshments when they went on 'views', and an occasional dinner.[25] Meetings of the General Courts varied in frequency from one Commission to another, and from time to time. During the greater part of the seventeenth century the Greenwich Commission seems only to have met when flooding occurred, but by the end of the century the need for at least one meeting a year was recognized, for an order was made on 10 January 1698/9 'that it be hereafter a Constant Rule amongst ye Jury yt ye Foreman summon his Brethren ye first week in October before ye Commission meet and walke ye Walls and Marshes and take a Deliberate tyme to Consider of their Presentments and carefully to prepare ym for ye Commissioners Examination and approvall'. The Westminster Commission, on the other hand, was by 1662 meeting fairly regularly every month, and it had a committee system in good working order by the second half of the eighteenth century. In all areas and at all periods Commissioners were expected personally to go and 'view' any sewers or embankments within their jurisdiction about which a serious complaint had been made.[26] The duties of the Commissioners,

[23] Robert Cantwell, who was also a member, was almost certainly the same as R—— Cantwell, architect, mentioned by H. M. Colvin in his *Dictionary of English Architects 1650–1840*. Joseph Cantwell had been a Commissioner in 1828.

[24] W.C.S. 64, p. 3.

[25] A long series of dinner bills for the Tower Hamlets Commissioners has survived.

[26] This entry from the minutes of the Westminster Commission of 23 January 1778 is typical of many:

'That the Cm[rs] being convened by Mr Wm Rhodes the Surveyor Viewed the Sewer in St Anns Court Dean Street Soho and found the Main Sewer two feet deep in Soil proceeding from the Small private drains in the Court adjacent and a drain from the Necessarys which emptied into the main Sewer, they therefore Ordained the said Sewer to be Cleansed and that the Proprietor of the Houses to which the small private drains belong be acquainted that he or they must immediately cleanse and repair them.

'They likewise ordered that the drains from the Necessarys be stopp'd up.

'They also found the Water Pipes which lay across the Sewer rotten and Ordered the Labourer in Trust to acquaint the Water Companys thereof.'

(W.C.S. 59, p. 122).

particularly of those who served in built-up areas, could therefore be quite onerous and time-consuming: nevertheless there seem to have been very few occasions on which a meeting failed to get a quorum.

The Jurors and their presentments

Whenever a new Commission was appointed by Letters Patent writs were sent to the Sheriff instructing him to receive the oaths of the Commissioners and to summon a Jury to report on the state of the sewers. From the beginning the view was accepted by the Commissioners that they could not take cognizance of any need for work on the sewers nor levy any rate without a Jurors' presentment. The procedure, though cumbersome, answered well enough in a rural area where the responsibility for the upkeep of banks and the scouring of ditches, etc., could with little difficulty be assigned to the owners of the land on either side, and the small farmers who made up the majority of the Jurors had some practical experience of drainage problems. In the town its deficiencies quickly became apparent.

If sewers flowed down the middle of a street of houses some elementary constructional work in the way of bottoming the channel to stop seepage and the formation of bridges for foot passengers was obviously essential, and as soon as the roadway was required for wheeled traffic requests to 'arch over' the sewers became frequent. The Jurors, mostly small tradesmen, unless they were connected with the building trade,[27] had no technical knowledge to help them in deciding how defects should be remedied, and it was not a simple matter to draw up a list of those who 'benefited' from the sewers, and should therefore pay for their repair, when they were flanked on either side by buildings all in separate occupations and ownerships.

In Westminster the extant series of presentments starts in 1668. The earliest report on the condition of particular sewers, but after 1695 they are almost entirely concerned with the names of owners or occupiers who should be assessed for the cost of necessary repairs.[28] An order of the Court of 1683[29] for a Jury 'to amend a Presentment by inserting severall names and Rents therein which were omitted, on paine of being fined 10 li. a peece' is a significant comment on the inadequacy of this means of assessment. In 1695 the Court ordered that the lists of names and rents taken by the Juries should be examined by the Commissioners living in the parishes affected before the presentments were ingrossed 'to the end none . . . may be over or under charged'. It was obvious that some method more official and efficient would have to be found, and in 1728[30] the Clerk was ordered to try to obtain from the Land Tax Books the names and rents of inhabitants of parishes to be assessed for the sewers 'for the better preparing the Presentments of the Jury'. It was not, however, till 1737 that a real solution of the difficulty was found. A large debt had accrued for work done on the Hartshorn Lane Sewer, and the Foreman of the Jury was ordered[31] to 'make due Presentments

---

[27] Although no detailed analysis has been made, it seems probable that from the mid-eighteenth century onwards Jurors for the Westminster area were selected from men in the building trade so far as possible; e.g. of the 16 members of a Jury called in January 1779, 4 were bricklayers and 8 were carpenters (W.C.S. 59). This may have been the case in other areas.

[28] For work required on the sewers, the Commissioners soon began to rely to a large extent on the advice of their technical officers, the Surveyors (see below), and they often went themselves to 'view' the situation. The Westminster Commission had tacitly dispensed with Presentments of a Jury for normal repair work long before the Act of 1833 declared that this was unneccssary in every case, though on occasion a jury was summoned as a useful means of dealing with an awkward landowner, e.g. in 1813 a Jury was returned to view a building erected on the wall of the open part of the King's Scholars' Pond Sewer in Pimlico (W.C.S. 63).

[29] W.C.S. 42, fo. 81. The same book contains an Order of Court 'for Moses Pitt to attend and answer his threatning the Jury'.

[30] W.C.S. 51.

[31] W.C.S. 53.

for the Work . . . together with the Christian and Surnames and Rents all of such Persons who by Law ought to Contribute . . . towards the Charge thereof and Exhibit such Presentments fairly written into Court. And that the Rents to be Returned in the said Presentments be taken from the Books for the Poors Rates in the Several Parishes'. From the middle of the eighteenth century onward, it can be assumed that the Presentments for Westminster were compiled from the Poor Rate Books, though the procedure was not authorized by statute until 1812.[32] By the end of the eighteenth century the Holborn and Finsbury, Surrey and Kent, and Tower Hamlets Commissions were also using the Poor Rate Books in the same way. So far as Westminster was concerned the Presentments for the levying of rates had outlived their administrative usefulness before the end of the eighteenth century, but they continued to be engrossed on parchment until 1847. They are all on rolls except those for the last six years which are in book form. Most of the Commissions had their Presentments engrossed on whole skins of parchment, and Westminster experimented with this form in 1775, on the suggestion of its Committee of Accounts, but quickly decided that the roll form was preferable but that in future the names should be listed in two columns on both sides of the roll. Probably because of their bulk very few of the later Presentments of the other Commissions have been preserved, but there are three very large bundles for the Tower Hamlets for 1831, 1836 and 1844.

The meeting places and offices of the Commissions

In the early days none of the Commissions had any permanent office, and they usually met either in a local Court house or in a convenient inn.[33] The Clerk therefore kept the books in his own house and carried them to and fro as required. In 1698 the Clerk of the Greenwich Level was provided with 'a strong Leather Bagg' for this purpose,[34] and doubtless similar provision was made for his opposite numbers in other levels. It was not until 1771 that the Westminster Commissioners began seriously to look for a permanent headquarters.[35] Their surveyor, William Rhodes, offered them a house in Great Marlborough Street, but they found that it would 'by no means answer the Purpose' and later in the year the Committee of Accounts recommended that a seven-year lease should be taken of the dwelling house of William Ogle, the Clerk, in King Square Court, Carlisle Street, 'to be used in the Business of the Commission', and an order was given for the making of a 'proper Repository' for safe custody of the books and records. From this time onward the provision of living accommodation became part of the emoluments of the Clerk, and he continued to live on the premises after the office was moved to a larger house in Carlisle Street. The Commissioners had agreed to pay for rates and repairs, but an order of 22 January 1808 'that no Furniture or Articles of that Description be in future provided or Repairs of the House occupied for the Office be undertaken without a particular Order of the Court'[36] suggests that some trouble had arisen in this connection. A proper Board Room was fitted up in this house for meetings of the Court and its Committees, and the place acquired a more official air when in the autumn of 1808 a brass plate was fixed to the street door with the inscription:

OFFICE OF THE COMMISSIONERS OF SEWERS
Applications to be made from 11 to 3 o'clock

The Clerk, or his assistant, was required to be on duty during these hours to attend to callers. In November 1810 the Court decided that the office was inadequate in size and an insecure place 'for

[32] Act 52 Geo. III c. 48 (local).
[33] During the reign of Charles II meetings of the Westminster Commission were held either in the 'Town Court House' at Westminster or in the Court of King's Bench in Westminster Hall.
[34] G.C.S. 5, 6 Jan. 1697/8.
[35] W.C.S. 58.
[36] W.C.S. 61.

the Preservation of the official Records' and asked the Clerk and the Surveyor to report on what accommodation they thought was requisite. Their report illustrates both the expansion of business which had taken place by that date and the more formal character which it had acquired.[37] They considered that the Commission needed:

For the Public: A Hall or Waiting Room sufficiently large to accommodate 40 or 50 Persons.

For Commissioners: A Board Room calculated for 60 Commissioners, being about one half of the whole Number . . . and about 90 having occasionally attended. A Room adjoining the Board Room sufficiently large to accommodate a Jury . . .

For the Clerk: An Office.

For the Surveyor, etc.: An Office for two Assistants to the Clerk, for the Surveyor, for two Clerks of the Works, for the Laborer in Trust, and other Persons necessarily employed under the Commission.

For Books Papers and Plans: A Strong Room for the purposes of securing the Records of the Court together with the various Plans and Drawings and other valuable Documents necessary for the Business of the Commissioners, with Access, if possible, only from the Principal Clerk's Office.

Stores: A Yard for the Convenience of depositing Stores, to be used for the Business of the Commission.

Apartments: for the Clerk to reside on the Premises for the Security of the Property and for being in readiness in Cases of Emergency.[38]

An offer was made of No. 1 Greek Street, at the corner of Soho Square, and, having viewed and approved it, the Commissioners began negotiations first for a lease and then for the purchase of the freehold at a cost of £5,000.[39] The plans drawn by the Surveyor in 1812 for the adaptation of the ground and first floors for the use of the Commission, the building of a strong room, etc., are still extant.[40] The house served as a Sewers Office for the remainder of the life of the Westminster Commission and then passed to the Metropolitan Commission of Sewers. It was also used by the Metropolitan Board of Works from 1855 until new offices were completed in Spring Gardens in 1861.[41] By 1800 some of the other Commissions were feeling the need for office accommodation, and a meeting place of their own. In December 1808 the Tower Hamlets Commissioners took a house in Osborne Street, Whitechapel, and appointed a hall keeper.[42] They moved to Great Alie Street in 1822 and remained there till 1847. The Holborn and Finsbury Commission occupied an office at No. 7 Hatton Garden from 1807 until 1847. The Surrey and Kent Commission, however, continued to use the Newington Sessions House as its headquarters, and the other smaller Commissions do not seem to have had permanent headquarters, though the Poplar Commission during its last year of existence established an office for its Works Foreman near Ferry Road, Poplar.

The Clerk and his records

Although the Clerk was not a permanent official in the modern sense it was obviously intended that he should provide some continuity between one Commission and the next since it was his duty both to make and keep the records and to apply for a new Commission when need arose. He was, therefore, the kingpin of the organization in each of the levels.

At first the Clerk's ability to write was his main requirement–Huntley Bigg, a scrivener, held the Clerkship of the Westminster Commission from 1701 to 1719–but as business increased,

---

[37] W.C.S. 62.

[38] W.C.S. P. 70.

[39] Statutory authority to purchase was given in 1812 (Act 52 Geo. III c. 48 (local)), the reason given being 'the prodigious increase of Buildings'.

[40] W.C.S. P. 70.

[41] In 1862 the house was purchased by the Charity for Distressed Persons in London, by whom it is still occupied. It is now known as the House of St Barnabas.

[42] T.H.C.S. 35.

so did the administrative work which largely devolved upon the Clerk, while the Treasurer, during the eighteenth century, gradually passed over most of the accounting work to him.

The 1531 Act authorized the payment to the Clerk of 2/– a day and 'reasonable Sums of Money . . . for writing of Books and Process'. In 1662 the 'Fees Due and Belonging to ye Clerke' of the Westminster Commission were listed in the Orders of Court. They were:[43]

	s	d
For every Sommons	1	0
For an Order	2	6
For every Report	2	6
For everyone Presented in this Court	2	4
For every Recognizance entered into upon a Travers	2	4
For a Venire and Returne upon a Travers	13	4
For entring a Judgement upon a Travers	3	4
For a Coppie of a Presentment (unless large–then 4d per sheete)	3	4
For every Warrant upon a Booke Rated and Assessed upon the Inhabitants	2	6
For every fine discharged	2	4
For every Decree passed (besides Ingrossing at 8d per sheete)	6	8
For a Warrant of Distresse	2	6

As money depreciated and the Clerk's work increased most of his income was derived from fees, and his rendered accounts occupied more and more space in the cash books. This was also true, though to a lesser extent, of the Bailiff and Cryer. In 1774, the Committee of Accounts made a series of recommendations to the Court with the object of reducing the amount of work involved in these accounts. Their report is worth quoting for the light it throws on the work of the Commission and of its Clerk at this date:[44]

They are of opinion That the Clerk be Allow'd for Keeping and Entring all the Accounts of the Commission into the different Books the usual Yearly Sum of £60.

For Attending All the General Courts and respective Committees, Entring the Minutes and Orders into the Books, Writing Receipts, and Attending on the Sheriffs, Summoning Juries on Views and to sign Presentments and attending them thereon, Writing Letters by Orders of Courts and Committees, Drawing Abstracts of Work done to the Sewers and of the Debts due therefrom for Courts and Committees to settle Rates, Drawing Engrossing and Attending the Execution of Contracts with Commissioners Workmen, and all other business relative to the Sewers except the undermentioned, the Yearly Sum of £60.

For attending the Vestry Clerks of each parish to obtain the names and Yearly Rents of the persons rateable to each Sewer, 10s. 6d.

For drawing and Engrossing each Decree and Parchment, £2. 2s.

For Drawing and Engrossing presentments on Rolls of parchment on both sides in double Columns each Roll containing 200 Lines, 5s. 0d.

For Copying Presentments into the Rate Books Includg Warrants to Coll[rs], Rates for whole and half Water Indexes, Summarys and making up of the Book, for every 90 pages containing 26 Lines in each page, £6. 6s.

For Coals and Candles for the use of Committees, Per Annum, £4.

Although in theory the Commissioners could appoint and dismiss their clerks at will, their knowledge and experience could not be dispensed with lightly, and in practice they usually held office so long as they were physically capable. Until the later part of the eighteenth century, appointments were normally made on the recommendation of one or more Commissioners, but the results were not always satisfactory; some clerks who were efficient were by no means disinterested, while others had few qualifications for what, in the larger Commissions, was a demanding occupation. An example of the latter was William Ogle, on whom, after twelve years' service with the West-

[43] W.C.S. 36.
[44] W.C.S. 57.

minster Commission, the Committee of Accounts reported bluntly that 'instead of forwarding the Business of the Board [he] greatly retards it'.[45] Ogle was asked to resign though he was temporarily kept on as an assistant with an allowance of £70 a year. The former assistant, William Wilmot, was appointed in his stead with a salary of £200 a year, the house to live in, and an allowance of £10 a year for coals and candles in the Committee Room. By 1813 the Clerk's salary had been increased to £400 a year plus an allowance of £200 for an assistant, but he was required to devote the whole of his time to the service of the Commissioners, and it was resolved that 'no Charges of any kind whatever; otherwise than as provided for by a settled annual allowance, shall be admitted or allowed'.[46] Nevertheless the Clerk continued to produce substantial expense accounts, e.g. that for the last quarter of 1827 amounted to £142 2 0.[47] After 1777 the Westminster Commission obtained candidates for the office by inserting advertisements in the press, and other Commissions gradually followed suit.

The most important business of the Clerk was to summon Commissioners to meetings of the Court and its Committees and to write up the minutes. From 1774 onward the Clerk drew up formal agendas of business for meetings of the Westminster Court; these were printed from 1836. The minute books are variously titled – Greenwich 'Orders and Proceedings'; Holborn and Finsbury and Tower Hamlets 'Minutes' or 'Registers'; Surrey and Kent 'Court Minutes and Orders'; Westminster 'Orders of Court' – and to some extent the titles reflect variations in form and content, e.g. copies of the presentments of the Jurors are included in the Minutes or Registers of the Tower Hamlets Commission right to the end, whereas the Westminster 'Orders of Court' consist almost entirely of the decisions of the Court on presentments, which were always separately engrossed, and on reports of the Committees and the officers.[48]

From 1777 onward the reports and papers which were 'presented', i.e. considered, by the Westminster Court, were kept in orderly fashion by the Clerk, and subsequently bound in chronological order; there are in all 64 volumes of these papers. This practice was taken over by the Metropolitan Commission of Sewers.[49]

One further function of the Clerk must be mentioned because of its value to searchers. All the Commissions realized at an early date the need for some means of easy reference to previous decisions. Most of the minute books, account books, etc., are indexed but from time to time the Clerk was ordered to prepare more comprehensive indexes. So, for example, in 1703 the Greenwich Commissioners ordered[50] Robert Watson, their Clerk, to examine the 'Books of Orders' and 'make a fit and proper Index . . . disposing the same Alphabetically in such order and under such proper heads that the Commissioners may readily turne to any Order', and in 1809 John Houseman, Clerk to the Westminster Commission, was paid £312 18 for indexing 'the Records of the Proceedings of the Commission' from 11 October 1659 to 11 April 1806.[51]

Finances

The Commissioners derived their income solely from the rates they were entitled to levy, and as soon as they started to carry out repairs to the sewers instead of forcing owners to do the work, they

---

[45] W.C.S. 59.

[46] W.C.S. 63.

[47] W.C.S. 70.

[48] In spite of having these quite detailed 'Orders of Court', an almost complete series of 'decrees' for the levying of rates has survived for the Westminster Commission, though not for any of the other Metropolitan Commissions. These decrees, which largely repeat the content of the presentments, were all engrossed on parchment until 1847, though the general Sewers Act of 1833 (3 and 4 Wm. IV c. 22) declared this to be inessential.

[49] The Metropolitan Board of Works continued it, and it was also followed by the London County Council.

[50] G.C.S. 5.

[51] W.C.S. 62. The index was later extended to 1826.

were up against the elementary difficulty of deciding whether to proceed with the work immediately and try to fend off the demands of workmen for payment until a rate was collected, or to brook the delay and opposition which would inevitably result from the attempt to collect a rate in advance. The former course was usually adopted, and until the device of raising loans on the security of future rates was hit upon[52] payments to officers and workmen were often months, and sometimes years, in arrear.

A further complication was the generally accepted theory that only those who gained direct benefit from any work on the sewers should contribute towards its cost, and by 'benefit' was implied improvement to the value of the property. In theory it was therefore the owners of property who paid, but the Commissioners soon found that the only practical arrangement was to collect from the tenants of houses and buildings and leave them to recover from the landlords. In 1662 the Westminster Commissioners ordered[53] that in the case of the landlords refusing to allow the rates the rents were to be sold. Three years later this was modified to a promise[53] to the tenants that, if the landlords refused to pay, the Court would do them justice. The liabilities of landlord and tenant remained a matter of controversy until the Commissions were superseded by the Metropolitan Board of Works, and continued to bedevil the financial arrangements of the Board. One useful result for the modern researcher is that the Sewer rate books often contain the names of owners as well as of occupiers of property.

Apart however from the respective liabilities of owners and occupiers was the question of which properties derived benefit from each sewer, or, even more particularly, from each work of repair or improvement, and how overhead charges should be allocated between the various sewer districts. In 1721 the Westminster Commissioners took the opinion of Counsel as to the legality of making a general rate on the district drained by each sewer to pay for the works in that district, but they were advised that they had no power to do this. [54] As late as 1820 a suit in the Court of King's Bench was brought by a resident of Knightsbridge against the Collector for seizure of goods for non-payment of Sewer Rate, the plea being that the property derived no benefit from the sewer.[55] Judgement was given in favour of the defendant, and from thenceforward the legality of a general rate for each district does not seem to have been questioned.[56] For accounting purposes the cost and income of each of the Westminster Districts were kept separate and are so shown in the printed annual accounts from 1824 to 1846.

Most of the work on the sewers was performed under contract. Until 1780 the Westminster Commissioners contracted separately with workmen of various trades, smiths, paviors, carpenters, etc., but from then onwards a general contract was made covering all the ordinary work, the first general contractor being Richard Holland. Prior to 1800 details of all payments both for work and materials used were entered in the Bill Books[57] and from 1836 to 1847 the vouchers survive. The detailed accounts of the contractors are extant from 1789 and largely bridge the gap between 1800 and 1836 when only the gross amounts were entered in the Bill Books.

In the other levels separate contracts seem to have been made for each of the more importa nt

---

[52] Statutory authority to borrow money on the security of the rates was given to the Westminster Commissioners by the Act of 52 Geo. III c. 48 (local), and provision was made for a form of lottery to determine the order in which creditors should be paid off as the rates came in.

[53] W.C.S. 38.

[54] W.C.S. 50.

[55] W.C.S. 38.

[56] A further question which was raised by the Westminster Commission in 1830–1 was the liability for rates of public buildings, churches, chapels, workhouses, etc., and royal palaces. They were advised against attempting to assess such buildings, but in the course of the investigation three useful books of plans were produced.

[57] There is a complete series of Bill Books from 1702 to 1847 (W.C.S. 502–21).

repair or constructional jobs carried out during the last thirty years or so of the Commissioners' existence.[58]

In 1770 the Westminster Court set up a new Committee of Accounts to bring more order into the accounting system. If the members took their duties over-seriously at first, as witness the minute of 13 December 1770 which relates that they 'cast the several Pages' of the Rate Book for the Essex Street Sewer and reached page 55 before they decided to adjourn 'the Completion of the same to the next Committee', they did manage in the course of the next few years to supersede most of the miscellaneous accounting books which had previously been kept by regular series of Journals and Ledgers. To these were added in 1809 Cash Books in which all receipts and payments were entered. The Clerk continued to be responsible for the accounts of the Westminster Commission until 1847.

In the other levels there are no regular series of Journals and Ledgers before the nineteenth century.

The Treasurers or Expenditors

Though this was not always the case with the other London Commissions, the Surrey and Kent and the Westminster Commissioners invariably elected one of themselves to serve as Treasurer.[59] Occasionally a second Treasurer, also a Commissioner, was appointed for some special purpose—thus in 1661 Emery Hill and Edmund Bury Godfrey were both serving the Westminster Commission in this capacity. Apparently some dispute arose on this matter for in 1707 the Westminster Court made an order that no one should be appointed Treasurer unless he was on the Commission. It was soon found that this was not necessarily a safeguard against loss, for in 1712 Richard Adams 'Treasurer for the Upper Liberty' failed in his payments. Even more serious, in 1745 Andrew Drummond (of Drummond's Bank), then Treasurer, stopped payment and the Clerk was ordered to enquire into the state of his affairs; nevertheless in December 1747, when a new Commission met, of which Andrew Drummond was a member, he was proposed by several Commissioners for the office of Treasurer and unanimously elected.[60] The need for a closer check on financial matters had become self-evident, and in August 1748 the Clerk was ordered to place before each meeting of the Court a statement of the amount of cash in the Treasurer's hands. It was not however till 1770 that the Court demanded a statement in writing from the Treasurer of the balance of money in his keeping. The Committee of Accounts appointed in that year to improve the financial administration of the Commission was ordered in October 1773 to balance the accounts with the Treasurer annually on 31 December and report thereon to the next meeting of the Court.

After Andrew Drummond ceased to act as Commissioner the Commission continued to use Drummond's Bank as Treasurer. In 1806 however a new Commission appointed William Mainwaring both as its Chairman and its Treasurer. He ceased to be Chairman in 1809, and Commissioner in 1812, but his banking-house continued as Treasurer until November 1841, when the Clerk reported that on presenting an Order to Mainwaring, Son, Chatteris and Co., he was informed that the bank had suspended payment. Several months elapsed before Mainwaring's affairs were settled. In the end the Commission, in common with his other creditors, had to accept a composition of 10/- in the pound. The loss involved had the effect of making the Commission again tighten up its financial controls, and Drummond's Bank, to whom the Treasurership was returned, were instructed to hand over vouchers for all payments made on behalf of the Commission.

---

[58] The original contracts made by the Surrey and Kent Commission from 1812 to 1847 have survived. There are only sporadic survivals for the other Commissions.

[59] In 1814 the Holborn and Finsbury Commission had a clause inserted in its amending Act (54 Geo. III c. 219 (local)) prohibiting the Treasurer from being a Commissioner or holding any other office.

[60] W.C.S. 54.

The Greenwich Commission adopted an entirely different method of fulfilling its statutory obligations. During the seventeenth century landowners were appointed in turn to hold the three offices of Bailiff, Expenditor (or Treasurer) and Collector. During their terms of office they had to ascertain what work was required and supervise its execution, to collect the money for it and to pay the bills. The arrangement had a sort of rough justice about it but did not lend itself to methodical accounting. In 1699 there was serious trouble, and the Commissioners made a standing order that for the future Expenditors were to 'distinguish what moneys are expended upon ye severall Ordainments enjoyned them to do And that they take distinct receipts from ye Workemen for ye performance of their several Ordainments And that they bring sufficient Receipts to vouch as their payments and leave no debt unpaid for ye year in which they serve as Expenditor'.[61]

A Mrs Granden was Expenditor for 1699, and her account was condemned as 'imperfect and trifling'. At the December meeting of the Court she was adjudged contumacious for breach of the standing order and fined £40, for which a distress warrant was issued. The Clerk added a footnote to the minute which brings home how small and closely-knit was the community of Greenwich Level at that time: 'Mr Dry, one of ye Commissioners . . . did concurr in ye above order but desired he might be excused from signeing ye same ye Expenditor being his daughter'.

The Collectors and the Rate Books

The rate collectors had by no means an enviable task particularly in the early days. In the country areas where only a small number of landowners were involved, it was fairly simple. The Greenwich Commissioners, for example, in the early seventeenth century expected the ratepayers to bring their money to the collector, who was required to be in the parish church to receive it between the hours of 8 and 11 a.m. In the town a house-to-house collection was necessary, and even so was by no means always successful, since occupiers tried to throw the onus for payment on to absentee landlords or to deny their liability on the ground that they would derive no benefit from the works proposed. On the other hand the Collectors were part-time officers whose integrity was not always to be relied upon. There was a long period of trial and error before anything like a watertight system was evolved.

In the seventeenth century the Westminster Commissioners alternated between threatening the Collectors with fines and imprisonment if they failed to collect arrears of rates and trying to find some practical solution of the difficulties. In 1677 they decided that if a tenant moved away without paying his rate they would issue a warrant 'to Levy the sayd Taxe by Distresse on the next occupant'. In 1682 they agreed that they would not decree any rate without prior notice to the inhabitants of the district, so that they could be present at the Court if they wished. In 1703 they ordered that appeals against the rates, except by peers of the realm, should be heard only in their Court, and they decided to consult Counsel as to their powers to decide what proportion of the Sewer Rate the ground landlords should pay. In 1706 they set up a Committee to meet once a month to audit the Collectors' accounts and to hear appeals against assessments. At the same time they authorized the employment of a constable 'to assist the Collectors in levying distress for rates' and the payment to him of 6d in the pound for his trouble; this sum was subsequently increased to a shilling in the pound, whether collected by means of distress or otherwise.

During the eighteenth century some of the administrative difficulties were ironed out. The Clerk was given instructions to defend any Collector who had an action brought against him for recovering rates by means of a distress warrant, and the Commissioners indemnified themselves against loss through defalcations of the Collectors by requiring the latter to produce securities at

---

[61] G.C.S. 2 Oct. 1699.

the time of their appointment.[62] The Collectors were also required to submit regular accounts at each Court. It was not until 1780 that Collectors were ordered to give check receipts to householders for payment of rates.

The Rate Book itself formed the Collector's warrant for asking householders for payment of the Sewer Rate.[63] It was essential therefore that it should be handed in when cleared and properly audited. In 1748 the Westminster Commission tried to regulate the number of Collectors so that each rate could be fully collected within a year but always the increase in building out-paced any increase in staff.

As has already been indicated, rates were levied not on parishes as a whole but on the sewer districts, which overlapped the parish boundaries and varied from time to time. The 1775 instruction that each book should have a proper index of the places mentioned in it must have been as useful to the Collectors as it is to a modern searcher. In 1818 the Westminster area was formed into three districts for rating purposes: Eastern and Western Divisions, and Counters Creek District. A fourth, Ranelagh District, was added in 1835.

The Rate Books themselves vary greatly in format. Many of the early ones are covered with parts of old parchment indentures or with portions of duplicate tax returns (window tax, carriage tax, etc.). There are many scribbled notes made by the Collector on his rounds in the margins, or on the interleaving which is a feature of some of the eighteenth century books: 'empty and going to be puld downe'; 'gave 2 receipts the 1st being lost'; 'very poor, nothing to be got'; 'seize pewter plates', etc.

The Surveyors

Under the provisions of the 1531 Act the position of the Surveyors was somewhat anomalous. It was obviously intended that the Commissioners should be able to obtain expert advice when they required it, but the statute put the onus for reporting defects on the Jurors and ordered the Commissioners 'to survey the . . . Walls, Streams, Ditches . . . and the same cause to be amended'. As a printed report of 1830 expressed it, prior to 1799 'no officer was required to notice the state of the sewers until specially ordered'.

The Surveyors were not engaged full time on work for the Commissioners; normally they carried on their private practice, only attending on the Commissioners when specifically required to do so. Until the latter part of the eighteenth century most of them seem to have looked on their work on the sewers as a minor side-line. It is no wonder that complaints concerning both their competence and diligence crop up from time to time. In April 1669, for example, Daniel Benson was discharged from the surveyorship of the Westminster Commission 'for his miscarryage in his sayd Imployment in Relacion to ye worke whiche was to be done in Reforming ye Dreynes . . . in Queenestreet . . .' In this instance Benson attributed his dismissal to the fact that Mr Wright, the occupant of a house in Queen Street affected by the drainage works, had used his position as a Commissioner to influence the Court because of a personal grievance. Benson was fined 20 shillings for his 'scandalous words', but there may have been some truth in them all the same; lack of professional status and insecurity of tenure of office left the surveyors very vulnerable to attack by individual Commissioners.

---

[62] In 1778 one of the Collectors absconded and Charles Hanbury Williams, who had stood security for him, was required to pay £120 indemnity.

[63] Several of the Commissions had duplicate copies made which remained in the Clerk's keeping and served as checks on the Collectors' books. In 1814 the Holborn and Finsbury Commission got detailed regulations as to the Rate Books inserted in their amending Act (54 Geo. III c. 219 (local)). These included the making of duplicates in every case and instructions to the Collectors to enter in their copies all sums collected, and all reasons for non-payment, to produce the book to any ratepayer if asked, and to give a receipt for all payments.

There were no recognized professional qualifications for surveyors until the end of the nineteenth century. In making appointments the Commissioners had to depend on recommendations. In 1691 the Westminster Commissioners 'taking notice that many extravagant Bills are brought in for work done to the public Sewers and Grates, for want of a faithfull and Skilfull Surveyor to make just Estimates of the Charge of such workes, and to see the well doing thereof, It is Ordered that the Clerk do wait upon Sir Christopher Wren knt Surveyor of their Maties workes, and desire him to think of a fit and able person to be Surveyor of the Sewers, and to recommend him to this Court'. Sir Christopher duly recommended John Scarborow, who was sworn in on 13 May 1691.

The surveyors were paid partly by salary and partly by fees, neither of which was on a fixed scale during the seventeenth century. Sir Christopher Wren himself served on the Committee appointed to audit Scarborow's accounts in May 1692. The Committee estimated that Scarborow had spent 107 complete days on the work during the year and had made 'Seventeen Estimates and eleaven Admeasurements', for which they reckoned he should be paid £46 5. The Court reduced this to a round £45, which they authorized to be paid 'out of the first Contingent moneys that shall be paid into the Treasurer's hands, or out of the Taxes [i.e. rates] now shortly to be set on foot'. It ordered that in future Scarborow should receive £30 a year.

The duties of the surveyor were only loosely defined in the Restoration period. On 9 April 1663 'the two Surveyors of this Court togeather with Mr John Davenport and Mr Richard Rider and Mr Lott Stalling' were ordered 'to meate togeather as occasion shall require for the Survey, Measuring and Estimating the charge of casting, scowring and cleansing the Towne Sewers as allso for Planking and bottoming the same As likewise to Indent and contract wth the seaverall Artificers and workemen . . .' Only three weeks later, however, it was ordered that 'ye care and speedie dispatch of the Towne Sewers of Westmr be whooly left to the Management of Mathew Child, gent., sworne Surveyor of this Court And the said Mathew Child is further required to Sommon all and every such Officer and Officers of Court togeather with his Assistants therein, at any time as ye necessity of ye service shall require, that soe the worke may not be retarded, and he to give account thereof unto the Court at their next sitting'. In November 1689 Thomas Brickland, the surveyor, was ordered that he 'upon all occasions summon the Jury to meet, the Court being informed it has for severall years belonged to his place so to do, and that he attend the Jury (when met) and assist them in their business'–in other words the Court made the Surveyor responsible for deciding when a Jury's report was necessary and for giving the Jury advice in making a report.

During the first half of the eighteenth century the surveyors to the Westminster Commission were very poorly paid for the amount of work and responsibility which devolved upon them. In 1748 the Commission considered that a salary of £50 a year was sufficient and insisted that the Surveyor should live 'within the Limit of the places where the work usually happens'.[64] In 1761 the only applicant for the place was John Smallwell, son of the previous occupant, and he died before the end of the year. In 1762 three applied, of whom one was rejected on the grounds that he was an undischarged bankrupt, and on a ballot being taken William Franks was appointed, still at a salary of £50. Franks resigned in the following year, and William Bacchus was appointed. It was not until 1768 that there was any competition for the position. William Rhodes, Samuel Drake, George Hewitt and Thomas Spencer all applied, and Rhodes was elected. Within a few months he got his salary increased to £80 on the ground that 'to do his duty therein almost takes up his whole time'.[65] Rhodes' term of office was a turning point in its development. He got a central store-room established for materials needed for repairs. He got assistants appointed to keep a closer watch on the condition of the sewers, and he undertook to make a plan of all the main sewers in the Westminster area–in fact

[64] W.C.S. 54.
[65] W.C.S. 55.

he took a more serious view of his responsibilities than his predecessors had done. Unfortunately he bit off more than he could chew. Payment of his bills was put off from month to month because he had not presented them, the plan was not completed, and finally, in 1778, a storm blew up over a contractor who was proved to have used faulty materials in a number of jobs. Rhodes admitted that he had not inspected the work himself but had relied on his labourer in trust in whom he had been 'exceedingly deceived', and he offered his resignation which was accepted.

Of the ten candidates for the vacancy Samuel Drake was elected by ballot of the Commissioners in February 1779. He undertook to relinquish all his private business and devote the whole of his time to the duties of the office save only 'the place of Surveyor under the Act of Parliament for regulating Buildings and party walls', and he offered to give that up also if the Commissioners thought it interfered with his duty to them. He held office until his death in 1806, and seems to have given satisfaction. He continued the series of 'reports of work done at the charge of the district' begun by his predecessor, and he prepared a few plans of sewers. In September 1795 the Commissioners unanimously agreed to increase his salary to £150 a year because of his long and faithful service.

Thomas Chawner and Henry Rhodes both applied for the surveyorship when it was advertised in 1806, but the successful candidate was William Treadgold. His advent coincided with the passing of the 1807 Act which, as already indicated, greatly extended the powers of the Commissioners. Treadgold immediately got to work to prepare a series of detailed maps of the sewers. These are still extant. A bigger staff was obviously required if a check was to be kept on all builders who wished to connect house drains to the sewers,[66] and in 1810 a second Clerk of Works was appointed. The area was divided into two districts, Northern and Southern, for the purposes of supervision, and a Clerk of the Works was appointed to each. They kept detailed records of the amount of time spent and the materials used in work on the sewers, which served as a check on contractors' bills. A third Clerk of Works was appointed in 1817 to supervise the Western District, i.e. the part of the Westminster area west of the King's Scholars' Pond Sewer. A further re-arrangement of districts followed the appointment of a fourth Clerk of Works in 1823.

What has been said as to the growth of the Surveyors' work under the Westminster Commission is, though to a lesser degree, also true of the other Commissions. The records contain a lot of material for the biographies of individual London surveyors as well as illustrating the development of surveying as a profession. The plans and proposals submitted by builders for new streets, squares or houses, and the reports on them, provide an enormous amount of detailed information both for the topographer and for students interested in building development in London during the first half of the nineteenth century.

Physical condition of the records

The bulk and the good condition of the surviving records bears witness to the care taken of them by their creators and successors. They have suffered more from damp during their well-meant evacuation to 'safe' storage during the 1939–45 war than from any other cause.

Of the maps and plans, of which there are about 1,000 in all dating from 1740 onward, the majority have been backed on linen and bound into strong if somewhat unwieldy volumes. Those which were too large for this treatment were mounted on rollers.[67]

---

[66] This had been done illicitly for many years. The 1807 Act first gave official sanction to the practice subject to the proviso that prior notification was given to the Commissioners and that each new drain should be 'made in such Manner and Form, and with such Materials and Workmanship, under the Survey and Control and according to the Direction of the said Commissioners of Sewers, their Surveyor or other Person by them duly authorised'.

[67] W.C.S. P. 13 includes a drawing and section made in 1817 of a 'cedar roller with brass rings at either end for drawings which are too large to be bound into books'.

In 1840 the Clerk of the Westminster Commission reported that 'under the direction of the Chairman [Thomas L. Donaldson] a great portion of the Records of the Court had been bound and put into good order'; the Chairman was therefore requested to see that the remainder (about 60 volumes) should also be treated at an estimated expense of £30. John Smith, stationer, seems to have carried out most of this work. His bills for 1839-41[68] include these items:

	£	s.	d.
Cases for Presentments	2	2	0
Rebinding, lettering and cleaning Books, etc., in Strong Room	77	3	9
Man at office Glueing on lettering, cleaning backs, etc. – 36 hours	1	4	0
6 demy folio Rate Books . . . rebound vellum and lettered vellum labels, etc.	5	2	0

It is a tribute to the excellence of John Smith's workmanship that most of his bindings are still strong and serviceable. In the 1890s the London County Council had some of the remaining unbound volumes bound in the same style. Some paper repairs were also carried out at this time by laminating with a transparent paper. The paper used in these repairs has retained its strength and the writing it covers is still clearly legible.

IDA DARLINGTON

---

[68] W.C.S. 498.

Index